AUTOCOURSE™

THE WORLD'S LEADING GRAND PRIX ANNUAL

CMG
PUBLISHING

TAGHeuer

WHAT ARE YOU MADE OF ?

JUAN PABLO MONTOYA and his Carrera Tachymetre Automatic Chronograph

SWISS AVANT-GARDE SINCE 1860

CONTENTS

AUTOCOURSE 2005–2006

is published by
Crash Media Group Ltd
Number One
The Innovation Centre
Silverstone Circuit
Silverstone
Northants NN12 8GX
United Kingdom
Tel: +44 (0)870 3505044
Fax: +44 (0)870 3505088
Email: info@crash.net
Website:www.crashmediagroup.com

Printed in England by
Butler and Tanner Ltd,
Frome, Somerset

ISBN: 1 905334 04 4

DISTRIBUTORS

Vine House
Waldenbury
Chailey
East Sussex BN8 4DR
Tel: +44 (0)1825 723398
Email: sales@vinehouseuk.co.uk

Menoshire Ltd
Unit 13
21 Wadsworth Road
Perivale
Middlesex UB6 7LQ
Tel: +44 (0)20 8566 7344
Fax: +44 (0)20 8991 2439

NORTH AMERICA
Motorbooks International
PO Box 1
729 Prospect Avenue
Osecola
Wisconsin 54020, USA
Tel: (1) 715 294 3345
Fax: (1) 715 294 4448

Dust-jacket: Fernando Alonso – at
just **24 years of age, the sport's
youngest-ever world champion.**
Photograph: Emily Davenport/XPB.cc

**Title page: Kimi Räikkönen
celebrating his brilliant victory
in the Japanese Grand Prix.**
Photograph: Laurent Charniaux/WRi

Editor's Acknowledgements

The editor of AUTOCOURSE wishes to thank the following for their assistance in compiling the 2005–2006 edition. **Eire:** Jordan Grand Prix (Ian Phillips, Charlotte Anderson and Annouck Heinrichs); **France:** ACO, Fédération Française du Sport Automobile; **FIA** (Max Mosley, Bernie Ecclestone, Alan Donnelly, Richard Woods, Christel Picot, Julia Brillard, Alexandra Scherin, Charlie Whiting, Herbie Blash and Pat Behar); Michelin (Pierre Dupasquier and Severine Ray); Renault F1 (Flavio Briatore, Pat Symonds, Patrizia Spinelli and Bradley Lord); **Germany:** Formula 3 Vereinigung; BMW Motorsport (Mario Theissen and Jorg Kottmeier); Mercedes-Benz (Norbert Haug, Wolfgang Schattling, Frank Reichert and Tanya Severin); Sabine Kehm; **Great Britain:** Autocar; British American Racing (Nick Fry, Geoff Willis, Hugh Chambers, Alastair Watkins, Tracy Novak, Emma Bearpark and Jane Chapman); Martin Brundle; Bob Constanduros; Maurice Hamilton; Emma Henry; Nick Henry; Cosworth Engineering (Bernard Ferguson); Ford (Jost Capito); Red Bull Racing (Helmut Marko, Christian Horner, Günther Steiner, Tina Sponer, Sophia Claughton-Wallin, Britta Roeske and Katie Tweedle); McLaren Racing (Ron Dennis, Martin Whitmarsh, Adrian Newey, Justine Blake, Beverley Keynes, Ellen Kolby, Clare Robertson, Claire Bateman, Lyndy Redding, Simon Points, Neil Oatley, Steve Hallam and Peter Stayner); Stan Piecha; Nigel Roebuck; Eric Silbermann; Sir Jackie Stewart; Jules Kulpinski; Professor Sid Watkins; WilliamsF1 (Sir Frank Williams, Patrick Head, Dickie Stanford, Sam Michael, Frank Dernie, Jonathan Williams, Claire Williams, Jim Wright, Silvia Hoffer Frangipane and Liam Clogger); **Italy:** Commisione Sportiva Automobilistica Italiana; Scuderia Ferrari (Jean Todt, Ross Brawn, Antonio Ghini, Luca Colajanni, Matteo Bonciani, Stefania Bocci and Regine Rettner); Minardi F1 Team (Paul Stoddart, Graham Jones and Fabiana Valenti); 'George' Piola; **Japan:** Bridgestone (Hirohide Hamashima, Hiroshi Yasukawa, Hisao Suganuma, Adrian Atkinson and Rachel Ingham); Honda Racing (Robert Watherston and Charlie Reid); Toyota (Tsutomu Tomita, John Howett, Mike Gascoyne, Andrea Ficarelli, Peter Innes, Fernanda Vilas, Marieluise Mammitsch and Chris Hughes); **Switzerland:** Sauber (Peter Sauber, Hans-Peter Brack and Ilka Wendlandt); **USA:** ChampCar; Daytona International Speedway; Indianapolis Motor Speedway; NASCAR; Roger Penske.

Publisher's Acknowledgements

The Publisher of Autocourse would like to add his sincere thanks to all of the above as well as the entire motorsport community and the motorsport enthusiasts and fans who have supported Autocourse in whatever shape or form throughout the years, without that support and passion our title would not be here today, thank you.
There are also a number of key people who have supported us and have been instrumental in making our first year as publishers a success. Simon Arkless, Suzanne Arnold, Simon Arron, Norman Barker, Henry Beaudette, Patrick Behar, Julian Bigg, Herbie Blash, Mark Blundell, Lyndon Bredenkamp, Mike Brown, Martin Brundle, Bob Constanduros, Rosanne Davis, Adrian Dean Stuart Dent, Bernie Ecclestone, Mike Fairholme, Angus Fleming, Maurice Hamilton, David Hayhoe, Alan Henry, Jeremy Lincoln, Pasquale Lattuneddu, Craig Llewellyn, Andy Marlor, Peter McLaren, Max Mosley, James Moy, Jo Nolan, Martin Nolan, James Reader, Nick Rose, Matt Salisbury, Wendy Salisbury, Michael Scott, Martin Sharp, Jeremy Shaw, Steve Small, Sir Jackie Stewart, Andy Stobart, David Tremayne, David Webb, Mike Weston, Martin Whitaker, Charlie Whiting, Rob Wilkins, David (DKW) Williams, Jerry Williams, Jo Wright and last but certainly not least Alex Wiliams, Ellie Williams, Jenny Williams, Jessie Williams and Lucy Williams, I salute and thank you all!

Photographs published in AUTOCOURSE 2005–2006 have been contributed by:

Chief photographer: James Moy of crash.net; *Chief contributing photographers:* Bryn Williams, Mike Weston and Rainer Ehrhardt of crash.net; Russell Batchelor, Emily Davenport and Marco Miltenberg of XPB.cc; Paul-Henri Cahier; Laurent Charniaux, Jean-François Galeron and Jad Sherif of World Racing Images; Jakob Ebrey Motorsport Images; Peter van Egmond; Lukas Gorys; GP2 Media Services; LAT Photographic; (Phil Abbott, Brad Bernstein, Richard Dole, Gregg Feistman, Mark Horsburgh, Michael Kim, Mike Levitt, Lesley-Ann Miller, Robert LeSieur, Dan Streck, Denis L Tanney); Peter Nygaard/GP Photo; Photo 4; Racepictures.com.

editor
ALAN HENRY

publisher
BRYN WILLIAMS

text editor
SUZANNE ARNOLD

results and statistics
DAVID HAYHOE
EMMA HENRY

sales promotion
STUART DENT

art editor
STEVE SMALL

design and production
ROSANNE DAVIS
MIKE WESTON

office manager
WENDY SALISBURY

chief photographer
JAMES MOY

chief contributing photographers
RUSSELL BATCHELOR
PAUL-HENRI CAHIER
LAURENT CHARNIAUX
EMILY DAVENPORT
PETER VAN EGMOND
JEAN-FRANÇOIS GALERON
LUKAS GORYS
MARCO MILTENBERG
PETER NYGAARD
JAD SHERIF
BRYN WILLIAMS

f1 illustrations
ADRIAN DEAN
f1artwork@blueyonder.co.uk

www.autocourse.com

FOREWORD

by FERNANDO ALONSO

'World champion.' I have been working for 20 years to hear those words. But each time I do, it reminds me that this title was not about me. It was a thank-you to my family and friends for their support. It was for my Renault team. We have grown up together and this year the team gave me a car with the speed and reliability to win. And it was for the fans.

It helps to know you are not racing alone and I hope their support will never stop. We had a plan for 2005. If a driver finishes on the podium at every race, it is hard to beat him. So we took the right risks and I got 15 podiums. There was a fantastic battle with Kimi Räikkönen and McLaren. And at the last grand prix, the proof that Renault had the speed. It was a complete year and I am very proud to be my country's first world champion.

Now, we have to focus on 2006. Becoming world champion is one thing; staying world champion is another. There is a mountain to climb between now and then. I can't wait!

Alonso

WELCOME TO THE HOME OF
MOTOR SPORT IN THE MIDDLE EAST

Bahrain International Circuit

To be part of the non-stop action,

Bahrain International Circuit is not just the No. 1 FIA certified track in the Middle East. It's a livewire of action and activity with a calendar year packed with races including the Gulf Air Bahrain Grand Prix, FIA International Drag Racing Festival, FIA GT Final, Formula BMW World Final, GP 2, V8 Supercar Championship Series and more. Are you ready for the non-stop action?

call +973 17 45 0000 or visit www.bahraingp.com

CHANGING THE GUARD
by ALAN HENRY

I T was back in 2003, just after Fernando Alonso scored his maiden F1 victory at Budapest, that team principal Flavio Briatore suggested that Renault would probably be ready to mount a world-championship challenge in 2005. A familiar mantra, some concluded – a case of upbeat team boss puts over-optimistic gloss on future potential, talking up the game as much as he could.

But Briatore knew what he was talking about. He could see that his team was maturing in tandem with Alonso's emergent status as one of the very best new drivers of his era. In 2005 the partnership blossomed with perfectly predicted timing and the 24-year-old Spaniard bagged seven out of 19 race victories to become the sport's youngest-ever world champion by the end of what was the longest season in the 56-year history of the official title contest.

Alonso and his team went wheel-to-wheel in a season-long battle for the crown with Kimi Räikkönen and his McLaren-Mercedes MP4-20. The Finn also won seven races. But whereas Alonso's season started steadily and built up a consistently formidable head of steam, Räikkönen's was more explosively unpredictable as McLaren failed to capitalise on its apparent performance edge early in the season and then fumbled a second chance to press home a counter-attack for the title mid-season with a rash of frustrating technical failures which either compromised Kimi's qualifying efforts

or neutralised his winning opportunities.

In many previous circumstances the combination of a driver such as Räikkönen and a team such as McLaren would still have held sway at the head of the points table, but not in a year when Alonso was countering their every move with such a rare blend of speed and consistency. All at McLaren consoled themselves with the notion that Räikkönen had the edge on pure speed, but this was debatable. Alonso ran just as quickly as he needed to clinch the drivers' crown in Brazil and then, with the pressure off, proved that he could certainly match Kimi's pace with two epic performances at Suzuka and Shanghai. Make no mistake, the new world champion certainly had the speed to get the job done at the very highest level.

Either way, the intense rivalry between Renault and McLaren-Mercedes made for an epic season of changing fortunes during which F1's established super team of the past five years was reduced to the role of also-ran. Ferrari and Bridgestone jointly dialled up the wrong number and the result was disastrous, yielding just a single victory for the still amazingly motivated Michael Schumacher in the ill-starred US GP at Indianapolis, where only the six Bridgestone runners took the start after the Michelin teams were obliged to withdraw prior to the start.

In the cool light of day, the Indianapolis débâcle was a thoroughly disreputable episode for the F1 business and Speedway boss Tony George could have been forgiven for telling

the tensions that simmered away beneath the sport's surface. Rivalling *Gone with the Wind* as one of the longest-running sagas in history, Bernie Ecclestone and the banks that controlled his SLEC commercial empire were continually burdened by the threat of a breakaway world championship organised by a posse of five car makers, which established another negotiating group under the banner Grand Prix Manufacturers' Association (GPMA).

This grouping of Renault, BMW, Honda, Toyota and DaimlerChrysler quietly went about the business of evaluating, assessing and developing every commercial and sporting option for the future beyond 2008, when the Concorde Agreement now controlling F1 expires. They want more administrative transparency from the FIA and a bigger, more equitable share of the sport's $800 million-plus annual commercial-rights income, the majority of which currently goes to Ecclestone's companies. The longer this issue remains unresolved, the bigger the potential for two series, given that Ferrari, Midland (formerly Jordan) and the two Red Bull-owned teams — formerly Jaguar and Minardi — seem to have lined up on Ecclestone's side of what is beginning to look like a disturbingly cavernous divide.

Left: Fernando Alonso and Kimi Räikkönen sharing the podium. The pair won 14 of the 17 races in 2005.
Photograph: James Moy/www.crash.net

Below: Energetic debate behind closed doors at Indianapolis between agitated team principals and drivers on race morning in a last-ditch attempt to resolve the apparent deadlock over whether a temporary chicane could enable the race to go ahead with a full field.
Photograph: Paul-Henri Cahier

Bottom: Down but not out. Michael Schumacher took the loss of his crown with the dignity of a great champion.
Photograph: James Moy/www.crash.net

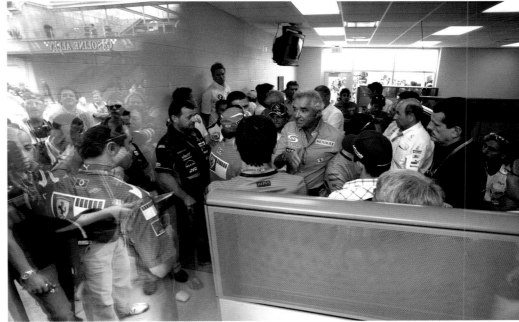

Bernie Ecclestone and his colleagues never to darken his door again. Admittedly, the whole issue of whether or not the Michelin teams competed after Ralf Schumacher's Toyota crashed due to tyre failure in Friday free practice was entirely shaped by legal considerations, but that cut no ice with some outraged spectators, who were heading for their attorneys' offices with the intention of suing the circuit almost before the exhaust notes had been stilled at the end of the race.

Michelin had certainly been lacking in bringing to the race tyres whose performance characteristics were not suited to the banked Turn 13, which leads onto the pit straight. These things happen when you are pushing the envelope of ultimate performance. It was hardly a hanging offence, but the manner in which the FIA pursued and criticised the French tyre maker in the wake of this episode seemed in some peoples' minds wholly out of proportion with the offence committed.

In the event, Michelin picked up the estimated $20-million cost of reimbursing the disappointed spectators and also bought a whole raft of tickets for the 2006 event. But from then on, even though Michelin won the championship with Alonso and Renault, the French tyre maker seemed to be on the back foot when it came to exchanges with the governing body, with the FIA's Max Mosley and Edouard Michelin indulging in progressively more barbed exchanges on various issues.

The Indianapolis issue was the most public manifestation of

Right: The distinctive colours of Sauber will disappear following the Swiss team's purchase by BMW.

Below: Jenson Button's phone bill must have been a hefty one after the British driver negotiated his way out of his Williams contract.
Photographs: James Moy/www.crash.net

Bottom: Dan Wheldon became one of only four British-born drivers to win the Indianapolis 500, but the achievement rated little attention in his native land.
Photograph: Mike Levitt/LAT Photographic

Talking of teams that changed hands, the arrival of Austrian Red Bull drinks billionaire Dietrich Mateschitz and his takeover of the Jaguar squad signalled just what commercial value can still be leveraged from this global sport. It took barely nine months for Mateschitz to decide 'more please' and acquire Minardi as a training ground for fledgling F1 talent. Russian-born Canadian businessman Alex Shnaider took a similarly upbeat, if lower-key, attitude to his takeover of the Jordan squad. Mateschitz and Shnaider were non-motor-industry outsiders investing in the business, but the car makers were not being left out of this acquisitive process by any manner or means. Having decided that the chemistry wasn't right in its partnership with Williams, BMW took a deep breath and decided to go the whole hog, purchasing the Swiss-based Sauber squad as a vehicle for its fully branded long-term ambitions. With Honda similarly taking total ownership of BAR, only DaimlerChrysler was left without 100-percent ownership of an F1 team, although with the 2005 season yielding an impressive tally of ten race wins, it must have been pretty satisfied with its 40-percent stake in McLaren.

If you had to put your finger on the two big disappointments of the 2005 season, they would have to be Williams and BAR Honda. Once BMW decided to opt for a different vision of its F1 future, it's hard to imagine that it was much inclined to develop intensively its V10 engine through to the end of the season, particularly with the development of a 2.4-litre V8 taking priority for 2006.

Similarly, BAR initially got lost aerodynamically and then was the subject of unwelcome attention from an FIA investigation, which led to its exclusion from the San Marino GP and suspension from the next two races for an apparent irregularity in its car's fuel system. Then came Jenson Button's decision that he didn't, after all, want to drive for Williams now that it had lost its BMW engines. He preferred to stay with BAR Honda, the team he had wanted to run away from 12 months earlier. Eventually Button had to pay through the nose for the privilege of not driving a Williams-Cosworth and he will be keeping his fingers crossed that he has made the right call.

Elsewhere on the international scene, there was plenty of colour. Dan Wheldon became only the fourth British-born driver to win the Indy 500, Sébastien Bourdais won a second straight Champ-car crown and, on this side of the Atlantic, former teenage karting team-mates Lewis Hamilton and Nico Rosberg clinched the Euro-F3 and GP2 championships respectively.

In summary, the international motor-sporting scene finished the 2005 season in generally fine fettle with F1 thriving at its very epicentre. Whether the governing body can really offer sufficiently wise long-term stewardship to give it a stable and secure future, with the interests of all its stakeholders properly protected, is one of the more exacting challenges by which Max Mosley – just embarking on another four years in office as the FIA's president – and his legacy to the sport will be judged.

Alan Henry
Tillingham, Essex
November, 2005

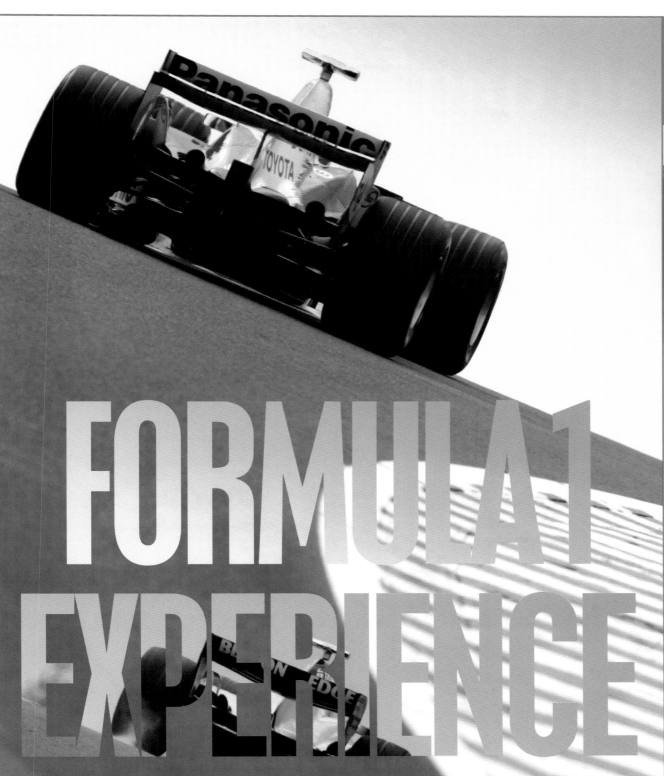

FORMULA 1 EXPERIENCE

Photograph: Peter Nygaard/GP Photo

TOP TEN DRIVERS

Chosen by the editor, taking into account their racing performances
and the equipment at their disposal

1

Date of birth: **29 July 1981**

Team: **Mild Seven Renault F1 Team**

GP starts in 2005: **19 (18 excluding the US GP)**

Championship placing in 2005: **1st**

Wins in 2005: **7**

Poles in 2005: **6**

Points in 2005: **133**

FERNANDO ALONSO

Photograph: James Moy/www.crash.net

FERNANDO ALONSO grew to maturity in 2005, emulating the achievements of previous greats such as Jackie Stewart, Alain Prost and Niki Lauda in the sense that his tactical racing savvy had matured to a level at which it now matched his supreme natural talent. Just 23 years old when the season began, the bright-eyed boy had suddenly grown into a modestly assured young man. That final piece of the jigsaw, the intense gratification generated by winning races, had slipped into place.

Lauda offered the most glowing endorsement of all. 'I have to say that Alonso is extraordinary,' said the retired triple world champion. 'The more pressure he has, the better he drives. I've never seen any driver of that age so completely composed and consistent. Okay, so he made one slip at Montreal [where he hit the wall] but, speaking for myself, I reckon that I would have made many more mistakes if I'd been in that position at that age.

'To be honest, I cannot find a single weakness in Alonso from any viewpoint. He's obviously a huge asset to the Renault team but, more important, a huge asset to the sport as a whole. I think he is perfect.'

Fernando became the youngest title holder in F1 history, claiming the distinction from Brazil's Emerson Fittipaldi, who was three months short of his 26th birthday when he clinched the 1972 championship at the wheel of his Lotus 72. Like Alonso, Fittipaldi was a thrusting young talent who emerged as a front runner over a similarly short period in the limelight.

On the strength of his 2005 efforts, it is difficult to identify a weak point in Alonso's armoury. All his race victories were earned on merit, whether it was through his sheer speed in Bahrain and Malaysia, his composure under intense pressure from Michael Schumacher at Imola or the relentlessness with which he kept hounding the hobbled Kimi Räikkönen at the Nürburgring. He raised the competitive bar to the point where his admittedly talented team-mate Giancarlo Fisichella was struggling to compete and the manner in which he nursed his bald rear Michelins to finish fourth through the unforgiving streets of Monte Carlo underlined the completeness of his rounded talent. His season was nothing less than brilliant.

Photograph: James Moy/www.crash.net

KIMI RÄIKKÖNEN

Date of birth: 17 October 1979

Team: Team McLaren Mercedes

GP starts in 2005: 19
(18 excluding the US GP)

Championship placing in 2005: 2nd

Wins in 2005: 7

Poles in 2005: 5

Points in 2005: 112

Making the decision between Fernando Alonso and Kimi Räikkönen for the number-one slot in this celebration of the 2005 world championship was the closest call for years, because if Alonso was the best driver of the season, then Kimi was the most pulsatingly exciting. His overtaking move on Giancarlo Fisichella going into the final lap of the Japanese GP at Suzuka will be remembered as one of the great moments in the sport's history, one of those heady episodes during which you could be forgiven for thinking you are witnessing the truly impossible.

Nevertheless, Kimi had a wobbly start to the season. He slid off the road at Melbourne, damaging his MP4-20's barge boards, suffered a blameless puncture in Malaysia and made a small, but crucial, slip in qualifying in Bahrain. Off-track, his seemingly boisterous private life also grabbed the headlines in some sections of the purple press to the point that, fleetingly, some observers felt he risked coming off the rails.

Yet the signs for potential on-track domination were there. He was walking away with the San Marino GP at Imola when a driveshaft broke, but he quickly made up for that acute disappointment by scoring decisive back-to-back victories at Barcelona and Monte Carlo.

His real racer's instinct went on public display at the Nürburgring when he pressed on hard regardless of a terrible front-suspension vibration caused by a flat-spotted tyre. The suspension broke going into the last lap – but it *might* have lasted the distance. For a real racer such as Kimi, it was well worth the gamble.

Räikkönen stole a lucky win at Montreal, but when the championship returned to Europe there followed that catalogue of mechanical misfortunes that terminally undermined his title challenge. Practice engine failures at Magny-Cours (bearing), Silverstone (oil-pump drive), Monza (piston) and – later – at Suzuka (connecting rod) all lost him ten places on those respective starting grids. Add to that a hydraulic leak causing his retirement from the lead at Hockenheim and a potential dominant tally of perhaps a dozen or more race wins, and a certain championship was squandered.

McLaren chairman Ron Dennis has suggested that the drivers' championship was lost through early-season problems. One might equally conclude that it slipped away during those frustrating summer months, as the dynamic and imperturbable Räikkönen will surely attest. From his personal perspective the Finn could hardly have done more.

MICHAEL SCHUMACHER

Date of birth: 3 January 1969

Team: Scuderia Ferrari Marlboro

GP starts in 2005: 19

Championship placing in 2005: 3rd

Wins in 2005: 1

Poles in 2005: 1

Points in 2005: 62

FOR the first time in five years, Michael Schumacher's Ferrari does not dominate the dust-jacket of AUTOCOURSE, yet nobody could conceivably have imagined at the start of the season just how far the greatest F1 star of the past decade would fall from his traditional pedestal. Historically, outgoing world champions have demonstrated gently fading form, yet from the touchlines you could have been forgiven for thinking that Michael, the Ferrari F2005 and Ferrari's partners at Bridgestone had conspired to drive over the edge of a precipice.

Yet it was not anywhere near as simple as that. If one accepts the principal that a competitor's real qualities are unmasked in conditions of adversity, 2005 was probably the most impressive single season of Schumacher's entire career. Here he was, statistically the most successful F1 driver of all time, apparently reduced to a walk-on, bit-part role on the stage he had previously regarded as his own private domain. Yet his approach to the business never changed. Each time he strapped himself into the cockpit of his Ferrari F2005 it was as if the very outcome of the title chase depended on that individual race.

How he tried! At Imola he slid off the road in qualifying and spent the opening phase of the race in the midfield ruck, conserving his Bridgestones as the fuel load was consumed. Then he picked up the pace dramatically, failing to win in front of Maranello's passionate fans only when he proved unable to out-fox the shrewd Fernando Alonso, who drove his Renault no quicker than he needed to in order to fend off the Ferrari. He qualified and finished second in Canada, claimed his sole win in the ersatz 'Indy 200', then bounced back to qualify on pole at Budapest, where he finished second ahead of his brother Ralf's Toyota.

If you want a snapshot of the real Michael Schumacher in 2005, watch the in-car coverage from Kimi Räikkönen's McLaren or Alonso's Renault during their stints behind the Ferrari at Suzuka. You witness total commitment and absolute precision from the oldest man on the F1 grid today. The flame of Schumacher's passion for racing clearly still burns with an overwhelming intensity.

JUAN PABLO MONTOYA

IT was the longest engagement in F1 history. Juan Pablo Montoya announced to the BMW Williams team shortly after the 2003 French GP that he would be leaving to join McLaren Mercedes for 2005 with the result that for the following 18 months the popular Colombian occupied a peculiar limbo land full of keen anticipation as to how he would manage his change of high-profile employer.

Coming in to tackle Kimi Räikkönen head-on in Kimi's own personal environment was never going to be easy and Montoya initially made heavy weather of the transition, clumsily finding himself forced to miss Bahrain and Imola after injuring his shoulder in either a fall on a tennis court or an accident on a mountain bike, depending on whether you accepted the official or unofficial explanation of an extremely unfortunate episode.

McLaren took a while to get Montoya's rather volatile temperament under control, but by the time he was sent to the back of the grid as a penalty for brake-testing his old nemesis Ralf Schumacher during free practice in Monaco, the team was starting to make definite progress. His integration into 'the McLaren way' wasn't helped by a strategic fumble on the pit wall at Montreal,

which led to Juan Pablo's disqualification and the win's falling into Räikkönen's lap. Montoya, fit to be tied, lost his cool in a big way and had to be placated with an apology from team chairman Ron Dennis.

Then Montoya caught his stride, having worked tirelessly to dial out the MP4-20's incipient mid-corner understeer with which he'd originally felt so uncomfortable. He won superbly at Silverstone, then spun off at Hockenheim in qualifying, but staged a brilliant come-back to finish second. He hit Tiago Monteiro's Jordan at Istanbul and tangled with Antonio Pizzonia's Williams at Spa, but triumphed superbly at both Monza and Interlagos, beating Kimi into second place at the last-named venue.

Juan Pablo's level of achievement in 2005 remained patchy, but he certainly proved that when he was on form he could deliver as one of the most formidable competitors on the contemporary starting grid. More than that, he arrived at McLaren wanting to learn, wanting to listen and hoping that the environment there could help him become a more rounded and consistent performer. Despite a few uncertain moments, that process looks as though it is beginning to pay off.

4

Date of birth: 20 September 1975

Team: Team McLaren Mercedes

GP starts in 2005: 17 (16 excluding the US GP)

Championship placing in 2005: 4th

Wins in 2005: 3

Poles in 2005: 2

Points: 60

Photograph: James Moy/www.crash.net

5

Date of birth: **14 January 1973**

Team: **Mild Seven Renault F1 Team**

GP starts in 2005: **19**
(18 excluding the US GP)

Championship placing in 2005: **5th**

Wins in 2005: **1**

Poles in 2005: **1**

Points in 2005: **58**

GIANCARLO FISICHELLA left the Sauber squad to rejoin Renault with high hopes. He knew from the outset that he was going to have a pretty good car in the R25, but he also knew that being measured against Fernando Alonso with the same equipment promised to be a pretty daunting experience. How right he was.

The season opened well for Giancarlo with a pole-to-flag victory in the Australian GP at Melbourne. He could have been forgiven for thinking that this was the start of something big in terms of his career progress. But, just as quickly, it all started to unravel for the pleasant Italian: he tangled with Mark Webber's Williams in Malaysia, suffered an engine failure in Bahrain and spun off with suspension failure at Imola. In Barcelona he ran strongly but dropped to fifth at the flag after an unscheduled stop to change the nose section.

Almost impossible to believe, but the man who dominated the opening race of the season had to wait until he finished third at Monza in September before next climbing the steps to the podium.

In Brazil he was beaten into fourth place by a strong-running Michael Schumacher's Ferrari, but his real heartbreak was to follow at Suzuka, where he just wasn't able to match the electrifying pace of Kimi Räikkönen's pursuing McLaren and suffered the public humiliation of being passed by the Finn going into the final lap of the race. Up on the rostrum, he stood between his own team-mate Alonso – who finished third – and Kimi, and what should have been a joyous occasion for Fisichella turned into an uncomfortable defining moment.

No matter how you explained it, Fisichella just should not have allowed a near-20-second advantage to dwindle into such an ignominious defeat. It was clear that the Italian had the talent, but on this occasion he lacked not only the luck but also the pace. He remains firmly contracted to Renault for 2006, during which season he really will be drinking at the last-chance saloon. Fisichella needs to demonstrate that he can rekindle the form that helped him win in Australia, otherwise his long-term future looks uncomfortably bleak.

GIANCARLO **FISICHELLA**

NICK HEIDFELD

Date of birth: 10 May 1977

Team: BMW WilliamsF1 Team

**GP starts in 2005: 14
(13 excluding the US GP)**

Championship placing in 2005: 11th

Wins in 2005: 0

Poles in 2005: 1

Points in 2005: 28

IT used to be the convention in AUTOCOURSE that no driver who failed to compete in all of a season's races would be eligible for inclusion in the Top Ten. This year we obviously could not adhere to that guideline, because it would have involved excluding Juan Pablo Montoya for his two-race absence at the start of the season and also debarred Nick Heidfeld from the list, which would clearly have made no sense at all.

At the start of the season, Williams followed the shoot-out format that had been used in 2000 to decide whether Jenson Button or Bruno Junqueira should be given the vacant seat alongside Ralf Schumacher. This time the contest was between Heidfeld and Antonio Pizzonia, with subliminal pressure being exerted by BMW and the Brazilian fuel company Petrobras, each of which supported one of the two candidates. As in 2000, the choice was almost too close to call, but Frank Williams eventually opted to please BMW – although while Heidfeld turned out to be an impressive choice, his selection didn't prevent the Munich car maker from cutting Williams adrift in favour of purchasing the rival Sauber team as a vehicle for its long-term F1 ambitions.

This was Heidfeld's first spell in a top-line F1 team and he certainly made the opportunity work for him, proving what the McLaren test team, Sauber and Jordan already knew in terms of his capability when it came to tyre selection and chassis set-up. His controlled pace through the streets of Monaco, where he beat team-mate Mark Webber into third place, was an indication of what the quiet young German driver was really capable of delivering and he raised more eyebrows by gaining pole position at the Nürburging, the first German driver using a German engine ever to have qualified at the top of the time sheets in a German round of the F1 world championship.

Heidfeld unfortunately crashed heavily in pre-Italian GP testing at Monza, badly shaking himself up and having to withdraw from the race. His recuperation was further complicated by a bicycle accident at home in Switzerland and he never drove for Williams again, although he'd done enough to earn a contract for BMW covering the 2006, 2007 and 2008 seasons. His future progress will be watched with interest, even though it could be said to be a little late in the day for the agreeable German driver.

7

Date of birth: **13 July 1974**

Team: **PanasonicToyota Racing**

GP starts in 2005: **19 (18 excluding the US GP)**

Championship placing in 2005: **7th**

Wins in 2005: **0**

Poles in 2005: **1**

Points in 2005: **43**

Photograph: James Moy/www.crash.net

JARNO TRULLI

AFTER scoring his maiden grand-prix victory in commanding style in Monaco in 2004, Jarno Trulli switched to Toyota for this season with a huge sense of burgeoning optimism. His recruitment, together with that of Ralf Schumacher, was seen as part of a major programme to raise the team's competitive level to such a point that it could compete consistently at the front of the field.

Jarno duly started the season on a highly promising note. He was on the front row of the grid at Melbourne alongside Giancarlo Fisichella – although he faded to ninth with tyre problems – he finished second in Malaysia to secure the team's first podium finish and then he delivered a repeat performance in Bahrain, raising hopes that the Japanese team's maiden GP victory might be just around the corner.

Yet the Toyota TF105 didn't quite make the hoped-for performance breakthrough, leaving Trulli in the role of regular points scorer and clearly the more convincing performer of the team's two drivers. He had a lucky escape in Canada when, running third, he suffered a brake-disc failure at the one point on the circuit where there was a sufficiently large run-off area to avoid the possibility of a big impact, then hit the headlines again with pole at Indianapolis. In reality, of course, Toyota suspected by that stage that it would not be able to take part in the race and had fuelled the Italian's car with an extremely light load to assist his headline-grabbing efforts.

From that point onwards, although Trulli qualified consistently strongly, he was unable to deliver the race pace necessary to gain a podium finish. Hopes that the revised TF105B would provide more pace came to a disappointing end for him in the Japanese GP at Suzuka when Takuma Sato rammed him out of the race in a quite absurdly ambitious overtaking effort. It effectively ended the season on a depressing note for the popular Italian driver, who had started the year hoping for a string of results that would dramatically enhance his status in the F1 community.

I N 2005 Jenson Button joined Michael Schumacher in having a career apparently in free fall and his commanding run to third place in the previous season's drivers' championship was receding fast in his personal rear-view mirror.

The BAR Honda squad got off to a slow start as it wrestled to get on top of the new 007's aerodynamics and the first few races were a performance disaster. These were followed all too quickly by Jenson's disqualification from the San Marino GP and the team's suspension from Spain and Monaco by the FIA Court of Appeal following the controversy over the configuration of the car's fuel system.

Disregarding whether or not one felt that BAR had come under legitimate scrutiny for this alleged offence, the long-term effects were unsettling for both driver and team. Button crashed out while running strongly at Montreal – a rare slip for a driver who usually demonstrated restraint and consistency – but began to claw things back with fourth in France, fifth at Silverstone, his first podium of the year with third at Hockenheim and then fifth places at Budapest and Istanbul. He posted his second podium finish of the season with another third in the Belgian GP at Spa-Francorchamps.

Off-track, Button's life was complicated by the need to unravel his 2006 contract with the WilliamsF1 team, a partnership he'd fought BAR to embrace only 12 months earlier but from which he now wanted to be liberated in the light of Williams' impending split from BMW. This turned into a protracted dispute, with Williams insisting that he required Jenson to abide by his contract for 2006, while the driver dug in his heels and made it very clear that he would consider sitting out that season on the sidelines unless he was released from his obligation.

This was hardly a state of affairs which could be expected to contribute positively to Button's mental equilibrium but if he allowed it to worry him at the races he concealed it well. Eventually a pragmatic solution was agreed and Jenson bought himself out of the Williams commitment. Let's hope staying with the newly branded Honda squad is worth it all.

Photograph: Russell Batchelor/XPB.cc

JENSON BUTTON

8

Date of birth: **19 January 1980**

Team: **Lucky Strike BAR Honda**

GP starts in 2005: **17 (16 excluding the US GP)**

Championship placing in 2005: **9th**

Wins in 2005: **0**

Poles in 2005: **1**

Points in 2005: **37**

9 DAVID COULTHARD

Date of birth: 27 March 1971

Team: Red Bull Racing

GP starts in 2005: 19
(18 excluding the US GP)

Championship placing in 2005: 12th

Wins in 2005: 0

Poles in 2005: 0

Points in 2005: 24

AFTER nine fruitful years with the McLaren Mercedes squad, David Coulthard found himself considering the need for gainful employment elsewhere for the 2005 season. Some observers felt that it would be wise to call it a day and retire to some off-track ambassadorial role that would enable him to maintain his links with the F1 pit lane while at the same time keeping his reputation intact.

Yet David saw the challenge ahead in more simply drawn terms. He loved driving, felt that he was as fit and motivated as ever he was and simply wasn't ready to hang up his helmet at the relatively early age of 33. Rightly, DC judged that the qualities he had showcased during his time at McLaren might be well employed elsewhere. He tried to get into the BMW Williams squad, but there was no deal available when it came to it. Then Red Bull shrewdly purchased the Jaguar F1 team as a going concern and a tailor-made opportunity suddenly opened out ahead of him.

Red Bull inherited the team's ongoing development programme and Coulthard was just the man to give it focus, direction and motivation. Vaulting from fifth on the grid to fourth ahead of Mark Webber's Williams on the run to the first corner at Melbourne gave the team a welcome early boost to its morale, although it quite outstripped the true comparative merits of the results achieved. That was followed by sixth in Malaysia and eighth in Bahrain, which gave the team an early momentum.

Coulthard struggled a little mid-season. The Cosworth V10 did not quite have the power to carry the necessary downforce and it was always tricky to work out the most comfortable handling balance as a result. But David still drove some really good races, most notably at the Nürburgring where, after a great first lap, he might have taken third place had it not been for a drive-through penalty and at Hockenheim, where he was a fine seventh. Coulthard was certainly right not to have retired.

Felipe Massa's good connections would eventually earn him a somewhat unexpected bonus for 2006 in the form of a contract to succeed Rubens Barrichello as Michael Schumacher's team-mate in the Ferrari squad. His credentials were earned, at least in part, during his spell as Ferrari test driver in 2003, but his past two seasons have been spent with Sauber, where he has compared very favourably with his team-mates during that period, respectively Giancarlo Fisichella and Jacques Villeneuve.

In 2005 he outqualified the Canadian driver 13–6, scoring his first points in Bahrain and then moving ahead to his personal best of the season, storming through to fourth at Montreal from 11th on the grid after fending off Mark Webber's Williams, which pressured him pretty closely for much of the race. During his second stint at Sauber, Massa developed into a consistent and assured performer, polishing off the rough edges of his talent to the point where Ferrari decided that it was worth the gamble to promote him to his next and most exacting role.

During the course of the season, Massa featured regularly on the fringes of the top ten when it came to the starting order, but rarely managed to parlay these grid positions into points-scoring race finishes. Even so, he came to be very highly regarded by Peter Sauber and his workforce. It remains to be seen whether the pleasant Brazilian driver has what it takes to climb the next rung of the ladder.

FELIPE MASSA

10

Date of birth: **25 April 1981**

Team: **Sauber Petronas**

GP starts in 2005: **19 (18 excluding the US GP)**

Championship placing in 2005: **13th**

Wins in 2005: **0**

Poles in 2005: **0**

Points in 2005: **11**

INTERVIEW WITH BERNIE ECCLESTONE
LITTLE BIG MAN
by NIGEL ROEBUCK – Grand Prix Editor, Autosport

NO question about it, the débâcle of the year was the six-car farce that passed for the US Grand Prix at Indianapolis. And once the recriminations had begun to subside, perhaps the most sobering fact was that here had been a problem – a crisis – that Bernie Ecclestone had not been able to resolve.

That, for many, was the clearest signal – if any were needed – that these are indeed changing days in F1. Time was when Ecclestone truly was lord of all he surveyed, when a word from him was all it took to put things to rights but now, while he remains the major power-broker in F1, his influence is no longer absolute and he knows it. 'In the good old days I'd have sorted it out,' he commented after Indy. So what had changed?

'Er... democracy! We had this problem with the Michelin tyres at Indy and I believe that the Michelin runners thought the FIA would back down and put a chicane in, before the quick turn that was causing the problem. I knew they never would – and, actually, I think it's lucky that didn't happen, because I don't think those tyres would have lasted the race anyway.

'Then you had the FIA's position – not because it was Ferrari – that someone [Bridgestone] had come with a tyre suitable for that circuit and someone else [Michelin] hadn't. Why should you change the circuit for somebody who's basically cocked it up?'

What Ecclestone says is unarguable but doesn't get around the fact that the race was ruined and the fans – in a massive market, still needing to be 'sold' on F1 – cheated. What, in 'the old days', would he have done to rescue the situation?

'I'd simply have said, "Why don't we tell Michelin that it has not done a very good job and the consequence is that we're in trouble – we've got 150,000 people out there who are going to be super-upset? We're in the entertainment business, as well as a sport. Why don't we ask Bridgestone if it will supply everyone? Okay, for sure, that'll put the Michelin teams at a disadvantage, because their cars obviously aren't set up for Bridgestones – but that's how it is." Whatever else, we couldn't cancel the race – it had been scheduled and practice and qualifying had taken place.'

As it was, Bernie concedes that he never discussed with Bridgestone the possibility of supplying all 20 cars. 'No, I didn't – because the teams wouldn't have wanted to hear about it. The Michelin runners were positive – almost up to the time of the start – that there was going to be a chicane. They thought, "We hold out and they'll put one in."'

That was never going to happen, according to Ecclestone, not least because this was America, the land of litigation. 'Think of the person who'd have been responsible for it – assume it was the safety delegate. Supposing he'd put a chicane in and then there'd been an accident there and someone got killed, or terminally injured. For sure, in America, that guy would have been six years lying on a bed somewhere, on a life-support machine, or whatever. So, nobody was going to say it was a good idea...

'I went to see the organisers and stewards and so on, but in the old days I'd have said to the guys, "Right, we're here and we've got to get this bloody race on. We've got a tyre problem –

Bernie always thought it unrealistic to expect any government help for Silverstone. 'Jackie was silly. He went on and on about how his close friend Tony Blair was going to supply all the money and I said, "Forget it – it will not happen. He'll find a bloody fortune for the Olympics – which are going to cost the country Christ knows what, anyway – but for something like this, you're not going to get a dollar from him."'

In the end, though, there was a British Grand Prix in 2005 and it will remain on the schedule for at least a while. 'I'd have been surprised,' says Ecclestone, 'if it hadn't been resolved in the short term, but that's all it is. There's a contract for five years, but I've told them, "If we still haven't got a circuit comparable with other European circuits, that's the end of it." It's a source of embarrassment – if they bought a bit of paint and tidied things up, it wouldn't hurt.

'The trouble is that Silverstone is run by a club and you can't have things run by clubs – particularly a 'gentlemen's club' that's devoid of gentlemen. I believe that what Jackie was trying

Left inset: Despite winning on-track, Pierre Dupasquier and Michelin had a troubled season embroiled with the authorities.
Photograph: Peter Nygaard/GP Photo

Below left inset: Ecclestone and his close ally Renault boss Flavio Briatore discussing their options during the shambolic US Grand Prix weekend.
Photograph: Paul-Henri Cahier

Bottom left inset: Bernie ploughing a furrow through the throng of photographers and journalists at Indy.
Photograph: James Moy/www.crash.net

sorry, but that's how it is. Let's try and get Bridgestone to supply everyone." In the days of Colin Chapman [Lotus], Teddy Mayer [McLaren] and all that lot, I'd have been able to do it, no problem. They didn't have any egos. And d'you know why they didn't have any egos? Because they had ability.'

For some months afterwards there was considerable doubt over whether another grand prix would be held at Indianapolis, but in September its date on the 2006 calendar was confirmed.

Silverstone, too, is on it, but for an endless time it seemed that the future of the British Grand Prix was in jeopardy and many believed a major stumbling-block was the 'difficult' personal relationship between Ecclestone and the president of the British Racing Drivers' Club, Jackie Stewart. Bernie said not.

'No, no, no. I'd been embarrassed about Silverstone for years. This is England and people more or less believe F1 is English. There'd be people saying they were interested in doing something and they were going to a race at Silverstone, to have a look. I'd say, "No, for now, why don't you go to Barcelona or the Nürburgring or somewhere? We're going to change Silverstone." But nothing happens – it never gets changed.

'Look at Turkey. It's supposed to be a third-world country, but I got it to spend the money – and it's probably now the best circuit in the world. Silverstone, though… They could do as they liked and their attitude is such that they don't lead you to believe they give a damn, anyway. I suppose if Spa wasn't Spa, we'd complain about it, wouldn't we? But it is Spa – a race circuit, rather than a Scalextric track.'

to do was genuine – and he was trying to do it for British motor sport. But look at the stick he got for doing it and not achieving it. People tried to vote him out – but he did go forward and try to do something.'

Aspects of the calendar are always going to cause controversy, not least because, as new countries host grands prix, other races must necessarily be shed. In 2005, there were 19 – including six, highly unpopular, back-to-back pairings – and many felt that was two or three too many. Time was when Ecclestone said he would never put on more than 16.

'I know – I'm a liar! No, it's not that I've changed my mind as much as a set of circumstances that have made that happen. There's been this big push to keep races in which we can run with tobacco branding. According to the law in Italy, for example, we can run branded there – so it means that we keep two races. Same in Germany. So we've got races that maybe we wouldn't have had otherwise.'

New grands prix on the horizon include Russian, South African and Mexican races, but they cannot be accommodated unless other events fall by the wayside. 'It's a bit of a strain on the teams,' acknowledges Bernie, 'to run all these races – especially the back-to-backs that we have to put together.

'On the other hand, these new areas are good for sponsors. If I say to them, "Would you get another sponsor because we have two races in Italy and Germany?" the answer is probably no – one's enough. So we ought to lose one Italian and one German, but realistically that would be difficult at the moment

Above: BRDC president Jackie Stewart's hopes of government help for the British GP were not supported by Ecclestone.

Top: Ecclestone wants Silverstone to be one of Europe's best circuits within years.
Photographs: James Moy/www.crash.net

Above: Ecclestone and FIA president Max Mosley have been kindred spirits for more than 30 years and the two most influential power-brokers on the F1 scene for much of that time.

Photograph: James Moy/www.crash.net

and I don't have the balls to put any more in there until that happens. In 2006 we'll have 19 races again, but after that we'll probably finish up with 18.'

Politically, F1 has endured a nightmare of a year, the animosity between the teams (save Ferrari) and Max Mosley, FIA president, reaching savage levels at times, although it was diluted to a point towards the end of the season. The spectre of a breakaway championship, from 2008, continues to loom.

'Every time,' says Ecclestone, 'the Concorde Agreement [by which F1 is run] comes up for renegotiation, we get all this trouble – they want more money, or whatever, more something.

'The Concorde Agreement has always been brought in by Ferrari, the FIA and myself – the first time, it was Mr Ferrari, [Jean-Marie] Balestre and me. And we followed the same procedure this time. We invited other people to sign, which some did and one or two others – as in the past – decided they wouldn't unless they got whatever it was they wanted. I'm not quite sure what they want, because they've never said, but…

'So this is commercial. Then we get to the sporting and technical regulations. The endless talks with the team owners drive you nuts – but this is what happens with democracy! You sit ten competitive people down, from different teams, and they all want to achieve the same thing – to win. You ask them to find a way to solve a problem and they're all thinking, "What's good for me and bad for the others?" You can't get them to agree to anything, because it doesn't suit them – and they're right, of course. But it's much worse than it used to be because the technical regulations are much more complicated and people invented things they don't want to un-invent. You need a dictator, really.

'In Monaco this year everyone agreed we had to find ways of reducing costs and it was more or less agreed that the right way to go about it, for a start, was to reduce the power – and that it was necessary, anyway, for safety.'

Did Bernie agree with that?

'No. But the engineers were asked, "What's the best way to reduce speeds?" and they said, "Reduce the power." So people agreed and then didn't agree and then wished they had agreed, or wished they hadn't. It went on and on and on. Then there were all the other things, to do with reducing the costs.

'When you think that today these people's gear ratios last for

400 km [250 miles]… it's a bit cranky, really, isn't it? You take one of those gearboxes to bits and it's like a Swiss watch. But people sitting in the grandstand haven't got the slightest idea about that – and if they had, they wouldn't care. Probably, if you asked them, "Do the cars have automatic or manual gearboxes?" most of them wouldn't know. If you asked them about most things, they wouldn't know – all they know is that, at the moment, the racing isn't very good.

'Actually, it's been good this year – but, prior to that, it wasn't, because there was only one super-competitive team. For several years Ferrari's cars were so good that the only person who could beat Michael Schumacher was someone else in a Ferrari and when that person wasn't allowed to beat him – and, worse than that, was riding shotgun in case somebody could get near him – people didn't have the respect for Michael that perhaps they should have done. I doubt that anyone would have beaten him, in equal cars, but we'll never know, will we?

'So Ferrari dominated everything, but now you've two or three teams that are up there together and that's good. Now what we have to do is save these people from spending astronomical amounts of money to be competitive.'

In the opinions of a growing number of people, the best way to cut costs would be to eliminate much of the sort of technology which drains resources but adds nothing – quite the opposite, in fact – to the fans' enjoyment of their sport.

Ecclestone agrees. 'For a start, that's why the teams have such massive wage bills – and why they've got a vested interest in keeping all this stuff. Really, what you need to do is sit all the aerodynamicists down and say, "We want you to find a way of doing things – so we can get rid of you!" In other words, find a way for us not to need you any more. Then you do the same with the electronics guys. Of course, the teams don't like getting rid of people and nor do we, but it's a fact of life. These things happen.

'I think, for example, we must have a one-tyre-manufacturer rule – if we don't, we're going to be in plenty of trouble. It's important to reduce the necessity for so much testing – most of the teams are testing Christ knows how much and that takes a big chunk out of their budgets. But if you had to reduce, say, a workforce of 1,000 to 300… that's not easy, is it?

'As for the 2.4-litre V8, I'm not in favour of a reduction in the horsepower – and yet, if you think, "When was F1 bloody good?" probably you answer, "When the horsepower was about 500." So, if we have 750 next year, is that terrible? But if we're going to have a 750-horsepower car, I'd like to see the weight limit reduced, I must say. Instead of sticking 90 kilos of ballast underneath, let's reduce the overall weight of the car.

'I'd also like to see smaller brakes – or less efficient brakes. And stop them putting on all these horrible-looking bits and pieces they stick on every day – so a car can be tucked in behind another through a corner.

'Look at the GP2 cars: they can race like F1 cars used to. With the F1 cars, as they've been developed, it's impossible to do that – if you really get behind someone, you lose your downforce.'

When the question of reducing horsepower first came up, Ecclestone suggested to Mosley that this should be achieved by reducing revs, rather than engine capacity, but the idea came to nought. 'Nobody wanted to do it – BMW, in particular, said no, because its technology would go out of the window. And in its case, and probably some others, that was right.

'Eventually we'll probably end up limiting the revs on the 2.4, because otherwise they're going to be revving like crazy, with people spending a fortune to get another seven horsepower. So we haven't really achieved anything – except, probably, putting the cost of engines up.'

Mosley has often spoken of his wish to get rid of traction control and other driver aids, but says the manufacturers won't accept a standard electronic control unit (ECU), which would be required. Does Ecclestone really believe that, if a standard ECU were imposed, the manufacturers would disappear?

'Well, they'll disappear when it suits them, anyway. They always have and they always will. When we had our original bust-up with them, at the Concorde Agreement signing, they said they couldn't sign for more than two years. Then they announced they were going to have their own series. I said, "Well, let's assume that all happens. Then, in two years you all go – what happens then?" For the teams themselves, F1 is their business – they have to stay in it. But the manufacturers will go when it suits them.'

If there are aspects of today's F1 cars that are not to Bernie's taste, he is rightly gratified that they are so much safer than they were. 'If you said to me today that I'd got to have an accident in a vehicle and I could choose it, I'd choose an F1 car.

'I think that, in the end, people like to see accidents but they don't like to see anyone hurt. Remember when [Nigel] Mansell had accidents? He'd get out of the car, limping, holding his arm or whatever – and then he'd forget and wave to the crowd with the wrong one! The public loved all that. There are no actors around today, are there? I mean, even if Nigel had never got a world championship, he certainly should have had an Oscar.'

Ecclestone remains apparently indefatigable, unaffected, he says, by the major heart surgery he underwent some years ago. 'They told me to stay at home for three months but I was in the office in ten days. It's not that I'm brave or anything like that; I just couldn't see the necessity of doing anything else. I never thought about it – and I don't think about it, although I'm a little bit more careful about what I eat. If I'd done that before, I wouldn't have had the problem in the first place. All that bread and dripping, in the good old days, when I was a kid…

'Do I still get the same buzz from the business? Absolutely. Maybe some of the guys today are more difficult to deal with than they were – but maybe I am, as well. We're all getting older, after all. And the one good thing about getting older – I'm 75 – is that you become more courageous. I mean, whatever I do, how much can I be punished? I haven't got that long to go!'

Below left: Although it still plays an important role in funding F1, the sport's reliance on cigarette sponsorship is gradually dwindling.

Below centre: Team owners such as Minardi's Paul Stoddart fought their own corners within the complex Concorde Agreement negotiations.

Below: F1 has embraced important countries such as China in developing the world championship.

Bottom: With costs ever escalating, testing has become a massive issue. David Coulthard is shown pounding around Barcelona in front of empty stands.
Photographs: James Moy/www.crash.net

ALONSO, THE

MAGICIAN WHO RULES IN F1

by PEDRO FERMÍN FLORES

On the podium after winning the title in
Brazil. Fernando Alonso took an early grip
on the championship and never relinquished it.
Photograph: Russell Batchelor/XPB.cc

SINCE he was a child, Fernando Alonso has had a clear target: to succeed and to be number one. At the age of three when he got his first go-kart, built by his father José Luís, he already used to raise his fingers, pointing to the sky to indicate imaginary victories in front of powerful rivals. Two years later, when he started to compete, he always had to win. At the end of a race, he always jumped out of his small machine to celebrate a victory, although often those wins were pure illusion and the innocent imaginings of a five-year-old child who competed against children quite a bit older than himself. He has carried along this passion along all these years to satisfy his life's ambition: to become F1 world champion.

There are many aspects of Fernando that we will never be able to know or analyse because of the privacy he always wishes to protect. Yet there are some aspects that he has no problem sharing with the people around him. Photography is one of his hobbies and, whenever he can, he immortalises anything that gets in front of his camera's lens.

He does not normally show his photos to many people, but you can be sure that if one day he decides to show them, we will see many amazing images obtained from the point of view of somebody who lives, daily, in front of thousands of flash lights and fish-eye lenses.

Something that he does happily show is his taste for tricks. Mainly card tricks or close-up magic tricks, which he buys anywhere in the world and then adapts with his personal touch before showing them publicly.

His grandmother Luisa is his great confidante. She is the protagonist in an anecdote about his first F1 win, in Hungary in 2003. She explains how Fernando, when leaving home, had told her, 'I'm going to win the next race, but don't tell anybody.'

The newly crowned king of F1 has gone around the globe many times since the end of 1999 when, with a fresh Formula Nissan championship title in his pocket, he had the chance to test an F1 car at Jerez, Spain. It was a modest Minardi and he did it, in heavy rain, as a prize for his recent title. On the pit wall of the Italian team, the then sporting manager Cesare Fiorio couldn't believe what he was seeing on the stopwatch and told Giancarlo Minardi that the Spaniard was much faster than expected.

At that time, the cost of Alonso's racing was around $500,000 and a thirsty Flavio Briatore – now Renault team principal – put this money on the table to beat an offer from Ferrari. Now, Alonso is worth his own weight in gold. His contract with Renault is worth much more than that sum from 1999 and sponsors are queuing to fill every little spot on his racing overalls or his cap.

Fernando has the ability to make appear easy what at first sight seems impossible. At his first grand prix, the 2001 Australian GP at Melbourne, he said what he thought of the F1 circus. 'It is nothing special,' he insisted. 'To me it is another test in which I have to set the car up and then do my best. It doesn't matter whether it is an F1 single-seater or a go-kart or any other car. The work is the same and when I go onto the track I do it always with the same thing in mind: to win.'

Now, five years after his début race (in which he drove a Minardi finished by the Italian mechanics just a few hours prior to the Friday free practice), this anecdote is only one of the thousands that the lad from Asturias has left behind him on his way to making history and becoming the youngest-ever F1 world champion. 'Of course I am happy. It is a dream I have always had since a child and that I have made real, finally. But I am still the same person and every time I put on

**Left: Alonso withstood immense pressure
to defeat Michael Schumacher at Imola.**
Photograph: Lukas Gorys

**Below: Fernando, every inch the
modern-day F1 star.**
Photograph: Jean-François Galeron

Above: Alonso crossing the finishing line at Shanghai to clinch the constructors' world championship for Renault.
Photograph: Bryn Williams/www.crash.net

my gloves and helmet, the only purpose I have is to win.'

To Fernando, it does not matter that his name shines among the most outstanding records of F1 history. What matters to him is to keep winning races. 'I do not race thinking of statistics,' he says. 'I race thinking about my rivals and how to beat them. This year, the duel between Kimi [Räikkönen] and me has been very nice. We respect each other a lot, on and off the track, despite what has been said by some people. I know him since long ago when we both were in karting and then we already had very exciting fights.'

Another driver with whom he maintains a special relationship is the deposed champion, Michael Schumacher, who was one of the first to embrace Alonso affectionately when the Spaniard celebrated the title in parc fermé at Interlagos. 'Schumi is a great driver and he can't be ruled out for the future even if this year he has not had any luck,' Alonso says. 'He has not forgotten how to win, but circumstances were against him. For instance, in San Marino he gave me a hard time on the last laps and it was quite hard to hold his pressure.'

The almost beardless teenager who appeared discreetly in the F1 paddock in 2001 is now the leader followed by almost everybody. 'Of course I have fond memories from my time at Minardi,' he smiles. 'Such as the first Friday free practice in Melbourne, when I left the pit and I nearly crashed into the back of [Heinz-Harald] Frentzen's car. He had stopped at the red light at the end of the pit lane and I did not remember which button I had to push to put the car in neutral.'

At those early grands prix with the Italian team, Fernando learned quickly what it meant to compete at the highest level. 'It was a very intense year; everything was new to me but the welcome at Minardi was fantastic,' he remembers. 'All was so familiar that we even travelled to the nearest races by road from

Faenza [in Italy, where Minardi is based]. We travelled smoothly in a convoy of vans, one behind the other. Then, later, Paul [Stoddart – team boss] thought it was a better idea to take all of us in one of his planes and we had always a great time.'

The departure from this team was not an easy move. Many people did not understand why Alonso agreed to spend a year without competing – despite offers – to be Renault test-driver in 2002. 'All was planned from the moment I signed the contract with Renault and I was loaned to Minardi,' he says.

'At one stage it was a possibility to stay one more year with Giancarlo or to go to another team, but in the end we did what had been planned at the beginning. I spent all season working closely with the engineers at Enstone [in England, where Renault's factory is]. I decided to move to Oxford to be closer to the factory to get the most of it. Every day I used to take my car and go to the factory to see how they were building the cars for [Jenson] Button and [Jarno] Trulli to learn as much as I could.'

This effort has paid off and Fernando now works alongside many of those mechanics and engineers whom he used to visit day after day back in 2002. 'In the team, we are as one,' he says. 'The success is shared by all of us, from the first person to the last one, although in the end it's me who's got the steering wheel in my hands.'

The announcement that Fernando Alonso would take Jenson Button's seat made for an uncomfortable situation. 'That day at Magny-Cours, all was ready for the announcement and the Renault managers told me that the best thing to do would be for me to come back home before the press conference that was scheduled for later that afternoon.

'So I took the car and came back without seeing all the media fuss when it was confirmed that Jenson would not stay and that I was the chosen driver to take his place in 2003.'

The road to success has involved occasional complicated and difficult moments. 'Maybe the accident in Brazil in 2003 was the worst of them all,' he says of his race-ending collision with the debris left by another accident. 'I remember how, that night, at the hospital the nurses were scared because when I sleep my pulse goes down quite a lot and all the alarms started to blast. I was all right but they didn't know.'

The person who spends the most time with the new world champion is Flavio Briatore, Alonso's manager and mentor since the day Flavio invited ex-racer Adrian Campos and Fernando for dinner at his London home, back in 2000.

'I met Flavio after winning the Open Nissan series,' Alonso says. 'Since then we have followed the same road and I am very grateful to him. Now our relationship is much warmer because I have more confidence in him. I have taught him to play cards and he and my physiotherapist, Eduardo, normally lose against Fisico [team-mate Giancarlo Fisichella] and me.'

Alonso has one more year contracted with Renault, during which time he will enjoy the champion's number one on the car and will consider the offers that are already starting to arrive.

'I have agreed to stay at Renault because I have always believed in this project that started in 2000, when the team signed me,' he says. 'All forecasts have been fulfilled and the team has clinched the manufacturers' world championship as well, which was the target set by Renault when it decided to come back into F1.

'Now we have one more year to stay fighting together and, in my case, to wait for new projects that may arrive. I will choose the one that I will consider the most positive one for my future.'

It really has been a dream year with all that Alonso has achieved on and off the track – including receiving Spain's prestigious Prince of Asturias award for sports.

'It has all been marvellous,' he reflects. 'I will always have near to my heart what I experienced this year. It has been very moving to share with all the fans a season so successful, in which millions of Spanish followers have supported me strongly. Every time I sat in the car I knew they were by me to push me. They are known everywhere as *marea azul* [blue tide] and I really expect they will be always there to support me.'

Left: Seven up. Fernando indicating his seventh win of the season.

Below left: A job well done. Alonso and Briatore shared the podium at Shanghai.
Photographs: Bryn Williams/www.crash.net

Below: Alonso's success has created a whole new fan-base for F1.
Photograph: James Moy/www.crash.net

Above: the first floor of the spectacular Red Bull 'Energy station', which made its first appearance in the paddock at Imola.

Right: Christian Klien's career has been nurtured by Red Bull.

Main photo: David Coulthard brought all his skill, experience and professionalism to bear in the team's maiden year.

Below: A striking image already ingrained on the F1 scene.

Bottom (left to right): Red Bull girls brightened up the paddock; the motor home floating in the harbour at Monaco; team owner Dietrich Mateschitz.

Photographs: James Moy/www.crash.net

Red Bull racing
FORMULA ONE TEAM

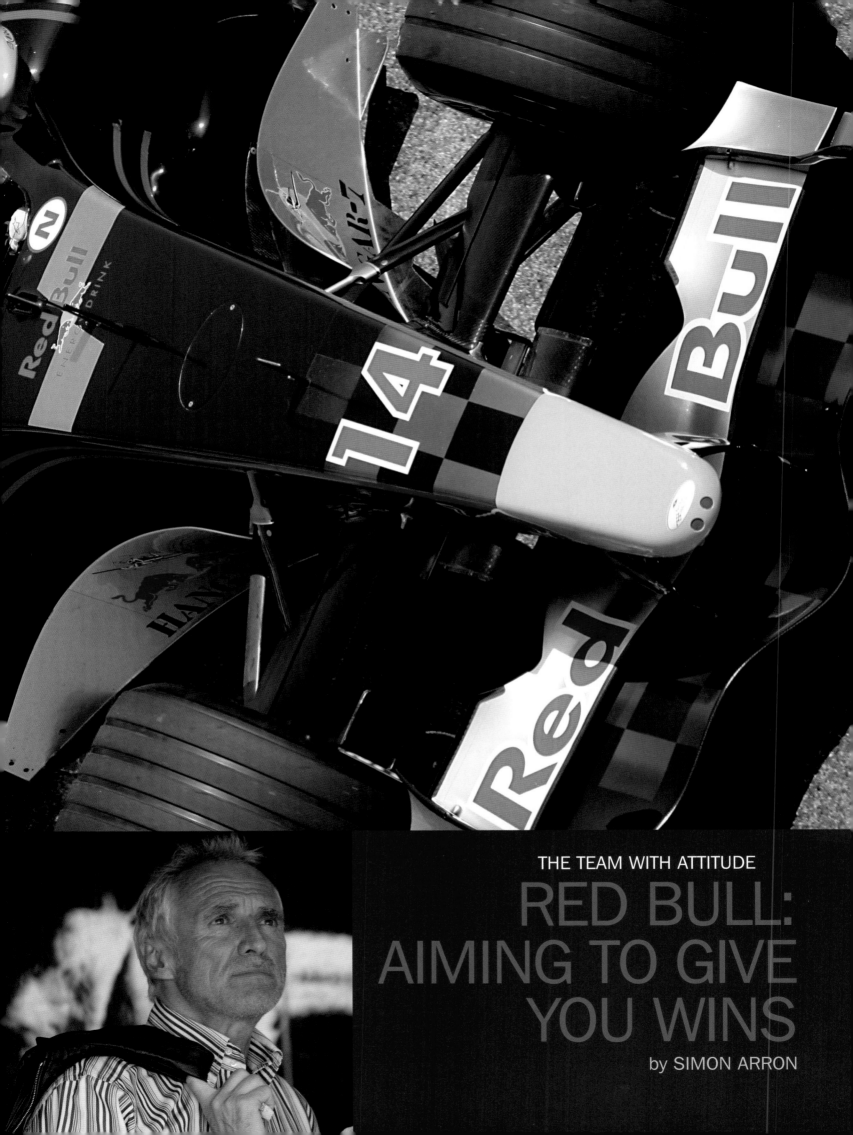

THE TEAM WITH ATTITUDE

RED BULL:
AIMING TO GIVE
YOU WINS

by SIMON ARRON

ALBERT PARK, Melbourne, Australia, 6 March, 2005. David Coulthard sprints from fifth to third at the first corner and spends the balance of the afternoon underlining the fact that F1 newcomer Red Bull Racing's brisk pre-season test pace has been no marketing-driven deceit. In his first grand prix at the wheel of anything other than an acknowledged top-line car, the Scot finishes fourth – as good as anything he managed with McLaren in 2004.

The paddock, Imola, Italy, 21 April. Peter Sauber pauses for a moment while hosting his team's media dinner. Storms are forecast and the rain is clearly gathering momentum. 'Is that thunder?' he asks as the clamour outside intensifies. No, he's told, that's just a party in the Red Bull motorhome. Towering above other paddock retreats, the imposing, three-tier structure renders many of its neighbours obsolete at a stroke. In addition to the usual wining and dining facilities, it features a dance floor, a choice of coloured lighting in the showers, bar-football tables and 48 plasma TV screens, including one in each bathroom.

The team may have started the campaign with little more than a reworked Jaguar sprayed in blue (something it evolved significantly during the next few months), but Red Bull Racing's first season as an entrant in its own right – rather than a high-profile sponsor, as it was for ten years – created ripples both on and off the track. It marked an extraordinary turnaround for

what used to be the forlorn, Ford-owned team that scraped just ten points from the previous campaign's 18 grands prix. Red Bull managed more than that within two races.

Jaguar had been plodding along for five largely unremarkable seasons by the time parent company Ford announced its wholesale withdrawal from F1 – along with the sale of engine-building subsidiary Cosworth – in September 2004. For the next two months, the future of its team's 300-plus staff hung in the balance, but by mid-November, shortly before the closure deadline, wealthy Austrian businessman Dietrich Mateschitz – Red Bull's founder – stepped in with a rescue package.

Mateschitz, who is rated 406th on the Forbes rich list, unlocked the key to his fortune in the early 1980s while on a trip to the Far East. Reading a magazine feature, he noticed that some of the highest-tax-payers in Asia produced a range of syrups – known as tonic drinks – that were sold over the counter at pharmacies. That set him wondering about the possibility of selling such a product in a more functional manner outside Asia. He met the manufacturer of a tonic known as Krating Daeng – Thai for Red Bull – and set up a deal to produce a carbonated version. The company was founded in 1984, launched its first energy drink – a term Mateschitz coined – in Austria three years later, cracked its first export market (Hungary) in 1992 and now sells more than a billion cans per annum all around the world. Red Bull's high-caffeine content initially made some countries wary, but regional bans simply added to its edgy reputation and acted as a catalyst for sales growth.

Is there any need to use motor sport as a promotional medium for something that apparently sells itself? Red Bull insiders point out that the company has a very different approach from that of other F1 teams, which are relatively small companies in the overall scheme of things. For Red Bull, whose core business has 1,850 employees, F1 is only one element in a global strategy – a piece in a large mosaic. While others concentrate on their sponsors' needs, Red Bull wants to focus on marketing opportunities that it believes its rivals neglect.

So is this a committed racing team or a fancy advertising caper? Christian Horner, head of successful FIA Formula 3000 team Arden International, joined as sporting director in January, after the previous, Ford-appointed, management had been shown the door. He says, 'There is a genuine passion to succeed here. F1 makes marketing sense because it offers a global platform 19 times a year, but this isn't just a promotional exercise. The objective is very clear: the team wants to be competitive – that's why I got involved. The goal is to start recording regular podium finishes within the next two seasons.

'In 2006 we want to be able to qualify consistently in the top eight with an eye on finishing in the top three – and there will be a chance to build on that in 2008, when wholesale regulation changes mean every team will start with a clean sheet of paper.'

At the beginning of the campaign, Horner outlined that the immediate ambition was for the team to 'punch above its weight', a mission he regards as accomplished. 'The objective was to seize any opportunity that came our way,' he says, 'and nine times out of ten I think we managed that. We have done the basics well and the results have exceeded expectations. We

have genuinely been on the pace on many occasions and I think we've looked a decent racing team.'

The outlandish motorhome wasn't the only surprise that Red Bull had for its rivals at Imola. That same weekend, it confirmed that it would run customer Ferrari engines from 2006. 'I was looking at various options,' Horner says, 'and first spoke to Ferrari's Jean Todt in Bahrain. We signed the deal three weeks later. Dietrich Mateschitz was totally supportive – and that's one of the benefits of an independent team such as ours. You don't have to report to a board of directors to obtain approval. One man makes the final call – and the swift conclusion of the Ferrari deal is a clear indication of our ambition.'

Study almost any career-minded sub-F1 single-seater series in global motor sport and you are likely to find at least one car festooned with Red Bull logos. The company's widespread sponsorship of emerging talent has earned it a reputation as a champion of youth – but such munificence can create bottlenecks. In recent years, many teams have discovered that grooming drivers from an early age is relatively straightforward initially but there comes a time when those drivers begin to congregate just south of F1, where drivers' ever-extending careers have slashed potential opportunities for the ambitious (collectively, Toyota's 2005 line-up has endured in F1 for 18 seasons, for instance, despite winning only seven races).

Red Bull already had one driver too many when it arrived in F1 – Jaguar refugee Christian Klien and F3000 champion Vitantonio Liuzzi ended up taking shifts in the second car – and a clutch of others, notably American Scott Speed, was champing at the bit. While Mercedes-Benz has a habit of keeping its juniors occupied in the Germany-based DTM touring-car series, Mateschitz solved the problem by sticking his hand in his pocket and buying Minardi, which will be rebranded as a Red Bull rookie team from 2006.

Below (left to right): Team principal Christian Horner and Formula One Management's Pasquale Lattuneddu making time for some table-top soccer in Hungary; may the force be with you – Horner and ex-racer Helmut Marko protected by a *Star Wars* trooper during the Monaco event, for which the team was allied to the film franchise; team personnel are well provided for in the culinary stakes.

Bottom: Christian Klien's Red Bull RB1 in a blur of colour at speed.
Photographs: James Moy/www.crash.net

Above: Coulthard did an excellent and secure job for Red Bull throughout its fledgling F1 season as a team owner.
Photograph: James Moy/www.crash.net

Horner says, 'Red Bull Racing's budget won't be affected by the arrival of a second team; that will be funded independently. My view is that the teams will be complementary rather than divisive – the rookie operation will be a great shop window for rising stars. Red Bull has the vision and commitment to back its young-driver programme and help recruits all the way to F1.'

The team gained personnel during the year – the head count rose to almost 400 – but essentially the improved results were achieved by the same core group that used to build Jaguars. 'The basics were all here before,' Horner says, 'but the system needed a little fine-tuning. We now have strong leadership in place in all departments. Obviously I was used to dealing with a smaller organisation in the past, in F3000, but it doesn't matter whether there are 14 people in a team or 400. The basics are the same; it's just the scale that's different.

'The keys to success are finding the best people, having a common goal, being able to solve problems within a short timescale, knowing when to change direction and being prepared to conduct honest self-appraisals. That's what we have tried to implement this year and I think a glance at the points table justifies our methods. The key change among the technical staff was the introduction of Mark Smith, formerly of Renault and Jordan. That has given us a big boost – and we also welcomed several others, including Paul Monaghan, previously Fernando Alonso's race engineer at Renault; Andrew Green, who used to be in charge of R&D at BAR Honda; and Anton Stepanovic, formerly of Ferrari. Anton is a good control-systems man – this year the cars have generally gone forwards off the grid, rather than backwards as they sometimes used to when they were Jaguars.

'We have managed to engender a good team spirit. Our core principle is that we want success – and everybody is focused on that. One year ago some potential recruits would have steered clear of the team, but things are clearly in the ascendant and people want to work here. The morale is excellent.'

Coulthard, too, has played a significant role. At the end of the 2004 campaign he was wondering whether he had driven his final GP and he faced his first winter of uncertainty for a decade. Red Bull gave him an opportunity to prolong his career, however, and by mid summer had already re-signed him for 2006. 'Melbourne immediately eliminated any doubts about whether the team and I were doing the right thing,' Coulthard says. 'We have gone forward since then and laid foundations for the coming years. I think the main thing I have been able to contribute is experience.

'I've worked with Williams and McLaren, two championship-winning teams, and have learned how to put systems in place to develop competitive cars. I have the benefit of knowing how to apply successful strategies and understanding how to deal with winning situations. This year's RB1 chassis has been very good balance-wise and with one or two extra elements would have been fantastic. I have won grands prix in cars that were less balanced. To take the next step we just need little bits of everything and to bring together the right design ideas – sometimes these work, sometimes they don't.

'There is no A-Z of how to win F1 races in your local library. You can't just open that and, hey presto, off you go. You have to get all the important bits working in harmony and it takes time. The worst-case scenario would have been to race at the level that Jaguar did, but we've gone smoothly, solidly forwards.'

Dietrich Mateschitz's germ of an idea for a fizzy drink has given him the keys, 23 years on, to two F1 teams. They are supported by the sport's plushest motorhome, a race-by-race parade of fashion models (the Formula Unas) and a mildly subversive magazine – the *Red Bulletin* – that is distributed within the paddock. The long-term plan is to sell this to spectators, with all proceeds going to the company's own Wings for Life charity, which finances research into spinal injuries.

'Red Bull has injected a little bit of missing atmosphere into a paddock that has recently been very corporate,' Coulthard says. 'There's nothing upsetting about having a few attractive girls around the place – it's more appealing than looking at sweaty racing drivers or oil-stained mechanics.

'The team operates in a very structured way, but in a balanced environment. There is no pressure pot of having to win yesterday. The target is to progress one step at a time and that's entirely realistic.' Winning, though, remains the ultimate, hard-nosed goal. 'We are facing a period of sustained growth,' Horner says. 'F1 is a people sport – and if you get the right people together you will get the right results. I believe we can compete for race victories within the next three years.'

Below: Christian Horner with technical operations director Günther Steiner. They will be joined by former McLaren technical director Adrian Newey for 2006, when he will take on the role of Red Bull Racing's chief technical officer.

Bottom: Red Bull among the Prancing Horses. For 2006 the team will enjoy Ferrari power.
Photographs: James Moy/www.crash.net

INSIGHT

ENGINEERING AN F1 WEEKEND

by GARY ANDERSON

F ROM the outside, the operation of a typical F1 team may seem slightly chaotic. Mechanics and engineers seem to be darting in all directions, but of course the reality is that the operation is extremely well drilled and scrupulously coordinated. Most of the time, in my experience, at any rate. In this feature I've drawn on my experience as technical director of the Jordan and Jaguar teams to offer the AUTOCOURSE reader a practical insight into the operational business of a contemporary F1 operation.

A typical medium-budget F1 team consists of two race cars plus a spare car. The engineering team required to look after these for such an organisation would consist of somewhere in the region of ten people. If the team has a test car, as most do, it will require another three engineers to prepare for testing. Their job is quite different from the race engineers', because test planning is one of their main functions. They will spend a lot of time accumulating test lists and having various set-ups available to be as efficient as possible at tests.

Just as the race engineer does while running the car, the test engineer will then study the data gathered by the car and try to find new set-up solutions that help the performance. He will also be responsible for cataloguing the huge amount of data gathered at a test in a prearranged format that allows the other engineers and various departments that are responsible for the development of the car to understand it and to interpret how the various test components performed.

In essence, the following job descriptions outline the key personnel involved. The chief race and test engineer oversees the group and makes sure all the relevant people are working as a team and not as individuals. It is very easy for a driver and his engineers to lose sight of the fact that the other teams are the enemies, not his own team-mates working on the other car. The engineer will also be responsible for acquiring information from suppliers such as the tyre, brake and damper companies and in setting up meetings to assist the engineers with a better understanding of the various products from outside suppliers which go to make up the package.

The senior race engineer carries the responsibility for his car's track-running and, as such, must ensure that his car complies with the technical regulations as laid down by the FIA at all times. He will be assisted by a data engineer and a control-systems engineer. This team of three will divide the workload for its car as required, but the senior race engineer will oversee it and make sure he has everything required to cover any situation thrown at him over a typical race weekend.

The main function of the data engineer is to analyse the data collected by the on-car data logger. On a typical F1 car there are some 400 channels collecting data while the car is going around the track. All of the areas measured can influence the car's performance or reliability and so channels have to be prioritised because it is almost impossible to check all this data.

The data engineer will be mainly responsible for the performance channels. He will be making sure that the car is working within the parameters defined by the set-up simulation and will be trying to find some sort of correlation between what the driver is saying and the data he has available to him, to improve the set-up of the car once the session is finished.

The control-systems engineer is responsible for the set-up of all the systems that are controlled by the 'black box', which in reality is a second driver and controls many functions such as throttle, clutch, start-function, gearchange, differential and the dreaded traction control. The driver has to put in the initial input but the black box is the brain behind carrying out that request.

All of these parameters will have a base map that can be altered by the driver using the various knobs and switches on his steering wheel. Again the different set-ups that are available need to be functional and set up in such a manner that the driver knows what to do to change the handling characteristics. For example, the differential setting might be in position five; the maps need to be configured in such a way that reducing the number position would give a reduction in understeer, whereas increasing the number would reduce oversteer.

Above: Ricardo Zonta's Toyota being pushed back to its pit after scrutineering.

Above right: Monitoring the track temperature is a crucial and continuing aspect of every GP weekend for all teams.

Right: Confined space – a Ferrari mechanic getting down to detailed business beneath the car.
Photographs: James Moy/www.crash.net

Far right: Changing a wishbone on the Williams-BMW.
Photograph: Marco Miltenberg/www.crash.net

PREPARING FOR THE RACE WEEKEND

As a starting point, the team needs to gather as much aerodynamic data as possible from the wind-tunnel engineers. Much of this will be based on the downforce level required for the circuit; that data will have been gained at the previous year's event and is in the format of an aero-map, which is a very large data file that includes the downforce, drag and centre of pressure of the car at about 40 different ride heights. There will also be a modification available for this file which takes the form of a plus or minus on the downforce level, which also alters the drag and the location of the centre of pressure. There will also be various engine and brake-cooling configurations, because each of these has an impact on the vehicle's performance.

This aero data is put into a one-lap simulation programme along with the engine data, tyre data and suspension set-up data, and a lap simulation is run. Modifications of the gear ratios, aerodynamic and mechanical set-up, either automated or by hand, are carried out until the best lap time is achieved; this can take thousands of simulations, so the more automated it is, the more solutions can be tried. When completed, this gives the team a base-line set-up to start the race weekend.

With the regulations as they currently are, the cars have to go into parc fermé after their qualifying laps. The team is not allowed to alter the rear-downforce levels or mechanical set-up prior to the race; this complication can alter the optimum set-up because the wing level required for the race, to allow some chance of overtaking, may not be as high a level as required to do the best lap time. This is one of the compromises that the engineer has to take into account when planning his weekend.

After this, a race simulation will be completed with various fuel loads, to give an indication of how many fuel stops would be the optimum. This is never black and white, because there are so many variables but, this early in the weekend, the engineer will opt for the optimum strategy and base his running on the fuel load required for this.

THURSDAY

After catching a flight at some God-forsaken hour – for European races – the engineering group arrives at the track around midday. The guys will get set up, see that everything is as planned and then have a meeting at about 4pm with the drivers, engine engineers, tyre engineers and so on. At this meeting, the plan for the first practice session on Friday will be discussed. For example, comparing two different fuel loads for a two- or three-stop strategy, comparing the different tyres and how many laps to do on each set, how the soft tyre might work with a three-stop strategy as opposed to the hard tyre on a two-stop strategy etc etc. By the end of this meeting, the hope is that a plan for the Friday-morning sessions will have evolved.

The race engineers will then have a short meeting with the chief mechanic and the mechanics on their respective cars to make sure that everyone is up to speed with the programme for the Friday sessions. With the regulations requiring an engine to do two race weekends, it is very important to cover the test plan while working within the allocated mileage for a given session.

FRIDAY

A short get-together at about 9am with all the engineering parties, just to make sure that nothing from any of the engineering areas has changed or that the weather has changed from the forecast of the day before.

SESSIONS ONE AND TWO

Hopefully, get through the allocated programme without any mechanical problems or driver errors such as visiting the gravel traps – things like that can really ruin your weekend. The objective is to gather as much data as possible.

Between session one and session two, the data will be analysed and a streamlined programme for session two evolved. You are always very tight for time between these sessions so a very short meeting will take place with the same group of people as before, to make sure everyone is up to speed with the session-two programme. Because time is limited, it is very important to have good communication between the various groups of people; if everyone is pulling in the same direction, a lot of work can be done during the sessions.

AFTER SESSIONS ONE AND TWO

After the Friday sessions are finished, the same engineering group will get together and discuss the outcome of the sessions and also what influence the other teams' running may have on their own programmes for the weekend. From the two types of tyre available for the Friday, one has to be chosen for the rest of the weekend. The tyre company may influence this choice, because it will have checked the tyres for blistering or any internal problems; if this is all satisfactory, it will just simply be down to performance.

After all this data is acquired, each car's race-engineering group will go off and look at more refined simulation, both for one-lap performance and for race strategy. The data gathered on the Friday will be used to confirm the inputs used for the pre-event simulations – various things may have changed since the previous year, such as the kerbs, bumps on the surface in the braking areas or even the surface grip level. All of these can alter the set-up required. After this is completed, a test programme will be defined for the Saturday-morning sessions.

Normally this workload means that the engineering group is at the circuit until late into the evening and usually the drivers will have gone to the hotel (hopefully for an early night but remember through my time in F1 I did work with the likes of James Hunt and Eddie Irvine, but I suppose that's a different story!) by the time any sort of programme is defined, so any consultation with the driver usually has to wait until the morning.

If the team is using a seven-post test rig (to simulate the forces experienced by a car) back at its technical headquarters, car-suspension and track-profile data will be sent back to the factory. The engineers working on this rig will normally work overnight doing suspension and damper set-up changes to see if they can get a better mechanical set-up for the car that would optimise the tyre-to-road-profile contact patch or optimise the ride-height variation during a lap. The data from this rig programme will be sent to the track early on Saturday morning, along with suggested alterations for the set-up, and the race engineer will then consider using or at least testing the variations during the Saturday-morning practice sessions.

SATURDAY

The day kicks off with a meeting between the driver and the engineering group at around 8am for the purpose of going through the plan for the Saturday-morning sessions, making sure that everyone is happy with it, and any input from anyone needs to be incorporated into the programme.

A short meeting will then follow with the chief mechanic and the mechanics on their respective cars to make sure that everyone is up to speed. As on Friday, a certain amount of mileage will be allocated for the sessions, so it is very important that the test programme is run through as efficiently as possible.

SESSIONS THREE AND FOUR

Again, hopefully these sessions go without a hitch and it is possible to complete the programme. After session three, time is starting to run out – if you are not able to achieve the test programme as defined, it is now time to start thinking on your feet. If the car set-up cannot be honed as required, it is time to adapt to what is known and get the best out of it in the short amount of time left before qualifying. This is really why two competitive drivers are required and, to be honest, a race-engineering group that is a team – if the guys work together and share the workload, an enormous amount of work can be done.

Above: **Ready for take off. The two
Jordan-Toyotas ready to roll and awaiting
their turns for qualifying.**
Photograph: James Moy/www.crash.net

DEBRIEF

The on-track running is now finished and it is about making sure
that the strategy that has been defined is the best for your given
situation. The break in the schedule before qualifying is very
limited and this is the time when the biggest decisions have to
made. After the sessions, a meeting will be held between
the engineering groups. The tyre compound has had to be
chosen prior to Saturday's running, so there is not much can
be done in that area. The main focus will be strategy: how many
stops and how the strategy affects tyre wear and condition.
As per the regulations, any changes on the fuel load have to be
carried out prior to the start of the qualifying session.

QUALIFYING

Over the past few years, this session has changed dramatically.
When it was a 12-lap session with everyone on-track at once, it
was much more exciting and for the driver and the engineers
it used to be the high-pressure part of the weekend. It was
possible to alter the car's set-up between runs and it was very
important not to get caught out in traffic. Also, that last lap late

in the session was something that got the heart pounding.

Now that qualifying is just one timed lap, it has to be more
disciplined, as we saw when the format was first introduced in
2003 – take too many risks and a mistake can cost a lot of
time. However, the drivers have become more accustomed to
this procedure and drive accordingly.

AFTER QUALIFYING

When the car comes back to the pits after its qualifying laps it
goes directly to parc fermé and is under the supervision of the
FIA officials. Other than adjusting the front wing, no changes
may be made to the car until after the race starts. In reality, it's
all over by this time but, if for any reason qualifying has been
worse – or, as happens sometimes, even better – than
expected, a close look at the strategy is required. Most races
are a two-stop strategy.

The car must start the race with the fuel load it carried during
qualifying. Nothing can be done about the lap on which the first
pit stop must be made, but the second-stop lap can be altered
and this is the area the engineers focus on – it is a lot easier to
pass cars when they are in the pit lane than it is on the track.

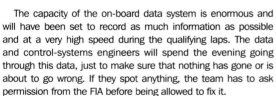

and fuel load will have been fed into the simulation programme. It is then possible to calculate when they will stop again and to alter your own second stop to optimise your finishing position. The only problem with this is that, all things being equal, the engineering group knows where it will finish by about lap 20 – sometimes that's good and sometimes it's not.

AFTER THE RACE

After – hopefully – going to the podium ceremony and cheering your driver as he stands proudly on the top step, the group will have a short post-race meeting with the tyre engineers and drivers and discuss what happened or, more important, what didn't happen.

Get the flight back to England on the Sunday night, usually about 8pm; arrive home around midnight. Back to work on Monday morning to file and catalogue all the data gathered over the weekend. Various meetings to sort problems. And start all over again for the next race weekend.

And to cap it all, your friends say what a wonderful lifestyle you have!

Below left: The Ferrari trio of team principal Jean Todt, Michael Schumacher and Schumi's race engineer Chris Dyer on the grid.

Below centre left: Ron Dennis follows matters via LCD screens on the pit wall.

Below: Christian Klien and technical chief Günther Steiner confer in the Red Bull enclave.
Photographs: James Moy/www.crash.net

Bottom: Last-minute systems checks for the BAR-Honda on the grid.
Photograph: Russell Batchelor/XPB.cc

The capacity of the on-board data system is enormous and will have been set to record as much information as possible and at a very high speed during the qualifying laps. The data and control-systems engineers will spend the evening going through this data, just to make sure that nothing has gone or is about to go wrong. If they spot anything, the team has to ask permission from the FIA before being allowed to fix it.

SUNDAY: THE RACE

As far as the engineering group is concerned, this is a living thing – these men will not only be tracking their own car, but they will be monitoring the other cars in the race. They will be feeding the simulation programme with car position, lap times and gaps to other cars, and altering their strategy constantly to try to optimise the finishing position.

As the first round of pit stops unfolds, you are hoping that your car is one of the last to stop. Not only does this allow your driver to put in some very fast laps because of his low fuel load against the others' higher fuel loads, and hopefully overtake a few cars; it also helps with your simulation for the second round of stops – because the other cars have stopped, their stop time

THE FUTURE DEVELOPMENT OF F1

WHERE DO WE GO FROM HERE?

by MARK HUGHES, F1 consultant editor – Autosport

WHEN Bernie Ecclestone first acquired control of F1, back in the 1970s, he did so on the back of apathy. The big players of those days – Colin Chapman (Lotus), Ken Tyrrell, Teddy Mayer (McLaren) – were addicted to the sport and in varying degrees displayed a lot of business nous, too. But it was used only to fuel their individual teams; none of them had any inclination towards developing the commercial interests of the sport on a macro scale. When arriviste team-owner Ecclestone (of Brabham) offered to do this, they happily gave him carte blanche. Ecclestone was addicted to business – that was his sport and the commercially underdeveloped F1 of the time provided a superb platform for its playing. Over the years, he made the team owners very rich men, but made himself much more so. It was the rightful prize of the entrepreneur.

For a long time, it worked beautifully – symbiotically, even. The teams got richer, invested yet more in being better, faster, slicker and Bernie was able to convert this into a better show as de facto promoter of the sport. With a better show he was able to charge more of race promoters and TV companies, making F1 yet richer and more successful. It couldn't go on.

The process received the first serious interruption in the early 1980s when the governing body, the FIA, got a feisty new president, Jean-Marie Balestre, whose mission it was to wrest control back from Ecclestone. To do this, Balestre targeted the road-car manufacturers that had recently been attracted to F1 by the Ecclestone-initiated marketing reach. He used them as a power base separate from Ecclestone's band of specialist constructors, stirred 'em up, one side against the other. Eventually they all kissed and made up. The FIA got to keep control of the championship and leased out the commercial rights to Ecclestone, while the manufacturers and the specialists got together to produce Brabham-BMWs, Williams-Hondas, Lotus-Renaults etc.

Meanwhile, to prevent a repetition, Ecclestone and cohort Max Mosley (of the March team) took over the governing body by infiltration and Max was successfully installed as president by 1991. With a united vision driving it all forward, by the mid 1990s F1's success dwarfed even that of the 1980s boom years and the manufacturers began to spend money in a way that made the 1980s' budgets look puny. Toyota's entering the fray in 2002 took the total number of manufacturers concurrently active in F1 to an unprecedented seven. They were flooding in – perhaps faster than Bernie and Max would have liked, in fact. Because with the manufacturers' overwhelming budgets came potential power – enough to threaten the iron fists of Max and Bernie.

With the covenant by which the sport is governed up for renewal at the end of 2007, for the past couple of years the two factions have been jockeying for position. Each has its own vision of what GP racing should look like from 2008 and the sport is sitting at this crossroads, scrutinising a very confusing road map and trying to decipher the correct way forward.

The manufacturers view F1 as a fantastic marketing platform for their products. They took a very dim view when an entity outside the automotive world – a German TV company – bought a controlling share in the sport from Ecclestone in the late 1990s. When that company went bust and its F1 shares ended up with the company's creditors – three commercial banks – it only reinforced the car manufacturers' view that, as the entities investing most in the sport, they should rightfully be entitled to a controlling role.

This is not a view shared by Ecclestone. 'Who are these manufacturers, anyway?' he has asked publicly, with the implicit message that he built up this championship and they chose to piggy-back onto its success for their own ends. Why should they therefore feel entitled to rob him of his control of the sport?

But not only do the manufacturers have money; they have allies, too. Key independent team owners such as Frank Williams and Ron Dennis (McLaren) have long harboured grudges about just how much income Ecclestone takes out of the sport. Only around one third of the income generated by F1 is distributed among the participants; the rest goes to Bernie's various companies. In theory, the sport could be almost self-financing. So when the manufacturers talk of a championship with a more equitable split of the profits and a more transparent management, these team owners are more than receptive.

For the past couple of years, the manufacturers have been threatening to form their own breakaway series from 2008 if they do not get what they want from any new F1 covenant. What they want includes not only income and power, however, but also a fairly technology-heavy F1. They can't apparently agree with each other about precisely which technology they want – only that they want lots of it. They see this as an essential justification for being involved, emphasising to potential customers their technical mastery and posing strong challenges for their engineers to grapple with.

So their future might involve stability control (managing the slip angle of a car into corners) in addition to the existing – and highly unpopular – traction control. It might mean CVT (continuously variable) transmissions with infinitely variable ratios that keep engines permanently at their peak speeds, active diffs (to prevent or reduce wheel-locking), four-wheel-steer, moveable aerodynamic devices, energy retention systems that re-use for additional acceleration energy otherwise lost to heat evaporation during braking... all features that are currently banned. Some manufacturers would favour hybrid power sources; at least one would prefer turbo-diesels; others would prefer to stick with the internal-combustion engine – albeit with fewer restrictions than apply to the new-for-2006 V8 formula.

All this would, in a way, be a continuation of what we have now – an F1 heavily technology-led with astronomical costs justified by the astronomical value placed on F1 as a marketing tool by the manufacturers. Left unchecked, rampant technology can also have a seriously negative effect on the quality of the racing and by definition it limits the importance of driver talent in the overall measure of lap time. Equally gravely, it can amplify differences in competitiveness between the cars and implicit in that possibility is the threat of key manufacturers' being continually beaten, thereby turning their F1 programmes from assets to liabilities.

Only so many teams can win races in one season and history suggests it's usually considerably fewer than six – the number of manufacturers currently involved. Other manufacturer-controlled series of the past – touring cars, rallying, sports cars, pre-war grand-prix racing – have historically followed a classic boom-and-bust cycle for this very reason. One manufacturer becomes dominant and key losers pull out, leaving only two or three players and thereby diminishing the value of remaining involved, and the series implodes. Once F1 became the preserve of independent teams (in the late 1950s and early 1960s) it became vastly more stable precisely because it was populated by those whose only source of income was this. No longer was the sport dependent upon the whim of companies whose core business was something else, who could pull out at a moment's notice at the stroke of a financial director's pen or the say-so of an impatient board.

The current F1 manufacturers recognise this structural weakness and say their vision accounts for it. The sport is so successful, they argue, that it could be profitable for all if there were no Ecclestone figure taking the money. The manufacturers could become stakeholders in it, part-owning it even if they elected not always to compete in it. For those manufacturers actively participating there would be some sort of contracted engine supply to independent teams, allowing the series' core to remain intact regardless of the comings and goings of the manufacturers. It's a grand vision, but there are real doubts about the ability of the manufacturers to deliver it.

The crossroads of conflicting financial interests and technical vision between the manufacturers and governing body is reflected in the very crossroads of the philosophy of what motor racing should be in the modern world. Should it be a simple contest to find the world's best racing driver? Should it be more sophisticated and multi-dimensional than that? For years now, F1 has put off that question, one made ever more awkward as the

Right: McLaren Mercedes pushed Renault all the way with Kimi Räikkönen and Juan Pablo Montoya (pictured in Brazil) taking a total of ten wins for the team.
Photographs: James Moy/www.crash.net

Below: Fernando Alonso took the world drivers' championship in Brazil. For Renault, it was the culmination of six seasons' relentless progress.
Photograph: Russell Batchelor/XPB.cc

Right: Toyota has yet to win in F1, but it certainly has the resources to tackle F1 seriously and is upbeat about the prospects for its forthcoming 2.4-litre V8 engine.
Photograph: James Moy/www.crash.net

technology progresses. Now the governing body has been pushed into grasping the nettle by the threat of the manufacturers.

As such, the FIA's vision of the future actually harks back to an earlier time – to the 'golden age' of unfettered Ecclestone-Mosley control in the days before the manufacturers began flooding in. It sees independent teams very much at the core of a future F1, ideally with independent specialist racing-engine manufacturers making their motors available to all. To enable such teams to be competitive with the factories – to limit how much lap-time advantage a bigger budget buys you once past a certain affordable point – technology has to be capped.

Cleverly, the FIA has already funnelled manufacturers towards its own vision with new and highly prescriptive engine regulations for the two years in which the current Concorde Agreement over F1 still has to run. Much against their instincts, the manufacturers have been obliged to meet an engine formula in which the weight, cylinder bore spacings, centre-of-gravity height, centre-of-gravity lateral position and crank height are pre-defined and in which such routine technology as variable inlet and exhaust geometries and variable valve timing are banned.

It's difficult to avoid the suspicion that the FIA has done this with the aim of limiting the advantage that manufacturer dollars will buy over a lower-budget specialist engine manufacturer such as, say, Cosworth. That way, independent teams will surely have a better chance of being competitive with the factory teams. Not coincidentally, Ecclestone has been busy encouraging new independent teams into the series, trying to build up a critical momentum of participants willing to sign up to his vision of low-tech/low-cost post-2007 F1 – and thereby stymie the threat of a manufacturer series. He has Ferrari and three tiddler teams on-side but, at the time of writing, the manufacturers and their allies are holding firm and ostensibly still pressing on with plans for their own 2008 series.

The prescriptive engine formula is just the beginning for the FIA. Its initial plans for 2008 and beyond outlined a 90-percent reduction in downforce, manual H-pattern gearshifts, FIA-supplied gears, control ECUs, control tyres and so on. Some teams did a little simulation work and came up with the answer that such cars would be around 15 seconds per lap slower than current GP2 machines – the cars racing in F1's junior series.

And therein lies the balancing point of the FIA's and Bernie's gamble in trying to bring the manufacturers to heel. To them the manufacturers are an inconvenience, a disruptive factor. But these companies will not simply go away, retire hurt, if Max and Bernie are nasty enough towards them. They'll set up their own series instead. Two competing series would be disastrous, would land the sport with the same credibility crisis as that faced by boxing when suddenly there was more than one world championship. If they push the manufacturers too hard, alienate them by being too uncompromising on the low-tech vision and the financial package, the danger is that the car makers will set up shop with high-tech cars that are massively faster than the FIA formula machines and with big budgets paying for the highest-profile drivers. That would in effect scupper the FIA series – working on the assumption that the manufacturers could get their collective act together.

There are other dangers implicit in the Mosley-Ecclestone vision, too. In order to encourage new independent teams, the previous stipulation that entrants must construct their own chassis will be dropped from 2006. In theory there is nothing to stop a new team from purchasing last year's McLaren and possibly using it to beat longer-established and better-funded teams. Take that to its logical conclusion and within a few seasons you could have a formula in which domination by two or three constructors has forced out the others and made F1 just another customer-chassis formula.

That would have serious implications for the long-term health of the racing-car industry. Already, control formulae (in which all the cars are the same) lower down the racing ladder – where the only competition between constructors is in who can tender the cheapest bid to supply the control chassis – has led to bankruptcies, redundancies and a dearth of starting opportunities for the F1 engineers of tomorrow.

There's also the matter of how businesses such as McLaren, Williams and others – developed exponentially during the 1990s thanks to the injection of previously undreamed-of investment from the car manufacturers – could possibly downsize to a dumbed-down, low-cost F1. Teams such as these typically employ up to 800 people and everything is geared to maintaining that. It's little wonder that the Ron Dennises and Frank Williamses of the paddock view an FIA-prescribed slashing of costs with a jaundiced eye when its logical conclusion would probably mean mass redundancies and a massive downscaling of their businesses – and when they know the sport's books would balance perfectly well at current expenditure if Ecclestone were not taking so much income from it. They would dearly love the manufacturers to get their act together and for them all to cut loose from Ecclestone. But even Dennis and Williams must have serious doubts about their ability to do this.

More likely is that a compromise will be reached – just as in the 1980s – and that some of the manufacturers' technology and commercial wishes will be accommodated. Regardless of the powerful cards in the hands of the manufacturers, it's difficult to envisage a collection of employees of six competing companies being sufficiently cohesive and heavy-hitting to outwit the combined intellect, savvy and experience of F1's dynamic duo.

A better financial deal for the participants is in the offing. Combine it with a little bit of technical leeway – maybe some agreement about energy retention systems on the grounds of their being environmentally useful – and it's easy to see how the car makers might be soothed into submission. Particularly when the alternative is slightly scary.

That still leaves the question of what happens after Bernie; of how the sport eases itself from an entrepreneurial to a management phase. That is more likely to be the time when the manufacturers' vision could come to the fore.

MAURICE TRINTIGNANT

MAURICE TRINTIGNANT, who died in February aged 87, twice won the Monaco Grand Prix, yet his successes in F1's most prestigious and charismatic event were achieved after races of attrition rather than being dominant wins from the front.

At Monaco in 1955 Trintignant performed reliably to inherit the lead after the Mercedes-Benz W196s of Juan Manuel Fangio and Stirling Moss succumbed to mechanical failures and Alberto Ascari crashed into the harbour in his Lancia D50. In the wake of these high-profile retirements, Trintignant's Ferrari 625 plodded around and kept out of trouble long enough to take the chequered flag ahead.

Three years later it would be Moss again, this time driving a British Vanwall, and Mike Hawthorn in a Ferrari who would retire while running first and second to hand Trintignant his second win through the streets of the Principality driving privateer Rob Walker's nimble Cooper-Climax.

Trintignant had started racing before the war with a Bugatti in which he won the 1939 Grand Prix des Frontières on the spectacular Chimay road circuit. The car was then laid up in a barn throughout hostilities and retrieved in time for its owner to take part in the first post-war motor race through the Bois de Bologne in Paris.

The Bugatti retired from the race due to rat droppings' – *les petoules* – blocking its fuel system, the result of its long years of inactivity. From then on Trintignant would be nicknamed *Le Petoulet,* an admittedly unfortunate but nonetheless affectionate soubriquet.

Through the decade that followed, Trintignant gained moderate success, winning Le Mans in 1954 sharing a 4.1-litre Ferrari with José Froilán González. After Stirling Moss was invalided out of racing after a crash at Goodwood on Easter Monday 1962, Trintignant was retained by Rob Walker in his team, but the pleasant Frenchman was a pale shadow compared with the dynamic British driver.

Trintignant drove his own BRM in 1964, which was to prove his final season in F1, after which he retired at the age of 47. In 1960 he was awarded the Légion d'Honneur for his services to French motor racing and he spent his retirement tending his thriving vineyard at Vergeze, near Nimes, where he also served a spell as mayor.

Right: The slight figure of Trintignant aboard the Reg Parnell Lola during practice for the 1963 Monaco Grand Prix.

CLIFF ALLISON

Photograph: LAT Photographic

CLIFF ALLISON was one of only nine British drivers to be hired by the Ferrari F1 team in the 56-season history of the official world championship. Yet the popular driver from rural Cumbria, who died in April aged 73, registered only a modest tally of achievement during the six races in which he competed for the Prancing Horse in 1959–60.

Allison's best result in a Ferrari was second place in a Dino 246, behind Bruce McLaren's mid-engined Cooper in the 1960 Argentine Grand Prix at Buenos Aires. Within another few months Allison became involved in a huge accident practising for the Monaco GP, which finished his top-line career for good.

Cliff came to prominence in 1957 when he shared a Lotus Eleven sports car with Keith Hall at Le Mans and finished an impressive 14th overall in this tiny 744-cc-engined machine, winning the prestigious Index of Performance handicap in the process. Allison's speed convinced Lotus team owner Colin Chapman to give him a drive in F1 alongside Graham Hill in 1958, which in turn led to the invitation to sign for Ferrari in 1959.

In fact Allison came closest to winning a world championship race at the wheel of a spindly little Lotus 12 in the 1958 Belgian GP on the challenging Spa-Francorchamps road circuit and he reflected in later life that if only the race had been one lap longer he would have beaten Stirling Moss to the distinction of becoming the first man to win a race for the British constructor.

Tony Brooks's Vanwall took the chequered flag to win despite slowing with a major gearbox problem, Hawthorn's Ferrari suffered an engine failure within sight of the finish and coasted over the line, while Stuart Lewis-Evans's Vanwall wobbled to a halt in third place just after the line with broken front suspension. Allison's Lotus, running fourth, was the first healthy car to finish.

Allison's career was abruptly interrupted by that crash in the Ferrari at Monaco's waterfront chicane, in which he was hurled from the cockpit onto the track. He recounted that he woke up in hospital 16 days later speaking French, 'which was strange because I didn't know any French.' Sidelined for a year with facial and arm injuries, he attempted a come-back in the 1961 Belgian Grand Prix, but rolled his UDT Laystall team Lotus 18 at the tricky Blanchimont corner and broke both his legs.

JOHN LOVE

Photograph: Autocourse Grand Prix Archive

Six-times winner of the prestigious South African F1 championship in the 1960s, JOHN LOVE died at the age of 80 in April after a long battle with cancer.

He was born in Bulawayo, Rhodesia – now Zimbabwe – in 1924 and originally shone as a member of Ken Tyrrell's Cooper-Austin Formula Junior team in 1961–62. A bad accident sustained in a crash at the Albi circuit unfortunately left him with a badly broken arm that prevented him from racing regularly in F1, although he came close when he was nominated to replace Phil Hill in the works Cooper team for the 1964 Italian Grand Prix.

Yet it was in the 1967 South African GP at Kyalami that Love was poised on the verge of the biggest success of his career, leading the race for 13 laps in his 2.7-litre Cooper-Climax before a misfire forced him to make a precautionary refuelling stop and he dropped to second behind Pedro Rodriguez's Cooper-Maserati.

He raced in another five South African GPs, his last being in 1972 when he crashed heavily, but thankfully without injury, in his Surtees TS9.

Above left: Love walks away unscathed from the wreckage after crashing his Surtees in the 1972 South African Grand Prix at Kyalami .

FORMULA 1 REVIEW

Photograph: James Moy/www.crash.net

Contributors

BOB CONSTANDUROS

MAURICE HAMILTON

ALAN HENRY

F1 illustrations

ADRIAN DEAN

SCUDERIA FERRARI MARLBORO

1
MICHAEL SCHUMACHER

2
RUBENS BARRICHELLO

Photographs: James Moy/www.crash.net

NEVER in Maranello's most tortured nightmares could F1's super-team of the new millennium ever have envisaged such a fall from grace as that suffered by the Prancing Horse in 2005. At a stroke, or so it seemed, Michael Schumacher and Rubens Barrichello found themselves reduced to the roles of bit-part players on the grand-prix stage, crucially let down by Bridgestone's inability to produce a tyre that would sustain its performance through the rigours of both qualifying and a full race distance as demanded by the latest rule change.

The net result was third place in the constructors' championship – although even that distinction might have been under threat from Toyota had not Ferrari enjoyed an 18-point boost to its fortunes from a one-two success in the US GP at Indianapolis, in which a threadbare six-car field competed in the absence of all the Michelin runners.

Technical director Ross Brawn believed that modifications to the new Ferrari, made as long ago as September 2004, delayed the team's development programme with the car. 'It was clear the gearbox we had wasn't the best from an aerodynamic point of view,' he explained. 'It was quite bulky in the wrong areas. So we made a decision to start again with the transmission. We felt, with all the other things going on – such as the one-race tyre and the two-race engine – that the first few races of the season would be so challenging that to take a version of the existing car [to those races] would be fine.

'We'd done it before and, looking back, everybody was keen to bring forward the new car, but the new car wasn't the solution. There were other issues involved, in the aerodynamic changes and the tyre situation.'

Initially things didn't seem too bad. Rubens Barrichello's Ferrari F2004M split the Renault R25s of Giancarlo Fisichella and Fernando Alonso in the opening race at Melbourne, although perhaps on reflection Michael Schumacher's performance was a more accurate touchstone for Ferrari's times. Heavy rain had frustrated Michael's qualifying efforts and he started from the back of the grid as a result. His race ended prematurely after a collision with Nick Heidfeld's Williams-BMW, for which the 2004 world champion later apologised.

By the time the team had completed the second round of the title chase in Malaysia – where Schumacher battled to seventh at the chequered flag from 13th on the starting grid and Barrichello had to withdraw, so badly worn were his tyres – all the warning bells at Maranello seemed to be ringing, all the evidence pointing to an urgent need to press the new F2005 into action as early as possible. It duly made its debut in

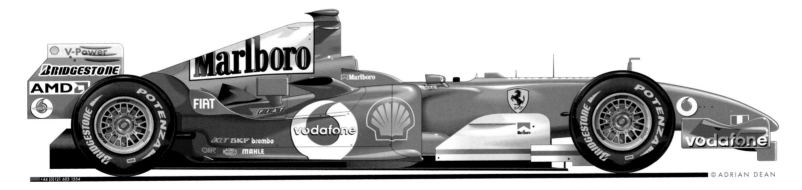

© ADRIAN DEAN

FERRARI F2005

SPONSORS	**Title sponsor: Marlboro** Major sponsors: **FIAT** • **Vodafone** • **Shell** • **Bridgestone** • **Olympus** • **AMD**
	Official suppliers: **Acer** • **Brembo** • **Magneti Marelli** • **Mahle** • **OMR** • **Puma** • **SKF** • **Beta Utensili** • **Europcar** • **Finmeccanica** • **Infineon** • **Iveco** • **NGK** • **Panerai** • **Sanbittèr** • **Tata Consultancy Services** • **ZF Sachs**
	Other suppliers: **BBS** • **Cima** • **Mecel** • **Parametric** • **Poggipolini** • **Sabelt** • **TRW** • **VeCa**
ENGINE	Type: **Ferrari 055** No. of cylinders (vee angle): **V10 (90°)** No. of valves: **40** Sparking plugs: **NGK** Electronics: **Magneti Marelli** Fuel: **Shell** Oil: **Shell**
TRANSMISSION	Gearbox: **Ferrari longitudinal gearbox, limited-slip differential; semi-automatic sequential electronically controlled gearbox**
	Number of gears: **7 plus reverse** Driveshaft: **Pankl** Clutch: **ZF Sachs**
CHASSIS	Front and rear suspension: **double wishbones, pushrod-activated torsion bars** Dampers: **Sachs**
	Wheel diameter: **330 mm front and rear** Wheels: **BBS** Tyres: **Bridgestone** Brake discs: **Brembo ventilated carbon-fibre disc brakes** Brake pads: **Brembo**
	Calipers: **Brembo** Steering: **Ferrari** Radiators: **Secan** Fuel tank: **ATL** Cockpit instruments: **Ferrari/Magneti Marelli**
DIMENSIONS	Wheelbase: **3,050 mm** Track, front: **1,470 mm** rear: **1,405 mm** Overall length: **4,545 mm** Overall height: **959 mm**
	Formula weight: **605 kg including driver**

FERRARI

President: **Luca di Montezemolo**
General director: **Jean Todt**
Technical director: **Ross Brawn**
Engine director: **Paolo Martinelli**
Team manager: **Stefano Domenicali**
Chief designer: **Aldo Costa**
Electronics: **Roberto Dalla**
Chief race engineer: **Luca Baldisserri**
Race and test technical manager:
Nigel Stepney
Race engineer, car no.1,
Michael Schumacher: **Christopher Dyer**
Chief mechanic, car no.1,
Michael Schumacher: **Francesco Barletto**
Race engineer, car no.2,
Rubens Barrichello: **Gabriele Delli Colli**
Chief mechanic, car no.2,
Rubens Barrichello: **Alessandro Palermo**
Chief race engineer: **Massimo Atzori**

Bahrain where, despite serious gearbox-bearing problems hobbling Barrichello's progress, Michael qualified second alongside Fernando Alonso, only to spin off early in the race due to hydraulic problems.

Imola was the high point. Had Schumacher been able to squeeze out one more lap before his final refuelling stop, he might well have pipped Alonso's Renault to an emotional victory in Ferrari's back yard. As it was, he had to be content with second place, his best result against a full field, matched only by his run to second from pole position at Budapest. Thereafter his results dwindled worryingly, despite the occasional flashes of optimism. 'There were some highlights and that's what makes me think that the car is actually quite good,' said Brawn of the F2005.

Yet in no way does he attach any blame for the new car's deficient performance to the team's new chief designer, Aldo Costa, who took over the role from the veteran Rory Byrne. 'It's been a bit of a transition from Rory to Aldo,' Brawn said. 'There's been a passing of the baton but they are both still running the race. Aldo and Rory have been key elements in the design on all the [recent] Ferraris and I know that Aldo wouldn't have done anything that Rory objected to. It is a much smoother transition than most people think. There were a lot of little flashes of promise which gave us encouragement and what's important for us from now to next year is not to disassemble what we have – it's just to clarify our thoughts a bit and ensure those flashes [of promise] become a consistent theme in 2006.'

Ferrari had certainly been hard hit by the fact that it was the prime team contracted to Bridgestone. That had for so long been one of the strongest cards in its competitive hand, when things were going well, but when things went wrong Brawn and his colleagues suddenly began to understand how potentially vulnerable their position really was. 'When you operate in isolation, as Ferrari does, as the main Bridgestone runner, you don't quite know where you are,' he said. 'You don't know whether you've got the best tyre or the worst tyre, but in a sense that doesn't matter because you're in a partnership

Top: Michael Schumacher's F2005 sweeping out of Casino Square in Monaco, where he set fastest race lap on his way to seventh place.

Above left: Team principal Jean Todt (left) and Ferrari chief Luca di Montezmolo took a philosophical and resilient stance over their team's disappointing loss of form.
Photographs: James Moy/www.crash.net

[with Bridgestone] and the aim is to win races. But there's no cross-reference point. We've done a huge amount of testing. It's been very frustrating.' Brawn is quick to add, 'We have had, and continue to have, a fantastic relationship with Bridgestone on both a professional and a personal level. We've gone in a little bit of a wrong direction this year, but we also accept a level of responsibility for this because we set the tyre direction. I don't think there was any intention behind the rule changes to handicap Bridgestone. I don't think anyone was clever enough to say, "If we do this, we'll favour Michelin." I think it was just good fortune that when the one-race tyre [rule] came along it suited Michelin down to the ground and it didn't suit Bridgestone.

'The whole Bridgestone philosophy over the past few years has been focused on a 20-lap tyre that's then finished. High degradation and high performance. We had different [tyre] characteristics that we could use to win races. Four pit stops at Magny-Cours in 2004, for example. Not a particularly logical strategy, you might think, but with the tyre we had we could create windows to use the car's performance.

'At that time Michelin often didn't change tyres, so for it to make the progression [to the 2005 rules] it didn't have to change much of its culture, but Ferrari and Bridgestone had to start again and perhaps we didn't appreciate this in the off-season.

'If you want to change direction with a tyre you've sometimes got to start again from first principals, go out and try compounds and constructions which won't necessarily give you lap times but which are parts of the building blocks to get you to where you want to be. And doing that when you're also trying to find some short-term solutions, because you are not winning races, is a difficult compromise to make.'

Despite this, Brawn had no criticism of Michael Schumacher and Rubens Barrichello, even though the Brazilian decided to join the BAR Honda team alongside Jenson Button for 2006. 'I have no complaints at all about the drivers,' Brawn said. 'In a difficult year, I think they showed their characters. I think Rubens' departure was inevitable if Michael wanted to keep driving. The pressure that a driver feels in a team with Michael Schumacher is very difficult to sustain and Rubens has done a fantastic job for six years.

'I know the cars are equal and I think we run a pretty balanced team. But obviously Rubens' crew wants to win as much as Michael's guys do. It's very rare we have to make a call [between the drivers]. This is a very well-resourced team and I can't recall the last time it gave Michael something Rubens hadn't had.'

For all that, it was clear that Barrichello was feeling slightly marginalised in the Ferrari set-up. Perhaps it was a manageable situation for the Brazilian when the team's fortunes were riding high, but the tensions worked their way closer to the surface when Ferrari was struggling.

Two moments stood out. Michael's last-lap lunge to grab seventh place from Rubens at Monaco may have been advanced by some as showcasing the then world champion's indomitable fighting spirit, but for Rubens it just seemed needlessly risky. Then at Indianapolis the two Ferraris came close to colliding when Michael rejoined the circuit after his second pit stop. Rubens clearly thought that was the German's fault as well and there was a palpable frostiness between the two men when they came face-to-face on the rostrum.

'But it's something Rubens now has to find out for himself, whether Michael has something special in terms of harmony with the team,' said Brawn. 'Maybe he thinks that he can recreate that for himself somewhere else, which is what Eddie Irvine wanted to do [when he left Ferrari at the end of 1999 after four years alongside Schumacher]. And I hope he does. I think Rubens will do okay. He's occasionally been able to beat Michael so it will be interesting to see how he fares against Jenson Button.'

Brawn also acknowledged that it would be a hard road back to winning form for Ferrari, but one that the team was poised willingly to tread. 'We had a year of dominating [in 2004] and we couldn't believe it was so easy, quite honestly,' he said. 'We'd turn up at a race, do a good job, win the race and wonder why everybody else was struggling so much. Suddenly when we were faced with the difficulties we had at the start of this season we were running around trying to solve the problems overnight when the situation needed recovering over a modest period of time.

'So that's the lesson everybody has learned. We have to have consistent steps to put ourselves back to where we want to be. There is no overnight switch we can turn, no magic key to the lock. There is no single thing we can do.'

Alan Henry

Top: Rubens Barrichello finally called time on his Ferrari career at the end of 2005.

Above centre: Technical director Ross Brawn had broad-enough shoulders to admit that the blame for such a poor year did not lie solely with Bridgestone.

Above: Paolo Martinelli's department produced reliable two-race engines.

Photographs: James Moy/www.crash.net

Opposite: Michael Schumacher continued to exert a dynamic influence on F1.

Photograph: Emily Davenport/XPB.cc

LUCKY STRIKE BAR HONDA

JENSON BUTTON

TAKUMA SATO

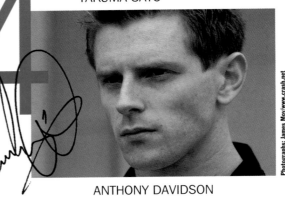

ANTHONY DAVIDSON

Photographs: James Moy/www.crash.net

© ADRIAN DEAN

© ADRIAN DEAN

BAR-HONDA 007

SPONSORS	BAT • Honda • Michelin • Eneos • Intercond • NITN • Celerant • Ray Ban • Seiko • Super H²O
ENGINE	Type: **Honda RA005E** No. of cylinders (vee angle): **V10 (90°)** Fuel: **Elf** Oil: **Eneos**
TRANSMISSION	Gearbox: **BAR-Honda maincase and internals; 7-speed unit** Clutch: **Carbon plate**
CHASSIS	Front and rear suspension: **Wishbone and pushrod-activated torsion springs and rockers; mechanical anti-roll bar** Dampers: **Showa** Wheel diameter, front: **312 mm** rear: **340 mm** Wheels: **BBS forged magnesium** Tyres: **Michelin** Brake discs: **Alcon carbon** Brake pads: **Alcon carbon** Steering: **BAR-Honda power-assisted rack and pinion** Fuel tank: **ATL** Instruments: **BAR-Honda steering-wheel dash display**
DIMENSIONS	Wheelbase: **3,140 mm** Track, front: **1,460 mm** rear: **1,420 mm** Overall length: **4,675 mm** Overall height: **950 mm** Overall width: **1,800 mm** Formula weight: **600 kg including driver**

60

HOW the mighty are fallen. BAR Honda dominated the pre-season feature stories in Britain: this was the team being touted as a possible challenger for the championship. The cover of *Autosport* claimed this was a 'Win or bust' situation. Even allowing for excessive editorial hype, no one believed it would be the latter. But it came alarmingly close.

BAR finished the year by fighting off Red Bull for sixth place. In the middle, a gaping and embarrassing hole created by a controversial exclusion from one race and a ban from the next two. Halfway through the season, BAR Honda – the team that had finished second in the 2004 constructors' championship – had not scored a single point. How the mighty are fallen, indeed.

Buoyed by 11 podium positions in 2004 and the potential for the team's first win, technical director Geoffrey Willis and his team produced a sophisticated car. A second generation of the neat carbon gearbox with a new shift mechanism was the most obvious step forward in improving performance and paring off even more weight. The aero department had produced BAR's interpretation of the wide-ranging rule changes. Honda, now an integral part of the company with its 45-percent share, continued development of the V10 while preparing for the massive step from one to two races per engine. The relationship with Michelin was blossoming into its second year. With Jenson Button and Takuma Sato remaining on the driving side of a team that was consolidating into a well-established unit, all seemed set for a strong season.

Then the car ran on the track. It was immediately apparent that the 007 lacked pace. Not even a package of aero improvements rushed through before the start of the season would raise the team's chances of running at the front.

'We thought we were well prepared for the 2005 season. As it turned out, I don't think we did a very good job initially in responding to the aero regulations,' said Willis. 'This really compromised a lot of our pre-season testing, in which we knew we had what looked to be an aerodynamic-characteristic problem. We struggled for quite a while to fix it.'

The mixed weather at the first race, in Australia, did not help to throw light on the team's true standing; nor did a disastrous pair of engine failures within seconds of each other at the next outing in Malaysia. By the time both cars retired from round three in Bahrain, another package of changes was ready to run at the next tests.

The team came away from Barcelona and Mugello excited by the test results and its optimism appeared to be vindicated by Button's running near the front at Imola. Then an already difficult season suddenly became much, much worse. Both cars were excluded from the Imola result and the team was banned from the next two races, in Spain and Monaco. Not only was BAR failing to win; it was not even getting the chance to lose with dignity.

'The car performed very well at Imola,' said Willis. 'We carried on developing it [during the team's racing ban] and went to the Nürburgring thinking we would be pretty strong. But not having raced at Barcelona and Monte Carlo, we couldn't gauge how we were relative to everyone else. We had quite a big shock at the 'Ring; we were really not happy with the car at all. As a result of that, we went back over our aero testing programme and we worked out what we had changed on the car that had made it poor.'

BAR was strong at Montreal but, unfortunately, Button hit the wall while running a competitive third. 'That was a very uncharacteristic mistake,' said Willis. 'Jenson is able to get on top of problems, get himself re-established on Saturday if we've had a difficult Friday. He makes almost no mistakes in the races and can be relied on to get the maximum out of the car every time. The team has a huge amount of confidence in him and knows that once it gives him the car, it's in a safe pair of hands.'

The same might not be said of Takuma Sato, who continued to have moments of brilliance which were too often clouded by dust from the gravel trap. 'He's a genuinely quick driver but he seems to find it difficult to be consistent,' said Willis. 'At some races he is confident right from the beginning, but at others he appears to be always on the back foot. He had a very good, solid drive at Imola, which is exactly the sort of thing we're looking for. It has to be said that Taku hasn't been helped by the car's not being quite quick enough.'

'There was a recurring theme. On relatively high-grip circuits, where we weren't using either maximum or minimum downforce, the car would work quite well. We had a wind-tunnel problem early in the season and we lost development because of trying to solve the initial problems. So things conspired against us in some ways. When the car was working well, we would get very good new-tyre performance from it and qualify well. If you look at the fuel-corrected times [lap times adjusted to take into account the weight of race fuel], it was a pretty strong car. But we also suffered from too much tyre-performance degradation; we were damaging the tyres. We had a number of theories and lots of discussion with Michelin about exactly what we were doing. You could see that some other fairly strong teams had a similar problem and others clearly didn't and could stay at the same level of performance during the race.'

On top of all this, BAR had to deal with the after-shock of the Imola affair. It was a daunting task for Nick Fry in his new role as replacement for David Richards as team principal. It was also a very tough baptism for Gil de Ferran, who had just joined the team as sporting director. 'Because the team pulled together, it was relatively easy to get over the Imola business,' said Fry. 'Straight after it happened, Jenson, Taku, Anthony [Davidson, third driver], Enrique [Bernoldi, test driver], Geoff, myself and Wada San [of Honda] stood before the entire factory and explained exactly what had happened. We explained where we were, why we didn't agree with the outcome, but that we couldn't carry on looking backwards; we had to look forwards. The day after we were banned really was a true turning point – "Forget what's happened; let's just push forward." And the interesting thing is that we are even closer as a team as a result. Honda has been fantastic. It is a tight-knit team. Imola is rarely, if ever, spoken about. It's not that anyone is ashamed of it. Over the course of motor-racing history, this sort of thing has happened to many great teams and we almost saw it as a rite of passage.

'This is not a team where anyone has any recriminations. We just get on with it. The team has been absolutely incredible from that point of view. Yes, the results have been disappointing but this has certainly been a character-building year and we can only be the better for it in the long run.'

Maurice Hamilton

BAR

Chief executive officer: **Nick Fry**

Technical director: **Geoffrey Willis**

Sporting director: **Gil de Ferran**

Head of Honda worldwide automobile racing
(F1 project leader): **Takeo Kiuchi**

Honda R&D, F1 executive technical adviser:
Ken Hashimoto

Honda R&D, head of F1 chassis
technology development
Yousuke Sekino

President, Honda Racing Development Ltd;
management board member, BAR Honda
Yasuhiro Wada

Senior adviser, Honda Racing
Development Ltd and BAR Honda
Shoichi Tanaka

Vice president, Honda Racing Development
Ltd; management board member, BAR Honda
Otmar Szafnauer

Engineering director, Honda Racing
Development Ltd
Shuhei Nakamoto

Chief race engineer: **Craig Wilson**

Race-team manager: **Ron Meadows**

Senior race engineer, car no. 9,
Jenson Button: **Andrew Shovlin**

Senior race engineer, car no. 10,
Takuma Sato **Jock Clear**

Top: **Team principal Nick Fry.**

Far left: **Sporting director Gil de Ferran.**

Left: **Geoff Willis struggled with the 007's aerodynamic balance during the early races.**

Below: **Jenson Button leading Takuma Sato at Monza.**
Photographs: James Moy/www.crash.net

FERNANDO ALONSO

GIANCARLO FISICHELLA

MILD SEVEN RENAULT F1 TEAM

Photographs: James Moy, www.crash.net

ON the basis that if a car looks right, it is right, Renault had a psychological advantage before the season had even started. The razzmatazz associated with the over-subscribed launch of the R25 in Monte Carlo on 1 February could not hide the fact that here was a quietly efficient organisation intent on continuing its patient and solidly productive march back to full competitiveness.

It was five years since the team had regrouped following Renault's absorption of its previous Benetton incarnation. With each successive season, there had been progress in terms of results. In 2004, Renault had second place snatched from its grasp at the last minute by BAR Honda. But, while the team was disappointed at the outcome, third was nevertheless a reasonable result. Particularly with a car that was not only more difficult to drive than 2003's R23 but one that was powered by a brand-new engine following the recent switch to a narrow-angle V10.

As ever, there had been room for improvement, as recognised by the experience and productive thinking of technical chiefs Pat Symonds, Bob Bell and Rob White. The result? A car that was beautifully and thoughtfully crafted, from the inventive vee-keel at the front to the swoopy bodywork and clever rear suspension.

'People had gone with the twin-keel idea, which is very good aerodynamically but terrible structurally,' said Symonds. 'Our guys rejected it initially and then someone came up with the vee-keel; a lovely solution to two conflicting requirements. It is a very nicely detailed car all the way through. The R24 [2004's car] was a difficult car to drive – and that's perhaps one of the hardest things to solve because you are dealing with a man-machine interface that none of us truly understands. But a lot of thought went into where the problems could lie and they were designed out of the R25.'

If the 2005 R25 had any weak points, they were that the McLaren MP4-20 was faster, particularly during qualifying, and that the Renault was harder on its rear tyres.

'I don't necessarily think the McLaren was a better car,' said Symonds. 'Everything is relative. The R25 was a superb car but, unfortunately, the McLaren was slightly quicker, so therefore there was room for improvement. We didn't use our tyres as well as McLaren did. We were a little bit hard on them, after years of maybe suffering the other way.

'Aerodynamically, I think we made full use of the new regulations – again, a sign of our lateral thinking. Whenever there is a change in regulations we always seem to be there. Despite being at a very high level to start with, our development

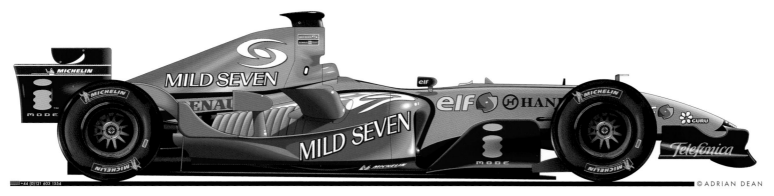

© ADRIAN DEAN

RENAULT R25

SPONSORS	**Mild Seven • Renault • Elf • Michelin • Hanjin • i-mode • Telefonica • Guru • Chronotech • Mutua Madrilena**
ENGINE	**Type: Renault RS25** No. of cylinders (vee angle): **V10 (72°)** Sparking plugs: **Champion** Electronics: **Magneti Marelli Step 11** Fuel: **Elf** Oil: **Elf**
TRANSMISSION	Gearbox: **Renault F1 6-speed longitudinal** Semi-auto: **Electro-hydraulic actuation of gearchange, clutch and differential** Hand-operated: **clutch and gearchange** Driveshafts: **Renault F1 integrated tri-lobe** Clutch: **AP Racing**
CHASSIS	Front and rear suspension: **Double wishbone/pushrod operating torsion bar** Dampers: **Penske** Wheel diameter: **330 mm front and rear** Wheels: **OZ** Tyres: **Michelin** Brake pads: **Hitco** Brake discs: **Hitco** Brake calipers: **AP Racing** Steering: **Renault F1 hydro-mechanical servo system (power-assisted)** Radiators: **Marston** Fuel tanks: **ATL** Instruments: **Renault F1 Team**
DIMENSIONS	Track, front: **1,450 mm** rear: **1,420mm** Gearbox weight: **40kg** Chassis weight (tub): **60kg** Formula weight: **605 kg including driver**

62

Sometimes you just want a car that's fun. Fun to drive. Look, there's a corner. Great, there's another. Quick, responsive, sporty. A car that's for... well, driving. And not much else. Our Renaultsport range satisfies that desire. The cars are powerful. They're controlled. They've been designed by people who love driving. With all sorts of innovations, and design details, formed in the white heat of F1. (Yes, we did win the FIA Formula 1 Constructors' Championship in 2005. Oh and yes, Fernando Alonso did become the youngest ever Drivers' World Champion.) As well as the kind of suspension that allows the driver to feel, you know, involved. Find out about the cars at www.renaultsport.co.uk. All work and no play... you've seen The Shining, haven't you?

Right: Flavio Briatore may have looked slightly world-weary on occasion, but those who worked with him in the Renault squad found his leadership inspirational as they battled their way to championship glory.

Below right: Giancarlo Fisichella's reputation took a few knocks in 2005 despite his superb victory at Melbourne.

Below: Renault F1 president Patrick Faure's commitment to the team's long-term stability led to a double title success.

Photographs: James Moy/www.crash.net

RENAULT

President: Patrick Faure
Managing director: Flavio Briatore
Deputy managing directors, France:
Rob White, André Lainé

Technical director: Bob Bell
Engine technical director: Rob White
Executive director of engineering:
Pat Symonds
Head of race engineering (engine):
Denis Chevrier
Chief designer: Tim Densham
Deputy chief designer: Martin Tolliday
Engine project leader (RS25):
Axel Plasse
Head of aerodynamics: Dino Toso
Sporting manager: Steve Nielsen
Chief mechanic: Jonathan Wheatley
Race engineers, car no. 5,
Fernando Alonso: Rod Nelson,
John McGill, Rémi Taffin
Race engineers, car no. 6,
Giancarlo Fisichella: Alan Permane,
David Greenwood, Fabrice Lom

slope is better than it has been for a long time – and the guys were still producing really good aero stuff at the end of the year.'

Good looks and inherent performance are ultimately useless if the car does not reach the end of the last lap. Renault had lost crucial ground in 2004 because of disastrous failures in Canada. That had heightened the search for technical perfection – which was pretty successful, judging by the succession of finishes in 2005. Fernando Alonso did not suffer a single failure, his only DNF being self-inflicted when he hit the barrier – in Canada, of all places.

Giancarlo Fisichella, meanwhile, was enduring the bulk of the few problems that were coming the team's way.

'Yes, we've improved reliability – but we haven't got enough!' said Symonds during the season. 'A lot of people had looked at 2004 and said we'd lost second place in the championship at the end of the year. I didn't see it that way at all. I thought we'd lost it earlier than that because of reliability. So that was the focus [going into 2005] and it continued right through the season as we expanded our reliability department yet again. Obviously I was pleased that we improved, but I'm not being silly when I say it's still not good enough.'

The Renault V10 scored highly when compared with the troublesome Mercedes. Fisichella had a failure in Bahrain and a precautionary engine change that knocked him back ten places on the grid at Spa. Otherwise, the engine division at Viry-Châtillon, France, under the control of Rob White, had done an excellent job when drawing that tricky line between performance and reliability in this two-race-per-engine era. And yet...

'We made a fabulous start to the year; absolutely superb,' said Symonds of the run of four successive wins. 'The RS25 was such an improvement on previous engines. But it's just a little bit unfortunate that the development didn't go quite as well as planned. You put in place certain investigations. But you can't be sure they're going to work. If you did know they were going to work, you'd have done them ages ago. So you set out certain areas where, obviously, you use your intelligence to look in the most productive areas, but you can't guarantee they're going to work. So let's say you spend two months investigating cylinder heads. You could come away with 15 more bhp – or you could have no more horsepower. But you don't know the answer until you get to the end of it.

'We have had a slightly unfortunate year in that respect. I'm not saying we've had no development; we've been through three major specs of engine and one of the things we really have done has been to pull the revs up. I think we are probably revving higher than anyone now compared with where we were a couple of years ago – which is a hell of an achievement. I feel one of the areas where McLaren made its big jump is that it was quite a way behind on engines and it has moved up as much as Renault has and maybe a bit more.'

That may be well and good but McLaren's failures at crucial moments perhaps indicated that Renault's rather more conservative policy had paid off. A case, perhaps, of never mind the qualifying performance; feel the winning width?

'Without a doubt,' said Symonds. 'If I went to Rob White [technical head on the engine side] and said, "We [the chassis guys] have done everything we can. We are behind McLaren but we can show by calculation that 30 horsepower will put us equal with them," he'd say, "Yes, of course. How long do you want this extra horsepower for? Friday? Friday *and* Saturday? Not Friday, Saturday *and* Sunday, surely? Two weeks! You must be mad!"'

If you like your driving to be, how shall we say, a little
on the raw side, then the Cup version of the 225
is for you. You'll notice the difference straight away.
Turning into a bend is that much sharper. Body roll? What body roll? The revised
front suspension helps here, of course. Then there are the powerful new brakes.
Or, as we affectionately call them, the drilled disc
brakes with Brembo callipers. If you can find
a nice straight road, the engine still produces the
225 hp the car is proud to name itself after.
Though if you're thinking of reaching the top speed
of 147 mph, please make sure it's a nice straight
private road. Find out more at renaultsport.co.uk.

MEGANE
RENAULT CRÉATEUR D'AUTOMOBILES

Right: The entire Renault team celebrated Fernando Alonso's championship in front of the photographic brigade at Interlagos.
Photograph: Paul-Henri Cahier

Bottom centre: Briatore (left) with executive director of engineering Pat Symonds, one of the team's most experienced and seasoned cornerstones.
Photograph: Russell Batchelor/XPB.cc

Bottom right: Alonso and the superb Renault R25 netted a total of seven wins together over the course of the season.

Bottom left: Fisichella and Alonso embraced each other after finishing first and third in Melbourne. The two men got on genuinely well and took pleasure in each other's company.

Below: Rob White and his department did a brilliant job on the Renault engine-development programme.
Photographs: James Moy/www.crash.net

'I find it a bit frustrating,' continued Symonds, speaking partway through the season, 'when I read that if McLaren doesn't win the championship, it will have lost it rather than Renault's having won it. That is just so untrue. It is taking a very narrow view of engineering. It is a very broad science and a very important part of that is reliability. It's like my saying, "Look, you can take this aircraft and it will get there 10 minutes quicker. Or maybe it won't." No contest, is there?'

Prior to the start of the season, you had the feeling that Alonso was the sort of driver who would take a chance on the quicker aircraft. Never usually giving anything less than 100 percent on every lap, the Spaniard had to modulate his approach as the season progressed and the title came within his grasp. Three early wins in succession – including a brilliant drive at Imola – provided the bedrock of a campaign that was helped by a deliberate policy to improve his one-lap qualifying and flawed only by one uncharacteristic mistake in Montreal.

'He didn't have an off-day,' said Symonds. 'He had an off-second and, unfortunately, that's all it takes. Up until that point in Canada he had been behind Fisi and he was clearly a lot quicker than Giancarlo. Fernando might have been rattled by that – he was certainly very aggressive on the radio, which is very unlike him. He's normally far from that; a very polite, nice person. Maybe that led to his hitting the wall; I don't know. But, if the guy goes for a season and that's his one lapse... well, I wish I could get through a year with just one mistake!'

Fisichella had a few more incidents; some his own fault, some not. Either way, they characterised a season that went from good to terrible as Giancarlo dominated the wet opening race of the season in Melbourne and then didn't visit the podium again for 14 races.

'I don't believe in luck but, when it comes to Fisi this year, sometimes I doubt myself,' said Symonds. 'Things like the fuel hose not going on [in France and Turkey]; we just can't explain it. Giancarlo is a damn good driver, smooth and consistent. We know him so well and he's just had a rotten year. The whole team has so much faith in him. It's a case of starting again afresh. We were so pleased when he won at Melbourne. Until then, I don't think I had really appreciated that the first race of the year is the most important because of what it does to people's spirits if they win. If I put on my mathematical head, I'll say it's ten points, just get on with it. But I saw this year what that meant to the whole team. It set the mood for what has been a really good year.'

Maurice Hamilton

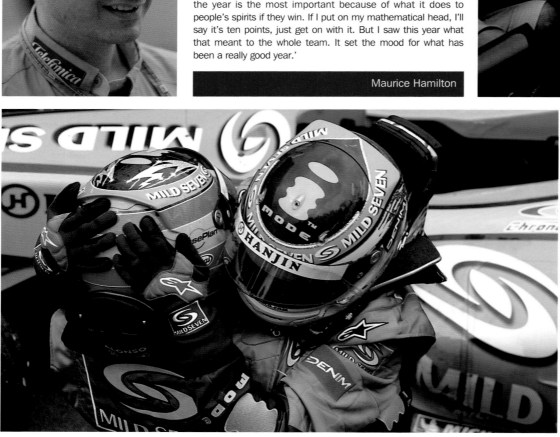

MARK WEBBER

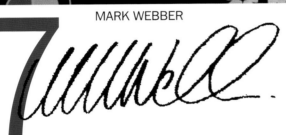

ANTONIO PIZZONIA

NICK HEIDFELD

© ADRIAN DEAN

WILLIAMS-BMW FW27

SPONSORS	Hewlett Packard • RBS • Accenture • Allianz • Budweiser • FedEx • Hamleys • Oris • Reuters • Castrol • Petrobras • Michelin • QinetiQ • Boysen • Dräxlmaier • Gore-tex • Man • O_2 • OZ Racing • PPG Industries • Puma • Würth
ENGINE	Type: **BMW P84/85** No. of cylinders (vee angle): **V10 (90°)** Sparking plugs: **Champion** Electronics: **BMW** Fuel: **Petrobras** Oil: **Castrol**
TRANSMISSION	Gearbox: **WilliamsF1 7-speed longitudinal semi-automatic** Driveshafts: **Pankl** Clutch: **AP Racing hand-operated**
CHASSIS	Front and rear suspension: **torsion bars** Dampers: **WilliamsF1** Wheel diameter: **330mm front and rear** Wheels: **OZ Racing** Tyres: **Michelin** Brake discs: **Carbone Industrie** Brake pads: **Carbone Industrie** Calipers: **AP Racing** Steering: **power-assisted** Radiators: **Marston** Fuel tank: **ATL** Fuel-tank capacity: **135 litres** Instruments: **WilliamsF1**
DIMENSIONS	Formula weight: **600 kg including driver**

IT was looking so good. After a season spent struggling to get up to speed, BMW WilliamsF1 appeared to be poised for better things when it finished 2004 with a second place for Ralf Schumacher in Japan and then a hard-earned win for Juan Pablo Montoya at the final round in Brazil. True, these two sometimes inconsistent drivers were leaving for richer (in the financial sense) pastures in 2005, but the team finally seemed to have sorted itself out. Aware that changes needed to be made, Sir Frank Williams and Patrick Head had promoted Sam Michael to technical director and given the young Australian the free rein he needed to knock certain areas of the team into shape.

Talking of shapes, the distinctive 'walrus nose' of 2004 had proved to be nothing more than a talking point and the aerodynamicist responsible for it had moved on to be replaced by the vastly experienced Frenchman Loïc Bigois. Michael, meanwhile, was continuing a process of realignment within the company while, at the same time, the team was preparing for two new drivers. While notification of Mark Webber's signing had been given before the 2004 season was over, the choice of the second driver turned out to be a typically long-winded affair as the team appeared to dither over Antonio Pizzonia, already a known quantity as test driver and occasional

substitute, and Nick Heidfeld, whose career at one point looked like being on the rocks. And, in the background, rumours continued to surface that the relationship between Williams and BMW was no better – indeed, probably worse – than before.

But all of that would become a minor series of issues when compared with two events that would have a far-reaching effect on the team's performance: commissioning a second wind tunnel at Grove and the late introduction of rule changes affecting the aerodynamic and bodywork configurations for 2005. The timing could not have been worse and this would knock Williams onto the back foot for the best part of 2005.

Despite a pessimistic forecast from Sir Frank, there seemed little cause for major concern when both cars were running up front in the second round in Malaysia (Heidfeld made it to the podium after Webber got himself tangled with Giancarlo Fisichella). Then the boys in blue and white finished second and third at Monaco two months later. The FW27 was on the pace at the Nürburgring and there was evidence of the necessary speed at Monza in September. But those were just four of 19 races. Elsewhere it was a constant struggle for balance and grip – as you might expect when the technical team has almost no data to work from.

'It was looking quite good at the end of last year and we

Above: Technical director Sam Michael could see light at the end of the team's development tunnel by the end of the year.

Centre: Antonio Pizzonia in the rain at Spa, where he had an unfortunate tangle with ex-Williams man Juan Pablo Montoya.

Top left: One-time Williams champion Nelson Piquet (left) with Frank Dernie, a consultant engineer, and Mark Webber.

Top right: Director of engineering Patrick Head was not satisfied with the season.

Photographs: James Moy/www.crash.net

thought we were back on track,' said Michael. 'Then the regulation changes hit us quite hard and we didn't recover from them as well as we would have liked to. At the same time, we commissioned the new tunnel and decommissioned the old one, so that was out of action for four months as well. It really hurt us; we didn't get as much development as we would have liked and we spent the year [2005] playing catch-up.

'There were points during the winter when we were getting one run per day in the tunnel and you normally get 25 to 30 runs per day. It was terrible. We were having to make design decisions on the car with no data. You can look back with hindsight and say it was bad timing but, actually, it's amazing how long it takes to commission a tunnel. The new one did its first run in April 2004 and, in reality, it became productive only in July and August of this year [2005]. Then it suddenly seemed worthwhile. The best thing is when you can see progress. And the changes we had towards the end of the season were massive. We signed off the last piece of development on the FW27 just before Brazil and then both tunnels were totally focused on the FW28, the 2006 car.'

That, it could be argued, was too late for the drivers – particularly Webber, for whom the move from Jaguar (and previously Minardi) was seen as a major step forward in his career path, one that would finally allow the Australian to show what he's worth. The frustration can be imagined when several promising qualifying performances came to nought through bad luck, the occasional error or, more often, a car that simply did not have the race performance.

'Mark came in with expectations of winning, so he was obviously disappointed,' said Michael. 'We were as well and we knew we were not doing a good-enough job. Mark was able to show his natural ability. He has a very good ability to feel the grip levels very quickly, which is why he is formidable in qualifying. Compared with his team-mate, that's pretty impressive and straight away it tells you about his talent. We have come a long way during the year and that can only strengthen Mark's relationship with the team, and vice versa.'

For Heidfeld, Williams represented the last-chance saloon – and the German just made it through the swing doors after a lengthy shoot-out with Pizzonia. Heidfeld had impressed at Jordan in 2004 and the trend continued with Williams. 'Nick had worked very hard over the winter and proved to Frank why he was worth having. But it was a very close call,' said Michael. 'Nick wasn't that special at Melbourne but Malaysia was different. To come through from 10th to a podium, fighting and attacking people, showed he had very good race-craft. Then there were fantastic drives in Monaco and at the Nürburgring. He really is a genuine guy – a lot of integrity, very intelligent – and I'm happy that he has resurrected his career and will continue to drive in F1.'

But not with Williams. BMW liked what it saw and lined up Heidfeld for its new liaison with Sauber for 2006, the split with Williams finally happening after six seasons together.

That, clearly, was another complication that Williams did not need. 'Once BMW decided to do its own team, it was pretty clear that the transfer of information had to stop so that we could protect our IPR [intellectual-property rights],' said Michael. 'There's no doubt that it's always worse for everyone when these things happen but that's what BMW wanted to do – and good luck to it. BMW will go its way and we'll go ours.'

And which direction is that for Williams? The restructuring continued through 2005 with Gavin Fisher leaving to be replaced as chief designer in September by Jörg Zander. Michael refuted the suggestion that the team would sometimes appear to be making change for change's sake. 'If something is wrong internally, you can't just sit there and not do anything,' he said. 'You have to change it. And keep changing it until you think it's right. We have an excellent partnership in place now; all the signs are that it looks very strong and we have no plans for further change. We're happy with what we've got and we plan to build on it after a very difficult time.'

Maurice Hamilton

BMW.WilliamsF1 Team
Official Sponsor

Stand still in Formula One and you go backwards fast. So, whilst the flag might have dropped on the 2005 season, the race for success in 2006 is well under way. As the international bank that likes to make it happen, we're looking forward to our next season in Formula One just as eagerly as we did our first.

Make it happen

RBS
The Royal Bank of Scotland Group

JUAN PABLO MONTOYA

TEAM McLAREN MERCEDES

KIMI RÄIKKÖNEN

ALEX WURZ

PEDRO DE LA ROSA

© ADRIAN DEAN

McLAREN-MERCEDES MP4-20

SPONSORS	Technology partners: **EXXONMobil • Siemens • Michelin • BAE SYSTEMS • Computer Associates Int'l, INC • Sun Microsystems, INC**
	Corporate partners: **SAP • AT&T • Johnnie Walker • HUGO BOSS • Hilton International • Schüco • TAG Heuer**
	Associate partners: **Steinmetz Diamond Group**
	Official suppliers: **Henkel • Nescafé Xpress • Sonax • Eisenmann • Advanced Composites Group • Charmilles • GS Yuasa • Yamazaki Mazak • Targetti • Enkei • Sports Marketing Surveys • Kenwood • 3D Systems • Sparco • Silicon Graphics**
ENGINE	Type: **Mercedes FO 110R** No. of cylinders: **V10** Electronics: **McLaren Electronics Systems** Fuel: **Mobil Unleaded** Lubricants: **Mobil 1 products**
TRANSMISSION	Gearbox: **7 forward speeds and 1 reverse; semi-auto** Driveshafts: **McLaren** Clutch: **Hand-operated**
CHASSIS	Front and rear suspension: **Inboard torsion bar/damper system operated by pushrod and bell crank with a double wishbone arrangement**
	Suspension dampers: **McLaren** Wheels: **Enkei** Tyres: **Michelin** Steering: **McLaren power-assisted** Battery: **GS Yuasa** Instruments: **McLaren Electronic Systems**
DIMENSIONS	Formula weight: **600 kg including driver**

'I suppose the school report would say, "Pretty good results but must try harder,' summarised McLaren chairman Ron Dennis just prior to the Chinese Grand Prix. At that stage, he knew that his man Kimi Räikkönen wouldn't win the drivers' title – that had gone to Fernando Alonso – but McLaren was still in with a shout in the constructors' series.

Dennis added, 'It is just so hard to get your mind around that when you have won ten races. While everybody [outside the team] wants to put the label of failure down to unreliability, that isn't where McLaren failed. It was a reason, part of a reason, but the main reason was that in the first four races we [the people who make up McLaren] really didn't extract the maximum out of the team and we were too cautious in our approach. That's where we lost this drivers' championship. Of course it would have helped if we had had a bit more reliability but the simple fact is that's where we felt we lost this year's world championship.'

There was no doubt that in pre-season testing and after those first four races McLaren was as quick as if not quicker than everyone else. Fernando Alonso went on to say that on a regular basis – although not at the last two races when Renault bounced back.

McLaren's MP4-20 was generally acknowledged to be the fastest car on the track for most of the middle part of the season, perhaps 14 races in total. 'But mistakes have been made in the team – by the mechanics, the engineers, the management and the drivers,' explained CEO Martin Whitmarsh and there, perhaps, is the crux of the matter. Something seemed to go wrong in nearly every race.

It started in Australia, where both drivers had off-track excursions, Juan Pablo Montoya finishing sixth, Räikkönen eighth after starting from the pit lane. In Malaysia a leaking right-rear tyre valve on Räikkönen's car caused a tyre failure and he wound up ninth; Montoya finished fourth after flat-spotting a tyre and suffering vibrations so bad that he could not see either his instruments or his pit signals.

In Bahrain Kimi posted the first podium finish with third after a mistake in qualifying, while test driver Pedro de la Rosa, standing in for the injured Montoya, was fifth. At Imola Räikkönen suffered a driveshaft failure while leading comfortably, leaving stand-in Alex Wurz to take third in his first race since Malaysia 2000.

Everything went right in Spain and Monaco, where Räikkönen led from start to finish. At Barcelona Montoya returned, not fully fit, and promptly crashed on Friday. He then qualified seventh and finished the race in seventh after a spin and two stops due to a fuel-rig malfunction.

At the Nürburgring Kimi led from pole until a suspension failure on the last lap, caused by a tyre flat-spotted when overtaking Jacques Villeneuve. He lucked into his third win of the season at Montreal, suffered engine failures in free practice at both Magny-Cours and Silverstone, which cost him ten-place penalties on the grids, then ground to a halt at Hockenheim with a hydraulic leak. Montoya scored his first McLaren win in the British GP.

That was followed by wins in Hungary and at the spectacular new Istanbul Park circuit. Then Montoya won again at Monza – where Räikkönen had *another* practice engine failure – and then handed Kimi the win at Spa-Francorchamps before being eliminated by a tangle with Antonio Pizzonia's lapped Williams. Finally, the pair scored McLaren's first one-two finish in five years, Montoya ahead, at Interlagos – but Alonso's superb third was enough to clinch the drivers' championship.

Everyone was looking for a Ferrari-beater after the 2004 season and McLaren hit the ground running. Having developed the MP4/18 and 18B the previous year, it was gratified to find the 18B a competitive car and a good basis for the MP4/19.

'We set out ambitious goals with the MP4/18,' said Whitmarsh. 'We were disappointed with where we were at the beginning of that season [meaning 2003]. Nonetheless, we did a good analysis of the problems and the issues that we had with that car.

'When we brought out the B-car, we made a good step forward. The timing of the 18B meant that we were already fixing principles of the 19 and our worst nightmare would have been if the direction we headed with the 18B was unsuccessful – then we would have had to revisit where we were on the 19. But it gave us a lot of confidence that the way we were heading with the 19 was the right direction. We learned lessons from 18 and 18B – a lot was the same, but there was sufficient change to make us believe we had the best performance package. The MP4-20 continued that. During the winter we were confident we had a quick car.'

New driver Montoya's size meant it was possible to build

McLAREN

Team principal: Ron Dennis

CEO, F1: Martin Whitmarsh

Vice president: Norbert Haug
(Mercedes-Benz Motorsport)

Managing director: Jonathan Neale

**Technical director (chassis):
Adrian Newey**

Technical director (engine): Mario Illien
(Mercedes-Benz High Performance Engines)

Team manager: Dave Ryan

Chief mechanic: Stephen Giles

**Race engineer, car no. 9,
Kimi Räikkönen:
Phil Prew**

**Race engineer, car no. 10,
Juan Pablo Montoya:
Mark Slade**

Below: Juan Pablo Montoya won in Brazil for McLaren just as he had done for Williams 12 months before.

Photograph: Paul-Henri Cahier

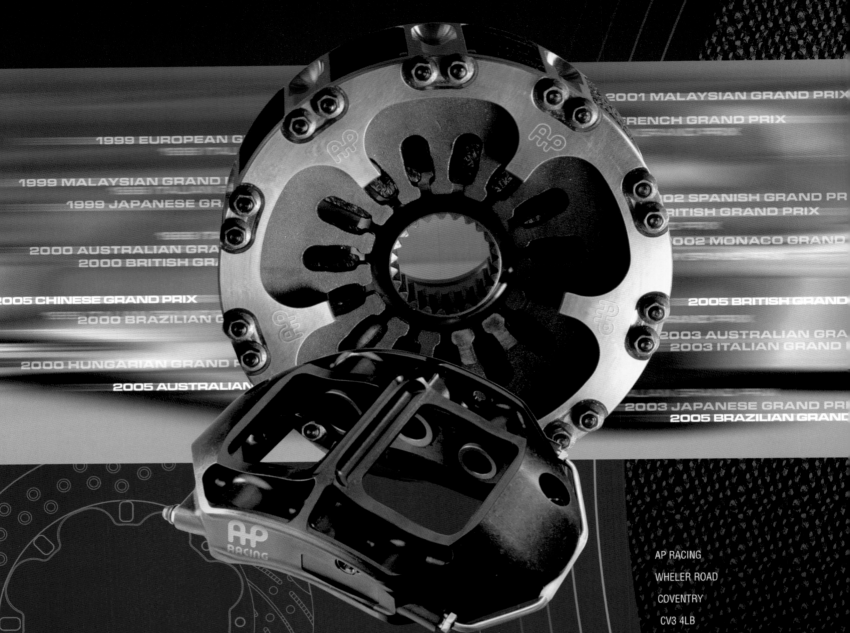

a new, smaller chassis – to third driver Alexander Wurz's detriment. Adrian Newey's design team was led by Mike Coughlan and once the chassis spec was defined, 3,600 hours of wind-tunnel work were begun by aerodynamicists Nicholas Tombazis and Peter Prodromou.

Up at the Mercedes-Ilmor engine facility at Brixworth, management and physical restructuring begun the previous year led to DaimlerChrysler's acquiring control and ownership of Ilmor. This allowed a realignment of resources and resulted in a spend-reduction for DaimlerChrysler by refocusing the efforts of the Mercedes-Benz High Performance Engines team.

It brought together two teams in one organisation. This was complicated by ownership, but that had now been restructured. There was now no competition between Mercedes-Benz and Ilmor and there was one clear, streamlined organisation, wholly owned by Mercedes. Ilmor IRL was now separated from F1.

Ola Kallenius became managing director; Mario Illien left to head Ilmor. The concept of alternating engineers was also introduced, so that Andy Cowell did the previous year's engine and Axel Wendorf did the 2005 two-race engine. 'Having said that, Axel didn't necessarily have the resources available because of demands last year,' said Whitmarsh. 'During the course of last year, we changed the processes and relationship between the engine and the chassis and that partnership is stronger than it's ever been, now, at the highest level of management and the technical working level.'

What did please the team was that chassis development brought results. It concentrated on two areas. The first was to adapt the car to Juan Pablo Montoya's driving style. Of course, it was interrupted by his broken shoulder after two races and perhaps he came back to racing a bit too soon. But suspension changes appeared to give him the steering feel that allowed him to iron out unfavourable mid-corner understeer.

The team also took a close look at its main rival, Renault. 'At the beginning of this year, McLaren had a car that had very good high-speed corner performance, but in terms of low-speed mid-corner understeer and traction it was slightly deficient to the Re-

nault,' said Whitmarsh, 'and we decided to work hard in that area and it's where we've improved the car in performance terms. Our goal there was to look at who was our strongest competitor and where we were strong in comparison and then consider the area in which to invest time and effort and identify a deficiency.'

The team made hundreds of changes to the car, according to Whitmarsh. 'Most of them were just refinements to improve efficiency, nothing that was significant,' he said. 'It was more a case of, "Here's a package; it's not bad, we've made good progress, but let's just grind away at enhancing the efficiency." It was satisfying that each of the small changes improved the performance of the car. It feels more in control, not chasing performance, not addressing a problem.'

McLaren, as a team, is no longer growing. 'It's been stable for some time now,' said Whitmarsh. 'That reflects the F1 business environment. The team hasn't grown now for two or three years. I think it was prudent that, during the buoyant phases, it was sensible in how it grew its investments and the scale of its enterprise.'

He added that the budget had remained pretty stable although the team lost West during the course of the year. 'It's going through a difficult phase of business maturing,' said Whitmarsh. 'The team has been used to year-on-year growth but the reality is that it has plateaued at the moment. World economic circumstances and political and commercial circumstances in F1 mean it's plateaued out. Structure can and will be stronger in the future. Tobacco is less significant. It's a much healthier situation now with high-technology, multinational brands and companies investing in F1. If McLaren improves the product, it can grow the company again.'

As far as Dennis and Whitmarsh were concerned, even if they had not taken the title in 2005 they had laid down the basis of an aggressive 2006 campaign. 'We won't make the same mistake next year,' was their clear message.

Bob Constanduros

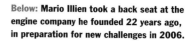

Below: Mario Illien took a back seat at the engine company he founded 22 years ago, in preparation for new challenges in 2006.

Below centre: Norbert Haug, the Mercedes Motorsport vice president, was frustrated by the engine failures that compromised Kimi Raikkonen's qualifying efforts.

Bottom right: Technical director Adrian Newey shocked the team with his decision not to renew his contract and take up a similar role with Red Bull in 2006.

Below left: Kimi Räikkönen displays his latest timepiece from TAG HEUER while sitting thoughtfully among the Michelins.
Photographs: James Moy/www.crash.net

JACQUES VILLENEUVE

FELIPE MASSA

SAUBER PETRONAS

EVERYBODY at Sauber realised that there had to be a major change in the team's financial situation for 2005. Another year with a dwindling budget would have resulted in having to reduce the personnel from the present ceiling of around 270 to perhaps 200 people, plus a move to the back of the field. So when it was announced on 22 June that BMW would take over the team at the end of the year, people recognised it as the perfect solution.

Several factors had hit Sauber hard, in spite of the first full year's operation of its wind tunnel. Red Bull had withdrawn all finance for obvious reasons and, despite several potential replacements, the budget was much reduced. The joint venture with Petronas also came to an end. There was no doubt that the team would need a new engine partner for 2006 because Red Bull had announced that it would be taking over the role of outside customer for Ferrari engines in 2006; the BMW solution was therefore again the perfect one for Sauber.

Thus reduced finance was already a severe problem in 2005. 'You cannot expect that our car is quicker than that of a team with twice the budget and twice the manpower,' said technical director Willy Rampf of near-rival Toyota. 'This would be dreaming. Overall, we can be quite satisfied because Sauber is still a private team and has to fight against all these big teams, but that's finally catching up on us. You cannot expect miracles. You have to be realistic.'

Having finished fourth in the 2001 constructors' championship, then fifth, then sixth the past two years, Sauber was finding it tough to maintain its position. Toyota had found pace and Red Bull had a good car from the start of the season and scored a lot of points in the first three races. 'It's quite disappointing to be finishing the season in eighth position, but that's how it is,' said team manager Beat Zehnder.

Two obvious results of the lack of budget slowed progress: reduced testing and having no third driver on Fridays. 'During the season, we have done a maximum of 20 one-car test days,' explained Rampf in September. 'Nearly everyone is doing two-car or sometimes three-car tests. If we have to do reliability and tyre testing and confirm aero configurations then we are running out of test kilometres. We have done 16,000 test kilometres [almost 10,000 miles] with the C24 since it was launched, at the beginning of the year. Some teams have done 60,000.'

Sauber was the only team that was allowed to run a third driver but didn't take advantage of that provision for Friday free-practice sessions. As in the past, the reason was financial. 'If we had more money, we would definitely have run a third car,' said

© ADRIAN DEAN

SAUBER-PETRONAS C24

SPONSORS	Petronas • Credit Suisse • Adelholzener • Adnovum Iinformatik AG • Advanced Micro Devices, INC • American Power Conversion • AS Lifts • Balzers AG • Brütsch/Rüegger AG • Catia/Enovia Solutions • Certina • Cisco Systems INC • DaimlerChrysler Schweiz AG • Dalco AG Switzerland • Egro Coffee Systems AG • Elektro Frauhiger AG • Emil Frey SA • Fluent • Gamatech Bottarlini AG • Italdesign/Giugario SpA. • Jacques Germanier • Kaeser Kompressoren • Klauke Industries • Lista Group • Magneti Marelli • Michelin • Mitsubishi Electric • Mobile Telesystems • MTS Systems Corporation • Paninfo AG • Philips • Pilatus Aircraft Ltd • Plenexis Group • Puma AG • Stoll Giroflex AG • Sun World AG • Supag Spichtig and Partners • Swisscom Mobile AG • TLT-Turbo GmbH • Vescal AG • Walter Meier AG • Winkler • Xerox Corporation
ENGINE	Type: **Petronas 05A** No. of cylinders: **V10** Sparking plugs: **NGK1/Cylinder** Electronics: **Magneti Marelli** Fuel: **Primax** Oil: **Syntium**
TRANSMISSION	Gearbox: **Longitudinally mounted, 7-speed Ferrari gearbox** Clutch: **AP Racing hand-operated carbon clutch**
CHASSIS	Damper front and rear suspension: **Sachs Race Engineering** Wheel diameter: **330 mm front and rear** Wheels: **OZ** Tyres: **Bridgestone** Brake pads and discs: **Brembo/Carbon Industrie** Brake calipers: **6-piston, Brembo** Steering: **power-assisted** Radiators: **Calsonic**
DIMENSIONS	Wheelbase: **3,100 mm** Track, front: **1,470 mm** rear: **1,410 mm** Formula weight: **600 kg including driver**

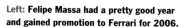

SAUBER

Team principal and CEO:
Peter Sauber

Technical director: **Willy Rampf**

Head of powertrain: **Osamu Goto**

Head of aerodynamics:
Seamus Mullarkey

Head of vehicle engineering:
Jacky Eeckelaert

Team manager: **Beat Zehnder**

Chief mechanic: **Urs Kuratle**

Race engineer, car no. 11,
Jacques Villeneuve: **Giampaolo Dall'Ara**

Race engineer, car no. 12,
Felipe Massa: **Mike Krack**

Rampf. 'It makes a difference, particularly now the race-engine mileage is limited because you have to run it for two weekends. Everybody is saving mileage. With a third car you can do proper long runs for tyre comparison, which helps define tyre choice.'

The tyres were something new for Sauber, which changed from Bridgestone to Michelin very soon after the end of the 2004 season. Why? 'One of the biggest motivations was that we would like to run the same tyres as our competitors, so if the tyre performance is not so great, it's the same for all of us, we are not falling back, we are maintaining the gap to the others,' said Rampf. 'This was the main issue; also the belief that Michelin would have a very strong development department.'

Sauber initially tested the Michelins on the 2004 C23 and was immediately impressed. 'Yes, that was quite a big surprise,' said Rampf. 'I did not expect that the step would be so good, how well the tyre was working on our car.' It was just as well – the C24 was already designed and it would have been very difficult to change the suspension. As it was, the C24 was about average when it came to tyre usage.

In other areas, Sauber's C24 was quite different from the 2003 C23, mainly due to the regulation changes. 'The front end of the monocoque was similar to that on last year's car,' continued Rampf, 'and also part of the front suspension, a few parts even carried over, but that's purely for cost reasons. The attitude was if we cannot get a big performance gain, let's keep the same part and concentrate on other areas where we can really improve the car's performance, which was mostly on the rear end. The monocoque from cockpit back was completely different from the C23. You can see the massive undercut that we have on the side pods. This was leading to quite different cooling and radiator installation. It was quite demanding because we needed the space. It made quite a difference.'

The C24 was the first car that was totally the produce of Sauber's own wind tunnel. However, for financial reasons the team could run only one shift with the tunnel – albeit a long one – five days a week: significantly less time than the big teams do. 'I think we are running the lowest amount of wind-tunnel hours except for Jordan and Minardi,' said Rampf. Having said that, there was still a constant stream of front-wing packages (Bahrain, Imola, Montreal, Magny-Cours, Silverstone), rear wings (Sepang, Imola, Montreal, Indianapolis, Silverstone), a new engine cover (Imola, Barcelona), turning vanes (Barcelona, Monaco, Nürburgring, Hockenheim, Budapest), cooling options (Sepang, Monaco, Magny-Cours) and so on.

'It wasn't all aero,' explained Rampf. 'We also tried to reduce weight during the year by introducing a few lighter components so we could run more ballast. We also worked on control systems but this was an ongoing development, with different techniques and different software versions.' In its final year as a Ferrari client, it got one engine update, at Magny-Cours. 'We started off with the same engine spec as Ferrari,' said Rampf, 'but maybe Ferrari had more updates than we did.'

There were four mechanical failures during the season: overheating in Spain for Jacques Villeneuve, a hydraulics failure in France for Felipe Massa, a coil failure for Villeneuve in Hungary and an engine failure for Massa in Turkey.

On the driving front, Jacques Villeneuve replaced Giancarlo Fisichella after almost a year of inactivity. At first, it seemed that Jacques had lost his touch. 'He was definitely struggling in the first two or three races,' said Zehnder. 'He had ideas as to how to set up the car which to us, at the beginning, weren't logical at all. Now we've found our way together. If you compare the two drivers, I would say that in five or six races Jacques was quicker than Felipe in qualifying if you take fuel into consideration.' Jacques spun in Malaysia, made another error in Monaco and lost a point at Magny-Cours when he spun after his pit stop. Massa, meanwhile, had a near-perfect season without a single mistake. Zehnder reckoned the last time he'd made a mistake was at Indianapolis the previous year.

Preparations for 2006 began even before the official announcement of the BMW takeover. There was little C24 development after the Nürburgring race because initial design of the C25 commenced, albeit with the existing technical team. The first planning meeting between Sauber and BMW took place after the French Grand Prix and initial contacts suggested that it would be a good coalition. It would also be the end of an era, of course. Sauber had been in F1 for 13 years; it was the Swiss national team. 'Everyone knows of Sauber in Switzerland,' said Zehnder. 'Peter Sauber is better known than our ministers – and we only have seven! But everybody realises that we are still in F1. With this joint venture, we have the tools with the financial background to be successful and now we have to fight hard for it.'

Bob Constanduros

RED BULL RACING

14

DAVID COULTHARD

CHRISTIAN KLIEN

15

VITANTONIO LIUZZI

Photographs: James Moy, www.crash.net

BY the time Mark Webber and Christian Klien competed in their final GP for the Jaguar F1 team at Interlagos in 2004 it looked very possible that the Milton Keynes-based team would have to be put into liquidation by its owner, Ford.

Yet if the Detroit car maker couldn't see that F1 gave a worthwhile 'bang for the buck', there was another man who most certainly did. As a result, more than 300 jobs at Jaguar Racing were saved when Dietrich Mateschitz, the billionaire owner of the Austrian Red Bull drinks company, agreed to take over the team. It is believed that Red Bull paid only a nominal amount for Jaguar Racing – possibly a symbolic one dollar – in return for taking on the team as a going concern with an estimated $400-million commitment to run the team for at least three years as part of an employee liability obligation on the part of Ford relating to the welfare of its existing staff.

Mateschitz and his lawyers had been negotiating behind the scenes to conclude a deal to buy the Jaguar team ever since Ford announced that it was up for sale in September 2004. However, the fact that the Jaguar workforce, under managing director David Pitchforth, had been working flat-out on an interim car to test from the start of December reflected just how optimistic Ford really was of completing the sale. Mateschitz was an experienced hand in the F1 business.

In 1995, Red Bull had bought a majority stake in the holding company which owned the Sauber team. Red Bull later split with Sauber over the hiring of Kimi Räikkönen in 2001 and Mateschitz sold his Sauber shares to Credit Suisse.

He could also spring surprises when he wanted to. Assurances that the former Jaguar management would be retained to run his newly acquired F1 team proved short-lived when Arden F3000 boss Christian Horner was appointed sporting director of Red Bull Racing in January 2005.

Team principal Tony Purnell and MD David Pitchforth would thus be leaving the team, which Horner would now run with a new technical director, Günther Steiner, the Austrian former WRC Ford Focus designer who originally left Jaguar in 2002 in the wake of Niki Lauda's departure as team principal. Horner's appointment strengthened the prospects for Vitantonio Liuzzi, signed up by Red Bull together with Christian Klien – although as things transpired it would be the young Austrian who would do the lion's share of the driving as number-two to David Coulthard, the Scot having his first change of F1 team since joining McLaren-Mercedes at the start of 1996.

Coulthard was an inspired choice for the emergent new

© ADRIAN DEAN

RED BULL-COSWORTH RB1

PARTNERS	Rauch • Bet & Win • Alpinstar • Michelin • Quehenberger • Amik
ENGINE	Type: **Cosworth TJ2005** No. of cylinders (vee angle): **V10 (90°)** Sparking plugs: **Champion** Electronics: **Pi VCS system** Fuel: **Castrol Race Fuel** Oil: **Castrol**
TRANSMISSION	Gearbox: **7-speed** Driveshafts: **Pankl** Clutch: **AP Racing triple-plate pull-type clutch**
CHASSIS	Front suspension: **Cast titanium uprights, upper and lower carbon wishbones, Koni damper** Rear suspension: **Cast titanium uprights, upper & lower carbon links, 7 pushrods, Koni damper** Dampers: **Koni** Wheels: **OZ** Wheel diameter, front: **373 mm** rear: **340 mm** Tyres: **Michelin** Brake discs: **AP Racing lithium alloy 6-piston calipers, Carbon incl, Hitco or Brembo** Brake discs and pads: **Carbon from Hitco or Brembo** Calipers: **AP Racing alloy 6-piston calipers** Steering: **Power-assisted** Radiators: **Marston** Fuel tank: **Castrol Racing Fuel** Instruments: **Red Bull Racing & Pi**
DIMENSIONS	Formula weight: **600 kg including driver**

Left: Christian Klien controlled the second Red Bull for much of the season in the face of a challenge from Vitantonio Liuzzi.

Below left: Scott Speed, Friday tester in North America, is expected to drive for the Red Bull-owned ex-Minardi squad in 2006.

Centre: Former F1 driver Helmut Marko was one of the closest advisors to Red Bull chief Dietrich Mateschitz.

Below: Sporting director Christian Horner.

Bottom: David Coulthard drove well to help bring Red Bull credibility and added status in its first year as an F1 team owner.

Photographs: James Moy/www.crash.net

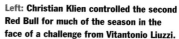

organisation. He brought a welcome stability and a crucial performance benchmark to Red Bull as it sought credibility. DC delivered that in spades, qualifying fifth in the opening race and finishing fourth. It was just the tonic the doctor ordered and David followed that up with points-scoring sixth and eighth places in Malaysia and Bahrain respectively, getting the programme off to a flying start.

Although David was an infrequent qualifier inside the top ten, his experience and racing savvy often worked in his favour. After qualifying 12th for the European GP at the Nürburgring, he shrewdly kept over to the right on the sprint to the first corner, neatly keeping clear of the customary multiple-car collision on the outside line. As a result, he completed the opening lap in fourth place and might well have posted a podium finish but for receiving a drive-through penalty for speeding in the pit lane.

The Red Bull RB1 – as the newly branded car was dubbed – lacked the ultimate edge in terms of Cosworth power, forcing the team to walk a particularly delicate tightrope between adequate downforce and excessive drag. Cosworth generally did a pretty good job given the level of uncertainty over its future going into the season, but early in the year Red Bull confirmed that it would be using Ferrari power in 2006, the first season of the new 2.4-litre V8 engine rules.

Technical director Mark Smith – who fleetingly joined Jordan at the start of the year before quickly switching to Red Bull – is conscious of the progress that has been made in getting the team into halfway competitive order. 'The team has come a reasonable way since I started here at the beginning of March,' he said. 'Many of the people here worked for Jaguar, but the engineering management has changed and the team has signed some very experienced people.

RED BULL

Team principal: **Dietrich Mateschitz**
Sporting director: **Christian Horner**
Technical director: **Mark Smith**
Head of vehicle design: **Rob Taylor**
Head of development:
Anton Stipinovich
Technical operations director:
Günther Steiner
Head of aerodynamics:
Ben Agathangelou
Head of R&D, rig testing and
vehicle dynamics: **Andrew Green**

'We were possibly a bit flattered at the start of the campaign, when BAR Honda and Ferrari were off form, but while others have moved forward, we have still been at a transitional stage in terms of the way we run the car. You don't make great strides overnight, but we know where we are and recognise what needs to be done to get to where we want to be. It is important to have people pulling together – and we have.'

Liuzzi took over the number-two seat alongside Coulthard starting at Imola but, despite some excellent set-up work and a fair turn of speed, was replaced by Klien for Montreal, after which the young Austrian remained in the seat, topping off the season with an excellent fifth place at Shanghai.

That left Red Bull seventh in the final constructors'-championship table, four points shy of BAR Honda. 'I'm satisfied with the job we've managed to achieve this year,' said Horner. 'Coming out of the last race of the season, our points tally was probably beyond many peoples' expectations and we had some very positive race performances spread across the whole season rather than just a peak here and there.

'I said at the beginning of the year that our target was to punch above our weight and grab all the opportunities as and when they presented themselves. I think we've managed to achieve that. We've laid some very solid foundations for the future and strengthened our technical base such that we've got some very promising things in the pipeline for next year.'

Alan Henry

JARNO TRULLI

RALF SCHUMACHER

RICARDO ZONTA

Photographs: James Moy, www.crash.net

WHEN Jarno Trulli put the Toyota TF105 on the front row of the grid alongside Giancarlo Fisichella's Renault R25 for the season-opening Australian GP at Melbourne, it was clear that the Japanese car maker's F1 programme had seriously gone up a gear. By the end of 2004 it had started to look as though Toyota had reached a glass ceiling in terms of hard results, mired in the midfield ruck and not quite sure how it was going to make the crucial breakthrough to the next level.

Yet armed with the first chassis completely evolved under technical director Mike Gascoyne's design stewardship, plus the all-new driver line-up of Trulli and Ralf Schumacher, Toyota grabbed plenty of early-season headlines and Trulli's strong second places in Malaysia and Bahrain raised hopes that Toyota's maiden victory might be just around the corner.

Yet with Fernando Alonso's catching his stride with the Renault and McLaren's superb MP4-20's picking up the pace dramatically after a wobbly start to the season, Toyota's ambitions had to be slightly recalibrated. After Trulli's strong start there were only three more podium finishes awaiting the team – the Italian driver pipped Ralf to third at Barcelona, and Ralf chased brother Michael's Ferrari home for a similar placing after a strong drive at Budapest and beat Giancarlo Fisichella to third in China.

Yet to a large extent the perception of Toyota's 2005 achievements was seriously coloured by the débâcle at Indianapolis, where it joined all the other Michelin runners in withdrawing from the race following the tyre failure that had sent Ralf into the wall during Friday free practice. Ferrari scored a one-two in the race at the head of a makeweight six-car pack, gathering 18 unchallenged points towards its tally in the constructors' championship. Three months later, Toyota went into the Brazilian GP just ten points behind Ferrari, wondering just how different things might have been if the team had been able to compete in the US GP.

'The TF105 was mechanically an evolution of the TF104B [which raced at the end of 2004],' explained Mike Gascoyne. 'Last year the TF104 lacked aerodynamic performance but we'd evolved it mechanically so it was a reasonably good package by the end of the season. So the TF105 was a carry-on from that. We started work on it pretty early from an aerodynamic point of view. We spent last year fixing the wind tunnel; when the new [aero] regulations were announced, it was about at the point where we were in a position to use the

© ADRIAN DEAN

+44 (0)121 603 1554

TOYOTA TF105/105B

SPONSORS	Panasonic • Denso • Karcher • BMW Software • Dassault Systemes • DEA • Ebbon-Dacs • EMC • Esso • Future Sports • Intel • KDDI • KTC • Magneti Marelli • MAN • Michelin • Nolan • Sparco • St Georges • Time Inc • Toyota Mitsui • Vuarnet
ENGINE	Type: **Toyota RVX-05** No. of cylinders (vee angle): **V10 (90°)** Sparking plugs: **Denso** Electronics: **Magneti Marelli** Fuel: **Esso** Oil: **Esso**
TRANSMISSION	Gearbox: **Toyota-Xtrack 7-speed semi-auto longitudinal** Driveshafts: **Toyota** Clutch: **AP Racing**
CHASSIS	Front and rear suspension: **Carbon-fibre double wishbone/pushrod** Dampers: **Penske/Toyota** Wheel diameter, front: **354 mm** rear: **330 mm** Wheels: **BBS** Tyres: **Michelin** Brake discs: **Hitco** Brake pads: **Hitco** Brake calipers: **Brembo** Steering: **Toyota power-assisted** Radiators: **Denso** Fuel tank: **ATL** Instruments: **Toyota/Marelli**
DIMENSIONS	Wheelbase: **3,090 mm** Overall length **4,530 mm** Overall height **950 mm** Overall width: **1,800 mm** Formula weight: **600 kg including driver**

Left: Jarno Trulli took pole at Indianapolis on the lightest of fuel loads.

Below left: Ralf Schumacher on his way to a strong third place behind his brother Michael at Budapest.

Below: Tsutomu Tomita was satisfied with podium finishes, but needs wins in future.
Photographs: James Moy/www.crash.net

TOYOTA

Team principal: **Tsutomu Tomita**

Team president: **John Howett**

Executive vice president:
Yoshiaki Kinoshita

Technical director (engine):
Luca Marmorini

Technical director (chassis):
Mike Gascoyne

Director, techical co-ordination:
Keizo Takahashi

Chief designer:
Gustav Brunner

General manager, operations:
Richard Cregan

Chief race engineer:
Dieter Gass

wind tunnel properly, so for us that was pretty convenient. So we switched all our efforts to the TF105 from that point.'

He continued, 'The TF105 was ready just before Christmas 2004, but with a very interim aerodynamic package. The intention had always been to update it just before Melbourne, the basic concept being that we would have the maximum time to evaluate the car mechanically. That meant putting new bodywork on the car for Melbourne, thereby giving ourselves the maximum time for development, although the downside was the fact that we had to throw away a load of stuff that we never raced.'

Despite media comments at the TF105's launch that the interim aero package made the car look pretty much like its predecessor, Gascoyne was confident about his development strategy and when Trulli qualified second at Albert Park it looked as though the year was off to a flying start. 'Pre-season testing went well and, knowing what was coming with the pre-season update, we were all very confident going into the first few races,' said Gascoyne. 'At Melbourne, we qualified on the front row and Jarno had a tyre problem after the first stint. People thought it was all a flash in the pan and we'd just dropped off the pace but for the next few races we were regularly qualifying on the front row and scoring podiums.

'Development-wise, the aero programme kept pace. The fact that we were able to score a podium in Hungary [with Ralf] indicated that we'd sustained our progress. I think overall the car was competitive at all types of circuit, but particularly high-downforce ones. I think we'd have been really strong in Monaco if it hadn't been for Ralf's accident in qualifying [and the knock-on effect on Trulli's run] and we were very competitive in Hungary – obviously quicker than Renault.

'I think the car was lacking a bit of aerodynamic efficiency; it needed less drag. Engine-wise, we've been incredibly reliable. If we'd actually managed to pull off third place in the constructors' championship I think everybody would have been well impressed.'

Trulli, the dominant winner at Monaco for Renault in 2004, came to Toyota as very much a known quantity. Ralf Schumacher, having experienced a patchy six years with Williams, was looking to reassert his F1 credentials and Toyota

had great expectations riding on his future form – it had coughed up a reputed stratospheric $24-million annual salary for his services, twice that earned by Trulli. But by any standards, Ralf had a disappointing year.

'I expected Jarno to outqualify Ralf and Ralf to outrace Jarno,' said Gascoyne. 'If that could bring each up to the others' level, in terms of their respective strengths, that would work well. Ralf has struggled more in qualifying; Jarno is exceptionally good at the one-lap formula. Ralf has had some strong, pretty good races, but often from lowly grid positions. He suffered from the knock-on effect of previous results. It just makes your life more difficult. He had a difficult season but he picked up a lot of points.

'The atmosphere in the team is very good; we've made the progress we've needed to make and we've got the platform we need to build on. I think we can do it quicker than Renault, thanks largely to the resources available at Toyota.'

Key aerodynamic updates came for Imola and Silverstone, and at the pre-Italian GP test at Monza the team assessed for the first time the TF105B, a heavily revised development car with McLaren-type front suspension. It was originally trailed as simply a development car for 2006 but was eventually raced by Trulli and Schumacher in the last two races of the year. It had been a good season, but not quite good enough.

Alan Henry

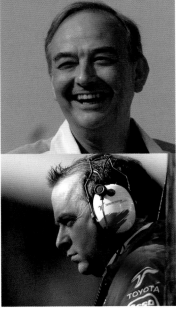

Above centre: John Howett had a calm and balanced attitude in all that he did.

Above: Chassis director Mike Gascoyne.
Photographs: James Moy/www.crash.net

Above left: Valued test driver Olivier Panis.
Photograph: XPB.cc

TIAGO MONTEIRO

JORDAN TOYOTA

NARAIN KARTHIKEYAN

THE 2005 season marked the end of one era for Jordan and the start of a new one for the Midland Group. After 14 years' ownership, founder Eddie Jordan sold his team to Alex Shnaider's Midland Group early in the year. Such takeovers are rarely painless – and this one proved to be no different. New team principal Colin Kolles admitted that his aim in 2005 was merely 'to survive'. The team did slightly better than that.

Shnaider is a Russian-born, Canadian-based industrialist who was approached by Romanian-born Kolles to finance a move for his German-based Formula 3 team into the DTM championship. However, ambitions grew and they instead decided to build up their own F1 team. Dallara would do the chassis and F3 boss Trevor Carlin would run the team from a new base at the former Dunsfold airfield in Surrey.

However, early in December 2004, F1 commercial-rights holder Bernie Ecclestone introduced Shnaider to Eddie Jordan. The latter wanted to sell his team. 'I was sent by Mr Schnaider to have a look,' said Kolles. 'I thought then that it would be the right way to go, so I called Mr Shnaider and said that we should rethink and maybe go this route. That's how the purchase of Jordan started. We made due diligence and signed a contract late in January and started work two days later.' However, the purchase came with an £11-million [$19.5-million] debt.

Fortunately for Shnaider and Kolles, the team had continued to operate during this period, so that components were being designed for the 2005 season, taking into account the new regulations. And part of Eddie Jordan's legacy was an engine deal with Toyota, negotiated on the typhoon-aborted Saturday of the Japanese Grand Prix the previous year.

Thus even though Kolles felt that he inherited nothing but four 2004 monocoques when he came in on that Monday in January, the car was able to run 15 days later. Coming in with Kolles were Carlin, who was appointed sporting director, and Adrian Burgess, who was originally team manager with Jordan's own Andy Stevenson.

Mark Smith was the technical director who oversaw the new car but, according to Kolles, he soon departed because he felt that the Dallara contact would destroy his reputation. It was to be the first of many departures, including Carlin, before the corner was turned and the team began recruiting again. Among those who came in to restore the team's character was former racer Johnny Herbert in mid-summer.

Technically, however, the team was run by James Key, who held the title of technical co-ordinator, formerly head of vehicle

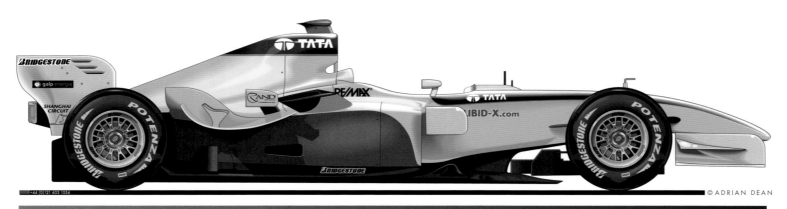

© ADRIAN DEAN

JORDAN-TOYOTA EJ15/15B

SPONSORS	Bridgestone • Benson & Hedges • TATA • Speed • Galp Energia • Portugal Tourism • Reimac • Libid-x.com • Steelbach Canadian beer • Liqui Moly • Libid-X • Trust • B&Q China • Beijing Chateau • Citibank China
ENGINE	Type: **Toyota RVX-05** No. of cylinders (vee angle): **V10 (90°)** Sparking plugs: **Denso** Electronics: **Magneti Marelli**
TRANSMISSION	Gearbox: **Jordan 7-speed longitudinal sequential semi-auto** Clutch: **Jordan/AP Racing triple-plate**
CHASSIS	Front and rear suspension: **carbon composite double wishbone/pushrod**
	Wheels: **BBS** Tyres: **Bridgestone** Brake discs: **Hitco/Brembo** Brake pads: **Hitco/Brembo** Calipers: **AP Racing** Steering: **Jordan** Radiators: **Oarston**
	Fuel tank: **ATL** Fuel-tank capacity: **over 95 kg** Instruments: **Jordan**
DIMENSIONS	Formula weight: **600 kg including driver**

science at Jordan for six years. Key oversaw the cars' running throughout the year. 'The car changed all the time,' said Kolles, 'but only small bits and pieces because the team was working on the B-version. When they [the people working on it] found something and had a comparison with the EJ15 and saw it was an improvement, they introduced it. The under-floor changed four times this year. The front wing and rear wing were constantly evolving.' The team developed the car during winter testing at Silverstone, Barcelona and Paul Ricard, but did a total of 18 days' testing during the year.

The B-version was finally run in Italy, in the hands of Tiago Monteiro. Its aim was to improve downforce, but it also incorporated suspension modifications. 'The EJ15 was very unstable under braking,' said Kolles. 'The B version had nothing to do with the car that was run in Melbourne. It had a new gearbox, new suspension... only the monocoque still existed, but even that had modifications. It had the small wings and new cooling ducts but we had to keep the basic monocoque because of the crash tests. We didn't want to make a new one because that would be an additional expense.' After initial cooling problems had been solved, the drivers reported improvements both in braking and downforce.

Throughout the year, Toyota updated Jordan's engines with just a few races' delay compared with the works team's receipt of upgrades. 'We introduced a couple of steps based on new port geometries,' said Toyota's Luca Marmorini, 'and we updated them [the engines for Jordan] continuously on the revs: 18,200 rpm for the first seven races, 18,500 rpm up to Germany and then 18,600 rpm. In qualifying they [Jordan's drivers] could use 200 rpm on top of the mentioned values, but these were still slightly below our own [drivers'] limits. We also introduced a slightly higher fuel-pressure system mid-season which they couldn't use because it needed a redesign of several car parts. Several updates for improved reliability were

introduced, as well, in parallel with the works engines. In total, Toyota supplied 33 engines to Jordan.'

The team used Bridgestone tyres again, Kolles citing loyalty to the Japanese company. 'The car is quicker on softer tyres,' he said, 'but then the problem is to finish races. For sure, we are struggling a bit with this.'

Apart from survival, Kolles had another aim: 'Right from the start, I said that we have to be reliable. That's the only thing that we wished for. By being reliable, if we were lucky we scored points and we were lucky and we scored points.'

Jordan's phenomenal reliability was a great credit to the team and the drivers. Narain Karthikeyan and Tiago Monteiro were rookies, both known to Kolles and Carlin. The Indian often looked the more spectacular but qualifying honours were almost equally divided between the two. However, Monteiro finished each of his first 16 races, a remarkable feat for driver and team.

How did Kolles see the difference between the two drivers? 'Tiago drives more with his brain. They both did a good job in my opinion, sometimes better, sometimes not so good, but in general they did a good job.

'I think that Narain is much better on high-speed circuits; and when it's very twisty, such as on the infield at Indianapolis, Tiago is better, so that also makes a little bit of a difference.' They both scored points at Indianapolis, of course, but Monteiro scored what he called 'a real point' when he finished eighth in Belgium. As with qualifying, race honours were equally divided between the two drivers.

The aim of Kolles and Shnaider in 2005 was to run Jordan efficiently. This, Kolles believed, they achieved. The team will become Midland for 2006. The only remnant of Jordan will be the type number in 2006 – M16.

Bob Constanduros

Top left: Tiago Monteiro drove well to score a point in the Belgian GP in treacherously slippery conditions.
Photograph: XPB.cc

Above left: Third-driver duties were handled by (from left to right) Sakon Yamamoto, Frank Montagny, Nicolas Kiesa and Robert Doornbos.

Above: (From top to bottom) Alex Shnaider, Dr Colin Kolles, Adrian Burgess and Johnny Herbert.
Photographs: James Moy/www.crash.net

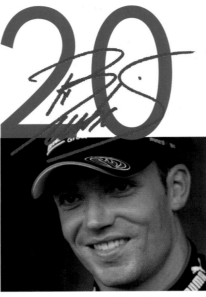

MINARDI COSWORTH

PATRICK FRIESACHER

ROBERT DOORNBOS

CHRISTIJAN ALBERS

Photographs: James Moy/crash.net

THERE were two momentous occasions in the history of Minardi during 2005. The first was that the team produced an entirely new car for the first time since 2002. The second was that Paul Stoddart sold the team to Red Bull GmbH in September, ending almost five years' ownership of it.

The birth of the new car was slow and painful. Stoddart had long campaigned to run his 2004 car for the first few races of 2005, despite changes in the technical regulations. It wouldn't upset the hierarchy, he argued, and it would save him money, vital because his budget was cut by a couple of million to $38 million in 2005.

He also believed that the new technical regulations were being improperly introduced. He therefore took his unmodified 2004-specification PS04s to Melbourne in a bid to reinforce his case. When the cars were refused a pass in scrutineering, he took the matter to the Australian courts. They ruled in his favour. The FIA threatened to cancel the grand prix and, indeed, for a while on the Friday evening the whole of Australian motor sport looked threatened.

This was not what Stoddart had intended and he reluctantly backed down. An all-nighter later, the cars had been converted to 2005 regulations. 'It caused us to waste a lot of good time and effort and money fixing up a dog of a car to do three races,' summarised Stoddart.

The cars ran in that form until the scheduled introduction of the PS05 at Imola, a massive undertaking for the small team. 'The technical department is [made up of] 17 people,' explained technical director Gabriele Tredozi. 'That includes drawing office, structural department and aero staff. But those people have been with me since the middle of 2001 and now they are experienced. But when you don't have a lot of time, you cannot invent anything.

'Before the first race we did 260 hours in the Lola wind tunnel and after that we've done another 200 hours. We've done a five-day, 12-hour session every two months.'

The layout of the car was similar to the previous year's one. 'The wheelbase is the same but the rear end is completely new,' said Tredozi. 'The gearbox and suspension plus the oil, water and hydraulic systems are all new and there was a great effort to improve engine mounting and gearbox stiffness.'

Once again, Minardi used Cosworth engines – in this case, the TJ2005 V10 that was used by Red Bull Racing for the first half of the season. 'Cosworth was fantastic, as always,' said Stoddart. 'Minardi's relationship with it is one of the best that I've ever had in business, never mind in F1. Minardi has

© ADRIAN DEAN

MINARDI-COSWORTH PS05

SPONSORS	**Muermans Group • Lost Boys • LB Icon • MD Helicopters • Garcia Jeanswear • NU.nl • JVC • ID&T • Media Republic • MAN • UPEX • SOL& MER • KPN • CO2 neutral.tv • SMP Bank • 4net.nl**
ENGINE	**Type: Cosworth TJ2005** No. of cylinders (vee angle): **V10 (90°)** Sparking plugs: **Champion** Electronics: **PI/Cosworth** Fuel: **Elf** Oil: **Silkolene**
TRANSMISSION	**Gearbox: Minardi 6-speed, semi-auto, titanium casing** Driveshafts: **Minardi** Clutch: **AP Racing triple-plate carbon**
CHASSIS	Front and rear suspension: **Upper/lower composite-reinforced wishbones, pushrod activated; torsion bars, rocker arms, mechanical anti-roll bars** Dampers: **Sachs** Wheel diameter: **330 mm front and rear** Wheels: **OZ forged magnesium** Tyres: **Bridgestone** Brake discs: **Hitco** Brake pads: **Hitco** Calipers: **Brembo** Steering: **Minardi power-assisted rack and pinion** Radiators: **Secan** Fuel tank: **ATL** Instruments: **Magneti Marelli in steering wheel**
DIMENSIONS	Wheelbase: **3,097 mm** Track, front: **1,451 mm** rear: **1,422 mm** Formula weight: **600 kg including driver**

84

Left: Christijan Albers demonstrated definite flashes of promise during his freshman F1 season.

Below far left: The Minardi crew watching proceedings with optimistic eyes.

Below left: Third-driver duties were handled on occasion by Chanoch Nissany (top) and Enrico Toccacelo.

Below: Paul Stoddart's five-year tenure ended in the sale of his team to Red Bull.

Bottom: Founder Gian Carlo Minardi can look back proudly on 20 years' involvement in F1.

Photographs: James Moy/www.crash.net

MINARDI

Team principal: **Paul Stoddart**

Technical director: **Gabriele Tredozi**

Director of young-driver development:
Gian Carlo Minardi

Administration director:
Stefano Sangiorgi

Chief engineer: **Andy Tilley**

Chief mechanics: **Paolo Piancastelli**
and Bruno Fagnocchi

Race engineer, car no. 20,
Patrick Friesacher/Robert Doornbos:
Riccardo Adami

Race engineer, car no. 21,
Christijan Albers: **Laurent Mekies**

had total reliability and a damn powerful engine.'

Plus-points were the engine's reliability and consistency, weight and low centre of gravity. Although there weren't many development steps, there were regular minor steps. However, it necessitated the new systems and titanium gearbox casing.

'The front suspension and the front axis of the car were slightly modified with some carry-over parts,' explained Tredozi. 'The nose was the same as last year's but otherwise it is a completely new car, partially because the 2005 rules involved a lot of change. Compared with last year we have good weight and carry a lot more ballast – this is also because the drivers are slightly lighter. We are quite happy with the weight distribution. I think it's an honest car.'

Stoddart explained, 'When we did introduce the new car on time, we were actually seriously stretched to get it into the condition we wanted it in so we had a lot of reliability issues. I think everybody will remember the two stillborn cars on the grid at Barcelona.'

Tredozi added, 'We broke the clutch shaft twice, but we solved the problem. After that, when the car stopped, it was for very stupid reasons. Twice was because of a cylinder in the power steering and at Magny-Cours there was the problem with the valve caps.

'The car simply wasn't finished when it first ran and Minardi has done only 1,400 km [about 870 miles] of testing during the year: 200 km before the first race, 200 afterwards and then 1,000 km before the race at Monza.'

By the time the teams reached Spa for the Belgian GP, Tredozi admitted, 'Now Minardi has a good package. I think the car is now complete following some evolution during the past few European races. There have been many new aero parts: the top wing, diffuser, side-pod inlets, front and rear ducts... Many many details and in the end you make gains everywhere. The car certainly seems quicker towards the end of the season.'

Once again Minardi used Bridgestone tyres but was very conservative in its choices. 'We don't dream; we use compounds that we know will work. Normally we use close to the compound that we used last year. It's better that we have a consistent set-up, because of the lack of testing.'

Paul Stoddart's target was always to be competitive with, or ahead of, Jordan. He felt that that aim had been accomplished in qualifying but in racing the Minardi suffered because 'on the longer runs, it deteriorates more quickly than the Jordan, particularly because it tends to "eat" its tyres'.

The team ran three race drivers and two third drivers. The eventual Dutch team-mates Christijan Albers and Robert Doornbos had both driven for Minardi before, as had Patrick Friesacher, whose sponsorship ran out after the British Grand Prix. All had been winners in other formulae and therefore certainly earned their seats. Friesacher usually outqualified Albers during the early part of the season and the pair scored points for Minardi at Indianapolis. Doornbos's arrival spurred Albers on, the newcomer outqualifying Albers a couple of times.

Finally, the team changed hands. There had been 32 offers over the years, nine in 2005, and at one time Stoddart had been dealing with seven individuals at once, including a syndicate headed by former F1 driver Eddie Irvine.

'I have always said, from day one, particularly after 9/11, that if ever an offer came along that would clearly allow the team to progress further and better than it could under my ownership, if the team could remain in Italy and the workforce be secure, I would take that offer,' said Stoddart at Spa, only a few minutes before the call came confirming that Red Bull would purchase the team. 'If that day has come, I leave Minardi an awful lot healthier than it was when I came into it. That can't be wrong.'

Bob Constanduros

GRANDS PRIX
2005

BY ALAN HENRY & DAVID TREMAYNE

MELBOURNE
AUSTRALIANGP

FIA F1 WORLD CHAMPIONSHIP/ROUND 1

Giancarlo Fisichella joined the Renault squad because he was convinced its moment had come. It certainly looked that way after he led almost every lap in Melbourne with the superb new R25, having started from pole position.
Photograph: James Moy/www.crash.net

Previously, the only restriction on tyres for race day was that whichever set was used in the single qualifying run on Saturday afternoon was also used at the start. Once the race got under way, tyres became an important element of pit-stop strategy and at the stops it was permissible to switch to either brand new tyres or scrubbed sets that had been used in practice or first qualifying.

For 2005 the set used in final qualifying had to last for the whole race distance. That meant up to four times longer than previously, depending on the number of stops normally made at a particular circuit. It represented a huge change in philosophy in terms of how tyres were developed.

There are specific challenges that have to be addressed as a tyre goes through its life cycle. Tyre temperature is maintained by a certain mass of rubber within the tread band itself. Without that you don't get the requisite movement of compound to generate the necessary heat or the thermal mass to retain it.

Under the new rules this now became a major issue after the final refuelling stops. With heavily worn tyres, the lack of tread mass could mean that teams found it difficult to regain temperature for the final stint to the chequered flag.

Just as the tyres had to last longer in 2005, so too did the engines. During the previous season they had a life of one race weekend. If a change was made during a GP weekend because of a failure or accident damage, the driver had to take a ten-place grid-slot penalty. Under the new

regulations, engines had to last for two full race weekends.

Other key technical changes for 2005 concerned aerodynamics. The one whose results were most obvious when the new cars were unveiled was raising the front wing, although the diffuser and rear wing had also been subject to changes designed to reduce ground effect.

The changes to the aero regulations were made very late and inevitably the teams then had to weigh up how much they could optimise in the limited time before the season began. No team had the time that it would have wanted in order to evaluate properly the opportunities that were afforded by the changes. The new rules triggered an initial loss of 20–25 percent in aero efficiency and everyone worked hard to erode that deficit.

For the third time in as many years, grand prix weekends would run to a new timetable in 2005. Following the unplanned experiment at Suzuka in 2004, when the threat of a typhoon meant that Saturday's qualifying was cancelled, there now would be a one-lap qualifying session on Sunday morning following the more familiar Saturday-afternoon session. For the first time in years, the grid would be formed by combining the times from both runs.

The key issue was that although on Sunday cars would run with race fuel, and could not be topped up before the race began, on Saturday the fuel load was free. And that meant that everyone would run in 'flat-out mode' with enough for one flying lap, just as in the past.

Top: The high nose on Jenson Button's BAR 007 reflected a shift of emphasis in the aerodynamic rules.

Above: Michelin rubber would dominate the 2005 season – although not without its problems, as things turned out.

Photographs: James Moy/www.crash.net

Right: Former DTM star Christijan Albers stepped up to F1 for 2005 with Minardi.

Photograph: Peter van Egmond

RUNNERS AND RIDERS FOR 2005

SCUDERIA FERRARI MARLBORO

Starting the season relying on an uprated F2004M version of last year's car for seven-times champion Michael Schumacher and his team-mate Rubens Barrichello. Debut of new F2005 initially shelved until Spanish GP, round five of the title chase. 'The new car is stiffer, lighter and more stable,' says technical director Ross Brawn. 'Fundamentally important in the light of the new regulations, it will place less stress on the tyres.' Aiding that quest is a brand new, light and compact carbon-fibre-skinned, titanium-cased gearbox which has enabled the rear of the car to be packaged for better aerodynamic effect.

LUCKY STRIKE BAR HONDA

Team now under the stewardship of former Prodrive MD Nick Fry following departure of David Richards. New BAR 007 a logical development of its predecessor, which carried Jenson Button to third place behind the Ferrari duo in the 2004 championship. Takuma Sato staying on as the British driver's team-mate for 2005. Power is provided by the latest Honda RA005E V10, a development of last year's impressive power unit.

MILD SEVEN RENAULT F1 TEAM

The team claimed that the new R25 for Fernando Alonso and returnee Giancarlo Fisichella was their best-optimised F1 car yet. Mechanically, the design group's priority had been to integrate every detail in the car around the new engine in terms of weight, stiffness and packaging. Powered by 72-degree RS25 V10, in which 98 percent of the components are new, and which had successfully completed 870 miles (1,400 km) without problems before Melbourne, boding well for the new season.

BMW WILLIAMSF1 TEAM

Under pressure to deliver in 2005 after two disappointing years. The Williams FW27 is an all-new contender with single-keel monocoque, abandoning twin-keel configuration and much-trumpeted 'twin tusk' nose section that delivered so little in 2004. Powered by a hybrid development of last year's BMW P84 V10 developed to last two races because FIA's late confirmation of the two-race rule meant all-new V10 for 2005 had to be scrapped. Fresh driver line-up of Mark Webber and Nick Heidfeld replacing Juan Pablo Montoya and Ralf Schumacher.

WEST McLAREN MERCEDES

Montoya joining Kimi Räikkönen in the cockpits of the striking new MP4-20 contenders, aerodynamically perhaps the most distinctive cars of the new 2005 generation. Seeking to bury disappointing memories of the MP4-18/19 forbears and having proved more than adequately quick in pre-race testing using the latest lower, lighter and stiffer Mercedes FO 110R V10 two-race engine.

SAUBER PETRONAS

Jacques Villeneuve and Felipe Massa are armed with the new Sauber C24, the first concept of which was outlined in May 2004, but detailed work deferred until August while FIA dithered over revised technical regulations. Aero profile shaped in dramatic new, but under-utilised, $45 million wind tunnel at Hinwil incorporating the most advanced technology available. Powered by the Petronas 05A V10, which is the latest state-of-the-art Ferrari type 054 V10 by any other name.

RED BULL RACING

Started in 1997 as Stewart Grand Prix, transformed into Jaguar Racing three years later and sold off by Ford to Red Bull for a nominal sum at the end of last year. Continuing to use Cosworth engines even though the famous Northamptonshire engine specialists had been sold to Champ car luminaries Kevin Kalkhoven and Gerald Forsythe. Red Bull RB1 started life as Jaguar R6, powered by latest Cosworth V10 upgrade of previous year's 90-degree V10 for new recruit David Coulthard and – initially, at least – Christian Klien.

PANSONIC TOYOTA RACING

Jarno Trulli and Ralf Schumacher relying on Toyota TF105, the first complete design for the Japanese constructor to be progressed from concept to completion by former Renault technical director Mike Gascoyne. Toyota RVX-05 90-degree V10 was expected to be the least of the team's problems. Last year the team had just a single failure during a race, which bodes well for reliability under the new two-race regulations.

JORDAN TOYOTA

Launched by extrovert Irish wild man Eddie Jordan with a suitably extrovert flourish in 1991, since when its form has varied from highly impressive to wildly unpredictable depending on EJ's mood and the company's bank balance. Purchased two months ago by the ascetic and pragmatic Russian-born Canadian steel billionaire Alex Shnaider. Freshman drivers Narain Karthikeyan and Tiago Monteiro using upgraded 2004 chassis now powered by bullet-proof customer Toyota V10s.

MINARDI COSWORTH

F1's survivor, getting by on a little over 10 percent of Ferrari's reputed $350 million budget. Starting the season with uprated version of Minardi PS04 with new PS05 ready for the first European race at Imola. Power from Cosworth's 72-degree CR3 V10, switching to the 90-degree TJ unit when the new car arrives. Financially qualified Christijan Albers and Patrick Friesacher replacing Gianmaria Bruni and Zsolt Baumgartner.

Under the newly introduced combined qualifying format, it inevitably emerged that the overwhelming priority was to produce one's defining lap time on a light fuel load in Saturday qualifying, because this session would inevitably play the major role in determining the grid order. On a heavier fuel load on Sunday morning, the priority would be to protect one's position achieved earlier. In a sense, you were less likely to make up places on the grid in the second session, but more likely to throw them away if you attacked with excessive zeal.

So it was with first qualifying, which set up Giancarlo Fisichella for his eventual dominant victory. The track was initially wet, then partially dried out in time for Giancarlo to post his 1m 33.171s best. Then it rained again, thwarting the efforts of high rollers such as Michael and Ralf Schumacher, Fernando Alonso, Kimi Räikkönen and Juan Pablo Montoya.

'I did a very good lap in difficult conditions,' said Fisichella. 'The track was still damp in lots of places and I had to push right to the limit without going over it. Running on dry tyres in the damp always makes it difficult to find enough grip, but the car was well balanced for my lap.'

By contrast, Alonso found his run to set 14th-fastest time was conducted in appallingly heavy rain. 'The conditions were almost impossible, even with full wet tyres, and the car was aquaplaning on the straight,' he reported.

Jarno Trulli was delighted with his second place on the grid in the Toyota TF105, but Ralf Schumacher's first outing for his new team proved 'a day to forget for me' as he could manage only 17th on the soaking track, but he pulled up by two places on Sunday morning to take an eventual 15th on the final grid.

Mark Webber did a fine job with the Williams FW27 to qualify third, but Jacques Villeneuve's fourth place in the Sauber C24 owed more to the rain's affecting his key rivals' efforts than any apparent inherent merit in his own track performance.

'The weather made things pretty difficult for us today,' said Jacques. 'When it was my turn it was a very tough decision which Michelin tyre to go for. It was a choice between intermediates and dries, and we went for the latter. It was slippery on them during my out lap and I was fortunate not to hit anything when I spun.

'After that I wasn't too aggressive on my qualifying lap. It was pretty good, so in the end I guess it was our lucky day.'

David Coulthard and Christian Klien lined up fifth and sixth for Red Bull, with Nick Heidfeld's Williams just easing out Jenson Button's BAR-Honda for seventh.

'The weather conditions haven't exactly given us the best start to the first qualifying session of the season,' said Button ruefully. 'Judging by the way the weather turned again after my run I was luckier than I thought I would be.'

Jenson was certainly luckier than his team-mate Takuma Sato, who slammed into the barrier on his out lap as the second rain shower of the afternoon dramatically intensified. That little slip guaranteed that he would be starting the race from the back of the grid. 'With intermediate tyres the car was just impossible to drive in those conditions,' he shrugged.

McLaren's duo also caught the eye of the second rainstorm, leaving new boy Juan Pablo Montoya and Kimi Räikkönen ninth and tenth, their only consolation being that they at least lined up ahead of Ferrari men Rubens Barrichello (11th) and a frustrated Michael Schumacher (19th).

'All I can say about today is that we were unlucky,' said Michael with masterly understatement. 'The weather has so often played in my favour that I can accept it was not the case this time.

'I had seen the rain clouds approaching and I hoped they would stay away a bit longer, but it didn't happen and we only just had enough time to fit the normal rain tyres when extreme wets would have been a better choice.'

Juan Pablo Montoya made the very best of things through the mist and murk of wet qualifying.

Photograph: Jean-François Galeron/WRI

DIARY 2004–05

November 2004

Red Bull concludes the purchase of the Jaguar F1 team, reputedly for a nominal sum on the condition that it stands by undertakings to run it for at least a further two years. Team principal Tony Purnell and MD David Pitchforth are fired a few weeks later, replaced by sporting director Christian Horner and technical director Günther Steiner.

December 2004

Anthony Davidson comes clean and frankly admits that he would have been delighted if Jenson Button had left BAR for Williams, clearing the path for him to inherit the BAR seat.

The British Racing Drivers' Club signs a five-year deal to guarantee the future of the British Grand Prix at Silverstone until 2009.

Ron Dennis denies speculation that he is considering retiring from the role of McLaren chairman.

January 2005

Michael Schumacher makes a donation of $10 million to the Asian tsunami disaster fund. One of his bodyguards was killed in the catastrophe.

Bernie Ecclestone loses landmark legal action with the three banks who control 75 percent of his SLEC empire, but still retains hands-on control. 'We would be badly advised if we were to exclude Ecclestone,' acknowledged SLEC chairman Gerhard Gribkowsky.

Newly recruited Jordan technical director Mark Smith resigns from the team only weeks after Eddie Jordan sells out to Canadian billionaire businessman Alex Shnaider.

Ferrari asks for an extra payment for competing in the 2005 French and British GPs because they are additional 18th and 19th races on the calendar.

February 2005

Jordan signs an all-new driver line-up of Narain Karthikeyan and Tiago Monteiro. Both are both former Nissan World Series competitors who drive for Carlin Motorsport, owned by Jordan's new sporting director Trevor Carlin.

Twice Monaco GP winner Maurice Trintignant dies aged 87.

Patrick Head slams the FIA's apparent pro-Ferrari stance, saying, 'We have to improve the governance of F1 rule-making in the future.'

Nick Heidfeld gets second BMW Williams seat alongside Mark Webber after a testing shoot-out with Antonio Pizzonia.

Right: Melbourne lit up to celebrate F1.

Centre left below: Professor Sid Watkins (left) and his successor as FIA medical delegate Gary Hartstein flanking former racer Jacques Laffite.
Photographs: James Moy/www.crash.net

Below: Slow off the mark: Michael was late for the pre-season school photograph.
Photograph: Paul-Henri Cahier

Above: Geoffrey Willis, technical director of BAR, and team principal Nick Fry.

Centre right above: Alex Shnaider, the Russian-born Canadian who recently purchased the Jordan team.

Left: Two images of Williams new boy Nick Heidfeld.
Photographs: James Moy/www.crash.net

Photograph: XPB.cc

MINARDI DOMINATES
OFF-TRACK DRAMA

Minardi team chief Paul Stoddart triggered a major crisis in Melbourne, his home city, by successfully obtaining a supreme-court injunction against the stewards of the Australian GP, who had ruled that the team's cars should not be permitted to compete in the opening round of the world championship.

Stoddart had come to Australia determined that he should be allowed to race the 2004 Minardi PS04s, claiming special dispensation despite the fact that the cars did not conform to the new aerodynamic regulations designed to reduce lap and cornering speeds.

Yet despite his getting agreement from the other nine competing teams that they had no objection to his racing the old cars, the three FIA stewards of the meeting decided it would be setting a dangerous precedent if cars which did not conform to the regulations were permitted to take part.

'It is the view of the stewards that it is inappropriate and unacceptable to alter the technical regulations with which all the other competitors comply in order to suit the individual needs and requirements of one competitor,' read a statement signed by stewards Tony Scott Andrews, Jacques Regis and Garth Wigston.

Stoddart was originally denied permission to run the old cars even though the new Minardi PS05 would not be ready before the San Marino GP, round four of the title chase.

However, the court decided that Minardi should be permitted to take part in Saturday practice and the first qualifying session.

WHEN Giancarlo Fisichella signed a contract with Renault boss Flavio Briatore in the summer of 2004, he just knew that this would be his best-ever chance of proving the critics wrong. A switch from Sauber for 2005 would bring him on board at the right time, according to Flav's long-stated prediction that this would be the season in which Renault could finally challenge for the world championship. Team bosses say that regularly, of course; next year, always next year. But Briatore wasn't talking hot air. As the beneficiary of that confidence, Fisichella decisively confirmed the Renault R25's pre-season testing form by producing a dominant victory at Albert Park, starting from pole position to beat Rubens Barrichello in the sole surviving Ferrari, who had climbed through from 11th on the grid, and Fernando Alonso in the other Renault, who came from 13th at the start to take the flag just 1.159s behind the Brazilian.

For the Italian veteran of 141 previous grands prix, this dominant performance represented a career breakthrough of considerable magnitude. It may have come rather late in the day, but it was a masterly performance played out at the front of the field in a car which used its Michelin rubber to brilliantly consistent effect – and tyre performance was the most crucial element in the F1 car's performance package now that one set of tyres had to last throughout two qualifying sessions and the race. In that respect, it stood as a spectacular contrast to his sole previous victory in the 2003 Brazilian GP at the wheel of a Jordan, the result of which was confirmed only five days later.

Intermittent heavy rain during Saturday's first qualifying meant that the grid order was scrambled by the time Sunday morning's second-session times had been aggregated in the new 2005 format to determine the overall starting line-up. One of the competitors to benefit from this chaos was David Coulthard, who qualified the Red Bull RB1 a fine fifth and then lunged up to third at the first corner. Thereafter the Scot drove brilliantly to finish fourth just ahead of the Williams-BMW of Mark Webber, the man who had left Jaguar before it was sold to Red Bull to sign with Frank's team.

The new qualifying format that led to this unfamiliar grid order was confusing in the extreme. Yet although he benefited from the situation, Coulthard was sufficiently honest to confirm that this was not what F1 should be about.

'If you want to see Michael Schumacher at the back of the grid then, yeah, go and clap your hands,' he said after qualifying was over. 'But that's not competition. I think it's shit, basically,

the way this session finished. We [Red Bull Racing's drivers] were fifth and sixth but we don't really deserve to be there. It's not what the sport stands for.'

With Kimi Räikkönen stalling his McLaren MP4-20 on the grid – and having to start from the pit lane as a result – the pack was given an extra formation lap and that lap was deducted from the overall race distance. When the starting signal was given, Fisichella got away cleanly to complete the opening lap already a dominant 1.4s ahead of Jarno Trulli's impressive Toyota TF105. Trulli had joined Fisi to make the first all-Italian front row since Michele Alboreto and Elio de Angelis at Rio in 1984.

Coulthard was next, ahead of Mark Webber's Williams FW27, Nick Heidfeld's sister car, the impressive Christian Klien's Red Bull, Juan Pablo Montoya's McLaren, Rubens Barrichello's Ferrari and Jacques Villeneuve's Sauber C24, which had qualified a fortuitous fourth only to be swallowed immediately by the rest of the pack. Fernando Alonso was tenth in the other Renault R25 while Michael Schumacher and Kimi Räikkönen were back in 15th and 16th.

Trulli kept the pace well in the opening stages and with ten laps completed was only 2.1s adrift. Jarno was running slightly lighter and made his first stop on lap 18. Coulthard moved into second and stayed out until lap 21, but Fisichella stayed out until lap 23 and, by the time the race settled back into its rhythm at the end of the first round of stops on lap 27, he was 12s ahead of the Toyota.

Trulli now found himself unable to sustain that early pace. 'I

had a good first stint fighting at the front,' he said. 'After my [first] pit stop, I had a problem with the rear tyres which dropped me out of the points and down the field. But we have certainly been encouraged by the TF105's performance over the weekend.' He wound up ninth at the chequered flag, admittedly three places and a lap better than his team-mate Ralf Schumacher, who was thwarted by the need for an extra stop early on to secure a loose seat harness. Even so, Trulli was pleased with the feel of the new car.

Barrichello's superb climb to second saved Ferrari's bacon. For once, Michael Schumacher not only failed to finish the Australian Grand Prix, but the multiple world champion's Ferrari F2004M was never a contender. Schumi was a bit-part player, consigned almost to the back of the starting grid after a heavy rain shower almost flooded the track during Saturday's first qualifying session.

Schumacher's demise came with 15 laps to go as he was battling for eighth place with Williams new boy Heidfeld, who ran into the back of him under braking for the tight right-hand Turn Three. Both cars spun into the gravel trap on the outside of the corner and, although Schumacher managed to extricate his car with the assistance of nearby marshals, its rear end was slightly damaged and he trailed back to the pits to retire.

'With this type of thing there are always different opinions,' said Schumacher, 'and mine is that it is impossible to blame either one of us. I saw him behind me just as I came out of the pits and I made it clear I was defending my position.'

Above: David Coulthard made an impressive start to his 2005 season with a strong run to fourth place in the Red Bull RB1.
Photograph: James Moy/www.crash.net

Left: Jacques Villeneuve qualified his Sauber C24 fourth on the grid and proved quite a challenge for Fernando Alonso to overtake in his Renault.
Photograph: Laurent Charniaux/WRI

Above: **Christian Klien acquitted himself well to score championship points in the opening race of the season.**
Photograph: James Moy/www.crash.net

Heidfeld was less philosophical about the whole episode. 'I think that I made a good move,' he said. 'Michael came out of the pits and obviously had a bad exit from the first chicane because he wasn't on the ideal line. I went alongside him and I could have outbraked him, but he didn't leave me any space and pushed me onto the grass, where braking is obviously impossible.'

Alonso, meanwhile, raced hard and fast all afternoon but just wasn't quite quick enough to keep Barrichello behind at the final round of refuelling stops. He led into his second stop on lap 45, but Rubens just squeezed into second as Fernando sprinted for the pit exit.

'For sure my 13th place on the grid was not my real position for the potential of the car this weekend,' said Alonso. 'I went through the slow traffic very easily, then followed Jacques [Villeneuve] for 17 laps with a very good fight, but lost 25s to the podium finishers in the process.' With a higher qualifying position, things could have been very different.

Barrichello proved that there wasn't much wrong with the Bridgestone-shod Ferrari, in cool conditions at least. 'Much was made after Melbourne of the fact that I climbed through the field to finish second,' he said modestly. 'But the fuel-stop strategy worked perfectly and, to be honest, I didn't really overtake many other cars. I drove seriously flat-out from the beginning while still giving the tyres sufficient care to ensure they were in good shape towards the end.

'But I did have a brake-balance problem which gave me a big percentage of the braking to the rear, handling like a kart. If it hadn't been for that I think I could have perhaps lapped a couple of tenths a lap quicker. But I was confident I had the pace to keep Alonso out for second, although I really wasn't doing anything that I hadn't done before many times.'

Meanwhile Coulthard was at his majestic best. Twice before he had won for McLaren at Melbourne and now there looked a slender possibility that he might post a third victory in remarkable circumstances. But it didn't work out. He locked up a couple of times and was lucky not to flat-spot his Michelins. He also lost a flap off his front wing while lapping one of the Minardi novices, but thankfully this didn't upset the car's handling balance.

For the 34-year-old Scot this was a red-letter day on three counts. He eclipsed Britain's F1 man of the moment Jenson Button, who had a simply miserable afternoon in the underperforming BAR-Honda. He also finished just under a second ahead of Mark Webber, the man who preceded him in the Jaguar squad before it was sold to Red Bull the previous November.

Webber, secretly nursing a painfully cracked rib sustained in pre-season testing at Barcelona, was not really happy with fifth place, but put a brave face on the outcome of the afternoon. 'Coming fifth is not a bad start [to the year] at all,' he said, 'but I think that we actually had an opportunity for a better result today.

'I lost one position to Coulthard at the first corner when I was looking after my tyres and trying not to lock my wheels. After that I was stuck behind him, which was a bit frustrating.'

Yet perhaps most satisfying for Coulthard was that he took the chequered flag 19s and two places ahead of Juan Pablo Montoya, the man who took his place in the McLaren Mercedes squad at the start of this season, ending David's nine-year partnership with the British team. JPM lost a barge board on his way to the finish, as did the eighth-placed Räikkönen, neither McLaren driver getting the best out of the obviously promising new MP4-20.

Ron Dennis, the McLaren chairman – who accused Montoya of throwing away a podium finish after he ran wide onto the grass trying to lap one of the tail-end Jordan-Toyotas – graciously offered Coulthard words of congratulation after a heady drive in which he ran second for part of the race.

'It is a young team but that car has been well developed,' he said. 'David had a good drive and I am happy for his fourth place, but let's just say the only people in front of us who concern us are the Renaults.'

Coulthard's efforts unexpectedly left Button in the shade. He was trailing disappointingly in 11th, three places ahead of his team-mate Takuma Sato, when the BARs were called in just before the finish to avail themselves of a loophole in the rules which permitted any car that failed to pass the chequered flag to have a new engine fitted in time for the next race. This was a dreadfully disappointing performance for the BAR Honda team, which was seeking to build on its 2004 record of second behind Ferrari in the constructors' championship.

'We were out of the points so on the last lap we decided to stop both cars, which gives us the opportunity to change engines for Malaysia without further penalty,' said the BAR technical director Geoff Willis. 'This could be an advantage at a race in which we normally encounter high temperatures.'

Trulli struggled home ninth ahead of Felipe Massa's Sauber, with Ralf Schumacher classified 12th ahead of the acutely disappointed Villeneuve, the stationary Sato and new boys Narain Karthikeyan, Tiago Monteiro and Patrick Friesacher, all of whom kept out of trouble on their GP debuts.

Renault had done a brilliantly impressive job, but we'd yet to see the new Ferrari F2005. Would Maranello accelerate its scheduled debut? Would things be different in the heat of Malaysia or Bahrain? Unquestionably there was a tantalising element of uncertainty about the way in which the new season might unfold.

Alan Henry

Right: **Fisichella was absolutely ecstatic on the rostrum after scoring the second grand prix victory of his career.**
Photograph: James Moy/www.crash.net

FOSTER'S AUSTRALIAN GRAND PRIX

MELBOURNE 4–6 MARCH 2005

MELBOURNE – ALBERT PARK

LAUDA 160/258 (5)
70/113 (3)
175/282 (6)
CLARK 60/97 (2)
MARINA
WAITE 130/209 (5)
HILL 180/290 (6)
180/290 (6)
WHITFORD 130/209 (5)
ASCARI 70/113 (3)
SENNA 45/72 (2)
50/81 (2)
BRABHAM
FANGIO 180/290 (6)
JONES CHICANE
185/298 (6)
PROST 80/129 (4)
STEWART 130/209 (4)

mph/km/h (gear)

CIRCUIT LENGTH: 3.295 miles/5.303 km

Photograph: Peter van Egmond

RACE DISTANCE: 57 laps, 187.822 miles/302.271 km   RACE WEATHER: Sunny/overcast (track 26–30°C, air 20–21°C)

Pos.	Driver	Nat.	No.	Entrant	Car/Engine	Tyres	Laps	Time/Retirement	Speed (mph/km/h)	Gap to leader	Fastest race lap	
1	Giancarlo Fisichella	I	6	Mild Seven Renault F1 Team	Renault R25-RS25 V10	M	57	1h 24m 17.336s	133.698/215.1		1m 25.994s	55
2	Rubens Barrichello	BR	2	Scuderia Ferrari Marlboro	Ferrari F2004M-054 V10	B	57	1h 24m 22.889s	133.552/214.931	+5.553s	1m 26.233s	54
3	Fernando Alonso	E	5	Mild Seven Renault F1 Team	Renault R25-RS25 V10	M	57	1h 24m 24.048s	133.521/214.882	+6.712s	1m 25.683s	24
4	David Coulthard	GB	14	Red Bull Racing	Red Bull RB1-Cosworth TJ2005/10 V10	M	57	1h 24m 33.467s	133.273/214.483	+16.131s	1m 26.690s	40
5	Mark Webber	AUS	7	BMW WilliamsF1 Team	Williams FW27-BMW P84/85 V10	M	57	1h 24m 34.244s	133.253/214.450	+16.908s	1m 26.493s	37
6	Juan Pablo Montoya	COL	10	West McLaren Mercedes	McLaren MP4-20-Mercedes FO 110R V10	M	57	1h 24m 52.369s	132.779/213.687	+35.033s	1m 26.393s	41
7	Christian Klien	A	15	Red Bull Racing	Red Bull RB1-Cosworth TJ2005/10 V10	M	57	1h 24m 56.333s	132.676/213.521	+38.997s	1m 26.627s	39
8	Kimi Räikkönen	FIN	9	West McLaren Mercedes	McLaren MP4-20-Mercedes FO 110R V10	M	57	1h 24m 56.969s	132.659/213.494	+39.633s	1m 26.255s	55
9	Jarno Trulli	I	16	Panasonic Toyota Racing	Toyota TF105-RVX-05 V10	M	57	1h 25m 20.444s	132.050/212.515	+63.108s	1m 27.116s	56
10	Felipe Massa	BR	12	Sauber Petronas	Sauber C24A-Petronas 05 V10	M	57	1h 25m 21.729s	132.018/212.462	+64.393s	1m 26.893s	55
11	Jenson Button	GB	3	Lucky Strike BAR Honda	BAR 007-Honda RA005E V10	M	56			DNF	1m 26.260s	55
12	Ralf Schumacher	D	17	Panasonic Toyota Racing	Toyota TF105-RVX-05 V10	M	56			+1 lap	1m 26.536s	56
13	Jacques Villeneuve	CDN	11	Sauber Petronas	Sauber C24A-Petronas 05 V10	M	56			+1 lap	1m 27.745s	54
14	Takuma Sato	J	4	Lucky Strike BAR Honda	BAR 007-Honda RA005E V10	M	55			DNF	1m 27.877s	36
15	Narain Karthikeyan	IND	19	Jordan Toyota	Jordan EJ15-Toyota RVX-05 V10	B	55			+2 laps	1m 27.970s	36
16	Tiago Monteiro	P	18	Jordan Toyota	Jordan EJ15-Toyota RVX-05 V10	B	55			+2 laps	1m 28.999s	16
17	Patrick Friesacher	A	20	Minardi Cosworth	Minardi PS04B-Cosworth CR3 V10	B	53			+4 laps	1m 32.852s	22
	Michael Schumacher	D	1	Scuderia Ferrari Marlboro	Ferrari F2004M-054 V10	B	42	Collision			1m 26.261s	38
	Nick Heidfeld	D	8	BMW WilliamsF1 Team	Williams FW27-BMW P84/85 V10	M	42	Collision			1m 26.854s	38
	Christijan Albers	NL	21	Minardi Cosworth	Minardi PS04B-Cosworth CR3 V10	B	16	Gearbox			1m 33.144s	1

All results and data © FOM 2005

Fastest lap: Fernando Alonso, on lap 24, 1m 25.683s, 138.446 mph/222.807 km/h.

Previous lap record: Michael Schumacher (Ferrari F2004-052 V10), 1m 24.125s, 141.009 mph/226.933 km/h (2004).

19th: M. SCHUMACHER Ferrari
Ten-place penalty for engine change

17th: ALBERS Minardi-Cosworth

15th: R. SCHUMACHER Toyota

13th: ALONSO Renault

11th: BARRICHELLO Ferrari

20th: SATO BAR-Honda
Ten-place penalty for engine change

18th: MASSA Sauber-Petronas

16th: FRIESACHER Minardi-Cosworth

14th: MONTEIRO Jordan-Toyota

12th: KARTHIKEYAN Jordan-Toyota

Grid order	1	2	3	4	5	6	7	8	9	10	11	12	13	14	15	16	17	18	19	20	21	22	23	24	25	26	27	28	29	30	31	32	33	34	35	36	37	38	39	40	41	42	43	44
6 FISICHELLA	6	6	6	6	6	6	6	6	6	6	6	6	6	6	6	6	6	6	6	6	6	6	2	6	6	6	6	6	6	6	6	6	6	6	6	6	6	6	6	6	6	6	5	5
16 TRULLI	16	16	16	16	16	16	16	16	16	16	16	16	16	16	16	16	14	14	14	10	10	2	6	2	14	14	14	14	14	14	14	14	14	14	14	14	14	14	14	2	6	6
7 WEBBER	14	14	14	14	14	14	14	14	14	14	14	14	14	14	14	14	7	7	10	2	5	14	7	7	7	7	7	7	7	7	7	7	7	7	7	7	7	7	2	2	5	2	2
11 VILLENEUVE	7	7	7	7	7	7	7	7	7	7	7	7	7	7	7	7	15	15	2	14	5	14	14	7	2	2	2	2	2	2	2	2	2	2	2	2	2	10	10	10	14	14	14
14 COULTHARD	8	8	8	8	8	8	8	8	8	8	8	8	8	8	8	8	8	10	10	7	5	14	7	7	5	10	10	10	10	10	10	10	10	10	10	10	5	5	5	10	7	7
15 KLIEN	15	15	15	15	15	15	15	15	15	15	15	15	15	15	15	15	2	2	5	7	10	10	10	16	16	16	16	5	5	5	5	5	5	5	5	4	5	7	7	7	10	10
8 HEIDFELD	10	10	10	10	10	10	10	10	10	10	10	10	10	10	10	16		5	5	5	16	16	16	16	5	5	5	16	16	16	16	15	15	15	15	1	1	15	15	15
3 BUTTON	2	2	2	2	2	2	2	2	2	2	2	2	2	2	2	2	16	15	11	15	15	15	15	15	15	15	15	15	15	15	15	9	8	8	15	15	1	9
10 MONTOYA	11	11	11	11	11	11	11	11	11	11	11	11	11	11	11	5	8	11	11	15	8	8	8	8	8	8	8	8	8	8	8	8	9	9	9	8	8	16	16
9 RÄIKKÖNEN	5	5	5	5	5	5	5	5	5	5	5	5	5	5	5	11	11	3	3	8	1	1	1	1	12	9	9	9	9	9	9	9	9	1	1	1	9	9	9	9	12	12
2 BARRICHELLO	3	3	3	3	3	3	3	3	3	3	3	3	3	3	3	3	3	8	12	9	9	9	12	1	1	1	1	1	1	1	1	16	16	16	16	3	16	16	3	3
19 KARTHIKEYAN	17	17	17	17	17	17	17	17	17	17	17	17	17	17	17	17	12	12	12	9	9	11	11	11	11	11	11	11	11	11	11	11	11	3	16	12	12	4	4
5 ALONSO	12	12	12	12	12	12	12	12	12	12	12	12	12	12	12	12	9	11	11	11	11	3	3	3	3	3	3	3	3	4	3	3	4	12	3	3	17	17
18 MONTEIRO	4	4	4	4	4	4	4	4	4	4	4	4	4	4	4	4	9	3	3	3	3	12	4	4	12	12	12	12	12	12	12	4	12	4	3	4	17	17
17 R SCHUMACHER	1	1	1	1	1	1	1	1	1	1	1	1	1	1	1	1	4	4	4	4	4	4	12	12	12	12	12	12	17	17	11	11	11	19
20 FRIESACHER	9	9	9	9	9	9	9	9	9	9	9	9	9	9	9	9	17	4	17	17	17	17	17	17	17	17	17	17	17	11	17	17	17	18	18
21 ALBERS	18	18	18	18	18	18	18	18	18	18	18	18	18	18	18	18	19	19	19	19	19	19	19	19	19	19	19	19	19	19	19	19	19	20	20
12 MASSA	19	19	19	19	19	19	19	19	19	19	19	19	19	19	19	18	18	18	18	18	18	18	18	18	18	18	18	18	18
1 M SCHUMACHER	20	20	20	20	20	20	20	20	20	20	20	20	20	20	21	20	20	20	20	20	20	20	20	20	20	20	20	20	20	20	20
4 SATO	21	21	21	21	21	21	21	21	21	21	21	21	20	20

QUALIFYING

SATURDAY: Windy/rainy (track 19–22°C, air 13–15°C)
SUNDAY: Cloudy/sunny (track 17–22°C, air 15–18°C)

Pos.	Driver	R/Order	1st qualifying	R/Order	2nd qualifying	Aggregate
1	Giancarlo Fisichella	12	1m 33.171s	20	1m 28.289s	3m 01.460s
2	Jarno Trulli	9	1m 35.270s	19	1m 29.159s	3m 04.429s
3	Mark Webber	7	1m 36.717s	18	1m 28.279s	3m 04.996s
4	Jacques Villeneuve	11	1m 36.984s	17	1m 29.862s	3m 06.846s
5	David Coulthard	10	1m 38.320s	15	1m 28.892s	3m 07.212s
6	Christian Klien	8	1m 37.486s	16	1m 29.991s	3m 07.477s
7	Nick Heidfeld	6	1m 39.717s	14	1m 29.413s	3m 09.130s
8	Jenson Button	5	1m 41.512s	13	1m 30.616s	3m 12.128s
9	Juan Pablo Montoya	19	1m 45.325s	10	1m 29.320s	3m 14.645s
10	Kimi Räikkönen	18	1m 44.997s	11	1m 30.561s	3m 15.558s
11	Rubens Barrichello	17	1m 45.481s	9	1m 31.341s	3m 16.822s
12	Narain Karthikeyan	3	1m 44.357s	12	1m 32.735s	3m 17.092s
13	Fernando Alonso	16	1m 47.708s	7	1m 29.758s	3m 17.466s
14	Tiago Monteiro	4	1m 46.846s	8	1m 33.483s	3m 20.329s
15	Ralf Schumacher	20	1m 51.495s	4	1m 31.222s	3m 22.717s
16	Patrick Friesacher	2	1m 50.864s	5	1m 37.499s	3m 28.363s
17	Christijan Albers	1	1m 49.230s	6	No time	No time
18	Michael Schumacher	14	1m 57.931s	3	No time	No time
19	Takuma Sato	15	No time	1	No time	No time
20	Felipe Massa	13	No time	2	No time	No time

CHASSIS LOG BOOK

	FERRARI				SAUBER-PETRONAS	
1	Michael Schumacher	F2004M/241		11	Jacques Villeneuve	C24/03
2	Rubens Barrichello	F2004M/240		12	Felipe Massa	C24/02
	Spare	F2004M/236			Spare	C24/01
	BAR-HONDA				RED BULL-COSWORTH	
3	Jenson Button	007/04		14	David Coulthard	RB1/2
4	Takuma Sato	007/02		15	Christian Klien	RB1/1
	Spare	007/03		37	Vitantonio Liuzzi	RB1/3
	RENAULT				Spare	RB1/3
5	Fernando Alonso	R25/04			TOYOTA	
6	Giancarlo Fisichella	R25/03		16	Jarno Trulli	TF105/03
	Spare	R25/02		17	Ralf Schumacher	TF105/04
	WILLIAMS-BMW			38	Ricardo Zonta	TF105/02
7	Mark Webber	FW27/03			Spare	TF105/02
8	Nick Heidfeld	FW27/04			JORDAN-TOYOTA	
	Spare	FW27/02		18	Tiago Monteiro	EJ15/03
	McLAREN-MERCEDES			19	Narain Karthikeyan	EJ15/02
9	Kimi Räikkönen	MP4-20/04		39	Robert Doornbos	EJ15/01
10	Juan Pablo Montoya	MP4-20/03			Spare	EJ15/01
35	Pedro de la Rosa	MP4-20/01			MINARDI-COSWORTH	
	Spare	MP4-20/01		20	Patrick Friesacher	PS04B/02
				21	Christijan Albers	PS04B/04
					Spare	PS04B/03

Photograph: James Moy/www.crash.net

PRACTICE 1 (FRIDAY)

Sunny/overcast (track 28–29°C, air 19–21°C)

Pos.	Driver	Laps	Time
1	Vitantonio Liuzzi	19	1m 25.967s
2	Pedro de la Rosa	19	1m 26.480s
3	Ricardo Zonta	2	1m 27.265s
4	Juan Pablo Montoya	5	1m 27.425s
5	David Coulthard	9	1m 27.573s
6	Felipe Massa	5	1m 27.971s
7	Mark Webber	10	1m 28.269s
8	Jarno Trulli	10	1m 28.366s
9	Jenson Button	10	1m 28.632s
10	Christian Klien	9	1m 28.834s
11	Nick Heidfeld	9	1m 29.172s
12	Rubens Barrichello	5	1m 29.227s
13	Ralf Schumacher	12	1m 29.285s
14	Jacques Villeneuve	7	1m 29.332s
15	Robert Doornbos	23	1m 29.370s
16	Takuma Sato	9	1m 31.364s
17	Tiago Monteiro	15	1m 32.348s
18	Narain Karthikeyan	6	1m 38.175s
19	Kimi Räikkönen	1	No time
20	Michael Schumacher	3	No time
21	Giancarlo Fisichella	2	No time
22	Fernando Alonso	2	No time

PRACTICE 2 (FRIDAY)

Sunny (track 32–34°C, air 20–21°C)

Pos.	Driver	Laps	Time
1	Pedro de la Rosa	28	1m 25.376s
2	Kimi Räikkönen	15	1m 25.676s
3	Nick Heidfeld	23	1m 25.940s
4	Michael Schumacher	15	1m 26.081s
5	Juan Pablo Montoya	14	1m 26.227s
6	Felipe Massa	19	1m 26.357s
7	Fernando Alonso	21	1m 26.562s
8	Jenson Button	26	1m 26.611s
9	Rubens Barrichello	14	1m 26.639s
10	Giancarlo Fisichella	23	1m 26.667s
11	Ricardo Zonta	31	1m 26.808s
12	David Coulthard	22	1m 27.017s
13	Ralf Schumacher	16	1m 27.162s
14	Jarno Trulli	24	1m 27.195s
15	Mark Webber	19	1m 27.329s
16	Jacques Villeneuve	18	1m 27.513s
17	Christian Klien	14	1m 27.544s
18	Takuma Sato	20	1m 27.891s
19	Narain Kathikeyan	29	1m 28.168s
20	Robert Doornbos	30	1m 28.620s
21	Vitantonio Liuzzi	7	1m 28.926s
22	Tiago Monteiro	23	1m 29.671s

PRACTICE 3 (SATURDAY)

Cloudy/rainy (track 15–16°C, air 13–14°C)

Pos.	Driver	Laps	Time
1	Michael Schumacher	5	1m 40.540s
2	Rubens Barrichello	4	1m 41.933s
3	Kimi Räikkönen	6	1m 43.526s
4	Narain Karthikeyan	10	1m 45.641s
5	Ralf Schumacher	6	1m 45.687s
6	Takuma Sato	3	1m 46.768s
7	David Coulthard	5	1m 48.369s
8	Christijan Albers	10	1m 48.566s
9	Jarno Trulli	8	1m 49.623s
10	Jenson Button	3	1m 51.364s
11	Tiago Monteiro	5	1m 53.457s
12	Patrick Friesacher	11	1m 53.507s
13	Jacques Villeneuve	3	No time
14	Christian Klien	1	No time
15	Felipe Massa	3	No time
16	Juan Pablo Montoya	1	No time
17	Nick Heidfeld	3	No time
18	Mark Webber	3	No time
19	Fernando Alonso	2	No time
20	Giancarlo Fisichella	2	No time

PRACTICE 4 (SATURDAY)

Cloudy/wet/drying (track 16–18°C, air 14–15°C)

Pos.	Driver	Laps	Time
1	Kimi Räikkönen	11	1m 27.297s
2	Fernando Alonso	14	1m 27.409s
3	Juan Pablo Montoya	11	1m 28.256s
4	Giancarlo Fisichella	13	1m 28.571s
5	Jenson Button	11	1m 29.577s
6	Mark Webber	10	1m 30.299s
7	Michael Schumacher	7	1m 30.533s
8	Takuma Sato	14	1m 30.554s
9	David Coulthard	14	1m 30.645s
10	Rubens Barrichello	7	1m 30.715s
11	Nick Heidfeld	7	1m 31.375s
12	Christian Klien	14	1m 31.671s
13	Jarno Trulli	18	1m 31.701s
14	Felipe Massa	14	1m 31.736s
15	Jacques Villeneuve	14	1m 32.031s
16	Ralf Schumacher	10	1m 32.924s
17	Christijan Albers	13	1m 32.975s
18	Patrick Friesacher	7	1m 40.045s
19	Tiago Monteiro	9	1m 40.802s
20	Narain Karthikeyan	6	1m 40.882s

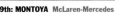
9th: MONTOYA McLaren-Mercedes

7th: HEIDFELD Williams-BMW

5th: COULTHARD Red Bull-Cosworth

3rd: WEBBER Williams-BMW

Pole: FISICHELLA Renault

0th: RÄIKKÖNEN McLaren-Mercedes
tarted from pit lane

8th: BUTTON BAR-Honda

6th: KLIEN Red Bull-Cosworth

4th: VILLENEUVE Sauber-Petronas

2nd: TRULLI Toyota

46	47	48	49	50	51	52	53	54	55	56	57	●
6	6	6	6	6	6	6	6	6	6	6	6	1
2	2	2	2	2	2	2	2	2	2	2	2	2
5	5	5	5	5	5	5	5	5	5	5	5	3
14	14	14	14	14	14	14	14	14	14	14	14	4
7	7	7	7	7	7	7	7	7	7	7	7	5
10	10	10	10	10	10	10	10	10	10	10	10	6
15	15	15	15	15	15	15	15	15	15	15	15	7
9	9	9	9	9	9	9	9	9	9	9	9	8
16	16	16	16	16	16	16	16	16	16	16	16	
12	12	12	12	12	12	12	12	12	12	12	12	
3	3	3	3	3	3	3	3	3	3	3		
4	4	4	4	4	4	4	4	17	17	17		
11	11	17	17	17	17	17	17	4	4	11		
17	17	11	11	11	11	11	11	11	11			
19	19	19	19	19	19	19	19	19				
18	18	18	18	18	18	18	18	18				
20	20	20	20	20	20	20	20					

it stop
ne lap or more behind leader

FOR THE RECORD

MELBOURNE GP 10 YEARS

FIRST GRAND PRIX START:
Christijan Albers, Patrick Friesacher,
Narain Karthikeyan, Tiago Monteiro,
Red Bull Racing
TENTH GRAND PRIX: Melbourne
FIRST POINTS: Red Bull Racing
20th FASTEST LAP: Renault

POINTS

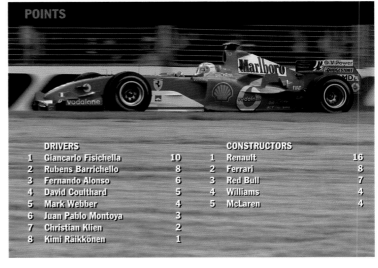

	DRIVERS			CONSTRUCTORS	
1	Giancarlo Fisichella	10	1	Renault	16
2	Rubens Barrichello	8	2	Ferrari	8
3	Fernando Alonso	6	3	Red Bull	7
4	David Coulthard	5	4	Williams	4
5	Mark Webber	5	5	McLaren	4
6	Juan Pablo Montoya	3			
7	Christian Klien	2			
8	Kimi Räikkönen	1			

Photographs: James Moy/www.crash.net

The strain of the effort in such sweltering conditions certainly seemed apparent in Jarno Trulli and Fernando Alonso, respectively second and first in the Malaysian Grand Prix.
Photograph: James Moy/www.crash.net

Above: The Renault garage was bathed in soft lighting as the mechanics worked late into the night.
Photograph: Peter Nygaard/GP Photo

Right: The BAR guys studied the Ferrari F2004M with thinly disguised interest.
Photograph: Jean-François Galeron/WRI

Centre right: Jenson Button was dreaming in vain of repeating his 2004 third place.

Below right: Anthony Davidson's maiden outing for BAR-Honda, subbing for the unwell Takuma Sato, turned into a fiasco.

Below: Sepang Sauber supporters.
Photographs: James Moy/www.crash.net

Fernando Alonso delivered a predictably controlled performance to ease Jarno Trulli's Toyota away from a potentially pole-winning effort. The young Spaniard demonstrated a supreme blend of car control and élan to take top slot on the grid by 0.253s, the engineers having successfully ironed out a handling imbalance about which he had complained the previous day.

'The car was quite difficult to drive yesterday [Friday] but the engineers did a really great job last night,' he said after first qualifying. 'The car was quick and easy to drive again. There was more grip than I'd been expecting for my timed lap and the car was well balanced, although I lost some time on the exit of Turn Six.'

Trulli was well satisfied to be on the front row again but, for Giancarlo Fisichella, the penny had well and truly dropped regarding just how formidable a team-mate he had on his hands in the Renault squad. His Saturday third place would be sustained through to the following day. 'I'm pleased to finish third,' he acknowledged after the first session. 'The car was understeering a bit on the timed lap. We learned yesterday that the R25 has the potential to be competitive on high fuel loads and I hope we can confirm this tomorrow in order to fight strongly in the race.' They did.

In the BMW Williams camp, Mark Webber lost valuable track time on Friday due to gear-selection problems, but he clawed back his lost laps to qualify a strong fourth. That lined him up ahead of Ralf Schumacher's Toyota and a slightly disappointed Kimi Räikkönen, who lost two grid positions in the second session due to an unwanted touch of understeer. Juan Pablo Montoya also made a mistake on his second run in the other McLaren; he judged it cost him 0.2s and dropped him out of contention to a lowly 11th.

Seventh and eighth were the Red Bull RB1s of Christian Klien and David Coulthard. 'I'm not unhappy with the lap, although it was a little bit messy in the last sector, where I ran into the kerb at the high-speed chicane and missed one shift pulling into Turn 14,' said Coulthard.

He added, 'It's going to be difficult, but reliability will be the key thing, as well as fuel strategy. This [season] is a journey of discovery and we will know a lot more about how this car functions after this grand prix.'

For his part, Jenson Button was obviously hoping for better after BAR's Melbourne débâcle and came to Sepang confident that the 007 would be a contender thanks to some new aero bits tested the previous week at Jerez while he went training in Brunei. As an ominous portent of things to come he suffered an engine oil leak in Saturday free practice which cost him valuable set-up time, obliging him to use data from his temporary team-mate Anthony Davidson, who was standing in for Takuma Sato after the Japanese driver was taken ill.

It was a disappointing qualifying effort for both the BAR boys. Button found that his friend's set-up was too oversteery for his taste and he wound up ninth, just behind the Williams of Nick Heidfeld. Davidson qualified too conservatively in 15th place after feeling unwilling to press too hard on a very dusty track surface on Saturday afternoon.

On this rare occasion, Michael Schumacher looked like just another driver. Consigned to 13th on the grid due to a combination of an ageing F2004M chassis and Bridgestone rubber that didn't want to work in the torrid Sepang conditions, Michael was destined to spend race afternoon struggling midfield in among cars that he usually sees only when a waved blue flag signals that they should get out of the way so he can lap them.

'Naturally I am not happy with the way things went,' said the world champion after Saturday qualifying. 'Yesterday, and after the first 45 minutes of today's practice, the situation seemed better, but already in the last free practice we began to understand that we would be struggling.

'It's clear that, on a quick lap with new tyres, our performance is not at the same level as our rivals'. But we know that over a distance things are different, as indeed we saw yesterday. And that's what counts, isn't it?'

DIARY

Michael Schumacher apologises to his colleagues at a meeting of the Grand Prix Drivers' Association for moving over on Nick Heidfeld and squeezing him onto the grass in the Australian GP.

Scott Speed and Neel Jani get F1 test opportunities with Red Bull Racing.

Renault veteran Bernard Dudot retires as managing director of the team's engine programme almost 30 years after starting work on the French company's turbocharged engine with which it made its F1 debut in 1977.

Sam Hornish Jnr heads Helio Castroneves to score Penske one-two in IRL round at Phoenix.

Emerson Fittipaldi says he might consider a racing return in the mooted Grand Prix Masters series.

FERRARI REMAINS ALOOF OVER TEST RESTRICTIONS

Ferrari boss Jean Todt made it clear in the aftermath of the Malaysian GP that he would not be having any further dialogue with the other F1 teams over any possible testing ban following his rivals' decision to write a letter of complaint about Ferrari's trenchant position to Luca di Montezemolo.

'We are more concerned at the moment with regaining Ferrari's competitive edge,' he said after eight of its rivals accused the team of acting in a manner 'highly disrespectful' to the sport by continuing to carry out unrestricted testing that thwarts any realistic efforts to cut costs.

'We have repeatedly made clear our position on this matter,' added a Ferrari spokesman. 'We have said we think that a limitation on the numbers of days' testing is unrealistic and it should be based on mileage. Consider the situation recently when Toyota and McLaren sat holding hands and wasting days at a test just waiting for the ideal weather conditions.

'In any event, if we are to have serious cost cutting in F1, that means everybody putting their cards on the table and making cuts in every area, not simply testing.'

As things stood post-Sepang, the other teams were still committed to the test limitations. And fuming about the situation.

FERNANDO Alonso vaulted into an early world championship lead after a Malaysian Grand Prix victory which was every bit as decisive and clear-cut as his Renault team-mate Giancarlo Fisichella's success in Melbourne a fortnight earlier. It was the 23-year-old's second career victory and came after a flawless drive in torrid conditions in which the track temperature topped the 50°C mark. During the course of this tour-de-force, Alonso broke an early challenge from his former team-mate Jarno Trulli's impressive Toyota TF105 to surge home the winner by 24.327s, confirming Renault's title credentials at a track where he had been the youngest pole winner in F1 history two years before.

'Physically it was a very demanding race and I really felt how hard it had been on the podium afterwards,' said Alonso, who scored his first grand prix victory in Hungary in 2003. 'But it is a great feeling to win here and the way I was able to do it demonstrated that we are competitive with our rivals this season on every type of circuit.'

The track temperature at Sepang was edging towards 54°C by the time the pack took up its position on the starting grid and Alonso accelerated cleanly away from pole position to head Trulli by a couple of lengths into the first right-hander. By the end of the opening lap Fernando was 0.8s ahead of the Toyota with Fisichella a strong third in front of Mark Webber's Williams, Ralf Schumacher's Toyota and Kimi Räikkönen's McLaren, past which Jenson Button decisively launched his BAR-Honda going into the first turn at the start of the second lap.

Button was already well clear of Räikkönen at the completion of the second lap, but the BAR driver's hopes that Malaysia would herald an upsurge in his fortunes were cruelly dashed midway around the third lap. Both he and his temporary team-mate Anthony Davidson skidded to a halt in a cloud of smoke from their Honda V10s, both of which had suffered oil-pressure sensor failures.

'It's an unbelievably small component failure to cause a double retirement,' said Otmar Szafnauer, the vice president of Honda Racing Developments. 'The only positive aspect is that it's easy to fix and not a fundamental problem with the engine.'

Button could hardly take such a benign and relaxed view. The 25-year-old was back in the BAR garage and changed out of his overalls long before Fernando Alonso made his first refuelling stop, let alone stormed past the chequered flag to win the second race of the season for Renault.

The ironies of this situation were certainly not lost on Button. In 2001 and 2002 he drove for Renault at a moment in the team's history when it was on the F1 ropes, often trailing around at the tail of the field and beset by seemingly endless technical problems.

The switch to BAR in 2003 was supposed to rejuvenate Button's career and the momentum certainly seemed to be building last year when he ended up third in the championship. Twelve months ago the celebrating British driver had been carried shoulder-high through the paddock by his adoring mechanics after speeding to a brilliant third place here at Sepang, the first podium finish of his grand prix career. Now the scene was painfully different indeed.

'Compared with last year, we've made a huge step back in every area,' fumed Button. 'It's just not good enough because we're quick. It's got to change and I don't think it'll change any time soon. I'm angry. I'm very angry.'

In second place, Trulli was doing a grand job, initially steadying Alonso's advantage at around 1.5s over the first few laps. Gradually, though, the Renault ace began to stamp his authority on proceedings. By lap six he was 3.9s ahead, then 4.3s, 4.7s, 5.8s... Clearly, assuming he didn't make a slip, there would be no catching him.

Alonso and Trulli made their first refuelling stops together at the end of lap 21, allowing Fisichella and Webber to take

Top: Kimi Räikkönen was robbed of a strong result by a punctured tyre.

Above: Bad day for Jacques Villeneuve: his race ended in a gravel trap.
Photographs: James Moy/www.crash.net

Left: A pit stop for Michael Schumacher's Ferrari on the way to one of the hardest seventh places of Michael's career.
Photograph: Jean-François Galeron/WRI

Main photo: Fernando Alonso took a brilliant victory for Renault.

Below: Ralf Schumacher worked hard for Toyota.
Photographs: James Moy/www.crash.net

fleeting first and second places before they pitted next time around. Unfortunately, early in his second stint, Fisichella thumped a kerb quite hard, slightly damaging his Renault's nose wing, which left him grappling with too much understeer. This caused him to drop back into the clutches of the BMW Williams duo Webber and Nick Heidfeld.

Ralf Schumacher was involved in what developed into an entertaining scrap for several laps, with both Williams drivers behaving as robustly and aggressively towards each other as they were towards their rivals from other teams. As the laps went by it seemed increasingly likely that the whole episode might end in tears – which it duly did.

Struggling with that handling imbalance, Fisichella found himself increasingly under pressure and Webber eventually took a run at him coming up to the final left-hander before the pits, his Williams drawing level with the Renault on the outside line.

Webber, who had left Fisichella enough room to manoeuvre, turned into the corner, but his rival kept coming and the Renault skidded into the Williams, spinning both cars around and leaving them damaged on the side of the track.

Fisichella didn't see it that way. 'As I was braking, the rear of the car slid and Mark had left no margin for error, so we collided,' he said. 'For me, it was a racing incident.'

This little drama allowed Nick Heidfeld to dodge through into third place, where he stayed to the finish ahead of Juan Pablo Montoya's McLaren, Ralf Schumacher's Toyota and the impressive David Coulthard, who turned in another fine performance for the Red Bull squad to claim another helping of championship points for the fledgling team.

Over in the McLaren Mercedes camp the MP4-20 drivers were unable to capitalise on their cars' undoubted pace to nail down a firm result. Kimi set the fastest lap of the race on lap

23 in 1m 35.483s and was actually in the lead when he came into the pits for his first stop at the end of lap 24 after a tactically astute long opening stint.

When he rejoined the race he almost immediately suffered a rear-tyre deflation, apparently due to a valve failure, briefly went off the track and then had to limp slowly around two thirds of the lap, front-left wheel pawing the air, to make another stop to fit a replacement wheel and tyre. He rejoined the race in 14th. Juan Pablo Montoya was now running seventh, but was unable to read either his pit signals or his instruments, so serious was the vibration he'd been grappling with after flat-spotting a tyre early on. 'Things like this make it difficult to get the best out of the car,' he said with masterly understatement.

Alonso made his second stop on lap 40, allowing Trulli two laps in the lead before he came in, and the status-quo was resumed at the head of the pack. Alonso reeled off the remaining laps to beat his Italian rival by 24.327s and grab the world-championship lead.

Trulli was delighted with his performance. 'I had an excellent start and was keeping my second place behind Fernando and extending my lead over Giancarlo,' he said. 'From there on I had an absolutely trouble-free race and could control those cars behind me. I want to thank everyone in the team for giving me the car with which I was able to score Toyota's first ever podium finish.'

Heidfeld was similarly satisfied with third, only the second podium finish of his F1 career. 'This was the most exciting race I ever had in F1,' he enthused. 'I pushed hard from the start, since I had to recover from my tenth-place starting position. It was real fun! Still, as usual in a hot race when it is the last thing you would like to happen, I had a problem with the drink bottle from the very first laps, which made my life more difficult.'

Ralf Schumacher's Toyota had touched Webber's Williams during the heat of their brief battle and the German driver fought poor tyre grip and some serious vibrations. The team fitted a replacement nose section at his second stop. 'But I am happy to have finished the race and contributed to that double helping of points,' he said.

As for Ferrari, the world champion constructor was totally out of play in Malaysia. Michael Schumacher qualified 13th and struggled through to finish seventh – splitting the Red Bull duo of Coulthard and Christian Klien – in a car which was simply not competitive on its Bridgestone tyres in these extreme conditions. Räikkönen was ninth ahead of Felipe Massa's sole surviving Sauber, Jacques Villeneuve having spun into a gravel trap after 26 laps.

As usual, with consummate diplomacy, Michael Schumacher refused to blame any element of the car's performance. At least he fared better than his team-mate Rubens Barrichello who, having thrown a piece of superfluous rubber foam out of his cockpit, had it lodge on the rear wing, upsetting the aerodynamics to the point where the Ferrari's rear tyres were worn smooth and he had no choice but to retire.

'He radioed in and said he thought he had a puncture,' said technical director Ross Brawn, 'but we could see from the pressure sensors that he didn't and we told him to stay out. Then we saw from the sensors that he'd lost a lot of rear downforce and we thought maybe the floor was broken. After five laps of that he said, "Look, I'm coming in. You'll have to fix it."' But there was nothing to be done.

Ferrari was certainly on the back foot. But the following Wednesday, Schumacher would travel to the Mugello track in Italy to test the new Ferrari F2005 for the first time. Only when he had assessed its performance fully would we know whether or not it was to be pressed into service for the Bahrain GP a fortnight after Sepang. And whether normal service would be resumed at the front of the F1 field.

Alan Henry

Below: Kimi couldn't quite bring himself to read Mika's words of wisdom!
Photograph: Laurent Charniaux/WRI

Bottom: Trulli's second place for Toyota was the Japanese team's best result ever.
Photograph: Paul-Henri Cahier

PETRONAS
MALAYSIAN GRAND PRIX
SEPANG 18–20 MARCH 2005

Photograph: James Moy/www.crash.net

SEPANG

TURN 4 65/105 (2)
TURN 3 140/225 (4)
TURN 6 130/209 (4)
TURN 2 55/89 (2)
TURN 5 135/216 (4)
180/290 (6)
TURN 1 65/105 (2)
50/81 (2)
PENANG STRAIGHT
TURN 14 65/105 (2)
180/290
TURN 7 100/161 (4)
TURN 12 110/176 (4)
TURN 9 45/72 (1)
TURN 8 100/161 (4)
TURN 13 104/166 (4)
TURN 11 80/129 (3)
mph/km/h (gear)

CIRCUIT LENGTH: 3.444 miles/5.543 km

RACE DISTANCE: 56 laps, 192.878 miles /310.408 km **RACE WEATHER:** Dry and sunny (track 46–52°C, air 34–37°C)

Pos.	Driver	Nat.	No.	Entrant	Car/Engine	Tyres	Laps	Time/Retirement	Speed (mph/km/h)	Gap to leader	Fastest race lap	
1	Fernando Alonso	E	5	Mild Seven Renault F1 Team	Renault R25-RS25 V10	M	56	1h 31m 33.736s	126.391/203.407		1m 35.899s	18
2	Jarno Trulli	I	16	Pansonic Toyota Racing	Toyota TF105-RVX-05 V10	M	56	1h 31m 58.063s	125.834/202.511	+24.327s	1m 35.816s	18
3	Nick Heidfeld	D	8	BMW WilliamsF1 Team	Williams FW27-BMW P84/85 V10	M	56	1h 32m 05.924s	125.654/202.222	+32.188s	1m 35.712s	40
4	Juan Pablo Montoya	COL	10	West McLaren Mercedes	McLaren MP4-20-Mercedes FO 110R V10	M	56	1h 32m 15.367s	125.440/201.877	+41.631s	1m 36.585s	42
5	Ralf Schumacher	D	17	Panasonic Toyota Racing	Toyota TF105-RVX-05 V10	M	56	1h 32m 25.590s	125.209/201.506	+51.854s	1m 36.321s	15
6	David Coulthard	GB	14	Red Bull Racing	Red Bull RB1-Cosworth TJ2005/10 V10	M	56	1h 32m 46.279s	124.743/200.756s	+72.543s	1m 36.790s	18
7	Michael Schumacher	D	1	Scuderia Ferrari Marlboro	Ferrari F2004M-054 V10	B	56	1h 32m 53.724s	124.577/200.488	+79.988s	1m 36.982s	41
8	Christian Klien	A	15	Red Bull Racing	Red Bull RB1-Cosworth TJ2005/10 V10	M	56	1h 32m 54.571s	124.558/200.458	+80.835s	1m 36.902s	17
9	Kimi Räikkönen	FIN	9	West McLaren Mercedes	McLaren MP4-20-Mercedes FO 110R V10	M	56	1h 32m 55.316s	124.541/200.431	+81.580s	1m 35.483s	23
10	Felipe Massa	BR	12	Sauber Petronas	Sauber C24-Petronas 05A V10	M	55			+1 lap	1m 37.212s	18
11	Narain Karthikeyan	IND	19	Jordan Toyota	Jordan EJ15-Toyota RVX-05 V10	B	54			+2 laps	1m 39.833s	18
12	Tiago Monteiro	P	18	Jordan Toyota	Jordan EJ15-Toyota RVX-05 V10	B	53			+3 laps	1m 40.432s	36
13	Christijan Albers	NL	21	Minardi Cosworth	Minardi PS04B-Cosworth CR3 V10	B	52			+4 laps	1m 42.485s	12
	Rubens Barrichello	BR	2	Scuderia Ferrari Marlboro	Ferrari F2004M-054 V10	B	49	Tyre wear; withdrew			1m 36.878s	22
	Giancarlo Fisichella	I	6	Mild Seven Renault F1 Team	Renault R25-RS25 V10	M	36	Collision			1m 36.182s	21
	Mark Webber	AUS	7	BMW WilliamsF1 Team	Williams FW27-BMW P84/85 V10	M	36	Collision			1m 35.899s	18
	Jacques Villeneuve	CDN	11	Sauber Petronas	Sauber C24-Petronas 05A V10	M	26	Spin			1m 38.058s	18
	Jenson Button	GB	3	Lucky Strike BAR Honda	BAR 007-Honda RA005E V10	M	2	Oil leak			1m 37.912s	2
	Anthony Davidson	GB	4	Lucky Strike BAR Honda	BAR 007-Honda RA005E V10	M	2	Oil leak			1m 41.470s	2
	Patrick Friesacher	A	20	Minardi Cosworth	Minardi PS04B-Cosworth CR3 V10	B	2	Accident			1m 43.558s	2

Fastest lap: Kimi Räikkönen, on lap 23, 1m 35.483s, 129.858mph/208.987s km/h (record).

Previous lap record: Juan Pablo Montoya (Williams FW26-BMW P84 V10), 1m 34.223s, 131.595 mph/211.782 km/h (2004).

All results and data © FOM 2005

19th: ALBERS Minardi-Cosworth

17th: KARTHIKEYAN Jordan-Toyota

15th: DAVIDSON BAR-Honda

13th: M. SCHUMACHER Ferrari

11th: MONTOYA McLaren-Mercedes

20th: FRIESACHER Minardi-Cosworth
Ten-place penalty for engine change

18th: MONTEIRO Jordan-Toyota

16th: VILLENEUVE Sauber-Petronas

14th: MASSA Sauber-Petronas

12th: BARRICHELLO Ferrari

Grid order	1	2	3	4	5	6	7	8	9	10	11	12	13	14	15	16	17	18	19	20	21	22	23	24	25	26	27	28	29	30	31	32	33	34	35	36	37	38	39	40	41	42	43
5 ALONSO	5	5	5	5	5	5	5	5	5	5	5	5	5	5	5	5	5	5	5	5	5	6	9	9	5	5	5	5	5	5	5	5	5	5	5	5	5	5	5	5	16	16	5
16 TRULLI	16	16	16	16	16	16	16	16	16	16	16	16	16	16	16	16	16	16	16	16	16	7	5	16	16	16	16	16	16	16	16	16	16	16	16	16	16	16	16	16	5	5	16
6 FISICHELLA	6	6	6	6	6	6	6	6	6	6	6	6	6	6	6	6	6	6	6	6	6	9	16	16	6	6	6	6	6	6	6	6	6	6	6	6	8	8	8	8	8	8	10
7 WEBBER	7	7	7	7	7	7	7	7	7	7	7	7	7	7	7	7	7	7	7	7	7	5	6	6	7	7	7	7	7	7	7	7	7	7	17	17	17	17	10	10	8		
17 R. SCHUMACHER	17	17	17	17	17	17	17	17	17	17	17	17	17	17	17	17	17	17	17	9	16	10	7	17	17	17	17	17	17	8	8	8	8	8	10	10	10	10	17	17	17		
9 RÄIKKÖNEN	9	3	9	9	9	9	9	9	9	9	9	9	9	9	9	9	9	9	9	9	9	10	10	7	2	2	8	8	8	8	8	8	17	17	17	17	14	14	14	14	14	1	1
15 KLIEN	3	9	8	8	8	8	8	8	8	8	8	8	8	8	8	8	8	8	8	9	2	2	2	17	8	10	10	10	10	10	10	10	10	10	15	15	15	15	1	14	14		
14 COULTHARD	8	8	14	14	14	14	14	14	14	14	14	14	14	14	14	14	14	14	14	17	17	1	10	2	2	2	2	2	2	14	14	14	1	1	1	1	9	9	15	15			
3 BUTTON	14	14	15	15	15	15	15	15	15	15	15	15	15	15	15	15	15	15	10	10	1	1	1	8	14	14	14	14	14	14	14	15	15	15	12	12	12	12	12	12			
8 HEIDFELD	15	15	10	10	10	10	10	10	10	10	10	10	10	10	10	10	10	10	15	2	2	12	8	8	10	15	15	15	15	15	15	15	2	1	1	9	9	9	9	12	9	9	
10 MONTOYA	10	10	2	2	2	2	2	2	2	2	2	2	2	2	2	2	2	2	12	12	8	14	14	14	1	1	1	1	1	1	1	1	1	12	12	2	2	2	2	2	2	2	
2 BARRICHELLO	2	2	12	12	12	12	12	12	12	12	12	12	12	12	12	12	12	1	1	14	11	11	15	12	12	12	12	12	12	12	12	2	9	19	19	19	19	19	19				
1 M. SCHUMACHER	12	12	1	1	1	1	1	1	1	1	1	1	1	1	1	1	1	11	11	11	15	15	12	9	9	9	9	9	9	9	9	2	18	18	18	18	18	18					
12 MASSA	1	1	11	11	11	11	11	11	11	11	11	11	11	11	11	11	15	15	15	12	12	11	9	19	19	19	19	19	19	19	21	21	21	21	21	21							
4 DAVIDSON	11	11	19	19	19	19	19	19	19	19	19	19	19	19	19	19	19	19	19	19	19	19	19	18	18	18	18	18															
11 VILLENEUVE	4	4	21	21	21	21	21	18	18	18	18	18	18	18	18	18	18	18	18	18	21	21	21	21	21	21	21	21															
19 KARTHIKEYAN	18	19	18	18	18	18	18	21	21	21	21	21	21	21	21	21	21	21	21	21	21																						
18 MONTEIRO	19	20																																									
21 ALBERS	21	21																																									
20 FRIESACHER	20	18																																									

QUALIFYING

SATURDAY: Sunny (track 48–50°C, air 35–36°C)
SUNDAY: Sunny (track 44–50°C, air 34–35°C)

Pos.	Driver	R/Order	1st qualifying	R/Order	2nd qualifying	Aggregate
1	Fernando Alonso	18	1m 32.582s	20	1m 35.090s	3m 07.672s
2	Jarno Trulli	12	1m 32.672s	19	1m 35.253s	3m 07.925s
3	Giancarlo Fisichella	20	1m 32.765s	18	1m 35.683s	3m 08.448s
4	Mark Webber	16	1m 33.204s	15	1m 35.700s	3m 08.904s
5	Ralf Schumacher	9	1m 33.106s	16	1m 35.901s	3m 09.007s
6	Kimi Räikkönen	13	1m 32.839s	17	1m 36.644s	3m 09.483s
7	Christian Klien	14	1m 33.724s	11	1m 35.865s	3m 09.589s
8	David Coulthard	17	1m 33.809s	10	1m 35.891s	3m 09.700s
9	Jenson Button	10	1m 33.616s	12	1m 36.216s	3m 09.832s
10	Nick Heidfeld	3	1m 33.464s	13	1m 36.453s	3m 09.917s
11	Juan Pablo Montoya	15	1m 33.333s	14	1m 36.757s	3m 10.090s
12	Rubens Barrichello	19	1m 34.162s	7	1m 37.340s	3m 11.502s
13	Michael Schumacher	4	1m 34.072s	9	1m 37.561s	3m 11.633s
14	Felipe Massa	11	1m 34.151s	8	1m 37.733s	3m 11.884s
15	Anthony Davidson	1	1m 34.866s	6	1m 37.024s	3m 11.890s
16	Jacques Villeneuve	8	1m 34.887s	5	1m 38.108s	3m 12.995s
17	Narain Karthikeyan	7	1m 37.806s	4	1m 39.850s	3m 17.656s
18	Tiago Monteiro	6	1m 37.856s	3	1m 40.106s	3m 17.962s
19	Patrick Friesacher	5	1m 39.268s	2	1m 41.918s	3m 21.186s
20	Christijan Albers	2	1m 40.432s	1	1m 42.569s	3m 23.001s

CHASSIS LOG BOOK

	FERRARI				SAUBER-PETRONAS	
1	Michael Schumacher	F2004M/241		11	Jacques Villeneuve	C24/03
2	Rubens Barrichello	F2004M/240		12	Felipe Massa	C24/02
	Spare	F2004M/236			Spare	C24/01
	BAR-HONDA				RED BULL-COSWORTH	
3	Jenson Button	007/04		14	David Coulthard	RB1/2
4	Takuma Sato/			15	Christian Klien	RB1/1
	Anthony Davidson	007/02		37	Vitantonio Liuzzi	RB1/3
	Spare	007/03			Spare	RB1/3
	RENAULT				TOYOTA	
5	Fernando Alonso	R25/04		16	Jarno Trulli	TF105/03
6	Giancarlo Fisichella	R25/03		17	Ralf Schumacher	TF105/04
	Spare	R25/02		38	Ricardo Zonta	TF105/02
	WILLIAMS-BMW				Spare	TF105/02
7	Mark Webber	FW27/03			JORDAN-TOYOTA	
8	Nick Heidfeld	FW27/04		18	Tiago Monteiro	EJ15/03
	Spare	FW27/02		19	Narain Karthikeyan	EJ15/02
	McLAREN-MERCEDES			39	Robert Doornbos	EJ15/01
9	Kimi Räikkönen	MP4-20/04			Spare	EJ15/01
10	Juan Pablo Montoya	MP4-20/03			MINARDI-COSWORTH	
35	Pedro de la Rosa	MP4-20/01		20	Patrick Friesacher	PS04B/02
	Spare	MP4-20/01		21	Christijan Albers	PS04B/04
					Spare	PS04B/03

Photograph: James Moy/www.crash.net

PRACTICE 1 (FRIDAY)

Cloudy/light wind (track 40–47°C, air 33–34°C)

Pos.	Driver	Laps	Time
1	Ricardo Zonta	17	1m 34.092s
2	Pedro de la Rosa	15	1m 35.144s
3	Vitantonio Liuzzi	18	1m 35.691s
4	Michael Schumacher	13	1m 36.011s
5	Jenson Button	9	1m 36.513s
6	Nick Heidfeld	7	1m 36.551s
7	Kimi Räikkönen	6	1m 36.563s
8	Juan Pablo Montoya	5	1m 36.610s
9	Felipe Massa	4	1m 36.963s
10	Mark Webber	8	1m 36.989s
11	Ralf Schumacher	5	1m 37.168s
12	David Coulthard	8	1m 37.338s
13	Takuma Sato	9	1m 37.366s
14	Christian Klien	9	1m 37.642s
15	Rubens Barrichello	4	1m 37.843s
16	Jacques Villeneuve	8	1m 38.416s
17	Tiago Monteiro	18	1m 39.571s
18	Robert Doornbos	20	1m 40.289s
19	Narain Karthikeyan	14	1m 40.375s
20	Patrick Friesacher	18	1m 43.574s
21	Christijan Albers	12	1m 43.691s
22	Giancarlo Fisichella	2	No time
23	Fernando Alonso	2	No time
24	Jarno Trulli	2	No time

PRACTICE 2 (FRIDAY)

Sunny (track 53–55°C, air 36–37°C)

Pos.	Driver	Laps	Time
1	Felipe Massa	19	1m 35.608s
2	Juan Pablo Montoya	13	1m 35.620s
3	Ricardo Zonta	30	1m 35.677s
4	Kimi Räikkönen	6	1m 35.719s
5	Ralf Schumacher	16	1m 35.838s
6	Giancarlo Fisichella	16	1m 35.841s
7	Rubens Barrichello	7	1m 35.949s
8	Jenson Button	19	1m 35.992s
9	Fernando Alonso	15	1m 36.103s
10	David Coulthard	20	1m 36.575s
11	Jarno Trulli	18	1m 36.841s
12	Christian Klien	19	1m 36.968s
13	Pedro de la Rosa	31	1m 37.033s
14	Takuma Sato	18	1m 37.044s
15	Nick Heidfeld	17	1m 37.067s
16	Michael Schumacher	22	1m 37.270s
17	Robert Doornbos	23	1m 37.878s
18	Jacques Villeneuve	19	1m 38.121s
19	Narain Karthikeyan	21	1m 38.855s
20	Vitantonio Liuzzi	11	1m 39.349s
21	Tiago Monteiro	21	1m 39.755s
22	Patrick Friesacher	19	1m 40.940s
23	Christijan Albers	16	1m 41.156s
24	Mark Webber	2	No time

PRACTICE 3 (SATURDAY)

Sunny (track 31–42°C, air 28–31°C)

Pos.	Driver	Laps	Time
1	Fernando Alonso	5	1m 34.715s
2	Michael Schumacher	10	1m 34.883s
3	Giancarlo Fisichella	6	1m 34.930s
4	Kimi Räikkönen	9	1m 35.054s
5	Jarno Trulli	6	1m 35.573s
6	Ralf Schumacher	10	1m 35.645s
7	Juan Pablo Montoya	8	1m 35.850s
8	Jenson Button	7	1m 36.162s
9	Nick Heidfeld	3	1m 36.434s
10	Mark Webber	5	1m 36.465s
11	David Coulthard	11	1m 36.888s
12	Rubens Barrichello	7	1m 36.903s
13	Felipe Massa	6	1m 36.987s
14	Anthony Davidson	12	1m 37.049s
15	Christian Klien	10	1m 37.204s
16	Jacques Villeneuve	6	1m 37.850s
17	Narain Karthikeyan	11	1m 38.444s
18	Tiago Monteiro	12	1m 39.349s
19	Patrick Friesacher	15	1m 41.398s
20	Christijan Albers	16	1m 42.023s

PRACTICE 4 (SATURDAY)

Sunny (track 36–42°C, air 31–35°C)

Pos.	Driver	Laps	Time
1	Jarno Trulli	12	1m 32.832s
2	Christian Klien	9	1m 32.870s
3	Fernando Alonso	11	1m 32.880s
4	Ralf Schumacher	11	1m 32.951s
5	David Coulthard	10	1m 33.092s
6	Giancarlo Fisichella	8	1m 33.349s
7	Kimi Räikkönen	12	1m 33.349s
8	Nick Heidfeld	5	1m 33.468s
9	Mark Webber	10	1m 33.517s
10	Anthony Davidson	15	1m 33.580s
11	Juan Pablo Montoya	10	1m 33.689s
12	Rubens Barrichello	11	1m 33.943s
13	Felipe Massa	10	1m 34.002s
14	Michael Schumacher	10	1m 34.102s
15	Jacques Villeneuve	9	1m 35.532s
16	Tiago Monteiro	10	1m 37.824s
17	Narain Karthikeyan	8	1m 38.126s
18	Christijan Albers	12	1m 38.673s
19	Patrick Friesacher	12	1m 38.974s

9th: BUTTON BAR-Honda

7th: KLIEN Red Bull-Cosworth

5th: R. SCHUMACHER Toyota

3rd: FISICHELLA Renault

Pole: ALONSO Renault

10th: HEIDFELD Williams-BMW

8th: COULTHARD Red Bull-Cosworth

6th: RÄIKKÖNEN McLaren-Mercedes

4th: WEBBER Williams-BMW

2nd: TRULLI Toyota

	45	46	47	48	49	50	51	52	53	54	55	56	
5	5	5	5	5	5	5	5	5	5	5	5	5	1
16	16	16	16	16	16	16	16	16	16	16	16	16	2
8	8	8	8	8	8	8	8	8	8	8	8	8	3
10	10	10	10	10	10	10	10	10	10	10	10	10	4
17	17	17	17	17	17	17	17	17	17	17	17		5
14	14	14	14	14	14	14	14	14	14	14	14		6
1	1	1	1	1	1	1	1	1	1	1	1		7
15	15	15	15	15	15	15	15	15	15	15	15		8
9	9	9	9	9	9	9	9	9	9	9	9		
12	12	12	12	12	12	12	12	12	12	12			
2	2	2	2	2	2	19	19	19	19	19			
19	19	19	19	18	18	18	18						
18	18	18	18	18	21	21	21						
21	21	21	21	21									

Pit stop
One lap or more behind leader

FOR THE RECORD

FIRST GRAND PRIX PODIUM: Toyota

POINTS

DRIVERS

1	Fernando Alonso	16
2	Giancarlo Fisichella	10
3	Jarno Trulli	8
4	Rubens Barrichello	8
5	Juan Pablo Montoya	8
6	David Coulthard	8
7	Nick Heidfeld	6
8	Ralf Schumacher	4
9	Mark Webber	4
10	Christian Klien	3
11	Michael Schumacher	2
12	Kimi Räikkönen	1

CONSTRUCTORS

1	Renault	26
2	Toyota	12
3	Red Bull	11
4	Ferrari	10
5	Williams	10
6	McLaren	9

Photographs: James Moy/www.crash.net

SAKHIR
BAHRAINGP

FIA F1 WORLD CHAMPIONSHIP/ROUND 3

An exultant Fernando Alonso gave the victory
salute from the cockpit of his Renault R25
after a faultess second win out of three races.
Photograph: James Moy/www.crash.net

MILD SEVEN
RENAULT F1 Team

MILD SEVEN

Chronotech

RENAULT

Fernando Alonso's pole run on Saturday was simply brilliant. Coming down to the final right-hander before the pits he had 0.5s in hand over his closest rival and, despite losing 0.3s with a mistake in the final turn, he nailed the overnight fastest time by 0.1s. On Sunday morning he was absolutely determined not to squander any more of his advantage and he clinched fastest overall time with 3m 1.902s.

Alongside him on the front row of the grid was Michael Schumacher (3m 2.357s) in the new Ferrari F2005, which had at least managed to squeeze out Jarno Trulli (3m 2.660s) for second-fastest time. Alonso and his Renault team-mate Giancarlo Fisichella, who lined up a disappointed tenth after a couple of small mistakes in qualifying, were the only Michelin runners not to feel it necessary to run the new tyres which had been tested after Malaysia and were, in the view of Nick Heidfeld, better on turn-in, traction and stability.

Heidfeld proved that his judgement about the new tyres had been absolutely correct when he placed his Williams FW27 firmly on the second row in fourth place with a 3m 3.217s aggregate, just one place ahead of team-mate Mark Webber, who had been sixth at the end of the Saturday session.

'It's pretty harsh to expect the drivers to do a perfect lap on Sunday morning since fuel load, track and wind conditions – especially here – have changed since Saturday afternoon,' said Webber. 'Some of the corners are very good for me, some others less good but, all in all, I had a fairly satisfying lap and I have improved one position from yesterday's qualifying.'

Over in the McLaren camp, Ron Dennis wasn't exactly delighted that the best Kimi Räikkönen and Pedro de la Rosa – standing in for Juan Pablo Montoya – could manage in first qualifying was seventh and ninth, but if anybody thought they could taunt the McLaren boss over the question of his two regular race drivers' recent newspaper publicity, they were going to be disappointed. He certainly wasn't biting.

No, he said firmly, he had no complaint that Montoya was absent from the Bahrain Grand Prix. Yes, it was unfortunate that he'd slipped and cracked a bone in his shoulder. No, he didn't care what the Colombian had been doing when he suffered the injury. Yes, JPM had told him it was a tennis accident and, yes, when he finally got around to asking Montoya the question to his face he would be well able to discern whether or not Montoya was telling the truth.

'Team discipline doesn't extend to our drivers' private lives,' he said. 'We don't have contractual restrictions on our drivers, nor have we ever done. I don't want to constrain them. I want free spirits to drive at McLaren.'

Kimi remained ninth on the grid at the end of second qualifying, having lost crucial fractions in the final corner in the Saturday session, but the guesting De la Rosa did a great job to move up to eighth, just behind the impressive Christian Klien, who outgunned David Coulthard comprehensively during qualifying with the Red Bull RB1, the Scot having struggled with poor handling balance from the very start of the weekend.

Jenson Button wound up 11th, two places ahead of his BAR Honda team-mate Takuma Sato, at the end of the second qualifying session, having made up a place on his first-session best. 'It was a reasonable lap on Saturday,' said Jenson, 'but the track was so hot that there was very little grip and I lost some time with a bit of oversteer at Turn Eight.'

Similarly, Felipe Massa and Jacques Villeneuve managed 12th and 16th places in their Sauber C24s, neither totally happy. Massa was satisfied that at least he didn't go off in the second session, as he had done on Saturday, and Jacques was another competitor to have fallen foul of the last corner.

DIARY

The Ferraris compete at Bahrain with black nose cones out of respect after the death of the Pope over the race weekend.

Former Indy 500 winner Gil de Ferran signs to join BAR Honda starting at the San Marino GP.

Vitantonio Liuzzi confirmed to take his turn as David Coulthard's team-mate in the Red Bull team from Imola.

Thieves steal two alloy wheels, worth $2,000, from Bernie Ecclestone's brand new Mercedes CL55 outside his Chelsea home.

FERNANDO Alonso dramatically extended his world championship points lead with another commanding victory from pole position, this one in the searing dry heat of Bahrain to keep Renault's 2005 winning record intact and round off the famous French marque's unprecedented hat trick of F1 victories.

Alonso's sheer poise and composure raised very clear echoes of Michael Schumacher's competitive demeanour back in the early 1990s, when the young German rising star was making his reputation as an F1 front runner, driving for the Benetton squad, now the Renault team that was setting the F1 agenda in the opening phase of 2005.

Little by little, lap by lap, as the season unfolded, the realisation was that the F1 business could be on the threshold of an epic era as Alonso, one of the most intelligent of the new generation, bid to topple Schumacher from his position as the sport's dominant master.

To be sure, Alonso's Renault R25 was up to this point in the year a more developed and reliable technical package than the fragile new Ferrari, which suffered minor teething troubles on its race debut in Bahrain, its undoubted pace notwithstanding.

As Alonso led the pack away from the starting grid, Michael Schumacher ruthlessly chopped across Jarno Trulli's third-placed Toyota TF105 to box the Italian out of the initial fight, then took a long, lingering look down the inside of the leading Renault as they went into the first corner.

For a moment it looked as though Schumacher might be tempted to risk all with an audacious lunge down the inside of the turn, but he wisely backed out of any premature confrontation. He finished the opening lap just 0.3s behind Alonso. Although the Renault driver stretched his advantage to 0.9s by lap three, that was as far away as he got.

Trulli was third at the end of the opening lap ahead of the Williams FW27s of Mark Webber and Nick Heidfeld, Ralf Schumacher's Toyota, Kimi Räikkönen's McLaren MP4-20 and Giancarlo Fisichella's Renault R25.

Already the race was collecting its first casualties. Christian Klien's Red Bull had stalled on the grid prior to the start and

was pushed to the pit lane for attention, but the mechanics were unable to rectify the apparent electronic failure and he was out almost before he started. Narain Karthikeyan was also out after two laps with electrical problems, while Fisichella's luck showed no signs of turning. After four laps he was called into the pits to retire after his engine lost power.

'It is normal that I feel extremely disappointed after retiring from a race where I could have scored a very strong result,' shrugged the Italian. 'The car felt great on the first lap when I gained positions and I felt I could gain even more. Then the engine lost power.'

Meanwhile Michael, who was running the softer Bridgestone tyre option – which could have been interpreted as a lack of confidence in the new car's durability – had faded slightly to 3.0s behind Alonso by the end of lap 11. Midway around the following lap it was all over for the world champion when he spun wildly after a hydraulic glitch interfered with the gearbox downchange. It was a big pirouette and Schumacher could offer thanks to the wide Sakhir run-off areas as he regained some semblance of control and limped back to the pits to retire.

'Today showed us in the opening laps that Ferrari will eventually be back challenging for victories,' said Alonso, 'but for the moment we don't have to worry too much. The results show that the Toyotas are currently our closest competitors.'

However he added, 'This weekend they [the Ferraris] were the only ones to put our victory at risk. In the opening laps I realised that Michael was probably running with a lighter fuel load, but he was all over my mirrors in the early stages. I knew, though, that my tyres were good over long runs and I was pretty confident that if he slipped ahead of me I would be able to get back ahead of him again.'

Now Alonso was left with a 2.7s edge over Trulli. Then came Webber, Ralf Schumacher, Heidfeld, Räikkönen, Takuma Sato and the impressive Pedro de la Rosa, filling in for the injured Juan Pablo Montoya. Jarno did his best but Alonso was just too strong for him. Fernando made his first refuelling stop in 8.4s at the end of lap 20, with the Toyota coming in for an 8.7s stop next time around. Webber also pitted at this time, leaving

Above: Pedro de la Rosa excelled himself as Juan Pablo Montoya's stand-in, setting the fastest lap on his way to an excellent fifth place in the McLaren MP4-20.
Photograph: Bryn Williams/www.crash.net

Left: Mark Webber had to work hard for sixth in the Williams FW27, battling tyre vibration after a spin.
Photographs: James Moy/www.crash.net

Right: The Red Bull crew at the ready with refuelling equipment.
Photograph: James Moy/www.crash.net

Below: Rubens Barrichello locks the brakes of his Ferrari F2005 to avoid the rear of Takuma Sato's BAR.
Photograph: Paul-Henri Cahier

Bottom: David Coulthard just managed to avoid running into the back of Felipe Massa's Sauber.
Photograph: Laurent Charniaux/WRI

Far right: The tightly bunched pack jostled for position on the first lap of the race.
Photograph: Jean-François Galeron/WRi

Bottom centre: Jarno Trulli was pretty satisfied with himself after another strong run to second place.
Photograph: Paul-Henri Cahier

Bottom right: The Sakhir paddock illuminated late in the evening.
Photograph: James Moy/www.crash.net

Main photo: Michael Schumacher gave the Ferrari F2005 a heartening debut for Maranello but eventually succumbed to hydraulic problems.
Photograph: Laurent Charniaux/WRi

Below: Jenson Button walking in after retiring his BAR-Honda at the end of the pit lane, a sad contrast to his third place and maiden podium 12 months earlier.
Photograph: James Moy/www.crash.net

Alonso briefly ahead of Heidfeld and Räikkönen but, when they made their stops, on laps 23 and 24 respectively, Trulli took back second place, 6.3s behind the leading Renault.

The race now settled down with Räikkönen piling on the pressure in fourth place. Webber buckled under the strain and spun back to fifth behind Ralf Schumacher on lap 34, comfortably elevating Kimi to third place, which he maintained to the finish to post McLaren's first podium of the season.

'It was a tough race for me,' confessed Webber. 'My tyres were in bad shape after I spun and the car was difficult to drive because of strong vibrations, so in the last few laps I lost another position to Pedro de la Rosa in the McLaren.'

McLaren's test driver handled himself well in his ferocious – but very clean and disciplined – wheel-to-wheel battle with the Australian for more than a dozen laps. De la Rosa finally made the passing move stick three laps from the chequered flag and also bagged the fastest race lap after a fine effort.

'I had a great time racing today,' enthused De la Rosa after taking the chequered flag. 'My lap times were consistently fast when I had an empty track ahead of me. It was certainly hard work to make my way through the field after a difficult first few laps, having to come up from ninth after the first lap.'

Jenson Button and his BAR team-mate Takuma Sato had another bitterly disappointing weekend, their world-

championship points score remaining firmly nailed on zero after both cars again failed to finish.

Sato had to stop when his brake-wear levels ran out of control and caution took the nod over the team's ambition. Button, after qualifying conservatively, was up to fourth place when he came in for his second refuelling stop with 11 laps left to run only to encounter major problems with his BAR's gearchange mechanism.

After an agonisingly long stop, Button was eventually push-started back into the fray, scattering a mechanic's jack in his wake as he accelerated away down the pit lane. Alas, it was all in vain and his BAR 007 ground to a halt before he could get back onto the circuit. Yet Button was philosophical about a season which seemed to be falling apart around his ears.

'I got a reasonable start, our car felt strong and we had good pace, so we were hoping for better things,' said Button. 'I tried to overtake Fisichella on lap two, but he moved across me and I lost three places behind him. From around lap 20 we were starting to experience some bad gear shifts and also signs of brake wear, so I had to look after the brakes a bit more.'

He added, 'The pit crew removed the tyre to inspect the front-left in the last pit stop and it seemed we would make it to the end of the race. When I tried to select first and pull away, though, the clutch problem recurred. The guys did a fantastic

job to try and get me back in the race, but then the car just stopped at the end of the pit lane.'

For BAR Honda it was particularly galling to watch their Japanese arch-rivals Toyota surge to another strong result: Jarno Trulli and Ralf Schumacher finished second and fourth, underlining Alonso's claim that they were the leading challengers to Renault, for the moment at least.

'I am so pleased with this result,' said an emotional Trulli after taking the chequered flag just 13.409s behind the winning Alonso. 'I thought we would be competitive and to claim our second successive podium is fantastic. I realised midway through the race that it was futile trying to catch Fernando and we were safely in second, which is tremendous for everybody in the team.'

Räikkönen was well satisfied with third and Ralf Schumacher managed to haul his way back to fourth after a good job to make up for a qualifying slip which consigned him to a distant 11th in the first qualifying session, although he managed to climb to an eventual sixth on the final grid.

Nick Heidfeld's strong run ended with an engine failure so it was Felipe Massa who climbed through to take the two points for seventh place in his Sauber C24.

'That was exactly what I had hoped for in my heart before the start of the race,' said Massa. 'The car was strong and consistent all the way through and I am sure that my hard-tyre choice was the right one. I think it was a good move I did on Rubens [Barrichello], but to be fair he was in trouble with his tyres, so it was not real overtaking.'

For his part, Barrichello drove a storming race from the back of the grid to run as high as sixth place before his tyres wore down badly and he slipped to ninth at the chequered flag between David Coulthard's Red Bull and Tiago Monteiro's Jordan. Jacques Villeneuve was classified 11th after retiring on lap 54 when Coulthard's car ran into the back of him.

'I could certainly have got a point today,' said the Canadian. 'It was only another lap and I would have passed Rubens, but then I got hit by David. I don't know why. I'll have to ask him.'

Alan Henry

NEW FERRARI F2005 NO APRIL FOOL

It was the most keenly anticipated moment of the new season so far. At a few minutes past 11 am on Friday, 1 April, Ferrari car number one chugged gently along the Sakhir pit lane before Michael Schumacher floored the throttle hard to launch his brand-new F2005 challenger into the braking area for the tight right-hand corner at the end of the start-line straight.

In a sense, 2005 started here. A gleaming scarlet symphony of curvaceous spats and spoilers, this was Ferrari's long-awaited new contender, representing the team's best interpretation of the new technical regulations and, it hoped, poised to make up for the disappointing performance delivered by the old updated F2004Ms which Schumacher and his team-mate Rubens Barrichello had been forced to use in the first two races.

'It was really nice to be driving the new car for the first time at a race meeting,' said Schumacher, who tested the F2005 for the first time at Mugello only ten days prior to Bahrain. 'It felt very good. We ran through our entire planned programme and everything went very smoothly.

'I did enough laps to have a good idea in which direction to work in terms of tyre choice and car set-up. It was a trouble-free day and so a pleasing debut for the new car and an encouraging start to the weekend.'

Yet if the new Ferrari was quick, it was also brittle. In Friday free practice, Rubens Barrichello's suffered a bearing failure on the left side of its carbon-fibre-skinned, titanium-cased, seven-speed gearbox. 'It was a catastrophic failure,' said Ferrari technical director Ross Brawn. More pertinently, there was no spare available in Bahrain – and no remaining direct flight from Italy to the Gulf kingdom over the race weekend.

This being Ferrari, the solution was simple. A private jet was chartered to whisk a replacement gearbox the five-hour journey from Bologna to Manama, accompanied by one of Maranello's transmission specialists. It arrived on Saturday night and, having passed FIA muster as an identical gearbox to the one that had failed, was duly installed in Barrichello's car for Sunday morning's second qualifying session.

Yet that wasn't the end of the team's problems. During second qualifying, Barrichello's new gearbox suffered another glitch, this time damaging its engine. That meant that a fresh V10 had to be installed together with the original, repaired gearbox – which now had to be reinstalled – and Rubens had to start from the back of the grid.

This latest Ferrari was the first to be built by the technical team directed by new chief designer Aldo Costa, who has taken over this key role from South African engineer Rory Byrne. Work started on the F2005 in August 2004 with all the factory's resources deployed on it to the exclusion of continued work on the F2004, the specification of which was frozen for the balance of the season.

Costa has impeccable credentials, having graduated in 1986 with a degree in mechanical engineering from the University of Bologna, the alma mater of many celebrated Ferrari technicians including Paolo Martinelli, who is currently head of the team's F1 engine department.

Costa wrote a thesis on F1 suspension systems and for 1988 was hired as chief designer of the Minardi team at the age of 27. He remained in charge of all technical matters at the tiny Faenza-based team until he left to join Ferrari at the end of 1995, since which time he has gradually assumed more responsibility for various aspects of its F1 chassis designs. First signs from the F2005 suggested that Costa had served his apprenticeship well.

GULF AIR
BAHRAIN GRAND PRIX
BAHRAIN 1–3 APRIL 2005

Photograph: James Moy/www.crash.net

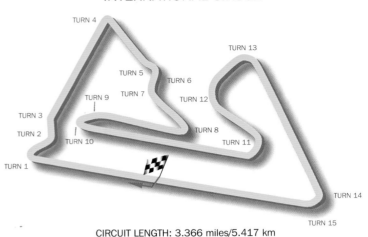

BAHRAIN
INTERNATIONAL CIRCUIT

TURN 4
TURN 13
TURN 5
TURN 6
TURN 9
TURN 7
TURN 12
TURN 3
TURN 8
TURN 2
TURN 10
TURN 11
TURN 1
TURN 14
TURN 15

CIRCUIT LENGTH: 3.366 miles/5.417 km

RACE DISTANCE: 57 laps, 191.716 miles/308.238 km   RACE WEATHER: Very hot and sunny (track 48–57°C, air 41–42°C)

All results and data © FOM 2005

Pos.	Driver	Nat.	No.	Entrant	Car/Engine	Tyres	Laps	Time/Retirement	Speed (mph/km/h)	Gap to leader	Fastest race lap	
1	Fernando Alonso	E	5	Mild Seven Renault F1 Team	Renault R25-RS25 V10	M	57	1h 29m 18.531s	128.674/207.082		1m 31.713s	39
2	Jarno Trulli	I	16	Panasonic Toyota Racing	Toyota TF105-RVX-05 V10	M	57	1h 29m 31.940s	128.353/206.565	+13.409s	1m 32.324s	41
3	Kimi Räikkönen	FIN	9	West McLaren Mercedes	McLaren MP4-20-Mercedes F0 110R V10	M	57	1h 29m 50.594s	127.909/205.850	+32.063s	1m 31.822s	41
4	Ralf Schumacher	D	17	Panasonic Toyota Racing	Toyota TF105-RVX-05 V10	M	57	1h 30m 11.083s	127.407/205.043	+53.272s	1m 32.683s	36
5	Pedro de la Rosa	E	10	West McLaren Mercedes	McLaren MP4-20-Mercedes F0 110R V10	M	57	1h 30m 23.519s	127.132/204.600	+64.988s	1m 31.447s	43
6	Mark Webber	AUS	7	BMW WilliamsF1 Team	Williams FW27-BMW P84/85 V10	M	57	1h 30m 33.232s	126.905/204.235	+74.701s	1m 33.087s	20
7	Felipe Massa	BR	12	Sauber Petronas	Sauber C24-Petronas 05A V10	M	56			+1 lap	1m 33.326s	40
8	David Coulthard	GB	14	Red Bull Racing	Red Bull RB1-Cosworth TJ2005/10 V10	M	56			+1 lap	1m 33.417s	42
9	Rubens Barrichello	BR	2	Scuderia Ferrari Marlboro	Ferrari F2005-055 V10	B	56			+1 lap	1m 32.976s	23
10	Tiago Monteiro	P	18	Jordan Toyota	Jordan EJ15-Toyota RVX-05 V10	B	55			+2 laps	1m 35.744s	18
11	Jacques Villeneuve	CDN	11	Sauber Petronas	Sauber C24-Petronas 05A V10	M	54			DNF	1m 33.458s	24
12	Patrick Friesacher	A	20	Minardi Cosworth	Minardi PS04B-Cosworth CR3 V10	B	54			+3 laps	1m 36.432s	16
13	Christijan Albers	NL	21	Minardi Cosworth	Minardi PS04B-Cosworth CR3 V10	B	56			+4 laps	1m 36.913s	3
	Jenson Button	GB	3	Lucky Strike BAR Honda	BAR 007-Honda RA005E V10	M	46	Clutch			1m 32.411s	45
	Takuma Sato	J	4	Lucky Strike BAR Honda	BAR 007-Honda RA005E V10	M	27	Brakes			1m 33.124s	23
	Nick Heidfeld	D	8	BMW WilliamsF1 Team	Williams FW27-BMW P84/85 V10	M	25	Engine			1m 33.055s	19
	Michael Schumacher	D	1	Scuderia Ferrari Marlboro	Ferrari F2005-055 V10	B	12	Hydraulics			1m 32.886s	7
	Giancarlo Fisichella	I	6	Mild Seven Renault F1 Team	Renault R25-RS25 V10	M	4	Engine			1m 37.036s	2
	Narain Karthikeyan	IND	19	Jordan Toyota	Jordan EJ15-Toyota RVX-05 V10	B	2	Electrical			1m 37.533s	2
	Christian Klien	A	15	Red Bull Racing	Red Bull RB1-Cosworth TJ2005/10 V10	M	0	Electrics on grid				

Fastest lap: Pedro de la Rosa, on lap 43, 1m 31.447s, 132.385 mph/213.054 km/h.

Lap record: Michael Schumacher (Ferrari F2004-052 V10), 1m 30.252s, 134.262 mph/216.074 km/h (2004).

19th: FRIESACHER Minardi-Cosworth
Ten-place penalty for engine change

17th: KARTHIKEYAN Jordan-Toyota

15th: VILLENEUVE Sauber-Petronas

13th: SATO BAR-Honda

11th: BUTTON BAR-Honda

20th: BARRICHELLO Ferrari
Ten-place penalty for engine change

18th: ALBERS Minardi-Cosworth
Ten-place penalty for engine change

16th: MONTEIRO Jordan-Toyota

14th: COULTHARD Red Bull-Cosworth

12th: MASSA Sauber-Petronas

Grid order	1	2	3	4	5	6	7	8	9	10	11	12	13	14	15	16	17	18	19	20	21	22	23	24	25	26	27	28	29	30	31	32	33	34	35	36	37	38	39	40	41	42	43	44	45
5 ALONSO	5	5	5	5	5	5	5	5	5	5	5	5	5	5	5	5	5	5	5	5	16	5	5	5	5	5	5	5	5	5	5	5	5	5	5	5	5	5	5	5	5	16	5	5	5
1 M. SCHUMACHER	1	1	1	1	1	1	1	1	1	1	1	1	16	16	16	16	16	16	16	16	7	8	9	16	16	16	16	16	16	16	16	16	16	16	16	16	16	16	16	16	16	5	16	16	16
16 TRULLI	16	16	16	16	16	16	16	16	16	16	16	16	7	7	7	7	7	7	7	7	5	9	8	16	4	7	7	7	7	7	7	7	9	9	9	9	9	9	9	9	9	10	9		9
8 HEIDFELD	8	7	7	7	7	7	7	7	7	7	7	7	17	17	17	17	17	17	17	8	8	16	16	4	9	9	9	9	9	9	17	17	17	17	17	17	17	17	17	7	10	9			
7 WEBBER	7	8	8	8	8	8	8	8	17	17	17	8	8	8	8	8	8	8	9	9	9	4	4	2	7	17	17	17	17	17	17	7	7	7	7	7	7	7	7	10	2	3	2		
17 R. SCHUMACHER	17	17	17	17	17	17	17	17	8	8	8	9	9	9	9	9	9	9	4	4	2	2	2	3	9	14	2	2	2	2	2	2	2	2	2	2	2	2	10	2	3	2	1		
15 KLIEN	9	9	9	9	9	9	9	9	9	9	9	4	4	4	4	4	4	4	10	10	2	3	3	7	11	2	3	3	3	3	10	10	10	10	10	10	10	10	2	3	17	17			
10 DE LA ROSA	6	6	4	4	4	4	4	4	4	4	4	10	10	10	10	10	10	10	2	2	3	10	10	11	8	3	10	10	10	10	3	3	3	3	3	3	3	3	17	12	7	10			
9 RÄIKKÖNEN	10	4	10	10	10	10	10	10	10	10	10	2	2	2	2	2	2	3	3	3	10	12	7	8	17	10	12	12	12	12	12	12	12	12	12	12	12	12	7	11	11				
6 FISICHELLA	3	10	2	2	2	2	2	2	2	2	2	3	3	3	3	3	3	12	12	12	7	11	17	14	4	11	11	11	11	11	11	11	11	11	11	11	11	11	14	14	12				
3 BUTTON	4	2	3	3	3	3	3	3	3	3	3	12	12	12	12	12	12	11	11	11	14	17	14	3	12	4	14	14	14	14	14	14	14	14	14	14	14	14	14	14	14	12	11		
12 MASSA	12	3	12	12	12	12	12	12	12	12	12	11	11	11	11	11	11	17	17	14	4	14	10	10	11	14	18	18	18	18	18	18	18	18	18	18	18	18	18	18	18	18	18		
4 SATO	2	12	11	11	11	11	11	11	11	11	11	14	14	14	14	14	14	14	14	14	18	18	20	20	20	20	20	20	20	20	21	21	20	20	20	20	20	20							
14 COULTHARD	11	11	6	14	14	14	14	14	14	14	14	1	20	20	20	20	18	18	18	18	20	20	20	20	20	21	21	20	21	21	21	21	21	21	21	21	21	21							
11 VILLENEUVE	19	19	14	18	18	18	18	18	18	18	20	20	18	18	18	18	20	20	20	20	20	20	21	21																					
18 MONTEIRO	14	14	18	20	20	20	20	20	20	18	18	18	21	21	21	21	21	21	21	21	21	21																							
19 KARTHIKEYAN	18	18	20	6	21	21	21	21	21	21	21	21																																	
21 ALBERS	20	20	21	21																																									
20 FRIESACHER	21	21																																											
2 BARRICHELLO																																													

TIME SHEETS

QUALIFYING

SATURDAY: Sunny (track 54°C, air 41–42°C)
SUNDAY: Cloudy/sunny (track 48°C, air 41°C)

Pos.	Driver	R/Order	1st qualifying	R/Order	2nd qualifying	Aggregate
1	Fernando Alonso	20	1m 29.848s	20	1m 32.054s	3m 01.902s
2	Michael Schumacher	15	1m 30.237s	18	1m 32.120s	3m 02.357s
3	Jarno Trulli	19	1m 29.993s	19	1m 32.667s	3m 02.660s
4	Nick Heidfeld	18	1m 30.390s	17	1m 32.827s	3m 03.217s
5	Mark Webber	6	1m 30.592s	15	1m 32.670s	3m 03.262s
6	Ralf Schumacher	17	1m 30.952s	10	1m 32.319s	3m 03.271s
7	Christian Klien	14	1m 30.646s	13	1m 32.723s	3m 03.369s
8	Pedro de la Rosa	1	1m 30.725s	12	1m 32.648s	3m 03.373s
9	Kimi Räikkönen	13	1m 30.594s	14	1m 32.930s	3m 03.524s
10	Giancarlo Fisichella	7	1m 30.445s	16	1m 33.320s	3m 03.765s
11	Jenson Button	4	1m 30.957s	9	1m 33.391s	3m 04.348s
12	Felipe Massa	12	1m 30.933s	11	1m 34.269s	3m 05.202s
13	Takuma Sato	2	1m 31.113s	8	1m 34.450s	3m 05.563s
14	David Coulthard	16	1m 31.211s	7	1m 34.633s	3m 05.844s
15	Rubens Barrichello	8	1m 31.826s	6	1m 35.867s	3m 07.693s
16	Jacques Villeneuve	5	1m 32.318s	5	1m 35.665s	3m 07.983s
17	Tiago Monteiro	10	1m 33.424s	3	1m 36.004s	3m 09.428s
18	Narain Karthikeyan	11	1m 33.190s	4	1m 36.953s	3m 10.143s
19	Christijan Albers	9	1m 34.005s	2	1m 36.417s	3m 10.422s
20	Patrick Friesacher	3	1m 38.848s	1	1m 36.413s	3m 11.261s

CHASSIS LOG BOOK

	FERRARI				SAUBER-PETRONAS	
1	Michael Schumacher	F2005/245		11	Jacques Villeneuve	C24/03
2	Rubens Barrichello	F2005/243		12	Felipe Massa	C24/02
	Spare	F2004M/236			Spare	C24/01
	BAR-HONDA				**RED BULL-COSWORTH**	
3	Jenson Button	007/04		14	David Coulthard	RB1/2
4	Takuma Sato	007/02		15	Christian Klien	RB1/1
	Spare	007/03		37	Vitantonio Liuzzi	RB1/3
	RENAULT				Spare	RB1/3
5	Fernando Alonso	R25/04			**TOYOTA**	
6	Giancarlo Fisichella	R25/03		16	Jarno Trulli	TF105/03
	Spare	R25/02		17	Ralf Schumacher	TF105/04
	WILLIAMS-BMW			38	Ricardo Zonta	TF105/02
7	Mark Webber	FW27/03			Spare	TF105/02
8	Nick Heidfeld	FW27/04			**JORDAN-TOYOTA**	
	Spare	FW27/02		18	Tiago Monteiro	EJ15/03
	McLAREN-MERCEDES			19	Narain Karthikeyan	EJ15/02
9	Kimi Räikkönen	MP4-20/04		39	Robert Doornbos	EJ15/01
10	Pedro de la Rosa	MP4-20/03			Spare	EJ15/01
35	Alex Wurz	MP4-20/01			**MINARDI-COSWORTH**	
	Spare	MP4-20/01		20	Patrick Friesacher	PS04B/02
				21	Christijan Albers	PS04B/04
					Spare	PS04B/03

Photograph: James Moy/www.crash.net

PRACTICE 1 (FRIDAY)

Sunny (track 36°C, air 45°C)

Pos.	Driver	Laps	Time
1	Ricardo Zonta	21	1m 31.449s
2	Michael Schumacher	5	1m 32.120s
3	Vitantonio Liuzzi	17	1m 32.509s
4	Alex Wurz	13	1m 33.106s
5	Rubens Barrichello	5	1m 33.111s
6	Pedro de la Rosa	9	1m 33.270s
7	Mark Webber	8	1m 33.427s
8	Kimi Räikkönen	5	1m 33.836s
9	Jenson Button	5	1m 34.002s
10	Nick Heidfeld	4	1m 34.722s
11	Christian Klien	8	1m 34.722s
12	Felipe Massa	6	1m 34.875s
13	David Coulthard	8	1m 34.984s
14	Robert Doornbos	23	1m 35.432s
15	Narain Karthikeyan	23	1m 35.766s
16	Tiago Monteiro	18	1m 36.534s
17	Jacques Villeneuve	8	1m 37.112s
18	Christijan Albers	15	1m 37.778s
19	Patrick Friesacher	16	1m 38.603s
20	Takuma Sato	2	No time
21	Giancarlo Fisichella	2	No time
22	Fernando Alonso	2	No time
23	Jarno Trulli	1	No time
24	Ralf Schumacher	1	No time

PRACTICE 2 (FRIDAY)

Sunny (track 38°C, air 54°C)

Pos.	Driver	Laps	Time
1	Alex Wurz	20	1m 30.695s
2	Fernando Alonso	24	1m 31.969s
3	Vitantonio Liuzzi	30	1m 32.319s
4	Pedro de la Rosa	13	1m 32.333s
5	Michael Schumacher	16	1m 32.431s
6	Jarno Trulli	22	1m 32.595s
7	Giancarlo Fisichella	24	1m 32.708s
8	Kimi Räikkönen	18	1m 32.988s
9	Jenson Button	23	1m 33.037s
10	Ralf Schumacher	19	1m 33.077s
11	Nick Heidfeld	20	1m 33.152s
12	Takuma Sato	13	1m 33.205s
13	Christian Klien	25	1m 33.436s
14	Ricardo Zonta	11	1m 33.443s
15	Mark Webber	16	1m 33.563s
16	David Coulthard	21	1m 33.708s
17	Felipe Massa	18	1m 33.726s
18	Narain Karthikeyan	16	1m 33.981s
19	Robert Doornbos	26	1m 34.222s
20	Jacques Villeneuve	19	1m 34.300s
21	Tiago Monteiro	18	1m 34.727s
22	Patrick Friesacher	21	1m 35.325s
23	Christijan Albers	22	1m 36.094s

PRACTICE 3 (SATURDAY)

Sunny (track 37–42°C, air 32–34°C)

Pos.	Driver	Laps	Time
1	Michael Schumacher	4	1m 30.552s
2	Fernando Alonso	6	1m 31.811s
3	Pedro de la Rosa	5	1m 32.766s
4	Jarno Trulli	8	1m 32.776s
5	Christian Klien	10	1m 32.941s
6	Ralf Schumacher	11	1m 32.868s
7	Giancarlo Fisichella	6	1m 32.877s
8	Narain Karthikeyan	8	1m 32.999s
9	Mark Webber	4	1m 33.276s
10	David Coulthard	10	1m 33.606s
11	Jenson Button	6	1m 33.683s
12	Nick Heidfeld	4	1m 34.133s
13	Takuma Sato	12	1m 34.163s
14	Felipe Massa	10	1m 34.232s
15	Tiago Monteiro	10	1m 34.392s
16	Jacques Villeneuve	6	1m 35.464s
17	Patrick Friesacher	15	1m 36.561s
18	Christijan Albers	13	1m 37.445s
19	Kimi Räikkönen	5	1m 37.949s

PRACTICE 4 (SATURDAY)

Sunny (track 44–48°C, air 35–37°C)

Pos.	Driver	Laps	Time
1	Mark Webber	10	1m 29.527s
2	Ralf Schumacher	12	1m 29.711s
3	Giancarlo Fisichella	15	1m 29.738s
4	Jarno Trulli	12	1m 29.798s
5	Kimi Räikkönen	10	1m 29.810s
6	Fernando Alonso	12	1m 29.825s
7	Pedro de la Rosa	10	1m 29.864s
8	Christian Klien	11	1m 29.896s
9	Michael Schumacher	8	1m 30.080s
10	Nick Heidfeld	6	1m 30.290s
11	Jenson Button	12	1m 30.324s
12	David Coulthard	11	1m 30.558s
13	Takuma Sato	15	1m 30.902s
14	Felipe Massa	11	1m 31.001s
15	Jacques Villeneuve	12	1m 31.126s
16	Narain Karthikeyan	10	1m 32.498s
17	Tiago Monteiro	12	1m 32.686s
18	Christijan Albers	12	1m 33.715s
19	Patrick Friesacher	12	1m 34.409s

9th: RÄIKKÖNEN McLaren-Mercedes

7th: KLIEN Red Bull-Cosworth
DNS: electrics on dummy grid

5th: WEBBER Williams-BMW

3rd: TRULLI Toyota

Pole: ALONSO Renault

10th: FISICHELLA Renault

8th: DE LA ROSA McLaren-Mercedes

6th: R. SCHUMACHER Toyota

4th: HEIDFELD Williams-BMW

2nd: M. SCHUMACHER Ferrari

46	47	48	49	50	51	52	53	54	55	56	57	
5	5	5	5	5	5	5	5	5	5	5	5	1
16	16	16	16	16	16	16	16	16	16	16	16	2
9	9	9	9	9	9	9	9	9	9	9	9	3
3	17	17	17	17	17	17	17	17	17	17	17	4
2	7	7	7	7	7	7	7	10	10	10		5
17	10	10	10	10	10	10	10	10	7	7	7	6
7	2	2	2	2	12	12	12	12	12	12		7
10	12	12	12	12	2	2	2	2	14			8
12	11	11	11	11	11	11	11	14	14	2		
11	14	14	14	14	14	14	14	11	18			
14	18	18	18	18	18	18	18					
18	20	20	20	20	20	20	20					
20	21	21	21	21	21	21	21					
21												

Pit stop
One lap or more behind leader

FOR THE RECORD

FIRST GRAND PRIX FASTEST LAP:
Pedro de la Rosa
20th GRAND PRIX WIN:
Renault
200th GRAND PRIX:
Sauber

POINTS

	DRIVERS	
1	Fernando Alonso	26
2	Jarno Trulli	16
3	Giancarlo Fisichella	10
4	Ralf Schumacher	9
5	David Coulthard	9
6	Rubens Barrichello	8
7	Juan Pablo Montoya	8
8	Kimi Räikkönen	7
9	Mark Webber	7
10	Nick Heidfeld	6
11	Pedro de la Rosa	4
12	Christian Klien	3
13	Felipe Massa	2
14	Michael Schumacher	2

	CONSTRUCTORS	
1	Renault	36
2	Toyota	25
3	McLaren	19
4	Williams	13
5	Red Bull	12
6	Ferrari	10
7	Sauber	2

Photographs: Bryn Williams/www.crash.net

Michael Schumacher could hardly have got
his Ferrari F2005 closer to Fernando Alonso's
Renault R25 as they battled for the lead in the
closing stages of the race. Alonso judged it
perfectly to deny Ferrari a win on its home turf.
Photograph: James Moy/www.crash.net

IMOLA
SAN MARINOGP
FIA F1 WORLD CHAMPIONSHIP/ROUND 4

Truth be told, Kimi Räikkönen did the business in decisive fashion to wrap up pole position on Saturday afternoon, then defended it with measured superiority on Sunday morning. Cumulatively, his McLaren MP4-20 wound up almost 0.6s faster than Fernando Alonso's Renault R25, which joined him on the front row.

'The car is much better than it was in Bahrain,' reported Räikkönen. 'The circuit seems to suit the car much better than the previous ones did. It was already good yesterday straight out of the box and I am pretty happy with it.'

Alonso was also pretty content and well able to consolidate his position on the outside of the front row in the second session, mindful of the fact that he needed to conserve his V10, which he'd already raced in Bahrain and about which there were some behind-the-scenes reliability concerns. This conservation-mode approach would duly kick forward into influencing just how Fernando tackled the race, adding a further impressive dimension to his weekend's performance.

Fresh from an intensive test programme at Barcelona and Paul Ricard, the BAR Honda squad arrived at Imola confident that it had unlocked some fresh aerodynamic secrets which would enable it to improve on the 007's disappointing form in the early races. Jenson Button (2m 44.105s) qualified third, his team-mate Takuma Sato (2m 44.658s) sixth, both men improving on their Saturday positions despite the fact that the second session started on a still-damp track surface after an overnight downpour.

Michael Schumacher had been a confident third fastest at the end of first practice but a slip at Rivazza on Sunday morning plummeted him back to 13th in the final order and benefited Mark Webber, whose Williams FW27 moved onto the second row on a 2m 44.511s, less than 0.1s faster than Jarno Trulli's Toyota TF105.

'From my perspective, I didn't make any mistakes across the lap,' said Webber on Saturday, 'but I could have done better in the first sector because I braked too early for Turn One. But I did a good last sector, which I feel balanced the lap.' Team-mate Nick Heidfeld had to make his run quite early, when conditions were not ideal, and would eventually wind up eighth on a cumulative 2m 45.196s, happy that back problems he'd suffered in testing were no longer causing him any anxiety.

'My lap was average,' Heidfeld reported. 'I lost a bit of grip towards the end, but it was reassuring that I didn't experience any back problems today. I feel that my muscles are now fully recovered.'

In the Toyota camp, Trulli was moderately content with what turned out to be fifth, but Ralf Schumacher was less happy with 12th on Saturday, even though he moved up two places on Sunday morning. 'It was a very tight Saturday qualifying session,' he said. 'It was obviously not a perfect lap for me and it ended up slightly slower than I would have liked. I took it slightly easier in the first sector, but apart from that it was a pretty clear lap with no real mistakes and I'm happy to report that the car feels pretty good whatever fuel load it is running.'

Seventh place fell to Alex Wurz, who was making his first visit to a GP starting grid since Sepang in 2000 – this time he was standing in for the injured Juan Pablo Montoya. After Pedro de la Rosa had taken this role in Bahrain it was decided to give the Imola opportunity to McLaren's longest-serving test driver, and Wurz was determined to grasp his opportunity with both hands. In qualifying he did a clean and competent job, never putting a wheel out of place or pushing too hard.

Jacques Villeneuve did well to qualify his Sauber 11th on 2m 46.259s, but his team-mate Felipe Massa's apparent eighth place took a hit with a ten-place penalty for an unscheduled engine change, dropping the Brazilian to the back between the Jordans and Minardis.

Another unlucky performer was Giancarlo Fisichella, who wound up a distant 12th after a disappointing Saturday session. 'We haven't found an explanation in the data yet,' he shrugged 'but going into Turn 15 the rear brakes locked, causing major oversteer. I did everything the same as I did in practice, braking in the same place, so I don't think it was a mistake but we are not sure yet.'

In 14th place, David Coulthard's 2m 48.070s best in the Red Bull RB1 was only just quick enough to beat his debutant team-mate Vitantonio Liuzzi's sister car because the Scot lost crucial time in Sunday's qualifying session.

'The lap started very badly,' said Coulthard. 'I lost the back end into Turn One so was all over the kerbs. I managed to pick up around the rest of the lap, but ultimately it wouldn't have made a huge difference to where we qualified. The others are ahead on pace and we were 0.6s down on Villeneuve, so it's now just a question of what luck we have in the race in terms of other people dropping out, otherwise it's probably going to be a quiet one.' It was.

Above: Vitantonio Liuzzi drove with restraint and maturity on his F1 race debut in the Red Bull RB1.

Far left: Narain Karthikeyan strapped tightly in the cockpit of his Jordan-Toyota EJ15 prior to the off.

Left: A beaming Luca di Montezemolo, Ferrari president, celebrated the continuation of his team's technical partnership with Shell by signing on the dotted line for the media.

Below left: GP2 competitors (from left) Mattias Lauda, Nelson Piquet Jr and Nico Rosberg pose with Niki Lauda and Keke Rosberg prior to the new series' first race.
Photographs: James Moy/www.crash.net

Right: Felipe Massa keeps a wary eye on the progress of his Sauber team-mate Jacques Villeneuve on the monitor.
Photograph: Jad Sherif/WRI

Above: Accelerating away from the start, Kimi glanced in his McLaren's right-hand mirror to check that Fernando Alonso was covered as the pack headed towards Tamburello. Kimi built up a commanding lead before suffering driveshaft failure.

Opposite: Peter Sauber watching some BAR team members busying themselves on the starting grid. It turned out to be a very bad day for the Brackley squad.

Photographs: James Moy/www.crash.net

Fernando Alonso steadfastly refused to be intimidated by the presence of Michael Schumacher's scarlet Ferrari filling his Renault's mirrors and drove the last few laps of the San Marino Grand Prix absolutely no faster than he needed to, depriving the capacity crowd at Imola's Autodromo Enzo e Dino Ferrari of the home victory it craved.

The heady cocktail of Schumacher's boiling determination and Alonso's unflappable resolve made the last 12 laps of this race one of the epic events in F1 history. The Renault driver held off everything Michael's Ferrari F2005 could throw at him from the moment the reigning world champion erupted out of his final refuelling stop on lap 50 and launched himself into a counter-attack against the young Spaniard – a battle in which they were never more than 0.4s apart all the way to the chequered flag.

'I knew that Michael was basically more than a second faster than me,' said Alonso, who had now won three of the four races to have taken place this season. 'So I had to hold him back slowly in the corners, which worked well. For the last ten laps we had a Red Bull and a Williams in front of us and in the slow corners I was braking a little early to protect my rear tyres and keep my edge over Michael.'

For Schumacher, the sheer brilliance of his relentless performance was highlighted by the fact that he'd started from 13th on the grid after running wide for the tricky downhill Rivazza left-hander during second qualifying. Heavy with his first stint of race fuel, Michael braked hard over a little bump on the approach to the corner and that was enough for the front-left wheel to become momentarily unloaded. He locked up, lurched onto the gravel and lost his momentum.

After the race, Michael was clearly disappointed that he didn't nail down another victory in front of the Ferrari faithful, yet the truth of the matter was that the F2005 – and, even more crucially, its Bridgestone tyres – had proved that Maranello was back in business. For the moment, at least, although it was clear that the relatively cool conditions played to the strengths of the Japanese tyres.

'Michael's pace for Ferrari was absolutely staggering,' said Jenson Button, who finished a strong third in the apparently rejuvenated BAR-Honda 007. 'But I'm very happy with the car and we've got a lot more in the pipeline to help us to keep in contention for the podium for the rest of the season.

'We lost out towards the end when I got a bad run up the hill from Acque Minerali and Michael was able to get beside me going into the Varianté Alta. Fighting him in that position could have put me out of the race, so I decided to play safe and ensure we got home and dry with a podium and our first points of the year to show for it.' As it turned out, Jenson's bright-eyed optimism on his descent from the podium was to prove sadly misplaced.

Yet from the start it seemed as though the fourth round of the championship might unfold in a very different fashion after Kimi Räikkönen's McLaren MP4-20 finally unlocked its pent-up promise to clinch pole position. Alonso might have professed not to be worried by the fact that Räikkönen opened a 3.5s lead by the end of lap eight, for the Spaniard believed his key rival would be stopping for fuel relatively early.

As things transpired, such speculation was academic. Midway around the ninth lap Kimi suddenly slowed and toured into the pits to retire, a driveshaft constant velocity joint having

GOOD DAY GOES BAD FOR BUTTON

Only hours after finishing third in the San Marino GP, Jenson Button and the BAR Honda team were enveloped in a storm of controversy after the FIA took the extraordinary decision to appeal against the stance of its own stewards, who gave the British driver's car a clean bill of health at the official post-race scrutineering.

The matter was now to be referred to the FIA court of appeal, which was scheduled to be convened in Paris on 4 May. If the court established that the car was not in conformity with the regulations, the decision would virtually guarantee exclusion from the Imola race at the very least.

Button's car spent a protracted six-hour spell in the scrutineering bay being examined in detail by FIA officials after finishing third in a dramatic race behind Fernando Alonso's Renault and Michael Schumacher's Ferrari. The car was weighed immediately after the race and tipped the scales at 606 kg, comfortably above the 600-kg minimum weight limit, but after it had been drained of fuel it weighed only 594 kg.

Despite this, it seemed that the team's explanation satisfied the race stewards and the provisional race results were duly confirmed. The FIA would not comment on the day after the race beyond issuing an official statement confirming the date of the appeal hearing.

Some F1 sources hinted that the BAR 007 may have been fitted with a concealed secondary fuel tank which could retain fuel pumped into the car at the final refuelling stop of the race.

However, BAR insiders claimed that this was merely a collector system for the Honda engine's high-pressure fuel pump, was very similar to systems used by many other contemporary F1 cars, was easy to see within the main fuel cell and was in no way hidden from view.

'While the scrutineers also wanted the fuel systems on [Fernando] Alonso's Renault and [Michael] Schumacher's Ferrari drained out, we couldn't help noticing that our car seemed to attract much more attention than the other two,' said a team member.

A statement from the BAR Honda headquarters at Brackley said that the team was surprised to have been contacted by the secretary general of the FIA's sporting department advising BAR that the governing body was proceeding with its appeal. It continued, 'In accordance with standard procedure, the FIA scrutineers all cars which have completed the race, which involves weighing and measuring the car, as well as performing random checks.

'During scrutineering of the BAR-Honda 007-04 race car (entry number car three) driven by Jenson Button, the FIA requested that the car be measured and weighed to ensure its compliance with the FIA technical regulations. The car was found to be compliant with all the regulations, including being above the weight limit.

'Thereafter, the FIA decided to perform a further check and requested that the team drain the fuel tank and then siphon out all the residual fuel remaining in the system. Once this had been completed, they determined that the car was below the required minimum weight.

'The FIA invited BAR Honda to explain its position and the team was able to demonstrate, using its own data and data gathered by the investigating stewards, that the car was above minimum weight at all times during the race.'

The clock was ticking in the countdown to developments of seismic significance for the BAR Honda squad.

failed. It was understandable under the circumstances that the Finn hurled his steering wheel across the garage in abject frustration. He'd not been due to stop until around lap 25 and the race was already in his pocket.

'Obviously I'm disappointed because I had a great start and was really building on my lead,' he shrugged once he'd regained his composure. 'At least we know that the car has the pace in qualifying as well as the race and with improvements due for Spain in two weeks I am looking forward to a good race there.'

That left Alonso leading comfortably from the assured Button, both of them steadily pulling clear of Jarno Trulli's Toyota TF105 which, in turn, was boxing in a great gaggle of cars including Mark Webber's slow-starting Williams FW27, Takuma Sato's BAR 007 and Alex Wurz's McLaren MP4-20. Then came Jacques Villeneuve's Sauber C24, Rubens Barrichello's Ferrari, Nick Heidfeld's Williams and the Schumacher brothers, Ralf just ahead of a disciplined Michael who was taking things easy on a heavy load of fuel, conserving his tyres and brakes until the car lightened up.

Yet if Alonso was relishing his spell at the head of the pack, Melbourne winner Giancarlo Fisichella was again frustrated in his efforts to rekindle the good times. Down in the pack the Italian lasted only five laps before pirouetting into the wall exiting the Tamburello chicane.

'I really don't know what happened,' said Fisichella. 'I made a good start and was much quicker than Heidfeld, so was just sitting behind him and waiting for the pit stop. Then going through Turn Two I lost control of the car and spun into the wall. Obviously it is extremely disappointing because we had the pace again today to score some points.' Renault later admitted that it

DIARY

Red Bull Racing signs a deal
to use Ferrari V8 engines for
the 2006 and 2007 seasons.
'This is an enormous boost for
the team and underlines our
commitment to compete in the
forefront of F1,' says sporting
director Christian Horner.

Flavio Briatore's contract to
remain managing director of the
Renault F1 team is extended to
the end of 2006.

Former Ferrari F1 driver Cliff
Allison dies at the age of 73.

Jean Todt hints strongly that
he is targeting Kimi Räikkönen,
rather than Fernando Alonso, as
a possible successor to Michael
Schumacher at Ferrari.

was difficult to pinpoint the precise cause of the accident, but
the team did subsequently reinforce some suspension elements
in order to counteract the possibility of its recurring. It was
eventually concluded that a right-rear track rod had failed.

Alonso led up to his first stop on lap 23, regaining his place
at the head of the field when Button made his routine stop next
time around. As the track gradually cleared in front of him,
Michael Schumacher duly picked up the pace, staying out until
lap 27 for his first fuel stop, by which time he was in third place
and well capable of retaining it on his return to the race.

While boxed in behind Ralf, Michael had been lapping in the
1m 24s bracket, but on a clear track he was able to raise his
game. Immediately before and after his first stop he clicked
down into the 1m 22s bracket and the chase was on. Having
disposed of Button for second place, he closed relentlessly on
Alonso. But Fernando was ready for him, determined to run the
balance of the contest at his own pace and his pace alone.

Fernando made his second stop on lap 42, Michael his on
lap 49. Had he been able to squeeze just a couple more miles
out of his second stint he might have made it to the end of lap
50, in which case he would have been home and dry. As it was,
Alonso just squeezed back into the lead.

This was a defining moment for the young Spaniard, the
moment when he either delivered a result to carry his
reputation to a fresh level or buckled under the strain. As things
unfolded he handled the situation perfectly, easing back to run
in the 1m 25s bracket for the last few laps to avoid getting
involved in the messy task of lapping some backmarkers, a
development which might expose him to vulnerability at the
hands of the ever-watchful Schumacher.

Alonso, ecstatic and wide-eyed, scraped home a length
ahead of the world champion. 'I am happy in one way and
excited after such a race,' said Schumacher, 'but on the other
hand I am disappointed that I made that mistake this morning
[in qualifying], without which it would have been a perfect day
for all of us. I could see that Fernando was not that quick,
but there was never a real opportunity to have a proper go at
passing him. Basically, he had a good race today and made no
mistakes. That's why he won and I did not.'

For his part, Barrichello failed to finish due to an electronic
problem, so was never in with a shout near the front of the
field. Behind Button at the chequered flag, Alex Wurz did a fine
job as Juan Pablo Montoya's stand-in to take fourth place in the
McLaren-Mercedes MP4-20. This meant that McLaren had
scored points with four different drivers in the first four races
of the year.

Yet it was a close call for the Austrian driver. At his last pit
stop the team noticed an apparent discrepancy between the
fuel-flow meter on the rig and the scales on which the rig is
mounted, sparking fears that Alex had been short-changed on
his fuel load. He was instructed to drive in fuel-conservation
mode as a precaution while the calculations were checked, but
eventually he got the green light to press on hard to the finish.

Takuma Sato took the chequered flag in fifth place with
Jacques Villeneuve next up after a heartening performance
in his Sauber. 'I thoroughly enjoyed my race,' said the
Canadian. 'I had a good fight with Webber and when he
ran wide he tried to come back on but I was able to get by.
If I had been another 10 cm further forward I would have
taken the risk with Wurz at the same time, but it was early

in the race and it would have been touch and go.'

Trulli took a disappointed seventh in the Toyota, having changed his chassis set-up just before qualifying and been saddled with too much oversteer as a result. Heidfeld and Webber spent most of the race frustratingly in traffic, finishing an unsatisfactory ninth and tenth, which at least became eighth and ninth soon after the race when Ralf Schumacher was awarded a time penalty for cutting in front of Heidfeld while rejoining from a refuelling stop.

As for Vitantonio Liuzzi, making his F1 debut for Red Bull, he overtook Michael at Tosa on the first lap before being repassed at Piratella. He also passed Webber at the Villeneuve corner on the last lap, but ran wide and was repassed. He reckoned he could have finished sixth if he'd been two seconds quicker up to his first stop, because he was being held up so much after that. He still set seventh-fastest race lap, three-tenths off Alonso's. Not bad for a new boy in front of his home crowd.

Alan Henry

Left: Alonso had both of his Renault's left-hand Michelins well up the kerb exiting the tight right-hander before the pits as he worked to defend his wafer-thin lead from the relentless Schumacher's Ferrari.
Photograph: Lukas Gorys

Below: Happy days! Alonso beamed with delight as Schumacher grinned broadly on the rostrum.

Bottom: Alex Wurz took a turn to stand in for Montoya at Imola and, in his first F1 race for almost five years, finished a fine fourth which turned into third after Button's BAR was excluded.
Photographs: James Moy/www.crash.net

5

FIA F1 WORLD CHAMPIONSHIP • ROUND 4

GRAN PREMIO FOSTER'S DI SAN MARINO

IMOLA 22–24 APRIL 2005

IMOLA – AUTODROMO DINO E ENZO FERRARI

PIRATELLA 105/169 (4)
TOSA 55/89 (2)
ACQUE MINERALI 70/113 (3)
VARIANTE ALTA 75/121 (3)
VILLENEUVE 85/137 (3)
mph/km/h (gear)
175/281 (6)
TRAGUARDO 55/89 (2)
RIVAZZA 65/105 (2)
TAMBURELLO 100/161 (3)
VARIANTE BASSA 180/290 (6)

CIRCUIT LENGTH: 3.065 miles/4.933 km

RACE DISTANCE: 62 laps, 189.898 miles /305.609 km   RACE WEATHER: Heavily cloudy (track 23–26°C, air 19°C)

Pos.	Driver	Nat.	No.	Entrant	Car/Engine	Tyres	Laps	Time/Retirement	Speed (mph/km/h)	Gap to leader	Fastest race lap	
1	Fernando Alonso	E	5	Mild Seven Renault F1 Team	Renault R25-RS25 V10	M	62	1h 27m 41.921s	129.919/209.085		1m 23.133s	22
2	Michael Schumacher	D	1	Scuderia Ferrari Marlboro	Ferrari F2005-055 V10	B	62	1h 27m 42.136s	129.914/209.077	+0.215s	1m 21.858s	48
3	Alex Wurz	A	10	West McLaren Mercedes	McLaren MP4-20-Mercedes F0 110R V10	M	62	1h 28m 09.475s	129.242/207.996	+27.554s	1m 23.023s	24
4	Jacques Villeneuve	CDN	11	Sauber Petronas	Sauber C24-Petronas 05A V10	M	62	1h 28m 46.363s	128.347/206.556	+64.442s	1m 24.017s	45
5	Jarno Trulli	I	16	Panasonic Toyota Racing	Toyota TF105-RVX-05 V10	M	62	1h 28m 52.179s	128.207/206.330	+70.258s	1m 24.022s	44
6	Nick Heidfeld	D	8	BMW WilliamsF1 Team	Williams FW27-BMW P84/85 V10	M	62	1h 28m 53.203s	128.183/206.291	+71.282s	1m 23.917s	54
7	Mark Webber	AUS	7	BMW WilliamsF1 Team	Williams FW27-BMW P84/85 V10	M	62	1h 29m 05.218s	127.895/205.827	+83.297s	1m 24.419s	17
8	Vitantonio Liuzzi	I	15	Red Bull Racing	Red Bull RB1-Cosworth TJ2005/10 V10	M	62	1h 29m 05.685s	127.884/205.809	+83.767s	1m 23.488s	46
9	Ralf Schumacher	D	17	Panasonic Toyota Racing	Toyota TF105-RVX-05 V10	M	62	+25s penalty	128.194/206.308	+70.841s	1m 24.230s	19
10	Felipe Massa	BR	12	Sauber Petronas	Sauber C24-Petronas 05A V10	M	61			+1 lap	1m 23.602s	37
11	David Coulthard	GB	14	Red Bull Racing	Red Bull RB1-Cosworth TJ2005/10 V10	M	61			+1 lap	1m 24.641s	22
12	Narain Karthikeyan	IND	19	Jordan Toyota	Jordan EJ15-Toyota RVX-05 V10	B	61			+1 lap	1m 24.094s	20
13	Tiago Monteiro	P	18	Jordan Toyota	Jordan EJ15-Toyota RVX-05 V10	B	60			+2 laps	1m 24.719s	19
	Christijan Albers	NL	21	Minardi Cosworth	Minardi PS05-Cosworth TJ2005 V10	B	20	Gearbox			1m 27.420s	18
	Rubens Barrichello	D	2	Scuderia Ferrari Marlboro	Ferrari F2005-055 V10	B	18	Electrics			1m 24.435s	13
	Kimi Räikkönen	FIN	9	West McLaren Mercedes	McLaren MP4-20-Mercedes F0 110R V10	M	9	Driveshaft			1m 23.296s	8
	Patrick Friesacher	A	20	Minardi Cosworth	Minardi PS05-Cosworth TJ2005 V10	B	8	Gearbox			1m 28.334s	5
	Giancarlo Fisichella	I	6	Mild Seven Renault F1 Team	Renault R25-RS25 V10	M	5	Mechanical failure			1m 25.665s	4
DQ	Jenson Button	GB	3	Lucky Strike BAR Honda	BAR 007-Honda RA005E V10	M	62				1m 22.604s	22
DQ	Takuma Sato	J	4	Lucky Strike BAR Honda	BAR 007-Honda RA005E V10	M	62				1m 23.368s	23

Fastest lap: Michael Schumacher, on lap 48, 1m 21.858s, 134.804 mph/216.946 km/h (record).

Previous lap record: Michael Schumacher (Ferrari F2004-052 V10), 1m 22.491s, 133.769 mph/215.281 km/h (2004).

19th: FRIESACHER Minardi-Cosworth

17th: MONTEIRO Jordan-Toyota

15th: LIUZZI Red Bull-Cosworth

13th: M. SCHUMACHER Ferrari

11th: VILLENEUVE Sauber-Petronas

20th: ALBERS Minardi-Cosworth

18th: MASSA Sauber-Petronas
Ten-place penalty for engine change

16th: KARTHIKEYAN Jordan-Toyota

14th: COULTHARD Red Bull-Cosworth

12th: FISICHELLA Renault

Grid order	1	2	3	4	5	6	7	8	9	10	11	12	13	14	15	16	17	18	19	20	21	22	23	24	25	26	27	28	29	30	31	32	33	34	35	36	37	38	39	40	41	42	43	44	45	46	47	4
9 RÄIKKÖNEN	9	9	9	9	9	9	9	9	5	5	5	5	5	5	5	5	5	5	5	5	5	5	5	3	5	5	5	5	5	5	5	5	5	5	5	5	5	5	5	5	5	5	3	3	3	3	1	
5 ALONSO	5	5	5	5	5	5	5	5	3	3	3	3	3	3	3	3	3	3	3	3	3	3	3	5	3	3	3	3	3	3	3	3	3	3	3	3	3	3	3	3	3	3	1	1	1	1	5	
3 BUTTON	3	3	3	3	16	16	16	16	16	16	16	16	16	16	16	16	16	16	16	16	16	4	4	10	1	1	1	1	1	1	1	1	1	1	1	1	1	1	1	1	1	1	5	5	5	5	5	
7 WEBBER	16	16	16	16	16	16	16	16	7	7	7	7	7	7	7	7	7	7	7	7	7	16	10	1	10	10	10	10	10	10	10	10	10	10	10	10	10	10	10	10	10	10	10	10	10	10	10	
16 TRULLI	7	7	7	7	7	7	7	7	4	4	4	4	4	4	4	4	4	4	4	4	4	7	1	4	4	4	4	4	4	4	4	4	4	4	4	4	4	4	4	4	4	4	4	4	4	4	4	
4 SATO	4	4	4	4	4	4	4	4	10	10	10	10	10	10	10	10	10	10	10	10	10	10	11	16	16	16	16	16	16	16	16	16	16	16	16	16	16	16	16	16	16	16	16	11	15	1		
10 WURZ	10	10	10	10	10	10	10	10	11	11	11	11	11	11	11	11	11	11	11	11	11	16	7	7	7	7	7	11	11	11	11	11	11	11	11	11	11	11	11	11	11	8	15	15	1			
8 HEIDFELD	11	11	11	11	11	11	11	11	2	2	2	2	2	2	2	2	2	2	8	8	8	1	15	11	11	11	11	7	7	7	7	7	7	7	7	7	7	7	7	7	8	15	16	16	11			
2 BARRICHELLO	2	2	2	2	2	2	2	2	8	8	8	8	8	8	8	8	17	17	17	17	15	15	11	15	15	15	8	8	8	8	8	8	8	8	8	8	8	8	17	17	17	17						
17 R. SCHUMACHER	8	8	8	8	8	8	8	8	17	17	17	17	17	17	17	17	1	1	1	14	14	14	14	8	17	17	17	17	17	17	17	17	17	17	17	17	17	15	15	8	8	8						
11 VILLENEUVE	6	6	6	6	17	17	17	1	1	1	1	1	1	15	15	15	8	8	17	17	15	15	15	15	15	15	15	15	15	15	15	15	7	7	7	7	1											
6 FISICHELLA	17	17	17	17	1	1	1	15	15	15	15	15	15	14	14	14	14	14	17	17	14	14	14	14	14	14	14	14	14	14	14	12	14	14	14	14	12											
1 M. SCHUMACHER	1	1	1	1	15	15	15	14	14	14	14	14	14	1	1	1	19	19	19	19	12	12	12	12	12	12	12	12	12	12	12	12	12	12	12	19	12	12	12	12	12	12	12					
14 COULTHARD	15	15	15	15	14	14	14	12	12	12	19	19	19	19	19	12	12	18	12	12	18	18	18	18	18	18	18	18	18	18	18	18	18	18	18	18	18											
15 LIUZZI	14	14	14	14	12	12	12	19	19	19	12	12	12	12	2	12	18	12	18	18	18	18	18	18	18	18	18	18	18	18	18	18	18	18	18	18	18											
19 KARTHIKEYAN	19	19	19	12	19	19	19	18	18	18	18	18	18	18	12	12	21	21																														
18 MONTEIRO	18	12	12	19	19	18	18	18	21	21	21	21	21	21	21	21																																
12 MASSA	12	18	18	18	18	20	20	20	9																																							
20 FRIESACHER	20	20	20	20	20	21	21	21																																								
21 ALBERS	21	21	21	21	21																																											

Pit stop
One lap or more behind leader

TIME SHEETS

QUALIFYING

SATURDAY: Overcast (track 25–31°C, air 19–20°C)
SUNDAY: Heavily cloudy (track 17–18°C, air 16–17°C)

Pos.	Driver	R/Order	1st qualifying	R/Order	2nd qualifying	Aggregate
1	Kimi Räikkönen	18	1m 19.886s	20	1m 22.994s	2m 42.880s
2	Fernando Alonso	20	1m 19.889s	19	1m 23.552s	2m 43.441s
3	Jenson Button	8	1m 20.464s	16	1m 23.641s	2m 44.105s
4	Mark Webber	16	1m 20.442s	17	1m 24.069s	2m 44.511s
5	Jarno Trulli	19	1m 20.492s	15	1m 24.026s	2m 44.518s
6	Takuma Sato	7	1m 20.851s	11	1m 23.807s	2m 44.658s
7	Alex Wurz	2	1m 20.632s	13	1m 24.057s	2m 44.689s
8	Felipe Massa	15	1m 20.593s	14	1m 24.337s	2m 44.930s
9	Nick Heidfeld	6	1m 20.807s	12	1m 24.389s	2m 45.196s
10	Rubens Barrichello	13	1m 20.892s	10	1m 24.351s	2m 45.243s
11	Ralf Schumacher	17	1m 20.994s	9	1m 24.422s	2m 45.416s
12	Jacques Villeneuve	11	1m 20.999s	8	1m 25.260s	2m 46.259s
13	Giancarlo Fisichella	4	1m 21.708s	6	1m 25.002s	2m 46.710s
14	Michael Schumacher	5	1m 20.260s	18	1m 26.984s	2m 47.244s
15	David Coulthard	14	1m 21.632s	7	1m 26.438s	2m 48.070s
16	Vitantonio Liuzzi	1	1m 21.804s	5	1m 26.351s	2m 48.155s
17	Narain Karthikeyan	3	1m 23.123s	4	1m 28.976s	2m 52.099s
18	Tiago Monteiro	12	1m 25.100s	3	1m 29.152s	2m 54.252s
19	Patrick Friesacher	10	1m 26.484s	1	1m 30.564s	2m 57.048s
20	Christijan Albers	9	1m 25.921s	2	No time	No time

CHASSIS LOG BOOK

	FERRARI				SAUBER-PETRONAS	
1	Michael Schumacher	F2005/245	11	Jacques Villeneuve	C24/04
2	Rubens Barrichello	F2005/246	12	Felipe Massa	C24/06
	Spare	F2005/243		Spare	C24/03

	BAR-HONDA				RED BULL-COSWORTH	
3	Jenson Button	007/04	14	David Coulthard	RB1/2
4	Takuma Sato	007/03	15	Vitantonio Liuzzi	RB1/1
	Spare	007/02	37	Christian Klien	RB1/3
				Spare	RB1/3

	RENAULT				TOYOTA	
5	Fernando Alonso	R25/04	16	Jarno Trulli	TF105/02
6	Giancarlo Fisichella	R25/05	17	Ralf Schumacher	TF105/04
	Spare	R25/02	38	Ricardo Zonta	TF105/05
				Spare	TF105/05

	WILLIAMS-BMW				JORDAN-TOYOTA	
7	Mark Webber	FW27/05	18	Tiago Monteiro	EJ15/03
8	Nick Heidfeld	FW27/04	19	Narain Karthikeyan	EJ15/02
	Spare	FW27/02	39	Robert Doornbos	EJ15/01
				Spare	EJ15/01

	McLAREN-MERCEDES				MINARDI-COSWORTH	
9	Kimi Räikkönen	MP4-20/04	20	Patrick Friesacher	PS05/02
10	Alex Wurz	MP4-20/05	21	Christijan Albers	PS05/01
35	Pedro de la Rosa	MP4-20/03		Spare	PS04B/03
	Spare	MP4-20/03			

Photograph: James Moy/www.crash.net

PRACTICE 1 (FRIDAY)

Sunny (track 23–28°C, air 15°C)

Pos.	Driver	Laps	Time
1	Pedro de la Rosa	17	1m 21.060s
2	Ricardo Zonta	21	1m 21.174s
3	Jenson Button	6	1m 21.805s
4	Michael Schumacher	14	1m 22.085s
5	Christian Klien	20	1m 22.736s
6	Takuma Sato	6	1m 22.945s
7	Kimi Räikkönen	5	1m 22.962s
8	Nick Heidfeld	8	1m 23.086s
9	Alex Wurz	5	1m 23.391s
10	Mark Webber	8	1m 23.532s
11	Rubens Barrichello	10	1m 23.797s
12	Vitantonio Liuzzi	22	1m 24.052s
13	David Coulthard	8	1m 24.126s
14	Felipe Massa	13	1m 24.175s
15	Jacques Villeneuve	8	1m 24.255s
16	Narain Karthikeyan	18	1m 24.512s
17	Tiago Monteiro	16	1m 25.257s
18	Robert Doornbos	26	1m 25.555s
19	Ralf Schumacher	4	1m 26.333s
20	Christijan Albers	10	1m 27.353s
21	Patrick Friesacher	13	1m 27.411s
22	Giancarlo Fisichella	2	No time
23	Fernando Alonso	2	No time
24	Jarno Trulli	1	No time

PRACTICE 2 (FRIDAY)

Sunny (track 29–32°C, air 17–18°C)

Pos.	Driver	Laps	Time
1	Pedro de la Rosa	31	1m 20.484s
2	Jenson Button	28	1m 21.052s
3	Kimi Räikkönen	16	1m 21.704s
4	Ricardo Zonta	35	1m 21.889s
5	Fernando Alonso	10	1m 21.899s
6	Michael Schumacher	24	1m 22.025s
7	Rubens Barrichello	22	1m 22.048s
8	Alex Wurz	17	1m 22.174s
9	Giancarlo Fisichella	23	1m 22.211s
10	Takuma Sato	27	1m 22.335s
11	Felipe Massa	23	1m 22.791s
12	Jacques Villeneuve	22	1m 22.955s
13	Jarno Trulli	20	1m 23.343s
14	Nick Heidfeld	16	1m 23.458s
15	Ralf Schumacher	21	1m 23.466s
16	David Coulthard	20	1m 23.815s
17	Narain Karthikeyan	16	1m 23.842s
18	Mark Webber	14	1m 23.964s
19	Christian Klien	38	1m 24.320s
20	Tiago Monteiro	21	1m 24.573s
21	Vitantonio Liuzzi	29	1m 24.626s
22	Robert Doornbos	15	1m 25.172s
23	Patrick Friesacher	14	1m 26.620s
24	Christijan Albers	1	No time

PRACTICE 3 (SATURDAY)

Sunny/cloudy (track 15–20°C, air 12–15°C)

Pos.	Driver	Laps	Time
1	Michael Schumacher	8	1m 21.356s
2	Rubens Barrichello	14	1m 22.885s
3	Felipe Massa	6	1m 22.971s
4	Kimi Räikkönen	6	1m 23.723s
5	Mark Webber	4	1m 23.788s
6	Vitantonio Liuzzi	17	1m 23.894s
7	Giancarlo Fisichella	3	1m 24.120s
8	Ralf Schumacher	4	1m 24.156s
9	Alex Wurz	7	1m 24.262s
10	Nick Heidfeld	4	1m 24.341s
11	David Coulthard	13	1m 24.523s
12	Jenson Button	5	1m 24.757s
13	Takuma Sato	6	1m 24.770s
14	Narain Karthikeyan	5	1m 25.148s
15	Tiago Monteiro	12	1m 25.197s
16	Jacques Villeneuve	6	1m 25.393s
17	Jarno Trulli	3	1m 25.730s
18	Christijan Albers	10	1m 27.658s
19	Patrick Friesacher	7	1m 27.854s

PRACTICE 4 (SATURDAY)

Light cloud (track 23–26°C, air 16–18°C)

Pos.	Driver	Laps	Time
1	Jenson Button	16	1m 20.058s
2	Fernando Alonso	8	1m 20.114s
3	Kimi Räikkönen	10	1m 20.209s
4	Michael Schumacher	13	1m 20.318s
5	Giancarlo Fisichella	18	1m 20.351s
6	Alex Wurz	11	1m 20.358s
7	Mark Webber	6	1m 20.424s
8	Nick Heidfeld	6	1m 20.431s
9	Takuma Sato	17	1m 20.450s
10	Felipe Massa	11	1m 20.506s
11	Ralf Schumacher	11	1m 20.802s
12	Jacques Villeneuve	12	1m 20.851s
13	Jarno Trulli	14	1m 21.105s
14	David Coulthard	12	1m 21.136s
15	Jacques Villeneuve	11	1m 21.543s
16	Vitantonio Liuzzi	13	1m 22.188s
17	Narain Karthikeyan	8	1m 22.964s
18	Tiago Monteiro	5	1m 24.910s

9th: BARRICHELLO Ferrari

7th: WURZ McLaren-Mercedes

5th: TRULLI Toyota

3rd: BUTTON BAR-Honda

Pole: RÄIKKÖNEN McLaren-Mercedes

10th: R. SCHUMACHER Toyota

8th: HEIDFELD Williams-BMW

6th: SATO BAR-Honda

4th: WEBBER Williams-BMW

2nd: ALONSO Renault

9	50	51	52	53	54	55	56	57	58	59	60	61	62	
1	5	5	5	5	5	5	5	5	5	5	5	5	5	1
5	1	1	1	1	1	1	1	1	1	1	1	1	1	2
3	3	3	3	3	3	3	3	3	3	3	3	3	3	3
10	10	10	10	10	10	10	10	10	10	10	10	10	10	4
4	4	4	4	4	4	4	4	4	4	4	4	4	4	5
1	11	11	11	11	11	11	11	11	11	11	11	11	11	6
6	16	16	16	16	16	16	16	16	16	16	16	16	16	7
7	17	17	17	17	17	17	17	17	17	17	17	17	17	8
8	8	8	8	8	8	8	8	8	8	8	8	8	8	
7	7	7	7	7	7	7	7	7	7	7	7	7	7	
5	15	15	15	15	15	15	15	15	15	15	15	15	15	
2	12	12	12	12	12	12	12	12	12	12	12	12	12	
4	14	14	14	14	14	14	14	14	14	14	14	14	14	
9	19	19	19	19	19	19	19	19	19	19	19	19	19	
8	18	18	18	18	18	18	18	18	18	18	18	18	18	

FOR THE RECORD

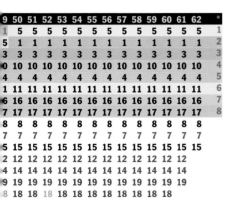

200th GRAND PRIX START:
Rubens Barrichello

FIRST GRAND PRIX POINT:
Vitantonio Liuzzi

POINTS

	DRIVERS			CONSTRUCTORS	
1	Fernando Alonso	36	1	Renault	46
2	Jarno Trulli	20	2	Toyota	29
3	Giancarlo Fisichella	10	3	McLaren	25
4	Michael Schumacher	10	4	Ferrari	18
5	Nick Heidfeld	9	5	Williams	18
6	Ralf Schumacher	9	6	Red Bull	13
7	David Coulthard	9	7	Sauber	7
8	Mark Webber	9			
9	Rubens Barrichello	8			
10	Juan Pablo Montoya	8			
11	Kimi Räikkönen	7			
12	Alex Wurz	6			
13	Jacques Villeneuve	5			
14	Pedro de la Rosa	4			
15	Christian Klien	3			
16	Felipe Massa	2			
17	Vitantonio Liuzzi	1			

Photographs: James Moy/www.crash.net

129

The drivers' parade in front of the fans prior to the start of the race at the Circuit de Catalunya, with the sea of blue signalling the crowd's allegiance to Spanish driver Fernando Alonso.
Photograph: Jad Sherif/WRi

GRAN PREMIO
MARLBORO
DE ESPAÑA
CATALUNYA 2005

BARCELONA
SPANISHGP

FIA F1 WORLD CHAMPIONSHIP/ROUND 5

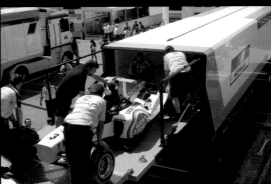

The BAR Honda team made the journey to Barcelona knowing full well that the FIA Court of Appeal would, on the Wednesday prior to the race, be adjudicating on the appeal made by the governing body against the decision of its stewards at the San Marino Grand Prix to give Jenson Button's car a clean bill of health after the race at Imola ten days earlier.

Yet when the verdict arrived it sent shock waves reverberating the length of the F1 paddock. The team was handed a three-race suspension, including disqualification from the San Marino event, plus a suspended six-race ban that could be triggered at any time over the remainder of the season should the team infringe any rules on another occasion.

Nick Fry, the BAR team principal, said the team was 'appalled' by the punishment meted out by the four-man court in Paris and was debating with its legal team, which includes the prominent British QC Michael Pannick, regarding its next step.

'We need to get some papers together today,' said Fry. 'I think if there is to be a hearing in court it will take place tomorrow. Our plan at the moment is to stay here. It's all in the hands of the legal experts. We've got the best people available working on this and they need to advise me.'

Fry added that the appeal-court hearing had disregarded the evidence presented to it. He said the FIA had inspected the fuel system in both Malaysia and Bahrain without question.

'The team proved that it complied with the current regulations and the FIA now acknowledges that the regulations are unclear,' he continued. 'We repeat that at no time did BAR Honda run underweight during the San Marino Grand Prix and this was also unchallenged by the FIA.'

However Bernie Ecclestone, the F1 commercial-rights holder, expressed the view that BAR might be well advised not to seek a remedy in the courts.

'I think they would be silly to do that,' he said. 'I think it would be bad for them. Other people might think they admitted they infringed the regulations. Anyone else is going to say they were warned at the start of the championship and they decided to ignore it.

'I wouldn't want to go to a civil court, personally. I think it's a big risk.'

Max Mosley, FIA president, added, 'Obviously the FIA cannot rule out the jurisdiction of a civil court, but they [civil courts] would not usually intervene unless there was something badly wrong with the procedure, which in this instance we are confident there was not.'

The Court of Appeal didn't exclude BAR Honda from the 2005 championship or impose a fine of at least a million euros ($1.2 million), as requested by the FIA, a decision which prompted Mosley to express the view that the team had got off lightly.

'The facts of the case are very clear,' he said. 'The team was asked to pump the fuel out of its car. It left 15 litres in the tank and told us it was empty. Under the circumstances, we feel BAR has been treated rather leniently.'

The court stopped short of endorsing the FIA's contention that BAR had committed a fraudulent act in concealing the details of an apparently hidden fuel tank on Button's car, but concluded that the team displayed 'a highly regrettable negligence and lack of transparency'.

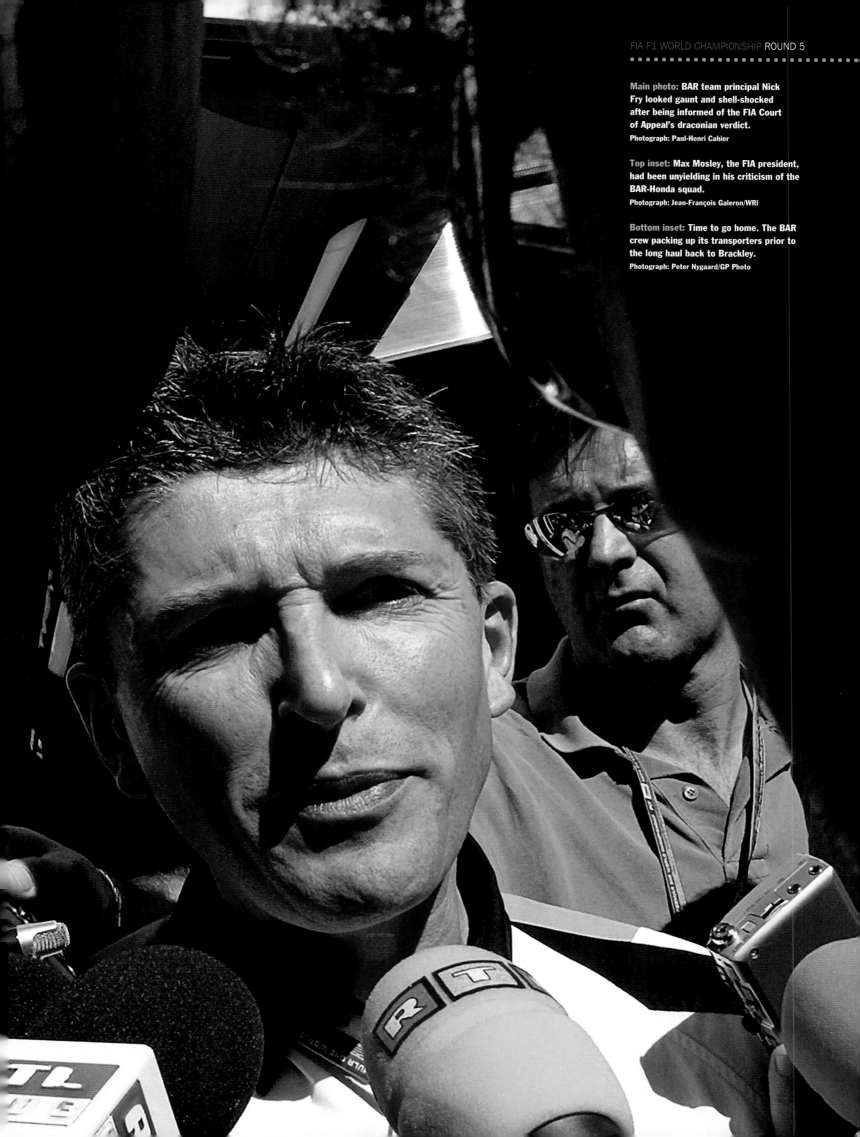

Main photo: BAR team principal Nick Fry looked gaunt and shell-shocked after being informed of the FIA Court of Appeal's draconian verdict.
Photograph: Paul-Henri Cahier

Top inset: Max Mosley, the FIA president, had been unyielding in his criticism of the BAR-Honda squad.
Photograph: Jean-François Galeron/WRi

Bottom inset: Time to go home. The BAR crew packing up its transporters prior to the long haul back to Brackley.
Photograph: Peter Nygaard/GP Photo

BARCELONA QUALIFYING

For Barcelona Juan Pablo Montoya had at last been given a clean bill of health after missing the previous two races recuperating from a shoulder injury, although the Colombian unfortunately celebrated his return to the cockpit by crashing his MP4-20 heavily in Friday free practice. The impact wrecked the radiators, exhausts and rear bodywork, but Juan Pablo stepped out unhurt and the car was duly repaired in time for the action on Saturday, the Colombian eventually lining up seventh for what was a crucially important come-back race.

Kimi Räikkönen clinched pole superbly, improving from third on Saturday after he lost 0.4s in what seemed like a crucial slip midway around his first qualifying lap. Kimi was joined on the front row by Mark Webber's Williams FW27. Mark delivered a fine performance after the team's early efforts were blighted by exhaust-valve problems which required BMW to ship in two new-spec V10s from Munich that the bleary eyed mechanics spent most of Friday night installing.

They must have wondered if it had all been worth the effort. Webber missed Friday practice to avoid taking an engine-change penalty and Nick Heidfeld started from the back after taking a penalty for changing his engine.

'I'm pleased to be on pole position, but there's still the race to go,' said Räikkönen, mindful of his initial dominance and eventual disappointment at Imola a fortnight earlier. 'Sunday's lap was good and my aggregate time would have been even better if I'd not made that mistake in yesterday's session.'

Fernando Alonso was obviously well satisfied with his third on the grid, three places ahead of team-mate Giancarlo Fisichella. Eighth in the first session, after what he confessed was a slightly conservative effort, and hampered by an early running slot as a result of his retirement at Imola a fortnight earlier, Fisi made another two places on Sunday morning to bag a position on the outside of the third row.

Meanwhile the BAR Honda team was licking its wounds, team principal Nick Fry pondering that its three-race exclusion would leave it facing costs of around £9 million ($16 million) in lost revenues. 'About half of this is sponsorship monies contracted which we will have to offer to pay

back due to failing to compete in Spain and Monaco,' he said. 'About a third of that figure is sponsorship which we are in the process of negotiating and are perhaps now not likely to get, and the balance is the income from Formula One Management which will now probably be lower in 2006 due to the problems we have experienced.'

Fourth and fifth in the final line-up were the Toyotas of Ralf Schumacher and Jarno Trulli, the Italian having at least enjoyed the overnight satisfaction of taking provisional pole thanks to his pace-setting efforts on Saturday afternoon. Ralf was fourth in the first session and maintained that place on race morning, admitting that on Saturday he'd perhaps been a touch conservative through the windy final sector of the lap.

In the Ferrari enclave, Michael Schumacher was tight-lipped with frustration over his F2005's struggle around the Circuit de Catalunya although he just pipped David Coulthard's Red Bull to take the outside of the fourth row.

Rubens Barrichello suffered a hydraulic glitch on Saturday morning and then an engine failure, the switch to a fresh V10 obviously costing him a move to the back of the grid. The Brazilian also reported that the car seemed difficult to drive over a quick lap even though the balance was not too bad.

Coulthard had been 10th on Saturday but dropped a place to Montoya, who moved from 12th to seventh in the Sunday-morning session. Nonetheless, he qualified ninth. 'The car went well, apart from some oversteer in the fast corners,' said DC. 'I expected to lose a place to Juan Pablo because he has a quicker car and made a mistake in yesterday's qualifying.' Coulthard's Red Bull team-mate Vitantonio Liuzzi did a tidy job to line up in 11th place on the grid.

Jacques Villeneuve was next up ahead of the Jordans of Narain Karthikeyan and Tiago Monteiro, although Monteiro later took an engine change and started last. Meanwhile, the Minardis of Christijan Albers and Patrick Friesacher had the bonus of qualifying on row nine after the misfortunes of Barrichello and Heidfeld put them firmly at the back of the grid. Friesacher had battled a handling imbalance from the outset and Albers spun in free practice, but the Faenza team was generally pretty encouraged by the PS05's performance on only its second outing.

KIMI Räikkönen delivered the McLaren Mercedes team's first victory of the season in impeccable style, dominating the fifth round of the title chase at the Circuit de Catalunya and seriously getting his own bid for the crown into top gear. It was a success which at last publicly showcased the potential of the MP4-20, which the McLaren top brass had been trailing since the start of the year, and the manner in which the Finn completed the race, inches ahead of his lapped team-mate Juan Pablo Montoya, raised speculation that one-two successes for the Silver Arrows may be just around the corner. Montoya had earlier lost time with a spin and needed an extra refuelling stop after a rig malfunction short-changed him a full tank load.

Räikkönen crossed the line 27.652s ahead of championship points leader Fernando Alonso's Renault R25. Alonso's F1 ascendancy ensured that the Circuit de Catalunya was packed to capacity with over 100,000 fans cramming in to offer their vocal support to the man they confidently hoped would be Spain's first F1 world champion. But on this occasion he simply

didn't have the sheer speed to live with the McLaren, his efforts frustrated by blistering rear tyres that he had to nurse carefully in the early stages of the race. Once the tyres cleaned up again the lad from Oviedo picked up the pace and still emerged on the podium wearing a spontaneous wall-to-wall grin to delight his supporters.

'The car was perfect all weekend and we knew we should be very strong,' said Räikkönen. He admitted he had a nasty moment at his first refuelling stop when some oil smoke indicated that lubricant might be recirculating into the airbox. Kimi was told to hold the car at a lower rev limit for the second stop and almost stalled as he sought to avoid the problem. Apart from that, everything was perfect.

Alonso said, 'I was a little bit conservative with the tyres in the early stages. The car wasn't very good up until about lap 25 but after that it was perfect and I was able to push hard, but by then Kimi was far ahead.'

Räikkönen accelerated into an immediate lead at the start to complete the opening lap 0.55s ahead of Alonso, an edge he

opened to 3.1s after only five laps. Ralf Schumacher's well-driven Toyota TF105 was next up ahead of Mark Webber's slow-starting Williams FW27, Jarno Trulli's Toyota and Giancarlo Fisichella's Renault R25.

Webber was in trouble almost from the start. He'd set only fifth-fastest time in the first qualifying session, then the team had decided to run a short opening stint on a three-stop strategy, giving him a relatively light fuel load for the second qualifying session, which at least enabled him to vault up to the front row alongside Räikkönen's McLaren.

'The start was tricky because I was on the dirty side of the track and I lost one position there,' he shrugged after eventually finishing the afternoon in a disappointed sixth place. 'I didn't want to risk too much at the first corner with Ralf Schumacher, to protect my position. Then I was stuck behind Ralf and Alonso, which was a shame because I was lighter than them.

'We decided to change strategy and go for two stops instead of three, but the fuel load was quite hard on the tyres then, causing quite a bit of deterioration and consequent vibrations in the car.'

Above: A fiery moment for Jarno Trulli's Toyota TF105 in the Barcelona pit lane passed without any serious damage.
Photograph: Peter van Egmond

Far left: A rare sighting of Bernard Charles Ecclestone trackside among the cameras.
Photograph: Jad Sherif/WRi

Webber thus made his first refuelling stop on lap 18 and then had to last through until lap 43 before making his second. Räikkönen stopped for the first time on lap 25, followed by Alonso two laps later, and Fisichella did not come in until lap 29, which enabled him to slot back into the queue ahead of Alonso.

Fisichella thought that second place was now his, but in the middle of the race he suddenly experienced a loss of front downforce and his second refuelling stop was brought forward for the team to change the car's nose section and to check for any damage to the floor. He came in on lap 40 and dropped back to 11th, now fuelled up for a non-stop run to the finish, and he eventually hauled his way back to fifth at the chequered flag.

'I have a mixture of emotions after the race,' said Fisichella. 'I am pleased to have finished in the points and I think we showed the pace we had in the car today. After I made my second stop it was just a case of picking off the cars in front of me as they made their stops. I was pleased to be able to pass Webber, though. I could see that I was quicker and then I got a run on him out of the last corner and did a good manoeuvre into Turn One.' Giancarlo also posted the fastest lap of the race on his very last tour.

The Toyota TF105s of Jarno Trulli and Ralf Schumacher were third and fourth, 0.772s apart, after a closely matched performance. Later, Trulli generously offered the view that his team-mate really deserved to be on the podium every bit as much as he did.

'This was one of the best races of my career,' he said, 'because I really had to fight for the whole race to keep ahead of Ralf. But I had a different strategy because my set-up meant that I was quicker with more fuel and a bit slower with less fuel in the car.

'It meant I had to push very hard throughout the race. I had a problem with the fuel rig at my first stop but in the end everything worked fine and it was a great feeling to finish on the podium again.'

For his part Ralf added, 'This was a long, hard race. It's great to score so many points again and in general the race went well. I gained a place at the start and kept pushing throughout the afternoon. It was a busy race, but I had no real problems with the car or tyres, so I'm happy with the way it went.'

Juan Pablo Montoya spun and recovered on lap seven without losing his position. The Colombian made his first stop on lap 29 only to suffer a problem with the refuelling rig and have to come in again to refuel on the next lap (10.0s). He came in for fuel for the last scheduled time on lap 56 and eventually finished seventh behind Webber.

'The car was working well throughout but we had not achieved the optimum set-up so I was struggling a bit with understeer to start with,' said Montoya. 'My shoulder was good but obviously it was tough, particularly at Turns Three and Nine and at the last two corners of the lap where you pull a lot of g-loadings.'

David Coulthard finished eighth in the Red Bull RB1 despite flat-spotting a tyre in the closing stages of the race, which left him grappling with a serious chassis vibration. This was so bad that he confessed he was having to judge his braking points from memory in the closing stages of the race, but at least he managed to make it to the chequered flag. Vitantonio Liuzzi, battling poor balance on the second Red Bull, eventually spun into a gravel trap and out of the race.

Sauber had a bad day. Jacques Villeneuve was quite happy with his car's balance but, early in the race, it began losing water and the consequent overheating further frustrated his efforts to lap competitively with a heavy fuel load aboard. Eventually the engine failed and that was that.

His team-mate Felipe Massa found that his C24 simply hadn't got the pace to run competitively and he eventually slithered to a halt coming down the start-finish straight after the left-rear wheel rim cracked, allowing its tyre to deflate.

It was much the same for Ferrari. The Prancing Horse had a

nightmare experience at Barcelona, blighted by two Bridgestone tyre failures which wiped out Michael Schumacher's chances of finishing on the podium and sent him scuttling into retirement. Rubens Barrichello started at the back after changing an engine, finishing ninth.

It was on lap 46 that Michael Schumacher's Ferrari F2005 limped into the pit lane, its left-front corner scuffing on the asphalt thanks to a deflated front tyre. The world champion didn't hesitate for a moment. Rather than braking to a halt in front of his eager mechanics, who had waited keenly for him to replace a deflated rear tyre a couple of laps earlier, this time the world champion simply swung tightly to the right and coasted into his team garage. He undid his harness, hopped from the cockpit and walked away without a backward glance.

Schumacher had qualified an average eighth at Barcelona, unable to squeeze a really quick single lap out of his Bridgestone tyres, which needed two or three laps to build up to their optimum operating temperature. Instead, he adopted the strategy that had served him so well in the San Marino Grand Prix a fortnight earlier, where Michael had taken a softly-softly approach, conserving his tyres with a heavy fuel load in the opening stages and then pressing harder as the car lightened up in the second part of the race.

It seemed as though it might pay off. At the end of the opening lap he was seventh, but by the time he came in for his first refuelling stop at the end of lap 32 he was second behind Räikkönen and had just posted the fastest lap of the race so far.

Schumacher resumed fourth, which became third after Alonso made his second stop on lap 40. But then it all began to fall apart for the seven-times champion.

'I think a third place would have been a realistic target,

seeing how the race was going,' he said, 'so it was very disappointing that I had those two problems. Already, on the lap before, I could feel the car becoming unbalanced, then suddenly the tyre pressure had gone. Then, after the rear tyre was changed, the same thing happened again. We have a lot of work to do across the entire package before Monaco.'

The great strength of Ferrari's relationship with its tyre supplier Bridgestone has traditionally been the two companies' reluctance to blame each other when mistakes are made and unexpected failures occur. On this occasion, both tyre failures were on the highly loaded left-hand tyres, which do most of the work on the right-hand corners at the Circuit de Catalunya – particularly in the hands of the fastest driver in the business.

Ferrari would now embark on an intensive programme of development testing as Bridgestone settled down to develop a new batch of tyres that would combine just the right blend of grip and good wear characteristics for the next few races on the championship calendar.

'Today's result was certainly disappointing,' said Hisao Suganuma, the technical manager of Bridgestone. 'Safety is of course our main priority and we have already started a thorough investigation into the cause of this loss of air. What we can say is that the wear on Michael's rear tyre was within acceptable boundaries.'

Truth be told, Bridgestone was working flat-out to play catch-up and the tyre company's problems at the Circuit de Catalunya were indicative of its determination to turn Ferrari's fortunes around. This meant walking the tightrope between success and failure, an experience others were to encounter to painful effect later in the season.

Alan Henry

Above: Ralf Schumacher drove a fine race to finish fourth for Toyota. He was only a length behind team-mate Jarno Trulli at the chequered flag and reckoned he could have lapped faster than the Italian if only he could have squeezed past.

Top left: At last! Kimi held aloft the victory trophy after that elusive and long overdue first win of the season.
Photographs: James Moy/www.crash.net

Left: Michael Schumacher scrambled his Ferrari over the kerbs as Giancarlo Fisichella's Renault made its escape.
Photograph: Laurent Charniaux/WRi

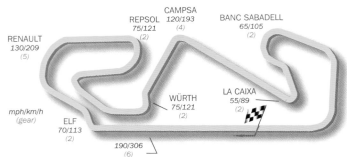

CATALUNYA CIRCUIT – BARCELONA

REPSOL 75/121 (2)
CAMPSA 120/193 (4)
BANC SABADELL 65/105 (2)
RENAULT 130/209 (5)
WÜRTH 75/121 (2)
LA CAIXA 55/89 (2)
mph/km/h (gear)
ELF 70/113 (2)
190/306 (6)

CIRCUIT LENGTH: 2.875 miles/4.627 km

FIA F1 WORLD CHAMPIONSHIP • ROUND 5

GRAN PREMIO
MARLBORO DE ESPAÑA
BARCELONA 6–8 MAY 2005

RACE DISTANCE: 66 laps, 189.677 miles /305.256 km   **RACE WEATHER:** Sunny (track 35–38°C, air 25°C)

Pos.	Driver	Nat.	No.	Entrant	Car/Engine	Tyres	Laps	Time/Retirement	Speed (mph/km/h)	Gap to leader	Fastest race lap	
1	Kimi Räikkönen	FIN	9	West McLaren Mercedes	McLaren MP4-20-Mercedes F0 110R V10	M	66	1h 27m 16.830s	130.391/209.844		1m 15.977s	41
2	Fernando Alonso	E	5	Mild Seven Renault F1 Team	Renault R25-RS25 V10	M	66	1h 27m 44.482s	129.706/208.742	+27.652s	1m 16.098s	59
3	Jarno Trulli	I	16	Panasonic Toyota Racing	Toyota TF105-RVX-05 V10	M	66	1h 28m 02.777s	129.257/208.019	+45.947s	1m 16.614s	63
4	Ralf Schumacher	D	17	Panasonic Toyota Racing	Toyota TF105-RVX-05 V10	M	66	1h 28m 03.549s	129.238/207.989	+46.719s	1m 16.469s	63
5	Giancarlo Fisichella	I	6	Mild Seven Renault F1 Team	Renault R25-RS25 V10	M	66	1h 28m 14.766s	128.964/207.548	+57.936s	1m 15.641s	66
6	Mark Webber	AUS	7	BMW WilliamsF1 Team	Williams FW27-BMW P84/85 V10	M	66	1h 28m 25.372s	128.706/207.133	+68.542s	1m 16.761s	62
7	Juan Pablo Montoya	COL	10	West McLaren Mercedes	McLaren MP4-20-Mercedes F0 110R V10	M	65			+1 lap	1m 15.771s	55
8	David Coulthard	GB	14	Red Bull Racing	Red Bull RB1-Cosworth TJ2005/10 V10	M	65			+1 lap	1m 16.947s	65
9	Rubens Barrichello	BR	2	Scuderia Ferrari Marlboro	Ferrari F2005-055 V10	B	65			+1 lap	1m 17.156s	64
10	Nick Heidfeld	D	8	BMW WilliamsF1 Team	Williams FW27-BMW P84/85 V10	M	65			+1 lap	1m 16.519s	60
11	Felipe Massa	BR	12	Sauber Petronas	Sauber C24-Petronas 05A V10	M	63	Split rear-wheel rim		DNF	1m 16.802s	51
12	Tiago Monteiro	P	18	Jordan Toyota	Jordan EJ15-Toyota RVX-05 V10	B	63			+3 laps	1m 18.998s	22
13	Narain Karthikeyan	IND	19	Jordan Toyota	Jordan EJ15-Toyota RVX-05 V10	B	63			+3 laps	1m 19.734s	16
	Jacques Villeneuve	CDN	11	Sauber Petronas	Sauber C24-Petronas 05A V10	M	51	Water leak/engine			1m 17.585s	43
	Michael Schumacher	D	1	Scuderia Ferrari Marlboro	Ferrari F2005-055 V10	B	46	Puncture			1m 15.648s	31
	Christijan Albers	NL	21	Minardi Cosworth	Minardi PS05-Cosworth TJ2005 V10	B	19	Gearbox			1m 20.124s	15
	Patrick Friesacher	A	20	Minardi Cosworth	Minardi PS05-Cosworth TJ2005 V10	B	11	Spin			1m 20.885s	10
	Vitantonio Liuzzi	I	15	Red Bull Racing	Red Bull RB1-Cosworth TJ2005/10 V10	M	9	Engine cut/spin			1m 19.435s	9

Fastest lap: Giancarlo Fisichella, on lap 66, 1m 15.641s, 136.834 mph/220.213 km/h (record).

Previous lap record: Michael Schumacher (Ferrari F2004-052 V10), 1m 17.450s, 132.023 mph/212.470 km/h (2004).

17th: HEIDFELD Williams-BMW
Ten-place penalty for engine change

15th: FRIESACHER Minardi-Cosworth

13th: KARTHIKEYAN Jordan-Toyota

11th: LIUZZI Red Bull-Cosworth

18th: MONTEIRO Jordan-Toyota
Ten-place penalty for engine change

16th: BARRICHELLO Ferrari
Ten-place penalty for engine change

14th: ALBERS Minardi-Cosworth

12th: VILLENEUVE Sauber-Petronas

Grid order	1	2	3	4	5	6	7	8	9	10	11	12	13	14	15	16	17	18	19	20	21	22	23	24	25	26	27	28	29	30	31	32	33	34	35	36	37	38	39	40	41	42	43	44	45	46	47	48	49	50
9 RÄIKKÖNEN	9	9	9	9	9	9	9	9	9	9	9	9	9	9	9	9	9	9	9	9	9	9	9	9	9	9	9	9	9	9	9	9	9	9	9	9	9	9	9	9	9	9	9	9	9	9	9	9	9	9
7 WEBBER	5	5	5	5	5	5	5	5	5	5	5	5	5	5	5	5	5	5	5	5	5	5	5	6	6	6	1	1	1	6	6	6	6	6	6	6	5	5	5	5	5	5	5	5	5	5	5	5	5	5
5 ALONSO	17	17	17	17	17	17	17	17	17	17	17	17	17	17	17	17	17	17	17	17	17	17	16	16	6	6	5	10	1	6	5	5	5	5	5	5	6	1	1	1	16	16	16	16	16	16	16	16	16	16
17 R. SCHUMACHER	7	7	7	7	7	7	7	7	7	7	7	7	7	7	7	7	16	16	16	16	16	16	10	10	1	10	5	5	5	1	1	1	1	1	1	1	16	16	16	1	17	17	17	17	17	17				
16 TRULLI	16	16	16	16	16	16	16	16	16	16	16	16	16	16	16	7	6	6	6	6	17	10	1	1	5	5	10	16	16	16	16	16	16	16	16	16	17	17	17	14	14	14	14	14	14	14				
6 FISICHELLA	6	6	6	6	6	6	6	6	6	6	6	6	6	6	6	6	10	10	10	10	10	1	14	14	16	16	16	17	17	17	17	17	17	17	17	17	7	7	7	12	12	12	12	12	12					
10 MONTOYA	1	1	10	10	10	10	10	10	10	10	10	10	10	10	10	10	1	1	1	1	14	12	12	17	7	7	7	7	7	7	7	7	14	14	12	10	10	10	10	10									
1 M. SCHUMACHER	10	10	1	1	1	1	1	1	1	1	1	1	1	1	1	14	14	14	14	14	12	16	16	7	7	2	2	2	7	14	14	14	14	12	12	10	1	7	7	7	7	7								
14 COULTHARD	14	14	14	14	14	14	14	14	14	14	14	14	14	14	14	12	12	12	12	12	17	17	11	11	11	11	14	14	12	12	12	12	12	10	10	10	7	7	8	8	8	8	8							
12 MASSA	12	12	12	12	12	12	12	12	12	12	12	12	12	12	12	7	7	7	7	7	7	8	2	2	14	12	12	10	10	10	10	10	10	8	8	8	8	8	6	6	6	6	6							
15 LIUZZI	11	11	11	11	11	11	11	11	11	11	11	11	11	11	11	11	11	2	8	14	12	10	10	10	8	8	8	8	8	6	6	6	6	2	2	2	2	2												
11 VILLENEUVE	8	8	8	8	8	8	8	8	8	8	8	8	8	8	8	8	14	14	12	10	8	8	8	2	2	2	2	2	2	2	11	11	11	11	11	11														
19 KARTHIKEYAN	15	15	15	15	15	15	15	15	15	2	2	2	2	2	2	2	8	8	2	2	2	2	12	12	8	11	11	11	11	11	11	11	11	11	1	18	18	18												
21 ALBERS	2	2	2	2	2	2	2	2	19	19	19	18	18	18	18	18	18	18	18	18	18	19	19	18	18	18	18	18	18	18	18	18	18	18	18	18	18	19	19	19	19									
20 FRIESACHER	19	19	19	19	19	19	19	19	18	18	18	19	19	19	19	19	19	19	19	19	19	18	18	19	19	19	19	19	19	19	19	19	19	19	19	19	19	19												
2 BARRICHELLO	18	18	18	18	18	18	18	18	18	18	21	21	21	21	21	21	21	21	21																															
8 HEIDFELD	21	21	21	21	21	21	21	21	21	20	20																																							
18 MONTEIRO	20	20	20	20	20	20	20	20	20																																									

Pit stop
One lap or more behind leader

TIME SHEETS

QUALIFYING

SATURDAY: Sunny (track 34–36°C, air 23–24°C)
SUNDAY: Sunny (track 25–29°C, air 19–22°C)

Pos.	Driver	R/Order	1st qualifying	R/Order	2nd qualifying	Aggregate
1	Kimi Räikkönen	4	1m 14.819s	16	1m 16.602s	2m 31.421s
2	Mark Webber	13	1m 15.042s	13	1m 16.626s	2m 31.668s
3	Fernando Alonso	18	1m 14.811s	17	1m 16.880s	2m 31.691s
4	Ralf Schumacher	11	1m 14.870s	15	1m 17.047s	2m 31.917s
5	Jarno Trulli	15	1m 14.795s	18	1m 17.200s	2m 31.995s
6	Giancarlo Fisichella	2	1m 15.601s	11	1m 17.229s	2m 32.830s
7	Juan Pablo Montoya	1	1m 15.902s	7	1m 17.570s	2m 33.472s
8	Michael Schumacher	17	1m 15.398s	12	1m 18.153s	2m 33.551s
9	David Coulthard	9	1m 15.795s	9	1m 18.373s	2m 34.168s
10	Felipe Massa	10	1m 15.863s	8	1m 18.361s	2m 34.224s
11	Vitantonio Liuzzi	12	1m 16.288s	6	1m 19.014s	2m 35.302s
12	Jacques Villeneuve	16	1m 16.794s	5	1m 19.686s	2m 36.480s
13	Narain Karthikeyan	8	1m 18.557s	4	1m 20.711s	2m 39.268s
14	Tiago Monteiro	7	1m 19.040s	3	1m 20.903s	2m 39.943s
15	Christijan Albers	6	1m 19.563s	2	1m 21.578s	2m 41.141s
16	Patrick Friesacher	3	1m 20.306s	1	1m 22.453s	2m 42.759s
17	Nick Heidfeld	14	1m 15.038s	14	No time	No time
18	Rubens Barrichello	5	1m 15.746s	10	No time	No time

PRACTICE 1 (FRIDAY)

Sunny (track 27–32°C, air 21–23°C)

Pos.	Driver	Laps	Time
1	Pedro de la Rosa	15	1m 15.675s
2	Christian Klien	25	1m 16.821s
3	Nick Heidfeld	12	1m 17.047s
4	Michael Schumacher	14	1m 17.574s
5	Kimi Räikkönen	7	1m 17.851s
6	David Coulthard	7	1m 17.977s
7	Ricardo Zonta	9	1m 18.103s
8	Vitantonio Liuzzi	12	1m 18.112s
9	Ralf Schumacher	6	1m 18.204s
10	Juan Pablo Montoya	9	1m 18.402s
11	Felipe Massa	11	1m 19.328s
12	Jacques Villeneuve	8	1m 20.621s
13	Tiago Monteiro	12	1m 20.773s
14	Robert Doornbos	23	1m 20.912s
15	Narain Karthikeyan	12	1m 21.628s
16	Christijan Albers	11	1m 21.635s
17	Patrick Friesacher	14	1m 22.454s
18	Rubens Barrichello	2	No time
19	Giancarlo Fisichella	2	No time
20	Fernando Alonso	2	No time
21	Jarno Trulli	2	No time

PRACTICE 2 (FRIDAY)

Sunny (track 36–39°C, air 25–27°C)

Pos.	Driver	Laps	Time
1	Pedro de la Rosa	28	1m 15.062s
2	Ricardo Zonta	34	1m 16.220s
3	Nick Heidfeld	30	1m 16.527s
4	Kimi Räikkönen	17	1m 16.586s
5	Jarno Trulli	26	1m 16.653s
6	David Coulthard	24	1m 16.797s
7	Giancarlo Fisichella	24	1m 17.200s
8	Ralf Schumacher	22	1m 17.264s
9	Fernando Alonso	24	1m 17.356s
10	Juan Pablo Montoya	10	1m 17.555s
11	Rubens Barrichello	22	1m 17.702s
12	Felipe Massa	24	1m 17.931s
13	Michael Schumacher	22	1m 18.042s
14	Jacques Villeneuve	27	1m 18.336s
15	Vitantonio Liuzzi	26	1m 18.444s
16	Christian Klien	23	1m 18.802s
17	Narain Karthikeyan	24	1m 18.858s
18	Robert Doornbos	28	1m 19.125s
19	Tiago Monteiro	27	1m 19.140s
20	Christijan Albers	17	1m 19.581s
21	Patrick Friesacher	23	1m 20.686s

PRACTICE 3 (SATURDAY)

Sunny (track 21°C, air 16–18°C)

Pos.	Driver	Laps	Time
1	Giancarlo Fisichella	6	1m 15.605s
2	Michael Schumacher	10	1m 15.631s
3	Ralf Schumacher	10	1m 15.860s
4	Rubens Barrichello	10	1m 16.004s
5	Vitantonio Liuzzi	16	1m 16.241s
6	David Coulthard	12	1m 16.323s
7	Juan Pablo Montoya	4	1m 16.560s
8	Kimi Räikkönen	5	1m 17.363s
9	Nick Heidfeld	7	1m 17.615s
10	Mark Webber	15	1m 17.701s
11	Tiago Monteiro	12	1m 17.870s
12	Narain Karthikeyan	7	1m 18.198s
13	Felipe Massa	7	1m 18.209s
14	Jarno Trulli	3	1m 18.215s
15	Jacques Villeneuve	6	1m 18.686s
16	Patrick Friesacher	15	1m 20.417s
17	Christijan Albers	10	1m 21.145s
18	Fernando Alonso	2	No time

PRACTICE 4 (SATURDAY)

Sunny (track 26–28°C, air 19–20°C)

Pos.	Driver	Laps	Time
1	Ralf Schumacher	13	1m 14.280s
2	Kimi Räikkönen	11	1m 14.462s
3	Juan Pablo Montoya	12	1m 14.672s
4	Mark Webber	11	1m 14.689s
5	Fernando Alonso	9	1m 15.030s
6	Giancarlo Fisichella	19	1m 15.048s
7	Jarno Trulli	13	1m 15.087s
8	Nick Heidfeld	6	1m 15.253s
9	David Coulthard	15	1m 15.339s
10	Rubens Barrichello	12	1m 15.374s
11	Michael Schumacher	12	1m 15.378s
12	Felipe Massa	16	1m 15.511s
13	Vitantonio Liuzzi	14	1m 15.546s
14	Jacques Villeneuve	11	1m 16.291s
15	Narain Karthikeyan	14	1m 17.569s
16	Tiago Monteiro	12	1m 17.848s
17	Christijan Albers	14	1m 19.031s
18	Patrick Friesacher	14	1m 19.296s

CHASSIS LOG BOOK

FERRARI
1	Michael Schumacher	F2005/245
2	Rubens Barrichello	F2005/246
	Spare	F2005/243

RENAULT
5	Fernando Alonso	R25/04
6	Giancarlo Fisichella	R25/06
	Spare	R25/02

WILLIAMS-BMW
7	Mark Webber	FW27/05
8	Nick Heidfeld	FW27/06
	Spare	FW27/04

McLAREN-MERCEDES
9	Kimi Räikkönen	MP4-20/04
10	Juan Pablo Montoya	MP4-20/05
35	Pedro de la Rosa	MP4-20/06
	Spare	MP4-20/06

SAUBER-PETRONAS
11	Jacques Villeneuve	C24/04
12	Felipe Massa	C24/06
	Spare	C24/03

RED BULL-COSWORTH
14	David Coulthard	RB1/3
15	Vitantonio Liuzzi	RB1/1
37	Christian Klien	RB1/2
	Spare	RB1/2

TOYOTA
16	Jarno Trulli	TF105/02
17	Ralf Schumacher	TF105/04
38	Ricardo Zonta	TF105/05
	Spare	TF105/05

JORDAN-TOYOTA
18	Tiago Monteiro	EJ15/03
19	Narain Karthikeyan	EJ15/02
39	Robert Doornbos	EJ15/01
	Spare	EJ15/01

MINARDI-COSWORTH
20	Patrick Friesacher	PS05/02
21	Christijan Albers	PS05/01
	Spare	PS04B/04

9th: COULTHARD Red Bull-Cosworth

7th: MONTOYA McLaren-Mercedes

5th: TRULLI Toyota

3rd: ALONSO Renault

Pole: RÄIKKÖNEN McLaren-Mercedes

10th: MASSA Sauber-Petronas

8th: M. SCHUMACHER Ferrari

6th: FISICHELLA Renault

4th: R. SCHUMACHER Toyota

2nd: WEBBER Williams-BMW

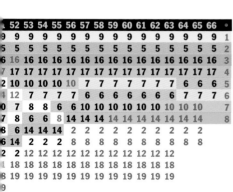

	52	53	54	55	56	57	58	59	60	61	62	63	64	65	66		
9	9	9	9	9	9	9	9	9	9	9	9	9	9	9	9	1
5	5	5	5	5	5	5	5	5	5	5	5	5	5	5	5	2
6	16	16	16	16	16	16	16	16	16	16	16	16	16	16	16	3
7	17	17	17	17	17	17	17	17	17	17	17	17	17	17	17	4
2	10	10	10	10	10	7	7	7	7	7	7	6	6	6	5	5
4	12	7	7	7	6	6	6	6	6	6	7	7	7	7	6	
0		7	8	8	6	10	10	10	10	10	10	10	10	10	10	7
7	8	6	6	8	14	14	14	14	14	14	14	14	14	14	14	8
8	6	14	14	14		2	2	2	2	2	2	2	2	2	2	
6	14	2	2	2	8	8	8	8	8	8	8	8	8	8		
2	12	12	12	12	12	12	12	12	12	12	12	12	12			
8	18	18	18	18	18	18	18	18	18	18	18	18	18			
4	19	19	19	19	19	19	19	19	19	19	19	19	19			
9																

POINTS

DRIVERS
1	Fernando Alonso	44
2	Jarno Trulli	26
3	Kimi Räikkönen	17
4	Giancarlo Fisichella	14
5	Ralf Schumacher	14
6	Mark Webber	12
7	Michael Schumacher	10
8	David Coulthard	10
9	Juan Pablo Montoya	10
10	Nick Heidfeld	9
11	Rubens Barrichello	8
12	Alex Wurz	6
13	Jacques Villeneuve	5
14	Pedro de la Rosa	4
15	Christian Klien	3
16	Felipe Massa	2
17	Vitantonio Liuzzi	1

CONSTRUCTORS
1	Renault	58
2	Toyota	40
3	McLaren	37
4	Williams	21
5	Ferrari	18
6	Red Bull	14
7	Sauber	7

MONTE CARLO
MONACOGP

FIA F1 WORLD CHAMPIONSHIP/ROUND 6

The magical vista that never ceases to impress: Kimi Räikkönen leading the field down towards Portier and the waterfront on the opening lap of the race.
Photograph: Peter van Egmond

The status and future of the Jordan F1 team was the subject of frenzied speculation over the Monaco weekend, with suggestions that Eddie Irvine (above), who made his grand prix debut driving for the team in 1993, might return to the pit wall as the front man for a group of investors keen on buying the Silverstone-based operation from Russian-born Canadian Alex Shnaider.

Word had it that Irvine, who appeared in the paddock at Monaco, was scouting on behalf of millionaire Roustam Tariko, who has interests in banking and a vodka company. Tariko was reputedly hoping to pay as little as £12 million ($21 million) for the cash-strapped team, which supposedly cost Shnaider around £24 million, including assuming responsibility for around £11 million of debt.

'I think I could do it,' said Irvine, who finished second to Mika Häkkinen in the 1999 world championship. 'I've seen the best in Jean Todt [Ferrari's sporting director] and even the worst in the Ford motor company [which owned Jaguar, for whom Irvine raced in 2000–2002].

'I think I learned a lot more from how badly Ford did it because Todt took such great care of everything. With Todt it went pretty much the way it should have done. You learn from your mistakes. Ford showed me how to make mistakes. The Ford experience with Jaguar was much more enlightening – but you need to have both.'

Irvine would not be drawn on the issue, but said he believed there was still a place for small independent teams such as Jordan alongside the major manufacturer-backed organisations.

'Look what Red Bull is doing,' he said. 'Okay, it's not getting the results, but it's doing a good job, biting at the tails of the big guys, which is all it can be expected to do – which I think is great for F1. I think the manufacturers are a bit stuffy to a certain extent.'

DIARY

McLaren boss Ron Dennis says he will help Lewis Hamilton to secure an F1 future after the young British driver wins both the Monaco F3 races.

The FIA confirms that the aggregate qualifying format will be ditched in favour of a single session in time for the European GP a week after Monaco.

Mercedes vice president Norbert Haug warns that the new generation of high-revving 2.4-litre V8s will be 'extremely expensive'.

The Champ Car World Series secures the future of the Long Beach GP by acquiring the complete assets of the street race through the Californian coastal city.

MONTE CARLO QUALIFYING

Ralf Schumacher was at the centre of the action on Saturday. In free practice Juan Pablo Montoya's McLaren suddenly slowed in front of him going up the hill to Massenet. David Coulthard slowed to avoid them both, only for Jacques Villeneuve to slam his Sauber into the back of the Red Bull. This, in turn, threw DC's car into Ralf's, which pirouetted into the barrier.

All the cars were repaired for qualifying, although the Red Bull suffered most damage and an indignant Coulthard called for Montoya to be penalised for apparently brake-testing Ralf, Montoya's unloved former Williams team-mate.

The stewards duly summoned all four drivers, together with their team representatives. Coulthard and Schumacher gave evidence which matched and confirmed that Montoya, running on a quick lap, had pulled in front of the Toyota and suddenly backed off 180 metres before his usual braking point.

After corroborating this evidence with data downloaded from Montoya's car, the stewards deleted Montoya's qualifying time, thereby consigning him to the back of the grid. Irony of ironies, he was joined there by Ralf's Toyota after the German driver crashed heavily at Tabac on his qualifying run, scattering oil and debris across the track as a result.

This hadn't been the only setback experienced by Ralf. In Thursday's free practice, he'd used an unauthorised left-front tyre and the stewards decreed that a 0.5s penalty should be added to his aggregate qualifying time. After he shunted on Saturday, failing to post a time, that penalty became academic.

Across the two qualifying sessions McLaren judged perfectly the balance between cramming in enough fuel to give Kimi Räikkönen a long opening stint on his soft Michelin rubber – a giant stride towards a victorious strategy – and having enough speed to hang on to pole position. Kimi did the rest, his aggregate 2m 30.323s enough to take pole by less than a tenth on this circuit where starting from the front is more of a priority than it is anywhere else on the calendar. At the opposite end of the grid was Montoya, who lined up 16th in a field reduced in number by BAR's enforced absence, ahead of Narain Karthikeyan's Jordan, which had taken an engine-change penalty, and the hapless Ralf.

If Fernando Alonso was disappointed, he kept it to himself. 'There's a good gap back to Mark [Webber],' he noted after a stellar performance to set what looked like fastest time in the dying moments of Saturday qualifying, only to be pipped by the inspired Räikkönen on the final lap of the day. He followed that up with the fastest lap on Sunday morning, but just failed to wrest pole from the Finn.

He added, 'I have always been very quick here, partly because I like Monaco and partly because the car has always been very competitive here – and this year more so. So these days are the best moments in my career, for sure.'

On the second row, Mark Webber muscled his way to an aggregate 2m 31.656s, picking up the pace nicely after losing time on Saturday morning due to a failed brake master cylinder. His team-mate Nick Heidfeld wound up three places farther back, separated from the Australian by Giancarlo Fisichella – grappling with a touch of understeer – and Jarno Trulli, whose efforts with the Toyota TF105 were spoiled when he was the first car to take to the track after Ralf's shunt interrupted proceedings in Saturday qualifying.

'I'm happy that Ralf is okay after such a big accident,' said the 2004 Monaco winner. 'For me, though, it was tough to be the first driver out after an accident like that. Because of the wait, the track temperature went down a lot. On my warm-up lap I also found that the track was dusty and slippery. I had no problems with the car but I didn't have enough faith to push as hard as usual, especially through the second sector.'

David Coulthard's efforts to qualify the Red Bull seventh accurately reflected his proven skill and ability at Monaco, easing out Michael Schumacher, Jacques Villeneuve and Rubens Barrichello.

In the Ferrari camp it was difficult to imagine how it could get a lot worse. The two F2005 drivers were still struggling desperately to get the best of the latest Bridgestone tyres and were way off the pace on Saturday as a result, Michael dropping almost three seconds to Räikkönen thanks to making his first run on a dirty track.

Felipe Massa's Sauber was 11th ahead of Vitantonio Liuzzi's Red Bull and the dynamic Patrick Friesacher, whose pace and sheer verve in the Minardi PS05 revived flickering memories of Fernando Alonso's similarly gutsy driving for the Faenza squad on this very same asphalt back in 2001.

Main photo: Räikkönen guiding his McLaren around the houses, inches from the unyielding barriers.
Photograph: James Moy/www.crash.net

Above: Ralf Schumacher and David Coulthard walk in after their skirmish with Juan Pablo Montoya during practice.
Photograph: Laurent Charniaux/WRi

Left: Patrick Friesacher impressed with his boldness and precision.
Photograph: James Moy/www.crash.net

KIMI Räikkönen raised the world championship stakes in dramatic fashion in Monaco by demonstrating yet again that the McLaren-Mercedes MP4-20 had now consolidated its position as the fastest car in the F1 business. The tortuous streets of Monte Carlo, with their tight corners and high kerbs, could hardly offer more of a contrast to the wide open spaces of Barcelona's Circuit de Catalunya on which the Finn had emerged similarly victorious a fortnight before.

It was the familiar Räikkönen mix: a crushing run to pole position, a blistering opening lap and the sheer speed enabling him to dictate the pace of the race with total authority, even when the cards appeared briefly to be stacked against him.

Räikkönen started from pole and broke Fernando Alonso's challenge almost from the end of the opening lap, by which he was already 1.2s ahead of the Spaniard's Renault R25 with Giancarlo Fisichella up to third in the other French machine.

With 20 laps completed, Räikkönen had extended his lead to 5.4s but when Christijan Albers spun his Minardi at the tricky downhill Mirabeau right-hander on lap 24, causing a queue of cars to judder to a halt behind him, the safety car was deployed just too late for Räikkönen to dive into the pits to refuel, a tactical option which both Renault drivers, both Williams drivers and Sauber's Felipe Massa promptly took advantage of.

Caught up in the incident, Michael Schumacher's Ferrari tapped the back of David Coulthard's Red Bull, breaking the nose of the Italian machine and the rear suspension of its rival. Schumacher continued after a stop for a replacement nose cone but Coulthard limped back to his pit to retire.

Main photo: Mayhem at Mirabeau: Christijan Albers spun his Minardi and brought most of the field to a standstill in a close call which might have resulted in the race's being red-flagged, but fortunately didn't.

Inset: Mark Webber muscled his way past Fernando Alonso to claim the first podium finish of his F1 career.

Photographs: Bryn Williams/www.crash.net

'There's not much to say,' shrugged Coulthard. 'Albers spun going into the corner, so I slowed down to avoid him. However, Michael couldn't see me and he hit my car, which damaged the rear wing and suspension.' It was the second time Coulthard had been involved in such an incident over the weekend.

Albers' spin, meanwhile, had left Räikkönen slightly concerned. 'I was a bit worried when the safety car came out because I'd just missed the entry to the pit lane as my team was telling me to come in,' he said. 'But the team told me I'd just have to build up a lead of 20s before I made my refuelling stop. This was the crucial period for us and the car really worked well this weekend.' McLaren's pit-wall decision to keep him out was buttressed by the team's in-house strategists back in Woking who, carefully monitoring Kimi's progress, sent a crisp confirmatory email saying that they were doing the right thing.

The safety car was duly withdrawn at the end of lap 28, after which Kimi simply erupted into action. With Jarno Trulli's Toyota between him and key rival Alonso, he stretched his advantage to an amazing 34.7s by the time he made his single 11.0s stop at the end of lap 42. This was the defining moment of the race and Räikkönen resumed still 13s ahead of the Renault as he accelerated back onto the asphalt.

Alonso, meanwhile, had his hands full as his hard-compound Michelin rear tyres were losing grip and wearing heavily, his lap times dropping away as a result, and he fell back into the clutches of the two Williams drivers.

Räikkönen won by 13.877s from Nick Heidfeld's Williams-BMW. This was Heidfeld's best-ever F1 result. He crossed the line ahead of his team-mate Mark Webber, for whom the satisfaction of a similarly career-best result was tempered by the fact that Williams had called Heidfeld in first for his second refuelling stop, even though he was running fourth at that moment behind Alonso and Webber.

This enabled Heidfeld to leapfrog Webber and, although they both got ahead of Alonso in the closing stages, the Australian

driver was clearly unamused that he had been apparently disadvantaged in this way.

The manner in which Heidfeld despatched Alonso from second place under braking for the waterfront chicane on lap 71 was as impressive as it was decisive. The German driver gained some breathing space for the next couple of laps until Webber also squeezed ahead of Alonso after they both made a mess at the chicane, but the issue was eventually resolved as the tough Australian sat it out wheel-to-wheel with Alonso going down to the next corner and Alonso had no choice but to concede the line.

'It's my first podium finish in F1 and it's very good [for Williams] to have two cars on the podium here,' said Webber. 'Apart from McLaren, we were much faster today than anybody else, but I was stuck behind Jarno Trulli's Toyota in the opening stages of the race, then unfortunately Nick passed me at the second pit stops and we were held up by Alonso, who was struggling with his tyres. I just wish I could have driven in some clean air today.'

Alonso scrabbled home fourth a few feet ahead of Juan Pablo Montoya's strongly driven McLaren. Alonso admitted it had been a struggle for him for most of the afternoon. 'It was a really tough race for me,' he said. 'I tried to look after the tyres at the start of the race, so I didn't worry too much about the fact that Räikkönen was pulling away, but for the last 20 laps things became really difficult.

'I did all I could to keep the Williams cars behind me, but I couldn't hold them off because my rear tyres were in a poor condition and they [the Williams drivers] could brake much later into the chicane. But we've got to look at the positive side. At least we managed to score points on an afternoon when it would have been very easy to score none at all.'

Ralf Schumacher was next up in sixth ahead of his brother Michael, who forced his way past his Ferrari team-mate Rubens Barrichello to take seventh place on the last lap. Seldom can he have put so much effort into a meagre tally of two

championship points on this epic track where his five victories to date now seemed little more than flickering memories.

Michael almost interlocked his wheels with Ralf's as they sprinted from the final corner to the chequered flag, prompting the younger sibling to brand his brother 'brainless', although the spat didn't last long and within a couple of days the Schumachers were delivering saccharine-coated pledges of mutual affection and consideration.

Michael was clearly every bit as exasperated as Alonso. 'Everything that could go wrong seemed to go wrong,' he said. 'I got stuck behind the Minardi that blocked the track and then I had to pit to change the nose on the car.

'It is clear when you look at the [lap] times that we had a very competitive race pace. It is a shame that we were not able to get the most out of it. But given everything that happened, I have to be reasonably content with two points.'

Meanwhile Barrichello tempered his initial criticism of his team-mate. 'If this would have happened two or three years ago I would keep my mouth shut, but not now. I don't think anything will change, because of the way I behaved over these five years,' said the Brazilian, who believed that only his prompt manoeuvring prevented a shunt at the chicane on the final lap as Michael muscled his way through on a tight line.

'I put up with a few things but I throw away the things that are not positive and I keep in my mind the good things.' It should be noted that Rubens was at the end of a stressful race during which he'd stalled in one refuelling stop and collected a drive-through penalty for speeding in the pit lane.

Ferrari chairman Jean Todt said, 'Rubens was understandably disappointed but this will not change at all the harmony inside the team. We have bigger problems to deal with.'

Farther back, Jacques Villeneuve ended the race in a disappointing 11th place, facing the prospect of a dressing down from the Sauber team management. He was duly summoned to the team's Hinwil base the following week.

Peter Sauber was absolutely furious after Villeneuve attempted to barge past Massa as they raced for eighth place, bouncing over the kerb at the Ste Devote right-hander in a bid to pass the Brazilian.

'We had a perfect strategy for the race,' he said, reflecting on the fact that the two cars would almost certainly have finished sixth and seventh. 'However, the incident caused by Jacques cost us five valuable [constructors'] championship points that would have enabled us to close the gap to our direct competitor, Red Bull. What happened today is the most depressing thing a team could experience.'

He added, 'I told both drivers that I don't want to discuss this issue with them in the paddock, because there are too many emotions at the surface at the moment. So we will meet in Hinwil this week to discuss the situation.

'They don't normally come to the factory after the races, but this is a very serious situation and we have to speak together.'

Villeneuve admitted that, after watching what he took to be the deteriorating state of Massa's rear tyres, he 'tried something which unfortunately didn't work'. For his part, Massa was more robust.

'The team called me in to refuel as the safety car came out and that was a brilliant plan because I'd just managed to squeeze through a small hole between Coulthard and Michael Schumacher,' recounted the Brazilian.

'After that I was running strongly behind Heidfeld and was able to make a second stop later on, on lap 50, without losing much time. Unfortunately my tyres were losing grip and Montoya passed me, and then there was the incident with Jacques. I think it was wrong on his side, but now I am just focusing on the next race.'

For the moment, however, Räikkönen basked in the feeling of a job well done. He'd ramped up his title challenge and it was easy to conclude that Alonso and Renault were on the back foot. Yet as events unfolded, it would prove to be an erroneous conclusion.

Alan Henry

Top: Nick Heidfeld leading a gaggle of cars down through Mirabeau on his way to a career-best second place in the Williams-BMW FW27.
Photograph: Bryn Williams/www.crash.net

Above: There was not much tread – or grip – left in this worn rear Michelin from Alonso's Renault.
Photograph: Jean-François Galeron/WRI

GRAND PRIX DE MONACO
MONACO 20–22 MAY 2005

MONACO – MONTE CARLO
GRAND PRIX CIRCUIT

GRAND HOTEL HAIRPIN 20/32 (1)
STE DÉVOTE 50/81 (2)
160/258 (6)
175/282 (6)
MONTÉE de BEAU RIVAGE 160/258 (6)
CASINO
MIRABEAU 40/64 (2)
VIRAGE du PORTIER 45/72 (2)
NOUVELLE CHICANE 30/48 (2)
TABAC 95/153 (3)
TUNNEL
VIRAGE ANTHONY NOGHES 50/81 (2)
La RASCASSE 30/48 (2)
mph/km/h (gear)

CIRCUIT LENGTH: 2.075 miles/3.340 km

Photograph: James Moy/www.crash.net

RACE DISTANCE: 78 laps, 161.879 miles /260.520 km **RACE WEATHER:** Sunny/scattered cloud (track 36–37°C, air 22–23°C)

Pos.	Driver	Nat.	No.	Entrant	Car/Engine	Tyres	Laps	Time/Retirement	Speed (mph/km/h)	Gap to leader	Fastest race lap	
1	Kimi Räikkönen	FIN	9	West McLaren Mercedes	McLaren MP4-20-Mercedes F0 110R V10	M	78	1h 45m 15.556s	92.274/148.501		1m 15.921s	41
2	Nick Heidfeld	D	8	BMW WilliamsF1 Team	Williams FW27-BMW P84/85 V10	M	78	1h 45m 29.433s	92.072/148.176	+13.877s	1m 17.159s	15
3	Mark Webber	AUS	7	BMW WilliamsF1 Team	Williams FW26-BMW P84/85 V10	M	78	1h 45m 34.040s	92.005/148.068	+18.484s	1m 16.971s	77
4	Fernando Alonso	E	5	Mild Seven Renault F1 Team	Renault R25-RS25 V10	M	78	1h 45m 52.043s	91.744/147.648	+36.487s	1m 16.600s	19
5	Juan Pablo Montoya	COL	10	West McLaren Mercedes	McLaren MP4-20-Mercedes F0 110R V10	M	78	1h 45m 52.203s	91.742/147.645	+36.647s	1m 17.403s	50
6	Ralf Schumacher	D	17	Panasonic Toyota Racing	Toyota TF105-RVX-05 V10	M	78	1h 45m 52.733s	91.734/147.632	+37.177s	1m 17.070s	11
7	Michael Schumacher	D	1	Scuderia Ferrari Marlboro	Ferrari F2005-055 V10	B	78	1h 45m 52.779s	91.733/147.631	+37.223s	1m 15.842s	40
8	Rubens Barrichello	BR	2	Scuderia Ferrari Marlboro	Ferrari F2005-055 V10	B	78	1h 45m 53.126s	91.729/147.623	+37.570s	1m 16.916s	51
9	Felipe Massa	BR	12	Sauber Petronas	Sauber C24-Petronas 05A V10	M	77			+1 lap	1m 17.799s	16
10	Jarno Trulli	I	16	Panasonic Toyota Racing	Toyota TF105-RVX-05 V10	M	77			+1 lap	1m 16.812s	38
11	Jacques Villeneuve	CDN	11	Sauber Petronas	Sauber C24-Petronas 05A V10	M	77			+1 lap	1m 17.482s	17
12	Giancarlo Fisichella	I	6	Mild Seven Renault F1 Team	Renault R25-RS25 V10	M	77			+1 lap	1m 16.776s	20
13	Tiago Monteiro	P	18	Jordan Toyota	Jordan EJ15-Toyota RVX-05 V10	B	75			+3 laps	1m 20.747s	12
14	Christijan Albers	NL	21	Minardi Cosworth	Minardi PS05-Cosworth TJ2005 V10	B	73			+5 laps	1m 20.237s	22
	Vitantonio Liuzzi	I	15	Red Bull Racing	Red Bull RB1-Cosworth TJ2005/10 V10	M	59	Accident damage/tyres			1m 18.030s	43
	Patrick Friesacher	A	20	Minardi Cosworth	Minardi PS05-Cosworth TJ2005 V10	B	29	Accident			1m 19.037s	19
	David Coulthard	GB	14	Red Bull Racing	Red Bull RB1-Cosworth TJ2005/10 V10	M	23	Accident damage/suspension			1m 17.693s	15
	Narain Karthikeyan	IND	19	Jordan Toyota	Jordan EJ15-Toyota RVX-05 V10	B	18	Accident damage/hydraulics			1m 22.019s	14

All results and data © FOM 2005

Fastest lap: Michael Schumacher, on lap 40, 1m 15.842s, 98.512 mph/158.540 km/h.

Previous lap record: Michael Schumacher (Ferrari F2004-052 V10), 1m 14.439s, 100.369 mph/161.528 km/h (2004).

17th: R. SCHUMACHER Toyota
Ten-place penalty for engine change

15th: MONTEIRO Jordan-Toyota

13th: FRIESACHER Minardi-Cosworth

11th: MASSA Sauber-Petronas

16th: KARTHIKEYAN Jordan-Toyota
Ten-place penalty for engine change

18th: MONTOYA McLaren-Mercedes
Sent to back after practice incident

14th: ALBERS Minardi-Cosworth

12th: LIUZZI Red Bull-Cosworth

Grid order	1	2	3	4	5	6	7	8	9	10	11	12	13	14	15	16	17	18	19	20	21	22	23	24	25	26	27	28	29	30	31	32	33	34	35	36	37	38	39	40	41	42	43	44	45	46	47	48	49	50	51	52	53	54	55	56	57	58	59	60
9 RÄIKKÖNEN	9	9	9	9	9	9	9	9	9	9	9	9	9	9	9	9	9	9	9	9	9	9	9	9	9	9	9	9	9	9	9	9	9	9	9	9	9	9	9	9	9	9	9	9	9	9	9	9	9	9	9	9	9	9	9	9	9	9	9	9
5 ALONSO	5	5	5	5	5	5	5	5	5	5	5	5	5	5	5	5	5	5	5	5	5	5	5	5	16	16	16	16	16	16	16	16	16	16	16	16	16	16	5	5	5	5	5	5	5	5	5	5	5	5	5	5	5	5	5	5	5	5	5	5
7 WEBBER	6	6	6	6	6	6	6	6	6	6	6	6	6	6	6	6	6	6	6	6	6	6	6	6	5	5	5	5	5	5	5	5	5	5	5	7	7	7	7	7	7	7	7	7	7	7	7	7	7	7	7	7	7	7	7	8	8	8	8	8
6 FISICHELLA	16	16	16	16	6	16	16	16	16	16	16	16	16	16	16	16	16	16	16	16	16	16	16	16	7	7	7	7	7	7	7	7	7	7	7	8	8	8	8	8	8	8	8	8	8	8	8	8	8	8	8	8	8	8	7	7	7
16 TRULLI	7	7	7	7	7	7	7	7	7	7	7	7	7	7	7	7	7	7	7	7	7	7	7	7	8	8	8	8	8	8	8	8	8	8	8	12	12	12	12	12	12	12	12	12	12	6	6	6	6	6	6	6	6	6	6	6
8 HEIDFELD	8	8	8	8	8	8	8	8	8	8	8	8	8	8	8	8	8	8	8	8	8	8	8	8	6	12	12	12	12	12	12	12	12	12	12	6	6	6	6	6	6	6	6	6	16	16	16	16	16	16	16	16	16	16
14 COULTHARD	14	14	14	14	14	14	14	14	14	14	14	14	14	14	14	14	14	14	14	12	12	11	11	11	11	11	11	11	11	11	11	6	2	2	2	2	2	10	16	16	16	16	12	12	12	12	12	12	12	12
1 M. SCHUMACHER	1	1	1	1	1	1	1	1	1	1	1	1	1	1	1	1	1	1	1	11	11	6	6	6	6	6	6	6	6	2	10	10	10	10	10	10	10	10	10	10	10	10	10	10	10	10	10	10	10	10	10	11
11 VILLENEUVE	12	12	12	12	12	12	12	12	12	12	12	12	12	12	12	12	12	12	12	2	2	2	2	2	2	2	2	2	10	16	15	15	15	15	15	11	11	11	11	11	11	11	11	11	11	11
2 BARRICHELLO	11	11	11	11	11	11	11	11	11	11	11	11	11	11	11	11	11	11	11	10	10	10	10	10	10	10	10	10	2	10	16	16	16	16	16	17	17	17	17	17	17	17	17	17	17	17
12 MASSA	2	2	2	2	2	2	2	2	2	2	2	2	2	2	2	2	2	2	2	15	15	15	15	15	15	15	15	15	17	17	16	17	11	11	11	1	1	1	1	1	1	1	1	1	1	2	2
15 LIUZZI	10	10	10	10	10	10	10	10	10	10	10	10	10	10	10	10	10	10	10	17	17	17	17	17	17	17	11	11	11	11	17	17	1	15	15	15	15	15	15	15	2	2	15	1
20 FRIESACHER	15	15	15	15	15	15	15	15	15	15	15	15	15	15	15	15	15	15	15	1	1	1	1	1	1	1	1	1	1	1	1	2	2	2	2	2	2	2	2
21 ALBERS	20	20	20	20	20	20	20	17	17	17	17	17	17	17	17	17	17	17	17	20	20	20	20	20	18	18	18	18	18	18	18	18	18	18	18	18	18	18	18	18	18	18	18	18	18	18
18 MONTEIRO	21	21	21	17	17	17	17	20	20	20	20	20	20	20	20	20	20	20	20	18	18	18	18	18	21	21	21	21	21	21	21	21	21	21	21	21	21	21	21	21	21	21	21	21	21
10 MONTOYA	18	18	17	21	21	21	21	21	21	21	21	21	21	21	21	21	21	21	21
17 R. SCHUMACHER	17	17	18	18	18	18	18	18	18	18	18	18	18	18	18	18	18	18	18	21
19 KARTHIKEYAN	19	19	19	19	19	19	19	19	19	19	19	19	19	19	19	19	19

Pit stop
One lap or more behind leader

QUALIFYING

SATURDAY: Scattered cloud (track 35–36°C, air 22–24°C)
SUNDAY: Sunny (track 28–31°C, air 21–23°C)

Pos.	Driver	R/Order	1st qualifying	R/Order	2nd qualifying	Aggregate
1	Kimi Räikkönen	18	1m 13.644s	18	1m 16.679s	2m 30.323s
2	Fernando Alonso	17	1m 14.125s	17	1m 16.281s	2m 30.406s
3	Mark Webber	13	1m 14.584s	16	1m 17.072s	2m 31.656s
4	Giancarlo Fisichella	14	1m 14.783s	15	1m 17.317s	2m 32.100s
5	Jarno Trulli	16	1m 15.189s	13	1m 17.401s	2m 32.590s
6	Nick Heidfeld	9	1m 15.128s	14	1m 17.755s	2m 32.883s
7	David Coulthard	11	1m 15.329s	12	1m 18.538s	2m 32.867s
8	Michael Schumacher	4	1m 16.186s	9	1m 18.550s	2m 34.736s
9	Jacques Villeneuve	5	1m 15.921s	11	1m 19.015s	2m 34.936s
10	Rubens Barrichello	10	1m 16.142s	10	1m 18.841s	2m 34.983s
11	Felipe Massa	8	1m 16.218s	8	1m 18.902s	2m 35.120s
12	Vitantonio Liuzzi	1	1m 16.817s	7	1m 20.335s	2m 37.152s
13	Patrick Friesacher	2	1m 18.574s	6	1m 22.236s	2m 40.810s
14	Christijan Albers	3	1m 19.229s	5	1m 22.977s	2m 42.206s
15	Tiago Monteiro	7	1m 19.408s	4	1m 23.670s	2m 43.078s
16	Narain Karthikeyan	6	1m 19.474s	3	1m 23.968s	2m 43.442s
17	Juan Pablo Montoya	12	1m 14.858s	1	No time	No time
18	Ralf Schumacher	15	No time	2	No time	No time

FERRARI				RED BULL-COSWORTH		
1	Michael Schumacher	F2005/245	14	David Coulthard	RB1/3
2	Rubens Barrichello	F2005/246	15	Vitantonio Liuzzi	RB1/1
	Spare	F2005/243	37	Christian Klien	RB1/2
				Spare	RB1/2
RENAULT				TOYOTA		
5	Fernando Alonso	R25/04	16	Jarno Trulli	TF105/02
6	Giancarlo Fisichella	R25/06	17	Ralf Schumacher	TF105/04
	Spare	R25/02	38	Ricardo Zonta	TF105/05
				Spare	TF105/05
WILLIAMS-BMW				JORDAN-TOYOTA		
7	Mark Webber	FW27/05	18	Tiago Monteiro	EJ15/03
8	Nick Heidfeld	FW27/06	19	Narain Karthikeyan	EJ15/02
	Spare	FW27/04	39	Robert Doornbos	EJ15/01
				Spare	EJ15/01
McLAREN-MERCEDES				MINARDI-COSWORTH		
9	Kimi Räikkönen	MP4-20/04	20	Patrick Friesacher	PS05/02
10	Juan Pablo Montoya	MP4-20/05	21	Christijan Albers	PS05/01
35	Pedro de la Rosa	MP4-20/03, 06		Spare	PS04B/03
	Spare	MP4-20/03, 06			
SAUBER-PETRONAS						
11	Jacques Villeneuve	C24/04			
12	Felipe Massa	C24/02			
	Spare	C24/03			

Photograph: Bryn Williams/www.crash.net

PRACTICE 1 (THURSDAY)

Sunny (track 31–37°C, air 23–24°C)

Pos.	Driver	Laps	Time
1	Juan Pablo Montoya	14	1m 17.152s
2	Fernando Alonso	14	1m 17.301s
3	Christian Klien	21	1m 17.511s
4	Michael Schumacher	16	1m 17.640s
5	Giancarlo Fisichella	19	1m 17.869s
6	Alex Wurz	26	1m 18.059s
7	Mark Webber	18	1m 18.244s
8	Ralf Schumacher	14	1m 18.482s
9	David Coulthard	15	1m 18.669s
10	Rubens Barrichello	16	1m 18.838s
11	Nick Heidfeld	17	1m 18.859s
12	Kimi Räikkönen	16	1m 19.055s
13	Jarno Trulli	13	1m 19.255s
14	Jacques Villeneuve	20	1m 19.755s
15	Vitantonio Liuzzi	21	1m 19.844s
16	Felipe Massa	15	1m 20.180s
17	Ricardo Zonta	21	1m 20.979s
18	Robert Doornbos	28	1m 21.511s
19	Patrick Friesacher	17	1m 21.968s
20	Tiago Monteiro	25	1m 22.388s
21	Narain Karthikeyan	20	1m 23.521s
22	Christijan Albers	17	1m 25.664s

PRACTICE 2 (THURSDAY)

Sunny (track 40–42°C, air 25–27°C)

Pos.	Driver	Laps	Time
1	Fernando Alonso	27	1m 15.836s
2	Alex Wurz	24	1m 15.912s
3	David Coulthard	21	1m 16.184s
4	Giancarlo Fisichella	32	1m 16.519s
5	Juan Pablo Montoya	21	1m 16.534s
6	Kimi Räikkönen	26	1m 16.558s
7	Vitantonio Liuzzi	27	1m 16.640s
8	Felipe Massa	19	1m 16.914s
9	Ralf Schumacher	24	1m 16.917s
10	Ricardo Zonta	35	1m 17.046s
11	Michael Schumacher	11	1m 17.170s
12	Mark Webber	30	1m 17.422s
13	Jarno Trulli	28	1m 17.487s
14	Jacques Villeneuve	27	1m 17.506s
15	Rubens Barrichello	25	1m 17.663s
16	Nick Heidfeld	29	1m 17.667s
17	Christian Klien	23	1m 18.815s
18	Robert Doornbos	26	1m 19.526s
19	Patrick Friesacher	26	1m 19.587s
20	Tiago Monteiro	31	1m 20.284s
21	Narain Karthikeyan	12	1m 21.879s
22	Christijan Albers	15	1m 22.162s

PRACTICE 3 (SATURDAY)

Sunny with scattered cloud (track 26–28°C, air 21–22°C)

Pos.	Driver	Laps	Time
1	Juan Pablo Montoya	16	1m 16.197s
2	Giancarlo Fisichella	12	1m 16.403s
3	Ralf Schumacher	16	1m 16.508s
4	Fernando Alonso	12	1m 16.513s
5	Michael Schumacher	14	1m 16.803s
6	Kimi Räikkönen	15	1m 16.875s
7	Nick Heidfeld	12	1m 16.935s
8	David Coulthard	13	1m 17.180s
9	Rubens Barrichello	12	1m 17.475s
10	Mark Webber	8	1m 18.065s
11	Jarno Trulli	12	1m 18.215s
12	Vitantonio Liuzzi	15	1m 18.259s
13	Jacques Villeneuve	9	1m 18.640s
14	Patrick Friesacher	13	1m 19.271s
15	Tiago Monteiro	15	1m 20.215s
16	Narain Karthikeyan	18	1m 20.348s
17	Christijan Albers	18	1m 21.563s
18	Felipe Massa	1	No time

PRACTICE 4 (SATURDAY)

Sunny with scattered cloud (track 28–29°C, air 21–22°C)

Pos.	Driver	Laps	Time
1	Giancarlo Fisichella	18	1m 13.988s
2	Fernando Alonso	14	1m 14.047s
3	Kimi Räikkönen	10	1m 14.258s
4	Jarno Trulli	11	1m 14.322s
5	Mark Webber	10	1m 14.418s
6	Ralf Schumacher	10	1m 14.459s
7	Juan Pablo Montoya	7	1m 14.543s
8	David Coulthard	16	1m 14.582s
9	Jacques Villeneuve	14	1m 14.961s
10	Vitantonio Liuzzi	16	1m 14.998s
11	Nick Heidfeld	10	1m 15.196s
12	Rubens Barrichello	8	1m 15.637s
13	Felipe Massa	17	1m 16.123s
14	Jacques Villeneuve	10	1m 16.148s
15	Patrick Friesacher	12	1m 18.506s
16	Tiago Monteiro	7	1m 19.034s
17	Narain Karthikeyan	10	1m 19.606s
18	Christijan Albers	10	1m 19.700s

9th: VILLENEUVE Sauber-Petronas

7th: COULTHARD Red Bull-Cosworth

5th: TRULLI Toyota

3rd: WEBBER Williams-BMW

Pole: RÄIKKÖNEN McLaren-Mercedes

10th: BARRICHELLO Ferrari

8th: M. SCHUMACHER Ferrari

6th: HEIDFELD Williams-BMW

4th: FISICHELLA Renault

2nd: ALONSO Renault

---

61 62 63 64 65 66 67 68 69 70 71 72 73 74 75 76 77 78	●	
9 9 9 9 9 9 9 9 9 9 9 9 9 9 9 9 9 9	1
5 5 5 5 5 5 5 5 5 8 8 8 8 8 8 8 8	2
8 8 8 8 8 8 8 8 8 5 5 5 7 7 7 7 7 3	
7 7 7 7 7 7 7 7 7 7 7 5 5 5 5 5 5	4
6 6 6 10 10 10 10 10 10 10 10 10 10 10 10 10 10 10	5
16 16 16 17 17 17 17 17 17 17 17 17 17 17 17 17 17 17	6
10 10 10 2 2 2 2 2 2 2 2 2 2 2 2 2 2 1	7
12 12 17 1 1 1 1 1 1 1 1 1 1 1 1 1 1 1	
11 11 2 16 6 6 6 6 6 6 12 12 12 12 12 12 12	
17 17 1 6 12 12 12 12 12 12 12 6 6 6 16 16 16	
2 2 12 12 16 16 16 16 16 16 16 16 16 11 11 11 11	
1 1 11 11 11 11 11 11 11 11 11 11 11 11 6 6 6	
18 18 18 18 18 18 18 18 18 18 18 18 18 18	
21 21 21 21 21 21 21 21 21 21 21 21	

Photograph: James Moy/www.crash.net

FIRST GP PODIUM: Mark Webber

	DRIVERS			CONSTRUCTORS	
1	Fernando Alonso	49	1	Renault	63
2	Kimi Räikkönen	27	2	McLaren	51
3	Jarno Trulli	26	3	Toyota	43
4	Mark Webber	18	4	Williams	35
5	Nick Heidfeld	17	5	Ferrari	21
6	Ralf Schumacher	17	6	Red Bull	14
7	Giancarlo Fisichella	14	7	Sauber	7
8	Juan Pablo Montoya	14			
9	Michael Schumacher	12			
10	David Coulthard	10			
11	Rubens Barrichello	9			
12	Alex Wurz	6			
13	Jacques Villeneuve	5			
14	Pedro de la Rosa	4			
15	Christian Klien	3			
16	Felipe Massa	2			
17	Vitantonio Liuzzi	1			

Photograph: Jad Sherif/WRI

NÜRBURGRING
EUROPEANGP
FIA F1 WORLD CHAMPIONSHIP/ROUND 7

Fernando Alonso celebrated his fourth win
of the season as he cruised around his
slowing-down lap. He pressed hard when
he needed to and reaped the reward with
Kimi Räikkönen's last-lap retirement.
Photograph: Paul-Henri Cahier

NÜRBURGRING QUALIFYING

Recent rule changes restored a single hour's qualifying on Saturday afternoon, with no F1 action on Sunday morning prior to the race. This was generally accepted as a positive development from the standpoint of the sport's PR and promotion. It did, however, deprive fans of the sight of the cars running in low-fuel configuration in first qualifying.

So it was back to the old guessing game when it came to assessing how much fuel the leading competitors had in their tanks during their qualifying runs. Thus when Nick Heidfeld did an excellent job in his Williams-BMW FW27 to steal pole position from Kimi Räikkönen, it was reasonable to conclude that the 28-year-old from nearby Mönchengladbach was running with a lighter fuel load than the winner of the two previous races, opting for a three-stop strategy to the Finn's two-stopper.

Heidfeld was delighted. 'Yes, it's fantastic,' he said. 'I thought after Monaco it would be a bit more difficult for us here but, luckily, I was wrong. I thought we could be on the front row, but I'm surprised to be on pole position.'

Räikkönen was pleased to be second on the grid, 0.116s away from Heidfeld's best, with Mark Webber a satisfied third in the other Williams FW27. The Australian lined up alongside Jarno Trulli's Toyota TF105, the Italian managing a 1m 30.700s best despite running quite a heavy fuel load. The Toyotas had an aerodynamic upgrade for this race but Trulli was alone in benefiting from a slightly more powerful engine, which was not available to team-mate Ralf Schumacher because he was in the second race of his current engine cycle.

Juan Pablo Montoya complained of poor grip in qualifying, but his 1m 30.890s gave him a place on the clean side of the grid after a slight mistake at the high-speed chicane cost him a few crucial tenths. That at least placed him ahead of Fernando Alonso's Renault and Rubens Barrichello (1m 31.249s). Barrichello, in the fastest of the two Ferrari F2005s, had opted for a three-stop race strategy in contrast to the two-stopping Michael Schumacher, who was a disappointed three places farther back on the grid.

'At least the balance of the car seemed good,' said Rubens. 'We definitely look better than last weekend. My qualifying lap was quite good, but it could even have been a bit better.' For his part, Schumacher admitted that his qualifying lap was spoiled by a touch too much understeer.

Both Renault drivers were planning long opening stints in the race and their cars were heavier than their immediate rivals', leaving Alonso (1m 31.056s) and Giancarlo Fisichella (1m 31.566s) to start sixth and ninth respectively.

'I did a good lap, the car balance was reasonable and we have had no problems today,' said Fernando. 'It was a little bit surprising to end up sixth after being among the fastest cars in practice this morning, especially because our day has run smoothly. But I believe the difference between us and pole position is down to different strategies.'

Farther back, Jenson Button and the BAR Honda team were in upbeat mood. They had been running fresh Honda engines five weeks earlier at Imola, so those engines had been sealed and stored away at Honda's Bracknell base before reappearing installed in the BAR 007s at the Nürburgring.

'It's not much fun being one of the first cars out in the session,' said Button. 'There was very little grip and the balance was not what we expected at all. It's a shame, because in free practice the car felt pretty good, but I am confident that we can make up some ground and be strong in the race.'

Takuma Sato and Button had to make their qualifying runs first on a dusty track. Jenson, fuel-heavy for a long opening stint and with an extra 6 kg of lead ballast in the under-tray to make doubly sure there would be no scrutineering problems, was unable to better 13th on the grid.

'TO finish first, first you have to finish.' It's the oldest motor-racing adage in the book and over the past decade it's been shrewdly adapted by the McLaren team to say, 'To finish first, first you have to be Finnish' in recognition of the achievements of first Mika Häkkinen and now Kimi Räikkönen. Yet on this occasion at the new Nürburgring, Räikkönen's luck was most certainly out. Instead Fernando Alonso scored his fourth win of the season for Renault in a nail-biting European Grand Prix in which Räikkönen's leading McLaren-Mercedes MP4-20 crashed off the track at 170 mph going into the final lap after a vibrating front wheel caused a catastrophic failure of the car's right-front suspension.

Räikkönen had dominated the race from the start but, as he grappled with his tyre problem in the closing stages, he was forced to ease his pace and Alonso was only just over a second adrift as they sped into that fateful final lap.

Under the new regulations introduced this year, one set of tyres must last a competitor through qualifying and the race, but if a tyre is in a dangerous condition it can be changed without penalty. McLaren is in the winning business and team boss Ron Dennis made no apology for leaving Räikkönen out on the track in a bid to secure the team's third win of the year.

'Kimi flat-spotted a tyre in going past [Jacques] Villeneuve,' said Dennis. 'He had to go off-line. It's a little bit bumpy at the entrance to that corner and he locked a wheel – it was the right-front. We looked at the tyre in the final pit-stop and we did not consider it to be dangerous.

'But from that moment on, of course, it had a tendency to lock on that particular point, so we started to really look after the tyre from about ten laps into the final part of the race. We discussed it with Kimi on the radio; he was obviously struggling a little bit with visibility but was not unduly worried about that discomfort, and he was able to keep a pace that would enable him to win the race.'

Asked if he felt the team should have called Räikkönen in, he added, 'We did consider it, but... The issues you're thinking about are, "Is the tyre unsafe?" and, "Is the driver's level of discomfort detrimental to his ability to finish?" And neither of those two things was judged to be an issue.

'Inevitably, this sort of rule has to be interpreted according to what you feel the circumstances are. And from our perspective the tyre was not unsafe and Kimi was able to cope with the vibration. So we took a calculated risk and paid the price.

'This is part of motor racing and looking after your tyres and

making sure you don't flat-spot them is part of the skill expected of the team in setting up the car and of the driver in driving it.'

Alonso was delighted with his win, particularly because he survived being hit from behind by Ralf Schumacher's Toyota in a first-corner accident that eliminated Mark Webber's Williams-BMW from the fray and delayed the Ferraris of Rubens Barrichello and Michael Schumacher.

'The car was beautiful to drive,' said Alonso. 'I pushed hard all the way and our strategy was perfect. In the early stages I was tucked in behind David Coulthard's Red Bull and decided to take it a bit easy, conserving fuel, brakes and tyres. The car seemed to get better and better every lap and in the closing stages the team came on the radio and said, "Push. Push – we're faster than McLaren," and I did.'

Nick Heidfeld, who had achieved an F1 milestone by becoming the first German driver in the 56-year history of the official world championship to qualify on pole position in a German race in a car powered by a German engine, finished runner-up 16.567s behind Alonso.

Heidfeld completed the opening lap 1.9s behind the dominant Räikkönen, the two of them having successfully

Above: Michael Schumacher and Juan Pablo Montoya rubbed wheels as they climbed back through the field following their delays at the first corner.
Photograph: James Moy/www.crash.net

Left: Thumbs up from Nick Heidfeld after he became the first German driver ever to take pole position in a German round of the F1 world championship in a car powered by a German engine.
Photograph: Laurent Charniaux/WRi

Main photograph: Heading for trouble as the pack jostled for position into the braking area for the tight right-hander immediately after the start. Fernando Alonso's Renault was already slightly out of shape as he and Rubens Barrichello tried to avoid touching the rear of Mark Webber's disappearing Williams-BMW.
Photograph: James Moy/www.crash.net

Right: A frustrated Juan Pablo Montoya gesticulated at Webber after being pitched into a spin and the Schumacher brothers skirted the disaster area on a wide line.
Photograph: Laurent Charniaux/WRi

Top left: **Felipe Massa's front left tyre shows severe damage as he works to keep his Sauber ahead of Jarno Trulli's Toyota.**
Photograph: Miltenberg/XPB.cc

Bottom left: **Kimi Räikkönen spun into retirement with front-suspension failure, the legacy of vibrations caused by a flat-spotted right-front tyre.**
Photograph: Laurent Charniaux/WRi

MOSLEY WARNS TEAMS ABOUT TYRE SAFETY

Five days after Kimi Räikkönen crashed out of the European GP, FIA president Max Mosley pointedly warned all the F1 teams that they should take the initiative to withdraw from a race any car about which they may have safety concerns.

'It should not be forgotten that a mechanical failure at high speed may involve a degree of risk to the spectating public,' Mosley wrote in a letter to all the F1 team principals. 'If you are in any doubt about your car, you should always call it in [to the pits]. If you are still in doubt after checking the car in the pits, you should retire it from the race.'

Mosley also wrote identical letters to Michelin and Bridgestone, requesting that they be mindful of the possible risk to spectators of any tyre failures, and published a copy of the letter he sent to Pierre Dupasquier, the competitions director of Michelin. It read, 'It is impossible for the FIA to assess the structural integrity, wear resistance or strength of a tyre. The FIA has neither the technical resources nor the necessary knowledge. F1 is therefore totally dependent on the tyre suppliers to ensure that no risks are taken in the pursuit of performance.

'Tyres should be built to be reliable under all circumstances, including prolonged periods under the safety car, off-road excursions, abuse on kerbs, contact with other cars and contact with debris on the track.

'A tyre failure may put the driver at risk but may also endanger members of the public. We are confident that we can rely on you to make every effort to see that there are no more tyre failures this season.'

The FIA was understood to be particularly concerned about the recent 200-mph tyre failure in testing at Paul Ricard involving McLaren driver Alex Wurz and caused by a Michelin tyre's inadvertently being fitted the wrong way around.

DIARY

Dan Wheldon becomes only the fourth British-born winner of the Indianapolis 500 after his success for Andretti Green Racing.

Heikki Kovalainen is nominated for the role of third Renault driver for the Canadian and US Grands Prix.

David Coulthard opens negotiations to extend his contract with Red Bull Racing into 2006.

Bruno Junqueira suffers spinal injuries after crashing heavily in the Indy 500.

---

avoided the first corner mêlée that sent cars spinning in all directions. Ralf Schumacher's Toyota plunged into the back of Alonso's Renault, Felipe Massa's Sauber slid into Takuma Sato's BAR and Mark Webber tipped Juan Pablo Montoya into a time-consuming spin, the Australian's FW27 ending up beached in the gravel trap and out of the race.

Alonso feared that his race might already be terminally damaged. 'I was afraid from the start of the race after Ralf hit me,' he admitted. 'I thought the car might have been damaged and that I would have to retire. After a few corners, though, it was clear that everything was okay, so then it was a case of pushing hard, doing the strategy and trying to get a good finish.'

For his part, Ralf was frustrated and apologetic. 'This was a very difficult day for me,' he said. 'I made a reasonably good start but as I went into Turn One I was very close behind Alonso, when suddenly he came almost to a complete stop. Because I was so close behind him I couldn't see what was happening in front and so I became involved in the accident. It was a pity, because it meant I had to replace my nose cone, which left me over a minute adrift.'

During the opening stages it seemed as though Räikkönen had the race in his pocket, nursing a 2s lead for the first ten laps or so without seriously pushing to keep ahead of Heidfeld. Jarno Trulli's Toyota TF105 held third ahead of David Coulthard's Red Bull, which the Scot had dodged through the debris at the first corner, making up a lot of places. Alonso was fifth ahead of Felipe Massa and the rest of the pack.

On lap eight it was announced that Trulli would receive a drive-through penalty because his mechanics had remained on the start-line within the prohibited 15s window prior to the start of the formation lap. Jarno was left seething, even though he managed to climb back to eighth by the finish and at least claim one hard-earned point.

'After an afternoon like that, a point is certainly better than nothing, but it could have been much more,' he reflected. 'Unfortunately we had a problem firing up the engine on the grid, and because of those few seconds we earned a drive-through penalty which completely spoiled my race. I pitted earlier than we intended because I was stuck in traffic and after that my race was fairly anonymous because it is nearly impossible to overtake here.'

Heidfeld made his first stop on lap 12, leaving Räikkönen with a 19.9s lead over Coulthard, Alonso and Massa. Kimi made his first stop (8.7s) on lap 18, allowing Coulthard to lead for a couple of laps before he too came in, and that left Alonso 5.6s ahead of Räikkönen at the head of the field with Heidfeld now third. Alonso duly made his first stop on lap 23, which left Räikkönen leading by 4s from Heidfeld with Alonso in third.

Heidfeld refuelled for the second time on lap 31, allowing Kimi back into the lead from Alonso and Rubens Barrichello's Ferrari, which made its second stop on lap 33, allowing Nick's Williams back to third. Ralf Schumacher's dismal afternoon ended when he spun off on the same lap.

It looked as though Räikkönen had got it in the bag until the view from the McLaren's in-car camera alerted outsiders to his problem. What started as a very conspicuous flat spot on his right-front Michelin gradually seemed to get bigger and, as it did so, the vibration became clear for all. At Kimi's second refuelling stop, on lap 43, the pit crew took a close look and their brief examination confirmed the general view that it would be safe to continue.

Yet Räikkönen was easing his pace and the Renault camp quickly homed in onto that reality, urging Alonso to press hard. Going into the final lap there was just 1.5s between them and no scope for Kimi to ease off. Then the suspension broke and the Finn slammed off the track at the first corner, the one good thing being that the safety cables successfully prevented

the wayward right-front wheel from parting company with the gyrating MP4-20.

Alonso, understandably elated, completed the final lap to post a fortuitous victory. 'I was quite happy to settle for second before the last pit stop,' he confessed. 'But then the team said Räikkönen had a problem and that I should push. That was when I briefly went off the road because I was trying 100 percent and made a mistake.

'But even so, I was catching Kimi and then I saw him crash at the first corner. For me, the big worry was that I would get caught up in the debris. Then I just had to stay calm for the final lap and take the chequered flag.'

Barrichello recovered well to take a strong third ahead of David Coulthard's Red Bull RB1, Michael Schumacher's Ferrari and the other Renault of Giancarlo Fisichella, who climbed back through the pack after stalling on the grid and being forced to start from the pit lane. Montoya also staged a great recovery to finish seventh despite grappling with a floor badly broken in his brush with Webber.

Ferrari came to the Nürburgring hoping for cool and wet conditions which might have allowed Michael Schumacher to capitalise on the potential of the Bridgestone rubber. Yet the weather gods in the Eifel mountains delivered an untypical weekend of sweltering track conditions that played to the strength of the rival Michelin tyres, which were at their best operating in the 38–46°C track-temperature range.

In the event the Ferraris delivered slightly better results than of late but, for the red-capped fans who crowded the grandstands in ritual obeisance to the seven-times champion, this was thin milk indeed.

Coulthard, by contrast, produced one of the best drives of the day, a success made all the more remarkable by the fact that he experienced a drive-through penalty for exceeding the pit-lane speed limit when he came in for his first refuelling stop.

'I was very happy with the start of the race,' said Coulthard. 'I'd said to the team beforehand that I was aiming to stay on the inside of the first corner because we've had incidents at that corner in previous years. We had a very good first sector [of the race] and I was disappointed that I made a mistake in trying to get out in front of a Minardi in the pit lane.

'I came off the speed limiter fractionally early and picked up a penalty which, I think, probably cost us a podium. But we've got to be satisfied with what we've done here today and I'm happy with the result.'

Yet while Coulthard basked in the knowledge of a job well done, Jenson Button and the BAR Honda team had a bruising return after their three-race suspension, proving off the pace and distinctly uncompetitive.

Button was never in the hunt and eventually finished 10th, two places ahead of his team-mate Takuma Sato, which was far from the come-back performance they had been hoping for.

'We thought that we would be reasonably strong here, so today's race has taken us by surprise,' said Button. 'We had a lot of oversteer in the car but also in turn-in we had huge amounts of understeer, so I don't really understand what was going on. I struggled a lot, but at least we made enough progress to move a bit farther up the grid for Canada.

'We have a few new aero parts coming for the next race, so that will help us there, I'm sure. We have a lot of work to do in testing next week and hopefully we will be able to make a bit more of an impact on the grid at Montreal.'

The BAR sporting director Gil de Ferran expressed his views more starkly. 'Our car just wasn't fast enough,' he said. 'At this stage we do not fully understand why, but we will investigate this during tests at Monza and Silverstone this week. Basically, it looks like a case of back to the drawing board.'

Alan Henry

ALLIANZ
GRAND PRIX OF EUROPE

Photograph: Peter van Egmond

NÜRBURGRING 27–29 MAY 2005

NÜRBURGRING – GRAND PRIX CIRCUIT

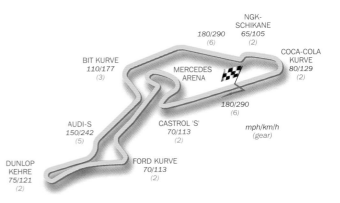

NGK-SCHIKANE 65/105 (2)
BIT KURVE 110/177 (3)
180/290 (6)
COCA-COLA KURVE 80/129 (2)
MERCEDES ARENA
180/290 (6)
AUDI-S 150/242 (5)
CASTROL 'S' 70/113 (2)
mph/km/h (gear)
DUNLOP KEHRE 75/121 (2)
FORD KURVE 70/113 (2)

CIRCUIT LENGTH: 3.199 miles/5.148 km

RACE DISTANCE: 59 laps, 188.199 miles /303.715 km   RACE WEATHER: Sunny with scattered cloud (track 35–36°C, air 24–25°C)

Pos.	Driver	Nat.	No.	Entrant	Car/Engine	Tyres	Laps	Time/Retirement	Speed (mph/km/h)	Gap to leader	Fastest race lap	
1	Fernando Alonso	E	5	Mild Seven Renault F1 Team	Renault R25-RS25 V10	M	59	1h 31m 46.648s	123.376/198.555		1m 30.711s	44
2	Nick Heidfeld	D	8	BMW WilliamsF1 Team	Williams FW27-BMW P84/85 V10	M	59	1h 32m 03.215s	123.006/197.959	+16.567s	1m 31.124s	9
3	Rubens Barrichello	BR	2	Scuderia Ferrari Marlboro	Ferrari F2005-055 V10	B	59	1h 32m 05.197s	122.962/197.888	+18.549s	1m 31.028s	44
4	David Coulthard	GB	14	Red Bull Racing	Red Bull RB1-Cosworth TJ2005/10 V10	M	59	1h 32m 18.236s	122.672/197.422	+31.588s	1m 31.306s	19
5	Michael Schumacher	D	1	Scuderia Ferrari Marlboro	Ferrari F2005-055 V10	B	59	1h 32m 37.093s	122.256/196.752	+50.445s	1m 31.503s	19
6	Giancarlo Fisichella	I	6	Mild Seven Renault F1 Team	Renault R25-RS25 V10	M	59	1h 32m 38.580s	122.224/196.700	+51.932s	1m 31.708s	47
7	Juan Pablo Montoya	COL	10	West McLaren Mercedes	McLaren MP4-20-Mercedes F0 110R V10	M	59	1h 32m 44.821s	122.086/196.479	+58.173s	1m 31.807s	42
8	Jarno Trulli	I	16	Panasonic Toyota Racing	Toyota TF105-RVX-05 V10	M	59	1h 32m 57.739s	121.803/196.024	+71.091s	1m 31.779s	43
9	Vitantonio Liuzzi	I	15	Red Bull Racing	Red Bull RB1-Cosworth TJ2005/10 V10	M	59	1h 32m 58.177s	121.794/196.009	+71.529s	1m 31.971s	43
10	Jenson Button	GB	3	Lucky Strike BAR Honda	BAR 007-Honda RA005E V10	M	59	1h 33m 22.434s	121.267/195.160	+95.786	1m 31.955s	20
11	Kimi Räikkönen	FIN	9	West McLaren Mercedes	McLaren MP4-20-Mercedes F0 110R V10	M	58	Suspension		DNF	1m 30.940s	9
12	Takuma Sato	J	4	Lucky Strike BAR Honda	BAR 007-Honda RA005E V10	M	58			+1 lap	1m 31.889s	26
13	Jacques Villeneuve	CDN	11	Sauber Petronas	Sauber C24-Petronas 05A V10	M	58			+1 lap	1m 32.583s	41
14	Felipe Massa	BR	12	Sauber Petronas	Sauber C24-Petronas 05A V10	M	58			+1 lap	1m 32.329s	18
15	Tiago Monteiro	P	18	Jordan Toyota	Jordan EJ15-Toyota RVX-05 V10	B	58			+1 lap	1m 33.425s	39
16	Narain Karthikeyan	IND	19	Jordan Toyota	Jordan EJ15-Toyota RVX-05 V10	B	58			+1 lap	1m 33.292s	21
17	Christijan Albers	NL	21	Minardi Cosworth	Minardi PS05-Cosworth TJ2005 V10	B	57			+2 laps	1m 35.047s	18
18	Patrick Friesacher	A	20	Minardi Cosworth	Minardi PS05-Cosworth TJ2005 V10	B	56			+3 laps	1m 35.536s	18
	Ralf Schumacher	D	17	Panasonic Toyota Racing	Toyota TF105-RVX-05 V10	M	33	Accident			1m 31.724s	25
	Mark Webber	AUS	7	BMW WilliamsF1 Team	Williams FW26-BMW P84/85 V10	M	0	Accident				

Fastest lap: Fernando Alonso, on lap 44, 1m 30.711s, 126.949 mph/204.305 km/h.

Lap record: Michael Schumacher (Ferrari F2004-052 V10), 1m 29.468s, 128.713 mph/207.144 km/h (2004).

All results and data © FOM 2005

19th: KARTHIKEYAN Jordan-Toyota

17th: MONTEIRO Jordan-Toyota

15th: VILLENEUVE Sauber-Petronas

13th: BUTTON BAR-Honda

11th: MASSA Sauber-Petronas

20th: ALBERS Minardi-Cosworth

18th: FRIESACHER Minardi-Cosworth

16th: SATO BAR-Honda

14th: LIUZZI Red Bull-Cosworth

12th: COULTHARD Red Bull-Cosworth

Grid order	1	2	3	4	5	6	7	8	9	10	11	12	13	14	15	16	17	18	19	20	21	22	23	24	25	26	27	28	29	30	31	32	33	34	35	36	37	38	39	40	41	42	43	44	45	46	4
8 HEIDFELD	9	9	9	9	9	9	9	9	9	9	9	9	9	9	9	9	9	9	9	14	5	5	5	5	9	9	9	9	9	9	9	9	9	9	9	9	9	9	9	9	9	9	9	9	5	5	5
9 RÄIKKÖNEN	8	8	8	8	8	8	8	8	8	14	14	14	14	14	14	5	14	9	9	9	8	8	8	8	8	8	8	9	8	5	5	5	5	5	5	5	5	5	5	9	9	9
7 WEBBER	16	16	16	16	16	16	16	14	14	14	14	14	5	5	5	5	5	9	9	8	8	5	5	5	5	5	5	2	8	8	8	8	8	8	8	8	8	8	5	9	9	9
16 TRULLI	14	14	14	14	14	14	14	5	5	5	5	5	8	8	8	8	8	8	8	14	14	14	2	2	2	2	2	2	2	8	2	2	2	2	2	2	2	2	2	2	2	2
10 MONTOYA	5	5	5	5	5	5	5	16	12	12	12	12	12	12	12	12	12	12	12	1	3	3	3	14	14	14	14	14	14	14	14	14	14	14	14	14	14	14	14	14	14	14	1
5 ALONSO	12	12	12	12	12	12	12	12	2	2	2	15	15	15	15	15	15	15	1	3	6	2	12	12	12	12	12	12	12	12	12	12	12	12	12	12	12	1	1	1
2 BARRICHELLO	15	15	15	15	15	15	2	15	15	15	10	10	10	10	10	10	10	15	6	2	2	12	1	1	1	1	1	1	1	1	1	1	1	1	1	1	1	1	1	12	10	6
17 R. SCHUMACHER	3	3	3	3	3	2	15	10	10	10	16	16	16	16	16	10	1	10	2	12	12	1	10	10	10	10	10	10	10	10	10	10	10	10	10	10	10	10	10	16	3	1
6 FISICHELLA	2	2	2	2	10	10	10	16	16	16	1	1	1	1	1	16	3	12	1	10	15	15	15	15	15	15	15	15	15	15	15	15	15	15	15	15	16	3	12	3
1 M. SCHUMACHER	18	10	10	10	10	3	3	3	3	3	1	3	3	3	3	3	6	10	10	15	16	16	16	16	16	16	16	16	16	16	16	16	16	16	16	16	15	6	10	1
12 MASSA	19	18	1	1	1	1	1	1	3	6	6	6	6	2	15	15	3	3	3	3	3	3	3	3	3	3	3	3	3	3	3	3	12	16	1
14 COULTHARD	11	1	18	6	6	6	6	6	6	2	2	2	2	16	16	6	6	6	6	6	6	6	6	6	6	6	6	6	6	6	15	15
3 BUTTON	10	19	19	18	18	18	18	18	6	18	18	18	18	11	11	11	11	11	4	4	4	4	4	4	4	4	4	4	4	4	4	4
15 LIUZZI	1	11	11	19	19	19	19	19	19	11	11	11	11	11	19	4	17	17	17	17	17	17	11	11	11	11	11	11	11	11	11
11 VILLENEUVE	20	20	6	11	11	11	11	11	19	19	11	19	19	19	4	4	11	11	11	11	11	11	19	19	19	19	19	19	18	18	19
4 SATO	21	6	20	20	20	20	20	20	21	21	21	4	4	4	4	17	19	19	19	19	19	19	18	18	18	18	19	19	19	19	1
18 MONTEIRO	6	21	21	21	21	21	21	20	4	21	17	17	17	17	18	18	18	18	21	21	21	21	21	21	21	21	12
20 FRIESACHER	4	4	4	4	4	4	4	4	17	4	4	21	21	21	17	17	17	17	20	20	20	20	20	20	20	20	20
19 KARTHIKEYAN	17	17	17	17	17	17	17	17	18	17	20	20	20	20	20	20	20	20	20
21 ALBERS																			

QUALIFYING

WEATHER: Sunny (track 41–44°C, air 29–30°C)

Pos.	Driver	R/Order	Sector 1	Sector 2	Sector 3	Time
1	Nick Heidfeld	19	29.737s	37.300s	23.044s	1m 30.081s
2	Kimi Räikkönen	20	29.860s	37.415s	22.922s	1m 30.197s
3	Mark Webber	18	29.767s	37.389s	23.212s	1m 30.368s
4	Jarno Trulli	11	29.793s	37.740s	23.167s	1m 30.700s
5	Juan Pablo Montoya	16	30.019s	37.708s	23.163s	1m 30.890s
6	Fernando Alonso	17	29.987s	37.905s	23.164s	1m 31.056s
7	Rubens Barrichello	13	30.182s	37.701s	23.366s	1m 31.249s
8	Ralf Schumacher	15	29.924s	38.026s	23.442s	1m 31.392s
9	Giancarlo Fisichella	9	30.270s	38.000s	23.296s	1m 31.566s
10	Michael Schumacher	14	29.896s	38.211s	23.478s	1m 31.585s
11	Felipe Massa	12	30.312s	38.267s	23.626s	1m 32.205s
12	David Coulthard	4	30.596s	38.454s	25.503s	1m 32.553s
13	Jenson Button	2	30.336s	38.392s	23.866s	1m 32.594s
14	Vitantonio Liuzzi	6	30.319s	38.278s	24.045s	1m 32.642s
15	Jacques Villeneuve	10	30.594s	38.744s	23.553s	1m 32.891s
16	Takuma Sato	1	30.433s	38.267s	24.226s	1m 32.926s
17	Tiago Monteiro	8	31.198s	39.555s	24.294s	1m 35.047s
18	Patrick Friesacher	5	31.337s	40.254s	24.363s	1m 35.954s
19	Narain Karthikeyan	3	31.521s	40.267s	24.404s	1m 36.192s
20	Christijan Albers	7	31.334s	40.407s	24.498s	1m 36.239s

FERRARI
1	Michael Schumacher	F2005/245
2	Rubens Barrichello	F2005/246
	Spare	F2005/243

BAR-HONDA
3	Jenson Button	007/04
4	Takuma Sato	007/02
	Spare	007/05

RENAULT
5	Fernando Alonso	R25/04
6	Giancarlo Fisichella	R25/06
	Spare	R25/02

WILLIAMS-BMW
7	Mark Webber	FW27/05
8	Nick Heidfeld	FW27/06
	Spare	FW27/04

McLAREN-MERCEDES
9	Kimi Räikkönen	MP4-20/04
10	Juan Pablo Montoya	MP4-20/05
35	Alex Wurz	MP4-20/03
	Spare	MP4-20/06

SAUBER-PETRONAS
11	Jacques Villeneuve	C24/04
12	Felipe Massa	C24/02
	Spare	C24/03

RED BULL-COSWORTH
14	David Coulthard	RB1/3
15	Vitantonio Liuzzi	RB1/1
37	Christian Klien	RB1/2
	Spare	RB1/2

TOYOTA
16	Jarno Trulli	TF105/02
17	Ralf Schumacher	TF105/03
38	Ricardo Zonta	TF105/05
	Spare	TF105/05

JORDAN-TOYOTA
18	Tiago Monteiro	EJ15/03
19	Narain Karthikeyan	EJ15/02
39	Franck Montagny	EJ15/01
	Spare	EJ15/01

MINARDI-COSWORTH
20	Patrick Friesacher	PS05/02
21	Christijan Albers	PS05/01
	Spare	PS04B/03

Photographs: James moy/www.crash.net

PRACTICE 1 (FRIDAY)

Sunny (track 34–38°C, air 26°C)

Pos.	Driver	Laps	Time
1	Alex Wurz	1	1m 31.670s
2	Michael Schumacher	10	1m 32.578s
3	Ricardo Zonta	21	1m 32.726s
4	Juan Pablo Montoya	7	1m 32.873s
5	Rubens Barrichello	11	1m 32.984s
6	Kimi Räikkönen	6	1m 32.988s
7	Nick Heidfeld	5	1m 33.142s
8	Mark Webber	5	1m 33.248s
9	Christian Klien	19	1m 33.304s
10	Ralf Schumacher	11	1m 34.018s
11	Jarno Trulli	9	1m 34.212s
12	Felipe Massa	8	1m 35.142s
13	David Coulthard	7	1m 35.413s
14	Jacques Villeneuve	9	1m 35.716s
15	Vitantonio Liuzzi	12	1m 36.129s
16	Tiago Monteiro	19	1m 37.021s
17	Christijan Albers	15	1m 37.406s
18	Narain Karthikeyan	16	1m 37.474s
19	Patrick Friesacher	15	1m 37.538s
20	Franck Montagny	23	1m 37.725s
21	Takuma Sato	2	No time
22	Jenson Button	2	No time
23	Giancarlo Fisichella	2	No time
24	Fernando Alonso	2	No time

PRACTICE 2 (FRIDAY)

Sunny (track 43–44°C, air 26°C)

Pos.	Driver	Laps	Time
1	Alex Wurz	31	1m 30.623s
2	Ricardo Zonta	33	1m 30.630s
3	Nick Heidfeld	13	1m 31.813s
4	Juan Pablo Montoya	13	1m 31.841s
5	Kimi Räikkönen	16	1m 31.870s
6	Mark Webber	7	1m 32.088s
7	Rubens Barrichello	19	1m 32.143s
8	Fernando Alonso	25	1m 32.335s
9	Giancarlo Fisichella	27	1m 32.842s
10	Ralf Schumacher	17	1m 33.098s
11	Jarno Trulli	20	1m 33.168s
12	Christian Klien	32	1m 33.174s
13	Michael Schumacher	5	1m 33.252s
14	David Coulthard	22	1m 33.430s
15	Takuma Sato	20	1m 33.514s
16	Jenson Button	22	1m 33.753s
17	Franck Montagny	27	1m 34.090s
18	Felipe Massa	26	1m 34.274s
19	Jacques Villeneuve	22	1m 34.645s
20	Tiago Monteiro	17	1m 34.702s
21	Vitantonio Liuzzi	16	1m 34.842s
22	Christijan Albers	19	1m 35.311s
23	Patrick Friesacher	5	1m 35.791s
24	Narain Karthikeyan	8	1m 36.702s

PRACTICE 3 (SATURDAY)

Sunny/windy (track 27–31°C, air 22–24°C)

Pos.	Driver	Laps	Time
1	Fernando Alonso	10	1m 30.615s
2	Juan Pablo Montoya	10	1m 31.278s
3	Kimi Räikkönen	10	1m 31.573s
4	Giancarlo Fisichella	9	1m 31.778s
5	Rubens Barrichello	8	1m 31.794s
6	Michael Schumacher	15	1m 32.097s
7	Mark Webber	9	1m 32.266s
8	Nick Heidfeld	7	1m 32.304s
9	Ralf Schumacher	13	1m 32.432s
10	Takuma Sato	7	1m 32.483s
11	Jenson Button	4	1m 32.501s
12	Jarno Trulli	5	1m 32.719s
13	Felipe Massa	7	1m 33.212s
14	David Coulthard	9	1m 33.365s
15	Vitantonio Liuzzi	5	1m 33.414s
16	Narain Karthikeyan	12	1m 33.681s
17	Jacques Villeneuve	6	1m 33.731s
18	Tiago Monteiro	7	1m 34.407s
19	Christijan Albers	15	1m 34.871s
20	Patrick Friesacher	11	1m 35.067s

PRACTICE 4 (SATURDAY)

Sunny (track 32–36°C, air 25–26°C)

Pos.	Driver	Laps	Time
1	Kimi Räikkönen	11	1m 29.680s
2	Juan Pablo Montoya	13	1m 29.789s
3	Fernando Alonso	15	1m 29.987s
4	Giancarlo Fisichella	14	1m 30.071s
5	Jarno Trulli	12	1m 30.552s
6	Nick Heidfeld	9	1m 30.559s
7	Takuma Sato	12	1m 30.645s
8	Ralf Schumacher	14	1m 30.692s
9	Jenson Button	13	1m 30.773s
10	Michael Schumacher	14	1m 31.026s
11	Rubens Barrichello	10	1m 31.449s
12	Vitantonio Liuzzi	17	1m 31.572s
13	Mark Webber	9	1m 32.054s
14	Felipe Massa	11	1m 32.079s
15	David Coulthard	14	1m 32.172s
16	Jacques Villeneuve	14	1m 33.140s
17	Christijan Albers	16	1m 33.977s
18	Tiago Monteiro	17	1m 34.527s
19	Narain Karthikeyan	12	1m 34.640s
20	Patrick Friesacher	14	1m 35.087s

9th: FISICHELLA Renault
Started from pit lane

7th: BARRICHELLO Ferrari

5th: MONTOYA McLaren-Mercedes

3rd: WEBBER Williams-BMW

Pole: HEIDFELD Williams-BMW

10th: M. SCHUMACHER Ferrari

8th: R. SCHUMACHER Toyota

6th: ALONSO Renault

4th: TRULLI Toyota

2nd: RÄIKKÖNEN McLaren-Mercedes

8	49	50	51	52	53	54	55	56	57	58	59	
9	9	9	9	9	9	9	9	9	9	9	5	1
8	8	8	5	5	5	5	5	5	5	5	8	2
2	5	5	8	8	8	8	8	8	8	8	2	3
5	2	2	2	2	2	2	2	2	2	2	14	4
14	14	14	14	14	14	14	14	14	14	14	1	5
6	6	6	1	1	1	1	1	1	1	6	6	6
1	1	1	6	6	6	6	6	6	6	10	10	7
12	12	10	10	10	10	10	10	10	10	10	16	8
10	10	12	12	16	16	16	16	16	16	16	15	
16	16	16	16	12	12	15	15	15	15	15	3	
15	15	15	15	15	15	3	3	3	3	3		
3	3	3	3	3	3	4	4	4	4			
4	4	4	4	4	4	12	11	11	11	11		
11	11	11	11	11	11	11	12	12	12	12		
19	19	19	19	19	19	19	19	19	18	18		
18	18	18	18	18	18	18	18	19	19	19		
21	21	21	21	21	21	21	21	21	21			
20	20	20	20	20	20	20	20					

Pit stop

One lap or more behind leader

FIRST LEAD LAP, FIRST GRAND PRIX POLE, 50th POINT: Nick Heidfeld

Photograph: James Moy/www.crash.net

DRIVERS
1	Fernando Alonso	59
2	Kimi Räikkönen	27
3	Jarno Trulli	27
4	Nick Heidfeld	25
5	Mark Webber	18
6	Giancarlo Fisichella	17
7	Ralf Schumacher	17
8	Michael Schumacher	16
9	Juan Pablo Montoya	16
10	Rubens Barrichello	15
11	David Coulthard	15
12	Alex Wurz	6
13	Jacques Villeneuve	6
14	Pedro de la Rosa	4
15	Christian Klien	3
16	Felipe Massa	2
17	Vitantonio Liuzzi	1

CONSTRUCTORS
1	Renault	76
2	McLaren	53
3	Toyota	44
4	Williams	43
5	Ferrari	31
6	Red Bull	19
7	Sauber	7

Photograph: Peter van Egmond

Kimi Räikkönen got his championship
hopes back on track at Montreal with a
close win ahead of Michael Schumacher
after a race in which the safety car helped
the German driver make up a lot of time.
Photograph: James Moy/www.crash.net

MONTREAL
CANADIANGP

FIA F1 WORLD CHAMPIONSHIP/ROUND 8

Right: Jenson and his father John Button celebrated the boy's pole-winning efforts.
Photograph: Paul-Henri Cahier

Centre right: Scott Speed, the young American GP2 driver, made his F1 debut as Red Bull's third driver on the Friday.
Photograph: James Moy/www.crash.net

Bottom left: Sir Frank Williams found himself in a politically delicate situation over his team's relationship with BMW.
Photograph: Jean-François Galeron/WRi

MONTREAL QUALIFYING

Jenson Button's run to pole on this circuit was achieved despite running higher levels of downforce than one might have expected, a tactic intended to protect his choice of hard-compound Michelin tyres from excessive wear in the gruelling conditions. Giancarlo Fisichella's Renault R25, which qualified fourth, registered the highest top speed, 205 mph (330 km/h), with Button 16th out of the 20 runners on 198 mph (318 km/h).

The BAR team's return to competitive form after the humiliation of a three-race ban for a fuel-system rule infringement had involved a certain amount of technical back-tracking. Prior to the San Marino GP, where Button had finished third before being disqualified, the team had enjoyed a highly productive test at the Mugello circuit, but it had since lost its way aerodynamically. At the recent Silverstone and Monza tests, the team returned to that Mugello baseline and it now seemed to be paying off.

'I'm thrilled to be back on pole,' said Button. 'The past few months have been difficult for all of us at BAR Honda and everyone has worked so hard to turn our performance around. It felt like a good lap but the circuit had quite low grip, so I was a little surprised, to be honest. I don't know if we are quick enough yet for the victory, but it will be interesting to see how far we can take today's result.'

For Michael Schumacher, second-fastest qualifying time meant that he returned the Ferrari F2005 to the front row of the starting grid for the first time since its debut race in Bahrain over two months earlier. He was happy that the Ferrari at last seemed to be making progress, but he was concerned about its potential reliability after both he and team-mate Rubens Barrichello suffered gearbox failures, the Brazilian driver's breakage thwarting his qualifying run and pushing him to the back of the grid.

Together on the second row were the well-matched Renault R25s of Fernando Alonso (1m 15.561s) and Giancarlo Fisichella (1m 15.577s). 'It was a good Saturday practice this morning with very good long runs and a good pace,' said Alonso. 'Then in qualifying it was obviously very difficult to know about the fuel loads of other people, but we are quite happy with our strategy, I think, for the race. Everything is going well for the team – we are third and fourth, we are very confident with everything in the car and at the moment it all looks perfect for us.'

In fifth and seventh places, sandwiching the BAR-Honda of Takuma Sato, were the McLaren MP4-20s of Juan Pablo Montoya (1m 15.669s) and Kimi Räikkönen (1m 15.923s). 'I am quite pleased with my lap and I'm sure that we will have a good race, because the strategy should be strong,' said Montoya. 'The aim is to have a nice, quiet and uneventful grand prix and get on the podium.' Some hope, as things turned out.

Räikkönen was looking forward to the points battle with Alonso. 'Of course I would have liked a better grid position, but we have a strong race strategy which will give us every opportunity to get a good result,' said Kimi. 'My battle is with Fernando, so I need to make sure I finish in front of him. Unlike this morning, I struggled slightly to get my tyres up to working temperature during my qualifying lap, but the package has been working well so far this weekend, so I'm reasonably optimistic.'

In eighth place, Jacques Villeneuve delivered what he reckoned was his personal best qualifying effort of the season so far, his 1m 16.116s slotting him in ahead of the Toyota duo Jarno Trulli (1m 16.201s) and Ralf Schumacher (1m 16.362s).

'I missed out on some running in the morning sessions due to an electronics problem,' said Trulli, 'so I'm satisfied with the lap, which was a pretty good one. I was struggling to get heat into the tyres on my warm-up lap, but I did my best.'

In a lowly 13th and 14th, behind David Coulthard's Red Bull, were the hapless Williams-BMWs of Nick Heidfeld (1m 17.081s) and Mark Webber (1m 17.749s), both of whom were struggling for handling balance and grip on this low-drag circuit.

In the Minardi camp there were broad grins all around after Christijan Albers stormed his PS05 to a superb 15th fastest (1m 18.214s) after a performance which impressed even Barrichello with the Cosworth-engined car's straight-line speed.

'We were struggling a little bit at the start of the weekend on worn tyres and saving the engine, but then this afternoon we got it together over one lap on new tyres and with maximum power,' said Albers. 'The team did a great job.'

By contrast his team-mate Patrick Friesacher was hobbled by what he felt was excessive oversteer, and managed only 19th on 1m 19.574s. Separating the Minardis were Christian Klien's Red Bull and the Jordans of Narain Karthikeyan and Tiago Monteiro. Klien had run first in qualifying on a dirty track and both Jordan lads reckoned their cars felt okay, but not really quick enough.

DIARY

David Richards dismisses speculation that he is considering standing against Max Mosley in the forthcoming FIA presidential election.

Indy 500 winner Dan Wheldon indicates that he would like the chance of an F1 test should the opportunity present itself.

WILLIAMS-BMW ALLIANCE IN STORMY WATER

Over the Montreal weekend, Frank Williams moved diplomatically to dissociate himself from comments reportedly made by his engineering chief Patrick Head accusing BMW of having 'a dishonest approach'.

'The remarks made by Patrick were private and absolutely do not reflect the position of this company in respect to Mario Theissen [BMW motorsport director] or to BMW,' said Williams. 'One particular remark was taken slightly out of context.'

He added, 'I have frequently said BMW are tough, hard people and that is why they have a rich and very profitable company. How many pushovers in life do you know who are multi-millionaires or billionaires? They are all hard people; that is how you get the job done.'

However, sources close to BMW confirmed the damage to the relationship with Williams was now terminal and it was just a question of when, and not if, the relationship came to an end. Speculation intensified that BMW was close to agreeing a buyout of the Sauber team, but spokesmen for both sides said at the Canadian Grand Prix that rumours of a $270-million takeover's being agreed were unfounded.

Theissen admitted he was surprised to hear of Head's criticism. 'I heard about this interview [containing the comment] when I arrived here,' he said at the Circuit Gilles Villeneuve. 'I have not spoken to Patrick. He has not called me. What do you expect me to say?'

KIMI Räikkönen dramatically reversed the course of the world championship battle when he stormed to victory in the Canadian Grand Prix at the Circuit Gilles Villeneuve. His McLaren-Mercedes MP4-20 took the chequered flag 1.137s ahead of Michael Schumacher's Ferrari F2005, which had dramatically made up 31s at a stroke after pressuring Jenson Button's BAR-Honda to the point where the British driver crashed into the wall and the safety car was deployed.

The Finn scored his third win of the year at the expense of his team-mate Juan Pablo Montoya, who seemed as though he was cruising to an easy victory when the safety car went out, but a scrambled strategy left him out a lap longer than was ideal. Agitated and annoyed, Montoya came in the next time around, only to ignore the red warning light at the exit of the pit lane, a transgression which resulted in his being black-flagged and excluded, a penalty which certainly took the edge off the McLaren team's subsequent victory celebrations.

Despite this, McLaren was delighted with Räikkönen's success and the fact that he had reduced Fernando Alonso's championship lead by ten points to just 22 points on a day when the Spanish driver made a rare error while leading the race – he glanced a wall and broke his right-rear suspension in the impact.

It was a bitter day for the Renault team. Giancarlo Fisichella led the opening stages ahead of Alonso, then succumbed to mechanical problems a few laps before Alonso made his slip. The high rate of attrition enabled Rubens Barrichello to finish a fantastic third in the second Ferrari, having started from the pit lane behind the whole field after suffering a gearbox breakage during qualifying.

With track temperatures nudging the 46°C mark, and in front of a capacity crowd, Button confidently took up his place on pole position and, as the starting lights went out, cleanly accelerated away on the racing line to take an immediate, if momentary, lead.

Yet as the BAR driver chopped right to cover Schumacher's Ferrari, the front-row cars were swamped from both sides by the fast-starting Renaults of Fisichella and Alonso, who simply rocketed into first and second places as they jostled for position into the first tight left-hander.

As the rest of the pack sorted itself out in a great jumble of cars at the first turn, the two Renaults streaked out onto the back straight in tight formation and Fisichella duly burst through the final ess-bend before the pits to complete the opening lap already 0.7s ahead of Alonso. Button was third ahead of the two McLarens, Montoya just ahead of Räikkönen, and Schumacher's Ferrari, which simply didn't have a hope of matching the Renault or McLaren pace at the front of the field.

For the opening phase the Renaults' sheer pace left onlookers speculating over precisely what refuelling strategy the leading runners had adopted. Button was hanging on well for the first few laps and even though he could not match the pace of the dominant French machines it became clear that this was not because the BAR was heavy with fuel. Button would last only until lap 15, when he made an early stop to refuel for the first time, dropping him to sixth place and allowing the two McLaren drivers a clear track on which to target the Renaults ahead of them.

Alonso made his first refuelling stop from second place at the end of lap 24, while Fisichella and Montoya came in to top up from first and second places next time around. Giancarlo resumed in the lead with Alonso back in second place, but he managed only another seven laps at the head of the field before his car slowed dramatically and he cruised in to retire.

'I am obviously very disappointed,' said Fisichella, who had yet again been thwarted in his bid to revive his winning form. 'I had a fantastic start, then I pushed only reasonably hard in order to save my brakes and my tyres. When I pitted [for the first stop], we put a lot of fuel on board – this was the best strategy for us.

'Unfortunately, a few laps later, the gearbox started not working properly. It was a hydraulic failure and the only thing I could do was go back to the pits to retire. This is particularly frustrating because I feel I could have won today. Moreover, I'll be among the first drivers to take to the track in qualifying at Indianapolis and that will be tough.'

Above: Juan Pablo Montoya looked on course for a win until a mistimed pit call triggered a sequence of events that eventually left him excluded for leaving the pits against a red warning light.
Photograph: James Moy/www.crash.net

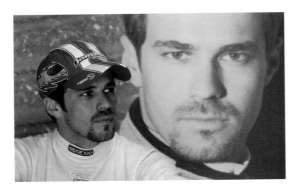

That put Alonso back into the lead. On lap 33 he was 1.52s ahead of Montoya, but Juan Pablo cut that back to 0.98s next time around. Yet Fernando seemed well up to the challenge, extending his edge to 1.2s, 1.3s, 2.3s and 2.6s on successive laps. Then on lap 39 Montoya came through in the lead, 4.88s ahead of Räikkönen. Alonso had glanced the wall at Turn Four and was out of the battle.

'Not a good day for me,' said the championship leader. 'When the [starting] light went off, the electronic system on my car had a problem and I lost a bit of time. Then, during my pit stop, the fuel rig had a problem. In the end, I went too wide. I touched the wall and damaged the car. It's a very disappointing result, because the weekend was almost perfect until then.'

Montoya was now left cruising confidently at the head of the field, a couple of seconds clear of his team-mate and eventual winner Kimi Räikkönen. Then the safety car was deployed on lap 47, after Jenson Button crashed his BAR-Honda on the fast left-hander in front of the pits while battling with Michael Schumacher's Ferrari for third place behind the two McLarens.

From the BBC Five Live radio commentary box overlooking the final corner, BAR test driver Anthony Davidson heard the flat burble of Button's traction control cutting in unexpectedly as Button's car skipped over the inside kerb, which immediately threw him out too wide to make the exit of the turn.

Davidson had the words out of his mouth in warning almost before the car slammed off the track, leaving Button with his world-championship points score still firmly stuck on zero and his own personal ambitions again apparently thwarted.

'It was completely my mistake,' said Button, 'and was very frustrating because we were looking good. My start wasn't great and the Renaults got better traction off the line, which allowed them to leapfrog me. To end the day with no points is frustrating but we have to look at the positives from the weekend. We have made real progress and now have to work hard to make the most of that at Indy.'

A closer analysis of the Montreal race suggested that Button's assessment of his car's competitive level might be optimistic. He was running third only after the retirement of both Renault R25s and it was clear that the BAR 007 simply did not yet have the speed to get on terms with either the Renault or the McLaren Mercedes teams in a straight fight characterised by total consistency and reliability.

'We are disappointed not to finish the race,' said Gil de Ferran, BAR Honda's sporting director. 'However, that's racing and the overwhelming feeling as we leave Canada and head to the US is a very positive one. Overall, our performance was much improved from the last race and we were challenging at the front of the field throughout the weekend. Hopefully that's where we will be at Indianapolis.'

At the moment the safety car was sent out, Montoya's McLaren was about ten seconds short of the pit lane and the decision was immediately made to call him in from the lead to refuel before the safety car accelerated out onto the track.

Unfortunately the engineers did not warn him in time, with the result that he missed the pit entrance and had to do an extra lap before stopping. Meanwhile Räikkönen did come in to

refuel. Montoya accidentally left the pits following his own stop while the red light was showing at the exit. Shortly afterwards, Montoya was black-flagged and disqualified from the race.

'We decided to slow the pace of both cars after Kimi's developed an apparent slight steering problem,' said Ron Dennis, McLaren chairman. 'After the Renaults went out of the race, Juan Pablo and Kimi were driving for a one-two finish and were not racing one another. Managing that is not as simple as you might think, because there were two guys who wanted to race and that inevitably put a bit of tension onto the pit wall.

'The team personnel who managed Juan Pablo's car just missed the call, with the result that he did not come in as we intended him to. He then exited the pits under a red light, but it is the stewards who determine the penalty. At the end of the day, a black flag is disqualification and we have to accept it.

'As a team, we have to apologise to Juan Pablo, but perhaps that is balanced by his rejoining the circuit against the red light.'

All this drama with the McLarens helped move Michael Schumacher into second place ahead of Jarno Trulli's Toyota TF105 and the other Ferrari F2005 of Rubens Barrichello. Trulli's hopes of a podium finish were dashed when a front brake disc exploded on lap 62, as he was approaching the braking area for the ess-bend before the pits, fortunately where there is a large run-off area available.

'That was a real pity for me and the team,' shrugged Jarno. 'We were looking quite good and all set for the podium when I suffered the brake failure. The brakes had been fine up to that point and there was no wear problem. It was just a failure. It's disappointing to lose out on three podiums in three races, but that's motor racing.'

Räikkönen, meanwhile, was left to cruise home to the chequered flag 1.137s ahead of Schumacher, with Barrichello joining them on the podium in third place. The battle for fourth was a close one, Felipe Massa's Sauber C24 just fending off Mark Webber's Williams-BMW by 0.640s, these two being the last unlapped runners at the chequered flag.

'I just couldn't generate enough heat in the rear tyres after the safety car went in,' said Massa, 'and I had Webber right behind me all the way. They were the toughest 15 laps of my life. In the last corner I could see he was going to try something but I was able to discourage that and hold him off.' Earlier, Nick Heidfeld had spent too long running close up in Massa's slipstream, with the result that the BMW engine overheated and eventually failed, despite his efforts to keep in clear air for as much of the time as possible.

Ralf Schumacher climbed back to sixth after a slow start, moderately satisfied with his efforts, while the Red Bull RB1s of David Coulthard and Christian Klien completed the list of points scorers. DC found the race tough and challenging throughout, having struggled for much of the day with too much oversteer, but was otherwise happy to have kept up a reasonable pace. Klien judged it one of the toughest races he'd ever experienced, battling with indifferent grip and excessive understeer.

A disappointed ninth was Jacques Villeneuve, who proved unable to capitalise on his high grid position. 'At the start, the grip was poorer than I expected and the car just didn't want to get off the line, so I lost ground immediately,' he reported.

'Then in the first corner, [Takuma] Sato came across me and damaged the front wing, so I had to pit for a replacement nose section. That was a great pity because the car was fast today. At the end I could attack Klien, but he was exiting the corners well and I could never quite get close enough to challenge him.'

For his part, Sato ran eighth from the start after the contact with Villeneuve's Sauber damaged his diffuser and rear wing. Later, he made a lengthy stop to change his gearbox and resumed many laps down to gather data, but then spun off when the rear end locked up.

Montoya had calmed down by the time he left Montreal, Ron Dennis's soothing words having struck precisely the right note. After all, Indianapolis now beckoned, a few days down the road. Things would be better there, surely?

Alan Henry

Above: **Mark Webber tried hard in his Williams-BMW FW27, but couldn't quite get on terms with Felipe Massa and had to settle for a slightly disappointed fifth at the chequered flag.**
Photograph: James Moy/www.crash.net

Michael Schumacher and Rubens Barrichello shook hands after finishing strongly in second and third places.
Photograph: James Moy/www.crash.net

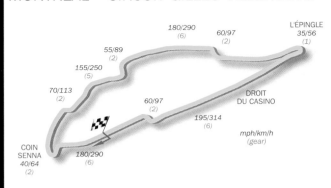

MONTREAL – CIRCUIT GILLES VILLENEUVE

L'ÉPINGLE 35/56 (1)
180/290 (6)
60/97 (2)
55/89 (2)
155/250 (5)
70/113 (2)
60/97 (2)
DROIT DU CASINO
195/314 (6)
mph/km/h (gear)
COIN SENNA 40/64 (2)
180/290 (6)

CIRCUIT LENGTH: 2.709 miles/4.361 km

Photograph: James Moy/www.crash.net

FIA F1 WORLD CHAMPIONSHIP • ROUND 8

GRAND PRIX DU CANADA
MONTREAL 10–12 JUNE 2005

RACE DISTANCE: 70 laps, 189.686 miles /305.270 km   RACE WEATHER: Sunny with high cloud (track 41–42°C, air 31–32°C)

All results and data © FOM 2005

Pos.	Driver	Nat.	No.	Entrant	Car/Engine	Tyres	Laps	Time/Retirement	Speed (mph/km/h)	Gap to leader	Fastest race lap	
1	Kimi Räikkönen	FIN	9	West McLaren Mercedes	McLaren MP4-20-Mercedes FO 110R V10	M	70	1h 32m 09.290s	123.500/198.754		1m 14.384s	23
2	Michael Schumacher	D	1	Scuderia Ferrari Marlboro	Ferrari F2005-055 V10	B	70	1h 32m 10.427s	123.474/198.713	+1.137s	1m 14.868s	32
3	Rubens Barrichello	BR	2	Scuderia Ferrari Marlboro	Ferrari F2005-055 V10	B	70	1h 32m 49.773s	122.602/197.309	+40.483s	1m 15.480s	46
4	Felipe Massa	BR	12	Sauber Petronas	Sauber C24-Petronas 05A V10	M	70	1h 33m 04.429s	122.281/196.792	+55.139s	1m 16.008s	18
5	Mark Webber	AUS	7	BMW WilliamsF1 Team	Williams FW27-BMW P84/85 V10	M	70	1h 33m 05.069s	122.266/196.769	+55.779s	1m 15.401s	23
6	Ralf Schumacher	D	17	Panasonic Toyota Racing	Toyota TF105-RVX-05 V10	M	69			+1 lap	1m 15.827s	44
7	David Coulthard	GB	14	Red Bull Racing	Red Bull RB1-Cosworth TJ2005/10 V10	M	69			+1 lap	1m 16.414s	17
8	Christian Klien	A	15	Red Bull Racing	Red Bull RB1-Cosworth TJ2005/10 V10	M	69			+1 lap	1m 16.299s	46
9	Jacques Villeneuve	CDN	11	Sauber Petronas	Sauber C24-Petronas 05A V10	M	69			+1 lap	1m 15.945s	26
10	Tiago Monteiro	P	18	Jordan Toyota	Jordan EJ15-Toyota RVX-05 V10	B	67			+3 laps	1m 17.344s	19
11	Christijan Albers	NL	21	Minardi Cosworth	Minardi PS05-Cosworth TJ2005 V10	B	67			+3 laps	1m 18.462s	15
	Jarno Trulli	I	16	Panasonic Toyota Racing	Toyota TF105-RVX05 V10	M	62	Brakes			1m 15.872s	43
	Jenson Button	GB	3	Lucky Strike BAR Honda	BAR 007-Honda RA005E V10	M	46	Accident			1m 15.189s	30
	Nick Heidfeld	D	8	BMW WilliamsF1 Team	Williams FW27-BMW P84/85 V10	M	43	Engine			1m 15.752s	20
	Takuma Sato	J	4	Lucky Strike BAR Honda	BAR 007-Honda RA005E V10	M	40	Gearbox			1m 16.044s	14
	Patrick Friesacher	A	20	Minardi Cosworth	Minardi PS05-Cosworth TJ2005 V10	B	39	Hydraulics			1m 18.709s	33
	Fernando Alonso	E	5	Mild Seven Renault F1 Team	Renault R25-RS25 V10	M	38	Accident			1m 14.727s	38
	Giancarlo Fisichella	I	6	Mild Seven Renault F1 Team	Renault R25-RS25 V10	M	32	Hydraulics			1m 14.890s	24
	Narain Karthikeyan	IND	19	Jordan Toyota	Jordan EJ15-Toyota RVX-05 V10	B	24	Electronics			1m 17.015s	20
DQ	Juan Pablo Montoya	COL	10	West McLaren Mercedes	McLaren MP4-20-Mercedes FO 110R V10	M	52	left pitlane against red light			1m 14.576s	24

Fastest lap: Kimi Räikkönen, on lap 23, 1m 14.384s, 131.147 mph/211.061 km/h.

Lap record: Rubens Barrichello (Ferrari F2004-052 V10), 1m 13.622s, 132.505 mph/206.682 km/h (2004).

19th: FRIESACHER Minardi-Cosworth

17th: KARTHIKEYAN Jordan-Toyota

15th: ALBERS Minardi-Cosworth

13th: HEIDFELD Williams-BMW

11th: MASSA Sauber-Petronas

20th: BARRICHELLO Ferrari
Started from pit lane

18th: MONTEIRO Jordan-Toyota

16th: KLIEN Red Bull-Cosworth

14th: WEBBER Williams-BMW

12th: COULTHARD Red Bull-Cosworth

Grid order	1	2	3	4	5	6	7	8	9	10	11	12	13	14	15	16	17	18	19	20	21	22	23	24	25	26	27	28	29	30	31	32	33	34	35	36	37	38	39	40	41	42	43	44	45	46	47	48	49	50	51	52	53	54
3 BUTTON	6	6	6	6	6	6	6	6	6	6	6	6	6	6	6	6	6	6	6	6	6	6	6	6	6	6	6	6	6	6	6	6	6	5	5	5	5	5	10	10	10	10	10	10	10	10	10	9	9	9	9	9	9	9
1 M. SCHUMACHER	5	5	5	5	5	5	5	5	5	5	5	5	5	5	5	5	5	5	5	5	5	5	5	10	10	5	5	5	5	5	5	10	10	10	10	10	10	9	9	9	9	9	9	9	9	9	10	10	10	10	1	1		
5 ALONSO	3	3	3	3	3	3	3	3	3	3	3	3	3	3	10	10	10	10	10	10	10	10	10	5	10	10	10	10	10	10	10	9	9	9	9	9	3	3	3	3	3	3	3	3	1	1	1	1	1	1	16	16		
6 FISICHELLA	10	10	10	10	10	10	10	10	10	10	10	10	10	9	9	9	9	9	9	9	9	9	9	9	9	9	9	9	9	9	9	3	3	3	3	3	1	1	1	1	1	1	1	1	16	16	16	16	16	16	2	2		
10 MONTOYA	9	9	9	9	9	9	9	9	9	9	9	9	9	16	16	16	16	16	16	16	16	16	3	3	3	3	3	3	3	3	3	1	1	1	1	1	16	16	16	16	16	16	16	12	7	7	7	7	2	12	12			
4 SATO	1	1	1	1	1	1	1	1	1	1	1	16	16	16	4	3	3	3	3	3	1	1	1	1	1	1	1	1	1	1	16	16	16	16	16	12	12	12	12	12	12	12	7	12	12	12	12	12	7					
9 RÄIKKÖNEN	16	16	16	16	16	16	16	16	16	16	4	4	4	3	12	12	12	12	12	1	1	7	7	7	7	7	16	16	16	16	12	12	12	12	12	8	8	8	8	17	17	7	17	2	17	17	17	17	17					
11 VILLENEUVE	4	4	4	4	4	4	4	4	4	4	12	12	12	12	8	8	8	7	7	16	16	16	16	16	2	2	2	12	12	8	8	8	8	17	17	17	17	17	7	7	7	17	2	17	17	17	17	17	14	14				
16 TRULLI	12	12	12	12	12	12	12	12	12	12	8	8	8	8	14	14	1	1	1	4	2	2	2	2	2	7	7	12	8	17	17	17	17	17	7	7	7	8	2	17	17	14	14	14	14	14	15	15						
17 R. SCHUMACHER	8	8	8	8	8	8	8	8	8	8	17	17	17	14	1	1	7	7	12	12	12	12	12	12	12	12	8	17	7	7	7	7	7	2	2	2	2	14	14	14	15	15	15	15	15	15	11	11						
12 MASSA	14	17	17	17	17	17	17	17	14	14	14	14	14	7	4	4	4	8	8	8	8	8	8	8	8	17	2	2	2	2	2	2	14	14	14	15	15	15	11	11	11	11	11	11	18									
14 COULTHARD	17	14	14	14	14	14	14	14	14	14	1	1	1	7	4	15	15	2	17	17	17	17	17	17	17	2	14	14	14	14	14	15	15	15	11	11	11	11	18	18	18	18	21	21	21									
8 HEIDFELD	11	7	7	7	7	7	7	7	7	7	7	7	7	2	2	17	17	17	14	14	14	14	14	14	14	14	11	11	11	11	11	11	11	11	18	18	21	21	21	21	21	21												
7 WEBBER	7	15	15	15	15	15	15	15	15	15	15	15	15	2	2	2	17	14	15	15	15	15	15	15	15	11	11	11	11	11	11	18	18	21	21	21	21	21																
21 ALBERS	15	21	21	21	21	21	2	2	2	2	2	2	17	17	14	14	15	11	11	11	11	11	11	11	18	18	18	18	18	18	21	21	21																				
15 KLIEN	21	19	19	19	2	2	2	21	21	21	21	21	2	15	15	15	11	19	19	18	18	18	18	18	21	21	21	21	21	20	4																						
19 KARTHIKEYAN	20	2	2	2	19	19	19	18	18	18	18	18	19	19	19	11	19	19	11	19	19	11	11	18	21	21	21	21	20	20	20	20	20	4																			
18 MONTEIRO	19	20	20	20	18	18	18	19	19	19	19	19	11	18	18	18	11	18	21	21	21	21	20	20	20	20	4	4	4	4	4	4																					
20 FRIESACHER	2	18	18	18	20	20	20	20	20	20	11	11	11	11	21	21	21	21	21	21	21	20	20	4	4	4	4	4	4	4																								
2 BARRICHELLO	18	11	11	11	11	11	11	11	11	11	20	20	20	20	20	20	20	4	4	4																																		

Pit stop
One lap or more behind leader

QUALIFYING

WEATHER: Sunny with high cloud (track 46–47°C, air 31–32°C)

Pos.	Driver	R/Order	Sector 1	Sector 2	Sector 3	Time
1	Jenson Button	12	21.109s	24.005s	30.103s	1m 15.217s
2	Michael Schumacher	16	21.349s	24.076s	30.050s	1m 15.475s
3	Fernando Alonso	20	21.302s	24.276s	29.983s	1m 15.561s
4	Giancarlo Fisichella	15	21.219s	24.324s	30.034s	1m 15.577s
5	Juan Pablo Montoya	14	21.432s	24.094s	30.143s	1m 15.669s
6	Takuma Sato	10	21.331s	24.125s	30.273s	1m 15.729s
7	Kimi Räikkönen	11	21.379s	24.214s	30.330s	1m 15.923s
8	Jacques Villeneuve	9	21.538s	24.404s	30.174s	1m 16.116s
9	Jarno Trulli	13	21.470s	24.341s	30.390s	1m 16.201s
10	Ralf Schumacher	3	21.481s	24.437s	30.444s	1m 16.362s
11	Felipe Massa	8	21.616s	24.518s	30.527s	1m 16.661s
12	David Coulthard	17	21.853s	24.550s	30.487s	1m 16.890s
13	Nick Heidfeld	19	21.585s	24.535s	30.961s	1m 17.081s
14	Mark Webber	2	21.694s	25.351s	30.704s	1m 17.749s
15	Christijan Albers	5	22.022s	25.093s	31.099s	1m 18.214s
16	Christian Klien	1	22.015s	24.992s	31.242s	1m 18.249s
17	Narain Karthikeyan	6	22.228s	25.259s	31.177s	1m 18.664s
18	Tiago Monteiro	7	22.476s	25.209s	31.349s	1m 19.034s
19	Patrick Friesacher	4	22.497s	25.546s	31.531s	1m 19.574s
20	Rubens Barrichello	18	25.469s	26.674s	-	No time

FERRARI
1	Michael Schumacher	F2005/245
2	Rubens Barrichello	F2005/246
	Spare	F2005/243

BAR-HONDA
3	Jenson Button	007/04
4	Takuma Sato	007/05
	Spare	007/02

RENAULT
5	Fernando Alonso	R25/04
6	Giancarlo Fisichella	R25/06
	Spare	R25/02

WILLIAMS-BMW
7	Mark Webber	FW27/05
8	Nick Heidfeld	FW27/06
	Spare	FW27/04

McLAREN-MERCEDES
9	Kimi Räikkönen	MP4-20/04
10	Juan Pablo Montoya	MP4-20/05
35	Alex Wurz	MP4-20/03
	Spare	MP4-20/03

SAUBER-PETRONAS
11	Jacques Villeneuve	C24/04
12	Felipe Massa	C24/06
	Spare	C24/03

RED BULL-COSWORTH
14	David Coulthard	RB1/3
15	Christian Klien	RB1/1
37	Scott Speed	RB1/2
	Spare	RB1/2

TOYOTA
16	Jarno Trulli	TF105/02
17	Ralf Schumacher	TF105/03
38	Ricardo Zonta	TF105/05
	Spare	TF105/05

JORDAN-TOYOTA
18	Tiago Monteiro	EJ15/03
19	Narain Karthikeyan	EJ15/02
	Spare	EJ15/01

MINARDI-COSWORTH
20	Patrick Friesacher	PS05/02
21	Christijan Albers	PS05/01
	Spare	PS04B/03

Photograph: James Moy/www.crash.net

PRACTICE 1 (FRIDAY)
Sunny, breezy (track 36–37°C, air 28°C)

Pos.	Driver	Laps	Time
1	Pedro de la Rosa	26	1m 16.415s
2	Ricardo Zonta	27	1m 16.584s
3	Kimi Räikkönen	10	1m 16.677s
4	Jenson Button	11	1m 16.710s
5	Michael Schumacher	12	1m 16.872s
6	Juan Pablo Montoya	10	1m 16.945s
7	Giancarlo Fisichella	6	1m 17.281s
8	Takuma Sato	10	1m 17.458s
9	Ralf Schumacher	10	1m 17.497s
10	Rubens Barrichello	11	1m 17.541s
11	Nick Heidfeld	5	1m 17.739s
12	Jarno Trulli	6	1m 18.049s
13	Mark Webber	6	1m 18.138s
14	Felipe Massa	8	1m 18.252s
15	Scott Speed	22	1m 18.499s
16	Jacques Villeneuve	7	1m 18.732s
17	Christian Klien	10	1m 19.212s
18	David Coulthard	10	1m 19.694s
19	Narain Karthikeyan	21	1m 19.791s
20	Patrick Friesacher	12	1m 21.990s
21	Christijan Albers	18	1m 22.452s
22	Tiago Monteiro	5	1m 23.152s
23	Fernando Alonso	2	No time

PRACTICE 2 (FRIDAY)
Sunny, windy (track 41–43°C, air 30–31°C)

Pos.	Driver	Laps	Time
1	Pedro de la Rosa	30	1m 14.662s
2	Ricardo Zonta	33	1m 14.858s
3	Fernando Alonso	33	1m 15.376s
4	Juan Pablo Montoya	18	1m 15.625s
5	Kimi Räikkönen	21	1m 15.679s
6	Giancarlo Fisichella	32	1m 15.846s
7	Jenson Button	32	1m 16.190s
8	Takuma Sato	32	1m 16.313s
9	Ralf Schumacher	23	1m 16.364s
10	Rubens Barrichello	23	1m 16.459s
11	Jarno Trulli	26	1m 16.638s
12	Mark Webber	30	1m 16.661s
13	Jacques Villeneuve	23	1m 16.718s
14	Felipe Massa	29	1m 16.727s
15	Nick Heidfeld	26	1m 16.826s
16	Michael Schumacher	26	1m 17.200s
17	David Coulthard	27	1m 17.299s
18	Christian Klien	26	1m 17.922s
19	Patrick Friesacher	25	1m 18.115s
20	Narain Karthikeyan	28	1m 18.234s
21	Christijan Albers	22	1m 18.463s
22	Tiago Monteiro	30	1m 19.186s
23	Scott Speed	15	1m 19.270s

PRACTICE 3 (SATURDAY)
Sunny (track 32–34°C, air 26–27°C)

Pos.	Driver	Laps	Time
1	Fernando Alonso	13	1m 15.582s
2	Giancarlo Fisichella	8	1m 15.758s
3	Kimi Räikkönen	9	1m 15.826s
4	Takuma Sato	10	1m 16.109s
5	Jenson Button	5	1m 16.386s
6	Mark Webber	9	1m 16.463s
7	Michael Schumacher	9	1m 16.538s
8	Nick Heidfeld	8	1m 16.569s
9	Juan Pablo Montoya	8	1m 16.749s
10	Felipe Massa	5	1m 16.816s
11	Ralf Schumacher	9	1m 16.999s
12	Jarno Trulli	5	1m 17.441s
13	Jacques Villeneuve	6	1m 17.469s
14	Christian Klien	9	1m 17.595s
15	Rubens Barrichello	10	1m 17.908s
16	David Coulthard	9	1m 17.992s
17	Narain Karthikeyan	11	1m 18.338s
18	Tiago Monteiro	15	1m 18.710s
19	Patrick Friesacher	14	1m 21.031s
20	Christijan Albers	7	1m 21.882s

PRACTICE 4 (SATURDAY)
High cloud (track 35–36°C, air 26–27°C)

Pos.	Driver	Laps	Time
1	Kimi Räikkönen	12	1m 14.232s
2	Fernando Alonso	15	1m 14.670s
3	Juan Pablo Montoya	13	1m 14.745s
4	Giancarlo Fisichella	19	1m 14.746s
5	Takuma Sato	16	1m 14.883s
6	Ralf Schumacher	12	1m 15.280s
7	Jenson Button	13	1m 15.282s
8	Michael Schumacher	13	1m 15.316s
9	Nick Heidfeld	11	1m 15.723s
10	Mark Webber	14	1m 15.894s
11	Rubens Barrichello	14	1m 15.995s
12	Felipe Massa	13	1m 16.020s
13	Jarno Trulli	8	1m 16.063s
14	David Coulthard	15	1m 16.341s
15	Jacques Villeneuve	13	1m 16.355s
16	Christian Klien	15	1m 16.355s
17	Narain Karthikeyan	12	1m 17.215s
18	Tiago Monteiro	19	1m 17.618s
19	Patrick Friesacher	13	1m 17.621s
20	Christijan Albers	14	1m 17.725s

9th: TRULLI Toyota

7th: RÄIKKÖNEN McLaren-Mercedes

5th: MONTOYA McLaren-Mercedes

3rd: ALONSO Renault

Pole: BUTTON BAR-Honda

10th: R. SCHUMACHER Toyota

8th: VILLENEUVE Sauber-Petronas

6th: SATO BAR-Honda

4th: FISICHELLA Renault

2nd: M. SCHUMACHER Ferrari

	5	56	57	58	59	60	61	62	63	64	65	66	67	68	69	70	•
9	9	9	9	9	9	9	9	9	9	9	9	9	9	9	9	9	1
1	1	1	1	1	1	1	1	1	1	1	1	1	1	1	1	1	2
6	16	16	16	16	16	16	16		2	2	2	2	2	2	2	2	3
2	2	2	2	2	2	2	12	12	12	12	12	12	12	12	12		4
2	12	12	12	12	12	12	7	7	7	7	7	7	7	7			5
7	7	7	7	7	7	7	17	17	17	17	17	17	17				6
7	17	17	17	17	17	17	14	14	14	14	14	14	14				7
4	14	14	14	14	14	14	14	15	15	15	15	15	15				8
5	15	15	15	15	15	15	15	11	11	11	11	11	11				9
1	11	11	11	11	11	11	11	18	18	18	18	18					10
8	18	18	18	18	18	18	18	21	21	21	21	21					11
1	21	21	21	21	21	21											

200th GRAND PRIX POINT:
Kimi Räikkönen

100th LEAD LAP: Giancarlo Fisichella

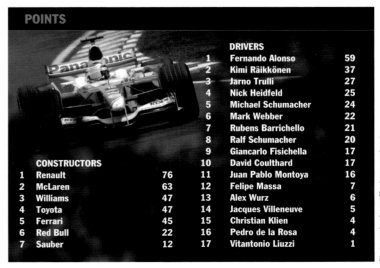

DRIVERS
1	Fernando Alonso	59
2	Kimi Räikkönen	37
3	Jarno Trulli	27
4	Nick Heidfeld	25
5	Michael Schumacher	24
6	Mark Webber	22
7	Rubens Barrichello	21
8	Ralf Schumacher	20
9	Giancarlo Fisichella	17
10	David Coulthard	17
11	Juan Pablo Montoya	16
12	Felipe Massa	7
13	Alex Wurz	6
14	Jacques Villeneuve	5
15	Christian Klien	4
16	Pedro de la Rosa	4
17	Vitantonio Liuzzi	1

CONSTRUCTORS
1	Renault	76
2	McLaren	63
3	Williams	47
4	Toyota	47
5	Ferrari	45
6	Red Bull	22
7	Sauber	12

Photographs: James Moy/www.crash.net

INDIANAPOLIS
UNITED STATESGP
FIA F1 WORLD CHAMPIONSHIP/ROUND 9

Left: Bernie Ecclestone under pressure with events spiralling out of control. He was unable to take charge of the situation and resolve it as he once would have.
Photograph: Jean-François Galeron

Below: A disgruntled race fan's gesture of disdain, tearing up his Indy entry ticket.

Bottom left: Only two Ferraris occupied the front half of the depleted starting grid.

Bottom right: Another member of the paying crowd showing his disapproval.
Photographs: Peter van Egmond

INDIANAPOLIS QUALIFYING

When F1 first came to Indianapolis, much was made of the fact that the final two corners of the road course, Turns 12 and 13, would comprise the first two corners of the famed two-and-a-half-mile oval, the lap direction being reversed. F1 cars on banking! It hadn't happened since the non-title Questor Grand Prix at Ontario in 1971 or Mexico City in 1992. But it didn't take long for everyone to be dismissive about it. 'Turn 13 isn't a corner at all,' the drivers would say. 'It's easy flat.'

But not in 2005. Not, that is, if you were driving a car shod with Michelin's rubber.

With the single-tyre rule introduced for 2005, Bridgestone and Michelin faced new challenges, not the least of which was to produce tyres that combined competitive performance with the ability to last through qualifying and the race. In the previous eight races Michelin had done this better than Bridgestone, but at Indianapolis it came unstuck in the most embarrassing way possible. The trouble started on Friday morning, when Toyota test driver Ricardo Zonta suddenly spun in Turn Five and ended up beached in Turn Six. His left-rear tyre had failed. That afternoon team-mate Ralf Schumacher suffered a similar problem, in exactly the same place that he had crashed his Williams in the 2004 race. The red-and-white car hit the outside wall in Turn 13 very heavily and again it was soon clear that a rear-tyre failure had been responsible.

'Lightning is not supposed to strike twice in the same place,' Ralf Schumacher said, 'but I guess that does not apply to me. I felt something go wrong on the left-hand side. I've never had much luck here.' Subsequently, he would be ruled out of further participation by FIA medical delegate Dr Gary Hartstein, who was worried about the possible effects of a secondary concussion if the German crashed again.

Overnight, everybody was talking about the problem. One possible reason for it was that the banked corners had been resurfaced, with special diamond glazing grooves that had caused Firestone some headaches at the Indianapolis 500 the previous month. 'We did our homework on that,' said Bridgestone's senior engineer, Kees van der Grint, 'because we knew from Firestone that the IRL cars had been having trouble here. The problem is the loading on the tyres, which is greater here than it is anywhere else we run, allied with the same heat and track temperature we get in Malaysia.'

Michelin either had not done its homework or had not done it so effectively.

Then there was the matter of Toyota's under-inflating its rear tyres and running steeper camber angles, in search of greater rear-end grip. Michelin advised its runners on precise settings and everyone in the French camp went into Saturday with their fingers crossed. There were no more failures and qualifying proved to be an exciting hour.

By the end of it, Toyota had taken pole position for the first time, courtesy of Jarno Trulli, who lapped his TF105 in 1m 10.625s. The Italian was the 10th driver to venture out and was delighted with his performance. 'It's been a day of mixed emotions for the whole Toyota team,' he said, 'after all the troubles we had yesterday, so that makes the result all the sweeter. I did a good job and put in a great, clear lap, but I was still very happy to keep hold of the position right up until the end of the session.'

Everyone at Toyota made similar clucking noises, but only later would it transpire that it was a sham; the team subsequently admitted that it had gone for pole to assuage the bad publicity from Friday. Knowing that he probably would not be racing, Trulli had fuel for very few laps.

The one man who might have displaced him was Canadian GP victor Kimi Räikkönen in the McLaren, who had a very good lap that, at 1m 10.694s, came up just 0.069s short. 'I think that was a pretty good lap, and I was very close to getting pole position,' the Finn said, 'but at least we got the front row.' And then he added, 'It will be interesting to see what strategies the other drivers are using.' He had the clear mien of a man who knows that he is in very good shape.

Third place for Jenson Button was a major boost for BAR Honda after the Englishman's crash in Montreal, but he admitted that he was surprised because he had been the ninth man out. 'It wasn't a great lap. I really struggled a lot with very low grip so it's great to be third. I think we can do some great things tomorrow.'

Renault was the leading team, with two cars in the top six, and this time Giancarlo Fisichella had the upper hand over Fernando Alonso. Both drivers had clean laps, but whereas the Italian's car was neutral, the Spaniard's had deliberately been set up to understeer a little because Alonso had the race in mind all along. 'We are clearly not as competitive as we were in Canada,' Alonso admitted. 'But having qualified early, I think a position on the third row is a good starting point.'

Michael Schumacher was pleased to split the blue-and-yellow cars and put a brave face on the gap to McLaren. 'Fifth place is better than fourth on this grid because the other side is dirtier. Although I am not really sure why, it was already clear yesterday that we seem to be more competitive here than at some other tracks. I hope that we will find out tomorrow that we qualified with a heavier fuel load than our rivals did, or at least are closer in terms of fuel load than we were in Canada.'

Team-mate Rubens Barrichello was also cautiously optimistic after qualifying seventh and, like Schumacher, he went to the grid confident that Ferrari had a

His partner on row four, Takuma Sato, lost out when BAR split its set-up strategy trying to find more speed. Sato suffered most where it mattered – on the long straight. His lap of 1m 11.497s was enough to keep Mark Webber in the Williams and Felipe Massa in the Sauber at bay, however. The atmosphere in the BMW Williams camp was tense all weekend following the comments made by the Williams management prior to Canada – director of engineering Patrick Head had criticised BMW's understanding of the word 'partnership' – and the Australian was rather downbeat after lapping in 1m 11.527s. 'It was reasonable and I couldn't have got much more out of it,' he said matter-of-factly.

Massa and team-mate Jacques Villeneuve experienced loss of grip towards the end of their otherwise clean laps, but the former champion admitted he should have pushed harder. 'I guess I wasn't aggressive enough,' he confessed. 'The lap was too clean. We thought we could get Juan Pablo [Montoya].'

Montoya was sandwiched between them and was not at all happy about it after the speed he had shown while dominating on Friday and Saturday morning. Having to start the session as second man out really hurt his chances and was the final kick from

Main photo: Amid a shower of debris, Ralf Schumacher revived memories of his 2004 accident at Turn 13.

Far left: Schumacher's left-rear Michelin was already coming off the rim as the Toyota spun towards the wall.
Photographs: Lukas Gorys

Left: Ralf was shaken but not unduly stirred by this unfortunate episode.
Photograph: Peter Nygaard/GP Photo

Above: The remains of the tyre that failed.
Photograph: Paul-Henri Cahier

early, but it was not until I got out there that I realised how challenging it would be. There was no grip and I was sliding all over the place. I believe the car is quick enough to win the race, but starting so far back it's going to be extremely challenging.'

Half a second covered the 11 cars from third place down to 13th, for which position Ralf Schumacher's stand-in, Zonta, had pushed his TF105 around in 1m 11.754s despite being the first man out.

Nick Heidfeld was very unhappy with his qualifying effort and was sandwiched between the Red Bulls in 15th place in a car that was difficult to drive and had no grip. Christian Klien and David Coulthard were a little disappointed that their new Cosworth TJ2005 series-12 engines, with an extra 35 bhp, had not led to the overall performance improvement they had been expecting, despite greater speed down the straight, but it would transpire in testing the following week at Jerez that more optimal fuelling settings would improve things.

At Jordan, Tiago Monteiro had the upper hand over team-mate Narain Karthikeyan, who suffered from having to run early, and they were separated by Christijan Albers, who ran a light fuel load in his Minardi. Monteiro lapped in 1m 13.462s, Albers 1m 13.632s and Karthikeyan in 1m 13.776s. Patrick Friesacher was at the back

on 1m 14.494s, struggling with understeer on his PS05. 'We will have to see what happens tommorrow with strategy and with the big story concerning tyres,' Albers said, adding with some prescience, 'Maybe events will play into our hands a little bit.'

It seemed that all was well on the tyre front, but behind the scenes there was major concern. In addition to the Toyotas, one McLaren, one Red Bull and one Sauber had shown signs of tyre distress and Michelin told its runners that the tyres it had brought to Indianapolis were not suitable for racing unless speeds in Turn 13 could be curtailed. Back at the factory in Clermont-Ferrand, France, Michelin had tried all sorts of tests on its dynamometers to duplicate the failures, without conclusive success. As it flew out a batch of tyres previously intended for Barcelona, with stiffer sidewalls to resist the loads at the Speedway, disaster was looming.

Later that evening, Bernie Ecclestone walked the paddock. 'They'll be all right,' he said, when Michelin's tyre problem was raised. 'They're bringing some new tyres in tomorrow and they'll all have to use them.' Then he paused, patted his listener's arm and added, 'It's nice to have some problems, isn't it?' That, of course, depended upon your vantage point. If you were looking in from IRL, CART or NASCAR, maybe so, but the following day even Bernie would discover that not all problems are soluble.

Above: Red Devil: dressed for the occasion, complete with FerrariFone.
Photograph: Jean-François Galeron/WRI

Top: The bizarre sight of the six-car grid waiting for the off as the other cars returned to their pit-lane garages.
Photograph: James Moy/www.crash.net

Above right: New Indy star Danica Patrick chatting with Jenson Button.
Photograph: James Moy/www.crash.net

Bottom right: Tiago Monteiro was best of the rest with third place in his Jordan.
Photograph: Laurent Charniaux/WRi

TONY George and his team at the Indianapolis Motor Speedway worked tirelessly to promote the US Grand Prix, now in its sixth year. As a result of their efforts, 130,000 spectators flocked to the Brickyard on Sunday, 19 June, Father's Day. There were delays for some cars leaving the pits as the minutes before the start clicked away, but few of them paid that much attention. The level of anticipation was ratcheting up, as it always does prior to that great moment when a gridful of cars accelerates towards the first corner. In their seats in the grandstands the spectators settled down in readiness. Eventually, the grid filled up and the 20 cars came under starter's orders and set off on their final formation lap. Jarno Trulli was a surprise pole-sitter ahead of favourite Kimi Räikkönen, followed by Jenson Button. Michael Schumacher split the Renaults of Giancarlo Fisichella and Fernando Alonso.

There was nothing grand about the prix that followed, however. Those spectators, and millions of others watching on television around the globe, stared in complete disbelief as car after car peeled into the pit lane at the end of that lap. All 14 Michelin runners parked up, leaving only the six Bridgestone-shod cars – two Ferraris, two Jordans and two Minardis – to take the start. All six of them finished, the two red cars staging a flypast. The US Grand Prix was a farce.

Fans booed, turned down their thumbs, scrawled their disgust in pen upon their faces. Some even threw bottles onto the track. The scandalous and wholly inappropriate use of politics and power, rather than any sort of sensible judgement or consideration and respect for those who ultimately pay for the sport – the spectators – ruled on one of the bleakest days in F1's history.

Behind the scenes, there had been civil war in the paddock. By Sunday morning it was clear that Michelin had advised all of its runners that the tyres it had brought were suitable only if speeds were slowed through Turn 13. Without that, they could not risk racing. As the hours passed, it became increasingly clear that the statesmanship from the FIA that would have overcome this unexpected drama and enabled the Michelin teams to run would not be forthcoming. However you cut and diced it, the teams were left with no option but to withdraw their cars at the end of the formation lap. Talk of a deliberate boycott was deeply unfair. To a man, they wanted to race. Indeed, David Coulthard and Alonso, to name but two, were desperately trying to persuade their teams all around that lap. Räikkönen had to be told in no uncertain terms by McLaren chairman Ron Dennis that he had better not go to the grid.

And so, as 14 cars trailed into the pits and were immediately pushed away, the other six lined up on the grid. From fifth, Michael Schumacher now found himself on pole; from seventh, Rubens Barrichello was second. Tiago Monteiro, 17th, was actually third, Christijan Albers was fourth from 18th, Narain Karthikeyan fifth from 19th and Patrick Friesacher sixth from 20th. What made it all the more ludicrous was that they all had to start from their original grid slots.

The starts were clean but, as his car smoked alarmingly, Karthikeyan got very close to team-mate Monteiro and lost out to Albers, so by the end of the opening lap Schumacher led Barrichello, Monteiro, Albers, Karthikeyan and Friesacher. Lap charts were not difficult but keeping awake was.

Karthikeyan moved up to fourth when three-stopping Albers made his first stop on lap 10 and the next change came when Albers moved up to fifth as Friesacher pitted on lap 19. Both Jordans were able to stop without losing places, Karthikeyan on lap 20 and Monteiro on lap 22. Barrichello came in on lap 24 and it was not until Schumacher pitted on lap 26 that the first real drama unfolded. The team closely inspected his car's left-rear Bridgestone and he was stationary for 16.8s.

Barrichello assumed the lead. After angry spectators had shown their disdain for the mandarins of the sport by hurling beer bottles onto the track, Ferrari's line was that inspection was the safe route. Perhaps it was true. Perhaps it was just a shallow attempt to make a race out of the farce.

Whatever, Michael was behind and had to chase Rubens. It seemed like they were racing, until you checked the lap times and saw that for much of the time the red cars were not running much faster than the Jordans, which had the Minardis tucked up behind them. On lap 49 Barrichello made his final stop, handing the lead to Schumacher. Two laps later, the champion was in. He exited the pit lane and headed for Turn One, and arrived there at precisely the same moment as his team-mate, but crucially he perforce had the inside line. He stayed there. Barrichello kept coming without trying to tighten his line. As his bluff failed, he sailed off onto the grass on the outside and that was that. Game over. On what passed for the podium ceremony (the nominated officials refused to present the awards and Allsport management executive David Warren was obliged to officiate instead), Barrichello's body language said it all. He would not even look at Schumacher.

DIARY

Danica Patrick's visit to the Speedway on the Thursday overshadows all of her IRL rivals'. While winner Dan Wheldon is able to walk around unmolested, the first woman ever to lead the Indy 500 is mobbed wherever she goes.

BAR confirms that 2004 IRL champion Tony Kanaan will test for the team later in the season.

In the week prior to the US GP, Sports Marketing Surveys reveals that the audience for Canadian GP qualifying has risen 50 percent since 2004 and that audiences have risen two percent in Germany, 10 percent in Italy and 50 percent in Spain.

McLaren's Technology Centre in Woking is awarded the Royal Fine Art Commission's Building of the Year Award.

Three days after the US GP, BMW officially announces that it will have its own F1 team in 2006 after acquiring Credit Suisse's shareholding in Sauber and some of owner Peter Sauber's share.

Of course Tiago Monteiro was delighted to finish third and who could truly blame him? He was there thanks to circumstances entirely beyond his control and he had made the most of them. Karthikeyan had generally had the upper hand all season but, in the one race that really mattered, Monteiro had produced the goods. 'I have mixed feelings today, because it was a strange race with no one being there,' he said with some dignity. 'However, for me, it was still a race. The most important thing was to finish. This is my ninth consecutive race finish this season and now I have scored some points, so I am very pleased with that. I know these were weird conditions, but nobody can take this away from me.'

Minardi's Paul Stoddart had run his cars only because Bridgestone had instructed him to and because he was a marked man who did not need to give the FIA any further ammunition against him, but the title of Minardi's post-race press release summarised his feelings: 'Racing the FIA way'.

And so ended a hugely damaging day for the sport.

'This was our first win and our first one-two [finish] of the season, obtained under very unusual circumstances,' Ferrari sporting director Jean Todt crowed. 'To put this result in boxing terms, we and Bridgestone won with a technical knock-out.'

Others believed that the only apposite boxing analogy for what F1 did to itself at Indianapolis was Mike Tyson's biting off Evander Holyfield's ear.

As the shadows lengthened in the paddock, Michael Schumacher sat with friends and hangers-on, savouring one of his trademark victory cigars. His 84th win had been a hollow triumph and all around him F1 in the US seemed to be dying, but he exuded the serenity of a contented man. The North-American tour might have brought the sport to its knees, but it had been highly profitable for Ferrari and for him. The team had netted 32 points in eight days, compared with zero for Renault and 10 for McLaren, and suddenly was back in contention in joint second place with McLaren on 63 points, only 13 adrift of Renault. He himself had scored 18 and was only three behind Räikkönen for second place in the drivers' championship.

Not quite everyone left the Indianapolis Motor Speedway feeling tainted by their involvement with F1.

David Tremayne

TYRE BATTLE CRIPPLES US GP

The overriding perception among fans and those involved in F1 is that the FIA adopted a high-handed attitude to the Michelin tyre problem and chose to make political capital out of it instead of ensuring that statesmanship shaped a suitable answer to a situation that nobody could have foreseen.

The FIA's immediate answer to Michelin's clear, hands-up admission that its tyres were unsuitable for the Indianapolis Motor Speedway was a patronising rebuke which began, 'We are very surprised that this difficulty has arisen.' Yet such things are inevitable from time to time when competition obliges everyone to push limits.

Michelin wanted a chicane to slow cars through Turn 13 and precedent for this existed from Spain 1994, when drivers threatened to strike unless one was installed on the back straight. The FIA did not want to build a chicane and instead suggested alternatives such as a race held behind the safety car, Michelin runners' using the pit lane rather than Turn 13, or a voluntary speed limit for them through that corner. It suggested that a chicane would be dangerous and that a collision there might 'send a car into the crowd'.

Yet with its own suggestion of a speed limit for the Michelin cars it was not difficult to envisage, say, Jacques Villeneuve arriving in Turn 13 under attack from the Jordans and suddenly remembering that he had to back off from 200 mph (320 km/h) to 175 mph (280 km/h). The French-Canadian has always claimed that Ralf Schumacher's doing something similar to him in Australia in 2001 led to their accident in which marshal Graham Beveridge lost his life.

The biggest concern among the Michelin runners was not just that their drivers might crash in Turn 13 if a tyre failed, but that the driver might then be tee-boned by an approaching car. They had not forgotten the Champ car accident at the Lausitzring in 2001 in which Alex Zanardi lost his legs, even if the FIA appeared to have forgotten.

'We lost Piers Courage and Ayrton Senna in our cars and for a while in 2004 we thought we had lost a third driver,' Sir Frank Williams said, referring to Ralf Schumacher's crash in the previous year's race. Team principals also had liability issues to consider in a country renowned for its litigious nature. Indiana state law simply forbade them from racing and they would have faced criminal prosecution had they done so, even if there had not been an accident. They also remembered that Mark Donohue's widow Eden had successfully sued Goodyear after the tyre failure that led to the accident that ultimately claimed Donohue's life in Austria in 1975.

The problem was exacerbated by the fact that Barcelona-spec tyres, flown in specially by Michelin for Sunday morning, were of the same construction but a different compound from the Indy tyres. By the time they arrived, Michelin had done further simulation and an MRI scan on Indy tyres in South Carolina and knew that the Barcelona tyres were not, after all, the answer at a time when it was telling its teams that the maximum acceptable load for its tyres was what they would experience in Turn Five, a 140-mph (230-km/h), fourth-gear right-hander.

In the end, the FIA resolutely refused to agree to a chicane, despite proposals that the Michelin runners would not race for points if one were built. FIA president Max Mosley's subsequent summons to all of the Michelin teams to appear before the World Motor Sport Council in Paris the following week only served to harden their belief that, by putting them in an invidious position, he was pursuing his political agenda against them for rebelling against the proposed 2008 Concorde Agreement, while simultaneously exploiting the situation to achieve his wish to see F1 return to a single tyre supplier.

The TV monitor told the sorry story of the grand prix.

Photograph: Laurent Charniaux/WRI

			GAP	INT		21.9	29.6	19.4
1	1	M. SCHUMACHER	LAP	73	1:14.600	22.8	30.4	21.2
2	2	R. BARRICHELLO	1.5	1.5	1:12.475	22.4	29.9	20.0
3	18	T. MONTEIRO	1L	1L	1:14.210	23.4	30.3	20.3
4	19	N. KARTHIKEYAN	1L	31.1	1:14.095	23.1	30.4	20.4
5	21	C. ALBERS	2L	1L	1:15.011	23.6	30.4	20.6
6	20	P. FRIESACHER	2L	15.5	1:15.564	23.8	31.0	20.7
	16	J. TRULLI	RETIRED					
	9	K. RAIKKONEN	RETIRED					
	3	J. BUTTON	RETIRED					
	6	G. FISICHELLA	RETIRED					
	5	F. ALONSO	RETIRED					
	4	T. SATO	RETIRED					
	7	M. WEBBER	RETIRED					
	12	F. MASSA	RETIRED					
	10	J. MONTOYA	RETIRED					
	11	J. VILLENEUVE	RETIRED					
	17	R. ZONTA	RETIRED					
	15	C. KLIEN	RETIRED					
	8	N. HEIDFELD	RETIRED					
	14	D. COULTHARD	RETIRED					

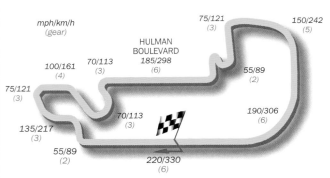

Photograph: James Moy/www.crash.net

FIA F1 WORLD CHAMPIONSHIP • ROUND 9

FOSTER'S UNITED STATES GRAND PRIX

INDIANAPOLIS 17–19 JUNE 2005

INDIANAPOLIS – GRAND PRIX CIRCUIT

mph/km/h (gear)

75/121 (3)

150/242 (5)

100/161 (4)

70/113 (3)

HULMAN BOULEVARD 185/298 (6)

55/89 (2)

75/121 (3)

70/113 (3)

190/306 (6)

135/217 (3)

55/89 (2)

220/330 (6)

CIRCUIT LENGTH: 2.605 miles/4.192 km

RACE DISTANCE: 73 laps, 190.150 miles /306.016 km   **RACE WEATHER:** Heavily cloudy (track 33–35°C, air 25–26°C)

Pos.	Driver	Nat.	No.	Entrant	Car/Engine	Tyres	Laps	Time/Retirement	Speed (mph/km/h)	Gap to leader	Fastest race lap	
1	Michael Schumacher	D	1	Scuderia Ferrari Marlboro	Ferrari F2005-055 V10	B	73	1h 29m 43.181s	127.162/204.648		1m 11.497s	48
2	Rubens Barrichello	BR	2	Scuderia Ferrari Marlboro	Ferrari F2005-055 V10	B	73	1h 29m 44.703s	127.126/204.590	+1.522s	1m 11.649s	48
3	Tiago Monteiro	P	18	Jordan Toyota	Jordan EJ15-Toyota RVX-05 V10	B	72			+1 lap	1m 13.237s	44
4	Narain Karthikeyan	IND	19	Jordan Toyota	Jordan EJ15-Toyota RVX-05 V10	B	72			+1 lap	1m 13.370s	65
5	Christijan Albers	NL	21	Minardi Cosworth	Minardi PS05-Cosworth TJ2005 V10	B	71			+2 laps	1m 13.907s	2
6	Patrick Friesacher	A	20	Minardi Cosworth	Minardi PS05-Cosworth TJ2005 V10	B	71			+2 laps	1m 14.490s	43
	Jarno Trulli	I	16	Panasonic Toyota Racing	Toyota TF105-RVX-05 V10	M	0	Withdrew after parade lap				
	Kimi Räikkönen	FIN	9	West McLaren Mercedes	McLaren MP4-20-Mercedes F0 110R V10	M	0	Withdrew after parade lap				
	Jenson Button	GB	3	Lucky Strike BAR Honda	BAR 007-Honda RA005E V10	M	0	Withdrew after parade lap				
	Giancarlo Fisichella	I	6	Mild Seven Renault F1 Team	Renault R25-RS25 V10	M	0	Withdrew after parade lap				
	Fernando Alonso	E	5	Mild Seven Renault F1 Team	Renault R25-RS25 V10	M	0	Withdrew after parade lap				
	Takuma Sato	J	4	Lucky Strike BAR Honda	BAR 007-Honda RA005E V10	M	0	Withdrew after parade lap				
	Mark Webber	AUS	7	BMW WilliamsF1 Team	Williams FW27-BMW P84/85 V10	M	0	Withdrew after parade lap				
	Felipe Massa	BR	12	Sauber Petronas	Sauber C24-Petronas 05A V10	M	0	Withdrew after parade lap				
	Juan Pablo Montoya	COL	10	West McLaren Mercedes	McLaren MP4-20-Mercedes F0 110R V10	M	0	Withdrew after parade lap				
	Jacques Villeneuve	CDN	11	Sauber Petronas	Sauber C24-Petronas 05A V10	M	0	Withdrew after parade lap				
	Ricardo Zonta	BR	17	Panasonic Toyota Racing	Toyota TF105-RVX-05 V10	M	0	Withdrew after parade lap				
	Christian Klien	A	15	Red Bull Racing	Red Bull RB1-Cosworth TJ2005/12 V10	M	0	Withdrew after parade lap				
	Nick Heidfeld	D	8	BMW WilliamsF1 Team	Williams FW27-BMW P84/85 V10	M	0	Withdrew after parade lap				
	David Coulthard	GB	14	Red Bull Racing	Red Bull RB1-Cosworth TJ2005/12 V10	M	0	Withdrew after parade lap				

Fastest lap: Michael Schumacher, on lap 48, 1m 11.497s, 131.155 mph/211.074 km/h.

Lap record: Rubens Barrichello (Ferrari F2004-052 V10), 1m 10.399s, 133.201 mph/214.366 km/h (2004).

All results and data © FOM 2005

19th: KARTHIKEYAN Jordan-Toyota

17th: MONTEIRO Jordan-Toyota

15th: HEIDFELD Williams-BMW
Withdrew after parade lap

13th: ZONTA Toyota
Withdrew after parade lap

11th: MONTOYA McLaren-Mercedes
Withdrew after parade lap

20th: FRIESACHER Minardi-Cosworth

18th: ALBERS Minardi-Cosworth

16th: COULTHARD Red Bull-Cosworth
Withdrew after parade lap

14th: KLIEN Red Bull-Cosworth
Withdrew after parade lap

12th: VILLENEUVE Sauber-Petronas
Withdrew after parade lap

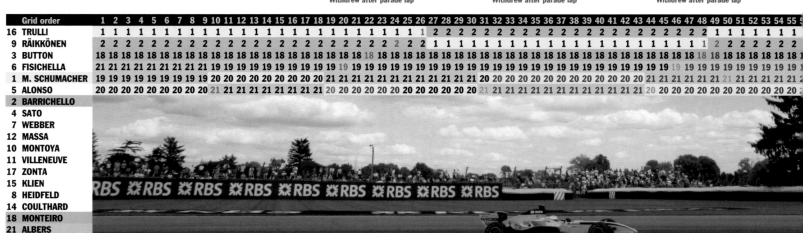

Grid order	1 2 3 4 5 6 7 8 9 10 11 12 13 14 15 16 17 18 19 20 21 22 23 24 25 26 27 28 29 30 31 32 33 34 35 36 37 38 39 40 41 42 43 44 45 46 47 48 49 50 51 52 53 54 55 5
16 TRULLI	1 1 1 1 1 1 1 1 1 1 1 1 1 1 1 1 1 1 1 1 1 1 1 1 1 1 1 2 2 2 2 2 2 2 2 2 2 2 2 2 2 2 2 2 2 2 2 2 2 1 1 1 1 1 1
9 RÄIKKÖNEN	2 2 2 2 2 2 2 2 2 2 2 2 2 2 2 2 2 2 2 2 2 2 2 2 2 2 2 1 1 1 1 1 1 1 1 1 1 1 1 1 1 1 1 1 1 1 1 1 1 2 2 2 2 2 2
3 BUTTON	18 18 18 18 18 18 18 18 18 18 18 18 18 18 18 18 18 18 18 18 18 18 18 18 18 18 18 18 18 18 18 18 18 18 18 18 18 18 18 18 18 18 18 18 18 18 18 18 18 18 18 18 18 18 18
6 FISICHELLA	21 21 21 21 21 21 21 21 21 19 19 19 19 19 19 19 19 19 19 19 19 19 19 19 19 19 19 19 19 19 19 19 19 19 19 19 19 19 19 19 19 19 19 19 19 19 19 19 19 19 19 19 19 19 19
1 M. SCHUMACHER	19 19 19 19 19 19 19 19 19 20 20 20 20 20 20 20 21 21 21 21 21 21 21 21 21 21 21 21 20 20 20 20 20 20 20 20 20 20 20 21 21 21 21 21 21 21 21 21 21 21 21 21 21 21 21
5 ALONSO	20 20 20 20 20 20 20 20 20 21 21 21 21 21 21 21 20 20 20 20 20 20 20 20 20 20 21 21 21 21 21 21 21 21 21 20 20 20 20 20 20 20 20 20 20
2 BARRICHELLO	
4 SATO	
7 WEBBER	
12 MASSA	
10 MONTOYA	
11 VILLENEUVE	
17 ZONTA	
15 KLIEN	
8 HEIDFELD	
14 COULTHARD	
18 MONTEIRO	
21 ALBERS	
19 KARTHIKEYAN	
20 FRIESACHER	

QUALIFYING

WEATHER: Heavily cloudy (track 31–32°C, air 23–24°C)

Pos	Driver	R/Order	Sector 1	Sector 2	Sector 3	Time
1	Jarno Trulli	9	21.790s	29.443s	19.392s	1m 10.625s
2	Kimi Räikkönen	20	21.883s	29.254s	19.557s	1m 10.694s
3	Jenson Button	8	22.052s	29.359s	19.866s	1m 11.277s
4	Giancarlo Fisichella	3	22.083s	29.489s	19.718s	1m 11.290s
5	Michael Schumacher	19	22.021s	29.477s	19.871s	1m 11.369s
6	Fernando Alonso	4	22.183s	29.519s	19.678s	1m 11.380s
7	Rubens Barrichello	18	22.119s	29.563s	19.749s	1m 11.431s
8	Takuma Sato	6	22.162s	29.412s	19.923s	1m 11.497s
9	Mark Webber	16	22.307s	29.266s	19.954s	1m 11.527s
10	Felipe Massa	17	22.170s	29.388s	19.997s	1m 11.555s
11	Juan Pablo Montoya	1	22.218s	29.607s	19.856s	1m 11.681s
12	Jacques Villeneuve	12	22.139s	29.643s	19.909s	1m 11.691s
13	Ricardo Zonta	15	22.167s	29.923s	19.664s	1m 11.754s
14	Christian Klien	13	22.437s	29.770s	19.925s	1m 12.132s
15	Nick Heidfeld	7	22.549s	29.776s	20.105s	1m 12.430s
16	David Coulthard	14	22.392s	30.281s	19.965s	1m 12.682s
17	Tiago Monteiro	11	22.962s	30.174s	20.326s	1m 13.462s
18	Christijan Albers	10	22.938s	30.296s	20.398s	1m 13.632s
19	Narain Karthikeyan	2	22.790s	30.670s	20.316s	1m 13.776s
20	Patrick Friesacher	5	23.199s	30.793s	20.477s	1m 14.494s

CHASSIS LOG BOOK

FERRARI
1 Michael Schumacher F2005/245
2 Rubens Barrichello F2005/246
Spare F2005/243

BAR-HONDA
3 Jenson Button 007/04
4 Takuma Sato 007/05
Spare 007/02

RENAULT
5 Fernando Alonso R25/04
6 Giancarlo Fisichella R25/06
Spare R25/02

WILLIAMS-BMW
7 Mark Webber FW27/05
8 Nick Heidfeld FW27/06
Spare FW27/04

McLAREN-MERCEDES
9 Kimi Räikkönen MP4-20/04
10 Juan Pablo Montoya MP4-20/05
35 Alex Wurz MP4-20/03
Spare MP4-20/03

SAUBER-PETRONAS
11 Jacques Villeneuve C24/04
12 Felipe Massa C24/06
Spare C24/03

RED BULL-COSWORTH
14 David Coulthard RB1/3
15 Christian Klien RB1/1
16 Scott Speed RB1/2
Spare RB1/2

TOYOTA
16 Jarno Trulli TF105/02
17 Ralf Schumacher TF105/03
38 Ricardo Zonta TF105/05
Spare TF105/05

JORDAN-TOYOTA
18 Tiago Monteiro EJ15/03
19 Narain Karthikeyan EJ15/02
Spare EJ15/01

MINARDI-COSWORTH
20 Patrick Friesacher PS05/02
21 Christijan Albers PS05/01
Spare PS04B/03

Photograph: James Moy/www.crash.net

PRACTICE 1 (FRIDAY)

Sunny with scattered cloud (track 34–35°C, air 23–24°C)

Pos.	Driver	Laps	Time
1	Juan Pablo Montoya	6	1m 12.027s
2	Ricardo Zonta	18	1m 12.085s
3	Fernando Alonso	10	1m 12.666s
4	Nick Heidfeld	9	1m 12.804s
5	Jenson Button	11	1m 12.865s
6	Pedro de la Rosa	4	1m 12.913s
7	Takuma Sato	9	1m 13.013s
8	Giancarlo Fisichella	10	1m 13.024s
9	Mark Webber	10	1m 13.082s
10	Michael Schumacher	12	1m 13.242s
11	Rubens Barrichello	12	1m 13.245s
12	Ralf Schumacher	7	1m 13.461s
13	Jarno Trulli	7	1m 13.683s
14	David Coulthard	8	1m 13.740s
15	Scott Speed	21	1m 13.846s
16	Christian Klien	8	1m 14.444s
17	Felipe Massa	7	1m 14.637s
18	Jacques Villeneuve	6	1m 14.696s
19	Narain Karthikeyan	18	1m 14.803s
20	Tiago Monteiro	20	1m 14.978s
21	Robert Doornbos	27	1m 15.791s
22	Patrick Friesacher	16	1m 16.343s
23	Christian Albers	12	1m 16.357s
24	Kimi Räikkönen	3	No time

PRACTICE 2 (FRIDAY)

Scattered cloud–cloudy (track 32–37°C, air 23–24°C)

Pos.	Driver	Laps	Time
1	Juan Pablo Montoya	21	1m 11.118s
2	Kimi Räikkönen	24	1m 11.228s
3	Rubens Barrichello	22	1m 11.746s
4	Michael Schumacher	22	1m 11.758s
5	Nick Heidfeld	24	1m 11.825s
6	David Coulthard	9	1m 12.076s
7	Pedro de la Rosa	37	1m 12.119s
8	Scott Speed	34	1m 12.143s
9	Fernando Alonso	28	1m 12.265s
10	Jarno Trulli	10	1m 12.344s
11	Giancarlo Fisichella	29	1m 12.384s
12	Felipe Massa	25	1m 12.464s
13	Mark Webber	24	1m 12.578s
14	Christian Klien	20	1m 12.664s
15	Jenson Button	24	1m 12.803s
16	Takuma Sato	26	1m 13.037s
17	Jacques Villeneuve	23	1m 13.079s
18	Robert Doornbos	36	1m 13.361s
19	Ricardo Zonta	6	1m 13.567s
20	Patrick Friesacher	16	1m 13.783s
21	Christian Albers	24	1m 13.963s
22	Narain Karthikeyan	31	1m 14.008s
23	Tiago Monteiro	35	1m 14.336s
24	Ralf Schumacher	2	No time

PRACTICE 3 (SATURDAY)

Sunny (track 27–32°C, air 21–22°C)

Pos.	Driver	Laps	Time
1	Juan Pablo Montoya	4	1m 10.726s
2	Michael Schumacher	11	1m 11.769s
3	Rubens Barrichello	9	1m 11.838s
4	David Coulthard	7	1m 12.409s
5	Tiago Monteiro	12	1m 13.399s
6	Narain Karthikeyan	12	1m 13.764s
7	Patrick Friesacher	16	1m 14.572s
8	Christian Albers	6	1m 15.164s
9	Jacques Villeneuve	7	No time
10	Kimi Räikkönen	6	No time
11	Jenson Button	7	No time
12	Takuma Sato	6	No time
13	Nick Heidfeld	5	No time
14	Giancarlo Fisichella	6	No time
15	Mark Webber	4	No time
16	Felipe Massa	7	No time
17	Fernando Alonso	4	No time
18	Christian Klien	4	No time
19	Ricardo Zonta	1	No time

PRACTICE 4 (SATURDAY)

Sunny and cloudy (track 34–35°C, air 24°C)

Pos.	Driver	Laps	Time
1	Kimi Räikkönen	12	1m 10.643s
2	Jenson Button	15	1m 10.844s
3	Fernando Alonso	10	1m 10.920s
4	Michael Schumacher	12	1m 11.203s
5	Takuma Sato	16	1m 11.324s
6	Giancarlo Fisichella	10	1m 11.375s
7	Jarno Trulli	7	1m 11.457s
8	Juan Pablo Montoya	7	1m 11.574s
9	Ricardo Zonta	10	1m 11.760s
10	Rubens Barrichello	13	1m 11.794s
11	Christian Klien	13	1m 11.806s
12	Jacques Villeneuve	10	1m 11.875s
13	Felipe Massa	10	1m 11.915s
14	Mark Webber	9	1m 12.080s
15	Nick Heidfeld	10	1m 12.186s
16	David Coulthard	7	1m 12.914s
17	Christijan Albers	16	1m 13.024s
18	Tiago Monteiro	14	1m 13.051s
19	Narain Karthikeyan	11	1m 13.161s
20	Patrick Friesacher	16	1m 13.501s

9th: WEBBER Williams-BMW
Withdrew after parade lap

7th: BARRICHELLO Ferrari

5th: M. SCHUMACHER Ferrari

3rd: BUTTON BAR-Honda
Withdrew after parade lap

Pole: **TRULLI** Toyota
Withdrew after parade lap

10th: MASSA Sauber-Petronas
Withdrew after parade lap

8th: SATO BAR-Honda
Withdrew after parade lap

6th: ALONSO Renault
Withdrew after parade lap

4th: FISICHELLA Renault
Withdrew after parade lap

2nd: RÄIKKÖNEN McLaren-Mercedes
Withdrew after parade lap

57	58	59	60	61	62	63	64	65	66	67	68	69	70	71	72	73	•
1	1	1	1	1	1	1	1	1	1	1	1	1	1	1	1	1	1
2	2	2	2	2	2	2	2	2	2	2	2	2	2	2	2	2	2
18	18	18	18	18	18	18	18	18	18	18	18	18	18	18	18		3
19	19	19	19	19	19	19	19	19	19	19	19	19	19	19	19	19	4
21	21	21	21	21	21	21	21	21	21	21	21	21	21	21			5
20	20	20	20	20	20	20	20	20	20	20	20	20	20				6
																	7
																	8

Pit stop
One lap or more behind leader

FOR THE RECORD

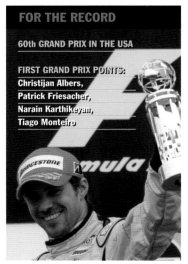

60th GRAND PRIX IN THE USA

FIRST GRAND PRIX POINTS:
Christijan Albers,
Patrick Friesacher,
Narain Karthikeyan,
Tiago Monteiro

POINTS

DRIVERS

1	Fernando Alonso	59	17	Christijan Albers	4
2	Kimi Räikkönen	37	18	Pedro de la Rosa	4
3	Michael Schumacher	34	19	Christian Klien	4
4	Rubens Barrichello	29	20	Patrick Friesacher	3
5	Jarno Trulli	27	21	Vitantonio Liuzzi	1
6	Nick Heidfeld	25			
7	Mark Webber	22		**CONSTRUCTORS**	
8	Ralf Schumacher	20	1	Renault	76
9	Giancarlo Fisichella	17	2	McLaren	63
10	David Coulthard	17	3	Ferrari	63
11	Juan Pablo Montoya	16	4	Williams	47
12	Felipe Massa	7	5	Toyota	47
13	Tiago Monteiro	6	6	Red Bull	22
14	Alex Wurz	6	7	Sauber	12
15	Jacques Villeneuve	5	8	Jordan	11
16	Narain Karthikeyan	5	9	Minardi	7

Photographs: James Moy/www.crash.net

GRAND
DE FRAN

MAGN

Fernando Alonso looked ecstatic after
giving Renault its first French-GP victory
in 22 years, ahead of a frustrated Kimi
Räikkönen (left). Michael Schumacher just
looked relieved to be on the podium.
Photograph: James Moy/www.crash.net

MAGNY-COURS QUALIFYING

The efforts of McLaren chairman Ron Dennis and his colleagues to move on from
the Indianapolis fiasco (see over page) came at the end of a day on which McLaren
team leader Kimi Räikkönen's championship prospects encountered a setback due
to a rare Mercedes engine failure in one of Friday's free-practice sessions.

This meant that Räikkönen, who went into the race second in the title chase, 22
points behind Fernando Alonso but only three ahead of Michael Schumacher, would
have to take a ten-place penalty on the grid position he achieved in qualifying.

Meanwhile, Fernando Alonso delivered a flawless performance to take pole
position on 1m 14.412s, a decisive 0.109s ahead of Jarno Trulli's Toyota TF105.
'The car felt really good all weekend after our testing last week at Jerez,' said
Alonso, 'and the balance was very stable on my [qualifying] lap, so I could attack
all the way without any mistakes.'

Alonso had done a superb job to bag his first pole since Bahrain, but the
ominous presence of Michael Schumacher's Ferrari F2005 on the second row of
the grid indicated just how much progress Bridgestone had made with the one-lap
qualifying performance of its tyres over the previous month or so.

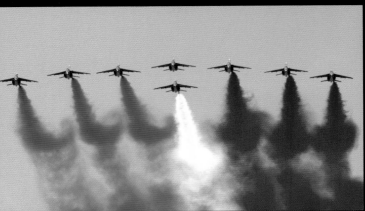

The world champion qualified fourth but moved up to third behind Jarno Trulli's
front-row Toyota TF105 after Räikkönen took his ten-place penalty, which demoted
Kimi to 13th.

Schumacher was mildly satisfied. 'We felt we could do well here and I will now be
starting from third place on the grid, which is a good position, even though I had
hoped to be fighting for pole,' he said. In the race he pressed on strongly, but an
eventual third was clearly a lot less than he had been hoping for.

Schumacher had set third-fastest time on Friday, giving a familiar tone to a day
on which he hoped to strengthen his bid for an eighth world championship after a
disappointing first half to the season.

'This has been a productive Friday and I am quite happy with what we have
achieved,' said Schumacher. 'The car seems to behave quite well, as do the tyres,
which probably explains why I have the impression the car is sliding around less
than usual on this track.

'I think we can be fighting for the win this weekend. The team has worked very
hard over the past months and it seems that all this work is beginning to pay off
now.' Well, almost.

Alonso's team-mate Giancarlo Fisichella had to satisfy himself with a lowly
seventh on 1m 14.887s, another acute disappointment in a season which now
seemed to be unravelling terminally. 'Obviously I am a little bit disappointed about
my position,' he shrugged with measured understatement. 'The first and second
sectors were quite good for me,' he said, 'but then I lost three or four tenths in the
final corner, which pushed me farther down the grid.'

Unhappy with his set-up on Friday, Trulli initially felt he was struggling for grip
and balance. He made some changes which paid off in Saturday's free practice and
then kicked forward to a confident qualifying in which he reported much higher
grip levels on his way to second place on the grid.

It all looked pretty gloomy for Ralf Schumacher in the other TF105. He had
to make his qualifying run first as the consequence of his practice accident at
Indianapolis but he did well to gain places on the starting grid, lining up 12th. Ralf
was also distraught after the apparent dog-napping of his pet chihuahua.

For Juan Pablo Montoya, qualifying at Magny-Cours was a disappointment
because he had to run early and he ended up ninth behind Jenson Button's
BAR-Honda with a 1m 15.406s best.

'My lap time pretty much matches what I did in practice,' said Juan Pablo. 'I
haven't had the pleasure of starting late in the qualifying sessions this year, which
always makes it more challenging. However, so far I've always been able to improve
in the race. I think we should have a strong race because the car is behaving well
and we have a good strategy.

The Saubers qualified tenth and 11th, Felipe Massa (1m 15.566s) ahead of
Jacques Villeneuve (1m 15.699s). Both were pretty happy, although Villeneuve was
coping with a touch more understeer than he would ideally like. 'The car really went
well,' he reported.

That could hardly have been the view of either Williams driver, neither of whom
was getting the best out of the latest FW27 aero updates. 'We have been trying to
make the car go faster every session, but we clearly don't have the pace to be at
the front here,' said Mark Webber after qualifying one place ahead of team-mate
Nick Heidfeld. 'The car is reliable and doesn't feel too bad, which is clearly positive,
but this weekend so far has been a tough one for us.' The only thing clear was that
it wouldn't get any easier.

FERNANDO Alonso took another giant step towards becoming F1's youngest ever world champion with a flawless display of precision driving that dominated the French Grand Prix in his Renault R25, delighting the 80,000 patriotic fans who turned out to cheer him on his way. In torrid conditions with track temperatures soaring to over 50°C, the 23-year-old Spaniard delivered the French car maker its first French victory since Alain Prost's similarly decisive run to victory at Paul Ricard 22 years ago.

Prost, now 50, was watching in the pits as Alonso took victory with an economy of style like that the Frenchman had made his personal hallmark a generation ago. Alonso now led the championship by 24 points ahead of McLaren team leader Kimi Räikkönen, who finished second after climbing through from 13th on the grid following a ten-place qualifying penalty, the legacy of an engine failure in Friday's free practice.

Alonso accelerated straight into the lead at the start, completing the opening lap 1.4s ahead of Jarno Trulli's Toyota. His advantage grew to 2.8s second time around, then 4.1s, 5.5s, 7.0s and 8.4s on consecutive laps, ensuring that even before the ten-lap mark he had built up a cushion from which he could dictate the pace for the remainder of the afternoon. Michael Schumacher could only look on wistfully and remember the glory days when he did just the same.

'The race was quite easy,' said Alonso with a cheeky grin which in no way appeared conceited. 'I pushed until the first round of refuelling stops and then controlled the gap, making only small adjustments to the car. I am really pleased to win, but this still does not change anything for the championship. I have quite a good gap to Kimi, but there is still a long way to go.'

Had Räikkönen started from third place on the grid, Alonso might have been forced to work harder for his success. The Finn used the softer Michelin tyre option and a two-stop refuelling strategy to compensate for his strategic disadvantage, but the

sheer pace and consistency of the McLaren MP4-20 while carrying a heavy fuel load was one of the most impressive aspects of the gruelling 70-lap race.

Räikkönen and his team-mate Juan Pablo Montoya, who was using the harder Michelin compound, had two stints of running second and third: the Colombian was ahead from lap 20 to lap 25, then Räikkönen reversed the order after Montoya made a scheduled pit stop. The prospect of McLaren's claiming a healthy tally of constructors' points was, however, thwarted when Montoya stopped after a hydraulic failure sent his car's gearchange haywire. This left Räikkönen to reel off the laps to the chequered flag largely unchallenged.

Räikkönen had no doubts about his winning potential. 'The car was working well and if I could have started third, which is where my qualifying time would have put me, I could definitely have won the race,' he said calmly.

'Our strategists got things right and it was an interesting race. I suffered a bit from traffic and lost too much time early on working my way through the field. When I had clear air it really was too late to make any significant impact on the gap to Alonso.'

For Ferrari, there were at last signs of a recovery, although whether it had come soon enough to revive the team's championship chances was another matter altogether. Michael Schumacher brought his F2005 home in third place, making the best of the latest Bridgestone tyre compound, which the Japanese company had developed progressively over the previous two races and which certainly offered a much better one-lap qualifying performance.

'I think third was the best I could have done today,' said Schumacher. 'I lost a lot of time stuck behind Trulli for 18 laps in the opening stages and that allowed Montoya to get past me. So, I had some problems in traffic. Without that delay our strategy might have put me ahead of Kimi. In fact, this race was all about different drivers on different strategies, but today we

Above: Jenson Button got his rather fraught 2005 campaign into gear with a solid and consistent run to fourth in the BAR-Honda 007. He is pictured leading Giancarlo Fisichella's Renault R25, which started sixth and finished fifth.

Left: Juan Pablo Montoya looked preoccupied with life on the starting grid prior to another race that would deliver him nothing but more disappointment.

Bottom left: Four-times world champion Alain Prost on the grid in company with Renault chief Carlos Ghosn.
Photographs: James Moy/www.crash.net

DIARY

did not quite match the pace of the leaders. I had one moment when I ran wide at Turn Three and then I also came under a bit of pressure from [Giancarlo] Fisichella when he was running lighter than me, but he never got too close.'

For his part, Fisichella had a disappointing day after running sixth from the start in a strong opening stint. He was briefly up to second behind Alonso when he made his first refuelling stop at the end of lap 19, but a problem with his refuelling rig dropped him way down the running order.

'Then the support for the under-tray broke, which cost me a lot of grip and downforce,' he shrugged, 'and at the last stop the engine cut out as I tried to pull away.' He rightly judged that, under the circumstances, sixth place was a pretty respectable result – even though he believed he should have wound up on the podium.

Jenson Button took heart from at last getting his points score off the ground with a lapped fourth in his BAR-Honda 007. 'It's great finally to get some points on the board after such a difficult first half of the season,' he said. 'This is a great result for the team and things can only get better for us during the rest of the year.

'It's also a real boost as we prepare for our home grand prix at Silverstone next week. I think we had a very good strategy here and the team has worked very hard all weekend to achieve fourth position today.'

Unfortunately his team-mate, Takuma Sato, was unable to match Button's success. The Japanese driver made a poor start and was overtaken by Rubens Barrichello's Ferrari as they jostled away from the grid. Sato's race was blighted by a couple of off-track excursions after which he struggled for traction, which gradually deteriorated through to the chequered flag.

As for Trulli, he faded to fifth by the end. 'After the miracle in qualifying yesterday, the race was much harder,' he grinned ruefully. 'I made a strong start and held everybody behind me, but then I couldn't keep up the pace because the car was sliding, particularly at the rear. After the first pit stop the problem became worse, but we balanced the car better at the second stop and it improved slightly.'

Ralf Schumacher ensured that Fisichella was the meat in a Toyota sandwich by bringing the other TF105 home seventh, which was reflective of a pretty satisfactory performance when one considered where he had started his weekend: he had had to run first in qualifying because of not having raced at Indianapolis. The team had changed his strategy to three stops and his progress through the field was assisted by Jacques Villeneuve's Sauber's briefly sliding off near the end of the race, handing Ralf an unexpected last-minute bonus.

Despite this slip, Villeneuve was upbeat after claiming the final point on offer. 'That was not bad at all,' he said. 'The car was good from start to finish, quite driveable, and I was able to push hard all the way. My only concern was when it was running on a full fuel load after my second stop, because it began bottoming in Turn One and I ran out of road there. That corner had been flat for me all weekend but I had to lift a bit after that.'

Barrichello grappled with brake problems throughout and trailed home 3.7s behind Villeneuve and 2.3s clear of David

Left: Pierre Dupasquier had a busy weekend defending Michelin's position in the aftermath of theIndianapolis race controversy.
Photograph: Jean-François Galeron/WRi

Below: Ron Dennis tried to explain the legal details of the Indianapolis débâcle. Onlookers including Bernie Ecclestone, Michelin's Pierre Dupasquier and team heads Nick Fry, Frank Williams and Flavio Briatore seemed glad the job fell to him.
Photograph: James Moy/www.crash.net

THE MICHELIN SAGA RUMBLES ON

The lingering spectre of the troubled US grand prix at Indianapolis continued to hang over the F1 community when it arrived in France and the press became aware that the seven Michelin teams would have been prosecuted under the state laws of Indiana had they competed in the race against the advice of the French tyre company, even if no accident had resulted.

'The legal information communicated to us indicated that not only would we be subject to legal actions if we raced and there had been an accident,' McLaren's Ron Dennis said, 'but we would also have been prosecuted criminally even if there had not been an accident, under a law which renders you liable to conviction if you carry out an act you know could be dangerous.'

Together with the other team principals, Dennis was emphasising the point that, given the legal advice, the discussions about running the race at reduced speeds – whether through the installation of a temporary chicane or with a speed-limited section of track – would have been valid only if the teams received a formal notification from Michelin that its original warning had been rescinded.

'We did everything we could to satisfy the crowds, but ultimately we were constrained by this legal aspect,' said John Howett, the Toyota team principal. 'We have a responsibility to the paying public but we were in a very difficult position.'

Michelin, meanwhile, felt the full force of FIA president Max Mosley's displeasure immediately prior to the French GP when the governing body's World Motor Sport Council deferred a decision regarding the penalties to be applied to the seven teams who failed to take the start of the US GP.

'I think it doesn't need me to launch into an attack on Michelin after what we have seen of it and what it can do and its responses over the past ten days,' said Mosley, who confirmed that he was not ruling out the eventual adoption of a one-tyre-supplier arrangement for F1 unless Michelin could satisfy the sport's governing body that it could supply safe and dependable tyres in the future. He added, 'The facts speak for themselves. It was a disastrous performance and the company should be deeply ashamed.' The WMSC, he said, would reconvene to decide on penalties on 14 September.

The seven teams – McLaren Mercedes, Renault, BMW Williams, Sauber, BAR Honda, Red Bull and Toyota – had been summoned before the World Motor Sport Council to answer five charges that they had brought the sport into disrepute. They were eventually found guilty on only two of the counts: failing to ensure that they were in possession of suitable tyres at Indianapolis and wrongfully refusing to allow their cars to start the race.

They were acquitted of the charges of refusing to race subject to a speed restriction, combining to make a demonstration and failing to inform the stewards that they did not intend to start. This would not, however, be the end of the matter.

Coulthard's Red Bull RB1. 'It was a terrible race for me,' said Rubens. 'After four or five laps I began to have a problem with the brakes and after my first stop I was unable to get ahead of Trulli, so I was always finding myself behind cars that were potentially slower than mine. The brake problem got worse so I wasn't able to score a point. I'm very disappointed.'

Behind Coulthard and Sato, Mark Webber struggled home two laps down in 12th place after an absolute nightmare of a race. After only a few laps the FW27's cockpit temperature had soared to such a height that water had to be poured around the seat area at his pit stops.

'It was very uncomfortable to race in that condition and, as a result, I have a large burn on my right hip which the doctor has treated,' he said after the race. It was later discovered that a rubber grommet, fitted to block an aperture through which electronic cabling had previously been routed, had dropped out, allowing the heat build-up from an electronic box outside the cockpit to trigger this unusual problem.

Nick Heidfeld, in the other Williams, finished 14th between the two Jordans. The young German was spooked by the car's unpredictable handling, which he feared might be a suspension problem but which he was assured by the guys in the pits was a slight glitch with the differential.

It was certainly a disappointing day for the outfit that was once regarded as Britain's blue-riband F1 team and a far cry from those dominant wins for Nigel Mansell in the first two GPs staged at Magny-Cours over a decade earlier. Times change.

Alan Henry

True Grit. Despite the severe discomfort from an overheating cockpit, Mark Webber gamely brought his Williams-BMW home to the finish.
Photograph: Jean-François Galeron

FIA F1 WORLD CHAMPIONSHIP • ROUND 10
GRAND PRIX DE FRANCE
MAGNY-COURS 1–3 JULY 2005

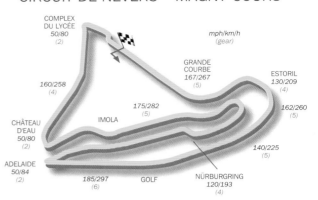

CIRCUIT DE NEVERS – MAGNY-COURS

COMPLEX DU LYCÉE 50/80 (2)
mph/km/h (gear)
GRANDE COURBE 167/267 (5)
160/258 (4)
ESTORIL 130/209 (4)
175/282 (5)
162/260 (5)
CHÂTEAU D'EAU 50/80 (2)
IMOLA
140/225 (5)
ADELAIDE 50/84 (2)
185/297 (6)
GOLF
NÜRBURGRING 120/193 (4)

CIRCUIT LENGTH: 2.741 miles/4.411 km

RACE DISTANCE: 70 laps, 191.746 miles /308.586 km RACE WEATHER: Sunny and dry (track 50–51°C, air 30–32°C)

Pos.	Driver	Nat.	No.	Entrant	Car/Engine	Tyres	Laps	Time/Retirement	Speed (mph/km/h)	Gap to leader	Fastest race lap	
1	Fernando Alonso	E	5	Mild Seven Renault F1 Team	Renault R25-RS25 V10	M	70	1h 31m 22.333s	125.913/202.638		1m 16.502s	5
2	Kimi Räikkönen	FIN	9	West McLaren Mercedes	McLaren MP4-20-Mercedes F0 110R V10	M	70	1h 31m 34.038s	124.642/202.202	+11.805s	1m 16.423s	25
3	Michael Schumacher	D	1	Scuderia Ferrari Marlboro	Ferrari F2005-055 V10	B	70	1h 32m 44.147	124.059/199.654	+81.914s	1m 17.714s	22
4	Jenson Button	GB	3	Lucky Strike BAR Honda	BAR 007-Honda RA005E V10	M	69			+1 lap	1m 17.408s	18
5	Jarno Trulli	I	16	Panasonic Toyota Racing	Toyota TF105-RVX-05 V10	M	69			+1 lap	1m 17.792s	67
6	Giancarlo Fisichella	I	6	Mild Seven Renault F1 Team	Renault R25-RS25 V10	M	69			+1 lap	1m 17.511s	18
7	Ralf Schumacher	D	17	Panasonic Toyota Racing	Toyota TF105-RVX-05 V10	M	69			+1 lap	1m 18.103s	36
8	Jacques Villeneuve	CDN	11	Sauber Petronas	Sauber C24-Petronas 05A V10	M	69			+1 lap	1m 17.841s	17
9	Rubens Barrichello	BR	2	Scuderia Ferrari Marlboro	Ferrari F2005-055 V10	B	69			+1 lap	1m 17.960s	4
10	David Coulthard	GB	14	Red Bull Racing	Red Bull RB1-Cosworth TJ2005/12 V10	M	69			+1 lap	1m 17.611s	39
11	Takuma Sato	J	4	Lucky Strike BAR Honda	BAR 007-Honda RA005E V10	M	69			+1 lap	1m 17.929s	8
12	Mark Webber	AUS	7	BMW WilliamsF1 Team	Williams FW27-BMW P84/85 V10	M	68			+2 laps	1m 18.395s	17
13	Tiago Monteiro	P	18	Jordan Toyota	Jordan EJ15-Toyota RVX-05 V10	B	67			+3 laps	1m 20.004s	32
14	Nick Heidfeld	D	8	BMW WilliamsF1 Team	Williams FW27-BMW P84/85 V10	M	66			+4 laps	1m 18.102s	36
15	Narain Karthikeyan	IND	19	Jordan Toyota	Jordan EJ15-Toyota RVX-05 V10	B	66			+4 laps	1m 20.156s	9
	Juan Pablo Montoya	COL	10	West McLaren Mercedes	McLaren MP4-20-Mercedes F0 110R V10	M	46	Hydraulics			1m 16.656s	24
	Christijan Albers	NL	21	Minardi Cosworth	Minardi PS05-Cosworth TJ2005 V10	B	37	Wrongly fitted tyre-valve caps			1m 21.077s	8
	Patrick Friesacher	A	20	Minardi Cosworth	Minardi PS05-Cosworth TJ2005 V10	B	33	Wrongly fitted tyre-valve caps			1m 21.451s	4
	Felipe Massa	BR	12	Sauber Petronas	Sauber C24-Petronas 05A V10	M	30	Hydraulics			1m 17.805s	11
	Christian Klien	A	15	Red Bull Racing	Red Bull RB1-Cosworth TJ2005/12 V10	M	1	Fuel pressure				

Fastest lap: Kimi Räikkönen, on lap 25, 1m 16.423s, 129.111 mph/207.785 km/h.

Lap record: Michael Schumacher (Ferrari F2004-052 V10), 1m 15.377s, 130.903 mph/210.669 km/h (2004).

19th: MONTEIRO Jordan-Toyota

17th: KARTHIKEYAN Jordan-Toyota

15th: COULTHARD Red Bull-Cosworth

13th: RÄIKKÖNEN McLaren-Mercedes
Ten-place penalty for engine change

11th: R. SCHUMACHER Toyota

20th: ALBERS Minardi-Cosworth

18th: FRIESACHER Minardi-Cosworth

16th: KLIEN Red Bull-Cosworth

14th: HEIDFELD Williams-BMW

12th: WEBBER Williams-BMW

Grid order / Lap chart

```
Grid order        1  2  3  4  5  6  7  8  9 10 11 12 13 14 15 16 17 18 19 20 21 22 23 24 25 26 27 28 29 30 31 32 33 34 35 36 37 38 39 40 41 42 43 44 45 46 47 48 49 50 51 52 53 54
 5 ALONSO         5  5  5  5  5  5  5  5  5  5  5  5  5  5  5  5  5  5  5  5  5  5  5  5  5  5  5  5  5  5  5  5  5  5  5  5  5  5  5  5  5  5  5  5  5  5  5  5  5  5  5  5  5  5
16 TRULLI        16 16 16 16 16 16 16 16 16 16 16 16 16 16 16 16 16 16 16 16 16  6 10 10 10 10 10 10 10  9  9  9  9  9  9  9  9  9  9  9  9  9  9  9  9  9  9  9  9  9  9  9  9  9
 1 M. SCHUMACHER  1  1  1  1  1  1  1  1  1  1  1  1  1  1  1  1  1  1  1 10  9  9  9  9  9  9  9 10 10 10 10 10 10 10 10 10 10 10 10 10 10 10 10 10 10 10 10 10 10  1  1  1  1  1
 4 SATO           2  2  2  2  2  2  2  2  2  2  2  2  2  2  2  2  2  6  3  1  1  1  1  1  1  1  1  1  1  1  1  1  1  1  1  1  1  1  1  1  1  1  1  1  1  1  1  1 11 11  6  6  6  6
 2 BARRICHELLO    4  4  4  4  4  4  4  4  4  4  4  4  4  6  6 10  9 16 16 16 16 16 16 16 16 16 16 16 16 16 16 16 16 16 16 16 16 16 16 16 16 16 16 16 16  3  6  6  3  3  3  3
 6 FISICHELLA     6  6  6  6  6  6  6  6  6  6  6  6  6  6 10 10  3 11  2  2  4  4  4  4  4  2  2  2  2  2  2  2  2  2  2  2  3  3  3  3  3  3 11  3  3 16 16 16 16 16  1
 3 BUTTON        10 10 10 10 10 10 10 10 10 10 10 10 10 10  3  3  9  1  4  4  2  2  2  2  2  3  3  3  3  3  3  3  3  6  6  6  6 11  6 16 16  2  2  2  2
10 MONTOYA        3  3  3  3  3  3  3  3  3  3  3  3  3  3  9  9 11 16  3  3  3  3  6  6  6  6  6  6  6  6  6 11 11 11 11  6 16  2  2 11 17 17 17 17 17  1
12 MASSA         12 12 12 12 12 12 12 12 12 12 12 12 12 11  2  2 14 14  6  6  6  6  6 12  4  4  4  4  4  4 11 11 11 11 17 17 17 17  2  2  2 17 17 11 11 11 11 11 11  1
11 VILLENEUVE    11  9  9  9  9  9  9  9  9  9  9  9  9  7  7  7  6 12 12 12 12 12  4 11 11 11 11 11 11 17 17 17 17  2  2  2 17 17 17  4  4  4 14 14 14 14  1
17 R. SCHUMACHER  9 11 11 11 11 11 11 11 11 11 11 11 11  4  4  4 12 12 17 17 17 17 17 17 17 17 17  8  8  8 14 14 14  4  4  4  4 14 14  4  4  4  4
 7 WEBBER        17 17 17 17 17 17 17 17 17 17 17 17 17 17 17  7  7  7  7  7  8  8  8 14 14 14 14  4  4  4  4 14 14 14  8  7  7  7  7  7  7
 9 RÄIKKÖNEN      7  7  7  7  7  7  7  7  7  7  7  7  7 14 14  8 12 17 17  7  7  7  8  8  8 14  4  4  4 14 14  4  8  8  8  8  8  8  7  7  7  7  7 18 18 18  8  8  8
 8 HEIDFELD       8  8  8  8  8  8  8  8  8  8  8  8  8 12 12 12 17  7  7  8  8  8 14 14  7  7  7  7  7  7  7  7  7  7  7  7  7 18 18 18 18  8  8  8
14 COULTHARD     14 14 14 14 14 14 14 14 14 14 14 14 14 17 17 17  8  8 14 14 14 14 14 14 12 18 18 18 18 18 18 18 18 18 18 18 18 18 19 19 19 19 19 19 19 19 19  1
15 KLIEN         19 19 19 19 19 19 19 19 19 19 19 19 19 19 19 19 18 18 18 18 18 18 18 18 19 19 19 19 19 19 19 19 19 19 19 19 19
19 KARTHIKEYAN   15 15 15 15 15 15 15 15 15 15 15 15 18 18 18 18 18 18 21 21 21 21 21 21 21 21 21 21 21 21 21 21
20 FRIESACHER    21 18 18 18 18 18 18 18 18 18 18 18 21 21 21 21 21 21 20 20 20 20 20 20 20 20 20
18 MONTEIRO      18 20 20 20 20 20 20 20 20 20 20 20 20 21 21 21 21 21 21 12
21 ALBERS        20
```

Pit stop
One lap or more behind leader

TIME SHEETS

QUALIFYING

WEATHER: Overcast (track 26°C, air 21°C)

Pos.	Driver	R/Order	Sector 1	Sector 2	Sector 3	Time
1	Fernando Alonso	10	24.262s	25.961s	24.189s	1m 14.412s
2	Jarno Trulli	14	24.301s	26.016s	24.204s	1m 14.521s
3	Kimi Räikkönen	13	24.374s	25.924s	24.261s	1m 14.559s
4	Michael Schumacher	20	24.105s	26.150s	24.317s	1m 14.572s
5	Takuma Sato	9	24.258s	26.113s	24.284s	1m 14.655s
6	Rubens Barrichello	19	24.250s	25.944s	24.638s	1m 14.832s
7	Giancarlo Fisichella	11	24.252s	26.096s	24.539s	1m 14.887s
8	Jenson Button	12	24.425s	26.280s	24.346s	1m 15.051s
9	Juan Pablo Montoya	6	24.493s	26.298s	24.615s	1m 15.406s
10	Felipe Massa	7	24.448s	26.466s	24.652s	1m 15.566s
11	Jacques Villeneuve	5	24.675s	26.359s	24.665s	1m 15.699s
12	Ralf Schumacher	1	24.316s	26.912s	24.543s	1m 15.771s
13	Mark Webber	8	24.636s	26.485s	24.764s	1m 15.885s
14	Nick Heidfeld	3	24.641s	26.645s	24.921s	1m 16.207s
15	David Coulthard	2	24.680s	26.735s	25.019s	1m 16.434s
16	Christian Klien	4	24.774s	26.776s	24.997s	1m 16.547s
17	Narain Karthikeyan	17	25.036s	27.220s	25.542s	1m 17.857s
18	Patrick Friesacher	15	25.307s	27.175s	25.478s	1m 17.960s
19	Tiago Monteiro	18	25.308s	26.953s	25.786s	1m 18.047s
20	Christijan Albers	16	25.305s	27.233s	25.797s	1m 18.335s

Photograph: James Moy/www.crash.net

CHASSIS LOG BOOK

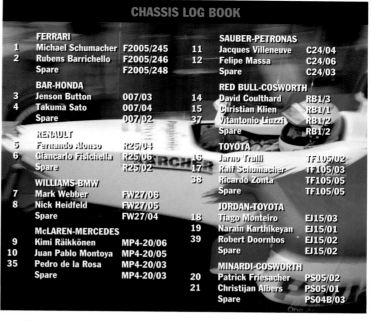

	FERRARI				
1	Michael Schumacher	F2005/245			
2	Rubens Barrichello	F2005/246			
	Spare	F2005/248			

SAUBER-PETRONAS
11 Jacques Villeneuve C24/04
12 Felipe Massa C24/06
Spare C24/03

BAR-HONDA
3 Jenson Button 007/03
4 Takuma Sato 007/04
Spare 007/02

RED BULL-COSWORTH
14 David Coulthard RB1/3
15 Christian Klien RB1/1
37 Vitantonio Liuzzi RB1/2
Spare RB1/2

RENAULT
5 Fernando Alonso R25/04
6 Giancarlo Fisichella R25/06
Spare R25/02

TOYOTA
16 Jarno Trulli TF105/02
17 Ralf Schumacher TF105/03
38 Ricardo Zonta TF105/05
Spare TF105/05

WILLIAMS-BMW
7 Mark Webber FW27/06
8 Nick Heidfeld FW27/05
Spare FW27/04

JORDAN-TOYOTA
18 Tiago Monteiro EJ15/03
19 Narain Karthikeyan EJ15/01
39 Robert Doornbos EJ15/02
Spare EJ15/02

McLAREN-MERCEDES
9 Kimi Räikkönen MP4-20/06
10 Juan Pablo Montoya MP4-20/05
35 Pedro de la Rosa MP4-20/03
Spare MP4-20/03

MINARDI-COSWORTH
20 Patrick Friesacher PS05/02
21 Christijan Albers PS05/01
Spare PS04B/03

Photograph: James Moy/www.crash.net

PRACTICE 1 (FRIDAY)

Sunny (track 27–31°C, air 21–22°C)

Pos.	Driver	Laps	Time
1	Pedro de la Rosa	21	1m 14.778s
2	Fernando Alonso	10	1m 15.183s
3	Giancarlo Fisichella	10	1m 15.255s
4	Takuma Sato	10	1m 15.530s
5	Kimi Räikkönen	10	1m 15.877s
6	Jenson Button	11	1m 16.038s
7	Olivier Panis	24	1m 16.146s
8	Juan Pablo Montoya	11	1m 16.366s
9	Ralf Schumacher	6	1m 16.731s
10	Nick Heidfeld	11	1m 16.758s
11	Michael Schumacher	11	1m 16.838s
12	David Coulthard	7	1m 17.168s
13	Christian Klien	10	1m 17.343s
14	Rubens Barrichello	10	1m 17.389s
15	Mark Webber	11	1m 17.451s
16	Felipe Massa	7	1m 17.777s
17	Jacques Villeneuve	6	1m 18.192s
18	Vitantonio Liuzzi	16	1m 18.876s
19	Robert Doornbos	20	1m 19.001s
20	Narain Karthikeyan	13	1m 20.067s
21	Christijan Albers	17	1m 20.382s
22	Patrick Friesacher	16	1m 20.725s
23	Tiago Monteiro	6	1m 21.725s
24	Jarno Trulli	1	No time

PRACTICE 2 (FRIDAY)

Sunny (track 37°C, air 24–25°C)

Pos.	Driver	Laps	Time
1	Pedro de la Rosa	35	1m 14.460s
2	Juan Pablo Montoya	21	1m 15.129s
3	Michael Schumacher	24	1m 15.204s
4	Fernando Alonso	23	1m 15.242s
5	Giancarlo Fisichella	27	1m 15.380s
6	Olivier Panis	37	1m 15.483s
7	Rubens Barrichello	27	1m 15.605s
8	Jarno Trulli	24	1m 15.774s
9	Ralf Schumacher	24	1m 15.925s
10	David Coulthard	26	1m 16.371s
11	Jacques Villeneuve	25	1m 16.430s
12	Jenson Button	29	1m 16.597s
13	Felipe Massa	27	1m 16.753s
14	Takuma Sato	28	1m 16.890s
15	Vitantonio Liuzzi	25	1m 16.987s
16	Mark Webber	27	1m 17.107s
17	Nick Heidfeld	28	1m 17.192s
18	Robert Doornbos	25	1m 17.574s
19	Narain Karthikeyan	23	1m 17.790s
20	Christijan Albers	14	1m 18.508s
21	Patrick Friesacher	25	1m 18.814s
22	Christian Klien	5	1m 18.897s
23	Tiago Monteiro	18	1m 19.186s
24	Kimi Räikkönen	2	No time

PRACTICE 3 (SATURDAY)

Warm and dry but overcast (track 18–20°C, air 17–19°C)

Pos.	Driver	Laps	Time
1	Fernando Alonso	11	1m 23.939s
2	Giancarlo Fisichella	10	1m 24.922s
3	Kimi Räikkönen	5	1m 26.483s
4	David Coulthard	3	1m 27.019s
5	Jenson Button	6	1m 27.276s
6	Mark Webber	8	1m 27.313s
7	Nick Heidfeld	7	1m 27.510s
8	Patrick Friesacher	5	1m 27.166s
9	Christijan Albers	6	1m 30.872s
10	Jarno Trulli	3	No time
11	Juan Pablo Montoya	1	No time
12	Tiago Monteiro	1	No time
13	Takuma Sato	1	No time
14	Ralf Schumacher	2	No time
15	Narain Karthikeyan	2	No time
16	Felipe Massa	1	No time
17	Jacques Villeneuve	1	No time
18	Christian Klien	1	No time

PRACTICE 4 (SATURDAY)

Warm and dry but overcast (track 21–31°C, air 19–20°C)

Pos.	Driver	Laps	Time
1	Giancarlo Fisichella	16	1m 14.466s
2	Ralf Schumacher	13	1m 14.603s
3	Kimi Räikkönen	14	1m 14.649s
4	Fernando Alonso	12	1m 14.792s
5	Michael Schumacher	14	1m 14.979s
6	Takuma Sato	18	1m 15.177s
7	Rubens Barrichello	15	1m 15.218s
8	Juan Pablo Montoya	15	1m 15.223s
9	Jenson Button	18	1m 15.228s
10	Jarno Trulli	15	1m 15.249s
11	David Coulthard	16	1m 15.305s
12	Mark Webber	12	1m 16.080s
13	Christian Klien	17	1m 16.095s
14	Jacques Villeneuve	15	1m 16.125s
15	Nick Heidfeld	12	1m 16.372s
16	Felipe Massa	17	1m 16.454s
17	Christijan Albers	14	1m 17.846s
18	Patrick Friesacher	16	1m 17.929s
19	Narain Karthikeyan	14	1m 18.195s
20	Tiago Monteiro	14	1m 18.310s

9th: MASSA Sauber-Petronas

7th: BUTTON BAR-Honda

5th: BARRICHELLO Ferrari

3rd: M. SCHUMACHER Ferrari

Pole: ALONSO Renault

10th: VILLENEUVE Sauber-Petronas

8th: MONTOYA McLaren-Mercedes

6th: FISICHELLA Renault

4th: SATO BAR-Honda

2nd: TRULLI Toyota

55	56	57	58	59	60	61	62	63	64	65	66	67	68	69	70	
5	5	5	5	5	5	5	5	5	5	5	5	5	5	5	5	1
9	9	9	9	9	9	9	9	9	9	9	9	9	9	9	9	2
1	1	1	1	1	1	1	1	1	1	1	1	1	1	1	1	3
6	6	6	6	3	3	3	3	3	3	3	3	3	3	3	3	4
3	3	3	3	16	16	16	16	16	16	16	16	16	16	16	16	5
16	16	16	16	6	6	6	6	6	6	6	6	6	6	6	6	6
17	17	17	17	17	17	17	17	17	17	17	17	17	17	17	17	7
11	11	11	11	11	11	11	11	11	11	11	11	11	11	11	11	8
14	14	14	14	2	2	2	2	2	2	2	2	2	2	2	2	
2	2	2	2	14	14	14	14	14	14	14	14	14	14	14	14	
4	4	4	4	4	4	4	4	4	4	4	4	4	4	4	4	
7	7	7	7	7	7	7	7	7	7	7	7	7	7	7	7	
18	18	18	18	18	18	18	18	18	18	18	18	18	18			
8	8	8	8	8	8	8	8	8	8	8	8					
19	19	19	19	19	19	19	19	19	19	19	19					

FOR THE RECORD

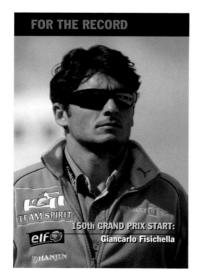

150th GRAND PRIX START:
Giancarlo Fisichella

POINTS

DRIVERS

1	Fernando Alonso	69	18	Christijan Albers	4
2	Kimi Räikkönen	45	19	Pedro de la Rosa	4
3	Michael Schumacher	40	20	Christian Klien	4
4	Jarno Trulli	31	21	Patrick Friesacher	3
5	Rubens Barrichello	29	22	Vitantonio Liuzzi	1
6	Nick Heidfeld	25			
7	Mark Webber	22			
8	Ralf Schumacher	22			
9	Giancarlo Fisichella	20			
10	David Coulthard	17			
11	Juan Pablo Montoya	16			
12	Felipe Massa	6			
13	Tiago Monteiro	6			
14	Alex Wurz	6			
15	Jacques Villeneuve	6			
16	Jenson Button	5			
17	Narain Karthikeyan	5			

CONSTRUCTORS

1	Renault	89
2	McLaren	71
3	Ferrari	69
4	Toyota	53
5	Williams	47
6	Red Bull	22
7	Sauber	13
8	Jordan	11
9	Minardi	7
10	BAR	5

Photographs: James Moy/www.crash.net

Above: A relieved Juan Pablo Montoya on the podium after his first win for McLaren.
Photograph: Peter Nygaard/GP Photo

Above right: The drivers formed up on the start line to observe one minute's silence for the victims of the London bombings.

Right: Journalist Bob McKenzie vowed to 'run around Silverstone naked' if McLaren won a race in 2004. Kimi Räikkönen won at Spa, so Bob made good his promise.

Top right: Fosters once again sponsored this highly successful event.

Far right: Crucial moment at Copse on the opening lap as Juan Pablo Montoya aimed his McLaren-Mercedes towards the outside line around Fernando Alonso's Renault, successfully grabbing the lead through the next left-hander.
Photographs: James Moy/www.crash.net

SILVERSTONE
BRITISHGP

FIA F1 WORLD CHAMPIONSHIP/ROUND 11

Right: A clear message from track-side fans to the governing body, the FIA, suggested it was a little too meddlesome.
Photograph: James Moy/www.crash.net

Below: FIA president Max Mosley took a robust stance over Michelin's US tyres.
Photograph: Laurent Charniaux/WRI

SILVERSTONE QUALIFYING

The pattern of qualifying for Kimi Räikkönen and ten of his rivals was set before the session even began. To be precise, at the start of Saturday morning's second practice session. That was when, for the second race in succession, the Finn suffered an engine failure. This time, it was an oil-pump failure that obliged Mercedes-Benz to change the unit, and Räikkönen was not amused.

'It's not a question of bad luck; it's a question of bad preparation,' he said. 'It was a huge disappointment and it's depressing to know that however perfectly you do a lap in qualifying, you still can't start from where you should. We are going in the wrong direction in the championship fight.'

That, of course, meant that whatever Räikkönen did, he was going to be lucky to start as high as 11th. In the event, however, he would not have secured pole even without that problem. Fernando Alonso was on superb form with a Renault that had the latest specification engine with a little bit more power. After their respective first and second places in Magny-Cours, Alonso and Räikkönen were the last two men to run in qualifying and when Räikkönen went out the man he had to beat was local hero Jenson Button.

All week the Englishman had assiduously played down BAR Honda's chances, yet here he was, setting what was then the fastest time of 1m 20. 207s. 'We got everything we could out of the car for qualifying,' he reported with a big smile. 'The car has struggled a little through Copse and Becketts, which has been a bit of a worry, but it is working very well in the low-speed corners.'

Räikkönen soon wiped away some smiles at BAR when he pushed the McLaren around in 1m 19.932s. Being unable to hone it on new rubber that morning because of the engine failure had compromised him a little bit. And a little bit was all Alonso needed as he rushed around in 1m 19.905s to snatch the pole.

'Aha!' everyone said. Kimi will have been running loads of fuel, just like he did at Magny-Cours. Indeed, the race would prove that the Finn had three laps' more juice than the Spaniard, but this was nonetheless a great performance from the series leader, who said the balance of his Renault was 'really nice'. He also admitted that the success was unexpected and he thanked the team for the overnight work that had improved the R25. It also meant that Räikkönen would now start 12th rather than 11th.

The first sign of what was to come in the race from Juan Pablo Montoya could be seen in his fourth-fastest qualifying lap of 1m 20.382s, since his hydraulic failure at Magny-Cours had left him as the fifth man out in the session, when the track was still not at its best. 'I could have been one or two tenths quicker,' he confessed, 'but I was careful coming into the first corner because of the wind and all of a sudden I lost a lot of grip when I turned in at Becketts. But the rest of the lap was pretty good and I pushed like crazy.'

Behind Montoya, Jarno Trulli had a clean lap in his Toyota for 1m 20.459s, and Rubens Barrichello completed the runners below 1m 21s with 1m 20.906s for Ferrari and Bridgestone.

Giancarlo Fisichella set a momentary fastest time in the first sector, but lost out in the second and was actually three tenths slower in the third than he had been on his out lap. There was less understeer, but he complained of a general lack of grip. 'It wasn't a perfect lap this afternoon,' he said glumly as 1m 21.010s left him seventh overall.

Takuma Sato and Ralf Schumacher shared row four, with laps of 1m 21.114s and 1m 21.191s respectively, while the fifth contained old enemies Michael Schumacher and Jacques Villeneuve. The reigning champion spoiled his run with a dirty moment exiting Stowe and could not recover the lost momentum on his way to a disappointing 1m 21.275s; the former champion was much happier with his Sauber's aerodynamic balance thanks to a new front wing that had been fitted for Saturday's sessions and he recorded 1m 21.352s.

Mark Webber was on row six with Räikkönen, but BMW Williams was all at sea on the aero front. Webber used the new MkII package for 1m 21.997s, while team-mate Nick Heidfeld kept his car with the old bodywork as it had run that morning and posted 1m 22.117s. Having been halted with an electronic problem in the morning, David Coulthard pipped Heidfeld, and his team-mate Christian Klien lined up on row eight alongside Sauber's Felipe Massa. Since the Brazilian had to start the session second, the team opted to give him plenty of fuel, so he didn't better 1m 22.495s. Narain Karthikeyan brought up the rear ahead of the Minardis of Christijan Albers and Patrick Friesacher. Following an engine failure, Tiago Monteiro simply did an installation lap to check out his Jordan's new Toyota V10.

MOSLEY STANDS FIRM

Max Mosley braved the fans at Silverstone in his first appearance at a race since the fiasco of the US Grand Prix at Indianapolis. Addressing selected journalists, he brushed aside the drivers' accusation that he had tried to influence them by threatening to withdraw from safety discussions. He was soon banging the table and reiterating the position of strength from which he operates at the FIA, while at the same time pouring scorn on the idea of any breakaway world championship.

As the weekend progressed, however, word filtered through of a mood for reconciliation. On the Thursday after the race, Ron Dennis of McLaren and Christian Horner of Red Bull Racing were invited to attend an FIA Senate meeting in Monaco. Later that day the sport moved a critical step closer to an end to its civil war when disciplinary proceedings against the seven Michelin teams who did not take part in the US Grand Prix were dropped.

The teams – McLaren Mercedes, Renault, BMW Williams, Sauber, BAR Honda, Red Bull and Toyota – had provided the Senate with a dossier supposedly, according to the FIA, of 'new evidence' relating to Indianapolis. The governing body then issued a statement which said, 'Having examined the new evidence and discussed it with Mr Dennis and Mr Horner, the Senate was satisfied that the teams were contractually bound to follow the instructions of their tyre supplier and that their tyre supplier had expressly prohibited them from racing at the Indianapolis Motor Speedway in its licensed configuration. Recognising that for both sporting and legal reasons it was impossible for the FIA to authorise a change to the circuit configuration and that both the FIA and the teams could have faced serious legal difficulties in the United States had they not observed to the letter their respective rules and contractual obligations (particularly had there been any kind of accident), the Senate was of the view that having regard to this new evidence, disciplinary proceedings against the teams had ceased to be appropriate and were no longer in the interest of the sport.'

The Senate, which meets when the World Motor Sport Council is unable to schedule a meeting, proposed to the WMSC that the guilty verdict returned against the teams in Paris on 29 June should be cancelled and a fax vote was put in motion to facilitate this.

In F1 circles the decision was hailed as an overdue victory for common sense and a climb-down by Mosley as the sport pulled back from the brink just as it appeared bent on self-destruction.

I F you wanted to be cynical, you might suggest that Juan Pablo Montoya's victory at Silverstone was the worst possible scenario for McLaren as far as the drivers' championship was concerned, but the best for its quest for the constructors' crown. But on a day when the best that Montoya's team-mate Kimi Räikkönen could do was third place after an engine failure had given him yet another ten-place grid penalty, the Colombian got a monkey off his back and prevented series leader Fernando Alonso from adding more than eight points to his tally.

Räikkönen really needed to win this British Grand Prix to keep his title hopes alive; so too Montoya needed to win it, for different reasons. Since he joined McLaren, his luck had been appalling and he needed something to demonstrate his true ability.

With Alonso and Jenson Button on the front row, Montoya knew that a good start was essential. His was pluperfect. Button and the other potential danger, habitual fast-starter Jarno Trulli, suffered on the dirty side of the track. Alonso went quickly, but Montoya was quicker and had greater momentum as they headed through Copse and out to the fast sweeps.

'I knew that I needed to get Fernando before Becketts,' Montoya said. 'I knew he couldn't risk too much and I was willing to risk a bit more and it really paid off. I think that's where the race was won. We were going to go side-by-side into Becketts. Either one of us was going to back off or we were going to go off, and the chances were that he was going to back off before me. He's got a fight for the world

championship and I haven't. I just wanted to win the race.'

The boldness paid off as Alonso took the sensible route. Why squander eight points? It soon became clear, however, that Montoya couldn't just drop the blue car because his McLaren began to understeer a little. So Montoya settled into a rhythm and waited for the first pit stops. As his crew saw mounting traffic ahead on lap 22 it called him in. But it was going to be close and there was plenty of urging over the radio prior to the stop as McLaren pushed its man to open the 1.5s gap he needed. Alonso stopped a lap later and it was nip and tuck as the McLaren swept around the outside of the Renault at Copse as the latter came out of the pit exit.

Now Alonso continued to hound Montoya. 'We put a lot of fuel on board to go very long in the second stint,' he revealed. 'I think the strategy was good. The four or five laps longer I had should have helped me to win the race but unfortunately I had some traffic after Juan Pablo stopped.'

Montoya came in for the second and final time on lap 44. This was the point at which the race could – possibly even should – have gone Renault's way. Alonso had a lighter car and several laps in which to squeeze the maximum from it. He hit traffic. One of the worst offenders was Trulli, who inadvertently got in the way and cost Alonso a crucial chunk of time.

'Those six or seven laps I had to really push and I lost two or three seconds. I lost a lot of time behind Trulli but it wasn't his fault because they were not showing any blue flags,' an aggrieved Alonso said. 'Even with that we were still close at the

disappointed Italian said. 'The strategy was excellent and I was in the fight at the front of the race. When we came here we knew that McLaren would be quicker than us but, honestly, it was very close indeed.'

Fisichella could be forgiven for being disappointed, for he had been within a second and a half of Alonso at the end of lap 45, with both men due to make one more pit stop. For a while now Renault had been getting rather upset by doubt of its support for Fisichella and here it was outraged by suggestions that his racing was being sacrificed for the good of Alonso's title campaign. But that did not explain why Fisichella, due to run until lap 50 if you figured out the maths of their stops and respective fuel loads, was called in on lap 46. Whatever, his delay allowed Räikkönen through to snatch another great podium finish. Fisichella had to be content with fourth.

As an indication of how tough F1 is these days, Räikkönen could do nothing in the early laps but follow Michael Schumacher's Ferrari as they ran in seventh and eighth places, and that was where he lost the time that would ultimately cost him any shot at second place. Once the German refuelled on lap 24, Räikkönen climbed up to second with a beautiful pass on fuel-heavy Alonso going into Stowe corner on the 26th lap before immediately peeling in to refuel. That little moment of drama was something else that helped Montoya. Subsequently Räikkönen resumed in fifth place behind Montoya, Alonso, Fisichella and Button, but he hunted down the BAR until the Englishman made his final stop on lap 43. After Fisichella's problem three laps later, Räikkönen was home and dry for third and cemented that by setting that fastest lap on the last tour.

'I think I did the best I could today,' he said with a resigned air. 'But if I hadn't had the penalty, the result would have been different.'

Button, pushed back to third and under pressure from Rubens Barrichello and Giancarlo Fisichella right from the start, knew that this would not be the day he could deliver the home win that his fans wanted. 'It was evident that we couldn't expect any more from the car,' he said. 'We came here hoping that we would benefit from our improvements but they obviously didn't go far enough and we are still some way behind. I'm just sorry that we couldn't get the podium that we all wanted.'

BAR's best was better than either of the Schumacher

DIARY

Jenson Button denies spurious rumours that he is entertaining a $20-million offer to join Michael Schumacher at Ferrari for 2006. Other rumours suggest that he is keen to stay with BAR rather than move to Williams.

Button is presented with the Mike Hawthorn Trophy by sports minister Richard Caborn in recognition of his performances for BAR in 2004. The award is made annually to the most successful British or Commonwealth driver in F1.

At the British Grand Prix the FIA and AMD publish the results of a survey of 93,000 F1 fans. According to the feedback, 94 percent want more overtaking, 74 percent want more emphasis on driver skill, 69 percent want more teams, and 84 percent want 18 or more races each season. The fans also say they want hi-technology to continue as a key part of the sport.

While Juan Pablo Montoya is breaking through for McLaren at Silverstone, former Jaguar F1 driver Justin Wilson celebrates his first Champ-car victory after winning in Toronto for his RuSPORT team.

pit exit.' But not close enough. As Alonso came out of the pit exit at the start of his 50th lap, Montoya had responded to more radio messages to increase his pace again and had enough in hand to sweep back into the lead at Copse. Just as McLaren's communication had failed so disastrously in Canada, so it worked to perfection here. Alonso closed to within a second of the lead in the final stint, but then settled for his eight-point haul. 'It's a bit frustrating to lose a win through traffic,' he said, 'but this is still a great result for us.'

One step higher on the podium, Montoya was delighted. 'It's a great feeling winning my first grand prix for McLaren. My start was perfect and I managed to get by Fernando in a wheel-to-wheel dice. It was then all about staying ahead and our strategy, combined with two excellent pit stops, really helped me to manage that.'

It was best described as a tense rather than an out-and-out exciting race and the McLaren had the speed when it was needed. The fastest laps told the tale. Kimi Räikkönen was fastest with 1m 20.502s and Montoya next with 1m 20.700s. Giancarlo Fisichella was third with 1m 21.159s, Alonso fourth on 1m 21.228s. Not a bad margin for the Silver Arrows.

Other than Montoya and Alonso, the only drivers in contention for the podium were Fisichella and Räikkönen. The Italian drove his usual fast but unobtrusive race and appeared to have a lock on third place as he made his second and last pit stop on lap 46. Then the engine stalled again, as it had at Magny-Cours. 'It was a very strong race for me,' the

Jenson Button's BAR held off Rubens Barrichello's Ferrari. Jenson finished fifth, the Brazilian two places farther back.
Photograph: Emily Davenport/XPB.cc

brothers managed on their way to sixth and eighth places as they sandwiched Barrichello. Ferrari had hoped, as it went through practice and qualifying, that everything would somehow come together for the race. It didn't. Michael Schumacher set the fifth-fastest lap with 1m 21.675s, but that was nearly a second off Räikkönen's best.

'I cannot be happy to have finished sixth,' Michael Schumacher said. 'Clearly, we are simply not fast enough at the moment. If I had not been delayed by Trulli, I might have been able to fight Button, but I am not keen on using "if" as an excuse. If you compare our performances in the two North-American races with these past two, we appear to be going backwards instead of forwards.' To make things worse, Barrichello's attempt to run the only three-stop strategy was stymied by the mysterious braking problems that beset him at Magny-Cours.

Interestingly, Ralf Schumacher set the sixth-fastest lap (1m 21.960s) despite being very unhappy with his tyre choice. One insider at Toyota revealed, 'To begin with, our cars were complete shit! They were sliding around all over the place, but gradually just got better and better.'

Trulli, however, was bitterly disappointed to come away with only ninth place. 'We made a mistake with our strategy and I lost positions because I was always in traffic or being held up by blue flags.' There was one note of encouragement, however: both drivers were using their V10s for the third time, relying on the units they had installed at Indianapolis. As the source said, 'The engine is one thing we really don't worry about.'

A fine 10th place fell to Felipe Massa after his strategy of a fuel-heavy first stint was rendered even more difficult when his car went into anti-stall mode at the start, requiring him to reset it quickly and repass both Jordans on the opening lap. 'When I was alone on the track the car was very good, very consistent,' he said. 'If I'd been able to start higher I could have taken points, for sure.'

So too should team-mate Jacques Villeneuve, who started 10th. But the French-Canadian had a disastrous first pit stop on lap 19. 'I screwed up,' he admitted. 'I got distracted by what was happening in the Red Bull pit [where David Coulthard was being serviced] and when I saw movement out of the corner of my eye I mistakenly thought it was my lollipop signal to go and moved too soon.' Refueller Silvan Ruegg still had the hose attached and got one of his feet run over.

'I gave him [Villeneuve] a few bangs on the helmet and eventually he stopped,' Ruegg said. He later had medical treatment but was okay apart from a sore limb, and Villeneuve lost time that he was never able to recover. Over the last stages of the race he was embroiled in a tight battle with Nick Heidfeld, Coulthard and Christian Klien, the quartet running wheel-to-wheel for some time before finishing less than five seconds apart.

It was a very poor race for Williams, with Mark Webber a lonely 11th ahead of Heidfeld, the FW27's aerodynamics clearly not working well.

The Red Bull drivers both enjoyed their fight but were critical of their RB1s' inconsistency. The tyre choice had been made on Friday by third driver Tonio Liuzzi, who said that for some reason the best tyre in Michelin's range (which some other teams had gone for) had not been chosen during the previous test by chief engineer Jerry Hughes, who had since been supplanted by former Renault man Paul Monaghan. The Italian said that the tyre he chose from the two that were available to the team felt worse for the first three laps but was then much better than the alternative.

Takuma Sato's contribution to proceedings had been to bring out the safety car for the opening two laps after pressing the kill switch on his BAR instead of resetting the engine controls as he went to the grid. He finished an undistinguished 16th ahead of Tiago Monteiro, who maintained his record of finishing every grand prix. Minardi runners Christijan Albers and Patrick Friesacher were 18th and 19th, both suffering from the need to be vigilant for faster cars and getting their tyres dirty as a result of having to move off-line so often. The only retiree was Narain Karthikeyan, with electronic failure on lap 11. The Indian was even more annoyed later when a Jordan source suggested the reason was 'finger trouble'.

The glorious British summer day was poignant in light of the bombings in London the previous Thursday and the drivers and dignitaries – who included Bernie Ecclestone, leader of the Commons Geoff Hoon and sports minister Richard Caborn – heard no official notification of the minute's silence on the grid and were still talking and laughing as spectators completed their tribute. Sadly it was the only part of the organisation of this oft-criticised event that did not run with clockwork precision.

David Tremayne

FIA F1 WORLD CHAMPIONSHIP • ROUND 11
FOSTER'S
BRITISH GRAND PRIX
SILVERSTONE 8–10 JULY 2005

Photograph: James Moy/www.crash.net

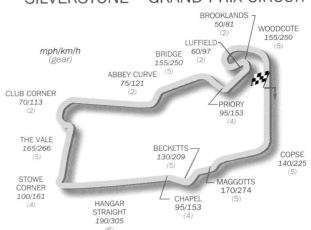

SILVERSTONE – GRAND PRIX CIRCUIT

mph/km/h (gear)

BROOKLANDS 50/81 (2)
WOODCOTE 155/250 (5)
LUFFIELD 60/97 (2)
BRIDGE 155/250 (5)
ABBEY CURVE 75/121 (2)
PRIORY 95/153 (4)
CLUB CORNER 70/113 (2)
THE VALE 165/266 (5)
BECKETTS 130/209 (5)
COPSE 140/225 (5)
STOWE CORNER 100/161 (4)
MAGGOTTS 170/274 (5)
CHAPEL 95/153 (4)
HANGAR STRAIGHT 190/305 (6)

RACE DISTANCE: 60 laps, 191.746 miles /308.586 km   RACE WEATHER: Sunny (track 30–31°C, air 20–21°C)

All results and data © FOM 2005

Pos.	Driver	Nat.	No.	Entrant	Car/Engine	Tyres	Laps	Time/Retirement	Speed (mph/km/h)	Gap to leader	Fastest race lap	
1	Juan Pablo Montoya	COL	10	West McLaren Mercedes	McLaren MP4-20-Mercedes F0 110R V10	M	60	1h 24m 29.588s	136.060/218.968		1m 20.700s	41
2	Fernando Alonso	E	5	Mild Seven Renault F1 Team	Renault R25-RS25 V10	M	60	1h 24m 32.327s	135.986/218.849	+2.739s	1m 21.228s	40
3	Kimi Räikkönen	FIN	9	West McLaren Mercedes	McLaren MP4-20-Mercedes F0 110R V10	M	60	1h 24m 44.024s	135.674/218.346	+14.436s	1m 20.502s	60
4	Giancarlo Fisichella	I	6	Mild Seven Renault F1 Team	Renault R25-RS25 V10	M	60	1h 24m 47.502s	135.581/218.197	+17.914s	1m 21.159s	43
5	Jenson Button	GB	3	Lucky Strike BAR Honda	BAR 007-Honda RA005E V10	M	60	1h 25m 09.852s	134.988/217.242	+40.264s	1m 21.993s	42
6	Michael Schumacher	D	1	Scuderia Ferrari Marlboro	Ferrari F2005-055 V10	B	60	1h 25m 44.910s	134.068/215.762	+75.322s	1m 21.675s	23
7	Rubens Barrichello	BR	2	Scuderia Ferrari Marlboro	Ferrari F2005-055 V10	B	60	1h 25m 46.155s	134.036/215.710	+76.567s	1m 22.302s	41
8	Ralf Schumacher	D	17	Panasonic Toyota Racing	Toyota TF105-RVX-05 V10	M	60	1h 25m 48.800s	133.967/215.599	+79.212s	1m 21.960s	46
9	Jarno Trulli	I	16	Panasonic Toyota Racing	Toyota TF105-RVX-05 V10	M	60	1h 25m 50.439s	133.924/215.530	+80.851s	1m 22.112s	56
10	Felipe Massa	BR	12	Sauber Petronas	Sauber C24-Petronas 05A V10	M	59			+1 lap	1m 22.466s	45
11	Mark Webber	AUS	7	BMW WilliamsF1 Team	Williams FW27-BMW P84/85 V10	M	59			+1 lap	1m 23.291s	16
12	Nick Heidfeld	D	8	BMW WilliamsF1 Team	Williams FW27-BMW P84/85 V10	M	59			+1 lap	1m 23.360s	58
13	David Coulthard	GB	14	Red Bull Racing	Red Bull RB1-Cosworth TJ2005/12 V10	M	59			+1 lap	1m 23.089s	44
14	Jacques Villeneuve	CDN	11	Sauber Petronas	Sauber C24-Petronas 05A V10	M	59			+1 lap	1m 23.210s	16
15	Christian Klien	A	15	Red Bull Racing	Red Bull RB1-Cosworth TJ2005/12 V10	M	59			+1 lap	1m 23.147s	58
16	Takuma Sato	J	4	Lucky Strike BAR Honda	BAR 007-Honda RA005E V10	M	58			+2 laps	1m 22.551s	54
17	Tiago Monteiro	P	18	Jordan Toyota	Jordan EJ15-Toyota RVX-05 V10	B	58			+2 laps	1m 24.247s	38
18	Christijan Albers	NL	21	Minardi Cosworth	Minardi PS05-Cosworth TJ2005 V10	B	57			+3 laps	1m 26.182s	53
19	Patrick Friesacher	A	20	Minardi Cosworth	Minardi PS05-Cosworth TJ2005 V10	B	56			+4 laps	1m 26.489s	37
	Narain Karthikeyan	IND	19	Jordan Toyota	Jordan EJ15-Toyota RVX-05 V10	B	10	Electrical failure			1m 25.257s	8

Fastest lap: Kimi Räikkönen, on lap 60, 1m 20.502s, 142.854 mph/229.902 km/h.

Lap record: Michael Schumacher (Ferrari F2004-052 V10), 1m 18.739, 146.052 mph/235.049 km/h (2004).

19th: FRIESACHER Minardi-Cosworth

17th: KARTHIKEYAN Jordan-Toyota

15th: KLIEN Red Bull-Cosworth

13th: COULTHARD Red Bull-Cosworth

11th: WEBBER Williams-BMW

20th: MONTEIRO Jordan-Toyota

18th: ALBERS Minardi-Cosworth

16th: MASSA Sauber-Petronas

14th: HEIDFELD Williams-BMW

12th: RÄIKKÖNEN McLaren-Mercedes
Ten-place penalty for engine change

Grid order	1	2	3	4	5	6	7	8	9	10	11	12	13	14	15	16	17	18	19	20	21	22	23	24	25	26	27	28	29	30	31	32	33	34	35	36	37	38	39	40	41	42	43	44	45	46	47
5 ALONSO	10	10	10	10	10	10	10	10	10	10	10	10	10	10	10	10	10	10	10	10	10	5	5	6	10	10	10	10	10	10	10	10	10	10	10	10	10	10	10	10	10	10	10	10	5	5	5
3 BUTTON	5	5	5	5	5	5	5	5	5	5	5	5	5	5	5	5	5	5	5	5	10	6	10	10	5	5	5	5	5	5	5	5	5	5	5	5	5	5	5	6	6	10					
10 MONTOYA	3	3	3	3	3	3	3	3	3	3	3	3	3	3	3	3	3	3	3	3	6	10	6	5	6	6	6	6	6	6	6	6	6	6	6	6	6	6	6	10	10	10					
16 TRULLI	2	2	2	2	2	2	2	2	2	2	2	2	2	2	2	6	1	1	9	9	9	3	3	3	3	3	3	3	3	3	3	3	3	3	3	3	3	9	9	9	9	6					
2 BARRICHELLO	6	6	6	6	6	6	6	6	6	6	6	6	6	6	6	2	16	16	1	9	9	9	1	3	2	2	2	9	9	9	9	9	9	9	9	9	3	3	3	3							
6 FISICHELLA	16	16	16	16	16	16	16	16	16	16	16	16	16	16	16	16	1	1	9	3	3	3	3	2	9	9	9	9	1	1	1	1	1	1	1	1	1	1	1	1	1	1	1	1	1	1	1
4 SATO	1	1	1	1	1	1	1	1	1	1	1	1	1	1	1	1	9	9	17	2	2	2	1	1	1	1	1	1	1	2	2	2	2	2	2	2	2	2	2	2	17						
17 R. SCHUMACHER	9	9	9	9	9	9	9	9	9	9	9	9	9	9	9	9	17	17	16	17	12	12	16	16	16	16	16	16	16	16	16	16	16	16	16	16	16	12	12	12	2						
1 M. SCHUMACHER	17	17	17	17	17	17	17	17	17	17	17	17	17	17	17	17	2	2	12	16	16	16	17	17	17	17	17	17	17	17	17	17	17	17	17	17	17	17	17	17	12	12	12	12			
11 VILLENEUVE	11	11	11	11	11	11	11	11	11	11	11	11	11	11	11	11	7	7	16	17	17	17	7	7	7	7	7	7	7	7	7	7	7	7	7	7	7	16	16	16	16						
7 WEBBER	7	7	7	7	7	7	7	7	7	7	7	7	7	7	7	7	11	12	7	7	12	12	12	12	12	12	12	12	12	12	12	12	12	12	12	7	7	7	7							
9 RÄIKKÖNEN	15	15	15	15	15	15	15	15	8	8	8	8	8	8	8	8	8	8	8	8	8	8	8	8	8	8	8	8	8	8	8	8	1	8	14	14	14	14	14							
14 COULTHARD	8	8	8	8	8	15	14	14	14	14	14	14	14	14	14	8	14	14	11	11	11	11	11	11	11	11	11	11	11	11	11	11	11	11	11	11	11	11	11							
8 HEIDFELD	14	14	14	14	14	14	14	14	12	12	12	12	12	12	14	14	14	14	14	14	14	14	15	15	15	15	15	15	15	15	15	15	11	11	11	11	11	11							
15 KLIEN	12	12	12	12	12	12	12	12	12	15	18	18	18	18	18	18	18	14	14	14	14	14	14	14	14	14	14	14	14	15	15	15	15	15	15												
12 MASSA	19	19	19	19	19	19	19	19	19	21	21	15	18	18	18	18	18	18	18	18	18	18	18	18	18	18	18	18	18	18	18	18	18	18	18	18	18	18									
19 KARTHKEYAN	18	18	18	18	18	18	18	18	18	21	20	20	20	15	21	20	21	21	21	21	21	21	21	21	21	21	21	21	4	4	4	4	4	4	4	4	4	4									
21 ALBERS	21	21	21	21	21	21	21	21	21	15	15	20	20	20	20	20	20	20	4	4	20	20	20	20	4	20	20	21	21	21	21	21	21	21	21	21											
20 FRIESACHER	20	20	20	20	20	20	20	20	20	20	4	4	4	4	4	4	4	4	20	20	4	4	20	20	20	4	20	21	20	20	20	20	20	20	20	20											
18 MONTEIRO	4	4	4	4	4	4	4	4	4	4																																				

TIME SHEETS

QUALIFYING

WEATHER: Sunny (track 21–23°C, air 28–30°C)

Pos.	Driver	R/Order	Sector 1	Sector 2	Sector 3	Time
1	Fernando Alonso	20	25.299s	34.388s	20.288s	1m 19.905s
2	Kimi Räikkönen	19	25.121s	34.513s	20.298s	1m 19.932s
3	Jenson Button	17	25.516s	34.487s	20.204s	1m 20.207s
4	Juan Pablo Montoya	5	25.374s	34.648s	20.360s	1m 20.382s
5	Jarno Trulli	16	25.404s	34.833s	20.222s	1m 20.459s
6	Rubens Barrichello	12	25.392s	34.820s	20.694s	1m 20.906s
7	Giancarlo Fisichella	15	25.356s	35.047s	20.323s	1m 21.010s
8	Takuma Sato	10	25.776s	34.828s	20.510s	1m 21.114s
9	Ralf Schumacher	14	25.614s	34.973s	20.604s	1m 21.191s
10	Michael Schumacher	18	25.517s	35.009s	20.749s	1m 21.275s
11	Jacques Villeneuve	13	25.901s	34.961s	20.490s	1m 21.352s
12	Mark Webber	9	25.882s	35.408s	20.707s	1m 21.997s
13	David Coulthard	11	25.787s	35.455s	20.866s	1m 22.108s
14	Nick Heidfeld	7	25.760s	35.652s	20.705s	1m 22.117s
15	Christian Klien	1	25.849s	35.582s	20.776s	1m 22.207s
16	Felipe Massa	2	25.991s	35.663s	20.841s	1m 22.495s
17	Narain Karthikeyan	6	26.462s	36.004s	21.117s	1m 23.583s
18	Christian Albers	4	26.867s	36.579s	21.130s	1m 24.576s
19	Patrick Friesacher	3	27.121s	36.935s	21.510s	1m 25.566s
20	Tiago Monteiro	8	-	-	-	No time

Photograph: James Moy/www.crash.net

CHASSIS LOG BOOK

	FERRARI	
1	Michael Schumacher	F2005/245
2	Rubens Barrichello	F2005/246
	Spare	F2005/248

	BAR-HONDA	
3	Jenson Button	007/03
4	Takuma Sato	007/04
	Spare	007/02

	RENAULT	
5	Fernando Alonso	R25/04
6	Giancarlo Fisichella	R25/06
	Spare	R25/02

	WILLIAMS-BMW	
7	Mark Webber	FW27/05
8	Nick Heidfeld	FW27/06
	Spare	FW27/04

	McLAREN-MERCEDES	
9	Kimi Räikkönen	MP4-20/04
10	Juan Pablo Montoya	MP4-20/07
35	Pedro de la Rosa	MP4-20/06
	Spare	MP4-20/06

	SAUBER-PETRONAS	
11	Jacques Villeneuve	C24/04
12	Felipe Massa	C24/06
	Spare	C24/03

	RED BULL-COSWORTH	
14	David Coulthard	RB1/3
15	Christian Klien	RB1/1
37	Vitantonio Liuzzi	RB1/2
	Spare	RB1/2

	TOYOTA	
16	Jarno Trulli	TF105/02
17	Ralf Schumacher	TF105/03
38	Ricardo Zonta	TF105/05
	Spare	TF105/05

	JORDAN-TOYOTA	
18	Tiago Monteiro	EJ15/03
19	Narain Karthikeyan	EJ15/01
39	Robert Doombos	EJ15/02
	Spare	EJ15/02

	MINARDI-COSWORTH	
20	Patrick Friesacher	PS05/02
21	Christijan Albers	PS05/01
	Spare	PS04B/03

PRACTICE 1 (FRIDAY)

Overcast (track 17–18°C, air 24–26°C)

Pos.	Driver	Laps	Time
1	Pedro de la Rosa	21	1m 19.205s
2	Ricardo Zonta	30	1m 20.139s
3	Jenson Button	10	1m 20.211s
4	Kimi Räikkönen	9	1m 20.411s
5	Ralf Schumacher	6	1m 21.080s
6	Juan Pablo Montoya	5	1m 21.091s
7	Michael Schumacher	9	1m 21.453s
8	Takuma Sato	10	1m 21.582s
9	Rubens Barrichello	9	1m 22.216s
10	Felipe Massa	11	1m 22.350s
11	David Coulthard	8	1m 22.403s
12	Christian Klien	8	1m 22.456s
13	Vitantonio Liuzzi	2	1m 22.615s
14	Jacques Villeneuve	7	1m 23.370s
15	Mark Webber	8	1m 23.394s
16	Nick Heidfeld	9	1m 24.321s
17	Narain Karthikeyan	10	1m 24.581s
18	Tiago Monteiro	17	1m 25.488s
19	Robert Doornbos	12	1m 25.560s
20	Christijan Albers	16	1m 25.897s
21	Patrick Friesacher	7	1m 27.246s
22	Giancarlo Fisichella	2	No time
23	Fernando Alonso	2	No time
24	Jarno Trulli	1	No time

PRACTICE 2 (FRIDAY)

Brightening (track 18–19°C, air 23–25°C)

Pos.	Driver	Laps	Time
1	Pedro de la Rosa	37	1m 18.530s
2	Ricardo Zonta	31	1m 18.964s
3	Juan Pablo Montoya	17	1m 20.252s
4	Kimi Räikkönen	15	1m 20.384s
5	Ralf Schumacher	23	1m 20.602s
6	Jarno Trulli	27	1m 20.816s
7	Fernando Alonso	21	1m 20.990s
8	Vitantonio Liuzzi	33	1m 21.004s
9	David Coulthard	19	1m 21.034s
10	Michael Schumacher	21	1m 21.044s
11	Jenson Button	28	1m 21.186s
12	Mark Webber	20	1m 21.235s
13	Giancarlo Fisichella	15	1m 21.279s
14	Christian Klien	21	1m 21.323s
15	Rubens Barrichello	21	1m 21.519s
16	Felipe Massa	28	1m 21.577s
17	Jacques Villeneuve	19	1m 22.180s
18	Nick Heidfeld	19	1m 22.500s
19	Takuma Sato	12	1m 22.795s
20	Robert Doornbos	20	1m 22.812s
21	Christijan Albers	22	1m 23.390s
22	Tiago Monteiro	22	1m 23.629s
23	Narain Karthikeyan	26	1m 23.891s
24	Patrick Friesacher	21	1m 24.594s

PRACTICE 3 (SATURDAY)

Sunny (track 20–22°C, air 25°C)

Pos.	Driver	Laps	Time
1	Kimi Räikkönen	7	1m 20.975s
2	Fernando Alonso	9	1m 21.402s
3	Jenson Button	6	1m 21.996s
4	Giancarlo Fisichella	9	1m 22.331s
5	Juan Pablo Montoya	5	1m 22.377s
6	Takuma Sato	12	1m 22.389s
7	Felipe Massa	14	1m 22.413s
8	Michael Schumacher	8	1m 22.496s
9	Christian Klien	6	1m 22.645s
10	Ralf Schumacher	7	1m 22.775s
11	David Coulthard	8	1m 23.026s
12	Rubens Barrichello	8	1m 23.182s
13	Jacques Villeneuve	12	1m 23.191s
14	Jarno Trulli	4	1m 23.458s
15	Nick Heidfeld	7	1m 23.480s
16	Mark Webber	5	1m 23.705s
17	Tiago Monteiro	13	1m 23.820s
18	Narain Karthikeyan	8	1m 24.230s
19	Christijan Albers	13	1m 25.007s
20	Patrick Friesacher	15	1m 25.696s

PRACTICE 4 (SATURDAY)

Sunny with light cloud (track 21-22°C, air 26°C)

Pos.	Driver	Laps	Time
1	Fernando Alonso	14	1m 20.077s
2	Juan Pablo Montoya	13	1m 20.128s
3	Jarno Trulli	13	1m 20.449s
4	Ralf Schumacher	12	1m 20.524s
5	Jenson Button	14	1m 20.763s
6	Giancarlo Fisichella	11	1m 20.798s
7	Michael Schumacher	12	1m 20.893s
8	Mark Webber	11	1m 21.004s
9	Nick Heidfeld	8	1m 21.052s
10	Christian Klien	9	1m 21.064s
11	Rubens Barrichello	10	1m 21.371s
12	Jacques Villeneuve	14	1m 21.476s
13	Felipe Massa	11	1m 21.704s
14	Takuma Sato	16	1m 21.931s
15	Tiago Monteiro	18	1m 22.036s
16	Narain Karthikeyan	8	1m 22.634s
17	David Coulthard	5	1m 23.165s
18	Christijan Albers	16	1m 23.444s
19	Patrick Friesacher	17	1m 23.586s
20	Kimi Räikkönen	2	No time

9th: M. SCHUMACHER Ferrari

7th: SATO BAR-Honda
Started from pit lane

5th: BARRICHELLO Ferrari

3rd: MONTOYA McLaren-Mercedes

Pole: ALONSO Renault

10th: VILLENEUVE Sauber-Petronas

8th: R. SCHUMACHER Toyota

6th: FISICHELLA Renault

4th: TRULLI Toyota

2nd: BUTTON BAR-Honda

48	49	50	51	52	53	54	55	56	57	58	59	60	
5	5	10	10	10	10	10	10	10	10	10	10	10	1
10	10	5	5	5	5	5	5	5	5	5	5	5	2
9	9	9	9	9	9	9	9	9	9	9	9	9	3
6	6	6	6	6	6	6	6	6	6	6	6	6	4
3	3	3	3	3	3	3	3	3	3	3	3	3	5
1	1	1	1	1	1	1	1	1	1	1	1	1	6
2	2	2	2	2	2	2	2	2	2	2	2	2	7
17	17	17	17	17	17	17	17	17	17	17	17	17	8
16	16	16	16	16	16	16	16	16	16	16	16	16	
12	12	12	12	12	12	12	12	12	12	12	12		
7	7	7	7	7	7	7	7	7	7	7	7		
8	8	8	8	8	8	8	8	8	8	8	8		
14	14	14	14	14	14	14	14	14	14	14	14		
11	11	11	11	11	11	11	11	11	11	11	11		
15	15	15	15	15	15	15	15	15	15	15	15		
18	18	18	4	4	4	4	4	4	4	4			
4	4	4	18	18	18	18	18	18	18	18			
21	21	21	21	21	21	21	21	21					
20	20	20	20	20	20	20	20	20					

 Pit stop
 One lap or more behind leader

POINTS

	DRIVERS					
1	Fernando Alonso	77		13	Felipe Massa	7
2	Kimi Räikkönen	51		14	Tiago Monteiro	6
3	Michael Schumacher	43		15	Alex Wurz	6
4	Rubens Barrichello	31		16	Jacques Villeneuve	6
5	Jarno Trulli	31		17	Narain Karthikeyan	5
6	Juan Pablo Montoya	26		18	Christijan Albers	4
7	Giancarlo Fisichella	25		19	Pedro de la Rosa	4
8	Nick Heidfeld	25		20	Christian Klien	4
9	Ralf Schumacher	23		21	Patrick Friesacher	3
10	Mark Webber	22		22	Vitantonio Liuzzi	1
11	David Coulthard	17				
12	Jenson Button	9				

	CONSTRUCTORS	
1	Renault	102
2	McLaren	87
3	Ferrari	74
4	Toyota	54
5	Williams	47
6	Red Bull	22
7	Sauber	13
8	Jordan	11
9	BAR	9
10	Minardi	7

Photograph: James Moy/www.crash.net

HOCKENHEIM
GERMANGP
FIA F1 WORLD CHAMPIONSHIP/ROUND 12

Mobil

PREIS VON
TSCHLAND
HO EIM 2005

Fernando Alonso was saturated in a
shower of Mumm champagne after
achieving his sixth victory of the
season for the Renault squad.
Photograph: James Moy/www.crash.net

Qualifying had promised to unlock the explosive rivalry between the two McLaren drivers, and Kimi Räikkönen – who made his qualifying run third from last – duly stamped his mastery on the proceedings by edging out Jenson Button's BAR-Honda to take pole position with a lap of 1m 14.320s, just 0.439s ahead of the Englishman.

Whether by accident or mischievous intent, the Finn ran wide on the first corner after the pits on his slowing-down lap, conveniently kicking some dirt onto the racing line immediately before Fernando Alonso and Juan Pablo Montoya went out onto the circuit as the final two qualifiers to make their bids.

Alonso duly lost time in the first sector and ended up posting third-fastest time (1m 14.904s). That left just Montoya to make his run and the Colombian looked on course to bump Button and join Räikkönen on an all-McLaren front row. But he pushed too hard into the final corner. The McLaren snapped out of line and spun smartly into the barrier, leaving Montoya with the frustrating prospect of starting from the back of the grid.

'There is no excuse, really,' said the apologetic Colombian. 'I made a mistake and simply lost the car. It was going to be a really quick lap, possibly pole, and I thought all that was left was to get a really good exit out of the last corner. As I lifted, I lost the rear and that was it.'

Meanwhile, Button was hugely satisfied that Montoya's slip had cemented his own claim for a front-row starting position. 'I'm obviously delighted to be on the front row for the second consecutive race,' he beamed.

'The team has done a fantastic job to make sure it took a step forward here after Silverstone and Honda has made good progress with the engine. It was a good lap for me today, although we did have a little bit too much front end [downforce] on the car, which meant I had a few moments, especially coming into the stadium. We have certainly made progress since Silverstone, but not quite enough to challenge the front runners yet, I think.'

In the Renault camp, Alonso (1m 14.904s) and Giancarlo Fisichella (1m 14.927s) were well satisfied with their efforts to button up the second row of the grid. 'I'm pretty pleased to be third this afternoon,' said Fernando. 'In fact I could have been on the front row, but it is actually quite good to be starting on the clean side of the track.

'I lost three or four tenths through the first corners. It was windier than this morning and the first corner is very quick and I was a bit unsettled. Then I didn't have the confidence to push into the braking zone for the next corner. I knew I was down after the first sector and really pushed after that to make up time, which I managed to do.'

Fisichella was similarly mindful of the problems posed by the crosswinds, but was particularly satisfied to have edged out Michael Schumacher's Ferrari F2005 (1m 15.006s) on the world champion's home turf.

'I had a clean lap,' reported Schumi, 'and I think I got the most out of the car, which behaved well. I don't think we ran with a particularly light fuel load compared with the other cars. Maybe I can battle with Button, but aiming for the top is unrealistic.'

In a strategic bet-hedging operation, Rubens Barrichello ran a heavier fuel load and harder tyres in the other Ferrari, ending up 15th with 1m 16.230s. The Brazilian was sanguine about his prospects. 'I took the second of the two options,' he said non-specifically, 'partly because this morning I did not feel the car was perfectly balanced and also I was bearing in mind that tomorrow may be tough on the tyres.'

Over at Williams, Mark Webber (1m 15.070s) and Nick Heidfeld (1m 15.403s) proved well matched in sixth and seventh places. 'My car wasn't too bad, even if I had to go out a bit early in the session,' said the Australian. 'We are doing okay here and are definitely better than our performances at Silverstone and Magny-Cours were. The track is much less sensitive and the car responds better.' Heidfeld added, 'It looks like our car has improved and that is encouraging.'

Takuma Sato (1m 15.501s) wound up eighth ahead of a brake-troubled Jarno Trulli's Toyota TF105, the Italian separated from his reasonably satisfied team-mate Ralf Schumacher (1m 15.689s) by the two Red Bull RB1s of Christian Klien (1m 15.635s) and David Coulthard (1m 15.679s). Coulthard admitted that he locked up at the hairpin, running a little wide as a result, but Klien reported feeling more confident with the car than at any time since Montreal.

At Sauber, meanwhile, Felipe Massa (1m 16.009s) and Jacques Villeneuve (1m 16.012s) slightly underdelivered. Massa admitted to 'a bad lap' plagued by unexpected oversteer and Jacques locked his front wheels, which also cost him some time.

Christijan Albers (1m 17.519s) and Minardi new boy Robert Doornbos (1m 18.313s) both did respectable jobs, lining up ahead of Tiago Monteiro's Jordan, the delayed Montoya and Narain Karthikeyan, who made a couple of mistakes and then aborted his lap to save his tyres.

DIARY

Michelin announces that it wants to reduce the number of teams it supplies in 2006 because it feels that its chances of winning may be hampered by servicing too many competitors.

McLaren protégé Lewis Hamilton moves close to winning the F3 Euroseries in his Dallara-Mercedes after bagging another two wins at the Norisring on 17 July.

Ferrari reaffirms that it will be continuing to test during the informal summer 'test-ban' period agreed by the other nine teams.

'No. I am not interested. I am going on holiday,' McLaren driver Kimi Räikkönen replies firmly after being asked whether he would attend FIA president Max Mosley's driver-safety meeting.

FERNANDO Alonso was gifted victory in the German Grand Prix after the fast but fragile McLaren-Mercedes of Kimi Räikkönen retired from a commanding lead with hydraulic problems, a failure which virtually wiped out any prospect of Kimi's winning the world championship.

In scoring his sixth win of the season, by 22.569s from Juan Pablo Montoya's McLaren, Alonso took another giant step towards becoming the sport's youngest ever world champion, a milestone he could theoretically reach as early as the first Turkish GP, to be held at the new Istanbul circuit on 21 August.

Third place fell to Jenson Button after a fine attacking drive in his BAR-Honda to battle his way ahead of Michael Schumacher's Ferrari, which eventually dropped to fifth behind Giancarlo Fisichella's Renault.

'I am delighted with this victory,' said Alonso. 'We saw McLaren dominate this weekend and we knew it would be tough to beat them even though our [race] pace was much closer [to theirs] than our qualifying pace. So to win here in Germany is a good surprise, but we all know that the race is 67 laps long and you don't get any prizes for being fastest until half distance.

'The car was reliable all weekend, as it has been throughout the season, and we know we have to find some more performance. That will start with some new pieces for Hungary [next Sunday]. In terms of the race it was quite straightforward. The biggest problem, as at Silverstone, was with the blue flags not being shown to the lapped traffic.'

Räikkönen had accelerated into an immediate lead to complete the opening lap 1.5s ahead of Alonso, who came through from the second row of the grid to lead the pursuit of the McLaren. Alonso knew he did not have to press too hard in an over-zealous bid to challenge Räikkönen's superior machine in the opening stages, mindful that with a 36-point lead in the title chase he would drop only another two points if he were to settle for a tactically comfortable second place.

As always on the truncated Hockenheim track, it was a wild opening lap, with Takuma Sato again at the centre of the action. Going into the first right-hander, the BAR-Honda driver skidded into the back of Mark Webber's Williams. Mark in turn lurched wide, his rear suspension broken, pushing Jarno Trulli's Toyota wide and causing it to pick up a front-left puncture. All three cars duly pitted at the end of the opening lap.

'I don't know what I've got to do this season to get some luck,' said an obviously exasperated Webber. 'The mechanics replaced the damaged rear-suspension component as quickly as they could, but by the time I went out on the track again I was 11 laps down. It not only compromised my race but also affected my qualifying in the next race [Hungary] because I will have a very early slot.'

Not that Sato had finished with his first-lap action – a few corners later he touched the back of Giancarlo Fisichella's

Above: Jenson Button drove a superb race in the BAR to finish third after an energetic and consistent performance.
Photograph: James Moy/www.crash.net

Left: Narain Karthikeyan locking up his Jordan's Bridgestone rubber in practice. He qualified 20th and finished 16th.
Photograph: Laurent Charniuax/WRI

Right: Jacques Villeneuve bounced his Sauber off Rubens Barrichello's Ferrari during their first-lap skirmish.
Photograph: Lukas Gorys

Below: Christian Klien would have needed rather more than wings to score points.
Photograph: James Moy/www.crash.net

Bottom: Jenson Button forced his way past Michael Schumacher's tyre-troubled Ferrari during his battle through to third.
Photograph: Ebener/XPB.cc

Renault and needed a replacement nose fitted. Giancarlo wasn't impressed. 'It knocked off part of the rear wing,' he explained, 'after which the handling felt strange for a few laps and I lost more places before I could start pushing.'

But wait; there's more. Rubens Barrichello's Ferrari and Jacques Villeneuve's Sauber also made contact. 'Rubens came into the side of me at the hairpin,' said Jacques. 'I think maybe somebody pushed him.' Barrichello explained, 'Just after the start another car came up the inside of me and I had no option but to move to the outside of the corner, which is how I collided with Villeneuve.'

By the end of the second lap Räikkönen had extended his advantage to 1.7s over Alonso and Jenson Button's BAR-Honda was running fourth behind Michael Schumacher's fast-starting

Ferrari. By lap four the flying Juan Pablo Montoya was up to ninth from last on the grid and Villeneuve was in the wars yet again when he tangled with Robert Doornbos's Minardi. 'He was being very over-aggressive in his first grand prix,' said Jacques. 'He moved over on me as we were braking, so we touched. That was Formula-Ford stuff – unnecessary.'

Nick Heidfeld was the first of the leading runners to pit, at the end of lap 15 from fifth place. Alonso and Michael Schumacher dived in for 9.3s stops on lap 22, but Kimi kept the leading McLaren out in the lead until lap 25, when he rejoined ahead of Alonso and the remarkable Montoya, who was carrying the heaviest fuel load in the whole field.

On the 36th lap, Räikkönen suddenly slowed up and skidded to a standstill at the side of the circuit, a victim of the same hydraulic failure as had sidelined his team-mate Montoya in the French Grand Prix earlier in the month. From then on Alonso could take things easy and conserve his equipment.

Montoya's climb through the field was undeniably impressive and he demonstrated a consistent speed which might well have enabled him to win in a straight fight with Räikkönen and, at the very least, to inherit a win when his team-mate's car wilted.

'It was a good day for me but a frustrating one for Kimi,' said Montoya. 'I hope the result made up a bit for the mistake I made yesterday [in qualifying]. I gained eight places on the first lap, which was very good, and then settled down behind the next four cars to save some fuel. There was no need to take any risks because I knew there would be a good chance to pass during the pit stops.

'The balance of my car was perfect and the strategy was spot on and allowed me to push during the race, especially when I

MORE TALK ABOUT A BREAKAWAY SERIES

The prospect of a breakaway world championship from 2008 hung in the balance at Hockenheim after a newly branded alliance of nine F1 teams and five car manufacturers offered the governing body a package of new proposals for the future development of the sport.

The Grand Prix Manufacturers' Association consisted of the BAR, Jordan, McLaren, Minardi, Red Bull, Renault, Sauber, Toyota and Williams teams in addition to manufacturers BMW, DaimlerChrysler, Honda, Renault and Toyota, all of whom wanted an early meeting with Max Mosley, the FIA president, to discuss their package of suggestions.

The group insisted that it expected Mosley to be receptive to its approach. 'Considering the fact that their alliance represents 90 percent of the current grid and views from key stakeholders such as circuits, broadcasters, sponsors and fans are included, the teams and manufacturers are confident that the FIA will consider their proposals carefully,' said a GPMA statement.

While the teams agreed with the governing body that costs in F1 must be reduced as a matter of some urgency, they opposed what they regarded as 'dumbing down' the sport's high-technology image in the FIA's proposals for the 2008 technical rules, which had been published the previous month.

They were concerned that standardisation of components risked undermining the sport's cutting-edge image, although with the running cost of a current F1 car averaging about £1,000 ($1,760) per lap, they appreciated that spending needed to be curtailed.

Their statement continued, 'Where possible, costs should be significantly reduced, providing that the sporting spectacle and competition are not compromised. The vision is for a fair and transparent sport with well-funded and highly competitive teams on every row of the grid, with the best drivers competing on the most exciting race tracks around the world.'

The team owners were reluctant to discuss the precise details of what their package of measures contained, but one senior team insider remarked that there was still an underlying nervousness about dealing with the FIA. 'I hope that Max will be receptive to these suggestions,' he said, 'and not dismiss them out of hand.'

An FIA spokesman tried to allay those fears. 'Our proposals were not a *fait accompli*,' he said. 'I think the two sides in this debate are much closer together than some outsiders might think.'

Mosley was due to stand for re-election to the FIA presidency in October and, although he would probably not be challenged, resolving F1's long-term problems would be seen as a feather in his cap.

had the chance to get by Button and Schumacher during their second stops. Without yesterday's mistake, which put me at the back of the grid, a race win would have been possible.'

Button was similarly delighted with third. 'It's fantastic to be back on the podium today after a great race for me and for the team,' he said. 'I don't need to tell anyone what a tough season this has been for us and it's a great feeling to come away from here with a trophy for the guys who've worked so hard to get us up there today.'

Michael Schumacher was less happy. The seven-times world champion struggled with dire lack of grip from his Bridgestone tyres and his eventual fifth place in front of his adoring home crowd was a painful disappointment. 'In the end, I guess you could say this was an interesting race,' he said ruefully, 'although I would have preferred to be fighting for a podium finish rather than the lower places. I struggled a lot with my tyres today, which is why I could not hold off Jenson.

'Later, Giancarlo got past me because I had a fuel-feed

problem. Fifth place is okay in that I did not lose any positions from where I started, but of course I was hoping to do something better for the fans, who were incredible all through the weekend. I am proud to have such support.'

The best of the Toyotas was Ralf Schumacher, whose TF105 was just half a second behind his elder brother's Ferrari at the chequered flag. 'That was an exciting race for the public and a good one for me as well,' said Ralf. 'I said yesterday we could have a good race today and so it proved. I didn't make the best of starts and I got crowded out, but it's always like that at Hockenheim. From then on our strategy was excellent, including a long stint to our first pit stop [he came in on lap 25, like Räikkönen]. 'We could even have ended up one or two places higher. Unfortunately when I came out of the pits after my first stop the tyres took a couple of laps to get the times back while I was struggling for grip.'

By contrast, after his early delay, Trulli collected a drive-through penalty for holding up Montoya, although Jarno pleaded

disappointed Heidfeld, who also struggled with a handling imbalance and reduced the engine power settings in the closing stages. Sato recovered to 12th after his early excursions and Christijan Albers took 13th after a bullish race, classified just ahead of the retired Trulli. Villeneuve was 15th ahead of Narain Karthikeyan and Tiago Monteiro, having had a minor collision with the Portuguese driver, his third brush of the afternoon.

It had been a weekend of if-onlys. If only the staff preparing Räikkönen's McLaren had given that hydraulic connection another half turn. If only the cards, for once, had fallen against the Renaults. But they didn't, and Alonso continued his steady march to his own well-moderated beat. McLaren could stop him. But would it?

Alan Henry

Left: Getting down to the job. Juan Pablo Montoya having just passed Christijan Albers' Minardi and Narain Karthikeyan's Jordan at the beginning of his superb charge through the field from the back of the grid to an eventual second.
Photograph: James Moy/www.crash.net

Below: Helmet on, visor still down in a bid to deter any questions, Kimi Räikkönen walked back through the paddock to the McLaren garage after retiring from the lead.
Photograph: XPB.cc

in mitigation that he was actually himself in the process of passing Nick Heidfeld at the time that the blue flags were waved. Not that it mattered either way in the end – he had to make yet another stop to top up the V10's pneumatic reservoir prior to the engine's eventually shutting down for good on the final lap.

David Coulthard and Christian Klien delivered seventh and ninth places in their Red Bull RB1s, DC never dropping below ninth at any point during the race. 'We felt we were well set up here to get points,' said the Scot. 'There are still some inconsistencies in the car which need attention, but we'll continue to work hard on it.'

Klien, who trailed Felipe Massa's Sauber home, was satisfied that he'd pulled a couple of good overtaking moves on Barrichello during the course of the race, but otherwise conceded that it had been an uneventful afternoon.

As for Rubens, he fought a battle against poor grip for most of the distance, but squeezed home 3.2s ahead of the equally

FIA F1 WORLD CHAMPIONSHIP • ROUND 12

GRÖSSER MOBIL 1 PREIS VON DEUTSCHLAND

HOCKENHEIM 22–24 JULY 2005

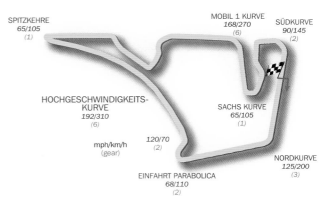

HOCKENHEIM

SPITZKEHRE
65/105
(1)

MOBIL 1 KURVE
168/270
(6)

SÜDKURVE
90/145
(2)

HOCHGESCHWINDIGKEITS-
KURVE
192/310
(6)

SACHS KURVE
65/105
(1)

mph/km/h
(gear)

120/70
(2)

NORDKURVE
125/200
(3)

EINFAHRT PARABOLICA
68/110
(2)

CIRCUIT LENGTH: 2.842 miles/4.574 km

RACE DISTANCE: 67 laps, 190.424 miles /306.458 km   RACE WEATHER: Heavily cloudy (track 27–30°C, air 23–24°C)

Pos.	Driver	Nat.	No.	Entrant	Car/Engine	Tyres	Laps	Time/Retirement	Speed (mph/km/h)	Gap to leader	Fastest race lap	
1	Fernando Alonso	E	5	Mild Seven Renault F1 Team	Renault R25-RS25 V10	M	67	1h 26m 28.599s	132.121/212.629		1m 15.235s	21
2	Juan Pablo Montoya	COL	10	West McLaren Mercedes	McLaren MP4-20-Mercedes F0 110R V10	M	67	1h 26m 51.168s	131.749/211.708	+22.569s	1m 15.878s	54
3	Jenson Button	GB	3	Lucky Strike BAR Honda	BAR 007-Honda RA005E V10	M	67	1h 26m 53.021s	131.502/211.633	+24.422s	1m 15.843s	19
4	Giancarlo Fisichella	I	6	Mild Seven Renault F1 Team	Renault R25-RS25 V10	M	67	1h 27m 19.186s	130.846/210.576	+50.587s	1m 15.890s	21
5	Michael Schumacher	D	1	Scuderia Ferrari Marlboro	Ferrari F2005-055 V10	B	67	1h 27m 20.289s	130.818/210.532	+51.690s	1m 16.099s	18
6	Ralf Schumacher	D	17	Panasonic Toyota Racing	Toyota TF105-RVX-05 V10	M	67	1h 27m 20.841s	130.804/210.509	+52.242s	1m 16.073s	23
7	David Coulthard	GB	14	Red Bull Racing	Red Bull RB1-Cosworth TJ2005/12 V10	M	67	1h 27m 21.299s	130.793/210.491	+52.700s	1m 16.233s	18
8	Felipe Massa	BR	12	Sauber Petronas	Sauber C24-Petronas 05A V10	M	67	1h 27m 25.169s	130.696/210.336	+56.570s	1m 16.288s	45
9	Christian Klien	A	15	Red Bull Racing	Red Bull RB1-Cosworth TJ2005/12 V10	M	67	1h 27m 38.417s	130.367/209.806	+69.818s	1m 16.236s	45
10	Rubens Barrichello	BR	2	Scuderia Ferrari Marlboro	Ferrari F2005-055 V10	B	66			+1 lap	1m 16.528s	47
11	Nick Heidfeld	D	8	BMW WilliamsF1 Team	Williams FW27-BMW P84/85 V10	M	66			+1 lap	1m 16.607s	10
12	Takuma Sato	J	4	Lucky Strike BAR Honda	BAR 007-Honda RA005E V10	M	66			+1 lap	1m 16.725s	27
13	Christijan Albers	NL	21	Minardi Cosworth	Minardi PS05-Cosworth TJ2005 V10	B	65			+2 laps	1m 18.425s	11
14	Jarno Trulli	I	16	Panasonic Toyota Racing	Toyota TF105-RVX-05 V10	M	64	Engine pneumatics		DNF	1m 16.474s	45
15	Jacques Villeneuve	CDN	11	Sauber Petronas	Sauber C24-Petronas 05A V10	M	64			+3 laps	1m 17.122s	26
16	Narain Karthikeyan	IND	19	Jordan Toyota	Jordan EJ15-Toyota RVX-05 V10	B	64			+3 laps	1m 18.212s	7
17	Tiago Monteiro	P	18	Jordan Toyota	Jordan EJ15-Toyota RVX-05 V10	B	64			+3 laps	1m 18.106s	12
18	Robert Doornbos	NL	20	Minardi Cosworth	Minardi PS05-Cosworth TJ2005 V10	B	63			+4 laps	1m 19.025s	44
	Mark Webber	AUS	7	BMW WilliamsF1 Team	Williams FW27-BMW P84/85 V10	M	55	Finished but not classified			1m 16.803s	46
	Kimi Räikkönen	FIN	9	West McLaren Mercedes	McLaren MP4-20-Mercedes F0 110R V10	M	35	Hydraulic leak			1m 14.873s	24

Fastest lap: Kimi Räikkönen, on lap 24, 1m 14.873s, 135.654 mph/219.924 km/h.

Lap record: Kimi Räikkönen (McLaren MP4/19B-Mercedes F0110P V10), 1m 13.780s, 138.679 mph/223.182 km/h (2004).

19th: KARTHIKEYAN Jordan-Toyota

17th: DOORNBOS Minardi-Cosworth

15th: BARRICHELLO Ferrari

13th: MASSA Sauber-Petronas

11th: COULTHARD Red Bull-Cosworth

20th: MONTOYA McLaren-Mercedes

18th: MONTEIRO Jordan-Toyota

16th: ALBERS Minardi-Cosworth

14th: VILLENEUVE Sauber-Petronas

12th: R. SCHUMACHER Toyota

Grid order	1	2	3	4	5	6	7	8	9	10	11	12	13	14	15	16	17	18	19	20	21	22	23	24	25	26	27	28	29	30	31	32	33	34	35	36	37	38	39	40	41	42	43	44	45	46	47	48	49	50
9 RÄIKKÖNEN	9	9	9	9	9	9	9	9	9	9	9	9	9	9	9	9	9	9	9	9	9	9	9	9		9	9	9	9	9	9	9	9	9	9	5	5	5	5	5	5	5	5	5	5		5	5	5	5
3 BUTTON	5	5	5	5	5	5	5	5	5	5	5	5	5	5	5	5	5	5	5	5	5	5	5	5	5	5	5	5	5	5	5	5	5	5	5	1	1	1	1	1	1	1	3	1	1	10	10			
5 ALONSO	1	1	1	1	1	1	1	1	1	1	1	1	1	1	1	1	1	1	1	1	1	1	1	10	10	10	10	10	1	1	1	1	1	1	1	3	3	3	3	3	3	3	1	10	10		1	6		
6 FISICHELLA	3	3	3	3	3	3	3	3	3	3	3	3	3	3	3	3	3	3	6	6	6	17	17	1	1	3	3	3	3	3	3	3	3	10	10	10	10	10	10	10	10	10	10	6	6	6	17			
1 M. SCHUMACHER	8	8	8	8	8	8	8	8	8	8	8	8	8	14	14	14	14	14	14	10	10	17	1	1	3	3	10	10	10	10	10	6	6	6	6	6	6	6	6	6	6	6	14	17	17	3				
7 WEBBER	14	14	14	14	14	14	14	14	14	14	14	14	14	8	12	12	12	6	6	17	17	1	3	2	6	6	6	6	6	6	6	14	14	14	14	14	14	14	14	14	14	17	3	3	1					
8 HEIDFELD	12	12	12	12	12	12	12	12	12	12	12	12	12	6	6	6	6	12	12	12	3	3	3	2	14	14	14	14	14	14	14	17	17	17	17	17	17	17	17	3	14	14	14							
4 SATO	6	6	6	6	6	6	6	6	6	6	6	6	6	10	10	10	10	17	2	2	6	14	17	17	17	17	17	17	17	12	12	12	12	12	12	12	12	12	12	12	2	2	2	12						
16 TRULLI	15	15	10	10	10	10	10	10	10	10	10	10	10	15	15	15	17	2	14	14	14	14	17	8	8	8	8	8	8	2	2	2	12	12	15	15	15	15	15	15	12	12	12							
15 KLIEN	17	10	15	15	15	15	15	15	15	15	15	15	15	17	17	17	15	8	8	8	8	8	12	12	12	12	12	12	12	15	15	15	2	2	2	2	2	2	2	2	15	15	15	2						
14 COULTHARD	10	17	17	17	17	17	17	17	17	17	17	17	17	2	2	2	2	12	12	12	12	12	2	2	2	2	2	2	2	8	8	8	8	8	8	8	8	8	8	8	8	8	8	8						
17 R. SCHUMACHER	21	2	2	2	2	2	2	2	2	2	2	2	2	15	15	15	15	15	15	15	15	15	15	15	15	15	16	16	16	16	16	16	16	16	16	16	16	16	16	16	16	4	4	4						
12 MASSA		21	21	21	21	21	21	21	21	21	21	21	21	21	21	21	4	4	4	4	4	16	16	16	16	16	4	4	4	4	4	4	21	21	21	21	21	21	21	21	19	19	19	19	19					
11 VILLENEUVE	20	20	20	19	19	19	19	19	19	19	19	19	19	19	19	4	16	16	16	16	16	4	4	4	4	4	21	21	21	21	21	21	4	4	4	4	4	21	19	19	21	21	21	21	19	21				
2 BARRICHELLO	11	11	11	18	18	18	18	18	18	18	18	18	18	18	4	16	16	21	21	18	18	21	21	21	21	21	19	19	19	19	19	19	19	19	19	19	19	19	21	19										
21 ALBERS	19	19	19	11	4	4	4	4	4	4	4	4	4	4	16	18	18	18	18	21	21	18	18	18	18	18	18	18	18	18	18	18	18	18	11	11	11	11	11	11	11	11	11	11						
20 DOORNBOS	18	18	18	4	16	16	16	16	16	16	16	16	16	16	18	20	21	20	20	20	20	20	18	18	18	18	18	18	18	18	18	18	18	18	18	18	18	18	18	18	18									
18 MONTEIRO	4	4	4	16	11	11	11	11	11	11	11	11	11	11	11	11	18	11	11	18	18	20	20	20	20	20	20	20	20	20	20	20	20	20	20	20	20	20	20	20	20									
19 KARTHIKEYAN	16	16	16	20	20	20	20	20	20	20	20	20	20	20	20	20	20	20	20	20	11	11	20	20	20	20	20	20	20	20	20	7	7	7	7	7	7	7	7	7	7	7								
10 MONTOYA	7	7	7	7	7	7	7	7	7	7	7	7	7	7	7	7	7	7	7	7	7	7	7	7	7	7	7	7	7	7	7	7	7																	

QUALIFYING

WEATHER: Sunny with scattered cloud (track 27–30°C, air 21–23°C)

Pos.	Driver	R/Order	Sector 1	Sector 2	Sector 3	Time
1	Kimi Räikkönen	18	16.349s	34.974s	22.997s	1m 14.320s
2	Jenson Button	16	16.487s	35.169s	23.103s	1m 14.759s
3	Fernando Alonso	19	16.722s	35.030s	23.152s	1m 14.904s
4	Giancarlo Fisichella	17	16.444s	35.344s	23.139s	1m 14.927s
5	Michael Schumacher	15	16.568s	35.409s	23.029s	1m 15.006s
6	Mark Webber	10	16.522s	35.536s	23.012s	1m 15.070s
7	Nick Heidfeld	9	16.609s	35.538s	23.256s	1m 15.403s
8	Takuma Sato	5	16.453s	35.796s	23.252s	1m 15.501s
9	Jarno Trulli	12	16.550s	35.520s	23.642s	1m 15.532s
10	Christian Klien	6	16.674s	35.507s	23.454s	1m 15.635s
11	David Coulthard	8	16.627s	35.561s	23.491s	1m 15.679s
12	Ralf Schumacher	13	16.713s	35.563s	23.413s	1m 15.689s
13	Felipe Massa	11	16.854s	35.587s	23.568s	1m 16.009s
14	Jacques Villeneuve	7	16.540s	35.839s	23.633s	1m 16.012s
15	Rubens Barrichello	14	16.658s	35.826s	23.746s	1m 16.230s
16	Christijan Albers	3	17.015s	36.213s	24.291s	1m 17.519s
17	Robert Doornbos	1	17.088s	36.773s	24.452s	1m 18.313s
18	Tiago Monteiro	4	17.322s	36.773s	24.504s	1m 18.599s
19	Juan Pablo Montoya	20	16.340s	35.079s	24.301s	No time
20	Narain Karthikeyan	2	17.613s	36.891s	24.614s	No time

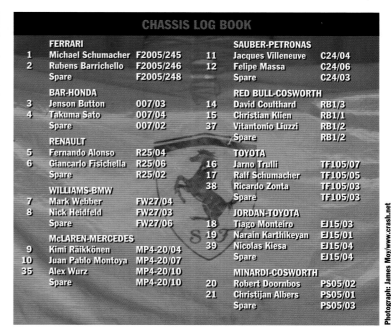

FERRARI		
1	Michael Schumacher	F2005/245
2	Rubens Barrichello	F2005/246
	Spare	F2005/248

BAR-HONDA		
3	Jenson Button	007/03
4	Takuma Sato	007/04
	Spare	007/02

RENAULT		
5	Fernando Alonso	R25/04
6	Giancarlo Fisichella	R25/06
	Spare	R25/02

WILLIAMS-BMW		
7	Mark Webber	FW27/04
8	Nick Heidfeld	FW27/03
	Spare	FW27/06

McLAREN-MERCEDES		
9	Kimi Räikkönen	MP4-20/04
10	Juan Pablo Montoya	MP4-20/07
35	Alex Wurz	MP4-20/10
	Spare	MP4-20/10

SAUBER-PETRONAS		
11	Jacques Villeneuve	C24/04
12	Felipe Massa	C24/06
	Spare	C24/03

RED BULL-COSWORTH		
14	David Coulthard	RB1/3
15	Christian Klien	RB1/1
37	Vitantonio Liuzzi	RB1/2
	Spare	RB1/2

TOYOTA		
16	Jarno Trulli	TF105/07
17	Ralf Schumacher	TF105/05
38	Ricardo Zonta	TF105/03
	Spare	TF105/03

JORDAN-TOYOTA		
18	Tiago Monteiro	EJ15/03
19	Narain Karthikeyan	EJ15/01
39	Nicolas Kiesa	EJ15/04
	Spare	EJ15/04

MINARDI-COSWORTH		
20	Robert Doornbos	PS05/02
21	Christijan Albers	PS05/01
	Spare	PS05/03

Photograph: James Moy/www.crash.net

PRACTICE 1 (FRIDAY)

Heavily cloudy (track 23–26°C, air 20–21°C)

Pos.	Driver	Laps	Time
1	Alex Wurz	21	1m 14.277s
2	Ricardo Zonta	27	1m 14.893s
3	Kimi Räikkönen	9	1m 15.634s
4	Jenson Button	16	1m 15.851s
5	Juan Pablo Montoya	9	1m 15.901s
6	Michael Schumacher	20	1m 16.259s
7	Rubens Barrichello	17	1m 16.280s
8	Vitantonio Liuzzi	26	1m 16.733s
9	Takuma Sato	16	1m 16.795s
10	Ralf Schumacher	14	1m 17.197s
11	David Coulthard	14	1m 17.277s
12	Jarno Trulli	14	1m 17.341s
13	Christian Klien	13	1m 17.423s
14	Felipe Massa	13	1m 17.442s
15	Nick Heidfeld	10	1m 17.665s
16	Mark Webber	10	1m 17.689s
17	Jacques Villeneuve	8	1m 18.132s
18	Narain Karthikeyan	21	1m 18.988s
19	Christijan Albers	19	1m 19.151s
20	Tiago Monteiro	19	1m 19.400s
21	Nicolas Kiesa	25	1m 19.933s
22	Robert Doornbos	17	1m 20.108s
23	Giancarlo Fisichella	2	No time
24	Fernando Alonso	2	No time

PRACTICE 2 (FRIDAY)

Scattered/heavy cloud (track 23–26°C, air 18–21°C)

Pos.	Driver	Laps	Time
1	Alex Wurz	37	1m 13.973s
2	Kimi Räikkönen	20	1m 14.576s
3	Fernando Alonso	34	1m 15.560s
4	Juan Pablo Montoya	18	1m 15.772s
5	Ricardo Zonta	34	1m 16.091s
6	Giancarlo Fisichella	28	1m 16.146s
7	Felipe Massa	24	1m 16.161s
8	Vitantonio Liuzzi	38	1m 16.297s
9	Jarno Trulli	23	1m 16.411s
10	Michael Schumacher	15	1m 16.474s
11	Ralf Schumacher	19	1m 16.575s
12	Christian Klien	14	1m 16.658s
13	Jenson Button	26	1m 16.752s
14	Mark Webber	17	1m 16.879s
15	Nick Heidfeld	18	1m 16.893s
16	Rubens Barrichello	17	1m 16.913s
17	Jacques Villeneuve	20	1m 16.938s
18	Takuma Sato	27	1m 16.992s
19	Narain Karthikeyan	25	1m 17.506s
20	Christijan Albers	17	1m 17.830s
21	Robert Doornbos	28	1m 17.978s
22	Tiago Monteiro	28	1m 18.227s
23	Nicolas Kiesa	19	1m 19.484s
24	David Coulthard	2	No time

PRACTICE 3 (SATURDAY)

Scattered cloud (track 23–24°C, air 10–20°C)

Pos.	Driver	Laps	Time
1	Kimi Räikkönen	10	1m 15.684s
2	Juan Pablo Montoya	5	1m 15.753s
3	Fernando Alonso	14	1m 16.477s
4	Christian Klien	7	1m 16.698s
5	Felipe Massa	7	1m 16.799s
6	David Coulthard	16	1m 16.926s
7	Mark Webber	7	1m 16.961s
8	Jarno Trulli	7	1m 17.053s
9	Giancarlo Fisichella	14	1m 17.061s
10	Takuma Sato	5	1m 17.331s
11	Jenson Button	8	1m 17.397s
12	Jacques Villeneuve	11	1m 17.408s
13	Nick Heidfeld	8	1m 17.536s
14	Rubens Barrichello	10	1m 17.599s
15	Michael Schumacher	9	1m 17.617s
16	Narain Karthikeyan	12	1m 18.102s
17	Christijan Albers	17	1m 18.217s
18	Ralf Schumacher	8	1m 18.229s
19	Robert Doornbos	17	1m 19.083s
20	Tiago Monteiro	14	1m 19.103s

PRACTICE 4 (SATURDAY)

Scattered cloud (track 26–27°C, air 19°C)

Pos.	Driver	Laps	Time
1	Kimi Räikkönen	11	1m 14.128s
2	Juan Pablo Montoya	16	1m 14.449s
3	Fernando Alonso	12	1m 14.758s
4	Giancarlo Fisichella	15	1m 14.958s
5	Jenson Button	15	1m 15.072s
6	Mark Webber	10	1m 15.111s
7	Michael Schumacher	12	1m 15.253s
8	Nick Heidfeld	10	1m 15.255s
9	Christian Klien	14	1m 15.388s
10	Jarno Trulli	14	1m 15.417s
11	David Coulthard	13	1m 15.491s
12	Ralf Schumacher	18	1m 15.585s
13	Takuma Sato	18	1m 15.699s
14	Felipe Massa	12	1m 15.781s
15	Jacques Villeneuve	13	1m 16.037s
16	Rubens Barrichello	11	1m 16.072s
17	Christijan Albers	14	1m 16.674s
18	Robert Doornbos	14	1m 16.912s
19	Narain Karthikeyan	16	1m 17.210s
20	Tiago Monteiro	11	1m 17.966s

9th: TRULLI Toyota

7th: HEIDFELD Williams-BMW

5th: M. SCHUMACHER Ferrari

3rd: ALONSO Renault

Pole: RÄIKKÖNEN McLaren-Mercedes

10th: KLIEN Red Bull-Cosworth

8th: SATO BAR-Honda

6th: WEBBER Williams-BMW

4th: FISICHELLA Renault

2nd: BUTTON BAR-Honda

2	53	54	55	56	57	58	59	60	61	62	63	64	65	66	67	
5	5	5	5	5	5	5	5	5	5	5	5	5	5	5	5	1
10	10	10	10	10	10	10	10	10	10	10	10	10	10	10	10	2
3	3	3	3	3	3	3	3	3	3	3	3	3	3	3	3	3
1	1	1	1	1	1	1	1	1	1	1	1	1	1	6	6	4
6	6	6	6	6	6	6	6	6	6	6	6	6	6	1	1	5
7	17	17	17	17	17	17	17	17	17	17	17	17	17	17		6
4	14	14	14	14	14	14	14	14	14	14	14	14	14	14	14	7
2	12	12	12	12	12	12	12	12	12	12	12	12	12	12	12	8
5	15	15	15	15	15	15	15	15	15	15	15	15	15	15		
2	2	2	2	2	2	2	2	2	2	2	2	2	2	2		
4	4	8	8	8	8	8	8	8	8	8	8	8	8	8		
8	8	4	4	4	4	4	4	4	4	4	4	4	4	4		
6	16	16	16	16	16	16	16	16	16	16	16	16	21			
1	21	21	21	21	21	21	21	21	21	21	21	21				
9	19	19	11	11	11	11	11	11	11	11	11	11				
1	11	11	19	19	19	19	19	19	19	19	19	19				
8	18	18	18	18	18	18	18	18	18	18	18					
0	20	20	20	20	20	20	20	20	20	20						
7	7	7	7													

Pit stop

One lap or more behind leader

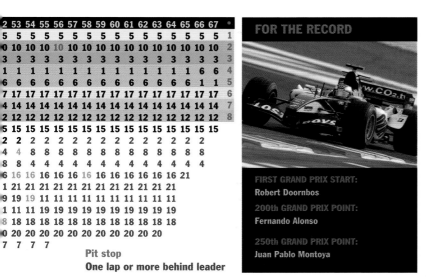

FIRST GRAND PRIX START:
Robert Doornbos

200th GRAND PRIX POINT:
Fernando Alonso

250th GRAND PRIX POINT:
Juan Pablo Montoya

DRIVERS

1	Fernando Alonso	87	18	Christijan Albers	4
2	Kimi Räikkönen	51	19	Pedro de la Rosa	4
3	Michael Schumacher	47	20	Christian Klien	4
4	Juan Pablo Montoya	34	21	Patrick Friesacher	3
5	Rubens Barrichello	31	22	Vitantonio Liuzzi	1
6	Jarno Trulli	31			
7	Giancarlo Fisichella	30			
8	Ralf Schumacher	26		CONSTRUCTORS	
9	Nick Heidfeld	25	1	Renault	117
10	Mark Webber	22	2	McLaren	95
11	David Coulthard	19	3	Ferrari	78
12	Jenson Button	15	4	Toyota	57
13	Felipe Massa	8	5	Williams	47
14	Tiago Monteiro	6	6	Red Bull	24
15	Alex Wurz	6	7	BAR	15
16	Jacques Villeneuve	6	8	Sauber	14
17	Narain Karthikeyan	5	9	Jordan	11
			10	Minardi	7

Photographs: James Moy/www.crash.net

HUNGARORING

HUNGARIANGP

FIA F1 WORLD CHAMPIONSHIP/ROUND 13

SIEMENS

Kimi Räikkönen steadied his challenge for
the championship by winning in Hungary
on a day when Fernando Alonso failed to
score any points after a first-corner brush
with Ralf Schumacher's Toyota.
Photograph: Jean-François Galeron

HUNGARORING QUALIFYING

DIARY

BAR sporting director Gil de Ferran lets slip during a Brazilian television interview that Rubens Barrichello will leave Ferrari at the end of 2005 to join BAR Honda.

Barrichello's departure from Ferrari clears the way for fellow Brazilian Felipe Massa, 24, to leave Sauber to join Maranello.

British secretary of state for health Patricia Hewitt informs Max Mosley that until a pending case before the European Court of Justice on the EU Tobacco Advertising Directive is resolved, the Tobacco Advertising and Promotion Act of 2002 does not apply to broadcasting, so teams can still run with cigarette branding in countries outside the European Union without fear of prosecution if images are relayed to the UK.

Johnny Herbert (below) makes a welcome return to the F1 paddock, having been appointed sporting-relations manager at Jordan.

How many laps would Michael Schumacher run before his first fuel stop?

After qualifying at the Hungaroring had ended with the world champion's taking his first pole position of the season, that was the question everyone else was asking. But there were plenty of supplementary questions, too. Had Ferrari finally found the target? Had Bridgestone really made the progress that Schumacher obliquely seemed to be suggesting, after introducing a new compound?

Or had Ferrari simply pulled a fast one and run its car in qualifying trim but with a fuel load that would get it through a very short first stint, on the basis that since it is almost impossible to overtake on the tight track Schumacher could open up a lead, stop and then defend a higher position against faster rivals in what is always a tough race?

The German was the only driver to dip below 1m 20s and came the closest to his 2004 pole time of 1m 19.146s when he wheeled his F2005 around in 1m 19.882s. This was a real surprise, for Ferrari had been off the pace for much of practice and had not hinted at such speed.

Before Schumacher's run, Jarno Trulli had been the fastest. The Italian had pushed his Toyota TF105 around in 1m 20.839s, which was good enough to displace the first man out in the session, Kimi Räikkönen. The Finn had that dubious honour courtesy of his early retirement from the German Grand Prix. It meant that he had to run when the track conditions were at their very worst. At the Hungaroring that always means when the track is dirty and dusty, as it habitually becomes after each session thanks to wind conditions which usually blow sand back onto the track after it has been displaced by the passage of cars in earlier sessions. The Finn lapped in 1m 20.891s, which was a fantastic time in the circumstances and would ultimately remain good enough for fourth slot on the grid. The very fact that Räikkönen was running first was a distraction and it was easy to miss the fact that McLaren had run him light, choosing the same race-opening tactics as Ferrari. Quite how clever the silver team had been would not really become apparent until Sunday afternoon.

Juan Pablo Montoya was the penultimate runner, having finished second to Fernando Alonso in Germany, and he lapped his McLaren in 1m 20.779s. While that was good enough for the second front-row slot it highlighted what was perceived to be

Ferrari's bold gamble in running lighter than anyone else.

Alonso was the only other runner who might have done something about Schumacher Sr, but Renault never quite got its act together in Hungary. It did not help that the Spaniard had a moment in the gravel on the exit to the last corner on his way to 1m 21.141s, but the real truth of the blues' weekend was that they had opted for the wrong tyre choice. The R25's inherent appetite for rear tyres persuaded Renault to go for the harder Michelin, which cost it lap time.

After Schumacher Sr, Montoya, Trulli and Räikkönen, Ralf Schumacher lined up fifth alongside Alonso. The German had had a pretty lacklustre season up until this point, but Hungary would prove to be one of his periodical good races and he kickstarted it by lapping his Toyota in 1m 20.964s. Rubens Barrichello and Jenson Button shared the fourth row with 1m 21.158s and 1m 21.302s respectively, and again the race would make clear their individual strategies. The Brazilian had low fuel while BAR, like Renault, opted for the harder Michelin. Both Barrichello and Button would be the subject of paddock gossip all weekend, the former amid rumours that he had signed for BAR Honda for 2006 (he had), the latter because of the clumsy manner in which he, his management and BAR Honda were handling his decision to renege on his contract with Williams and to try to stay after all with the Anglo-Japanese team.

Giancarlo Fisichella's conservative lap of 1m 21.333s left him ninth, just ahead of Takuma Sato on 1m 21.787s. Christian Klien was the final man below 1m 22s with 1m 21.937s and his Red Bull team-mate David Coulthard was 13th on 1m 22.279s as Nick Heidfeld slipped his Williams-BMW between them with 1m 22.086s.

Felipe Massa and Jacques Villeneuve struggled to squeeze any more speed out of their Sauber Petronases and ended up 14th and 15th, on 1m 22.565s and 1m 22.866s respectively, while Mark Webber, the second man out, took his Williams around in 1m 23.495s for 16th.

Christijan Albers was again the Minardi pace-setter with 1m 24.443s, which put him ahead of Narain Karthikeyan (1m 25.057s), Robert Doornbos (1m 25.484s) and Tiago Monteiro, who did a lap in his Jordan only to check out a new Toyota engine, changed that morning, because he would in any case be starting last as a result of the change.

Top left: Michael Schumacher hitched a ride back to the paddock with his Ferrari F2005 after it had been stranded on the circuit with electrical problems during Friday free practice.
Photograph: Peter Nygaard/GP Photo

IF the German Grand Prix had been a bitter blow for Kimi Räikkönen and McLaren, the Hungarian was a sugar-coated vitamin pill. With pluperfect performances from both driver and team, who got the strategy absolutely spot-on, they made the most of the worst weekend of Renault's season to claw back ten crucial points for the Finn. The major surprise, however, was just how competitive Michael Schumacher, Ferrari and Bridgestone were.

The champion jumped straight into the lead from pole position and for a while it seemed just like old times. But before the German could get comfortable, Räikkönen had gone past team-mate Juan Pablo Montoya to snatch second place. After Schumacher's surprise pole, everyone suspected that Ferrari was running him with a light fuel load but as he tried to sprint clear Räikkönen went with him and soon they were trading fastest laps. When the Finn was the first to refuel, on the 11th lap, it was clear that both teams were playing the same game. McLaren might have let him go another lap or two, but either way it was crucial to try and position Räikkönen in clear air so that he could really start to exploit the MP4-20's pace.

Schumacher pitted on lap 15, confirming all the qualifying suspicions, and now it was Montoya in the lead. Schumacher was still ahead of Räikkönen when he rejoined, but soon their absorbing duel was resumed. Montoya refuelled on lap 22 and dropped back to third again and now Räikkönen was less than a second adrift of Schumacher. It would all come down to who stopped first the second time around.

This time it was Schumacher, on lap 36. Räikkönen came in one lap later and, crucially, was able to get back out ahead of the red car. Cannily he had deliberately dropped back slightly after his second stop and had saved just enough fuel to go that one critical lap farther than the Ferrari. Now McLaren could let him

speed up again and Räikkönen began lapping in the 1m 21s compared to Schumacher's 1m 23s. The explanation came on lap 48 when Räikkönen refuelled for the final time after doing only an 11-lap stint and having made perfect use of his light load to build a lead of 24s. He rejoined still five seconds ahead of the Ferrari, which did not stop again until lap 57. By then McLaren's excellent strategy had put Räikkönen 30 seconds ahead and the game was over.

As it transpired, fate even aided Schumacher's path to second place, for it struck down Montoya with a driveshaft failure. The McLaren MP4-20 was so clearly the fastest car on the day, but its reliability remained its Achilles' heel. Montoya had moved into second place during Schumacher's second stop and then took the lead when his team-mate stopped. On his two-stop strategy he, too, was a genuine contender for the win and the last laps would almost certainly have involved the two McLaren drivers' fighting it out. But on lap 41, as Räikkönen was closing in fast on his light fuel load, Montoya suddenly slowed before pitting and retiring. McLaren thus lost eight crucial points which would have brought it within five of Renault's tally.

Räikkönen was nonetheless delighted and relieved to have won. 'This is a great result for the entire team,' he said. 'The car felt really good throughout and the tyres were perfect right up until the last lap.'

Schumacher, some 36 seconds adrift, was philosophical. 'If I could have come in at the same time as or later than Kimi, maybe, given how hard it is to overtake here, I might have been able to win. I was happy with the pace in the first stint, but then our tyres got slower. But I am happy with the result.'

Behind them, others had less to celebrate, but Toyota was happy. It makes strong cars and that certainly helped Ralf

Above: Felipe Massa was officially confirmed to be joining Ferrari for 2006.
Photograph: James Moy/www.crash.net

Below: Christian Klien made a spectacular exit at the first corner when his car was flipped over following contact with Jacques Villeneuve. Klien landed on his wheels and was unhurt.
Photograph: Russell Batchelor/XPB.cc

Schumacher and Jarno Trulli, because both were involved in collisions in the first corner. Ralf squeezed Fernando Alonso up the inner kerb and dislodged the Renault driver's front wing, while Jarno was hit from behind by Rubens Barrichello. Both Toyotas continued unabashed. Schumacher Jr took a useful third place, pressuring his big brother in the closing stages, while Trulli battled oversteer from a damaged diffuser courtesy of Barrichello and was a distant fourth.

Behind them Jenson Button had an uneventful run through to fifth for BAR Honda, his harder-compound Michelins lacking the grip of rivals' softer rubber. By the flag he was being chased energetically (and ironically, given Button's wish to stay with BAR in 2006) by BMW Williams' Nick Heidfeld.

Qualifying was a disaster for Williams, with Heidfeld only 12th and Mark Webber 16th, but a brilliant strategy and a two-stop plan elevated the German to sixth and the Australian to seventh by the time the chequered flag fell. The team made some definite progress with the FW27, a fact borne out by Heidfeld's fastest lap, which was within 0.8s of Räikkönen's and was the sixth-best overall. In fact, technical director Sam Michael thought that a three-stopper might have worked well enough to put Heidfeld ahead of Button in the final result, possibly even ahead of fourth-placed Trulli. Unfortunately, however, they had to wind down the revs on his BMW engine after it showed signs of overheating early on: Heidfeld's radiator ducts had become clogged with debris from Alonso's front wing. By the time that was cleared out in the pit stop he had lost too much ground.

With the same strategy helping Webber to seventh ahead of Takuma Sato, Sunday was better for the team than Saturday had been: it scored five more points and salvaged some pride.

Without question this was the worst race of Renault's season. Neither car finished in Canada, but at least they were competitive there. Here they were always struggling with their tyre choice. Alonso could finish only after stopping for a new nose and front wing at the end of the opening lap. He had started to have a look down the inside of Ralf Schumacher in the first corner but had clearly thought better of it and was backing off when the German locked his own front tyres under braking and then kept moving over on him. Alonso was forced up the inside kerb and, just as it seemed the Spaniard might be okay, the Toyota came over even more and its right-rear wheel swiped the Renault's wing askew. It fell off further around the lap. Hamstrung by Michelin's harder tyres and damage to his car's under-tray and therefore grip, where his departed wing had hit the car, Alonso soldiered on to finish as high as he could in order to get the best possible qualifying start-slot for Turkey. Afterwards, Renault's Pat Symonds calculated that the aerodynamic damage to Alonso's car, together with the initial need to turn down the revs because the radiator ducts were full of debris, cost him some 1.2s a lap until a proper repair could be made during his second pit stop.

The race was no better for Giancarlo Fisichella. He was trapped behind Heidfeld for a long time in a car that became increasingly difficult to drive on its hard rubber. A couple of

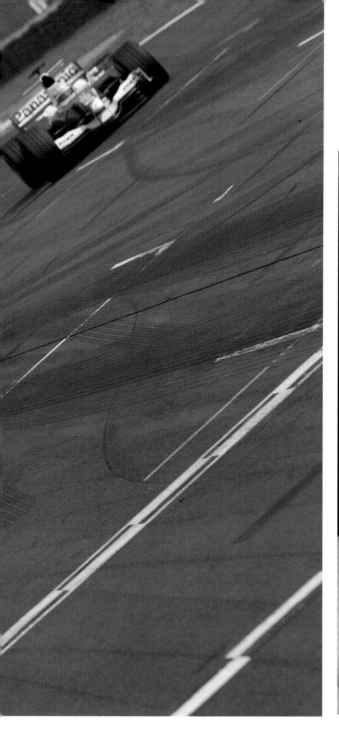

excursions hampered his pace and fluctuating fuel pressure necessitated a stop on the 68th lap out of 70 because a higher fuel load seemed to alleviate the problem. He finished ninth.

Barrichello ran into the back of Trulli at the start and the resultant pit stop for repairs ruined his chances. Later he so nearly struck one of the Jordans in the same place, in Turn One, as he was preparing to lap it. All he could look forward to was all the testing that Ferrari would do while everyone else was observing the summer test ban prior to Turkey.

Over at Jordan the surprise appearance of former racer Johnny Herbert as sporting-relations manager certainly improved the team's tarnished image in the paddock but naturally had little effect on its on-track performance. Narain Karthikeyan described the race as the toughest of his life but also the most consistent of his brief F1 career and was pleased to bring his EJ15 home 12th. Tiago Monteiro had one of his rear tyres punctured in the first corner mêlée just after he'd made up three places with a strong start, so a pit stop cost him plenty of time and he finished 13th, a lap down on his team-mate, after pushing hard for the whole race.

After several races in which nearly everyone had finished, Sauber Petronas, Minardi and Red Bull all failed to do so. Both Felipe Massa and Jacques Villeneuve were affected by an under-bonnet overheating problem which affected their cars' coils. Massa's problem was rectified by a change of coils when he came in on lap 43, but not before a fire beneath his Sauber-Petronas C24's engine cover had created a dramatic moment

JENSON BUTTONED UP BY WILLIAMS?

Twelve months after he had found himself in the spotlight while trying to leave BAR Honda for BMW Williams, Jenson Button was once again in the media's glare in Hungary – for seeking to renege on his Williams contract in order to stay with BAR.

'I suppose it is ironic,' Button admitted sheepishly. 'But I need to be in the best position that I can be, with the best team. I've been in F1 for six years and I haven't won a race. I want to win races and fight for the world championship and I cannot afford three years to build up another team. To be strong in F1 you need a works engine manufacturer. I found out that Honda was so committed and was going to buy 45 percent of the team only after I had made my decision to go for Williams last year. It was definitely a mistake to sign a contract so early and I was a little misguided, but that's ultimately my responsibility.'

Button admitted he was embarrassed, especially because Sir Frank Williams had given him his F1 chance back in 2000. 'We will keep discussing things,' he said. 'It's a sticky situation. We have always had a good friendship, but the fact that I am prepared to risk that shows him how serious I am about staying with BAR Honda. It's a crucial decision for my career.'

Williams was completely unimpressed and sent Button a clear message. 'No amount of money will make us [the people at Williams] change our minds,' he said. 'Jenson could have been better advised. Williams has a fully binding contract. There is no let-out clause. It is very clear and straightforward. There needs to be a clear understanding of the word "commitment". Once you give your word, you should keep your word.

'I recognise that where he presently is the team is doing well to very well. But then I look at the coming season and the order will almost certainly shuffle. Williams is a strong team with a strong past, a weak present and, certainly in my own mind, a strong future. It is as well resourced as any team and I do not overestimate. It will be back. And Jenson is a key part of that. Williams is looking forward to a British team with a British driver. And I remind you that it brought him in in 2000 and it looks forward to seeing him again, because it has a right – and a proper and correct legal right – to expect him to be here. English law is as clear as it comes.'

or two for his crew. He eventually got going again, but had lost so many laps that he could finish only 14th, a disappointment after he had been chasing Heidfeld from 10th place initially after making a great start. Like Massa, Villeneuve was on a two-stop strategy with a late first pit call and he too had a fire during his second stop, but the team's attempt to get him to the finish (and thus improve his qualifying start-position for Turkey) was stymied when the former champion stopped on the circuit on lap 57 because the fire had damaged other components.

Minardi failed to get either car home, which was a particular shame after Christijan Albers' impressive pace on Saturday morning. He got caught up with Webber and Monteiro in the first-corner fallout and as his car landed after a momentary flight it shed some of its aerodynamic appendages. Subsequently a hydraulic problem meant several pit stops and retirement. Team-mate Robert Doornbos raced well and was nursing his tyres nicely when he was struck down out on the circuit by the problem that would later afflict Albers.

Red Bull came to Hungary with two brand-new chassis for David Coulthard and Christian Klien and saw both destroyed within a lap of the race. In the first corner Villeneuve tipped Klien into a gentle rollover that ended his race, while Coulthard made a great start from the seventh row of the grid but got less than halfway around the opening lap. Alonso's Renault shed its damaged front wing on the approach to the top chicane.

Several drivers were able to dodge it as it lay in the middle of the road, but DC was unsighted behind Webber's Williams and was unable to avoid the debris. The modern front wing is a curved structure and weighs a lot, since most are ballasted with lead. When the Red Bull struck it at speed, the car's right-front wheel was smashed off and the Scot spun luridly to a halt in the chicane's run-off area before jumping out and starting to pick up some of the plentiful debris.

Coming so soon after the death the previous Wednesday of team chef Darren Hawker, who fell from a balcony at the Marriott Hotel, this weekend was a much-needed but bitter-sweet success for McLaren. On the podium neither Räikkönen nor team chief Ron Dennis, who received the winning constructors' trophy, took part in the traditional champagne-spraying activities with the Schumacher brothers.

This was an emotional victory that might yet play a crucial role in crowning Räikkönen as world champion. From 36 points after Hockenheim, the gap between him and Alonso was back down to 26. It was damage limitation at its best but was no less important for that. Days before, it had seemed all but over, the mountain just too high to scale; now, after Räikkönen had gone out first in qualifying and gone on to win a brilliant victory, McLaren could permit itself to hope once again. The title battle, perhaps, was far from over after all.

David Tremayne

BUDAPEST 2005

Above: Nick Heidfeld continued to impress in his unobtrusive way with a good run to sixth place in his Williams-BMW FW27.

Left: Takuma Sato may have had an action-packed race at Budapest, but it netted him what would be his only championship point of the season.

Below: Track-side snappers framing Rubens Barrichello as he headed for tenth at the end of a fraught race.

Photographs: James Moy/www.crash.net

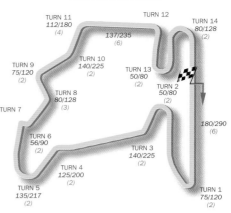

HUNGARORING

TURN 11 112/180 (4)
TURN 12 137/235 (6)
TURN 14 80/128 (2)
TURN 9 75/120 (2)
TURN 10 140/225 (2)
TURN 13 50/80 (2)
TURN 8 80/128 (3)
TURN 2 50/80 (2)
TURN 7
180/290 (6)
TURN 6 56/90 (2)
TURN 3 140/225 (2)
TURN 4 125/200 (2)
TURN 5 135/217 (2)
TURN 1 75/120 (2)

CIRCUIT LENGTH: 2.722miles/4.381 km

FIA F1 WORLD CHAMPIONSHIP • ROUND 13
MARLBORO
MAGYAR NAGYDIJ
HUNGARORING 29–31 JULY 2005

RACE DISTANCE: 70 laps, 190.551 miles /306.663 km | RACE WEATHER: Sunny (track 46–48°C, air 33–34°C)

Pos.	Driver	Nat.	No.	Entrant	Car/Engine	Tyres	Laps	Time/Retirement	Speed (mph/km/h)	Gap to leader	Fastest race lap	
1	Kimi Räikkönen	FIN	9	Team McLaren Mercedes	McLaren MP4-20-Mercedes F0 110R V10	M	70	1h 37m 25.552s	117.351/188.859		1m 21.219s	40
2	Michael Schumacher	D	1	Scuderia Ferrari Marlboro	Ferrari F2005-055 V10	B	70	1h 38m 01.133s	116.641/187.716	+35.581s	1m 21.476s	13
3	Ralf Schumacher	D	17	Panasonic Toyota Racing	Toyota TF105-RVX-05 V10	M	70	1h 38m 01.681s	116.631/187.699	+36.129s	1m 21.873s	13
4	Jarno Trulli	I	16	Panasonic Toyota Racing	Toyota TF105-RVX-05 V10	M	70	1h 38m 19.773s	116.273/187.123	+54.221s	1m 21.842s	32
5	Jenson Button	GB	3	Lucky Strike BAR Honda	BAR 007-Honda RA005E V10	M	70	1h 38m 24.384s	116.182/186.977	+58.832s	1m 22.406s	70
6	Nick Heidfeld	D	8	BMW WilliamsF1 Team	Williams FW27-BMW P84/85 V10	M	70	1h 38m 33.927s	115.994/186.675	+68.375s	1m 22.053s	53
7	Mark Webber	AUS	7	BMW WilliamsF1 Team	Williams FW27-BMW P84/85 V10	M	69			+1 lap	1m 22.453s	47
8	Takuma Sato	J	4	Lucky Strike BAR Honda	BAR 007-Honda RA005E V10	M	69			+1 lap	1m 22.399s	45
9	Giancarlo Fisichella	I	6	Mild Seven Renault F1 Team	Renault R25-RS25 V10	M	69			+1 lap	1m 22.506s	19
10	Rubens Barrichello	BR	2	Scuderia Ferrari Marlboro	Ferrari F2005-055 V10	B	69			+1 lap	1m 22.768s	20
11	Fernando Alonso	E	5	Mild Seven Renault F1 Team	Renault R25-RS25 V10	M	69			+1 lap	1m 22.884s	51
12	Narain Karthikeyan	IND	19	Jordan Toyota	Jordan EJ15-Toyota RVX-05 V10	B	67			+3 laps	1m 24.446s	17
13	Tiago Monteiro	P	18	Jordan Toyota	Jordan EJ15-Toyota RVX-05 V10	B	66			+4 laps	1m 24.774s	15
14	Felipe Massa	BR	12	Sauber Petronas	Sauber C24-Petronas 05A V10	M	63			+7 laps	1m 23.048s	22
	Christijan Albers	NL	21	Minardi Cosworth	Minardi PS05-Cosworth TJ2005 V10	B	59	Finished but not classified			1m 25.956s	8
	Jacques Villeneuve	CDN	11	Sauber Petronas	Sauber C24-Petronas 05A V10	M	56	Engine fire			1m 23.118s	23
	Juan Pablo Montoya	COL	10	Team McLaren Mercedes	McLaren MP4-20-Mercedes F0 110R V10	M	41	Drive shaft			1m 21.237s	20
	Robert Doornbos	NL	20	Minardi Cosworth	Minardi PS05-Cosworth TJ2005 V10	B	26	Hydraulics			1m 25.646s	16
	Christian Klien	A	15	Red Bull Racing	Red Bull RB1-Cosworth TJ2005/12 V10	M	0	Accident				
	David Coulthard	GB	14	Red Bull Racing	Red Bull RB1-Cosworth TJ2005/12 V10	M	0	Accident				

Fastest lap: Kimi Räikkönen, on lap 40, 1m 21.219, 120.661 mph/194.186 km/h.

Lap record: Michael Schumacher (Ferrari F2004-052 V10), 1m 19.071s, 123.939 mph/199.461 km/h (2004).

19th: DOORNBOS Minardi-Cosworth

17th: ALBERS Minardi-Cosworth

15th: VILLENEUVE Sauber-Petronas

13th: COULTHARD Red Bull-Cosworth

11th: KLIEN Red Bull-Cosworth

20th: MONTEIRO Jordan-Toyota

18th: KARTHIKEYAN Jordan-Toyota

16th: WEBBER Williams-BMW

14th: MASSA Sauber-Petronas

12th: HEIDFELD Williams-BMW

Grid order	1	2	3	4	5	6	7	8	9	10	11	12	13	14	15	16	17	18	19	20	21	22	23	24	25	26	27	28	29	30	31	32	33	34	35	36	37	38	39	40	41	42	43	44	45	46	47	48	49	50	51	52	53	54
1 M. SCHUMACHER	1	1	1	1	1	1	1	1	1	1	1	1	1	1	1	10	10	10	10	10	10	10	10		1	1	1	1	1	1	1	1	1	1	1	1	1	1	1	9	9	10	10	10	9	9	9	9	9	9	9	9	9	9
10 MONTOYA	9	9	9	9	9	9	9	9	9	9	9	10	10	10	10	1	1	1	1	1	1	1	9	9	9	9	9	9	9	9	9	9	9	1	10	9	9	1	1	1	1	1	1	1	1	1	1	1	1	1	1	1	1	1
16 TRULLI	10	10	10	10	10	10	9	10	10	10	10	16	17	17	17	9	9	9	9	9	9	9	10	10	10	10	10	10	10	10	10	10	10	10	1	1	1	10	17	17	17	17	17	17	17	17	17	17	17	17	17	17	17	17
9 RÄIKKÖNEN	16	16	16	16	16	16	16	16	16	16	17	16	9	9	3	3	3	3	3	3	3	3	17	17	17	17	17	17	17	17	17	17	17	17	17	17	16	16	16	16	16	16	16	16	16	16	16	16	16	16	16	16	8	8
17 R. SCHUMACHER	17	17	17	17	17	17	17	17	17	17	9	9	3	17	17	17	17	17	17	16	16	16	16	16	16	16	16	16	16	16	16	16	16	16	16	16	3	3	3	3	3	8	8	8	8	8	8	16	16
5 ALONSO	3	3	3	3	3	3	3	3	3	3	3	3	16	16	16	16	16	16	16	8		3	3	3	3	3	3	3	3	3	3	3	3	3	3	3	3	3	8	8	8	8	8	8	8	3	3	3	3	3	3	3	3	3
2 BARRICHELLO	4	4	4	4	4	4	4	4	4	4	4	4	4	4	4	4	4	8	4	3	7	8	8	8	8	8	8	8	8	8	8	8	8	4	4	4	4	4	4	4	4	4	7	7	7	4	4	4	4	4	4	4
3 BUTTON	8	8	8	8	8	8	8	8	8	8	8	8	8	8	8	8	6	12	3	12	11	7		4	4	4	4	4	4	4	4	4	4	4	6	7	7	7	7	7	4	6	4	4	4
6 FISICHELLA	6	6	6	6	6	6	6	6	6	6	6	6	6	6	6	6	6	6	12	6	11	11	7	11	4	4	6	6	6	6	6	6	6	6	7	6	6	6	6	6	6	4	6	6	6
4 SATO	5	12	12	12	12	12	12	12	12	12	12	12	12	12	2	11	11	7	7	4	4	6	2	2	2	2	7	7	7	7	7	7	2	2	2	2	2	2	2	2	2	2	2	2	2
15 KLIEN	12	11	11	11	11	11	11	11	11	11	11	11	11	11	11	11	11	11	11	11		4	6	6	6	2	7	7	7	11	2	2	5	5	5	5	5	5	5	5	5	5	5	5	5
8 HEIDFELD	11	7	7	7	7	7	7	7	7	7	7	7	7	7	7	7	7	7	7	4	4	2	6	2	2	11	11	11	12	11	11	11	11	11	11	11	11	11	11	11	11	11	11	11	11	11
14 COULTHARD	2	19	19	19	19	19	19	19	19	19	19	2	2	19	19	19	19	19	19	2	2	5	5	5	5	5	5	5	12	19	19	19	19	19	19	19	19	19	19	19
12 MASSA	7	21	21	21	21	21	21	21	21	21	2	19	19	5	5	5	5	5	5	5	5	12	12	12	12	12	12	12	5	12	12	12	12	12	21	21	21	21	21	18	18	18
11 VILLENEUVE	19	20	20	20	20	20	20	20	2	2	21	21	5	5	5	19	19	19	19	19	19	19	19	19	19	19	19	19	12	12	12	12	18	18	18	18	18	21	18	18
7 WEBBER	21	2	2	2	2	2	2	2	20	20	5	5	21	21	21	20	20	20	20	20	20	20	20	20	21	21	21	21	21	21	12	12	12	12	12	12	12	12	21	21
21 ALBERS	20	5	5	5	5	5	5	5	5	5	20	20	20	20	21	21	21	21	21	21	21	18	18	18	18	18	18	18	18	18	18	18	18	18
19 KARTHIKEYAN	18	18	18	18	18	18	18	18	18	18	18	18	18	18	18	18	18	18	18
20 DOORNBOS																				
18 MONTEIRO																				

Pit stop

One lap or more behind leader

TIME SHEETS

QUALIFYING

WEATHER: Sunny with a light wind (track 48–50°C, air 34–35°C)

Pos.	Driver	R/Order	Sector 1	Sector 2	Sector 3	Time
1	Michael Schumacher	16	28.354s	29.178s	22.350s	1m 19.882s
2	Juan Pablo Montoya	19	28.434s	29.668s	22.677s	1m 20.779s
3	Jarno Trulli	7	28.533s	29.805s	22.501s	1m 20.839s
4	Kimi Räikkönen	1	28.486s	29.674s	22.731s	1m 20.891s
5	Ralf Schumacher	15	28.769s	29.655s	22.540s	1m 20.964s
6	Fernando Alonso	20	28.497s	29.643s	23.001s	1m 21.141s
7	Rubens Barrichello	11	28.565s	29.835s	22.758s	1m 21.158s
8	Jenson Button	18	28.563s	29.824s	22.915s	1m 21.302s
9	Giancarlo Fisichella	17	28.616s	29.810s	22.907s	1m 21.333s
10	Takuma Sato	9	28.512s	30.300s	22.975s	1m 21.787s
11	Christian Klien	12	28.932s	30.109s	22.896s	1m 21.937s
12	Nick Heidfeld	10	28.609s	30.303s	23.174s	1m 22.086s
13	David Coulthard	14	28.876s	30.425s	22.978s	1m 22.279s
14	Felipe Massa	13	28.934s	30.463s	23.168s	1m 22.565s
15	Jacques Villeneuve	6	28.932s	30.604s	23.330s	1m 22.866s
16	Mark Webber	2	28.969s	30.769s	23.757s	1m 23.495s
17	Christijan Albers	8	29.247s	31.407s	23.789s	1m 24.443s
18	Narain Karthikeyan	5	29.726s	31.236s	24.095s	1m 25.057s
19	Robert Doornbos	3	29.886s	31.268s	24.169s	1m 25.484s
20	Tiago Monteiro	4	-	-	-	No time

PRACTICE 1 (FRIDAY)

Sunny (track 42–44°C, air 32–33°C)

Pos.	Driver	Laps	Time
1	Alex Wurz	20	1m 21.411s
2	Rubens Barrichello	8	1m 22.834s
3	Jenson Button	12	1m 23.028s
4	Kimi Räikkönen	7	1m 23.159s
5	Michael Schumacher	8	1m 23.234s
6	Felipe Massa	10	1m 23.375s
7	Nick Heidfeld	8	1m 23.384s
8	Juan Pablo Montoya	7	1m 23.558s
9	Takuma Sato	11	1m 23.679s
10	Ralf Schumacher	6	1m 23.706s
11	Jarno Trulli	8	1m 23.764s
12	Fernando Alonso	10	1m 23.833s
13	Mark Webber	8	1m 23.918s
14	Giancarlo Fisichella	9	1m 23.940s
15	Vitantonio Liuzzi	19	1m 24.174s
16	Ricardo Zonta	18	1m 24.270s
17	Jacques Villeneuve	10	1m 24.683s
18	Narain Karthikeyan	14	1m 26.130s
19	Robert Doornbos	16	1m 27.011s
20	Tiago Monteiro	8	1m 27.344s
21	Christijan Albers	8	1m 27.540s
22	Nicolas Kiesa	19	1m 28.230s
23	Channock Nissany	8	1m 34.319s
24	Christian Klien	1	No time
25	David Coulthard	1	No time

PRACTICE 2 (FRIDAY)

Sunny (track 47–49°C, air 34–35°C)

Pos.	Driver	Laps	Time
1	Ricardo Zonta	24	1m 20.409s
2	Alex Wurz	35	1m 20.519s
3	Kimi Räikkönen	18	1m 21.281s
4	Jarno Trulli	26	1m 21.410s
5	Ralf Schumacher	24	1m 21.631s
6	Juan Pablo Montoya	17	1m 21.662s
7	Rubens Barrichello	23	1m 21.914s
8	Fernando Alonso	21	1m 22.473s
9	Jenson Button	29	1m 22.544s
10	Christian Klien	23	1m 22.626s
11	Giancarlo Fisichella	21	1m 22.652s
12	Nick Heidfeld	16	1m 22.861s
13	David Coulthard	24	1m 22.886s
14	Vitantonio Liuzzi	15	1m 22.913s
15	Mark Webber	18	1m 22.935s
16	Jacques Villeneuve	23	1m 23.558s
17	Takuma Sato	12	1m 23.560s
18	Felipe Massa	25	1m 23.574s
19	Robert Doornbos	23	1m 23.670s
20	Christijan Albers	21	1m 24.093s
21	Tiago Monteiro	24	1m 24.862s
22	Narain Karthikeyan	2	1m 25.184s
23	Nicolas Kiesa	17	1m 25.269s
24	Michael Schumacher	1	No time

PRACTICE 3 (SATURDAY)

Sunny (track 35–37°C, air 28–30°C)

Pos.	Driver	Laps	Time
1	Kimi Räikkönen	7	1m 21.686s
2	Michael Schumacher	10	1m 21.842s
3	Juan Pablo Montoya	7	1m 21.980s
4	Ralf Schumacher	10	1m 22.712s
5	Fernando Alonso	8	1m 22.798s
6	Jarno Trulli	10	1m 22.888s
7	Nick Heidfeld	6	1m 23.167s
8	Rubens Barrichello	4	1m 23.583s
9	Mark Webber	7	1m 23.678s
10	Felipe Massa	10	1m 23.715s
11	Jenson Button	6	1m 23.902s
12	David Coulthard	7	1m 23.932s
13	Christian Klien	7	1m 24.006s
14	Takuma Sato	11	1m 24.070s
15	Jacques Villeneuve	11	1m 24.078s
16	Giancarlo Fisichella	6	1m 24.200s
17	Robert Doornbos	11	1m 25.691s
18	Narain Karthikeyan	10	1m 25.721s
19	Christijan Albers	11	1m 25.947s
20	Tiago Monteiro	12	1m 26.600s

PRACTICE 4 (SATURDAY)

Sunny (track 38–40°C, air 30–31°C)

Pos.	Driver	Laps	Time
1	Kimi Räikkönen	11	1m 20.203s
2	Juan Pablo Montoya	14	1m 20.517s
3	Michael Schumacher	17	1m 20.773s
4	Ralf Schumacher	13	1m 20.903s
5	Rubens Barrichello	7	1m 21.266s
6	Giancarlo Fisichella	14	1m 21.276s
7	Jenson Button	15	1m 21.301s
8	Fernando Alonso	12	1m 21.336s
9	Takuma Sato	17	1m 21.880s
10	Mark Webber	9	1m 21.889s
11	Nick Heidfeld	9	1m 21.918s
12	Christian Klien	13	1m 22.340s
13	David Coulthard	14	1m 22.534s
14	Jarno Trulli	6	1m 22.699s
15	Felipe Massa	11	1m 22.753s
16	Christijan Albers	11	1m 22.979s
17	Jacques Villeneuve	14	1m 22.985s
18	Robert Doornbos	8	1m 23.358s
19	Narain Karthikeyan	14	1m 24.265s
20	Tiago Monteiro	17	1m 24.628s

CHASSIS LOG BOOK

FERRARI
1	Michael Schumacher	F2005/245
2	Rubens Barrichello	F2005/246
	Spare	F2005/248

BAR-HONDA
3	Jenson Button	007/04
4	Takuma Sato	007/03
	Spare	007/02

RENAULT
5	Fernando Alonso	R25/04
6	Giancarlo Fisichella	R25/06
	Spare	R25/02

WILLIAMS-BMW
7	Mark Webber	FW27/04
8	Nick Heidfeld	FW27/03
	Spare	FW27/06

McLAREN-MERCEDES
9	Kimi Räikkönen	MP4-20/04
10	Juan Pablo Montoya	MP4-20/07
35	Alex Wurz	MP4-20/06
	Spare	MP4-20/06

SAUBER-PETRONAS
11	Jacques Villeneuve	C24/04
12	Felipe Massa	C24/06
	Spare	C24/03

RED BULL-COSWORTH
14	David Coulthard	RB1/3
15	Christian Klien	RB1/1
37	Vitantonio Liuzzi	RB1/2
	Spare	RB1/2

TOYOTA
16	Jarno Trulli	TF105/07
17	Ralf Schumacher	TF105/05
38	Ricardo Zonta	TF105/03
	Spare	TF105/03

JORDAN-TOYOTA
18	Tiago Monteiro	EJ15/03
19	Narain Karthikeyan	EJ15/01
39	Nicolas Kiesa	EJ15/04
	Spare	EJ15/04

MINARDI-COSWORTH
20	Robert Doornbos	PS05/02
21	Christijan Albers	PS05/01
40	Chanock Nissany	PS05/03
	Spare	PS05/03

9th: FISICHELLA Renault

7th: BARRICHELLO Ferrari

5th: R. SCHUMACHER Toyota

3rd: TRULLI Toyota

Pole: M. SCHUMACHER Ferrari

10th: SATO BAR-Honda

8th: BUTTON BAR-Honda

6th: ALONSO Renault

4th: RÄIKKÖNEN McLaren-Mercedes

2nd: MONTOYA McLaren-Mercedes

Lap chart (laps 55–70)

55	56	57	58	59	60	61	62	63	64	65	66	67	68	69	70	
9	9	9	9	9	9	9	9	9	9	9	9	9	9	9	9	1
1	1	1	1	1	1	1	1	1	1	1	1	1	1	1	1	2
17	17	17	17	17	17	17	17	17	17	17	17	17	17	17	17	3
16	16	16	16	16	16	16	16	16	16	16	16	16	16	16	16	4
3	3	3	3	3	3	3	3	3	3	3	3	3	3	3	3	5
8	8	8	8	8	8	8	8	8	8	8	8	8	8	8	8	6
7	7	7	7	7	7	7	7	7	7	7	7	7	7	7	7	7
4	4	4	4	4	4	4	4	4	4	4	4	4	4	4	4	8
6	6	6	6	6	6	6	6	6	6	6	6	6		6	6	
2	2	2	2	2	2	2	2	2	2	2	2	2	2			
5	5	5	5	5	5	5	5	5	5	5	5	5				
11	11	19	19	19	19	19	19	19	19	19	19					
19	19	18	18	18	18	18	18	18	18	18	18					
18	18	12	12	12	12	12	12	12								
12	12	21	21	21												
21	21															

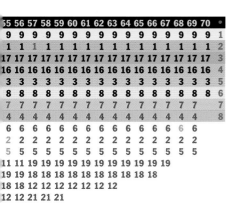

FOR THE RECORD

20th GRAND PRIX IN HUNGARY

150th GRAND PRIX POINT:
Jarno Trulli

50th GRAND PRIX POINT:
Mark Webber

500th LEAD LAP:
Kimi Räikkönen

POINTS

DRIVERS

1	Fernando Alonso	87	18	Christijan Albers	4
2	Kimi Räikkönen	61	19	Pedro de la Rosa	4
3	Michael Schumacher	55	20	Christian Klien	4
4	Jarno Trulli	36	21	Patrick Friesacher	3
5	Juan Pablo Montoya	34	22	Vitantonio Liuzzi	1
6	Ralf Schumacher	32	23	Takuma Sato	1
7	Rubens Barrichello	31			
8	Giancarlo Fisichella	30		**CONSTRUCTORS**	
9	Nick Heidfeld	28	1	Renault	117
10	Mark Webber	24	2	McLaren	105
11	Jenson Button	19	3	Ferrari	86
12	David Coulthard	19	4	Toyota	68
13	Felipe Massa	8	5	Williams	52
14	Tiago Monteiro	7	6	Red Bull	24
15	Alex Wurz	6	7	BAR	20
16	Jacques Villeneuve	6	8	Sauber	14
17	Narain Karthikeyan	5	9	Jordan	11
			10	Minardi	7

Photograph: James Moy/www.crash.net

Photographs: James Moy/www.crash.net

ISTANBUL
TURKISH GP

FIA F1 WORLD CHAMPIONSHIP/ROUND 14

ISTANBUL QUALIFYING

Kimi Räikkönen benefited from some crucial overnight set-up changes and the fact that he made his qualifying run last thanks to his victory in Hungary. Despite losing a fraction in the last sector of the lap, he confidently grabbed his eighth career pole.

'The lap was good but not perfect and I lost a little time in the last sector, but I knew I had some time in hand,' said the Finn. 'We had made some changes to the car overnight and it had worked really well in the morning, so we knew we had a strong chance of pole if everything worked well.'

Meanwhile Juan Pablo Montoya found himself positioned uncomfortably early in the qualifying queue as a result of his retirement at Budapest, but his efforts stood up well and he felt confident for the race, starting from the second row. 'My qualifying lap was okay,' he said, 'but I know my time would have been so much better if I'd done it later in the session. There is no reason why I can't be strong in the race.'

In the Renault camp, Giancarlo Fisichella was delighted to post what was briefly the fastest time and earned him second on the grid (1m 27.039s) alongside Räikkönen, despite claiming that he was slightly unsettled by Rubens Barrichello, who was finishing his in-lap just ahead of Fisichella.

'It's great to be on the front row,' he conceded. 'We have worked hard all this weekend to get a good set-up and the team has done a great job. My only problem was that I came up on Barrichello – we were very close through Turns 12 and 13 and it disrupted my concentration, costing me a few tenths.'

In taking third place on the inside of the second row, Fernando Alonso (1m 27.050s) admitted that he had struck a balance between speed and conservatism, but also found himself unsettled by a tail wind down the back straight, which caused him to miss an apex, costing him a sliver of time.

Jenson Button looked on course to put the BAR-Honda 007 right up with the high rollers but he got into a high-speed wobble at the challenging Turn Eight and wound up 13th on 1m 30.063s, just a tenth quicker than his team-mate Takuma Sato, with whom he provisionally shared the seventh row.

'It was a very disappointing qualifying lap,' Jenson confessed, because in practice today we didn't have any issues with the

high-speed corners but we could see that the other teams were struggling with the rear-end quite a bit. It's a shame because we've been quick here all weekend. But all is not lost.'

Button's slip left Jarno Trulli to bag fifth on the grid with a 1m 27.501s, extracting the maximum here from the Toyota TF105's improved aerodynamic package – introduced for this race – which included a revised floor and modified rear wing. 'This was another good lap,' said Trulli, 'because we have been struggling to finalise the set-up on my car this weekend.

'I was not happy with the balance this morning, so I changed the set-up completely for qualifying. It was a bit windier than before so the car was a bit more nervous and that made the run a little more difficult than usual.'

By contrast his team-mate Ralf Schumacher lost a little time at Turn Nine, admitting that he had perhaps been trying a bit too hard. He ended up ninth on 1m 28.594s.

Nick Heidfeld (1m 27.929s) and Mark Webber (1m 27.944s) proved well matched in their Williams FW27s, while in the Sauber camp Felipe Massa came out decisively on top with an eighth-fastest 1m 28.419s. Jacques Villeneuve spun off at the tricky Turn Eight and lined up 16th, sandwiched by the Minardis of Christijan Albers and Robert Doornbos. Doornbos had had to abort his run after a problem with an incorrectly fitted brake pipe 'which made it feel as though the handbrake was stuck on'.

As for the Ferrari drivers, Rubens Barrichello wound up 11th on 1m 29.369s, splitting the Red Bull RB1s of Christian Klien (1m 28.963s) and David Coulthard (1m 29.764s), but Michael Schumacher spun off and wound up starting 19th, having taken an engine penalty, ahead of the hapless Sato, who started from the pit lane because his time was disallowed by the stewards, who felt he had 'illegitimately impeded' Webber on his in-lap.

'In the race, all I can do is push hard and try to do my best,' said Schumacher. 'It is important to do as well as possible here, to help in qualifying at Monza. After our performances at Hockenheim and Budapest, this is clearly a step backwards.'

Narain Karthikeyan was another to take an engine penalty, which obliged him to start 18th while his team-mate Tiago Monteiro lined up 14th.

Above: Felipe Massa dutifully paid a courtesy call on his new employer for the 2006 season.
Photograph: James Moy/www.crash.net

Opening spread: Giancarlo Fisichella and Kimi Räikkönen raced wheel-to-wheel for the first turn at the start of the maiden Turkish GP at the spectacular new Istanbul Park circuit.
Photograph: Lukas Gorys

Far left: Busy time for Red Bull Racing in the pit lane during Friday free practice with RB1s for David Coulthard, Christian Klien and Vitantonio Liuzzi all in action.
Photograph: Jad Sherif/WRI

Top left: Ralf Schumacher featured on the cover of *The Red Bulletin*, the paddock's new satirical magazine.
Photograph: Lukas Gorys

Left: Eyedrops for Jenson Button-lookalike Jacques Villeneuve.

Below: The intensity of race control with its NASA-like levels of concentration.
Photographs: James Moy/www.crash.net

Above: Ah well, BAR next season. Rubens Barrichello had another weekend to forget at Istanbul.
Photograph: James Moy/www.crash.net

Right: Jenson Button (leading team-mate Takuma Sato past Tiago Monteiro's Jordan) drove a fine race. After a qualifying slip that dropped him to 13th on the grid, the Englishman pulled back to an excellent fifth by the chequered flag.
Photograph: XPB.cc

KIMI Räikkönen once again demonstrated that the McLaren-Mercedes MP4-20 was decisively the quickest car on the 2005 F1 championship trail when he totally dominated the inaugural Turkish Grand Prix at the spectacular new Istanbul Park circuit, decisively beating the world-championship leader Fernando Alonso's Renault R25 by 18.609s.

It was the poker-faced Finn's second straight victory and his fifth out of the season's 14 races so far. Yet the mathematics of the unfolding championship battle still suggested that Räikkönen and McLaren might have caught their stride a couple of races too late to retain anything but an outside chance of preventing 24-year-old Alonso from becoming the youngest world champion in the sport's history.

With five races left, Alonso emerged from the Turkish race nursing a 24-point lead over the McLaren team leader. There were 50 points left to race for and even if Räikkönen and his team-mate Juan Pablo Montoya finished first and second ahead of the Renault driver in all the remaining races, Alonso would still squeeze home with the championship by four points.

With that in mind, the McLaren team was understandably hoping that Räikkönen's team-mate Juan Pablo Montoya might hold on to the second place he had monopolised for much of the race, but he slid wide at the fastest corner on the circuit with just over a lap to go, allowing Alonso to overtake and claim what could be a crucially important second place.

To be fair, the Colombian was grappling with a handling imbalance caused by a damaged rear underbody diffuser, the result of Jordan driver Tiago Monteiro's having inadvertently nudged Montoya into a spin as the McLaren lapped him a short while earlier. Responsibility for this unfortunate incident was laid firmly at Monteiro's door by some observers, although others were baffled as to quite why Montoya felt it necessary to chop aggressively back in front of the Jordan after completing his passing manoeuvre.

'Yeah, it is a bit disappointing,' admitted Montoya thoughtfully. 'I was in a difficult position yesterday in qualifying and even with fuel the car had the speed for it so I thought I was looking really good for today.

'I had too much [tyre] graining at the start of the race so I couldn't really push because it was just wearing out the fronts. But when the fronts came up the car was very quick. I managed to set the fastest lap of the race and we were looking quite good. Towards the end we were just cruising, then I passed Monteiro and he just did a bit like what [Jos] Verstappen did to me a few years back [in Brazil in 2001]. I did the first few corners fine, then went into Turn Eight, had no rear grip and could not keep on line.'

Understandably, Monteiro saw things differently. 'Montoya overtook me and [then] shut the door in a braking zone,' he said firmly. 'I could not avoid pushing him because I was blinded and lost all the downforce. I am really sorry for him

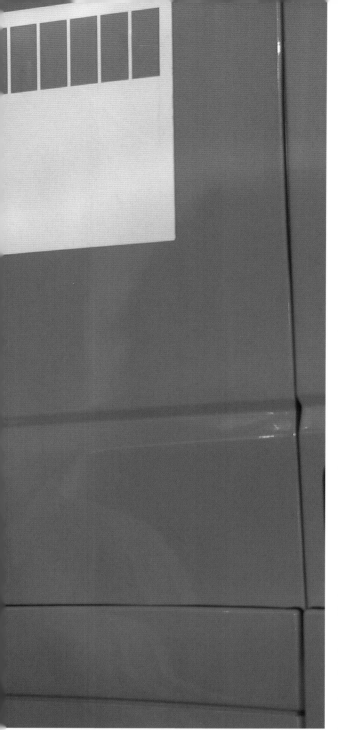

because he was fighting for a podium, but we talked a lot during the briefings about not moving positions in braking areas.

The start took place in front of huge new grandstands packed to capacity with almost 100,000 spectators after limousine-loads of Turkish government dignitaries had been escorted through the paddock and grid by a solicitous Bernie Ecclestone, the F1 commercial-rights holder who had sold the promoters this new race at an annual cost in the region of $20 million.

Security was understandably intense, with rifle-toting marksmen discreetly tucked away on top of grandstands and race-administration buildings. Happily there was no trouble and the crowds rose to their feet in delight as Giancarlo Fisichella just got the jump on Räikkönen to lead into the first left-hander.

'I didn't exactly get the best start,' said Räikkönen. 'I got a bit of wheelspin and then Fisichella got past me and Alonso got alongside me. But I was hoping and then on the first lap Fisichella ran wide at the exit of Turn Nine, I think, and I got beside him. But I didn't pass him because they [the Renaults] were much faster in a straight line, so I was actually behind them both braking into Turn 12, but then from the middle I could brake later and got first place.'

Alonso overtook Fisichella for second place at the end of lap two – responding to instructions from his pit that he was quicker and should therefore overtake the Italian – but although the Renault team leader steadied the Finn's advantage at little more than a second during the opening phase, Räikkönen stayed out nine laps longer than the Spaniard before making his first refuelling stop on lap 22, by which time the McLaren driver had such a cushion that he was able to dictate the pace of the race all the way to the finish.

'I knew the McLarens were faster,' said Alonso, 'so I concentrated on doing a race without any mistakes and driving consistently. The car was reliable again and I had some luck from Montoya's problems as well. But you know, sometimes you can make your own luck. I kept the pressure on and it paid off because I was close enough to take advantage.'

Fisichella finished a distant fourth after losing over ten seconds due to a problem with a refuelling rig at one of his pit stops, while Jenson Button took a strong fifth after his climb through the pack from 13th on the grid.

'I really enjoyed that,' said Button. 'I had a terrible start, but to work my way through the pack was fantastic. The result is a little disappointing because we had good pace all weekend. I've got to try not to make that mistake [the qualifying slip] again.'

Photograph: James Moy/www.crash.net

DIARY

Rubens Barrichello is confirmed to be leaving Ferrari for BAR Honda in 2006.

Jordan team principal Colin Kolles puts his dentistry skills to good use by carrying out emergency root-canal surgery on driver Tiago Monteiro on the eve of the race.

Michael Schumacher reveals that he will decide 'sometime next year' whether to continue racing beyond the end of 2006.

BMW makes it clear that it has made no decision about drivers for 2006, even though Jacques Villeneuve still has a contract in place with Peter Sauber.

Button was still in the throes of his contractual stand-off with Frank Williams, but the sight of the problems facing Mark Webber and Nick Heidfeld in the race must have made him shudder with apprehension. Both suffered two right-rear tyre failures, apparently caused by the under-tray's scuffing against the sidewalls, and were forced into ignominious retirements. There was also a close call for Heidfeld with Felipe Massa's Sauber in the first corner of the race and a later moment between Webber and Michael Schumacher's Ferrari shortly after the Australian had resumed following his first tyre change.

'I was a lap behind Michael, but much quicker,' explained Webber. 'I thought it was strange that he was moving around in the braking area because all the drivers agreed to try not to do that. Michael seemed quite keen to do it, so I didn't show much respect and we made contact.'

Unsurprisingly, Michael came back with an alternative view. 'I saw him closing on me and moved to the right,' he explained. 'As I began to brake I could no longer see him and, when I was in mid-corner, I felt a bang as he hit me with his nose. He was one lap down, so I don't know why he tried this.'

It was the low point of an appalling weekend for the once all-conquering Ferrari team, which was now in dire trouble. It had been planned that Schumacher and Rubens Barrichello should use the Bridgestone tyre compound they had used at Budapest three weeks earlier. But the team reverted to the compound and construction used at Magny-Cours, which it hoped would at least be consistent, if not necessarily super-quick.

Come qualifying, however, things could hardly have gone worse for Maranello. Barrichello grappled with graining tyres and consequent understeer in the final sector of the lap and Michael admitted he misjudged the effect of a tail wind on his braking performance and spun off.

After Michael's collision with the Williams, he spent 25 minutes in the pits having a damaged steering rack replaced. He rejoined the race, way back, in a bid to move himself up the qualifying order for Monza.

As for Barrichello, he had seldom been forced to work so hard to earn a lapped tenth place. 'This was a very, very tough race,' he explained. 'I drove flat-out from the start, but it had been obvious that we lacked performance since we started on Friday.

'After Hungary it is disappointing to be back in a situation such as this. We had no grip and we clearly made the wrong choice in terms of the tyres we brought to Turkey. Tenth place is not what we would have wanted in this inaugural Turkish race. We must keep on working and try to do better.'

David Coulthard and Christian Klien drove exceptionally well to take seventh and eighth places in their Red Bulls. 'I was happy with the overall performance of the car throughout the race,' said Coulthard, 'and although we still have some issues regarding the downforce level at top speed, the balance felt good. We had some understeer at the start but made a wing adjustment during the first pit stop to create more downforce and after that it was a lot better.'

Toyota had frankly hoped for more. Jarno Trulli drove hard all afternoon to claim sixth, admitting that he'd lost quite a bit of time in traffic. Ralf Schumacher got pushed wide at the first corner and ran over the front wing from Felipe Massa's Sauber, a car that later succumbed to engine problems. 'Basically, I lost it all then,' said Ralf. 'From then on it was always going to be a big struggle for me.' He wound up 12th behind Jacques Villeneuve's Sauber and ahead of Robert Doornbos's Minardi and the Jordans of Narain Karthikeyan and Monteiro.

Despite these individual problems, there was no doubt that the Turkish GP had been one of the outstanding new races to appear on the F1 calendar in recent years, proof positive that it is possible to develop an imaginative new track design within the context of contemporary safety and security requirements. By any objective standards it had been a magnificent success.

Alan Henry

SQUEEZING A NEW RACE INTO A HECTIC SCHEDULE

Fitting the Turkish GP into an already crowded world-championship schedule was always going to be a challenging task. Following an unprecedented helter-skelter of eight races in 11 weeks, the drivers had at least enjoyed a three-week break following the Hungarian race, but the opportunity to relax in the Mediterranean sunshine did not extend to most of the backroom boys, who were working flat-out to ready the cars in time for F1 to make its first trip to Istanbul.

'Istanbul in August is going to be punishingly hot, placing a great physical toll on the drivers, so we'll have to be at peak fitness,' said Mark Webber in the run-up to the race. 'The circuit looks longer than average with a lot of interesting corners and I think a lot of us will be practising it in advance on our computer-game circuit simulators.'

That's as maybe, but many team personnel were left wishing that the logistical challenge of attending the Turkish race were as straightforward as a computer game. For F1's foot soldiers, the Turkish GP marked the start of probably the most exacting spell of the year, stretching out to the season's finale in China on 16 October.

Immediately after Hungary, the cars returned to their various bases across Europe, a two-day journey back to the UK for the McLaren, Williams, Red Bull, BAR Honda, Jordan and Renault transporters. The cars then had to be stripped, serviced and rebuilt in five days before heading for the channel ferries and a two-day blast back across Europe to Trieste, where they met up with the European-based teams' transporters – Ferrari's from Maranello, Minardi's from Faenza, Sauber's from near Zurich and Toyota's from Cologne – to be loaded aboard a specially chartered ferry for the 72-hour voyage to Istanbul.

'After the race they'll be shipped back to Trieste, from where they'll go directly to Monza to park up in preparation for the Italian GP on 4 September,' explained Dickie Stanford, the Williams team manager. 'I imagine there will be van-loads of modifications being sent down from base if we need any upgrades.

'Then we'll go straight to Spa for the Belgian race the following weekend, after which the cars will be back at base in the UK for about five days before being despatched to Brazil and then on to Suzuka and Shanghai. It is one hell of a schedule.'

TURKIS
GRAND
NBUL 2005

NEW STANDARD FOR F1 VENUES

The Istanbul track shares its anti-clockwise configuration with only two other circuits on the F1 championship trail: Imola and Interlagos. Yet it was the constructional challenge to complete the new facility which really stretched Hermann Tilke and his design team to the limits.

'We needed to blast away a lot of rock,' said Tilke, 'but we were already experienced in that from our work in Bahrain. There, we moved approximately a million cubic metres of rock. Here, the excavation totalled about three million cubic metres. We even had to case a small river that now runs underneath the circuit in a concrete channel.'

Tilke, who has designed all of the most recent new circuits to join the F1 schedule, believes that it is important that each facility should reflect the traditions of the country concerned.

'It is very important to my team and I that our race tracks make it apparent which country is hosting F1,' he said. 'In Bahrain it was the desert; in Shanghai we made use of the river-delta environment, which is full of canals and bodies of water. For the Istanbul circuit, we used oriental elements that you no longer see all that often here because Turkey has also become a very modern country in respect of its architecture.'

Far left: Mechanics from the Williams (top) and McLaren teams preparing their cars prior to a race that unfolded very differently for the two British teams.

Top: Race promoter Thomas Franke (left) with track designer Hermann Tilke.

Left: Kimi Räikkönen on the rostrum, calmly hoping that his title chances might still be alive.

Photographs: James Moy/www.crash.net

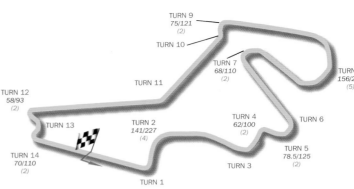

ISTANBUL PARK

TURN 9
75/121
(2)

TURN 10

TURN 7
68/110
(2)

TURN 11

TURN 8
156/250
(5)

TURN 12
58/93
(2)

TURN 13

TURN 2
141/227
(4)

TURN 4
62/100
(2)

TURN 6

TURN 5
78.5/125
(2)

TURN 14
70/110
(2)

TURN 3

TURN 1

CIRCUIT LENGTH: 3.337 miles/5.340 km

FIA F1 WORLD CHAMPIONSHIP • ROUND 14

MARLBORO
TURKISH GRAND PRIX
ISTANBUL 19–21 AUGUST 2005

RACE DISTANCE: 58 laps, 190.551 miles /306.663 km   RACE WEATHER: Scattered cloud (track 38–42°C, air 28–31°C)

Pos.	Driver	Nat.	No.	Entrant	Car/Engine	Tyres	Laps	Time/Retirement	Speed (mph/km/h)	Gap to leader	Fastest race l	
1	Kimi Räikkönen	FIN	9	Team McLaren Mercedes	McLaren MP4-20-Mercedes F0 110R V10	M	58	1h 24m 34.454s	136.388/219.496		1m 25.030s	40
2	Fernando Alonso	E	5	Mild Seven Renault F1 Team	Renault R25-RS25 V10	M	58	1h 24m 53.063s	135.890/218.694	+18.609s	1m 25.524s	58
3	Juan Pablo Montoya	COL	10	Team McLaren Mercedes	McLaren MP4-20-Mercedes F0 110R V10	M	58	1h 24m 54.089s	135.863/218.650	+19.635s	1m 24.770s	39
4	Giancarlo Fisichella	I	6	Mild Seven Renault F1 Team	Renault R25-RS25 V10	M	58	1h 25m 12.427s	135.375/217.866	+37.973s	1m 25.604s	34
5	Jenson Button	GB	3	Lucky Strike BAR Honda	BAR 007-Honda RA005E V10	M	58	1h 25m 13.758s	135.340/217.809	+39.304s	1m 25.790s	58
6	Jarno Trulli	I	16	Panasonic Toyota Racing	Toyota TF105-RVX-05 V10	M	58	1h 25m 29.874s	134.915/217.125	+55.420s	1m 26.178s	52
7	David Coulthard	GB	14	Red Bull Racing	Red Bull RB1-Cosworth TJ2005/12 V10	M	58	1h 25m 43.750s	134.551/216.539	+69.296s	1m 26.417s	58
8	Christian Klien	A	15	Red Bull Racing	Red Bull RB1-Cosworth TJ2005/12 V10	M	58	1h 25m 46.076s	134.490/216.441	+71.622s	1m 26.374s	58
9	Takuma Sato	J	4	Lucky Strike BAR Honda	BAR 007-Honda RA005E V10	M	58	1h 26m 24.441s	133.495/214.840	+109.987s	1m 25.858s	54
10	Rubens Barrichello	BR	2	Scuderia Ferrari Marlboro	Ferrari F2005-055 V10	B	57			+1 lap	1m 26.635s	45
11	Jacques Villeneuve	CDN	11	Sauber Petronas	Sauber C24-Petronas 05A V10	M	57			+1 lap	1m 26.967s	44
12	Ralf Schumacher	D	17	Panasonic Toyota Racing	Toyota TF105-RVX-05 V10	M	57			+1 lap	1m 27.025s	38
13	Robert Doornbos	NL	20	Minardi Cosworth	Minardi PS05-Cosworth TJ2005 V10	B	55			+3 laps	1m 29.229s	53
14	Narain Karthikeyan	IND	19	Jordan Toyota	Jordan EJ15-Toyota RVX-05 V10	B	55			+3 laps	1m 29.286s	42
15	Tiago Monteiro	P	18	Jordan Toyota	Jordan EJ15-Toyota RVX-05 V10	B	55			+3 laps	1m 29.035s	50
	Christijan Albers	NL	21	Minardi Cosworth	Minardi PS05-Cosworth TJ2005 V10	B	48	Hydraulics			1m 29.392s	13
	Michael Schumacher	D	1	Scuderia Ferrari Marlboro	Ferrari F2005-055 V10	B	32	Collision damage			1m 26.991s	21
	Nick Heidfeld	D	8	BMW WilliamsF1 Team	Williams FW27-BMW P84/85 V10	M	29	Tyres			1m 27.353s	25
	Felipe Massa	BR	12	Sauber Petronas	Sauber C24-Petronas 05A V10	M	28	Engine			1m 26.514s	27
	Mark Webber	AUS	7	BMW WilliamsF1 Team	Williams FW27-BMW P84/85 V10	M	20	Tyres			1m 26.791s	12

Fastest lap: Juan Pablo Montoya, on lap 39, 1m 24.770, 140.860 mph/226.693 km/h (record for new track).

19th: M. SCHUMACHER Ferrari
Ten-place penalty for engine change

17th: DOORNBOS Minardi-Cosworth

15th: ALBERS Minardi-Cosworth

13th: BUTTON BAR-Honda

11th: BARRICHELLO Ferrari

20th: SATO BAR-Honda
Started from pit lane

18th: KARTHIKEYAN Jordan-Toyota
Ten-place penalty for engine change

16th: VILLENEUVE Sauber-Petronas

14th: MONTEIRO Jordan-Toyota

12th: COULTHARD Red Bull-Cosworth

Grid order	1	2	3	4	5	6	7	8	9	10	11	12	13	14	15	16	17	18	19	20	21	22	23	24	25	26	27	28	29	30	31	32	33	34	35	36	37	38	39	40	41	42	43	44
9 RÄIKKÖNEN	9	9	9	9	9	9	9	9	9	9	9	9	9	9	9	9	9	9	9	9	9	9	9	9	9	9	9	9	9	9	9	9	9	9	9	9	9	9	9	9	9	9	9	9
6 FISICHELLA	6	5	5	5	5	5	5	5	5	5	5	5	6	10	10	10	10	10	10	10	10	10	10	10	10	10	10	10	10	10	10	10	10	10	10	10	10	10	10	10	10	10	10	10
5 ALONSO	5	6	6	6	6	6	6	6	6	6	6	6	10	16	16	16	16	5	3	3	5	5	5	5	5	5	5	5	5	5	5	5	5	6	6	5	5	5	5	5	5	5	5	5
10 MONTOYA	10	10	10	10	10	10	10	10	10	10	10	10	16	5	5	5	5	3	5	5	15	15	14	6	6	6	6	6	6	6	6	5	16	16	16	16	16	3	3					
16 TRULLI	16	16	16	16	16	16	16	16	16	16	16	16	5	3	3	3	15	15	14	14	16	16	16	16	16	16	16	16	16	16	3	3	3	3	3	3	16	6						
8 HEIDFELD	8	8	8	8	15	15	7	7	3	3	3	3	15	15	15	15	14	14	14	16	16	2	3	3	3	3	3	3	3	3	6	6	6	6	6	6	14							
7 WEBBER	15	15	15	15	7	7	15	15	15	15	15	14	14	14	14	14	16	16	2	2	6	4	4	4	4	14	14	14	14	14	14	14	14	14	14	15								
12 MASSA	14	14	7	7	14	14	14	14	14	14	14	14	2	2	2	2	6	3	14	14	14	15	15	15	15	15	15	15	15	15	15	15	15	16										
17 R. SCHUMACHER	7	7	14	14	3	3	3	2	2	2	2	2	6	6	6	6	6	3	4	15	15	15	15	2	2	2	2	2	2	2	2	2	2	2										
15 KLIEN	2	2	2	3	2	2	2	1	1	1	1	1	1	4	4	4	4	4	15	2	2	2	2	4	4	4	4	4	4	4	4	4	4	4										
2 BARRICHELLO	1	1	3	2	1	1	8	4	4	4	4	4	11	12	12	11	11	11	11	11	11	11	12	12	12	12	11	11	11	11	11	11	11	11	11	11	11							
14 COULTHARD	3	3	1	1	8	18	18	8	4	11	11	11	11	11	17	17	17	12	17	12	11	11	11	11	11	11	11	11	17	17	17	17	17	17										
3 BUTTON	18	18	18	11	4	11	4	11	11	18	17	17	17	17	21	12	12	17	12	17	17	17	17	19	20	20	20	20	19	19	19	19	17	19	19	19	20							
18 MONTEIRO	19	19	19	19	4	9	19	14	17	17	8	8	18	12	12	8	8	8	8	8	20	19	19	19	20	19	19	19	20	20	20	20	20	20	20	19								
21 ALBERS	21	21	11	11	11	4	11	18	18	21	20	8	19	18	18	18	18	18	18	18	18	18	18	18	18	18	18	18	18	18	18	18	18	18										
11 VILLENEUVE	11	11	11	21	17	17	21	3	8	8	21	21	20	8	19	19	19	19	19	19	19	18	21	21	21	21	21	21	21	21	21	21	21	21										
20 DOORNBOS	20	20	20	4	4	21	19	20	20	20	20	12	12	18	18	21	21	21	21	20	20	20	21	1	1	1																		
19 KARTHIKEYAN	17	4	4	17	7	20	8	8	12	12	19	19	20	20	20	20	21	21	21	21	1	1	1																					
1 M. SCHUMACHER	4	17	17	20	20	8	8	12	19	19	19	8	1	1	7	7	7	7	1	1	1	1																						
4 SATO	12	12	12	12	12	12	12	7	7	7	7	7	7	1	1	1	1	1																										

QUALIFYING

WEATHER: Sunny (track 29–30°C, air 37–41°C)

Pos.	Driver	R/Order	Sector 1	Sector 2	Sector 3	Time
1	Kimi Räikkönen	20	32.440s	30.532s	23.825s	1m 26.797s
2	Giancarlo Fisichella	12	32.629s	30.752s	23.658s	1m 27.039s
3	Fernando Alonso	10	32.582s	30.591s	23.658s	1m 27.050s
4	Juan Pablo Montoya	4	32.704s	30.856s	23.792s	1m 27.352s
5	Jarno Trulli	17	32.717s	30.744s	24.040s	1m 27.501s
6	Nick Heidfeld	15	32.838s	30.943s	24.148s	1m 27.929s
7	Mark Webber	14	32.804s	31.031s	24.109s	1m 27.944s
8	Felipe Massa	7	33.078s	31.218s	24.123s	1m 28.419s
9	Ralf Schumacher	18	32.739s	31.758s	24.097s	1m 28.594s
10	Christian Klien	1	33.447s	31.191s	24.325s	1m 28.963s
11	Rubens Barrichello	11	33.301s	31.587s	24.481s	1m 29.369s
12	David Coulthard	2	33.648s	31.854s	24.262s	1m 29.764s
13	Jenson Button	16	32.450s	32.176s	24.298s	1m 30.063s
14	Takuma Sato	13	32.839s	30.463s	23.168s	1m 30.175s
15	Tiago Monteiro	8	33.792s	32.383s	24.535s	1m 30.710s
16	Christijan Albers	6	34.682s	32.333s	25.171s	1m 32.186s
17	Michael Schumacher	19	-	-	-	No time
18	Jacques Villeneuve	5	-	-	-	No time
19	Narain Karthikeyan	9	-	-	-	No time
20	Robert Doornbos	3	-	-	-	No time

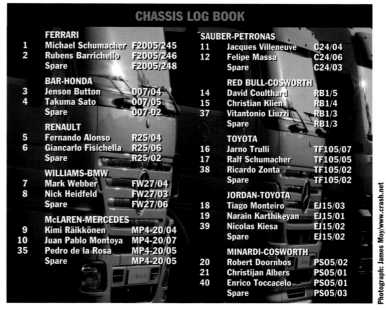

FERRARI
1	Michael Schumacher	F2005/245
2	Rubens Barrichello	F2005/246
	Spare	F2005/248

BAR-HONDA
3	Jenson Button	007/04
4	Takuma Sato	007/05
	Spare	007-02

RENAULT
5	Fernando Alonso	R25/04
6	Giancarlo Fisichella	R25/06
	Spare	R25/02

WILLIAMS-BMW
7	Mark Webber	FW27/04
8	Nick Heidfeld	FW27/03
	Spare	FW27/06

McLAREN-MERCEDES
9	Kimi Räikkönen	MP4-20/04
10	Juan Pablo Montoya	MP4-20/07
35	Pedro de la Rosa	MP4-20/05
	Spare	MP4-20/05

SAUBER-PETRONAS
11	Jacques Villeneuve	C24/04
12	Felipe Massa	C24/06
	Spare	C24/03

RED BULL-COSWORTH
14	David Coulthard	RB1/5
15	Christian Klien	RB1/4
37	Vitantonio Liuzzi	RB1/3
	Spare	RB1/3

TOYOTA
16	Jarno Trulli	TF105/07
17	Ralf Schumacher	TF105/05
38	Ricardo Zonta	TF105/02
	Spare	TF105/02

JORDAN-TOYOTA
18	Tiago Monteiro	EJ15/03
19	Narain Karthikeyan	EJ15/01
39	Nicolas Kiesa	EJ15/02
	Spare	EJ15/02

MINARDI-COSWORTH
20	Robert Doornbos	PS05/02
21	Christijan Albers	PS05/01
40	Enrico Toccacelo	PS05/01
	Spare	PS05/03

Photograph: James Moy/www.crash.net

PRACTICE 1 (FRIDAY)

Cloudy (track 37–38°C, air 27–28°C)

Pos.	Driver	Laps	Time
1	Pedro de la Rosa	16	1m 27.882s
2	Kimi Räikkönen	11	1m 28.453s
3	Mark Webber	8	1m 28.765s
4	Ricardo Zonta	25	1m 28.810s
5	Jenson Button	12	1m 28.968s
6	Juan Pablo Montoya	10	1m 29.183s
7	Fernando Alonso	13	1m 29.283s
8	Michael Schumacher	11	1m 29.766s
9	Takuma Sato	12	1m 30.050s
10	Giancarlo Fisichella	9	1m 30.106s
11	Felipe Massa	11	1m 30.368s
12	Ralf Schumacher	12	1m 30.563s
13	Jarno Trulli	11	1m 30.785s
14	Nick Heidfeld	10	1m 30.847s
15	Jacques Villeneuve	12	1m 30.847s
16	Christian Klien	10	1m 31.008s
17	Rubens Barrichello	11	1m 31.294s
18	David Coulthard	11	1m 31.306s
19	Vitantonio Liuzzi	20	1m 31.353s
20	Tiago Monteiro	15	1m 32.147s
21	Nicolas Kiesa	22	1m 32.501s
22	Narain Karthikeyan	12	1m 32.886s
23	Christijan Albers	13	1m 33.474s
24	Robert Doornbos	12	1m 35.367s
25	Enrico Toccacelo	15	1m 36.411s

PRACTICE 2 (FRIDAY)

Heavily cloudy (track 34–35°C, air 26–27°C)

Pos.	Driver	Laps	Time
1	Ricardo Zonta	32	1m 25.583s
2	Pedro de la Rosa	33	1m 26.196s
3	Juan Pablo Montoya	17	1m 26.525s
4	Kimi Räikkönen	18	1m 27.274s
5	Jenson Button	28	1m 27.346s
6	Vitantonio Liuzzi	28	1m 27.578s
7	Fernando Alonso	25	1m 27.579s
8	Giancarlo Fisichella	29	1m 27.673s
9	Jarno Trulli	22	1m 27.964s
10	Takuma Sato	25	1m 28.081s
11	Mark Webber	20	1m 28.120s
12	David Coulthard	25	1m 28.235s
13	Michael Schumacher	25	1m 28.293s
14	Jacques Villeneuve	26	1m 28.404s
15	Rubens Barrichello	25	1m 28.460s
16	Ralf Schumacher	22	1m 28.641s
17	Felipe Massa	27	1m 28.681s
18	Christian Klien	21	1m 28.828s
19	Nick Heidfeld	21	1m 28.959s
20	Tiago Monteiro	21	1m 30.626s
21	Robert Doornbos	16	1m 30.628s
22	Christijan Albers	22	1m 30.730s
23	Nicolas Kiesa	18	1m 30.884s
24	Narain Karthikeyan	12	1m 30.899s
25	Enrico Toccacelo	19	1m 32.813s

PRACTICE 3 (SATURDAY)

Scattered cloud then sunny (track 29–35°C, air 24–28°C)

Pos.	Driver	Laps	Time
1	Juan Pablo Montoya	8	1m 26.857s
2	Jenson Button	6	1m 27.031s
3	Fernando Alonso	8	1m 27.119s
4	Kimi Räikkönen	9	1m 27.134s
5	Takuma Sato	8	1m 27.159s
6	Nick Heidfeld	8	1m 27.471s
7	Mark Webber	8	1m 27.633s
8	Giancarlo Fisichella	8	1m 27.921s
9	David Coulthard	9	1m 27.953s
10	Felipe Massa	9	1m 28.018s
11	Ralf Schumacher	9	1m 28.049s
12	Christian Klien	9	1m 28.063s
13	Jarno Trulli	6	1m 28.468s
14	Michael Schumacher	14	1m 28.487s
15	Jacques Villeneuve	8	1m 28.740s
16	Rubens Barrichello	10	1m 28.854s
17	Tiago Monteiro	10	1m 30.216s
18	Christijan Albers	13	1m 30.837s
19	Robert Doornbos	13	1m 30.851s
20	Narain Karthikeyan	1	No time

PRACTICE 4 (SATURDAY)

Sunny (track 37–39°C, air 27–28°C)

Pos.	Driver	Laps	Time
1	Kimi Räikkönen	10	1m 26.120s
2	Jenson Button	15	1m 26.599s
3	Fernando Alonso	13	1m 26.627s
4	Juan Pablo Montoya	11	1m 26.748s
5	Giancarlo Fisichella	15	1m 27.240s
6	Takuma Sato	14	1m 27.308s
7	Mark Webber	7	1m 27.335s
8	Ralf Schumacher	13	1m 27.556s
9	David Coulthard	14	1m 27.796s
10	Felipe Massa	8	1m 27.829s
11	Christian Klien	14	1m 27.919s
12	Jarno Trulli	15	1m 27.921s
13	Nick Heidfeld	9	1m 27.951s
14	Michael Schumacher	16	1m 28.155s
15	Jacques Villeneuve	12	1m 28.534s
16	Rubens Barrichello	12	1m 28.615s
17	Tiago Monteiro	15	1m 28.830s
18	Robert Doornbos	14	1m 30.155s
19	Christijan Albers	13	1m 30.999s
20	Narain Karthikeyan	3	No time

9th: R. SCHUMACHER Toyota

7th: WEBBER Williams-BMW

5th: TRULLI Toyota

3rd: ALONSO Renault

Pole: RÄIKKÖNEN McLaren-Mercedes

10th: KLIEN Red Bull-Cosworth

8th: MASSA Sauber-Petronas

6th: HEIDFELD Williams-BMW

4th: MONTOYA McLaren-Mercedes

2nd: FISICHELLA Renault

	46	47	48	49	50	51	52	53	54	55	56	57	58	
	9	9	9	9	9	9	9	9	9	9	9	9	9	1
	10	10	10	10	10	10	10	10	10	10	10	5	5	2
	5	5	5	5	5	5	5	5	5	5	10	10	3
	3	3	6	6	6	6	6	6	6	6	6	6	6	4
	6	6	3	3	3	3	3	3	3	3	3	3	5
	16	16	16	16	16	16	16	16	16	16	16	16	6
	2	14	14	14	14	14	14	14	14	14	14	14	7
	14	15	15	15	15	15	15	15	15	15	15	15	8
	15	4	4	4	4	4	4	4	4	4	4	4	
	4	2	2	2	2	2	2	2	2	2	2		
	11	11	11	11	11	11	11	11	11	11	11	11	
	17	17	17	17	17	17	17	17	17	17	17		
	20	20	20	20	20	20	20	20	20	20			
	19	19	19	19	19	19	19	19	19				
	18	18	18	18	18	18	18	18	18				
	21	21	21										

Pit stop
One lap or more behind leader

FOR THE RECORD

FIRST GRAND PRIX IN TURKEY

40th GRAND PRIX WIN:
McLaren-Mercedes

150th GRAND PRIX POINT:
Jenson Button

500th GRAND PRIX LEAD LAP:
Juan Pablo Montoya

POINTS

DRIVERS
1	Fernando Alonso	95
2	Kimi Räikkönen	71
3	Michael Schumacher	55
4	Juan Pablo Montoya	40
5	Jarno Trulli	39
6	Giancarlo Fisichella	35
7	Ralf Schumacher	32
8	Rubens Barrichello	31
9	Nick Heidfeld	28
10	Mark Webber	24
11	Jenson Button	23
12	David Coulthard	21
13	Felipe Massa	8
14	Tiago Monteiro	6
15	Alex Wurz	6
16	Jacques Villeneuve	6
17	Narain Karthikeyan	5
18	Christian Klien	5

19	Christijan Albers	4
20	Pedro de la Rosa	4
21	Patrick Friesacher	3
22	Takuma Sato	1
23	Vitantonio Liuzzi	1

CONSTRUCTORS
1	Renault	130
2	McLaren-Mercedes	121
3	Ferrari	86
4	Toyota	71
5	Williams	52
6	Red Bull	27
7	BAR	24
8	Sauber	14
9	Jordan	11
10	Minardi	7

Photographs: James Moy/www.crash.net

MONZA
ITALIANGP

FIA F1 WORLD CHAMPIONSHIP/ROUND 15

Top: Kimi Räikkönen's Vodafone grid girl lined up ahead of his MP4-20.

Above: The seething tifosi always have smiles on their faces at Monza.

Right: The jubilant McLaren personnel let their hair down as Montoya took the chequered flag.
Photographs: James Moy/www.crash.net

Left: Juan Pablo Montoya enjoyed spraying the champagne as he celebrated his second win as a McLaren-Mercedes driver.
Photograph: Paul-Henri Cahier

MONZA QUALIFYING

Kimi Räikkönen had had more than his fair share of problems during the course of the season. Having waited since 2002 for the fastest car, he had now time and again been let down by its lack of reliability. At Monza another Mercedes V10 cried enough in Saturday morning's second practice session.

The sheer frustration he felt showed in his driving in qualifying, but in the best possible way. There were many long faces in the McLaren garage while the engine was changed, for weary engineers and mechanics had slaved for long hours honing the fast but quirky MP4-20s. But Räikkönen relieved his stresses and repaid the rest of the team with a stellar lap, the true value of which was not immediately apparent.

When the Finn went out, it was his team-mate Juan Pablo Montoya who had set the fastest time and Fernando Alonso's efforts to better it had come up short. The Colombian had lapped in 1m 21.054s, to which the Spaniard's response was 1m 21.319s. Renault was fast at the autodrome, but not quite fast enough.

Then came Räikkönen, driving with the controlled aggression that is his trademark. He stopped the clocks in 1m 20.878s and barely looked out of shape for a moment. But while one McLaren would start from pole, Räikkönen's would drop to 11th under the ten-grid-place-penalty rule covering engine changes.

It was not until later that it transpired that Räikkönen had done his stunning lap with a heavy fuel load. While Alonso would refuel on lap 19 and Montoya on 20, Räikkönen would run until lap 25. It was an absolutely electrifying performance.

Until Alonso set his time, Jenson Button had looked like a contender for the front row with 1m 21.369s, which had displaced BAR-Honda team-mate Takuma Sato's 1m 21.477s, which had been the fastest time for half the session. But, as the race would cruelly demonstrate, the Anglo-Japanese team was doing a spot of window dressing and was not half as competitive as it looked.

Giancarlo Fisichella should have been in the midst of this fight, but he made two key errors on his lap. The first came at the first chicane, the other in the first Lesmo and he was left only eighth on the corrected grid with 1m 22.068s. Ahead of him, besides Montoya, Alonso, Button and Sato, were Jarno Trulli, who pushed his Toyota TF105 around in 1m 21.640s, and the Ferraris of Michael Schumacher and Rubens Barrichello.

A year ago Ferrari had been untouchable on its home ground; now it was struggling and was confidently believed to be running light fuel loads when Michael Schumacher lapped in 1m 21.721s and Barrichello in 1m 21.962s.

Ralf Schumacher did not do as good a job as his team-mate on his way to ninth overall on 1m 22.266s, but he was carrying two laps' more fuel, which was worth around half a second. David Coulthard's 11th-fastest time for Red Bull (1m 22.304s) was sufficient for 10th in the corrected line-up and displaced team-mate Christian Klien (1m 22.532s), who yet again was racing instead of Tonio Liuzzi – who had beaten both his team-mates comfortably on Friday despite running with less horsepower. Jacques Villeneuve was the quicker Sauber-Petronas driver on 1m 22.356s, which left him 12th alongside Räikkönen.

BMW Williams showed good form in practice, but in qualifying that translated into a lap of only 1m 22.560s, which left Mark Webber 14th. The Australian had a new team-mate for the weekend after Nick Heidfeld complained of a severe headache on Saturday morning. The young German had had a major shunt at the second Lesmo in testing the previous week, when the rear suspension on his FW27 had failed. Racing in his place was test driver Antonio Pizzonia but because Williams had refused to let him test the previous week (technical director Sam Michael preferring to help fellow tester Nico Rosberg's GP2 campaign by giving him two days in the car) he understandably struggled. Through circumstance he had not driven the FW27 for three months. Added to that, he was the first man out for qualifying. His 1m 23.291s left him 16th.

Sauber's Felipe Massa likewise suffered from being one of the first three runners in the session and his lap of 1m 23.060s separated the Williams duo.

Tiago Monteiro and Narain Karthikeyan had tossed a coin to see who would drive the singleton Jordan EJ15B and the Portuguese driver won. The car appeared to be a significant improvement over the EJ15 and he lapped it in 1m 24.666s for 17th. Karthikeyan's 1m 25.859s left him 19th.

Once again Robert Doornbos drove his Minardi PS05 with commitment, for 1m 24.904s which split the Jordans, while team-mate Christijan Albers' over-adventurous attack in one of the Lesmos cost him dearly and left him last on 1m 26.964s.

ROSSI HOPES LIVEN FERRARI SPECULATION

Fevered speculation that the 26-year-old Superbike star Valentino Rossi (pictured below at Melbourne) might make the switch to F1 with Ferrari spiralled out of control in the run-up to the Italian GP following Rossi's test outings for the Prancing Horse at Fiorano.

Initially Ferrari technical director Ross Brawn fuelled the rumours by suggesting that Rossi would undertake a regular programme of F1 tests in 2006, hinting that this might lead to a firm arrangement later on. But Rossi was tantalisingly non-committal about his future plans, a stance which served merely to intensify interest in this possible switch.

Ferrari has pursued Rossi for a long time and his initial test in its F1 car took place as long ago as April 2004. 'When I got ready to drive an F1 car for the first time in my life,' he said, 'I hear the Ferrari engineers having bets about me. They say if you lap their track at Fiorano in 60 seconds it means you drive the Ferrari quite fast. If you are slower you are not an F1 racer. Most of the engineers bet money I never go under a minute. I keep on smiling but, inside, I wanted to show them.' In the end he did a 59.1s.

Brawn recalled, 'Rossi was quick, which came as no surprise, but what pleased us more were his understanding of the car's set-up and his intelligent analysis of its handling and balance. The test was highly encouraging.'

Having clinched his fifth successive MotoGP world championship in 2005 – over a hundred points clear of his rivals – Rossi admitted his motivation was waning. 'I have won with Honda and Yamaha,' he said, 'so maybe it is interesting to win with a third team, Ducati, which is Italian. But I could also start F1 or rallying. I love rallying much more.'

Perhaps so, but in the end most F1 insiders believe that Rossi would like to emulate the achievements of multiple bike champion John Surtees, who switched to cars and won the 1964 F1 world championship. In a Ferrari.

FORMULA 1™ GRAN PREMIO VODAFONE D'ITALIA

Above: FIA president Max Mosley (left) with Henri Richard, executive vice-president of AMD, the governing body's new technology partner.
Photograph: James Moy/www.crash.net

Left: Alex Zanardi (left) and BMW Motorsport boss Mario Theissen.
Photograph: Jean-François Galeron/WRI

Right: Looking to the future? Italian racing magazine *Autosprint* had Kimi Räikkönen dressed as a Ferrari driver for its cover.
Photograph: Lukas Gorys

Below: BAR at work in the garage.
Photograph: Paul-Henri Cahier

DIARY

Michelin boss Edouard Michelin makes it clear that his company does not like the FIA's aim to make F1 a single-tyre formula by 2008.

Speaking at a press conference at Monza, FIA president Max Mosley reveals that the AMD software company will collaborate with the governing body by supplying its computational-fluid-dynamics programmes for research into the optimum shape that the 2008 F1 car should take.

Red Bull confirms that American Scott Speed will be its test driver in 2006.

The F1 world is saddened by the death of Michèle Dubosc, who was well known as an indefatigable lap timer for Matra, Renault and Ligier in the pre-computer days of the 1970s.

Rumours in the media in the lead-up to the race suggest that Kimi Räikkönen has signed a binding agreement to join Ferrari in 2007.

Above: Juan Pablo Montoya gained the upper hand on Fernando Alonso as the field scrambled through the first chicane on the opening lap.

Photograph: Russell Batchelor/XPB.cc

WHAT McLaren Mercedes most desperately needed at Monza was a one-two finish. Kimi Räikkönen's practice engine failure and resultant grid-place penalty put paid to such hopes early in the weekend, but victory over Renault still seemed assured courtesy of the pace and consistency of Juan Pablo Montoya. Just as he had at Silverstone, the Colombian again rose to the occasion for his team and it appeared that another ten points were in the bank – until suddenly the team faced an agonising late-race replay of the nightmare of the Nürburgring that threatened to snatch defeat from the jaws of success.

Having started from pole position, Montoya had led all the way and stamped his authority on the race. Farther back, Räikkönen had staged a great recovery to push into the top four, but had been delayed by a cut tyre and then by a spin that so nearly left him beached in the gravel trap at the second chicane. Then, on lap 49 with only four more laps to go, Montoya began to feel the tell-tale signs of a delaminating left-rear tyre. That was exactly what had previously stymied Räikkönen and now the cakewalk in the beautiful park just outside Milan was to become yet another of the dramas to beset the team this year.

It was the Grand Prix of Europe dilemma all over again as McLaren faced a tough choice: to bring Montoya in for a new tyre and lose the win, or risk staying out on the circuit where in testing the previous week he had hit 231 mph (372 km/h) down the main straight? There were so few laps left, but that

had been the case in Germany, too, where Räikkönen had led into the final lap before the vibrations from a flat-spotted tyre finally led to the spectacular collapse of his front suspension with victory in sight.

It was a drama that enlivened what had hitherto been a rather dull race. Fernando Alonso had chased Montoya as best he could and was surprisingly competitive on a circuit that suited Renault's low-downforce efficiency, but the Spaniard lost vital time in his pit stops and was just under ten seconds behind when the team radioed to him the information about Montoya's tyre problem. As the Colombian began to ease his pace, the Spaniard began to give it everything he had got.

Montoya, however, was at the head of the queue when the things that make a man were being handed out. He has always been comfortable at very high speed, thanks to his experiences in America's Champ car series and his 2000 victory in the Indianapolis 500, and there was no way he was going to stop just because a tyre might let go. There were several factors that he might have taken into consideration – the fact that Monza has one of the highest full-throttle loadings on the calendar; a lap-speed close to 160 mph (256 km/h); three chicanes for which you have to scrub off speed from 224 mph (360 km/h) to 50 mph (80 km/h) and bounce your car inelegantly over tyre-punishing kerbs.

In these exacting circumstances, Montoya elected to gamble and it paid off. 'Towards the end I had a severe problem with my left-rear tyre,' he said matter-of-factly. 'This left me with very little

championship. 'I felt I had very bad grip coming out of the pits,' Alonso disclosed. 'Maybe the tyres were a little bit dirty and maybe they weren't ready on the first lap. I was penalised a little bit by this and on the first lap after the [first] pit stop I lost a little bit of time, but I was lucky that I wasn't fighting with anyone so I took the race quite easy.'

Alonso's nonchalant comments must have struck despair into team-mate Giancarlo Fisichella's heart, for the Italian was outpaced all afternoon by the Spaniard and was frequently exhorted over the team radio to push harder. He brought his R25 home third to score six valuable points for Renault but he was only five seconds ahead of Räikkönen by the finish.

For the Finn, the Italian Grand Prix was one of those races in which everything that could go wrong did just that.

First he got trapped behind Jacques Villeneuve's Sauber for the opening 14 laps. Once the former champion stopped to refuel, Räikkönen climbed as high as second during other drivers' stops before making his first pit visit on lap 25. That dropped him back to fifth, but three laps later he had to stop again. The outer shoulder of the left-rear tyre showed signs of stress, so a new Michelin was fitted and off he went. Now, because of the heavy fuel load with which he had qualified, he did not need to stop again, but his chances of beating Alonso had already been jeopardised twice.

The unscheduled stop put him back behind Villeneuve, where he had started, but when the French-Canadian was unfairly and incorrectly shown blue flags Villeneuve had no choice but to let the McLaren through. Thereafter Räikkönen charged back into contention to pass Jarno Trulli for fourth place by the 43rd of the 53 laps.

Two laps later, however, he made one of his rare errors and spun in the second chicane, so he had to repass the Toyota two laps later. That really killed his chances of challenging Fisichella but it was a fabulous performance in adversity that netted fastest lap and again showcased his talent.

Alonso, however, was not among those who cheered Räikkönen's efforts. The Spaniard was struggling on his Michelins after his first pit stop on lap 19 when he had an altercation with the Finn. 'I went out of the pits and he was behind me,' Alonso explained. 'I tried to stop him as much as I could but again I had this problem with the front tyres so I was very, very slow in one part.

'It was good because he was going slowly, too, but it was

Below: **Michael Schumacher finished tenth, out of the points. It was far less than he and the tifosi were used to on Maranello's home soil.**

Bottom: **Antonio Pizzonia stood in for Nick Heidfeld at Williams. He is pictured in a pit stop on the way to seventh place.**
Photographs: James Moy/www.crash.net

grip in the closing stages and I just couldn't go on pushing.'

Michelin's motorsport director Pierre Dupasquier admitted that he was surprised the McLarens should experience problems with the outer shoulders of their left-rear tyres. 'Normally it's the inside shoulder that bears the bulk of the load down the long straights,' he observed.

All afternoon Montoya had been complaining about oversteer, but playing with the differential controls on the steering wheel had merely led him to the conclusion that he could either live with it or have understeer. 'I was looking at the tyres constantly in the mirrors and could see a little bit on the left rear,' he revealed. 'Then I had a big moment going through the Parabolica. I was very close to spinning and I wondered what the heck happened. From then on it became undriveable. The thing was that I couldn't really push or lean on the tyre or anything. It was a case of going as slowly as I could.

'I had turned the engine down before that, so I brought it back up to full power and I think that helped me a little bit. I was calculating that I couldn't go any quicker, to be honest. Any quicker held a big risk of going off. When I had four seconds [to Alonso] with two laps to go I thought it would be okay, but I could probably have done only one more lap in the lead and that was about it.'

Over those final laps Alonso had cut the deficit to 2.479s, but once again he did not have to drive at the limit. Second place, and three more points than Räikkönen scored for fourth place, was good enough to keep him firmly in control of the

Above: **Kimi Räikkönen setting about passing Jacques Villeneuve while climbing through the field to fourth place.**
Photograph: Emily Davenport/XPB.cc

very easy to overtake me so he did in the end. I think he was a little bit unfair in the overtaking manoeuvre because he cut the first chicane and then he let me pass to recover the position, but he was still really in the tow and was able to overtake me again going into the second chicane. It was a little bit of a strange manoeuvre.'

Monza offered further endorsement of the inherent strength and reliability of Toyota's burgeoning campaign as fifth and sixth places for Jarno Trulli and Ralf Schumacher garnered another seven points and suddenly brought the team within eight points of Ferrari for third place in the constructors' championship.

After a disappointing time in qualifying, BMW Williams also had something to cheer when some sound strategic decisions bore fruit. Stand-in Antonio Pizzonia admitted that he made some silly little errors early on while re-acclimatising himself to the FW27, but seventh place with the sixth-fastest lap was a solid performance. Poor Mark Webber was the victim yet again in the inevitable first-chicane contretemps. David Coulthard

snagged the back of Fisichella's Renault (so lightly, it transpired, that the Italian didn't even notice) and then backed off, and Webber damaged his front wing on the back of Coulthard's Red Bull. After first-lap repairs the Australian and the Scot had a wonderful fight in which Webber came out on top on his way to 14th overall.

At BAR Honda there was nothing to cheer. Jenson Button ran third initially but went backwards the moment the race started, had problems with his refuelling rig – which forced him to make his second stop four laps sooner than planned (on lap 35) – and was generally unhappy with the 007's tardy performance in low-downforce configuration.

Takuma Sato had an even worse refuelling-rig problem, which obliged him to stop again a lap after his first call, and struggled with poor handling thereafter. While Williams was encouraged by its race pace, BAR was demoralised.

Sauber Petronas ended up buoyed, but was a victim of the remarkable reliability rate. If you discount the fluke of the six-car

US Grand Prix in June, this Italian GP was the first race since the 1961 Dutch Grand Prix at Zandvoort in which every starter had finished. Felipe Massa's strategy proved correct and the little Brazilian dragged an oversteery car home a sound ninth, while Villeneuve benefited less from his low-fuel qualifying strategy, fought a nervous car too, but lost out when he was unjustly obliged by blue-flag-waving marshals to concede track position to Räikkönen.

As for Ferrari, this was its worst race performance at Monza for years. Even qualifying the F2005s light failed to get them up the field and the inter-team fight between Rubens Barrichello and Michael Schumacher hindered rather than helped. The feisty Brazilian should have finished ninth but lost out when his left-rear Bridgestone picked up a puncture and had to be replaced on the 42nd lap.

Michael, meanwhile, dropped back to 10th after taking one risk too many trying to pass Button for eighth and falling off in a big way in the second Lesmo on lap 50.

Future engine partner Red Bull had nothing to get excited about, either. After Coulthard's race came apart in the first chicane, leaving him to a 15th-placed finish, Christian Klien brought his sister RB1 home an unremarkable 13th. Jordan, too, was compromised at the start after Christijan Albers hit Narain Karthikeyan's left-rear Bridgestone and punctured it.

The Indian lost more ground than he could make up, especially because a trip into the gravel on Saturday morning had obliged him to run a very old set of tyres. He finished 20th and last. Team-mate Tiago Monteiro lost some bodywork in the opening-lap kerfuffle and that hurt the handling of the new EJ15B, but at least the team got some useful mileage on the car in race trim.

Minardi took 18th and 19th places, Robert Doornbos again enjoying himself with a strong run. Albers lost time after the first-corner incident and ended up stopping four times: once for a new nose, twice for fuel and once for a drive-through penalty after ignoring blue flags waved to assist Massa.

Alonso's eight points and Räikkönen's five left the drivers' respective scores at 103 and 76 with four races left. It was still possible that incidents might reduce that 27-point deficit, but that was looking increasingly unlikely with Alonso's 'champion's luck' running so strongly. But the constructors' championship battle between Renault and McLaren – 144 points to 136 respectively – was another matter altogether.

Alan Henry

Main photograph: The splendour of Monza in the autumn sunshine.
Photograph: Paul-Henri Cahier

Top inset: Fernando Alonso (right) and Giancarlo Fisichella celebrate their second- and third-placed finishes.

Bottom inset: Takuma Sato and Mark Webber enjoyed an impromptu race along the pit lane.
Photographs: James Moy/www.crash.net

MONZA – GRAND PRIX CIRCUIT

PRIMA VARIANTE 71/115 (2)
218/350 (6)
CURVA PARABOLICA 155/250 (4)
CURVA GRANDE 181/290 (5)
RETTILINEO PARABOLICA 205/330 (6)
VARIANTE ASCARI 100/161 (3)
CURVA DEL VIALONE 90/145 (3)
SECONDA VARIANTE 70/113 (2)
mph/km/h (gear)
CURVA DEL SERRAGLIO 205/330 (6)
CURVA DI LESMOS 100/161 (3)

CIRCUIT LENGTH: 3.600 miles/5.793 km

FIA F1 WORLD CHAMPIONSHIP • ROUND 15

GRAN PREMIO
VODAFONE D'ITALIA
MONZA 2–4 SEPTEMBER 2005

RACE DISTANCE: 53 laps, 190.587 miles /306.720 km   RACE WEATHER: Sunny (track 40–41°C, air 28–29°C)

Pos.	Driver	Nat.	No.	Entrant	Car/Engine	Tyres	Laps	Time/Retirement	Speed (mph/km/h)	Gap to leader	Fastest race lap	
1	Juan Pablo Montoya	COL	10	Team McLaren Mercedes	McLaren MP4-20-Mercedes F0 110R V10	M	53	1h 14m 28.659s	153.538/247.096		1m 21.828s	15
2	Fernando Alonso	E	5	Mild Seven Renault F1 Team	Renault R25-RS25 V10	M	53	1h 14m 31.138s	153.453/246.959	+2.479s	1m 22.146s	16
3	Giancarlo Fisichella	I	6	Mild Seven Renault F1 Team	Renault R25-RS25 V10	M	53	1h 14m 46.634s	152.923/246.106	+17.975s	1m 22.587s	16
4	Kimi Räikkönen	FIN	9	Team McLaren Mercedes	McLaren MP4-20-Mercedes F0 110R V10	M	53	1h 14m 51.434s	152.759/245.843	+22.775s	1m 21.504s	51
5	Jarno Trulli	I	16	Panasonic Toyota Racing	Toyota TF105-RVX-05 V10	M	53	1h 15m 02.445s	152.386/245.242	+33.786s	1m 22.831s	19
6	Ralf Schumacher	D	17	Panasonic Toyota Racing	Toyota TF105-RVX-05 V10	M	53	1h 15m 12.584s	152.044/244.691	+43.925s	1m 23.076s	19
7	Antonio Pizzonia	BR	8	BMW WilliamsF1 Team	Williams FW27-BMW P84/85 V10	M	53	1h 15m 13.302s	152.019/244.652	+44.643s	1m 22.870s	21
8	Jenson Button	GB	3	Lucky Strike BAR Honda	BAR 007-Honda RA005E V10	M	53	1h 15m 32.294s	151.383/243.627	+63.635s	1m 23.161s	16
9	Felipe Massa	BR	12	Sauber Petronas	Sauber C24-Petronas 05A V10	M	53	1h 15m 44.072s	150.990/242.996	+75.413s	1m 23.365s	18
10	Michael Schumacher	D	1	Scuderia Ferrari Marlboro	Ferrari F2005-055 V10	B	53	1h 16m 04.729s	150.307/241.896	+96.070s	1m 23.584s	5
11	Jacques Villeneuve	CDN	11	Sauber Petronas	Sauber C24-Petronas 05A V10	M	52			+1 lap	1m 23.892s	13
12	Rubens Barrichello	BR	2	Scuderia Ferrari Marlboro	Ferrari F2005-055 V10	B	52			+1 lap	1m 23.466s	13
13	Christian Klien	A	15	Red Bull Racing	Red Bull RB1-Cosworth TJ2005/12 V10	M	52			+1 lap	1m 23.633s	17
14	Mark Webber	AUS	7	BMW WilliamsF1 Team	Williams FW27-BMW P84/85 V10	M	52			+1 lap	1m 22.935s	40
15	David Coulthard	GB	14	Red Bull Racing	Red Bull RB1-Cosworth TJ2005/12 V10	M	52			+1 lap	1m 23.867s	18
16	Takuma Sato	J	4	Lucky Strike BAR Honda	BAR 007-Honda RA005E V10	M	52			+1 lap	1m 23.341s	14
17	Tiago Monteiro	P	18	Jordan Toyota	Jordan EJ15B-Toyota RVX-05 V10	B	51			+2 laps	1m 24.810s	9
18	Robert Doornbos	NL	20	Minardi Cosworth	Minardi PS05-Cosworth TJ2005 V10	B	51			+2 laps	1m 25.193s	31
19	Christijan Albers	NL	21	Minardi Cosworth	Minardi PS05-Cosworth TJ2005 V10	B	51			+2 laps	1m 24.966s	33
20	Narain Karthikeyan	IND	19	Jordan Toyota	Jordan EJ15-Toyota RVX-05 V10	B	50			+3 laps	1m 25.146s	17

Fastest lap: Kimi Räikkönen, on lap 51, 1m 21.504s, 158.992 mph/255.874 km/h.

Lap record: Rubens Barrichello (Ferrari F2004-052 V10), 1m 21.046s, 159.891 mph/257.320 km/h (2004).

19th: KARTHIKEYAN Jordan-Toyota

17th: MONTEIRO Jordan-Toyota

15th: MASSA Sauber-Petronas

13th: KLIEN Red Bull-Cosworth

11th: RÄIKKÖNEN McLaren-Mercedes
Ten-place penalty for engine change

20th: ALBERS Minardi-Cosworth

18th: DOORNBOS Minardi-Cosworth

16th: PIZZONIA Williams-BMW

14th: WEBBER Williams-BMW

12th: VILLENEUVE Sauber-Petronas

Grid order	1	2	3	4	5	6	7	8	9	10	11	12	13	14	15	16	17	18	19	20	21	22	23	24	25	26	27	28	29	30	31	32	33	34	35	36	37	38	39	40	41
10 MONTOYA	10	10	10	10	10	10	10	10	10	10	10	10	10	10	10	10	10	10	10	10	10	10	10	10	10	10	10	10	10	10	10	10	10	10	10	10	10	10	10	10	10
5 ALONSO	5	5	5	5	5	5	5	5	5	5	5	5	5	5	5	5	6	6	9	9	9	9	9	5	5	5	5	5	5	5	5	5	5	5	5	5	5	5	6	6	
3 BUTTON	3	3	3	3	3	3	3	3	3	3	3	3	3	3	3	16	17	17	5	5	5	6	6	6	6	6	6	6	6	6	6	6	6	6	6	6	6	6	5	6	
4 SATO	4	4	4	4	4	4	4	4	4	4	4	4	4	4	16	6	6	6	17	9	5	8	6	16	16	16	16	16	16	16	16	16	16	16	16	16	16	16	16	12	
16 TRULLI	16	2	2	2	2	2	2	2	2	2	2	16	16	6	3	17	17	5	5	8	6	16	16	9	9	3	3	3	3	3	3	3	3	17	17	17	17	17			
1 M. SCHUMACHER	2	1	1	16	16	16	16	16	16	16	16	6	6	4	17	9	9	9	8	6	16	3	3	3	17	17	17	17	17	17	17	3	2	8	8	8	8	8			
2 BARRICHELLO	1	16	16	1	1	1	1	1	1	6	2	17	17	8	9	12	8	8	16	16	17	17	17	17	9	2	2	2	2	2	2	2	9	2	9	9					
6 FISICHELLA	6	6	6	6	6	6	6	6	6	1	17	9	8	12	8	8	12	3	3	2	2	2	2	1	1	1	1	1	1	1	9	12	12	12	12	12					
17 R. SCHUMACHER	17	17	17	17	17	17	17	17	17	17	9	12	12	15	15	3	2	2	2	1	1	1	1	8	8	8	8	8	9	12	11	11	11	11	2	2	3				
14 COULTHARD	11	11	11	11	11	11	11	11	11	11	15	15	8	3	2	1	1	1	12	12	12	12	12	12	12	9	12	11	2	2	3										
9 RÄIKKÖNEN	9	9	9	9	9	9	9	9	9	12	8	2	1	1	12	12	12	12	11	9	9	9	9	11	11	3	3	3	1												
11 VILLENEUVE	12	12	12	12	12	12	12	12	12	12	2	1	4	11	11	11	11	11	11	11	11	9	11	11	11	11	11	3	1	1	15	15									
15 KLIEN	15	15	15	15	15	15	15	15	15	8	1	11	11	14	14	14	14	14	14	14	14	15	15	15	15	15	15	15	15	4	4										
7 WEBBER	8	8	8	8	8	8	8	8	8	1	11	11	14	7	7	7	7	7	7	7	7	7	4	7	7	7	7	7	7	7	7	7	11	11							
12 MASSA	18	18	18	18	18	18	18	18	18	20	20	20	14	7	15	15	15	4	7	7	15	15	4	7	7	7	7	7	11	11											
8 PIZZONIA	20	20	20	20	20	20	20	20	20	14	14	14	7	4	4	4	4	4	4	7	14	14	14	14	14	14	14	14	14	14	14	14	14	14							
18 MONTEIRO	14	14	14	14	14	14	14	14	7	7	7	7	20	18	18	18	18	18	18	18	18	18	18	18	18	18	20	20	18	18	18	18	18	18	18						
20 DOORNBOS	7	7	7	7	7	7	7	7	18	18	18	18	18	20	20	20	20	20	20	20	20	20	20	20	20	20	18	18	20	20	20	20	20	20	20						
19 KARTHIKEYAN	21	21	21	21	21	21	21	21	21	21	21	21	21	21	21	21	21	21	21	21	21	21	21	21	21	21	21	21	21	21	21	21	21	21	21	21	21				
21 ALBERS	19	19	19	19	19	19	19	19	19	19	19	19	19	19	19	19	19	19	19	19	19	19	19	19	19	19	19	19	19	19	19	19	19	19	19	19	19				

TIME SHEETS

QUALIFYING

WEATHER: Sunny (track 40–41°C, air 30°C)

Pos.	Driver	R/Order	Sector 1	Sector 2	Sector 3	Time
1	Kimi Räikkönen	20	26.161s	27.543s	27.174s	1m 20.878s
2	Juan Pablo Montoya	18	26.107s	27.792s	27.155s	1m 21.054s
3	Fernando Alonso	19	26.121s	27.836s	27.362s	1m 21.319s
4	Jenson Button	16	26.408s	27.639s	37.322s	1m 21.369s
5	Takuma Sato	12	26.373s	27.875s	27.229s	1m 21.477s
6	Jarno Trulli	15	26.427s	27.819s	27.394s	1m 21.640s
7	Michael Schumacher	4	26.539s	27.878s	27.304s	1m 21.721s
8	Rubens Barrichello	11	26.311s	28.031s	27.620s	1m 21.962s
9	Giancarlo Fisichella	17	26.735s	27.855s	27.478s	1m 22.068s
10	Ralf Schumacher	9	26.583s	28.211s	27.472s	1m 22.266s
11	David Coulthard	14	26.618s	28.161s	27.525s	1m 22.304s
12	Jacques Villeneuve	10	26.625s	28.142s	27.589s	1m 22.356s
13	Christian Klien	13	26.442s	28.233s	27.867s	1m 22.532s
14	Mark Webber	2	26.508s	28.413s	27.639s	1m 22.560s
15	Felipe Massa	3	26.813s	28.404s	27.843s	1m 23.060s
16	Antonio Pizzonia	1	26.830s	28.708s	27.753s	1m 23.291s
17	Tiago Monteiro	6	27.053s	29.109s	28.504s	1m 24.666s
18	Robert Doornbos	8	27.042s	29.134s	28.728s	1m 24.904s
19	Narain Karthikeyan	7	27.087s	29.550s	29.222s	1m 25.859s
20	Christijan Albers	5	26.913s	29.577s	28.717s	1m 26.964s

CHASSIS LOG BOOK

	FERRARI				SAUBER-PETRONAS	
1	Michael Schumacher	F2005/249		11	Jacques Villeneuve	C24/04
2	Rubens Barrichello	F2005/248		12	Felipe Massa	C24/06
	Spare	F2005/245			Spare	C24/03
	BAR-HONDA				**RED BULL-COSWORTH**	
3	Jenson Button	007/04		14	David Coulthard	RB1/3
4	Takuma Sato	007/05		15	Christian Klien	RB1/1
	Spare	007/02		37	Vitantonio Liuzzi	RB1/5
	RENAULT				Spare	RB1/5
5	Fernando Alonso	R25/07			**TOYOTA**	
6	Giancarlo Fisichella	R25/06		16	Jarno Trulli	TF105/07
	Spare	R25/04		17	Ralf Schumacher	TF105/05
	WILLIAMS-BMW			38	Ricardo Zonta	TF105/02
7	Mark Webber	FW27/04			Spare	TF105/02
8	Nick Heidfeld	FW27/03			**JORDAN-TOYOTA**	
	Spare	FW27/06		18	Tiago Monteiro	EJ15B/02
	McLAREN-MERCEDES			19	Narain Karthikeyan	EJ15/01
9	Kimi Räikkönen	MP4-20/04		39	Nicolas Kiesa	EJ15/04
10	Juan Pablo Montoya	MP4-20/07			Spare	EJ15/04
35	Pedro de la Rosa	MP4-20/06			**MINARDI-COSWORTH**	
	Spare	MP4-20/05		20	Robert Doornbos	PS05/02
				21	Christijan Albers	PS05/01
				40	Enrico Toccacelo	PS05/03
					Spare	PS05/03

Photograph: James Moy/www.crash.net

PRACTICE 1 (FRIDAY)

Scattered cloud then sunny (track 31–33°C, air 27–28°C)

Pos.	Driver	Laps	Time
1	Pedro de la Rosa	21	1m 20.201s
2	Mark Webber	3	1m 21.816s
3	Kimi Räikkönen	5	1m 21.842s
4	Juan Pablo Montoya	6	1m 22.078s
5	Nick Heidfeld	3	1m 22.351s
6	Ricardo Zonta	25	1m 22.567s
7	Takuma Sato	13	1m 22.577s
8	Michael Schumacher	5	1m 23.739s
9	David Coulthard	4	1m 24.001s
10	Vitantonio Liuzzi	21	1m 24.166s
11	Rubens Barrichello	6	1m 24.196s
12	Tiago Monteiro	12	1m 25.134s
13	Nicolas Kiesa	23	1m 25.374s
14	Christijan Albers	11	1m 25.497s
15	Narain Karthikeyan	8	1m 25.611s
16	Robert Doornbos	11	1m 25.853s
17	Enrico Toccacelo	17	1m 25.896s
18	Jacques Villeneuve	3	No time
19	Jenson Button	2	No time
20	Felipe Massa	3	No time
21	Christian Klien	1	No time
22	Fernando Alonso	2	No time
23	Giancarlo Fisichella	2	No time
24	Jarno Trulli	1	No time
25	Ralf Schumacher	1	No time

PRACTICE 2 (FRIDAY)

Sunny (track 40–41°C, air 31–32°C)

Pos.	Driver	Laps	Time
1	Ricardo Zonta	28	1m 20.531s
2	Juan Pablo Montoya	10	1m 21.583s
3	Kimi Räikkönen	14	1m 21.735s
4	Pedro de la Rosa	24	1m 21.922s
5	Mark Webber	18	1m 22.032s
6	Nick Heidfeld	18	1m 22.107s
7	Vitantonio Liuzzi	26	1m 22.253s
8	Jarno Trulli	22	1m 22.278s
9	Giancarlo Fisichella	15	1m 22.440s
10	Fernando Alonso	10	1m 22.594s
11	Christian Klien	11	1m 22.600s
12	Michael Schumacher	9	1m 22.749s
13	Felipe Massa	21	1m 23.052s
14	Ralf Schumacher	18	1m 23.126s
15	Jacques Villeneuve	17	1m 23.208s
16	Rubens Barrichello	19	1m 23.213s
17	Takuma Sato	23	1m 23.223s
18	Jenson Button	26	1m 23.415s
19	David Coulthard	10	1m 23.506s
20	Tiago Monteiro	14	1m 23.994s
21	Narain Karthikeyan	18	1m 24.202s
22	Robert Doornbos	15	1m 24.233s
23	Christijan Albers	14	1m 24.264s
24	Enrico Toccacelo	2	1m 25.245s
25	Nicolas Kiesa	1	No time

PRACTICE 3 (SATURDAY)

Sunny (track 27–30°C, air 23–24°C)

Pos.	Driver	Laps	Time
1	Kimi Räikkönen	5	1m 22.415s
2	Michael Schumacher	5	1m 22.550s
3	Juan Pablo Montoya	5	1m 22.676s
4	Fernando Alonso	9	1m 22.867s
5	Giancarlo Fisichella	9	1m 22.900s
6	Mark Webber	4	1m 23.162s
7	Takuma Sato	10	1m 23.257s
8	Jenson Button	5	1m 23.875s
9	Ralf Schumacher	9	1m 23.898s
10	Rubens Barrichello	7	1m 23.942s
11	David Coulthard	8	1m 24.019s
12	Jarno Trulli	5	1m 24.129s
13	Antonio Pizzonia	7	1m 24.367s
14	Christian Klien	7	1m 24.390s
15	Felipe Massa	6	1m 24.447s
16	Tiago Monteiro	6	1m 24.668s
17	Jacques Villeneuve	5	1m 25.041s
18	Narain Karthikeyan	11	1m 25.172s
19	Robert Doornbos	8	1m 25.722s
20	Christijan Albers	5	1m 26.197s

PRACTICE 4 (SATURDAY)

Sunny (track 32–34°C, air 25–26°C)

Pos.	Driver	Laps	Time
1	Kimi Räikkönen	8	1m 20.916s
2	Juan Pablo Montoya	10	1m 21.318s
3	Takuma Sato	13	1m 21.399s
4	Fernando Alonso	13	1m 21.548s
5	Jarno Trulli	14	1m 21.884s
6	Giancarlo Fisichella	12	1m 21.951s
7	Mark Webber	7	1m 22.066s
8	David Coulthard	16	1m 22.291s
9	Christian Klien	12	1m 22.345s
10	Michael Schumacher	14	1m 22.395s
11	Rubens Barrichello	13	1m 22.437s
12	Jenson Button	13	1m 22.558s
13	Jacques Villeneuve	12	1m 22.701s
14	Ralf Schumacher	11	1m 22.710s
15	Antonio Pizzonia	10	1m 22.823s
16	Felipe Massa	12	1m 23.389s
17	Tiago Monteiro	15	1m 23.472s
18	Robert Doornbos	14	1m 23.676s
19	Christijan Albers	12	1m 24.104s
20	Narain Karthikeyan	11	1m 24.772s

9th: R. SCHUMACHER Toyota

7th: BARRICHELLO Ferrari

5th: TRULLI Toyota

3rd: BUTTON BAR-Honda

Pole: MONTOYA McLaren-Mercedes

10th: COULTHARD Red Bull-Cosworth

8th: FISICHELLA Renault

6th: M. SCHUMACHER Ferrari

4th: SATO BAR-Honda

2nd: ALONSO Renault

42	43	44	45	46	47	48	49	50	51	52	53	°
10	10	10	10	10	10	10	10	10	10	10	10	1
5	5	5	5	5	5	5	5	5	5	5	5	2
6	6	6	6	6	6	6	6	6	6	6	6	3
8	8	9	16	16	9	9	9	9	9	9	9	4
16	9	16	9	9	16	16	16	16	16	16	16	5
9	16	17	17	17	17	17	17	17	17	17		6
17	17	8	8	8	8	8	8	8	8	8	8	7
3	3	3	3	3	3	3	3	3	3	3	3	8
2	1	1	1	1	1	1	12	12	12	12		9
1	12	12	12	12	12	12	1	1	1	1		10
15	11	11	11	11	11	11	11	11	11			11
12	2	2	2	2	2	2	2	2				12
15	15	15	15	15	15	15	15	15				13
7	14	7	7	7	7	7	7	7				14
11	7	14	14	14	14	14	14	14	14			15
14	4	4	4	4	4	4	4	4				16
18	18	18	18	18	18	18	18	18				17
20	20	20	20	20	20	20	20	20				18
4	21	21	21	21	21	21	21	21				
19	19	19	19	19	19	19	19	19				

Pit stop
One lap or more behind leader

FOR THE RECORD

500th GRAND PRIX LEAD LAP:
Juan Pablo Montoya

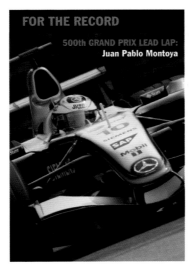

POINTS

DRIVERS

1	Fernando Alonso	103		19	Christijan Albers	4
2	Kimi Räikkönen	76		20	Pedro de la Rosa	4
3	Michael Schumacher	55		21	Patrick Friesacher	3
4	Juan Pablo Montoya	50		22	Antonio Pizzonia	2
5	Jarno Trulli	43		23	Takuma Sato	1
6	Giancarlo Fisichella	41		24	Vitantonio Liuzzi	1
7	Ralf Schumacher	35				
8	Rubens Barrichello	31			**CONSTRUCTORS**	
9	Nick Heidfeld	28		1	Renault	144
10	Jenson Button	24		2	McLaren	136
11	Mark Webber	24		3	Ferrari	86
12	David Coulthard	21		4	Toyota	78
13	Felipe Massa	8		5	Williams	54
14	Tiago Monteiro	6		6	Red Bull	27
15	Alex Wurz	6		7	BAR	25
16	Jacques Villeneuve	6		8	Sauber	14
17	Narain Karthikeyan	5		9	Jordan	11
18	Christian Klien	5		10	Minardi	7

Photographs: James Moy/www.crash.net

Kimi Räikkönen stormed to his third win in four races at Spa-Francorchamps, his second straight Belgian victory for the McLaren team.

Photograph: Laurent Charniaux/WRI

SPA-FRANCORCHAMPS

BELGIAN GP

FIA F1 WORLD CHAMPIONSHIP/ROUND 16

SPA-FRANCORCHAMPS QUALIFYING

When Saturday dawned cloudy but dry at Spa-Francorchamps there was a general sigh of relief in the paddock, for Friday's rain had created such unpleasant track conditions that David Coulthard and Michael Schumacher had openly suggested that the race might not go ahead if such poor weather continued to prevail.

In contrast, Saturday remained dry and, though there was a threat of rain partway through qualifying, nothing developed to cause the sort of upset for which the Hautes Fagnes district of Belgium has become notorious.

For McLaren, qualifying was a dream. The team wrapped up the front row, as had been expected, with Juan Pablo Montoya lapping in 1m 46.391s and Kimi Räikkönen in 1m 46.440s. As the victor in Italy, the Colombian was the last man to run and he made the most of the advantage. But it had been a slightly nerve-wracking wait. 'I was sitting in the car when I saw a few drops of rain and was thinking, "Oh no,"' he admitted. 'However, I think it just stopped when I went out and it didn't affect my lap, which was nice and smooth. The car seemed to be working well despite our having only limited time to work on the set-up.'

Like everyone else, McLaren had been obliged by Friday's conditions to postpone tyre selection until Saturday morning. Only Tonio Liuzzi – who crashed at Les Combes after Red Bull sent him out on intermediates – Robert Doornbos and Fernando Alonso (who, on wets, described the conditions as 'impossible') did a lap apiece on Friday afternoon, so everyone had to pack a lot of set-up work into Saturday's two practice sessions.

Räikkönen was happy enough with a front-row starting position and admitted that the few drops of rain had discouraged him from driving absolutely on the limit.

Fernando Alonso might have been expected to start third, given current form. But Toyota had opted for a light-fuel strategy, which allowed Jarno Trulli to jump into that position with a lap in 1m 46.596s. With Ralf Schumacher fifth on 1m 47.401s, the Japanese team looked in good shape. Trulli in particular did well, for the raindrops had been at their heaviest while he was on-track.

'I honestly think that was a great lap,' Trulli smiled. 'There were a few spots of rain during my first sector so I couldn't push quite as hard as I would have liked. But in general the car was well balanced so I could push hard elsewhere, right up

to the limit, and that's what I did.'

Renault had to be satisfied with Alonso's fourth spot, on 1m 46.760s, which was actually only the fifth-fastest time. Team-mate Giancarlo Fisichella had set the third-best lap with 1m 46.497s, but a rare Renault engine failure in the morning had handed him an obligatory ten-grid-place penalty, so he would start only 13th. Both drivers reported clean laps, but they were running low downforce to get their speed and that would hamper Fisichella particularly when the one thing he didn't want – a wet race – became a reality the following day.

Behind brother Ralf, Michael Schumacher appeared higher up the grid than Ferrari had expected. After Monza, a team representative had sat holding his head in his hands predicting dire problems at Spa – 'It has a lot more corners than Monza and that's where we have our problems' – yet there was the champion, sixth on the grid with a lap of 1m 47.476s. Schumacher, however, sounded glum and said he would rather have started seventh because it was on the inside line to La Source. Like his younger brother and Trulli, however, Michael was running relatively light.

Felipe Massa did an excellent job to place his Sauber-Petronas C24 seventh on the grid with 1m 47.867s, which put him ahead of Jenson Button's BAR-Honda. The Englishman admitted to caution as he lapped his 007 in 1m 47.978s. Right behind Button, Mark Webber was the quicker BMW Williams pilot on 1m 48.071s, then came Takuma Sato, who had set the early pace with 1m 48.383s.

David Coulthard was yet again the faster Red Bull driver, on 1m 48.508s. He just clung on to 11th on the grid after Rubens Barrichello (on a conservative strategy) narrowly failed to beat him with 1m 48.550s.

Jacques Villeneuve was on a longer first-stint strategy than Massa and complained of oversteer, which made his 1m 48.889s reasonable, while birthday boy Antonio Pizzonia, again standing in for Nick Heidfeld, complained of low grip and lapped his Williams in 1m 48.898s to pip Christian Klien. The Austrian was 16th fastest on 1m 48.994s.

Robert Doornbos used his circuit experience from his 2004 F3000 victory to outpace Minardi team-mate Christijan Albers, 1m 49.779s to 1m 49.842s, and at the back the Jordan drivers in their EJ15Bs were evenly matched on 1m 51.498s for Tiago Monteiro and 1m 51.575s for Narain Karthikeyan.

Fernando Alonso failed to clinch his world title at Spa-Francorchamps and thus to become history's youngest champion. But when McLaren yet again had a one-two result snatched from its grasp in the closing stages of a race, the Spaniard moved another inexorable step closer to his destiny even though Kimi Räikkönen did everything he needed to do to keep his own slim hopes alive.

This was no easy task, despite the Belgian Grand Prix's showing that the McLaren-Mercedes had indeed retained its customary advantage at the head of the field. The race began on a track that, while wet, was not so wet that a safety-car start was necessary. But it never really dried out until the final few laps. In retrospect, an intermediate tyre choice was obvious, but on the day it was a time for calculated gambling.

Everyone bar the two Minardi drivers (who started from the pit lane) went to the grid on intermediate rain tyres but, as the race progressed, the key became when to make the switch to dry-weather grooved rubber. Several teams mistimed things with spectacular results.

McLaren actually had that one down pat: Räikkönen and team-mate Juan Pablo Montoya stayed on intermediates throughout. Indeed, this was one of those pluperfect McLaren races in which the team deserved what would have been its first one-two since Austria 2000.

The Colombian did everything he could possibly have done to help Räikkönen's title campaign. He exploded into the lead from pole position and was holding it comfortably when Giancarlo Fisichella, fighting up from 13th on the grid, lost control of his low-downforce Renault at slippery Eau Rouge on

lap 11 and littered the track at the top of the famed climb with a lot of debris after hitting the tyre wall hard.

This was the signal for mass pit stops as the safety car was deployed; of the front runners, only Ralf Schumacher and Jacques Villeneuve kept going. This was where McLaren's cunning first manifested itself.

Räikkönen was instructed to slow down all around that lap so that McLaren could service Montoya and have time to get him back into the race before the Finn arrived. This ploy worked perfectly and Räikkönen led Jarno Trulli, Alonso, Michael Schumacher, Takuma Sato, Jenson Button, Felipe Massa, David Coulthard, Mark Webber, Christian Klien, Antonio Pizzonia, Rubens Barrichello and Narain Karthikeyan into the pit lane. Michael Schumacher, Sato, Button, Coulthard, Trulli, Webber and Pizzonia opted for dry tyres, but this was not the right time for them. All of them had to come in again a lap or two later to go back to intermediates.

'This is,' Jordan sporting-relations manager Johnny Herbert observed, 'the first time I can remember a wet Spa not really drying out before the end of the race.'

When the safety car pitted at the end of lap 13, Montoya was leading Ralf Schumacher. The German was on a low fuel load in qualifying and had climbed to second thanks to stopping to refuel on the 10th lap, before all the drama. At this stage, Toyota was looking good.

Montoya did a great job of surrendering his lead subtly; there were no team orders at McLaren but gradually he allowed the five-second lead he had built up over Räikkönen after that first stop to dwindle. Räikkönen by contrast was

running at full speed as he carved down the gap and after running two laps close beyond Montoya, who stopped again on lap 33, the Finn was able to reduce the deficit and retain the lead after his own refuelling call. Now all the McLarens had to do was cruise home first and second, and indeed this seemed the inevitable conclusion to the team's race.

Meanwhile, Michael Schumacher's downfall had come fast and early. As he braked for the La Source hairpin on the 14th lap, trying to make up the lost time from his extra pit stop, he was savaged from behind by Sato. The Japanese driver had been in feisty form before the Fisichella accident, climbing to sixth behind Michael Schumacher after passing team-mate Jenson Button, but either he misjudged things or Schumacher braked early; whatever, both the Ferrari and the BAR retired.

Schumacher was not amused and remonstrated with Sato while the latter still sat in the cockpit. 'We have often experienced Hari-kari reactions from him in the past and that was another today,' Schumacher said trenchantly. 'We have talked to him about it in the past. I don't know what sort of therapy might help him.'

Michael's brother was also in the wars. When he refuelled again on the 24th lap, Toyota switched him to dry tyres, but an immediate spin at Les Combes was sufficient to convince Ralf that it was too early and in he came again for intermediates on lap 25. That dropped him way back, so it was once again the imperturbable Alonso who chased along in a comfortable third place behind the McLarens. It wasn't enough to win him the title that afternoon, but it was yet further damage limitation.

Above: Juan Pablo Montoya took an immediate lead from Kimi Räikkönen as the pack scrambled into the La Source hairpin on a still-wet track surface at the start of the race.
Photograph: Photo 4

Far left: Shadows at La Source. The reflections of the photographers' hardware mingled with the colours of the cars during sunny practice.
Photograph: James Moy/www.crash.net

DIARY

Just before the Belgian GP, BMW confirms that Nick Heidfeld has been signed to a two-year deal to drive for its eponymous team from 2007.

King Juan Carlos of Spain announces that he will present Fernando Alonso with the Prince of Asturias award in October. It is Spain's most prestigious award, given annually to the sportsman who achieves the most during the year.

Michelin announces at Spa that it will supply only five teams in 2006, rather than seven: Renault, McLaren Mercedes, BAR Honda, BMW and Red Bull Ferrari.

Meanwhile, Bridgestone confirms that Williams will switch to its rubber in 2006; Toyota is expected to follow suit.

Behind the Spaniard, Villeneuve's glory of fourth place lasted until lap 20, when he refuelled (having opted for a one-stop strategy). He resumed in eighth, still in the hunt for points but now fighting a fuel-heavy car again. At this stage the other Sauber-Petronas, driven with equal spirit by Felipe Massa, was a solid fourth ahead of Rubens Barrichello's Ferrari, with Mark Webber chasing after them in his Williams-BMW. Massa held his position until he refuelled on lap 29 – and that was when an easy podium slipped away.

Technical director Willy Rampf wanted his driver to stick with intermediates; other members of the team, together with Massa, got their way and switched the Brazilian to dry tyres. It was a mistake. The track was still not good enough for them and Massa slumped down the order before stopping again for intermediates. He would finish a disappointed but philosophical tenth.

Farther back, Villeneuve just held on to his C24 as it twitched sideways through Eau Rouge on the 29th lap and then had a wheel-banging session with a hungry Narain Karthikeyan at Les Combes as the Indian sought successfully to take advantage of the former champion's lost momentum.

In all this, the man who benefited most was Button, who was able to recover the time he lost early on changing from intermediates to dries and back again, and by the time he made his second pit stop on lap 33 the Englishman was on target for an unexpected fourth place. His recovery drive included a great pass around the outside of Villeneuve at Pouhon on the 24th lap.

With nine laps left to run, Räikkönen and Montoya were comfortably ahead of Alonso, who equally was not going to be challenged by Barrichello, who had Button thirsting back after him following his fuel stop. Webber was also on the move. Button outbraked Barrichello for fourth place in the entry to the Bus Stop on lap 38 and that was when Webber and Williams cannily judged the time to be right for dry tyres. At last, the decision was the correct one. Red Bull had also put Christian Klien on to dries, on lap 31, and then Williams brought in Antonio Pizzonia for them on lap 39. That would prove to be a pivotal point in the race. Now the dry-shod cars were the fastest things on the track but, as Pizzonia tried to unlap himself on Montoya at Fagnes, each driver completely misread the other. The result was that they collided and both became instant retirements. Pizzonia was later fined $8,000 by the race stewards, but that was little consolation to either Montoya or McLaren.

The beneficiary, yet again, was Fernando Alonso, who pocketed two more points than he had expected. And Button suddenly found himself heading for the podium.

'It's always tough to retire from a race but when it's caused by matters out of your team's control it's even harder,' said Montoya. 'My disappointment is even greater because as a team we were doing a great job.' Privately, he was not impressed, but perhaps somebody at McLaren should have forewarned Montoya that Pizzonia was running a lot faster than Montoya was, albeit a lap down, and was fighting for the final point.

The Pizzonia business aside, BMW Williams had reason to be cheerful – Webber's charge on dries enabled him to clamber up to fourth place by the finish after catching and passing Rubens Barrichello. A good performance all around.

Frankly, Ferrari came to Belgium expecting little even if it was wet but, though it struggled, the four points for Barrichello's fifth place helped to maintain the Scuderia's third place over Toyota in the constructors' championship.

There was a high degree of luck involved there, however. But for that gaffe with dries early on, Ralf Schumacher should have finished much higher than his eventual seventh (with fastest lap, after a late-race switch to dries). And team-mate Trulli could have expected better, too. He ran third behind the McLarens initially, lost a lot of time with the premature switch to dries on lap 11 and resultant repeat stop on lap 13 to go back to intermediates, and was just coming back into the points picture when he tripped over Tiago Monteiro's Jordan-Toyota when the Portuguese driver inadvertently activated his pit-lane speed limiter on lap 35. Trulli hit the back of the yellow car, losing his front wing and crashing into a tyre wall.

That one mistake apart, Monteiro drove a great race and thoroughly deserved the final point, having been in the thick of the fighting all afternoon. Team-mate Karthikeyan was his usual feisty self, especially against Villeneuve, but could not better 11th behind Massa, having lost time in the pit queue on lap 11 while Monteiro was serviced.

Red Bull had a disappointing race: David Coulthard broke an engine on lap 19 when running 11th and Klien's pace on the drying track came too late for him to do better than ninth.

The Minardis started from the pit lane because, on Paul Stoddart's orders, Robert Doornbos and Christijan Albers qualified with such low fuel loads that neither car could complete the grid formation and opening lap before it would have run dry. Doornbos took over the spare PS05 and had it refuelled before the start; Albers likewise started from the pit lane and was thus able to refuel. Both made early stops for intermediates after starting on Bridgestone's full-wet tyre and in that early period Doornbos lost a crucial minute. Later, Albers lost second gear and after 12 laps did not use anything lower than third. He finished 12th, Doornbos 13th.

Higher up the order, Button and BAR were all smiles, salvaging a podium from an afternoon that at one stage seemed to court disaster. 'The first stint wasn't easy and I had such bad oversteer I barely had to turn into the corners,' Button revealed. But a key front-wing adjustment in his first stop helped things and gradually the race came back to him. His six points were sufficient to push BAR Honda ahead of Red Bull into sixth place overall in the constructors' table.

Räikkönen put a brave face on things as his title hopes grew dimmer in the Belgian shadows. 'I claimed the lead after the second stop because I could stay out longer than Juan Pablo and that was it,' he said. 'However, there are mixed emotions because we should have had a one-two today.'

Alan Henry

Jenson Button took the BAR to a strong third place after Juan Pablo Montoya's last-lap tangle with Antonio Pizzonia.
Photograph: Miltenberg/XPB.cc

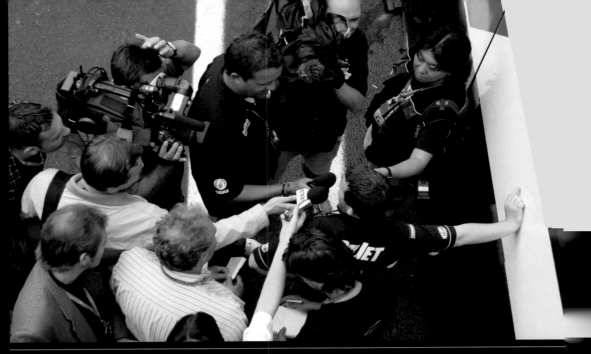

RED BULL DEAL TO BUY MINARDI CONFIRMED

Paul Stoddart announced on the Saturday of the Belgian GP weekend that he had finalised a deal with Dietrich Mateschitz to sell the Minardi squad to Red Bull in a move that will make the Austrian sports-drink company one of the most influential commercial powers in the pit lane from 2006.

Next year's Red Bull Ferrari squad had already signed David Coulthard as lead driver. Christian Klien, Vitantonio Liuzzi and Scott Speed were all under contract and were expected to be divided across the two Red Bull operations. The feeling at Spa was that Klien would remain as Coulthard's team-mate, and Liuzzi and Speed would use Cosworth power in the former Minardi squad.

Stoddart admitted that he had seriously mixed feelings about his decision to sell up and quit the sport he loves. 'The terrorist attacks of 9/11 hit my core business – aviation – so badly that I

was not able to go through with my investment plans for the team,' he said. 'From then on I always said I would sell if I could secure a better future for the team.'

He added, 'I was impressed by what I had seen of Red Bull since it took over Jaguar last year. Most of the same people are there and that was the most important thing to me – that the jobs of the staff at Faenza [the team's headquarters] would be protected. It was an emotional moment standing in front of the team last Saturday to tell everyone what had happened.'

More significantly, the acquisition of Minardi also gave Red Bull a second vote on F1 issues and aligned the team – alongside Ferrari, Jordan and the main Red Bull squad – behind Bernie Ecclestone's stance in the battle over the sport's future commercial-rights income.

FORMULA 1
BELGIAN GRAND PRIX

SPA-FRANCORCHAMPS 9–11 SEPTEMBER 2005

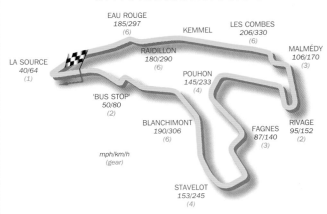

SPA-FRANCORCHAMPS

EAU ROUGE 185/297 (6)
RAIDILLON 180/290 (6)
KEMMEL
LES COMBES 206/330 (6)
MALMÉDY 106/170 (3)
LA SOURCE 40/64 (1)
POUHON 145/233 (4)
'BUS STOP' 50/80 (2)
BLANCHIMONT 190/306 (6)
FAGNES 87/140 (3)
RIVAGE 95/152 (2)
STAVELOT 153/245 (4)

mph/km/h (gear)

CIRCUIT LENGTH: 4.333 miles/6.973 km

Photograph: James Moy/www.crash.net

RACE DISTANCE: 44 laps, 190.715 miles /306.927 km   RACE WEATHER: Overcast (track 18–19°C, air 17–18°C)

Pos.	Driver	Nat.	No.	Entrant	Car/Engine	Tyres	Laps	Time/Retirement	Speed (mph/km/h)	Gap to leader	Fastest race lap	
1	Kimi Räikkönen	FIN	9	Team McLaren Mercedes	McLaren MP4-20-Mercedes F0 110R V10	M	44	1h 30m 01.295s	127.125/204.588		1m 53.810s	34
2	Fernando Alonso	E	5	Mild Seven Renault F1 Team	Renault R25-RS25 V10	M	44	1h 30m 29.689s	126.448/203.499	+28.394s	1m 56.131s	31
3	Jenson Button	GB	3	Lucky Strike BAR Honda	BAR 007-Honda RA005E V10	M	44	1h 30m 33.372s	126.362/203.361	+32.077s	1m 53.323s	44
4	Mark Webber	AUS	7	BMW WilliamsF1 Team	Williams FW27-BMW P84/85 V10	M	44	1h 31m 10.462s	125.506/201.982	+69.167s	1m 52.287s	44
5	Rubens Barrichello	BR	2	Scuderia Ferrari Marlboro	Ferrari F2005-055 V10	B	44	1h 31m 19.431s	125.300/201.651	+78.136s	1m 52.590s	44
6	Jacques Villeneuve	CDN	11	Sauber Petronas	Sauber C24-Petronas 05A V10	M	44	1h 31m 28.730s	125.088/201.310	+87.435s	1m 54.251s	44
7	Ralf Schumacher	D	17	Panasonic Toyota Racing	Toyota TF105-RVX-05 V10	M	44	1h 31m 28.869s	125.085/201.305	+87.574s	1m 51.453s	43
8	Tiago Monteiro	P	18	Jordan Toyota	Jordan EJ15B-Toyota RVX-05 V10	B	43			+1 lap	1m 57.886s	41
9	Christian Klien	A	15	Red Bull Racing	Red Bull RB1-Cosworth TJ2005/12 V10	M	43			+1 lap	1m 52.582s	43
10	Felipe Massa	BR	12	Sauber Petronas	Sauber C24-Petronas 05A V10	M	43			+1 lap	1m 57.748s	28
11	Narain Karthikeyan	IND	19	Jordan Toyota	Jordan EJ15B-Toyota RVX-05 V10	B	43			+1 lap	1m 55.885s	43
12	Christijan Albers	NL	21	Minardi Cosworth	Minardi PS05-Cosworth TJ2005 V10	B	42			+2 laps	2m 01.627s	6
13	Robert Doornbos	NL	20	Minardi Cosworth	Minardi PS05-Cosworth TJ2005 V10	B	41			+3 laps	2m 01.148s	38
14	Juan Pablo Montoya	COL	10	Team McLaren Mercedes	McLaren MP4-20-Mercedes F0 110R V10	M	40			DNF	1m 55.988s	14
15	Antonio Pizzonia	BR	8	BMW WilliamsF1 Team	Williams FW27-BMW P84/85 V10	M	39			DNF	1m 57.541s	32
	Jarno Trulli	I	16	Panasonic Toyota Racing	Toyota TF105-RVX-05 V10	M	34	Spun off			1m 56.953s	3
	David Coulthard	GB	14	Red Bull Racing	Red Bull RB1-Cosworth TJ2005 V10	M	18	Engine			1m 58.451s	8
	Michael Schumacher	D	1	Scuderia Ferrari Marlboro	Ferrari F2005-055 V10	B	13	Collision			1m 57.444s	10
	Takuma Sato	J	4	Lucky Strike BAR Honda	BAR 007-Honda RA005E V10	M	13	Collision			1m 57.534s	10
	Giancarlo Fisichella	I	6	Mild Seven Renault F1 Team	Renault R25-RS25 V10	M	10	Accident			1m 57.117s	9

All results and data © FOM 2005

Fastest lap: Ralf Schumacher, on lap 43, 1m 51.453, 140.013 mph/225.329 km/h.

Lap record: Kimi Räikkönen (McLarenMP4/19B-Mercedes F0110P V10), 1m 45.108s, 148.465 mph/238.931 km/h (2004).

19th: MONTEIRO Jordan-Toyota

17th: DOORNBOS Minardi-Cosworth
Started from pit lane

15th: PIZZONIA Williams-BMW
Ten-place penalty for engine change

13th: FISICHELLA Renault

11th: COULTHARD Red Bull-Cosworth

20th: KARTHIKEYAN Jordan-Toyota

18th: ALBERS Minardi-Cosworth
Started from pit lane

16th: KLIEN Red Bull-Cosworth

14th: VILLENEUVE Sauber-Petronas

12th: BARRICHELLO Ferrari

Grid order	1	2	3	4	5	6	7	8	9	10	11	12	13	14	15	16	17	18	19	20	21	22	23	24	25	26	27	28	29	30	31	32	33	34	35	36
10 MONTOYA	10	10	10	10	10	10	10	10	10	10	10	10	10	10	10	10	10	10	10	10	10	10	10	10	10	10	10	10	10	10	10	10	9	9	9	9
9 RÄIKKÖNEN	9	9	9	9	9	9	9	9	9	9	9	11	11	17	17	17	17	17	17	17	17	9	9	9	9	9	9	9	9	9	9	10	10	10	10	
16 TRULLI	16	16	16	16	16	16	16	16	16	16	16	17	17	9	9	9	9	9	9	9	9	17	5	5	5	5	5	5	5	5	5	5	5			
5 ALONSO	5	5	5	5	5	5	5	5	5	5	5	9	9	11	11	11	11	11	5	5	5	12	12	12	12	2	2	7	7	3	2	2	2			
17 R. SCHUMACHER	1	1	1	1	1	1	1	1	1	1	1	5	5	5	5	5	5	5	11	12	12	12	12	2	2	2	2	7	7	2	3	2	7	3	3	
1 M. SCHUMACHER	4	4	4	4	4	4	4	4	4	4	16	12	12	12	12	12	12	12	2	2	2	2	7	7	7	7	12	3	3	2	7	3	7	7		
12 MASSA	3	3	3	3	3	17	17	17	6	11	12	2	2	2	2	2	2	7	7	7	3	3	3	3	3	8	8	8	8	17	17	17				
3 BUTTON	17	17	17	17	17	3	3	6	3	12	18	18	7	7	7	7	7	11	11	3	11	11	18	18	12	19	17	17	8	8	8					
7 WEBBER	12	12	12	12	12	12	6	6	3	12	3	18	19	7	18	18	18	3	3	3	11	18	18	11	8	18	16	19	11	11	11	11				
4 SATO	7	14	14	14	14	6	12	12	12	14	12	1	3	3	3	3	18	18	18	18	18	8	8	11	19	19	17	16	18	18	18					
14 COULTHARD	14	6	6	6	6	14	14	14	7	14	4	4	14	14	14	14	8	8	8	19	19	19	11	11	16	11	11	16	16	12	12					
2 BARRICHELLO	6	7	7	7	7	7	7	7	17	7	15	7	8	8	8	19	19	19	19	17	16	16	16	16	17	15	18	19	15	15	15					
6 FISICHELLA	15	15	15	15	15	15	15	15	15	14	3	19	19	16	16	16	16	16	16	16	17	17	17	11	18	15	12	19								
11 VILLENEUVE	2	8	8	8	8	8	8	8	2	16	14	16	16	16	16	16	15	15	15	15	15	15	15	15	12	12	19	21	21							
8 PIZZONIA	8	2	2	2	2	2	2	2	2	8	7	8	15	15	15	21	21	20	20	21	21	21	21	21	21	21	21	20	20							
15 KLIEN	11	11	11	11	11	11	11	11	11	18	3	16	21	21	21	20	20	21	21	20	20	20	20	20	20	20	20	20	20							
20 DOORNBOS	18	18	18	18	18	18	18	18	18	19	8	15	20	20	20	20																				
21 ALBERS	19	19	19	19	19	19	19	19	19	21	21	21																								
18 MONTEIRO	20	20	20	20	20	20	20	21	21	21	20	20																								
19 KARTHIKEYAN	21	21	21	21	21	21	21	20	20	20																										

TIME SHEETS

QUALIFYING

WEATHER: Sunny then heavily cloudy (track 28–31°C, air 23–24°C)

Pos.	Driver	R/Order	Sector 1	Sector 2	Sector 3	Time
1	Juan Pablo Montoya	20	29.143s	47.183s	30.055s	1m 46.391s
2	Kimi Räikkönen	17	29.221s	47.154s	30.065s	1m 46.440s
3	Giancarlo Fisichella	18	28.821s	47.762s	29.914s	1m 46.497s
4	Jarno Trulli	16	29.412s	46.834s	30.350s	1m 46.596s
5	Fernando Alonso	19	29.026s	47.850s	29.884s	1m 46.760s
6	Ralf Schumacher	15	29.481s	47.468s	30.352s	1m 47.401s
7	Michael Schumacher	11	29.535s	47.383s	30.558s	1m 47.476s
8	Felipe Massa	12	29.285s	48.223s	30.359s	1m 47.867s
9	Jenson Button	13	29.645s	47.817s	30.516s	1m 47.978s
10	Mark Webber	7	29.459s	48.171s	30.441s	1m 48.071s
11	Takuma Sato	5	29.626s	48.286s	30.441s	1m 48.353s
12	David Coulthard	6	29.533s	48.581s	30.394s	1m 48.508s
13	Rubens Barrichello	9	29.564s	48.359s	30.627s	1m 48.550s
14	Jacques Villeneuve	10	29.353s	49.037s	30.499s	1m 48.889s
15	Antonio Pizzonia	14	29.576s	48.671s	30.651s	1m 48.898s
16	Christian Klien	8	29.575s	48.839s	30.580s	1m 48.994s
17	Robert Doornbos	3	29.623s	49.217s	30.939s	1m 49.779s
18	Christijan Albers	2	29.537s	49.711s	30.594s	1m 49.842s
19	Tiago Monteiro	4	30.039s	50.283s	31.176s	1m 51.498s
20	Narain Karthikeyan	1	30.129s	50.171s	31.375s	1m 51.675s

PRACTICE 1 (FRIDAY)

Cloudy then heavily rainy (track 24–25°C, air 21°C)

Pos.	Driver	Laps	Time
1	Kimi Räikkönen	5	1m 48.206s
2	Alex Wurz	18	1m 48.216s
3	Giancarlo Fisichella	6	1m 48.619s
4	Ricardo Zonta	22	1m 49.445s
5	Mark Webber	4	1m 49.692s
6	Jenson Button	7	1m 49.890s
7	Jarno Trulli	9	1m 50.542s
8	Michael Schumacher	4	1m 50.564s
9	Ralf Schumacher	8	1m 50.820s
10	Vitantonio Liuzzi	17	1m 50.951s
11	Takuma Sato	7	1m 51.003s
12	Rubens Barrichello	5	1m 51.177s
13	Jacques Villeneuve	7	1m 52.173s
14	Felipe Massa	9	1m 52.236s
15	Narain Karthikeyan	9	1m 53.148s
16	Antonio Pizzonia	4	1m 53.535s
17	Christijan Albers	9	1m 53.807s
18	Nicolas Kiesa	17	1m 54.437s
19	Robert Doornbos	8	1m 54.973s
20	Tiago Monteiro	7	1m 55.174s
21	Enrico Toccacelo	5	2m 02.502s
22	David Coulthard	1	No time
23	Christian Klien	1	No time

PRACTICE 2 (FRIDAY)

Light then heavy rain (track 21–23°C, air 18–20°C)

Pos.	Driver	Laps	Time
1	Vitantonio Liuzzi	1	No time
2	Robert Doornbos	1	No time
3	Fernando Alonso	1	No time

PRACTICE 3 (SATURDAY)

Heavily cloudy then sunny (track 17–21°C, air 15–18°C)

Pos.	Driver	Laps	Time
1	Kimi Räikkönen	7	1m 48.125s
2	Juan Pablo Montoya	9	1m 48.516s
3	Giancarlo Fisichella	8	1m 48.883s
4	Fernando Alonso	7	1m 49.286s
5	Michael Schumacher	11	1m 49.520s
6	Jenson Button	8	1m 49.780s
7	Mark Webber	5	1m 50.066s
8	David Coulthard	14	1m 50.139s
9	Ralf Schumacher	8	1m 50.403s
10	Antonio Pizzonia	9	1m 50.449s
11	Jarno Trulli	9	1m 50.451s
12	Takuma Sato	10	1m 50.750s
13	Felipe Massa	8	1m 50.877s
14	Christian Klien	14	1m 50.907s
15	Jacques Villeneuve	8	1m 51.655s
16	Tiago Monteiro	9	1m 51.953s
17	Christijan Albers	8	1m 53.250s
18	Robert Doornbos	8	1m 53.278s
19	Narain Karthikeyan	5	1m 53.480s
20	Rubens Barrichello	1	No time

PRACTICE 4 (SATURDAY)

Sunny (track 24–27°C, air 19–22°C)

Pos.	Driver	Laps	Time
1	Fernando Alonso	14	1m 46.307s
2	Kimi Räikkönen	11	1m 46.641s
3	Jarno Trulli	15	1m 46.681s
4	Juan Pablo Montoya	8	1m 46.858s
5	Giancarlo Fisichella	16	1m 47.049s
6	Ralf Schumacher	16	1m 47.054s
7	Jenson Button	14	1m 47.419s
8	Takuma Sato	15	1m 47.507s
9	Michael Schumacher	12	1m 47.773s
10	Rubens Barrichello	14	1m 47.991s
11	Antonio Pizzonia	13	1m 48.092s
12	Jacques Villeneuve	15	1m 48.204s
13	Mark Webber	11	1m 48.213s
14	Felipe Massa	16	1m 48.551s
15	David Coulthard	12	1m 48.866s
16	Christian Klien	11	1m 48.877s
17	Christijan Albers	12	1m 49.166s
18	Robert Doornbos	15	1m 49.208s
19	Tiago Monteiro	13	1m 50.740s
20	Narain Karthikeyan	14	1m 51.594s

CHASSIS LOG BOOK

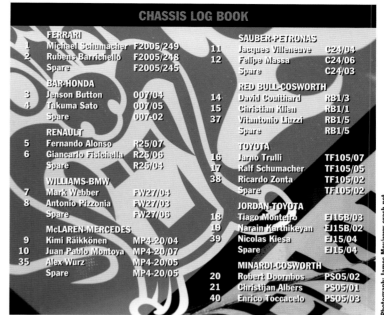

	FERRARI	
1	Michael Schumacher	F2005/249
2	Rubens Barrichello	F2005/248
	Spare	F2005/245

	BAR-HONDA	
3	Jenson Button	007/04
4	Takuma Sato	007/05
	Spare	007/02

	RENAULT	
5	Fernando Alonso	R25/07
6	Giancarlo Fisichella	R25/06
	Spare	R25/04

	WILLIAMS-BMW	
7	Mark Webber	FW27/04
8	Antonio Pizzonia	FW27/03
	Spare	FW27/06

	McLAREN-MERCEDES	
9	Kimi Räikkönen	MP4-20/04
10	Juan Pablo Montoya	MP4-20/07
35	Alex Wurz	MP4-20/05
	Spare	MP4-20/05

	SAUBER-PETRONAS	
11	Jacques Villeneuve	C24/04
12	Felipe Massa	C24/06
	Spare	C24/03

	RED BULL-COSWORTH	
14	David Coulthard	RB1/3
15	Christian Klien	RB1/1
37	Vitantonio Liuzzi	RB1/5
	Spare	RB1/5

	TOYOTA	
16	Jarno Trulli	TF105/07
17	Ralf Schumacher	TF105/05
38	Ricardo Zonta	TF105/02
	Spare	TF105/02

	JORDAN-TOYOTA	
18	Tiago Monteiro	EJ15B/03
19	Narain Karthikeyan	EJ15B/02
39	Nicolas Kiesa	EJ15/04
	Spare	EJ15/04

	MINARDI-COSWORTH	
20	Robert Doornbos	PS05/02
21	Christijan Albers	PS05/01
40	Enrico Toccacelo	PS05/03

Photograph: James Moy/www.crash.net

9th: WEBBER Williams-BMW

7th: MASSA Sauber-Petronas

5th: R. SCHUMACHER Toyota

3rd: TRULLI Toyota

Pole: MONTOYA McLaren-Mercedes

10th: SATO BAR-Honda

8th: BUTTON BAR-Honda

6th: M. SCHUMACHER Ferrari

4th: ALONSO Renault

2nd: RÄIKKÖNEN McLaren-Mercedes

37	38	39	40	41	42	43	44	•
9	9	9	9	9	9	9	9	1
10	10	10	10	5	5	5	5	2
5	5	5	5	3	3	3	3	3
2	3	3	3	7	7	7	7	4
3	2	2	2	2	2	2	2	5
7	7	17	7	11	11	11	11	6
17	17	7	17	17	17	17	17	7
8	11	11	11	18	18	18		8
11	8	18	18	15	15	15		
18	18	8	15	12	12	12		
15	15	15	12	19	19	19		
12	12	12	19	21	21			
19	19	19	21	20				
21	21	21	20					
20	20	20						

Pit stop
One lap or more behind leader

POINTS

	DRIVERS				
1	Fernando Alonso	111	19	Christijan Albers	4
2	Kimi Räikkönen	86	20	Pedro de la Rosa	4
3	Michael Schumacher	55	21	Patrick Friesacher	3
4	Juan Pablo Montoya	50	22	Antonio Pizzonia	2
5	Jarno Trulli	43	23	Takuma Sato	1
6	Giancarlo Fisichella	41	24	Vitantonio Liuzzi	1
7	Ralf Schumacher	37			
8	Rubens Barrichello	35		CONSTRUCTORS	
9	Jenson Button	30	1	Renault	152
10	Mark Webber	29	2	McLaren	146
11	Nick Heidfeld	28	3	Ferrari	90
12	David Coulthard	21	4	Toyota	80
13	Jacques Villeneuve	9	5	Williams	59
14	Felipe Massa	8	6	BAR	31
15	Tiago Monteiro	7	7	Red Bull	27
16	Alex Wurz	6	8	Sauber	17
17	Narain Karthikeyan	5	9	Jordan	12
18	Christian Klien	5	10	Minardi	7

Photograph: James Moy/www.crash.net

Juan Pablo Montoya was totally confident
he had the edge over his McLaren
team-mate Kimi Räikkönen at Interlagos
and dominated the Brazilian round of the
championship chase.
Photography James Moy/www.crash.net

INTERLAGOS
BRAZILIAN GP

FIA F1 WORLD CHAMPIONSHIP/ROUND 17

INTERLAGOS QUALIFYING

Yet again, it would transpire that qualifying revealed only part of a story that the race would ultimately relate.

McLaren went to Brazil ready to operate at what Ron Dennis called 'full ramming speed', meaning that every 'galley slave' was rowing his hardest. The MP4-20 was expected to continue its customary form and to take pole position, though the team knew it had its work cut out getting Juan Pablo Montoya up with Kimi Räikkönen because his retirement in Belgium had left the Colombian as the seventh man out in the session.

Renault also came loaded for bear. A huge amount of effort had gone into a new aerodynamic update, said to be 'the most significant step so far this season'. The plan was to enable Fernando Alonso and Giancarlo Fisichella to compete with McLaren. There was also the latest D-specification Renault RS25 V10 engine in both cars.

Alonso needed only six points, which he could get for a third-placed finish, to cement his title, but the blues were determined to win from the front if possible.

Fisichella was the first to run in qualifying, having been the first retiree at Spa. Up to that point, Renault had appeared to be pretty much on a par with McLaren all through the different stages of practice and his lap of 1m 12.558s was well received. Takuma Sato was next and did one installation lap in his BAR-Honda; he had a ten-grid-place penalty, levied for his clash with Michael Schumacher at Spa, but in any case needed an engine change on Saturday. Then Michael Schumacher lapped in 1m 12.976s, which was rather more competitive than Ferrari had been of late. David Coulthard posted 1m 13.844s for Red Bull, then Jarno Trulli took his Toyota around in 1m 13.041s and Antonio Pizzonia (still standing in for Nick Heidfeld at BMW Williams) lapped in 1m 13.581s.

The interest picked up when Montoya came out and the Colombian lost no time in cutting down to 1m 12.145s to put Fisichella's effort into fresh perspective. Montoya's lap resisted all challengers until Alonso came out. Jenson Button was the only man to come anywhere near close as he pushed the BAR-Honda to 1m 12.696s, enjoying the 007's aerodynamic update.

When Alonso ran after the Englishman, everyone had their ears pinned back as he lapped in 1m 11.988s to snatch the pole. This was something remarkable from Renault given McLaren's recent domination of qualifying, so everything came down to what Räikkönen could do.

Out came the Finn, set on taking pole, but, going into the Senna S, the first corner, he pushed a fraction too hard and immediately lost the better part of half a second as his McLaren understeered wide in the first section of the corner. The lap was thus ruined early and his eventual 1m 12.781s time left him only fifth on the grid.

Christian Klien's personal-record-matching sixth place on the grid, with a lap of 1m 12.889s for Red Bull, was confidently put down to a low-fuel run by sceptics, particularly because Coulthard was a second slower. But the Austrian's time proved to be correct insofar as he would run a long first stint in the race; Coulthard, it transpired, had just done a poor lap.

Schumacher Sr's time stood up for seventh with Trulli eighth, but the Italian was another to face a ten-grid-place penalty after changing an engine. Felipe Massa complained of understeer as he took ninth place for Sauber Petronas on 1m 13.151s, which was sufficient to pip fellow countryman and 2004 pole-sitter Rubens Barrichello in the second Ferrari, who managed 1m 13.183s. Ralf Schumacher was 11th on 1m 13.285s and Jacques Villeneuve was very satisfied with 1m 13.372s considering that he was on a one-stop strategy.

Tiago Monteiro surprised a few people with 1m 13.387s in his Jordan EJ15B, which was running low fuel, but while Mark Webber and Antonio Pizzonia appeared to be on single stops too for BMW Williams, they were in fact on two stops. The FW27s were just off the pace, with respective laps of 1m 13.538s and 1m 13.581s.

Coulthard's time left him 16th ahead of Narain Karthikeyan, who had more fuel than his team-mate en route to 1m 14.520s. That meant the Jordans outqualified the Minardis. Christijan Albers fought twitchy handling for 1m 14.763s but team-mate Robert Doornbos got caught out by it in Turn 12 and spun.

FERNANDO ALONSO always said that he wanted to make a race of it in Brazil and he staked his claim to the race by putting his Renault on pole position. He led initially, too, but once an early safety-car period had neutralised that and he had sat it out wheel-to-wheel with a hungry Juan Pablo Montoya down the back straight on the third lap, he conceded hopes of victory and instead followed home the Colombian and his team-mate Kimi Räikkönen – a McLaren one-two – to do all he needed to become the youngest world champion in F1 history.

All morning the question that had occupied most minds concerned the weather. Was it going to be 2003 all over again? The skies wore a dark hue. 'Our [Williams' and its advisers'] forecast says it will definitely rain today, but not until after the race,' said Williams' director of engineering Patrick Head. 'Knowing us, that means it will rain on the first lap!'

As the start time grew closer, however, the skies were relatively clear and everybody went to the line with dry-weather tyres. Well, almost everybody. In his 150th GP, Jacques Villeneuve found his hard-won 11th position on the grid nullified when the stewards discovered that for some unfathomable reason part of his Sauber's right-hand rear anti-roll bar had been changed in parc fermé. Since that is strictly forbidden, the French-Canadian was obliged to start from the pit lane. At the end of the grid formation lap, Tiago Monteiro joined him there. As a corollary of his quick qualifying time he had to come in for fuel and the team gambled by refilling his tank before the race actually started. It paid off.

From pole, Alonso boiled into the lead from Montoya, with Giancarlo Fisichella third from Räikkönen, and Jenson Button quickly falling back from fourth. Michael Schumacher gave the unfortunate Christian Klien a driving lesson in the Senna S, pushing alongside him on the outside and then squeezing the Red-Bull driver right up the inner kerb on the third, left-hand section of the corner where it leads to the back straight. The outgoing champion had clearly not forgotten how to be ruthless.

Throughout the lap Räikkönen and Fisichella had a real scrap, which eventually resulted in the Italian's losing sufficient momentum for Schumacher Sr to get a run on him, too, so in a matter of a few corners the second Renault went from third to fifth. Button was sixth from Klien, Rubens Barrichello, Ralf Schumacher and Felipe Massa, who had made an indifferent getaway.

Back on the grid, however, there had been chaos. Neither Williams driver made a good start, but David Coulthard did. The trouble developed when he tried to push his Red Bull into the closing gap between Mark Webber, on the left, and Antonio Pizzonia, on the right. Coulthard's right-front wheel hit Pizzonia's left-rear, damaging both cars and sending the Brazilian spinning across the road into his team-mate. Before they even got through the first corner, both Williamses were out (though Webber rejoined the race 25 laps down after a long stop for repairs), as was Coulthard. And so, too, was the safety car. It was deployed for two laps as the mess was cleared up and then the racing resumed on lap three.

The safety car had negated a small lead that the determined

Above: Juan Pablo Montoya led the pack into the first corner and Kimi Räikkönen was just eased out by Fernando Alonso's Renault. Farther back, Antonio Pizzonia's Williams was broadside in the pack after tangling with team-mate Mark Webber and David Coulthard's Red Bull.
Photograph: Peter Nygaard/GP Photo

Far left: Despite suffering consistently low grip levels, Michael Schumacher drove brilliantly to beat Giancarlo Fisichella's Renault for fourth place.

Near top left: Christian Klien telling ITV's Martin Brundle all about his storming lap in qualifying.

Near bottom left: Rubens Barrichello was appearing on his home ground with Ferrari for the last time.
Photographs: James Moy/www.crash.net

Alonso had built over Montoya. The Colombian was right with
the Spaniard as they went into the Senna S – where he had so
memorably passed Schumacher in 2001 – and as they headed
down the back straight Juan pulled level with Fernando, down
the inside. As for Renault's winning, that idea was over.

'I could see he was quicker,' Alonso said of Montoya, 'and
that he would try at the first opportunity, so I didn't fight it.
Today wasn't a day to fight.'

Nor was it a day, as Renault had initially hoped, on which the
R25 could match the McLaren MP4-20. Like most of the top
runners, McLaren and Renault had opted for Michelin's harder
compound in the interest of longevity (only the Saubers, the
Red Bulls and Ralf Schumacher opted for the softer tyre). But
even this early, the McLaren was using its tyres a little better
and that would prove decisive. Farther back, Jenson Button was
in all sorts of trouble with his BAR's rear Michelins graining and
once again all hope of his maiden triumph was put on hold.

Having taken the lead, Montoya surrendered it only during
the pit stops, each time to Räikkönen. And this was when
McLaren's true superiority became apparent. Alonso was the
first significant runner to stop, on lap 22, followed by Fisichella
a lap later. By contrast, Schumacher Sr and Button stopped on
lap 26, Montoya on 28 and Räikkönen not until lap 31.

This put a lot of things into perspective. Alonso had held
second until his stop, but Räikkönen's longer opening stint left
him comfortably in second place by the time things had settled
down again. Farther back, Schumacher Sr was still easily ahead
of Fisichella, having once or twice had to get ruthless again in
discouraging his attention. The Italian had struggled initially with
oversteer (suggesting that he had a similar graining problem to

Button's) and thereafter his race was, to say the least,
unconvincing at a time when Renault still needed to maximise
its points scoring. Even Fisichella admitted later that Renault
should have beaten Ferrari. It appeared to escape his
immediate attention that one of the R25s had.

As long as Alonso was third, Räikkönen's mathematical
chance of winning the crown had evaporated. Thus there
appeared to be little point in McLaren's doing anything to
persuade the fired-up Montoya to surrender his lead the way he
had in Belgium. Certainly Montoya would have done so had
it been necessary, but almost certainly it wasn't going to be.
Montoya refuelled again on lap 54 and again Räikkönen ran
a lot longer, not completing his final stop until lap 59. If there
was going to be any action between the McLaren drivers, this
was when it would have come, but Montoya came safely
through the Senna S and out onto the back straight as
Räikkönen exited the pits.

The game was up as far as the Finn was concerned. For a
while they went at it, but with eight laps to go it was clear that
both men had reduced their pace. Montoya duly won the race
for the second successive year and in doing so drew level on
points with Michael Schumacher, who was in third place in the
drivers' stakes. And at last McLaren got its first one-two finish
since Austria 2000. Nearly 25 seconds farther back, all Alonso
had to do was follow them home.

In their wake, Schumacher gave Ferrari a boost with fourth
place. This was an interesting result given that no development
had gone into the unloved F2005 since Spa, but it owed much
to the car's ability to run on Bridgestone's softer tyre. This made
the car look more competitive than it had of late. With

BUTTON DOES A DEAL WITH WILLIAMS – TO DRIVE FOR BAR

The major story prior to the Brazilian Grand Prix was that the long-running Jenson-Button saga had finally been resolved after the 25-year-old driver paid Sir Frank Williams an alleged $35 million to get out of his contract. The deal was struck on Friday 16 September and made official on Wednesday 21 September.

'The past few days have been the high point of my season,' Button said at a press conference in São Paulo's Grand Hyatt Hotel on the Thursday before the race. 'It is unbelievable how much more relaxed I feel after resolving this issue with Frank Williams. Now I am able to focus on what is important.

'I'm ecstatic that we have sorted the situation between Frank and me. The contract was between him and me and that was how we sorted it. We had as many meetings as possible and talked the situation through. It was down to me and not down to the people around me and I think that made the difference. It was not a nice situation to be in, but I'd like to say thank you to him because we were able to stop it before it went any further.'

Button refused to confirm the length of his new contract with BAR Honda beyond the quip, 'It's longer than a year,' and denied that the Japanese motor giant had helped him with the cost of the release. 'That situation was down to me and Frank. The contract was between the two of us and the deal we have done was done between the two of us. Trust me, it hurts.'

However, he stands to make $90 million on a five-year rights deal with Honda, whom he firmly believes to be the key to an eventual championship title. 'It is never 100 percent [sure] that any team can challenge for the world championship,' he acknowledged, 'but the determination and dedication of BAR Honda is beyond anything I have seen in F1, how the Japanese and British sides of the operation work together and how focused they are on our goals.'

DIARY

On the Wednesday after the Belgian Grand Prix, Williams confirms that it will not be taking up its 2006 option on Nick Heidfeld's services. BMW immediately responds by extending his two-year deal (from 2007) to three, to include 2006.

In the week leading up to the Brazilian GP, Mark Webber is voted off the board of the Grand Prix Drivers' Association.

As the teams gather at Interlagos, BAR is getting ready to take a cosmetically modified 007 F1 car to the Bonneville Salt Flats in Utah, where South African Alan van der Merwe is to attempt to set a new record for F1 cars of 400 km/h (250 mph).

It is revealed in Brazil that the first grand prix of 2006 will be in Bahrain, followed by Malaysia, because the Australian race in Melbourne needs to reschedule to April because Australia is hosting the Commonwealth Games on 15–26 March.

Indianapolis Motor Speedway owner Tony George confirms that there will be a US Grand Prix at Indianapolis in 2006, on 2 July.

Above: The McLaren pair Juan Pablo Montoya (bottom) and Kimi Räikkönen completed a one-two finish, but it was third-placed Fernando Alonso who attracted all the post-race attention.
Photograph: Jad Sherif/WRI

Right: The moment of release for Fernando Alonso as he became the sport's youngest-ever world champion.
Photograph: Laurent Charniaux/WRI

Barrichello taking sixth, a long way behind his team leader, Ferrari did enough to preserve its third place in the constructors' table after Toyota's challenge had brought it dangerously close. The Brazilian had a good battle with his 2006 team-mate Button, but later lost some edge when a power-steering problem made the Ferrari pull to the left.

Button's race was miserable and fourth place on the grid translated only into a seventh-placed finish. Button may have been delighted to escape from Williams, but he was not so ecstatic now. 'It was a difficult day for us [the BAR team],' he admitted. 'Our pace was slow and we suffered that graining problem right from the start. We were on the hard tyre as well, so we didn't expect that. In fact, that's why we took that tyre. I struggled, particularly on the last section, through the fast corner and onto the straight, where we had big oversteer.' Tenth-fastest lap was clear indication of his problems.

Team-mate Takuma Sato wasn't very quick either: he was on a single-stop strategy because of his engine change and resultant lowly grid position, and he also suffered from low grip. Altogether, a race to forget for the team.

Rival Toyota took the final point courtesy of Ralf Schumacher, who complained that his TF105 was difficult to drive for most of the race. Team-mate Jarno Trulli had a frustrating day that began with a lucky avoidance of the start-line shunt and ended after 69 laps with a pneumatic failure.

At least Red Bull was able to prove that Christian Klien's qualifying performance was not, as everyone had suspected, a result of a light fuel load. After having that bit of a first-lap kerfuffle with Schumacher Sr, he struggled home in a disappointed ninth place, just outside the points.

Sauber Petronas was very disappointed with 11th and 12th places for Felipe Massa and Jacques Villeneuve respectively. The Brazilian said his car was very nervous and had poor traction, even on the softer Michelins, and that by the time it improved towards the end it was too late to do anything useful. After starting from the pits, Villeneuve lost huge amounts of

time stuck behind the Minardis early in the race. The team changed him from a one-stop to a two-stop strategy to try and improve the situation, but it didn't really affect his result. 'My car was very fast today,' the former champion said, 'but not in a straight line. I just couldn't get a tow from Doornbos early on.'

Christijan Albers brought his Minardi home 14th as team-mate Robert Doornbos fell victim to engine failure on lap 35. Narain Karthikeyan lost time being lapped and later flat-spotted a tyre on his Jordan and had to make an extra stop just as he was catching the Dutchman. His team-mate, Tiago Monteiro, had his amazing run of 16 consecutive finishes finally come to an end after an engine failure on lap 56.

McLaren's success proved the one bitter-sweet moment for Renault. With 18 points for their afternoon's work, Montoya and Räikkönen moved their team into the lead of the constructors' championship for the first time this season, with 164 points to Renault's 162. Interestingly, while saluting the success of Renault in the drivers' championship, McLaren chairman Ron Dennis apologised to his drivers for the year's lost opportunities.

At Renault there were no regrets, just celebrations. In parc fermé, Fernando Alonso clambered from the cockpit and waved his arms aloft with the pure elation of a man who has realised his destiny. Then he ran to his delirious team and embraced it warmly. In turn, the guys showed him the pit board that said it all: 'Bravo Fernando Alonso, 2005 world champion'. As if symbolically to wash away the final traces of Michael Schumacher's tenancy of the title, a brief rain shower fell.

On the podium, Alonso poured the victory champagne into his trophy from a great height, celebrating the way that Spaniards do when they pour their cider in the Oviedo region. As he savoured his success he was gracious and calm.

'I come from a country that has no tradition in F1 and I had to fight alone – I had no help from anybody,' he said quietly. 'I think this is the maximum I can achieve in my career and it is thanks to three or four people. No more than that.'

David Tremayne

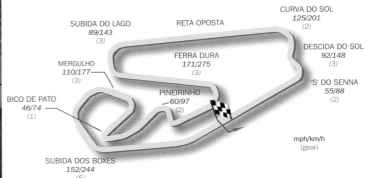

FIA F1 WORLD CHAMPIONSHIP • ROUND 17
GRAND PREMIO DO BRASIL

INTERLAGOS, SÃO PAULO
AUTODROMO CARLOS PACE

CURVA DO SOL
125/201
(2)

SUBIDA DO LAGO
89/143
(3)

RETA OPOSTA

DESCIDA DO SOL
92/148
(3)

MERGULHO
110/177
(3)

FERRA DURA
171/275
(3)

'S' DO SENNA
55/88
(2)

BICO DE PATO
46/74
(1)

PINEIRINHO
60/97
(2)

mph/km/h
(gear)

SUBIDA DOS BOXES
152/244
(5)

CIRCUIT LENGTH: 2.677 miles/4.309 km

INTERLAGOS 23–25 SEPTEMBER 2005

RACE DISTANCE: 71 laps, 190.083 miles /305.909 km RACE WEATHER: Overcast, light and rainy (track 23–24°C, air 22–23°C)

Photograph: James Moy/www.crash.net

All results and data © FOM 2005

Pos.	Driver	Nat.	No.	Entrant	Car/Engine	Tyres	Laps	Time/Retirement	Speed (mph/km/h)	Gap to leader	Fastest race lap	
1	Juan Pablo Montoya	COL	10	Team McLaren Mercedes	McLaren MP4-20-Mercedes F0 110R V10	M	71	1h 29m 20.574s	127.654/205.439		1m 12.650s	27
2	Kimi Räikkönen	FIN	9	Team McLaren Mercedes	McLaren MP4-20-Mercedes F0 110R V10	M	71	1h 29m 23.101s	127.593/205.342	+2.527s	1m 12.268s	29
3	Fernando Alonso	E	5	Mild Seven Renault F1 Team	Renault R25-RS25 V10	M	71	1h 29m 45.414s	127.065/204.491	+24.840s	1m 12.653s	21
4	Michael Schumacher	D	1	Scuderia Ferrari Marlboro	Ferrari F2005-055 V10	B	71	1h 29m 56.242s	126.810/204.081	+35.668s	1m 12.800s	25
5	Giancarlo Fisichella	I	6	Mild Seven Renault F1 Team	Renault R25-RS25 V10	M	71	1h 30m 00.792s	126.703/203.909	+40.218s	1m 13.190s	11
6	Rubens Barrichello	BR	2	Scuderia Ferrari Marlboro	Ferrari F2005-055 V10	B	71	1h 30m 29.747s	126.028/202.822	+69.173s	1m 13.192s	49
7	Jenson Button	GB	3	Lucky Strike BAR Honda	BAR 007-Honda RA005E V10	M	70			+1 lap	1m 13.746s	24
8	Ralf Schumacher	D	17	Panasonic Toyota Racing	Toyota TF105-RVX-05 V10	M	70			+1 lap	1m 13.724s	25
9	Christian Klien	A	15	Red Bull Racing	Red Bull RB1-Cosworth TJ2005/12 V10	M	70			+1 lap	1m 13.800s	50
10	Takuma Sato	J	4	Lucky Strike BAR Honda	BAR 007-Honda RA005E V10	M	70			+1 lap	1m 14.394s	32
11	Felipe Massa	BR	12	Sauber Petronas	Sauber C24-Petronas 05A V10	M	70			+1 lap	1m 14.343s	70
12	Jacques Villeneuve	CDN	11	Sauber Petronas	Sauber C24-Petronas 05A V10	M	70			+1 lap	1m 14.054s	25
13	Jarno Trulli	I	16	Panasonic Toyota Racing	Toyota TF105-RVX-05 V10	M	69			DNF	1m 13.570s	69
14	Christijan Albers	NL	21	Minardi Cosworth	Minardi PS05-Cosworth TJ2005 V10	B	69			+2 laps	1m 15.527s	19
15	Narain Karthikeyan	IND	19	Jordan Toyota	Jordan EJ15B-Toyota RVX-05 V10	B	68			+3 laps	1m 14.906s	41
	Tiago Monteiro	P	18	Jordan Toyota	Jordan EJ15B-Toyota RVX-05 V10	B	55	Engine			1m 15.113s	41
	Mark Webber	AUS	7	BMW WilliamsF1 Team	Williams FW27-BMW P84/85 V10	M	45				1m 13.590s	45
	Robert Doornbos	NL	20	Minardi Cosworth	Minardi PS05-Cosworth TJ2005 V10	B	34	Oil pipe			1m 15.792s	16
	Antonio Pizzonia	BR	8	BMW WilliamsF1 Team	Williams FW27-BMW P84/85 V10	M	0	Accident				
	David Coulthard	GB	14	Red Bull Racing	Red Bull RB1-Cosworth TJ2005/12 V10	M	0	Accident				

Fastest lap: Kimi Räikkönen, on lap 29, 1m 12.268s, 133.378 mph/214.651 km/h.

Lap record: Juan Pablo Montoya (Williams FW26-BMW P84 V10), 1m 11.473s, 134.861 mph/217.038 km/h (2004).

19th: SATO BAR-Honda
Ten-place penalty for Spa incident

17th: TRULLI Toyota
Ten-place penalty for engine change

15th: KARTHIKEYAN Jordan-Toyota

13th: PIZZONIA Williams-BMW

11th: MONTEIRO Jordan-Toyota
Started from pit lane

20th: VILLENEUVE Sauber-Petronas
Started from pit lane

18th: DOORNBOS Minardi-Cosworth

16th: ALBERS Minardi-Cosworth

14th: COULTHARD Red Bull-Cosworth

12th: WEBBER Williams-BMW

Grid order	1	2	3	4	5	6	7	8	9	10	11	12	13	14	15	16	17	18	19	20	21	22	23	24	25	26	27	28	29	30	31	32	33	34	35	36	37	38	39	40	41	42	43	44	45	46	47	48	49	50	51	52	53	54	55
5 ALONSO	5	5	10	10	10	10	10	10	10	10	10	10	10	10	10	10	10	10	10	10	10	10	10	10	10	10	10	10	9	9	9	10	10	10	10	10	10	10	10	10	10	10	10	10	10	10	10	10	10	10	10	10	10	10	9
10 MONTOYA	10	10	5	5	5	5	5	5	5	5	5	5	5	5	5	5	5	5	5	5	5	5	5	5	5	5	5	5	10	10	10	9	9	9	9	9	9	9	9	9	9	9	9	9	9	9	9	9	9	9	9	9	9	9	10
6 FISICHELLA	9	9	9	9	9	9	9	9	9	9	9	9	9	9	9	9	9	9	9	9	9	9	5	6	1	1	1	5	5	5	5	5	5	5	5	5	5	5	5	5	5	5	5	5	5	5	5	5	1	1	1	1	1	5	5
3 BUTTON	1	1	6	6	6	6	6	6	6	6	6	6	6	6	6	6	6	6	6	6	6	6	6	1	3	3	5	1	1	1	1	1	1	1	1	1	1	1	1	1	1	1	1	1	1	1	1	1	5	5	5	5	5	1	1
9 RÄIKKÖNEN	6	6	1	1	1	1	1	1	1	1	1	1	1	1	1	1	1	1	1	1	1	1	3	5	5	3	6	6	6	6	6	6	6	6	6	6	6	6	6	6	6	6	6	6	6	6	6	6	6	6	6	6	6	6	6
15 KLIEN	3	3	3	3	3	3	3	3	3	3	3	3	3	3	3	3	3	3	3	3	3	3	3	3	3	5	15	17	6	4	4	4	4	4	4	4	4	4	4	4	4	3	3	3	3	3	2	2	2	2	2	3	3	3	3
1 M. SCHUMACHER	15	15	15	15	15	15	15	15	15	15	15	15	15	15	15	15	15	15	15	15	15	15	15	15	15	15	6	17	17	3	3	3	3	3	3	3	3	3	2	2	2	2	2	3	3	3	3	3	3	3	3	15	15	17	17
12 MASSA	2	2	2	2	2	2	2	2	2	2	2	2	2	2	2	2	2	2	2	2	2	2	2	6	4	4	16	16	16	16	16	2	2	2	15	15	15	15	15	15	15	15	15	15	15	15	15	15	17	17	17	15	2		
2 BARRICHELLO	17	17	17	17	17	17	17	17	17	17	17	17	17	17	17	17	17	17	17	17	17	4	16	16	2	2	2	2	16	15	15	15	15	17	17	17	17	17	17	17	17	17	17	17	17	17	17	17	2	2	2	2	15		
17 R. SCHUMACHER	12	12	12	12	12	12	12	12	12	12	12	12	12	12	12	12	12	12	12	12	4	4	4	4	16	2	15	15	15	15	17	17	17	17	4	4	4	4	4	4	4	4	4	4	4	4	4	4	4	4	4	4	4		
18 MONTEIRO	4	4	4	4	4	4	4	4	4	4	4	4	4	4	4	4	16	16	16	16	2	15	15	17	17	17	17	17	11	11	16	16	16	16	16	16	16	16	16	16	16	16	16	16	16	16	16	16	11	11	11	12			
7 WEBBER	19	19	19	19	19	19	19	19	19	19	19	19	19	19	19	21	21	11	11	11	11	11	11	11	11	11	11	11	11	11	11	11	11	11	11	11	11	11	11	11	11	11	11	11	16	12	11								
8 PIZZONIA	7	21	16	16	16	16	16	16	16	16	16	16	16	16	16	19	20	20	20	12	12	12	11	11	11	11	11	11	12	12	12	12	12	12	12	12	12	12	12	12	12	12	12	12	12										
14 COULTHARD	21	16	21	21	21	21	21	21	21	21	21	21	21	21	21	20	11	12	12	20	21	21	21	21	21	21	21	21	21	21	21	21	21	21	21	21	21	21	21	18	18	18	18	18	18	18	18								
19 KARTHIKEYAN	16	20	20	20	20	20	20	20	20	20	20	20	20	20	20	11	12	18	18	18	18	18	18	18	18	18	18	18	18	18	18	18	18	18	18	18	18	18	18	21	21	21	21	21	21	21	21								
21 ALBERS	20	11	11	11	11	11	11	11	11	11	11	11	11	11	11	18	18	21	21	21	20	20	20	20	20	20	20	20	20	19	19	19	19	19	19	19	19	19	19	19	19	19	19	19	19	19	19								
16 TRULLI	11	18	18	18	18	18	18	18	18	18	18	18	18	18	18	16	19	19	19	19	19	19	19	19	19	19	19	19	20	7	7	7	7	7	7	7	7	7	7																
20 DOORNBOS	18	7	7	7	7	7	7	7	7	7	7	7	7	7	7	7	7	7	7	7	7	7	7	7	7	7	7	7	7																										
4 SATO																																																							
11 VILLENEUVE																																																							

Pit stop
One lap or more behind leader

QUALIFYING

WEATHER: Dry (track 33–34°C, air 24–26°C)

Pos.	Driver	R/Order	Sector 1	Sector 2	Sector 3	Time
1	Fernando Alonso	19	18.231s	36.724s	17.033s	1m 11.988s
2	Juan Pablo Montoya	7	18.323s	36.799s	17.023s	1m 12.145s
3	Giancarlo Fisichella	1	18.422s	37.109s	17.027s	1m 12.558s
4	Jenson Button	18	18.414s	36.950s	17.303s	1m 12.696s
5	Kimi Räikkönen	20	18.940s	36.790s	17.051s	1m 12.781s
6	Christian Klien	12	18.432s	37.193s	17.264s	1m 12.889s
7	Michael Schumacher	3	18.339s	37.367s	17.187s	1m 12.976s
8	Jarno Trulli	5	18.573s	37.184s	17.284s	1m 13.041s
9	Felipe Massa	11	18.534s	37.229s	17.248s	1m 13.151s
10	Rubens Barrichello	16	18.414s	37.450s	17.319s	1m 13.183s
11	Ralf Schumacher	14	18.670s	37.304s	17.311s	1m 13.285s
12	Jacques Villeneuve	15	18.634s	37.313s	17.425s	1m 13.372s
13	Tiago Monteiro	13	18.809s	37.264s	17.314s	1m 13.387s
14	Mark Webber	17	18.761s	37.450s	17.327s	1m 13.538s
15	Antonio Pizzonia	6	18.587s	37.805s	17.189s	1m 13.581s
16	David Coulthard	4	18.677s	37.777s	17.390s	1m 13.844s
17	Narain Karthikeyan	10	18.941s	38.077s	17.502s	1m 14.520s
18	Christijan Albers	9	18.923s	38.329s	17.511s	1m 14.763s
19	Takuma Sato	2	-	-	-	No time
20	Robert Doornbos	8	-	-	-	No time

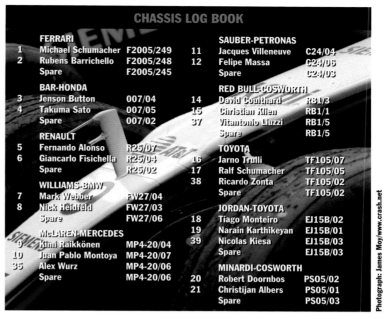

CHASSIS LOG BOOK

FERRARI
1	Michael Schumacher	F2005/249
2	Rubens Barrichello	F2005/248
	Spare	F2005/245

BAR-HONDA
3	Jenson Button	007/04
4	Takuma Sato	007/05
	Spare	007/02

RENAULT
5	Fernando Alonso	R25/07
6	Giancarlo Fisichella	R25/04
	Spare	R25/02

WILLIAMS-BMW
7	Mark Webber	FW27/04
8	Nick Heidfeld	FW27/03
	Spare	FW27/06

McLAREN-MERCEDES
9	Kimi Räikkönen	MP4-20/04
10	Juan Pablo Montoya	MP4-20/07
35	Alex Wurz	MP4-20/06
	Spare	MP4-20/06

SAUBER-PETRONAS
11	Jacques Villeneuve	C24/04
12	Felipe Massa	C24/06
	Spare	C24/03

RED BULL-COSWORTH
14	David Coulthard	RB1/3
15	Christian Klien	RB1/1
37	Vitantonio Liuzzi	RB1/5
	Spare	RB1/5

TOYOTA
16	Jarno Trulli	TF105/07
17	Ralf Schumacher	TF105/05
38	Ricardo Zonta	TF105/02
	Spare	TF105/02

JORDAN-TOYOTA
18	Tiago Monteiro	EJ15B/02
19	Narain Karthikeyan	EJ15B/01
39	Nicolas Kiesa	EJ15B/03
	Spare	EJ15B/03

MINARDI-COSWORTH
20	Robert Doornbos	PS05/02
21	Christijan Albers	PS05/01
	Spare	PS05/03

PRACTICE 1 (FRIDAY)

Scattered cloud/cloudy (track 30–34°C, air 23–24°C)

Pos.	Driver	Laps	Time
1	Alex Wurz	25	1m 11.701s
2	Takuma Sato	17	1m 12.738s
3	Fernando Alonso	10	1m 12.782s
4	Jenson Button	12	1m 12.918s
5	Kimi Räikkönen	7	1m 13.055s
6	Giancarlo Fisichella	10	1m 13.094s
7	Juan Pablo Montoya	6	1m 13.256s
8	Antonio Pizzonia	4	1m 13.427s
9	Mark Webber	4	1m 13.509s
10	Ricardo Zonta	31	1m 13.573s
11	Ralf Schumacher	6	1m 13.788s
12	Michael Schumacher	10	1m 14.154s
13	Rubens Barrichello	10	1m 14.282s
14	Christian Klien	7	1m 14.468s
15	Jarno Trulli	6	1m 14.504s
16	David Coulthard	7	1m 14.724s
17	Vitantonio Liuzzi	28	1m 14.842s
18	Jacques Villeneuve	14	1m 15.211s
19	Narain Karthikeyan	14	1m 16.230s
20	Tiago Monteiro	15	1m 16.230s
21	Nicolas Kiesa	23	1m 16.351s
22	Robert Doornbos	12	1m 16.769s
23	Christijan Albers	8	1m 17.180s
24	Felipe Massa	5	No time

PRACTICE 2 (FRIDAY)

Scattered cloud/cloudy (track 30–32°C, air 22–23°C)

Pos.	Driver	Laps	Time
1	Alex Wurz	38	1m 12.083s
2	Juan Pablo Montoya	13	1m 12.694s
3	Ricardo Zonta	36	1m 12.708s
4	Felipe Massa	28	1m 12.710s
5	Rubens Barrichello	21	1m 13.088s
6	Kimi Räikkönen	18	1m 13.172s
7	Jacques Villeneuve	21	1m 13.202s
8	Michael Schumacher	24	1m 13.205s
9	Jarno Trulli	26	1m 13.493s
10	Giancarlo Fisichella	29	1m 13.518s
11	Fernando Alonso	29	1m 13.545s
12	Mark Webber	18	1m 13.650s
13	Antonio Pizzonia	19	1m 13.828s
14	Robert Doornbos	28	1m 13.922s
15	David Coulthard	22	1m 14.006s
16	Vitantonio Liuzzi	29	1m 14.141s
17	Jenson Button	26	1m 14.189s
18	Ralf Schumacher	20	1m 14.427s
19	Christijan Albers	23	1m 14.563s
20	Takuma Sato	27	1m 14.584s
21	Tiago Monteiro	22	1m 14.671s
22	Christian Klien	7	1m 14.698s
23	Nicolas Kiesa	25	1m 15.094s
24	Narain Karthikeyan	19	1m 15.187s

PRACTICE 3 (SATURDAY)

Cloudy/sunny (track 25–26°C, air 22–23°C)

Pos.	Driver	Laps	Time
1	Fernando Alonso	7	1m 12.738s
2	Giancarlo Fisichella	9	1m 12.789s
3	Juan Pablo Montoya	10	1m 13.050s
4	Kimi Räikkönen	6	1m 13.088s
5	Jenson Button	9	1m 13.186s
6	Rubens Barrichello	8	1m 13.529s
7	Antonio Pizzonia	8	1m 13.795s
8	Jarno Trulli	12	1m 13.869s
9	Ralf Schumacher	9	1m 13.908s
10	Michael Schumacher	8	1m 13.952s
11	Takuma Sato	9	1m 14.042s
12	Christian Klien	12	1m 14.051s
13	Mark Webber	8	1m 14.112s
14	Felipe Massa	8	1m 14.255s
15	David Coulthard	5	1m 14.401s
16	Jacques Villeneuve	11	1m 14.479s
17	Tiago Monteiro	11	1m 14.851s
18	Narain Karthikeyan	9	1m 15.252s
19	Robert Doornbos	8	1m 15.772s
20	Christijan Albers	13	1m 15.815s

PRACTICE 4 (SATURDAY)

Cloudy (track 33–34°C, air 24–26°C)

Pos.	Driver	Laps	Time
1	Kimi Räikkönen	11	1m 11.929s
2	Fernando Alonso	13	1m 12.110s
3	Jenson Button	14	1m 12.148s
4	Giancarlo Fisichella	13	1m 12.158s
5	Juan Pablo Montoya	11	1m 12.292s
6	Rubens Barrichello	10	1m 12.382s
7	Michael Schumacher	15	1m 12.453s
8	Ralf Schumacher	18	1m 12.509s
9	Antonio Pizzonia	10	1m 12.752s
10	Felipe Massa	11	1m 12.799s
11	Christian Klien	12	1m 12.811s
12	David Coulthard	14	1m 13.199s
13	Jarno Trulli	14	1m 13.222s
14	Narain Karthikeyan	8	1m 13.242s
15	Tiago Monteiro	18	1m 13.305s
16	Jacques Villeneuve	18	1m 13.508s
17	Takuma Sato	5	1m 13.817s
18	Christijan Albers	16	1m 14.012s
19	Mark Webber	9	1m 14.114s
20	Robert Doornbos	17	1m 14.595s

9th: BARRICHELLO Ferrari

7th: M. SCHUMACHER Ferrari

5th: RÄIKKÖNEN McLaren-Mercedes

3rd: FISICHELLA Renault

Pole: ALONSO Renault

10th: R. SCHUMACHER Toyota

8th: MASSA Sauber-Petronas

6th: KLIEN Red Bull-Cosworth

4th: BUTTON BAR-Honda

2nd: MONTOYA McLaren-Mercedes

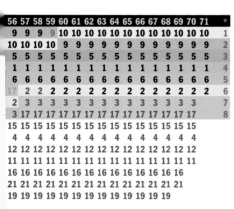

56	57	58	59	60	61	62	63	64	65	66	67	68	69	70	71	
9	9	9	9	10	10	10	10	10	10	10	10	10	10	10	10	1
10	10	10	10	9	9	9	9	9	9	9	9	9	9	9	9	2
5	5	5	5	5	5	5	5	5	5	5	5	5	5	5	5	3
1	1	1	1	1	1	1	1	1	1	1	1	1	1	1	1	4
6	6	6	6	6	6	6	6	6	6	6	6	6	6	6	6	5
2	2	2	2	2	2	2	2	2	2	2	2	2	2	2	2	6
3	3	3	3	3	3	3	3	3	3	3	3	3	3	3	3	7
3	17	17	17	17	17	17	17	17	17	17	17	17	17	17		8
15	15	15	15	15	15	15	15	15	15	15	15	15				
4	4	4	4	4	4	4	4	4	4	4	4	4	4			
12	12	12	12	12	12	12	12	12	12	12	12	12	12			
11	11	11	11	11	11	11	11	11	11	11	11					
16	16	16	16	16	16	16	16	16	16	16	16					
21	21	21	21	21	21	21	21	21	21	21	21	21				
19	19	19	19	19	19	19	19	19	19	19	19	19				

FOR THE RECORD

50th GRAND PRIX START:
Felipe Massa

POINTS

DRIVERS
1	Fernando Alonso	117
2	Kimi Räikkönen	94
3	Michael Schumacher	60
4	Juan Pablo Montoya	60
5	Giancarlo Fisichella	45
6	Jarno Trulli	43
7	Ralf Schumacher	38
8	Rubens Barrichello	38
9	Jenson Button	32
10	Mark Webber	29
11	Nick Heidfeld	28
12	David Coulthard	21
13	Jacques Villeneuve	9
14	Felipe Massa	8
15	Tiago Monteiro	7
16	Alex Wurz	6
17	Narain Karthikeyan	5
18	Christian Klien	5
19	Christijan Albers	4
20	Pedro de la Rosa	4
21	Patrick Friesacher	3
22	Antonio Pizzonia	2
23	Takuma Sato	1
24	Vitantonio Liuzzi	1

CONSTRUCTORS
1	McLaren	164
2	Renault	162
3	Ferrari	98
4	Toyota	81
5	Williams	59
6	BAR	33
7	Red Bull	27
8	Sauber	17
9	Jordan	11
10	Minardi	7

SUZUKA

GP

FIA F1 WORLD CHAMPIONSHIP/ROUND 18

The defining moment at Suzuka: Kimi Räikkönen launched his McLaren MP40-20 down the outside of Giancarlo Fisichella's Renault R25 to grab the lead going into the final lap of the race.
Photograph: Laurent Charniaux/WRI

The previous year it was the threat of a typhoon that had everyone talking at Suzuka, but this season all it took to set up a fantastic Japanese Grand Prix was some timely rain, which turned everything on its head.

At the end of qualifying Ralf Schumacher was on pole position and, since he was driving for the Japanese Toyota team, that was sufficient to make the encouragingly large crowd very happy. F1 is on the rise again in Japan and the crowd had even more to cheer when Jenson Button parked his BAR-Honda on the other front-row slot. Ralf Schumacher had run at the halfway mark and lapped the damp circuit in 1m 46.106s and the Englishman's lap took fractionally longer in 1m 46.141s, moments after Schumacher Jr had run.

The only time that Toyota had previously sat on pole was courtesy of Jarno Trulli at Indianapolis. That was a clear bit of window-dressing based on Toyota's knowledge that it would not be racing on the Sunday. Accordingly, Trulli's fuel tank was almost empty. So this time, it would transpire, was Schumacher's. He would run only 13 laps in the race before refuelling – and six of those would be behind the safety car. Button's performance was more kosher. Clearly, however, he too owed much to the shower of rain that fell right after Giancarlo Fisichella had pushed his Renault around in 1m 46.276s to take third spot. The Italian was the last man able to run intermediate tyres, before the wet track became suddenly saturated.

By that point all but the top four drivers in the championship had made their qualifying runs: Michael Schumacher, Fernando Alonso, Kimi Räikkönen and Juan Pablo Montoya were due to go in that order after the finishing positions in Brazil.

All around his lap, Michael Schumacher's Ferrari threw up a big rooster-tail and the outgoing champion lost a great deal of time at the hairpin on his way to 1m 52.676s. The fact that Fisichella had lapped six seconds faster only moments earlier was a graphic illustration of just how much conditions had deteriorated. Alonso fared even worse, struggling in worsening rain to 1m 54.667s.

Then Räikkönen did 2m 2.309s, but he was the least concerned because he already faced a ten-grid-place penalty after

yet another Mercedes-Benz engine failure on Friday. This time it was some sort of catastrophic bottom-end breakage. Montoya, the victor at Interlagos, received the cruellest reward for that success – the conditions were simply dire by the time he left the pits. He had nothing to lose or gain and pitted to save his engine.

All of this was excellent news for Christian Klien and Red Bull. Fresh from qualifying sixth in Brazil the Austrian wheeled his Red Bull RB1 around in 1m 46.464s, dislodging local hero Takuma Sato, who only moments earlier had set the fastest time thus far in the session with 1m 46.841s to delight his countrymen. David Coulthard, who had set the pace as the first man out, lined up sixth for Red Bull on 1m 46.892s.

Mark Webber was as fast as ever at Suzuka on his way to 1m 47.233s for BMW Williams, setting the fastest sector-one time up to that point. Jacques Villeneuve admitted that he was surprised to take eighth in his Sauber Petronas with 1m 47.440s despite coping with serious oversteer. Team-mate Felipe Massa had the opposite problem with massive understeer on his C24, but the Brazilian's 1m 48.278s held up for 10th. They were split by Rubens Barrichello, who lapped his Ferrari in 1m 48.248s.

Narain Karthikeyan had starred in wet morning practice and had actually been fastest when he took the chequered flag, only to have his time subsequently bettered by Fisichella. Now he continued that form, albeit with a light fuel load, to take 11th place for Jordan Toyota with 1m 48.718s, sharing row six with Antonio Pizzonia, who lapped his BMW Williams in 1m 48.898s. The BMW Williams driver was lucky to get away with a spin at Degner Two on his out lap.

Christijan Albers placed his Minardi PS05 a very good 13th on 1m 50.843s, which put him on row seven with Schumacher Sr. Robert Doornbos was two seconds slower than Albers but lined up 15th alongside Alonso. Räikkönen and Montoya shared row nine after catching what passed as a break in the circumstances when slippery Degner Two proved the undoing of Jarno Trulli and Tiago Monteiro. The Italian was going well when he spun his Toyota there and Monteiro fell victim to the surface there on his out lap. Trulli lined up 19th, Monteiro 20th.

I T began with both McLarens at the back of the grid and ended with Kimi Räikkönen winning on the last lap and team chairman Ron Dennis crying racer's tears. Small wonder that the Japanese Grand Prix was hailed as the race of the century.

It was, without doubt, the greatest victory of the Finn's burgeoning career and it came against all odds after his problems in qualifying. Yet it could have ended for him on the opening lap courtesy of his own team-mate, Juan Pablo Montoya.

Following the rain that had spoiled things for the top four championship runners during qualifying – leaving Michael Schumacher, Fernando Alonso and the two McLaren drivers down the back of the grid – the opening lap was always going to be tense. Ralf Schumacher led away from pole ahead of fast-starting Giancarlo Fisichella and Jenson Button, with Mark Webber making short work of Christian Klien to chase after fourth-placed David Coulthard.

Farther back there was mayhem as the four fast guys started carving their way through the rabbits. 'There was quite a lot happening,' Räikkönen said, after a brush with Montoya left him 12th at the end of the lap. 'I was turning in and Montoya touched my rear wheel and I got sideways and he went by me. Luckily we did not damage the cars.'

It did not take Montoya long to change that. At the chicane he tried to go around the outside of Jacques Villeneuve's ninth-placed Sauber and succeeded only in putting himself into a gap that had disappeared by the time he got there. The result was his McLaren's slithering onto the grass and into the tyre wall at very high speed. The left-rear wheel was torn off and wreckage strewn everywhere quickly prompted deployment of the safety car. Unfathomably, the race stewards later gave Villeneuve a post-race 25s penalty, even though he had

been ahead of Montoya throughout the incident.

While the debris was cleared away, the safety car trundled around. Toyota's game plan was already ruined, for Ralf Schumacher's hopes of sprinting away were well and truly damned – not that anyone outside the team really thought they were feasible in the first place. The track went green again on the eighth lap and Ralf gamely tried to open a gap as Button moved in on Fisichella.

Meanwhile, a feisty drive from Michael Schumacher had already enabled him to catch and pass Klien for sixth and Alonso had also moved ahead of the Austrian. However, in doing so the Spaniard had cut the chicane. He clearly slowed and let Klien repass him, before repassing Klien after the start-finish line. This was not good enough for the stewards, who informed Renault that Alonso had to let Klien by again. Just as Alonso did this, they said that he didn't have to do it, after all. This nonsense cost Alonso seven seconds and, Renault was adamant, that was instrumental in his being in the wrong place later on and thus losing his own chance of winning.

The upshot was that by lap 13 the order was Ralf Schumacher, Fisichella and Button, then a gap to Coulthard and Webber, with Schumacher Jr under serious threat from Alonso. Behind them, Räikkönen was sizing up Klien. It was the lap on which Toyota's publicity stunt was exposed as Ralf swept in for the first of three refuelling stops, and now the fight for the lead was between Fisichella and Button, with the Italian seeming in clear control. Behind them, the duel between Michael Schumacher and Alonso was simply electrifying.

Lap after lap Schumacher drove the wheels off his Ferrari to keep the Spaniard's faster car behind – and Kimi's, too, after Räikkönen jumped Klien on lap 14. Eventually, however, on lap 20, Alonso pulled a brilliant move on the former champion in

Above: What was he doing? Takuma Sato got himself excluded from the results after this heavy-handed collision with Jarno Trulli's Toyota.

Bottom left: Ralf Schumacher qualified on pole with his Toyota TF105B but his planned three-stop strategy was ruined by the early deployment of the safety car.

Top left: It was a sunny day by the time of the driver parade.

Above centre: Takuma Sato's BAR mechanics dressed up suitably for the occasion.

Bottom centre: Jarno Trulli also had a new livery on his headgear in practice.
Photographs: James Moy/www.crash.net

the entry to the notorious 130R corner. Moving up on the outside he cut neatly back across the Ferrari's nose, entering this most challenging corner at 206 mph and with 4.5g. It was fantastic stuff. Räikkönen was unable to follow suit at this stage – possibly because he was carrying a fair bit more fuel than Alonso.

Fisichella refuelled on lap 20, followed by leader Button and Alonso on lap 22 and new leader Coulthard and Webber on 23. By now Räikkönen was all over Michael Schumacher and clearly being held up, but this was Michael at his old best. Both of them pitted on lap 26 and when they rejoined Schumacher was still in front, though the overall order had shuffled again to Fisichella, Ralf Schumacher, Button, Webber, Schumacher Sr and Räikkönen, then Coulthard and Alonso, who had seriously lost out and had it all to do all over again.

On lap 30 it was Räikkönen's turn to make a superb passing move on Michael Schumacher by dragging up behind him down the pit straight and then, when Schumacher again defended the inside line, going around the outside of the Ferrari in Turn One. Räikkönen immediately set off after Webber and Button, who were now chasing leader Fisichella. Two laps later Alonso also swept by Schumacher Sr, going into the first corner.

The final drama was set up when Fisichella refuelled for the second time, on lap 38. That briefly put Button in the lead again from Webber, until they too refuelled on lap 41. Now Räikkönen finally had the lead, but he still had to refuel again. He did so on lap 45, three laps after Schumacher Sr had refuelled the Ferrari.

With only eight laps left, Fisichella appeared to have the race in the bag, holding a lead of 5.4s. But Räikkönen was far from done. A lap later he had slashed the deficit to 4.3s, another lap later to 3s, then 1.8s and the writing was on the wall. By lap 50, with three to run, the McLaren was only half a second behind the Renault. It stayed there for two more laps; the gap between the two cars was officially given as two-tenths and then only one.

Going into the final lap, Fisichella was too cautious in the chicane and Räikkönen got a run on him all down the pit straight. As they approached the braking area for Turn One, he was wheel-to-wheel with the hapless Italian and in a piece of totally committed racing he jinked around the outside of the Renault and into the lead. It was a classic demonstration of the real art of GP driving. Though there was traffic farther around the lap, which might have given him the chance to counterattack, Fisichella gave up and finished 1.633s adrift of his conqueror, and the race of the century was over. On the pit wall, Dennis had tears in his eyes as the excitement pushed everyone to fever pitch.

'I think it is one of the best for sure,' Räikkönen said of his victory, 'because I really had to fight for it and, after all the problems we had this weekend, it was very nice. There was a lot happening in the race all the time. When I came up behind Fisichella I was thinking which way I should go. Of course at the inside it is easier to overtake, but Fisichella went to the inside so I didn't have much choice but to go around the outside.'

The result certainly seemed to put a question mark over Fisichella's future because he lost what had at one time been a lead of 19 seconds. Team principal Flavio Briatore is not a man to tolerate such disappointment. 'He was just quicker than me on the straight,' Fisichella said lamely. 'I did my best but unfortunately I always try to keep my position but I could see there was the possibility of a collision.'

Some 16 seconds farther back, Alonso completed his remarkable race with third place after an equally impressive overtaking move on Mark Webber in the first corner, depriving the Australian of what should have been a podium position for BMW Williams.

'In the final laps I just couldn't keep him behind me,' Webber admitted and it was common knowledge that he had resisted a BMW order to turn down his engine for four laps before finally complying. He was not a happy man afterwards. Nevertheless he beat Button and BAR Honda fair and square as the

Englishman's car was again found wanting and lost its handling edge as the race progressed. Initially Button could stay with Fisichella, who had passed him at the start, but then his fuel flap failed to open during his refuelling stop on lap 22, which cost him six seconds because the team had to open the flap manually. Later, he lost another place to Webber in his second stop. The irony of the result was certainly not lost on Sir Frank Williams.

All that Michael Schumacher got for an afternoon on which he reminded everyone that his fire still burns was a paltry seventh place and the knowledge that he had squeezed every ounce of performance from his mount. He found the F2005 less competitive than it had been in Brazil and lost a place during his second pit stop when he asked for adjustments to improve the handling balance. But, if nothing else, the result secured third place for the team overall.

Rubens Barrichello had an off-track moment in the first corner on lap one and punctured his left-rear tyre after clobbering the right-front wheel of Takuma Sato's BAR as they headed for the gravel in separate incidents. That necessitated a slow lap for the Brazilian and a pit stop, and after the safety car was deployed Ferrari switched him to a single-stop strategy. By then he had lost too much time to make up any ground.

Ahead of Michael Schumacher, Coulthard was a disappointed sixth after losing his own hopes of a podium during his first refuelling stop, when Webber had jumped him. After that the extra fuel load upset the RB1's balance and the Scot began to lose ground. However, his three points for sixth place ensured that Peter Sauber's team could not realistically overhaul Red Bull Racing for seventh overall. Once again, Christian Klien's strong qualifying performance did not convert to a points finish and he had to be content with ninth place.

It was not a great race for Toyota, either, after Schumacher Jr's start from pole. The safety car prevented him from opening up the gap he needed to make a three-stop strategy work and cost him any chance of a decent finish. The team had to be content with just one more point, rather than the third or fourth place it had hoped for, and tempers were frayed after Takuma Sato's ill-judged overtaking attempt on Jarno Trulli wrecked Trulli's Toyota in the chicane on lap nine.

The Japanese driver had pitted for repairs after his first-corner gaffe and dropped to last. His error with Trulli merely compounded his recent run of mistakes and, having stopped again for a new nose and soldiered home 13th, he was excluded from the results by the stewards who, like everyone else, were getting tired of his antics.

Sauber Petronas was disappointed with the slow performance of its C24s. The cars were well balanced and after the safety-car deployment the team hedged its bets, with Felipe Massa's staying on a two-stop strategy and Jacques Villeneuve's switching to one stop. But the fact that they finished less than a second apart suggested that, whatever they did, 10th and 11th places were the best they could have hoped for. When Villeneuve's 25-second penalty was applied, he dropped to 12th behind Barrichello.

Tiago Monteiro took an undramatic (and corrected) 13th place for Jordan, but Narain Karthikeyan suffered a late stop on lap 43 to change the right-front tyre after flat-spotting it and thus dropped back to finish a corrected 15th. Minardi's Robert Doornbos had a good scrap with the Indian and was pleased with his race, but Christijan Albers lost time in his second pit stop on lap 34 after overshooting his stop marks. That led to a problem refuelling and a brief fire. He recovered to finish 16th and last.

The sensational race left everyone in the paddock buzzing and confirmed Räikkönen and Alonso as worthy pretenders to Schumacher's mantle as the best in the game. Somewhat overshadowed by the drama, Renault's haul of 14 points helped it to regain the constructors'-championship lead that it had lost to McLaren in Brazil. The two thus headed for the showdown in China separated by only two points.

David Tremayne

DIARY

Honda announces that it will buy out British American Tobacco's remaining 55-percent stake in the BAR Honda F1 team by 31 December, 2005, having acquired a 45-percent share-holding in 2004.

At the Bonneville Salt Flats in Utah, BAR Honda's Bonneville 400 attempt to reach 400 km/h (250 mph) in an F1 car is dealt a blow when rainstorms flood the course and prompt postponement until July 2006.

Plans to run a second Japanese F1 race in 2006, at Toyota's Fuji International Speedway, stumble, allegedly because the motor giant refuses to sign up to Bernie Ecclestone's 2008 Concorde Agreement.

Sauber Petronas's former race engineer-turned-head of vehicle engineering, Jacky Eeckelaert, leaves the team to take up a similar role with BAR Honda.

Top left: Michael Schumacher gave maximum effort as usual while Kimi Räikkönen loomed large in his mirrors.
Photograph: James Moy/www.crash.net

Left: David Coulthard added to Red Bull's tally of points once again.
Photograph: James Moy/www.crash.net

Right: **Even McLaren chairman Ron Dennis couldn't help but smile after McLaren's dramatic win.**
Photograph: Russell Batchelor/XPB.cc

Far right: **Fisichella looked shell-shocked as he stood on the podium alongside winner Kimi Räikkönen, whose trace of a smile revealed his genuine satisfaction with a job well done.**
Photograph: Paul-Henri Cahier

Below: **Takuma Sato fans turned out in their thousands to support their man.**

Below right: **Sato had a simply disastrous race in front of his huge fan base.**

Below far right: **Mark Webber had a promising and energetic race in the Williams FW27, proving a tough nut to overtake.**
Photographs: James Moy/www.crash.net

SATO'S B-TEAM MOVE

Speculation was rife in the paddock all weekend about the identity of the second team that Honda said it planned to set up in order to secure a drive for Takuma Sato, who would be dropped at the end of the season by BAR Honda in favour of Rubens Barrichello.

Honda confirmed earlier in the week that it would supply its forthcoming V8 engines to a second team. The favourite initially was the Dome Company, which manufactures Formula 3 cars and racing sports cars, but it was soon discounted after founder Minoru Hayashi and technical director Akiyoshi Okuto issued firm denials on the Thursday. Other candidates, as the paddock detectives got on the case, were former F1 racer Jean Alesi or IRL team owner Michael Andretti. Later the focus turned to the Japanese Super Aguri team, run by former Zakspeed, Larrousse and Footwork F1 racer Aguri Suzuki.

According to the stories, Suzuki would run BAR refugee Sato and the team's test driver Anthony Davidson, who was busily exploring avenues for a race seat with Williams, BMW and Jordan. The two drivers were paired together at Carlin Motorsport in their Formula 3 days in England in 2001. The team would be based in Brackley, near BAR Honda's factory.

At the same time, talk of a McLaren B-team also resurfaced and Alesi was also linked with overseeing an operation out of McLaren's old Albert Road factory in Woking.

'McLaren Racing is one company in a group of companies,' responded McLaren chief Ron Dennis. 'We initiated three years ago a strategy that led to the birth of McLaren Applied Technologies and this is a company that looks at the intellectual property that is emerging out of all the group companies and looks at whether we can turn that intellectual property into a moneymaking business strategy.'

So did this mean the project was still alive and was there a deadline of 22 October for a decision, as the rumours for some reason suggested?

'It means it is constantly under review and we are going through a period at the moment of evaluating another option that was presented to us over the past few months,' said Dennis.

More manufacturer-supported teams would give the so-called rebel teams a stronger hand in the ongoing war with Bernie Ecclestone's group – Ferrari, Jordan, Red Bull and Red Bull Junior (formerly Minardi) – which had already signed up to the new Concorde Agreement, which will take effect from 2008.

FIA F1 WORLD CHAMPIONSHIP · ROUND 18

SUZUKA JAPANESE GRAND PRIX

SUZUKA 7–9 OCTOBER 2005

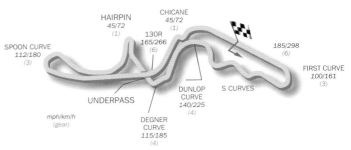

SUZUKA RACING CIRCUIT

HAIRPIN 45/72 (1)
CHICANE 45/72 (1)
130R 165/266 (6)
SPOON CURVE 112/180 (3)
185/298 (6)
FIRST CURVE 100/161 (3)
UNDERPASS
DUNLOP CURVE 140/225 (4)
S CURVES
DEGNER CURVE 115/185 (4)
mph/km/h (gear)

CIRCUIT LENGTH: 3.629 miles/5.807 km

RACE DISTANCE: 53 laps, 191.126 miles /307.573 km   **RACE WEATHER:** Scattered cloud but sunny (track 38–39°C, air 27–29°C)

Pos.	Driver	Nat.	No.	Entrant	Car/Engine	Tyres	Laps	Time/Retirement	Speed (mph/km/h)	Gap to leader	Fastest race lap	
1	Kimi Räikkönen	FIN	9	Team McLaren Mercedes	McLaren MP4-20-Mercedes F0 110R V10	M	53	1h 29m 02.212s	128.799/207.277		1m 31.540s	44
2	Giancarlo Fisichella	I	6	Mild Seven Renault F1 Team	Renault R25-RS25 V10	M	53	1h 29m 03.845s	128.753/207.203	+1.633s	1m 32.522s	19
3	Fernando Alonso	E	5	Mild Seven Renault F1 Team	Renault R25-RS25 V10	M	53	1h 29m 19.668s	128.373/206.591	+17.456s	1m 31.599s	21
4	Mark Webber	AUS	7	BMW WilliamsF1 Team	Williams FW27-BMW P84/85 V10	M	53	1h 29m 24.486s	128.258/206.406	+22.274s	1m 33.022s	21
5	Jenson Button	GB	3	Lucky Strike BAR Honda	BAR 007-Honda RA005E V10	M	53	1h 29m 31.719s	128.085/206.128	+29.507s	1m 32.754s	19
6	David Coulthard	GB	14	Red Bull Racing	Red Bull RB1-Cosworth TJ2005/12 V10	M	53	1h 29m 33.813s	128.035/206.047	+31.601s	1m 33.023s	18
7	Michael Schumacher	D	1	Scuderia Ferrari Marlboro	Ferrari F2005-055 V10	B	53	1h 29m 36.091s	127.981/205.960	+33.879s	1m 32.763s	25
8	Ralf Schumacher	D	17	Panasonic Toyota Racing	Toyota TF105B-RVX-05 V10	M	53	1h 29m 51.760s	127.609/205.362	+49.548s	1m 32.795s	9
9	Christian Klien	A	15	Red Bull Racing	Red Bull RB1-Cosworth TJ2005/12 V10	M	53	1h 29m 54.137s	127.553/205.271	+51.925s	1m 33.499s	49
10	Felipe Massa	BR	12	Sauber Petronas	Sauber C24-Petronas 05A V10	M	53	1h 29m 59.721s	127.421/205.059	+57.509s	1m 33.232s	43
11	Rubens Barrichello	BR	2	Scuderia Ferrari Marlboro	Ferrari F2005-055 V10	B	53	1h 30m 02.845s	127.347/204.940	+60.633s	1m 33.133s	52
12	Jacques Villeneuve	CDN	11	Sauber Petronas	Sauber C24-Petronas 05A V10	M	53	1h 30m 25.433s	126.817/204.087	+83.221s	1m 33.288s	50
13	Tiago Monteiro	P	20	Jordan Toyota	Jordan EJ15B-Toyota RVX-05 V10	B	52			+1 lap	1m 35.458s	17
14	Robert Doornbos	NL	18	Minardi Cosworth	Minardi PS05-Cosworth TJ2005 V!0	B	51			+2 laps	1m 36.574s	50
15	Narain Karthikeyan	IND	19	Jordan Toyota	Jordan EJ15B-Toyota RVX-05 V10	B	51			+2 laps	1m 35.887s	11
16	Christijan Albers	NL	21	Minardi Cosworth	Minardi PS05-Cosworth TJ2005 V10	B	49			+4 laps	1m 36.039s	33
	Antonio Pizzonia	BR	8	BMW Williams F1 Team	Williams FW27-BMW P84/85 V10	M	9	Spin		DNF	1m 36.711s	9
	Jarno Trulli	I	16	Scuderia Ferrari Marlboro	Toyota TF105B-RVX-05 V10	M	9	Collision		DNF	1m 57.444s	10
	Juan Pablo Montoya	COL	10	Team McLaren Mercedes	McLaren MP4-20-Mercedes F0 110R V10	M	0	Accident		DNF		
DQ	Takuma Sato	J	4	Lucky Strike BAR Honda	BAR 007-Honda RA005E V10	M	52			+1 lap	1m 34.186s	28

Fastest lap: Kimi Räikkönen on lap 44, 1m 31.450, 228.372 km/h (lap record).

Previous lap record: Rubens Barrichello (Ferrari F2004-054 V10), 1m 32.730s, 140.082 mph/225.299 km/h (2004).

19th: TRULLI Toyota
Started from pit lane

17th: RÄIKKÖNEN McLaren-Mercedes
Ten-place penalty for engine change

15th: DOORNBOS Minardi-Cosworth

13th: ALBERS Minardi-Cosworth

11th: KARTHIKEYAN Jordan-Toyota

20th: MONTEIRO Jordan-Toyota

18th: MONTOYA McLaren-Mercedes

16th: ALONSO Renault

14th: M. SCHUMACHER Ferrari

12th: PIZZONIA Williams-BMW

Grid order	1	2	3	4	5	6	7	8	9	10	11	12	13	14	15	16	17	18	19	20	21	22	23	24	25	26	27	28	29	30	31	32	33	34	35	36	37	38	39	40	4
17 R. SCHUMACHER	17	17	17	17	17	17	17	17	17	17	17	17	6	6	6	6	6	6	6	6	3	3	14	1	1	1	6	6	6	6	6	6	6	6	6	6	6	6	3	3	9
3 BUTTON	6	6	6	6	6	6	6	6	6	6	6	6	17	3	3	3	3	3	3	14	14	7	9	9	9	17	17	3	3	3	3	3	3	3	3	3	3	7	7		
6 FISICHELLA	3	3	3	3	3	3	3	3	3	3	3	3	14	14	14	14	14	14	14	7	7	1	6	6	6	3	3	7	7	7	7	7	7	7	7	7	7	9	9		
15 KLIEN	14	14	14	14	14	14	14	14	14	14	14	14	7	7	7	7	7	7	5	5	9	17	17	17	7	7	1	9	9	9	9	9	9	9	9	9	9	6	6		
4 SATO	7	7	7	7	7	7	7	7	7	7	7	7	1	1	1	1	5	1	1	6	3	3	1	1	1	1	5	5	5	1	1	1	5	5	5	1	1	1	1		
14 COULTHARD	15	15	15	15	15	15	15	1	1	1	1	1	1	5	5	5	5	5	9	9	17	7	7	7	9	9	5	5	5	5	1	1	1	1	14	14	14	14	1		
7 WEBBER	1	1	1	1	1	1	1	15	5	5	15	15	5	9	9	9	9	9	9	6	6	3	14	14	14	14	5	14	14	14	14	14	14	14	14	17	17	17	17		
11 VILLENEUVE	5	5	5	5	5	5	5	5	15	15	5	15	15	15	15	15	15	15	15	17	11	11	11	11	5	14	17	17	17	17	17	17	17	15	5	5	5	5	5		
2 BARRICHELLO	11	11	11	11	11	11	11	11	11	11	9	9	9	9	17	17	17	17	17	17	15	12	12	5	5	11	15	15	15	15	15	15	15	15	15	15	15	15			
12 MASSA	8	8	8	8	8	8	8	8	9	11	11	11	11	11	11	11	11	11	5	5	12	15	15	4	2	2	2	12	12	12	12	12	12	12	12	12	12	12	1		
19 KARTHIKEYAN	12	12	12	12	12	12	12	9	8	12	12	12	12	12	12	12	12	12	12	15	15	14	4	2	4	12	12	12	11	11	11	11	11	11	11	11	11	11			
8 PIZZONIA	9	9	9	9	9	9	9	12	12	19	19	19	19	21	21	18	18	18	4	4	4	4	2	12	12	11	11	11	2	2	2	2	2	2	2	2	2	2			
21 ALBERS	19	19	19	19	19	19	19	19	21	21	21	21	18	18	21	4	4	4	2	2	2	2	12	15	11	4	4	4	4	4	4	4	4	4	4	4	4	4			
1 M. SCHUMACHER	21	21	21	21	21	21	21	21	21	18	18	18	20	4	2	2	2	2	18	18	18	18	18	18	18	18	18	18	18	18	18	18	18	18	18	18	18	18			
20 DOORNBOS	18	18	18	18	18	18	18	18	18	20	20	20	4	2	19	19	19	19	19	19	19	19	19	19	19	19	19	21	21	19	19	19	19	19	19	19	19	19			
5 ALONSO	4	20	20	20	20	20	20	20	20	4	4	4	2	20	19	21	21	21	21	21	21	21	21	21	21	21	21	21	20	19	19	20	20	20	20	20	20				
9 RÄIKKÖNEN	20	4	16	16	16	16	16	16	16	2	2	2	19	19	20	20	20	20	20	20	20	20	20	20	20	20	20	20	19	20	20	21	21	21	21	21	21				
10 MONTOYA	16	16	4	4	4	4	4	4	4																																
16 TRULLI	2	2	2	2	2	4	2	2	2																																
18 MONTEIRO																																									

TIME SHEETS

QUALIFYING

WEATHER: Overcast with light rain (track 23–24°C, air 22–23°C)

Pos.	Driver	R/Order	Sector 1	Sector 2	Sector 3	Time
1	Ralf Schumacher	13	37.386s	47.501s	21.209s	1m 46.106s
2	Jenson Button	14	37.680s	47.441s	21.020s	1m 46.141s
3	Giancarlo Fisichella	16	37.327s	47.610s	21.339s	1m 46.276s
4	Christian Klien	12	37.908s	47.485s	21.071s	1m 46.464s
5	Takuma Sato	11	38.042s	47.728s	21.071s	1m 46.841s
6	David Coulthard	1	38.207s	47.506s	21.179s	1m 46.892s
7	Mark Webber	4	37.558s	48.002s	21.673s	1m 47.233s
8	Jacques Villeneuve	9	37.578s	48.250s	21.612s	1m 47.440s
9	Rubens Barrichello	15	38.383s	48.146s	21.719s	1m 48.248s
10	Felipe Massa	10	38.336s	48.461s	21.481s	1m 48.278s
11	Narain Karthikeyan	6	38.688s	48.256s	21.774s	1m 48.718s
12	Antonio Pizzonia	2	38.449s	48.298s	22.151s	1m 48.898s
13	Christijan Albers	7	39.222s	49.143s	22.478s	1m 50.843s
14	Michael Schumacher	17	37.897s	49.898s	22.660s	1m 52.676s
15	Robert Doornbos	3	39.566s	50.646s	22.650s	1m 52.894s
16	Fernando Alonso	18	39.719s	50.660s	23.496s	1m 54.667s
17	Kimi Räikkönen	19	41.420s	53.157s	24.655s	2m 02.309s
18	Juan Pablo Montoya	20	-	-	-	No time
19	Jarno Trulli	8	-	-	-	No time
20	Tiago Monteiro	5	-	-	-	No time

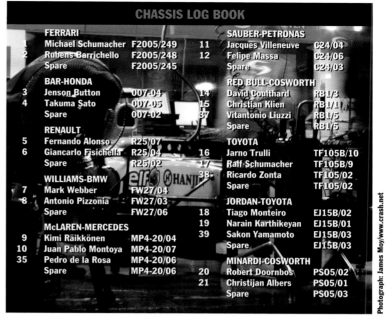

CHASSIS LOG BOOK

FERRARI			SAUBER-PETRONAS		
1	Michael Schumacher	F2005/249	11	Jacques Villeneuve	C24/04
2	Rubens Barrichello	F2005/248	12	Felipe Massa	C24/06
	Spare	F2005/245		Spare	C24/03
BAR-HONDA			**RED BULL-COSWORTH**		
3	Jenson Button	007-04	14	David Coulthard	RB1/3
4	Takuma Sato	007-05	15	Christian Klien	RB1/1
	Spare	007-02	37	Vitantonio Liuzzi	RB1/5
RENAULT				Spare	RB1/5
5	Fernando Alonso	R25/07	**TOYOTA**		
6	Giancarlo Fisichella	R25/04	16	Jarno Trulli	TF105B/10
	Spare	R25/02	17	Ralf Schumacher	TF105B/9
WILLIAMS-BMW			38	Ricardo Zonta	TF105/02
7	Mark Webber	FW27/04		Spare	TF105/02
8	Antonio Pizzonia	FW27/03	**JORDAN-TOYOTA**		
	Spare	FW27/06	18	Tiago Monteiro	EJ15B/02
McLAREN-MERCEDES			19	Narain Karthikeyan	EJ15B/01
9	Kimi Räikkönen	MP4-20/04	39	Sakon Yamamoto	EJ15B/03
10	Juan Pablo Montoya	MP4-20/07		Spare	EJ15B/03
35	Pedro de la Rosa	MP4-20/06	**MINARDI-COSWORTH**		
	Spare	MP4-20/06	20	Robert Doornbos	PS05/02
			21	Christijan Albers	PS05/01
				Spare	PS05/03

Photograph: James Moy/www.crash.net

PRACTICE 1 (FRIDAY)

Scattered cloud (track 27–31°C, air 23–26°C)

Pos.	Driver	Laps	Time
1	Pedro de la Rosa	22	1m 30.532s
2	Ricardo Zonta	16	1m 31.075s
3	Jenson Button	18	1m 32.043s
4	David Coulthard	23	1m 32.229s
5	Juan Pablo Montoya	9	1m 32.321s
6	Fernando Alonso	22	1m 32.370s
7	Giancarlo Fisichella	19	1m 32.470s
8	Takuma Sato	20	1m 32.791s
9	Mark Webber	13	1m 33.098s
10	Christian Klien	19	1m 33.139s
11	Felipe Massa	16	1m 33.257s
12	Vitantonio Liuzzi	22	1m 33.441s
13	Kimi Räikkönen	8	1m 33.486s
14	Antonio Pizzonia	22	1m 33.528s
15	Jacques Villeneuve	15	1m 33.645s
16	Rubens Barrichello	9	1m 33.700s
17	Ralf Schumacher	10	1m 33.735s
18	Michael Schumacher	9	1m 33.866s
19	Jarno Trulli	11	1m 34.535s
20	Sakon Yamamoto	23	1m 36.295s
21	Christijan Albers	16	1m 37.153s
22	Narain Karthikeyan	13	1m 37.154s
23	Robert Doornbos	17	1m 37.816s
24	Tiago Monteiro	17	1m 38.250s

PRACTICE 2 (FRIDAY)

Breezy, light rain (track 24–25°C, air 23°C)

Pos.	Driver	Laps	Time
1	Ricardo Zonta	21	1m 30.682s
2	Michael Schumacher	16	1m 31.716s
3	Pedro de la Rosa	28	1m 31.821s
4	Rubens Barrichello	15	1m 32.267s
5	Kimi Räikkönen	13	1m 32.849s
6	Ralf Schumacher	13	1m 32.917s
7	Jarno Trulli	13	1m 33.122s
8	Fernando Alonso	7	1m 33.259s
9	Jenson Button	20	1m 33.453s
10	Mark Webber	14	1m 33.520s
11	David Coulthard	11	1m 33.563s
12	Antonio Pizzonia	14	1m 33.679s
13	Takuma Sato	16	1m 34.330s
14	Giancarlo Fisichella	7	1m 34.400s
15	Felipe Massa	17	1m 34.421s
16	Christian Klien	17	1m 34.707s
17	Sakon Yamamoto	19	1m 34.829s
18	Jacques Villeneuve	18	1m 34.874s
19	Vitantonio Liuzzi	7	1m 34.977s
20	Robert Doornbos	8	1m 35.150s
21	Tiago Monteiro	12	1m 35.388s
22	Juan Pablo Montoya	5	1m 37.371s
23	Christijan Albers	7	1m 37.626s
24	Narain Karthikeyan	7	1m 38.034s

PRACTICE 3 (SATURDAY)

Rainy (track 23°C, air 21–22°C)

Pos.	Driver	Laps	Time
1	Michael Schumacher	3	1m 46.543s
2	Kimi Räikkönen	5	1m 48.729s
3	Juan Pablo Montoya	4	1m 49.097s
4	Mark Webber	3	1m 49.484s
5	Antonio Pizzonia	5	1m 50.537s
6	Narain Karthikeyan	8	1m 50.811s
7	Rubens Barrichello	4	1m 50.846s
8	Jenson Button	4	1m 51.884s
9	Tiago Monteiro	7	1m 52.023s
10	Christijan Albers	6	1m 52.700s
11	David Coulthard	10	1m 53.346s
12	Takuma Sato	5	1m 53.454s
13	Christian Klien	4	1m 54.348s
14	Jarno Trulli	3	No time
15	Robert Doornbos	5	No time
16	Ralf Schumacher	1	No time
17	Felipe Massa	1	No time
18	Jacques Villeneuve	1	No time

PRACTICE 4 (SATURDAY)

Overcast/rainy (track 23–25°C, air 22–24°C)

Pos.	Driver	Laps	Time
1	Giancarlo Fisichella	9	1m 50.136s
2	Narain Karthikeyan	6	1m 50.150s
3	Ralf Schumacher	8	1m 50.369s
4	Jenson Button	7	1m 50.920s
5	Christijan Albers	8	1m 50.994s
6	Tiago Monteiro	6	1m 51.223s
7	Mark Webber	5	1m 51.274s
8	Jarno Trulli	8	1m 51.503s
9	David Coulthard	9	1m 51.710s
10	Robert Doornbos	10	1m 51.971s
11	Fernando Alonso	9	1m 52.667s
12	Christian Klien	4	1m 52.897s
13	Jacques Villeneuve	8	1m 53.460s
14	Rubens Barrichello	5	1m 53.739s
15	Felipe Massa	8	1m 53.842s
16	Takuma Sato	8	1m 54.307s
17	Antonio Pizzonia	4	2m 01.075s

9th: BARRICHELLO Ferrari   7th: WEBBER Williams-BMW   5th: SATO BAR-Honda   3rd: FISICHELLA Renault   Pole: R. SCHUMACHER Toyota

10th: MASSA Sauber-Petronas   8th: VILLENEUVE Sauber-Petronas   6th: COULTHARD Red Bull-Cosworth   4th: KLIEN Red Bull-Cosworth   2nd: BUTTON BAR-Honda

42	43	44	45	46	47	48	49	50	51	52	53	●
9	9	9	9	6	6	6	6	6	6	6	6	1
6	6	6	6	9	9	9	9	9	9	9	6	2
1	14	14	7	7	7	7	5	5	5	5	5	3
14	17	17	5	5	5	5	7	7	7	7	7	4
17	7	7	3	3	3	3	3	3	3	3	3	5
7	5	5	14	14	14	14	14	14	14	14	14	6
3	3	3	1	1	1	1	1	1	1	1	1	7
5	1	1	17	17	17	17	17	17	17	17	17	8
12	12	12	15	15	15	15	15	15	15	15	15	
15	15	15	12	12	12	12	12	12	12	12	12	
11	11	11	11	11	11	11	11	11	11	11	11	
2	2	2	2	2	2	2	2	2	2	2	2	
4	4	4	4	4	4	4	4	4	4	4		
18	18	18	18	18	18	18	18	18	18	18		
20	20	20	20	20	20	20	20	20	20			
19	19	19	19	19	19	19	19	19				
21	21	21	21	21	21	21	21					

Pit stop

One lap or more behind leader

FOR THE RECORD

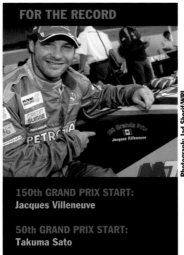

Photograph: Jad Sherif/WRI

150th GRAND PRIX START:
Jacques Villeneuve

50th GRAND PRIX START:
Takuma Sato

POINTS

DRIVERS

1	Fernando Alonso	123	19	Christijan Albers	4
2	Kimi Räikkönen	104	20	Pedro de la Rosa	4
3	Michael Schumacher	62	21	Patrick Friesacher	3
4	Juan Pablo Montoya	60	22	Antonio Pizzonia	2
5	Giancarlo Fisichella	53	23	Takuma Sato	1
6	Jarno Trulli	43	24	Vitantonio Liuzzi	1
7	Ralf Schumacher	39			
8	Rubens Barrichello	38		**CONSTRUCTORS**	
9	Jenson Button	36	1	Renault	176
10	Mark Webber	34	2	McLaren	174
11	Nick Heidfeld	28	3	Ferrari	100
12	David Coulthard	24	4	Toyota	82
13	Jacques Villeneuve	9	5	Williams	64
14	Felipe Massa	8	6	BAR	37
15	Tiago Monteiro	7	7	Red Bull	30
16	Alex Wurz	6	8	Sauber	17
17	Narain Karthikeyan	5	9	Jordan	12
18	Christian Klien	5	10	Minardi	7

Photograph: James Moy/www.crash.net

SHANGHAI
CHINESEGP

FIA F1 WORLD CHAMPIONSHIP/ROUND 19

A jubilant Fernando Alonso and Flavio Briatore acknowledged the plaudits after dominating the final race of the 2005 championship campaign.

Photograph: Bryn Williams/www.crash.net

Did Renault lull McLaren into a false sense of security in qualifying? That was the burning question long after the dust of the Chinese Grand Prix had finally settled and the Anglo-French team had walked off with a constructors' championship that almost everyone else believed would fall to its Anglo-German rival.

The 'deception' began in free practice on Friday and matured during a qualifying session that involved Fernando Alonso's taking pole position and Giancarlo Fisichella's backing him perfectly by annexing second place to give Renault its only front-row of the season. Even before the red lights went out at the start, McLaren, third and fifth courtesy of Kimi Räikkönen and Juan Pablo Montoya, knew it had a race on its hands.

The track surface confused some teams, with differing levels of grip in practice and qualifying. On Friday some dipped way below Rubens Barrichello's 2004 pole time of 1m 34.012s. This was unusual by 2005 standards and the fastest runner that day was McLaren's Pedro de la Rosa, who worked down to 1m 32.834s. But come qualifying and the grip level had dropped off. Where the Renaults had front-end grip aplenty, the McLarens did not.

Takuma Sato started qualifying first, having been disqualified in Japan. His 555-liveried BAR-Honda was fitted with the final iteration of the Honda V10, which boasted 965 bhp, but he also had a heavy fuel load and his lap of 1m 37.083s was soon thrown into perspective when Montoya took his McLaren around in 1m 35.188s. This remained the target until the final quarter of the session, which contained Jenson Button, Mark Webber, the Renault drivers and Räikkönen. Button, running fifth from the end, redefined things with 1m 34.801s and said afterwards that the BAR was going much better than it had in Japan the previous week, apart from a bit too much understeer. Webber got nowhere near that with 1m 35.739s, but Alonso unleashed a remarkable 1m 34.080s lap. That, it transpired, would be enough for pole.

The R25 looked smooth and fast, turning in nicely and taking fastest time in all three sectors, and it was undoubtedly helped by Renault's producing a special one-race, E-specification version of its V10, which was cleared by engine guru Rob White to rev to 19,200 rpm for qualifying.

Giancarlo Fisichella, in his similarly powered sister car, also displaced Button, with 1m 34.401s. Then it was down to Räikkönen, but right from the first corner it was evident that the Finn was fighting his McLaren. The first apex was not pretty and

thereafter a couple of small mistakes robbed him of speed. His 1m 34.488s left him third on the grid, alongside Button and ahead of Montoya and Michael Schumacher.

Alonso described his Renault as 'almost perfect', while Fisichella was surprised to be so far up after struggling with his R25's balance. Räikkönen admitted that he was unsurprised not to have pole and knew only too well that on this unusual surface the MP4-20's bugbear of failing to generate sufficient heat in its tyres over a single qualifying lap – not a factor since Imola – had come back when he least needed it.

When it was all over on Sunday evening, Renault engineering chief Pat Symonds suggested, 'We sold them [the McLaren guys] a dummy and it worked pretty well. We didn't show our true pace in practice or qualifying because we were pretty confident with what we had.'

Michael Schumacher's performance in taking sixth on the grid seemed encouraging for Ferrari. First, Rubens Barrichello had taken the second-fastest slot behind Montoya with 1m 35.610s, which his team-mate subsequently reduced to 1m 35.301s. Barrichello's time stood up for eighth and he and Schumacher quietly suggested that they might be in good shape for the race. Between them, David Coulthard was back on strong form for Red Bull as he lapped in 1m 35.428s to take seventh, but team-mate Christian Klien's run of good qualifying positions came to an end and he managed only 14th position after a lap of 1m 36.472s.

Ralf Schumacher's lap of 1m 35.723s put him in ninth place ahead of Webber, and Felipe Massa was the final sub-1m-36s runner on 1m 35.898s. The Brazilian, like Alonso, described his lap as 'almost perfect' after a gamble on set-up changes had dramatically improved the balance of his Sauber-Petronas C24 since morning practice.

Those who had to run early tended to suffer as usual because the track had yet to reach its best. Jarno Trulli was the third man out and could not better 1m 36.044s in his Toyota for 12th, with Antonio Pizzonia next up on 1m 36.445s for BMW Williams. Behind Klien was Narain Karthikeyan, who took his Jordan around in 1m 36.707s to beat Jacques Villeneuve. The former champion admitted to a poor lap because his Sauber lacked grip on the way to 1m 36.788s and 16th place. He had not adopted Massa's changes. Sato's time stood up for only 17th, ahead of Christijan Albers, who squeezed 1m 39.105s out of his Minardi. Team-mate Robert Doornbos did 1m 39.460s, which left Tiago Monteiro the meat in the Minardi sandwich on 1m 39.233s.

Left: Minardi held a farewell party in the Shanghai paddock. The fish waiting to be gutted on the slab was called Max.
Photograph: Peter Nygaard/GP Photo

Far left: Peter Sauber's team posed in Swiss-emblemed T-shirts for a farewell photo to mark its final appearance.

Below left: The end of an era for Jordan.
Photographs: Jad Sherif/WRI

Centre right: Minardi's goodbye photo.

Centre left: Pierre Dupasquier received a memento to mark his retirement from race duties at Michelin.
Photographs: Lukas Gorys

Bottom far left: In the shadows. Will Jacques Villeneuve be retained by BMW?
Photograph: Jean-François Galeron

NEW RULES FROM MOSLEY

FIA president Max Mosley sparked much debate in the paddock in China when he cancelled a press conference on Saturday morning in which he had been due, among other things, to outline his vision for the future shape of the F1 car. This caused some embarrassment to technology partner AMD, whose top brass had flown in specially, but a week later, back in London, details were leaked to selected areas of the media the day before the F1 Commission met.

It was Mosley who once offered the opinion that too much overtaking would be 'confusing' for spectators and television viewers, but Mosley performed a neat U-turn in July, following the survey conducted by the FIA in conjunction with the computer-chip company AMD, which revealed what fans of the sport already knew: the majority (94 percent) wanted to see more of it.

Now Mosley argued that the existing cars created so much aerodynamic turbulence that overtaking was almost impossible because the 'dirty air' robbed following cars of much of their vital front-end downforce. Designers, he said, made their cars as aerodynamically efficient as possible while creating maximum turbulence in their wake so they couldn't be overtaken.

The result of all this debate was the centreline downwash-generating (CDG) wing, which in effect comprises two narrower conventional rear wings, one mounted aft of each rear wheel, with a clear gap between them. The airflow between the two wings is much cleaner and therefore following cars will be able to retain their own aerodynamic efficiency and will thus have a better chance of passing.

Mosley initially intended that the CDG wing would form part of a package for the 2008 FIA F1 technical regulations, but hoped that it could be adopted as early as 2007 if the teams were in favour.

'This new research is important for the future of F1,' Mosley said. 'By introducing the CDG wing, we can give motor-sport fans exactly what they have asked for – wheel-to-wheel racing with much more overtaking.

'It is our hope that the teams will collaborate with us in the optimisation of this radical new idea so that the aerodynamic benefits can be introduced into F1 in 2007 rather than having to wait until 2008.'

That is precisely what happened when the proposal was presented to the F1 Commission. The CGD wing was approved in principle by team owners (subject to consultation with the Technical Working Group) for introduction in 2007.

The other key elements of Mosley's package were also approved. One featured another U-turn from the man who introduced grooved tyres for 1998: a return to slick tyres, to give drivers greater mechanical grip and further enhance the likelihood of overtaking. Another proposal called for a single tyre supplier by 2007.

More controversial was the proposal to reintroduce tyre changes during races in 2006. The Michelin teams were in favour of retaining the system wherein teams had to qualify and race on one set of tyres and the racing was much better as a result. Ferrari and Bridgestone, predictably, wanted a return to tyre changes, which had been allowed before 2005. It was, after all, only a week since Michael Schumacher's worn tyres had sent him spinning ignominiously into retirement with less than half of the Chinese GP run.

Commission members also agreed on a new format for qualifying devised by commercial-rights holder Bernie Ecclestone. From 2006, qualifying would be split, with the slowest five drivers eliminated after each of two 15-minute sessions. The remaining ten drivers would then fight for pole position during the final 20 minutes.

Right: Climb every mountain. Michael Schumacher was forced to find an unusual route back to the pits after his pre-race collision with Cristijan Albers. Photograph: XPB.cc

Below: Out with a whimper. Rubens Barrichello ended his Ferrari career with a distant 12th place.

Bottom: Ralf Schumacher took the Toyota TF105B to a lucky third place after Giancarlo Fisichella had to take a drive-through penalty late in the race. Photographs: Bryn Williams/www.crash.net

IT was a race that almost everyone had expected McLaren to dominate. Instead, it fell to Fernando Alonso in such a style that the new world champion described it as the easiest of the season. Kimi Räikkönen finished a game second for McLaren, fairly beaten on a day on which the safety car was twice deployed, but fourth place for Giancarlo Fisichella added further points to Renault's impressive tally. As Alonso's success drew the score to seven-all with Räikkönen, the *Régie* for the first time as a manufacturer rather than an engine supplier found itself crowned constructors' world champion.

It was always unlikely that the Chinese Grand Prix would be able to emulate the Japanese for sheer excitement, but there was plenty of drama and some of it came before the race even started. Michael Schumacher appeared to be in a world of his own as he took his Ferrari out on the recognition lap and then wandered across the path of the faster Christijan Albers in a style more suited to the worst sort of motorway mimser. The Minardi flew over the left-hand side of the Ferrari, narrowly avoiding being launched upside down, and one very angry Dutchman headed back to the pits to take over a spare Minardi that, among other things, lacked his intended race car's power-steering.

When the red lights went out, Alonso leaped straight into the lead. Fisichella also made a strong getaway and proceeded to manage his pace to contain the challenge of Räikkönen and his McLaren team-mate Juan Pablo Montoya. That order prevailed until lap 17, which was when Montoya ran over a dislodged drain cover in Turn Ten. Back in June 2004, Australian saloon-car racer Mark Winterbottom had the underside of his car torn out after a similar problem, so it was clear that despite their multi-million-dollar investment, the Shanghai International Circuit owners still had further work to do.

The Colombian continued for another lap and a half before pitting to investigate possible damage on lap 18. Under the rules he could not also refuel, so he came back in a lap later for that while the safety car was deployed so that the errant cover could be retrieved and others inspected. He would keep going

until lap 24, when he retired in the pits with a Mercedes-engine problem said not to be connected to the drain-cover incident. As one disgruntled team member said, 'How is it everyone else can avoid the damn thing?' meaning Alonso and Räikkönen, who dodged the cover that Montoya hit.

The deployment prompted a rash of pit stops: Alonso, Fisichella, Räikkönen, Rubens Barrichello, Ralf Schumacher, Mark Webber, Felipe Massa, Antonio Pizzonia and Jacques Villeneuve also took advantage and came in.

The safety car stayed out until lap 24 and when the racing resumed on lap 25 Alonso was still in front. But the period of slow running had wiped out his hard-won 17.5s lead. However, he had been quite close to his refuelling window (Fisichella had been due on lap 21, Alonso on 23) so he was able to maintain his lead over Fisichella and Räikkönen. Unfortunately we would not now know the lap on which Räikkönen had been due to stop, but sources suggested it would have been 25 or 26. It was academic, but knowing it would have put qualifying into further perspective. As it was, McLaren's much-fancied chances of the constructors' title were now looking weak.

The stops had juggled the order farther down the pack. Jenson Button, having pitted on lap 18, dropped from fifth to seventh and David Coulthard also lost out as he dropped from sixth to eighth and had Massa and Christian Klien on his tail. Both Button and Coulthard felt aggrieved.

'Unfortunately for David,' Red Bull sporting director Christian Horner said, 'he picked up the pace car at just the wrong time, which cost him significantly because it allowed other cars to pass, while David had in effect to complete another lap to catch the safety car. That ultimately cost him points.'

Alonso quickly opened up a lead again over Fisichella, but Räikkönen was not yet able to challenge the second Renault. Farther back, fourth-placed Barrichello came under attack from Ralf Schumacher, Webber, Button and Coulthard.

The next drama unfolded on lap 29 when Narain Karthikeyan crashed his Jordan very heavily in Turn 13 after losing front-end

Above: Fernando Alonso strode onto the podium after taking the win that ensured that Renault clinched the constructors' title.

Photograph: Jean-François Galeron/WRI

Far right: How was it for you? End-of-term discussion for David Coulthard and Jenson Button, who disputed the final point on offer.

Photograph: Bryn Williams/www.crash.net

downforce and getting sucked onto the grass while following Jarno Trulli's Toyota. Jacques Villeneuve had a very lucky escape as he just avoided the wreckage and there was so much debris on the track that another safety-car period was inevitable. This time the field queued up behind it until lap 34.

Crucially, however, Toyota, Sauber and Red Bull respectively kept Schumacher Jr, Massa and Klien out as all of the other leading runners pitted again. When the race resumed on lap 35 they were suddenly running second, third and fourth behind Alonso. Each really had to get the hammer down now in order to open up a sufficient margin over the others to make his own second refuelling stop later on.

Räikkönen overtook Fisichella during this round of pit stops and the Italian's ploy of trying to hold up everyone as he came into the pits, as Räikkönen had done in Belgium, backfired badly. Since Spa, FIA race director Charlie Whiting had made it clear (though Fisichella tried to protest ignorance and innocence later) that such tactics would no longer be tolerated. Accordingly, the stewards handed the Italian a drive-through penalty. As the television showed, there was nothing subtle in the way that Fisichella slowed Räikkönen.

When Massa, Klien and Schumacher Jr finally pitted on laps 44, 45 and 47 respectively, Räikkönen at last had a clear road

to Alonso. Now, it seemed, we would learn the truth of the whole affair. But the Spaniard was 13.1s ahead and had detuned his Renault's engine. Räikkönen set two fastest laps, but it was all too late. The disruptions of the safety car had worked against McLaren but, in truth, Alonso and Renault had always had everything firmly under control. The Spaniard's seventh win of the year was a sweet success that evened the seasonal win tally with the Finn. Renault was the champion and, despite winning ten races, McLaren left with nothing.

'The race itself did not unfold as expected,' said Renault's executive director of engineering, Pat Symonds. 'In all honesty, I wish the safety-car periods had not happened because that would have allowed us to show the true performance we have gained in the past few weeks. To win the championship with a dominant performance is the perfect way to round off an amazing season.'

Over at McLaren, a philosophical insider admitted, 'Renault has made some very impressive progress since Brazil. The team was bloody quick this weekend.'

According to Räikkönen, his MP4-20 didn't come on until late in the race. That was mystifying for everyone in the team because he had been quick all weekend – except when it really mattered. Certainly the safety-car periods meant that the

Behind the Australian, Jenson Button was an unhappy eighth after BAR Honda had yet another disappointing race. It began badly when Takuma Sato blatantly jumped the start – and later he was forced into retirement when ongoing gearbox problems worsened. Button reported that his 007 initially felt good, but towards the end it was no better than it had been in Japan the previous week.

Michael Schumacher's appalling day ended in the gravel trap when he lost control of his Ferrari and slid off the road on lap 23 during the first safety-car period. The former champion blamed worn Bridgestone tyres for his second embarrassing incident of the afternoon.

'This weird ending pretty much summed up our season,' he said. 'I spun simply because my tyres were completely worn and very cold, so when someone braked ahead of me I had to brake as well and went off the track. Actually, I'm not sure I would have finished anyway because of the condition of the tyres.'

Jacques Villeneuve said his race was compromised by the safety cars. Antonio Pizzonia lost out when the Williams team refuelled both cars on lap 30, as the second safety-car period began, and he too lacked straight-line speed. At the end he dropped from 11th to 13th when a right-rear puncture brought him to a halt on the last lap. In its 250th and final race, Jordan lost Karthikeyan's EJ15B in his hefty shunt, but team-mate Tiago Monteiro had no problems on his way to an 11th-placed finish. A late stop for fresh rubber on lap 46 dropped Barrichello to a lowly 12th in his final race for Ferrari and, behind Pizzonia, Robert Doornbos and Albers in their Minardis sandwiched Trulli's Toyota, which was another to fall foul of the first safety car because Trulli had already made his first pit stop when it was deployed. Albers actually failed to finish after his left-rear wheel-nut came loose and flew off the car down the back straight.

Down the back of the field there was much post-race emotion as Sauber, Minardi and Jordan all prepared to change identity for 2006. All of the elation was at the sharp end, in the Renault camp. 'This is a fantastic feeling,' beamed Alonso as the champagne corks popped. 'I didn't think anything could equal winning the drivers' championship, but seeing our people celebrating, it's just as good! I am really so happy today and there is only one thing to say to them: thank you!

'The race was actually very easy. We used full power only in the first part and we saw we were quicker than everybody so we turned things down and went conservative for the second part. Honestly, it was like the opening races, when we had an advantage and could manage our pace.'

It was, by any standard, a wonderful season for the blue-and-yellow team and its final performance could not have been better: it silenced the critics who had accused Renault of lucking into the drivers' title by stealth.

David Tremayne

DIARY

Williams reveals that it will offer some of the most important cars in its history for sale in a Bonhams auction. They include Nigel Mansell's race-winning FW10 from 1985, one of Alain Prost's six-times winning 1993 FW15Cs and Damon Hill's four-times winning FW16B from 1994.

To send him on his way as he leaves the team's marketing department to take up a new role with RBS, Williams mechanics tape the Queen's grandson, Peter Phillips, to a trolley and then decorate him with oil and fire-extinguisher foam shortly after the end of the Chinese Grand Prix.

McLaren's design guru Adrian Newey, who got itchy feet and actually signed a contract with Jaguar back in 2001, admits in Shanghai that he is contracted to McLaren only until the end of 2005.

Credit Suisse confirms that it will stay on as a major sponsor of the Sauber team when the team becomes BMW for 2006.

---

strategic advantage of being able to run a few laps longer couldn't be exploited, but there was a feeling in some quarters of McLaren that the team just wasn't quite there in China.

'Today was not our day and finishing second was the best we could do,' Räikkönen said as he shifted his focus to 2006.

'It's frustrating not to achieve the result we wanted at the end of a season in which we have finished on the podium 18 times and claimed 10 victories,' said team chairman Ron Dennis and it was impossible not to sympathise with him.

Fisichella's drive-through penalty on lap 52 dropped him to fourth place and promoted Ralf Schumacher to a solid third to finish Toyota's great season in style, while Klien finished a strong fifth for Red Bull and Massa maintained sixth despite a flat-spotted right-front tyre that allowed Webber to challenge him as he had in Canada. Massa's final performance for Sauber earned him a race car of his own – departing team principal Peter Sauber promised him the reward as the driver crossed the finish line.

Webber pushed hard for points all afternoon, but the Williams-BMW lacked pace down the long straights. While Webber was fast in the corners, Barrichello was fast down the straights, so Webber had to tolerate a stalemate for a long time until the Brazilian made a mistake at the hairpin on lap 44.

SHANGHAI INTERNATIONAL CIRCUIT
CIRCUIT LENGTH: 3.387 miles/5.451 km

TURN 1 135/217 (2)
TURN 3
TURN 2
TURN 5
TURN 6 63/102 (2)
TURN 4
TURN 7
TURN 9 85/137 (2)
TURN 8
TURN 12
TURN 16 113/181 (3)
TURN 15
TURN 11
TURN 13
TURN 14 55/88 (2)
TURN 10

FIA F1 WORLD CHAMPIONSHIP • ROUND 19
FORMULA 1 SINOPEC
CHINESE GRAND PRIX
SHANGHAI 14–16 OCTOBER 2005

RACE DISTANCE: 56 laps, 189.559 miles /305.066 km   RACE WEATHER: Bright and sunny (track 32–33°C, air 23–25°C)

Pos.	Driver	Nat.	No.	Entrant	Car/Engine	Tyres	Laps	Time/Retirement	Speed (mph/km/h)	Gap to leader	Best time	Lap
1	Fernando Alonso	E	5	Mild Seven Renault F1 Team	Renault R25-RS25 V10	M	56	1h 39m 53.618s	113.862/183.234		1m 33.536s	45
2	Kimi Räikkönen	FIN	9	Team McLaren Mercedes	McLaren MP4-20-Mercedes F0 110R V10	M	56	1h 39m 57.633s	113.785/183.111	+4.015s	1m 33.242s	56
3	Ralf Schumacher	D	17	Panasonic Toyota Racing	Toyota TF105B-Toyota RVX-05 V10	M	56	1h 40m 18.994s	113.381/182.461	+25.376s	1m 34.035s	44
4	Giancarlo Fisichella	I	6	Mild Seven Renault F1 Team	Renault R25-RS25 V10	M	56	1h 40m 19.732s	113.368/182.439	+26.114s	1m 33.563s	54
5	Christian Klien	A	15	Red Bull Racing	Red Bull RB1-Cosworth TJ2005/12 V10	M	56	1h 40m 25.457s	113.260/182.266	+31.839s	1m 33.727s	43
6	Felipe Massa	BR	12	Sauber Petronas	Sauber C24-Petronas 05A V10	M	56	1h 40m 30.018s	113.174/182.128	+36.400s	1m 34.094s	43
7	Mark Webber	AUS	7	BMW WilliamsF1 Team	Williams FW27-BMW P84/85 V10	M	56	1h 40m 30.460s	113.166/182.115	+36.842s	1m 34.271s	53
8	Jenson Button	GB	3	Lucky Strike BAR Honda	BAR 007-Honda RA005E V10	M	56	1h 40m 34.867s	113.084/181.982	+41.249s	1m 34.766s	53
9	David Coulthard	GB	14	Red Bull Racing	Red Bull RB1-Cosworth TJ2005/12 V10	M	56	1h 40m 37.865s	113.027/181.891	+44.247s	1m 34.585s	54
10	Jacques Villeneuve	CDN	11	Sauber Petronas	Sauber C24-Petronas 05A V10	M	56	1h 40m 53.595s	112.734/181.419	+59.977s	1m 34.713s	53
11	Tiago Monteiro	P	18	Jordan Toyota	Jordan EJ15B-Toyota RVX-05 V10	B	56	1h 41m 18.266s	112.276/180.682	+84.648s	1m 36.563s	13
12	Rubens Barrichello	BR	2	Scuderia Ferrari Marlboro	Ferrari F2005-055 V10	B	56	1h 41m 26.430s	112.125/180.440	+92.812s	1m 35.011s	18
13	Antonio Pizzonia	BR	8	BMW WilliamsF1 Team	Williams FW27-BMW P84/85 V10	M	55	In pit		DNF	1m 34.560s	52
14	Robert Doornbos	NL	20	Minardi Cosworth	Minardi PS05-Cosworth TJ2005 V10	B	55			DNF	1m 36.894s	54
15	Jarno Trulli	I	16	Panasonic Toyota Racing	Toyota TF105B-Toyota RVX-05	M	55			+1 lap	1m 35.347s	16
16	Christijan Albers	NL	21	Minardi Cosworth	Minardi PS05-Cosworth TJ2005 V10	B	51	Loose wheel		DNF	1m 37.215s	48
	Takuma Sato	J	4	Lucky Strike BAR Honda	BAR 007-Honda RA005E V10	M	34	Gearbox			1m 35.587s	17
	Narain Karthikeyan	IND	19	Jordan Toyota	Jordan EJ15B-Toyota RVX-05	B	28	Accident			1m 37.398s	17
	Juan Pablo Montoya	COL	10	Team McLaren Mercedes	McLaren MP4-20-Mercedes FO 110R V10	M	24	Engine			1m 34.501s	15
	Michael Schumacher	D	1	Scuderia Ferrari Marlboro	Ferrari F2005-055 V10	B	22	Spin			1m 35.877s	16

Fastest lap: Kimi Räikkönen on lap 56, 1m 33.242s, 130.779 mph/210.458 km/h.

Lap record: Michael Schumacher (Ferrari F2004-054 V10), 1m 32.238s, 132.196 mph/212.749 km/h (2004).

19th: MONTEIRO Jordan-Toyota

17th: SATO BAR-Honda

15th: KARTHIKEYAN Jordan-Toyota
Started from pit lane

13th: PIZZONIA Williams-BMW

11th: MASSA Sauber-Petronas

20th: DOORNBOS Minardi-Cosworth

18th: ALBERS Minardi-Cosworth
Started from pit lane

16th: VILLENEUVE Sauber-Petronas

14th: KLIEN Red Bull-Cosworth

12th: TRULLI Toyota

Grid order	1	2	3	4	5	6	7	8	9	10	11	12	13	14	15	16	17	18	19	20	21	22	23	24	25	26	27	28	29	30	31	32	33	34	35	36	37	38	39	40	41	42	43	44	45
5 ALONSO	5	5	5	5	5	5	5	5	5	5	5	5	5	5	5	5	5	5	5	5	5	5	5	5	5	5	5	5	5	5	5	5	5	5	5	5	5	5	5	5	5	5	5	5	5
6 FISICHELLA	6	6	6	6	6	6	6	6	6	6	6	6	6	6	6	6	6	6	6	6	6	6	6	6	6	6	6	6	6	6	17	17	17	17	17	17	17	17	17	17	17	17	17	17	17
9 RÄIKKÖNEN	9	9	9	9	9	9	9	9	9	9	9	9	9	9	9	9	9	9	9	9	9	9	9	9	9	9	9	9	9	9	12	15	12	12	12	12	12	12	12	12	12	15	15	12	12
3 BUTTON	10	10	10	10	10	10	10	10	10	10	10	10	10	10	10	10	10	10	10	2	2	2	2	2	2	2	2	2	2	2	15	15	15	15	15	15	15	15	15	15	15	12			
10 MONTOYA	3	3	3	3	3	3	3	3	3	3	3	3	3	3	3	3	3	3	3	17	17	17	17	17	17	17	17	17	17	17	9	9	9	9	9	9	9	9	9	9	9	9	9	9	9
1 M. SCHUMACHER	14	14	14	14	14	14	14	14	14	14	14	14	14	14	14	14	14	2	7	7	7	7	7	7	7	7	7	7	7	6	6	6	6	6	6	6	6	6	6	6	6	6	12		
14 COULTHARD	2	2	2	2	2	2	2	2	2	2	2	2	2	2	2	2	17	12	3	3	3	3	3	3	3	3	3	3	3	12	2	2	2	2	2	2	2	2	2	2	2	2	7		
2 BARRICHELLO	17	17	17	17	17	17	17	17	17	17	17	17	17	17	17	17	7	15	14	14	14	14	14	14	14	14	14	14	15	4	4	4	4	7	7	7	7	7	7	7	7	3			
17 R. SCHUMACHER	7	7	7	7	7	7	7	7	7	7	7	7	7	7	7	7	8	12	12	12	12	12	12	12	12	12	12	12	3	3	3	3	3	3	3	3	3	3	3	3	3	2	1	14	
7 WEBBER	16	16	16	16	16	16	16	16	16	16	16	16	16	16	16	12	15	11	1	1	1	15	15	15	15	15	15	15	14	18	18	3	3	18	14	14	14	14	14	14	14	14	14		
12 MASSA	12	12	12	12	12	12	12	12	12	12	12	12	12	12	12	16	8	3	15	15	8	8	8	8	8	8	8	8	3	3	18	18	14	18	18	18	18	18	18	18	18	18	18		
16 TRULLI	4	4	4	15	15	15	15	15	15	15	15	15	15	15	15	11	11	8	11	8	11	11	11	11	11	11	11	11	16	16	14	14	14	14	11	11	11	16	11	11	11	11	11		
8 PIZZONIA	15	15	15	8	8	8	8	8	8	8	8	8	8	8	8	14	10	11	11	11	10	11	11	11	11	19	19	19	20	20	16	11	11	11	11	11	11	11	16	8					
15 KLIEN	8	8	8	11	11	11	11	11	11	11	11	11	11	11	11	8	1	1	16	16	16	16	16	16	4	11	20	20	20	11	4	20	20	20	20	8	20	20	20	20	20	20	20		
19 KARTHIKEYAN	11	11	11	18	18	18	18	18	18	18	18	18	18	18	18	1	1	16	16	16	16	16	4	11	20	20	20	11	4	11	8	8	8	8	8	8	8	8	20	20	20	20	20		
11 VILLENEUVE	18	18	18	4	1	1	1	1	1	1	1	1	1	1	18	4	4	4	4	4	18	19	20	11	11	4	18	10	20	20	20	20	21	21	21	21	21	21	21	21	21	21	21		
4 SATO	1	1	1	1	20	20	20	4	4	4	4	4	4	4	20	19	19	4	4	4	20	18	18	18	18	21	21	21	21	21															
21 ALBERS	20	20	20	20	19	19	19	4	20	20	20	20	20	20	4	20	18	19	19	19	18	10	21	21	21	21																			
18 MONTEIRO	21	21	21	19	21	21	4	19	19	19	19	19	19	19	19	18	18	20	20	20	20	21	21																						
20 DOORNBOS	19	19	19	21	4	4	21	21	21	21	21	21	21	21	21	21	21	21	21	21	21																								

QUALIFYING

WEATHER: Sunny with scattered cloud (track 32–33°C, air 24°C)

Pos.	Driver	R/Order	Sector 1	Sector 2	Sector 3	Time
1	Fernando Alonso	18	24.873s	28.488s	40.719s	1m 34.080s
2	Giancarlo Fisichella	19	25.126s	28.487s	40.788s	1m 34.401s
3	Kimi Räikkönen	20	25.052s	28.528s	40.908s	1m 34.488s
4	Jenson Button	16	25.197s	28.565s	41.039s	1m 34.801s
5	Juan Pablo Montoya	2	25.301s	28.677s	41.210s	1m 35.188s
6	Michael Schumacher	14	25.539s	28.782s	40.980s	1m 35.301s
7	David Coulthard	15	25.588s	28.716s	41.124s	1m 35.428s
8	Rubens Barrichello	10	25.593s	28.857s	41.160s	1m 35.610s
9	Ralf Schumacher	13	25.488s	28.699s	41.536s	1m 35.723s
10	Mark Webber	17	25.278s	28.737s	41.724s	1m 35.739s
11	Felipe Massa	11	25.561s	28.915s	41.422s	1m 35.898s
12	Jarno Trulli	3	25.618s	28.813S	41.613S	1m 36.044S
13	Antonio Pizzonia	4	25.617s	29.153s	41.675s	1m 34.445s
14	Christian Klien	12	25.787s	29.026s	41.659s	1m 36.472s
15	Narain Karthikeyan	6	25.681s	29.215s	41.778s	1m 36.707s
16	Jacques Villeneuve	9	25.700s	29.482s	41.606s	1m 36.788s
17	Takuma Sato	1	25.785s	29.544s	41.754s	1m 37.083s
18	Christijan Albers	5	26.484s	30.295s	42.268s	1m 39.105s
19	Tiago Monteiro	8	26.109s	30.595s	42.469s	1m 39.233s
20	Robert Doornbos	7	26.008s	30.283s	43.169s	1m 39.460s

CHASSIS LOG BOOK

FERRARI
1	Michael Schumacher	F2005/249
2	Rubens Barrichello	F2005/248
	Spare	F2005/245

BAR-HONDA
3	Jenson Button	007-04
4	Takuma Sato	007-05
	Spare	007-02

RENAULT
5	Fernando Alonso	R25/07
6	Giancarlo Fisichella	R25/04
	Spare	R25/02

WILLIAMS-BMW
7	Mark Webber	FW27/04
8	Antonio Pizzonia	FW27/03
	Spare	FW27/06

McLAREN-MERCEDES
9	Kimi Räikkönen	MP4-20/04
10	Juan Pablo Montoya	MP4-20/07
35	Pedro de la Rosa	MP4-20/06
	Spare	MP4-20/06

SAUBER-PETRONAS
11	Jacques Villeneuve	C24/04
12	Felipe Massa	C24/06
	Spare	C24/03

RED BULL-COSWORTH
14	David Coulthard	RB1/3
15	Christian Klien	RB1/1
37	Vitantonio Liuzzi	RB1/5
	Spare	RB1/5

TOYOTA
16	Jarno Trulli	TF105B/10
17	Ralf Schumacher	TF105B/9
38	Ricardo Zonta	TF105B/2
	Spare	TF105B/2

JORDAN-TOYOTA
18	Tiago Monteiro	EJ15B/02
19	Narain Karthikeyan	EJ15B/01
39	Nicolas Kiesa	EJ15/03
	Spare	EJ15/03

MINARDI-COSWORTH
20	Robert Doornbos	PS05/02
21	Christijan Albers	PS05/01
	Spare	PS05/03

Photograph: James Moy/www.crash.net

PRACTICE 1 (FRIDAY)

Hazy sunshine (track 25–26°C, air 23°C)

Pos.	Driver	Laps	Time
1	Pedro de la Rosa	20	1m 33.463s
2	Rubens Barrichello	13	1m 35.303s
3	Ricardo Zonta	24	1m 35.373s
4	Kimi Räikkönen	5	1m 35.481s
5	Michael Schumacher	12	1m 35.494s
6	Juan Pablo Montoya	9	1m 35.521s
7	Fernando Alonso	10	1m 35.605s
8	Mark Webber	13	1m 35.945s
9	David Coulthard	10	1m 36.089s
10	Jenson Button	11	1m 36.096s
11	Antonio Pizzonia	12	1m 36.208s
12	Takuma Sato	11	1m 36.829s
13	Ralf Schumacher	13	1m 36.866s
14	Vitantonio Liuzzi	24	1m 37.119s
15	Felipe Massa	11	1m 37.123s
16	Giancarlo Fisichella	5	1m 37.143s
17	Christian Klien	8	1m 37.480s
18	Jacques Villeneuve	7	1m 37.688s
19	Jarno Trulli	9	1m 37.764s
20	Narain Karthikeyan	15	1m 38.308s
21	Tiago Monteiro	11	1m 39.088s
22	Nicolas Kiesa	21	1m 39.687s
23	Robert Doornbos	14	1m 40.724s
24	Christijan Albers	13	1m 40.787s

PRACTICE 2 (FRIDAY)

Light, overcast, hazy (track 25–26°C, air 22–23°C)

Pos.	Driver	Laps	Time
1	Pedro de la Rosa	30	1m 32.834s
2	Ricardo Zonta	29	1m 32.977s
3	Kimi Räikkönen	14	1m 34.092s
4	Fernando Alonso	24	1m 34.226s
5	Juan Pablo Montoya	16	1m 34.351s
6	Rubens Barrichello	24	1m 34.618s
7	Giancarlo Fisichella	28	1m 34.932s
8	Mark Webber	24	1m 35.035s
9	Jenson Button	25	1m 35.072s
10	Felipe Massa	26	1m 35.196s
11	David Coulthard	19	1m 35.201s
12	Vitantonio Liuzzi	26	1m 35.306s
13	Takuma Sato	24	1m 35.397s
14	Michael Schumacher	24	1m 35.567s
15	Christian Klien	19	1m 35.613s
16	Antonio Pizzonia	13	1m 35.709s
17	Jacques Villeneuve	21	1m 35.894s
18	Ralf Schumacher	20	1m 36.051s
19	Jarno Trulli	26	1m 36.079s
20	Nicolas Kiesa	25	1m 36.644s
21	Robert Doornbos	22	1m 36.993s
22	Christijan Albers	21	1m 37.173s
23	Tiago Monteiro	11	1m 37.435s
24	Narain Karthikeyan	18	1m 37.467s

PRACTICE 3 (SATURDAY)

Sunny (track 32–33°C, air 24°C)

Pos.	Driver	Laps	Time
1	Kimi Räikkönen	6	1m 34.253s
2	Juan Pablo Montoya	6	1m 34.446s
3	Giancarlo Fisichella	8	1m 34.472s
4	Fernando Alonso	4	1m 34.631s
5	Mark Webber	12	1m 34.749s
6	Jenson Button	6	1m 35.004s
7	David Coulthard	9	1m 35.296s
8	Takuma Sato	9	1m 35.461s
9	Felipe Massa	8	1m 35.532s
10	Antonio Pizzonia	13	1m 35.675s
11	Michael Schumacher	10	1m 35.981s
12	Jacques Villeneuve	8	1m 35.982s
13	Rubens Barrichello	10	1m 35.994s
14	Jarno Trulli	13	1m 36.100s
15	Ralf Schumacher	10	1m 36.251s
16	Tiago Monteiro	6	1m 37.555s
17	Narain Karthikeyan	10	1m 37.563s
18	Robert Doornbos	6	1m 38.072s
19	Christijan Albers	10	1m 38.697s

PRACTICE 4 (SATURDAY)

Sunny (track 34°C, air 24°C)

Pos.	Driver	Laps	Time
1	Kimi Räikkönen	12	1m 33.212s
2	Juan Pablo Montoya	12	1m 33.554s
3	Fernando Alonso	13	1m 33.793s
4	Giancarlo Fisichella	11	1m 34.392s
5	David Coulthard	14	1m 34.453s
6	Rubens Barrichello	12	1m 34.535s
7	Jenson Button	12	1m 34.729s
8	Michael Schumacher	11	1m 34.807s
9	Antonio Pizzonia	10	1m 34.835s
10	Mark Webber	8	1m 35.004s
11	Jarno Trulli	13	1m 35.107s
12	Christian Klien	13	1m 35.179s
13	Takuma Sato	17	1m 35.280s
14	Narain Karthikeyan	3	1m 35.310s
15	Ralf Schumacher	15	1m 35.371s
16	Tiago Monteiro	8	1m 35.488s
17	Felipe Massa	13	1m 35.693s
18	Christijan Albers	15	1m 36.397s
19	Jacques Villeneuve	11	1m 36.417s
20	Robert Doornbos	14	1m 36.558s

9th: R. SCHUMACHER Toyota

7th: COULTHARD Red Bull-Cosworth

5th: MONTOYA McLaren-Mercedes

3rd: RÄIKKÖNEN McLaren-Mercedes

Pole: ALONSO Renault

10th: WEBBER Williams-BMW

8th: BARRICHELLO Ferrari

6th: M. SCHUMACHER Ferrari
Started from pit lane

4th: BUTTON BAR-Honda

2nd: FISICHELLA Renault

46	47	48	49	50	51	52	53	54	55	56	
5	5	5	5	5	5	5	5	5	5	5	1
17	17	9	9	9	9	9	9	9	9	9	2
9	9	6	6	6	6	6	17	17	17	17	3
6	6	17	17	17	17	17	6	6	6	6	4
15	15	15	15	15	15	15	15	15	15	15	5
12	12	12	12	12	12	12	12	12	12	12	6
7	7	7	7	7	7	7	7	7	7	7	7
3	3	3	3	3	3	3	3	3	3	3	8
14	14	14	14	14	14	14	14	14	14	14	
2	11	11	11	11	11	11	11	11	11	11	
11	8	8	8	8	8	8	8	8	8	18	
18	18	18	18	18	18	18	18	18	18	2	
8	16	16	16	16	16	16	2	2	2		
16	2	2	2	2	2	20	20	20			
20	20	20	20	20	20	16	16				
21	21	21	21	21	21						

Pit stop
One lap or more behind leader

FOR THE RECORD

Photograph: Bryn Williams/www.crash.net

300th GRAND PRIX POINT:
Ralf Schumacher

100th GRAND PRIX START:
Jenson Button

POINTS

DRIVERS
1	Fernando Alonso	133
2	Kimi Räikkönen	112
3	Michael Schumacher	62
4	Juan Pablo Montoya	60
5	Giancarlo Fisichella	58
6	Ralf Schumacher	45
7	Jarno Trulli	43
8	Rubens Barrichello	38
9	Jenson Button	37
10	Mark Webber	36
11	Nick Heidfeld	28
12	David Coulthard	24
13	Felipe Massa	11
14	Jacques Villeneuve	9
15	Christian Klien	9
16	Tiago Monteiro	7
17	Alex Wurz	6
18	Narain Karthikeyan	5
19	Christijan Albers	4
20	Pedro de la Rosa	4
21	Patrick Friesacher	3
22	Antonio Pizzonia	2
23	Takuma Sato	1
24	Vitantonio Liuzzi	1

CONSTRUCTORS
1	Renault	191
2	McLaren	182
3	Ferrari	100
4	Toyota	88
5	Williams	66
6	BAR	38
7	Red Bull	34
8	Sauber	20
9	Jordan	12
10	Minardi	7

Photograph: James Moy/www.crash.net

STATISTICS: 2005 DRIVERS' POINTS TABLE Compiled by DAVID HAYHOE

Place	Driver	Nationality	Date of birth	Car	Australia	Malaysia	Bahrain	San Marino	Spain	Monaco	Europe	Canada	USA	France	Britain	Germany	Hungary	Turkey	Italy	Belgium	Brazil	Japan	China	Points total
1	Fernando ALONSO	E	29/7/81	Renault	3f	1p	1p	1	2	4	1f	R	NS	1p	2p	1	11	2	2	2	3p	3	1p	133
2	Kimi RÄIKKÖNEN	FIN	17/10/79	McLaren-Mercedes	8	9f	3	Rp	1p	1p	11*	1f	NS	2f	3f	Rpf	1f	1p	4f	1	2f	1f	2f	112
3	Michael SCHUMACHER	D	3/1/69	Ferrari	R	7	R	2f	R	7f	5	2	1f	3	6	5	2p	R	10	R	4	7	R	62
4	Juan Pablo MONTOYA	CO	20/9/75	McLaren-Mercedes	6	4	-	-	7	5	7	R	NS	R	1	2	R	3f	1p	14*p	1	R	R	60
5	Giancarlo FISICHELLA	I	14/1/73	Renault	1p	R	R	R	5f	12	6	R	NS	6	4	4	9	4	3	R	5	2	4	58
6	Ralf SCHUMACHER	D	30/6/75	Toyota	12	5	4	9	4	6	R	6	NS	7	8	6	3	12	6	7f	8	8p	3	45
7	Jarno TRULLI	I	13/7/74	Toyota	9	2	2	5	3	10	8	R	NSp	5	9	14*	4	6	5	R	13	R	15	43
8	Rubens BARRICHELLO	BR	23/5/72	Ferrari	2	R	R	R	9	8	3	3	2	9	7	10	10	10	12	5	6	11	12	38
9	Jenson BUTTON	GB	19/1/80	BAR-Honda	11*	R	R	DQ	-	-	10	Rp	NS	4	5	3	5	5	8	3	7	5	8	37
10	Mark WEBBER	AUS	27/8/76	Williams-BMW	5	R	6	7	6	3	R	5	NS	12	11	NC	7	R	14	4	NC	4	7	36
11	Nick HEIDFELD	D	10/5/77	Williams-BMW	R	3	R	6	10	2	2p	R	NS	14	12	11	6	R	-	-	-	-	-	28
12	David COULTHARD	GB	27/3/71	Red Bull-Cosworth	4	6	8	11	8	R	4	7	NS	10	13	7	R	7	15	R	6	9	9	24
13	Felipe MASSA	BR	25/4/81	Sauber-Petronas	10	10	7	10	11*	9	14	4	NS	R	10	8	14	R	9	10	11	10	6	11
14=	Jacques VILLENEUVE	CDN	9/4/71	Sauber-Petronas	13	R	11*	4	R	11	13	9	NS	8	14	15	R	11	11	6	12	12	10	9
14=	Christian KLIEN	A	7/2/83	Red Bull-Cosworth	7	8	-	-	-	-	-	8	NS	R	15	9	R	8	13	9	9	9	5	9
16	Tiago MONTEIRO	P	24/7/76	Jordan-Toyota	16	12	10	13	12	13	15	10	3	13	17	17	13	15	17	8	R	13	11	7
17	Alex WURZ	A	15/2/74	McLaren-Mercedes	-	-	-	3	-	-	-	-	-	-	-	-	-	-	-	-	-	-	-	6
18	Narain KARTHIKEYAN	IND	14/1/77	Jordan-Toyota	15	11	R	12	13	R	16	R	4	15	R	16	12	14	20	11	15	15	R	5
19=	Christijan ALBERS	NL	16/4/79	Minardi-Cosworth	R	13	13	R	R	14	17	11	5	R	18	13	R	R	19	12	14	16	16	4
19=	Pedro de la ROSA	E	24/2/71	McLaren-Mercedes	-	-	5f	-	-	-	-	-	-	-	-	-	-	-	-	-	-	-	-	4
21	Patrick FREISACHER	A	26/9/80	Minardi-Cosworth	17	R	12	R	R	R	18	R	6	R	19	-	-	-	-	-	-	-	-	3
22	Antonio PIZZONIA	BR	11/9/80	Williams-BMW	-	-	-	-	-	-	-	-	-	-	-	-	-	-	7	15*	R	R	13	2
23=	Vitantonio LIUZZI	I	6/8/80	Red Bull-Cosworth	-	-	-	8	R	R	9	-	-	-	-	-	-	-	-	-	-	-	-	1
23=	Takuma SATO	J	28/1/77	BAR-Honda	14*	-	R	DQ	-	-	12	R	NS	11	16	12	8	9	16	R	10	DQ	R	1
25=	Anthony DAVIDSON	GB	18/4/79	BAR-Honda	-	R	-	-	-	-	-	-	-	-	-	-	-	-	-	-	-	-	-	0
25=	Robert DOORNBOS	NL	23/9/81	Minardi-Cosworth	-	-	-	-	-	-	-	-	-	-	-	18	R	13	18	13	R	14	14	0
25=	Ricardo ZONTA	BR	233/76	Toyota	-	-	-	-	-	-	-	-	NS	-	-	-	-	-	-	-	-	-	-	0

The following drivers took part in Friday practice sessions at grand prix meetings but not in official qualifying or the race:

Nicolas KIESA	DK	3/3/78	Jordan-Toyota
Franck MONTAGNY	F	5/1/78	Jordan-Toyota
Chanoch NISSANY	IL	29/7/63	Minardi-Cosworth
Olivier PANIS	F	2/9/66	Toyota
Scott SPEED	USA	24/1/83	Red Bull-Cosworth
Enrico TOCCACELO	I	12/12/78	Minardi-Cosworth
Sakon YAMAMOTO	J	9/7/82	Jordan-Toyota

KEY

p	pole position	f	fastest lap
R	retired	DQ	disqualified
*	classified, but not running at the finish		
NC	not classified	NS	did not start

POINTS & PERCENTAGES
Compiled by DAVID HAYHOE

GRID POSITIONS: 2005

Pos.	Driver	Starts	Best	Worst	Average
1	Fernando Alonso	18	1	16	3.83
2	Giancarlo Fisichella	18	1	13	5.83
3	Kimi Räikkönen	18	1	17	5.89
4	Jenson Button	16	1	13	6.12
5	Jarno Trulli	18	2	19	6.33
6	Alexander Wurz	1	7	7	7.00
7	Juan Pablo Montoya	16	1	20	7.31
8	Mark Webber	18	2	16	7.89
9	Pedro de la Rosa	1	8	8	8.00
10	Michael Schumacher	19	1	19	8.21
11	Ralf Schumacher	18	1	18	8.61
12	Nick Heidfeld	13	1	17	9.15
13	Rubens Barrichello	19	5	20	10.53
14	David Coulthard	18	5	15	10.72
15	Takuma Sato	15	4	20	11.00
16	Christian Klien	13	4	16	11.08
17	Felipe Massa	18	7	18	12.00
18	Jacques Villeneuve	18	4	20	12.50
19	Vitantonio Liuzzi	4	11	15	13.00
20	Antonio Pizzonia	5	12	16	13.80
21	Anthony Davidson	1	15	15	15.00
22	Narain Karthikeyan	19	11	20	16.63
23	Christijan Albers	19	13	20	17.16
24	Tiago Monteiro	19	11	20	17.21
25	Robert Doornbos	8	15	20	17.62
26	Patrick Friesacher	11	13	20	17.82
27	Ricardo Zonta	-	-	-	-

Additionally, Nicolas Kiesa, Franck Montagny, Chanoch Nissany, Olivier Panis, Scott Speed, Enrico Toccacelo and Sakon Yamamoto tested at grand prix meetings, but did not participate in qualifying.

CAREER PERFORMANCES: 2005 DRIVERS

Driver	Nationality	Races	Championships	Wins	2nd places	3rd places	4th places	5th places	6th places	7th places	8th places	Pole positions	Fastest laps	Points
Christijan Albers	NL	19	-	-	-	-	-	1	-	-	-	-	-	4
Fernando Alonso	E	69	1	8	7	8	8	3	2	2	1	9	3	247
Rubens Barrichello	BR	215	-	9	26	26	15	14	6	7	4	13	15	489
Jenson Button	GB	100	-	-	4	8	7	14	4	6	8	2	-	167
David Coulthard	GB	193	-	13	26	21	11	16	13	14	4	12	18	499
Anthony Davidson	GB	3	-	-	-	-	-	-	-	-	-	-	-	-
Pedro de la Rosa	E	64	-	-	-	-	-	2	4	-	4	-	1	10
Robert Doornbos	NL	8	-	-	-	-	-	-	-	-	-	-	-	-
Giancarlo Fisichella	I	159	-	2	6	5	10	11	9	11	10	2	2	174
Patrick Friesacher	A	11	-	-	-	-	-	-	1	-	-	-	-	3
Nick Heidfeld	D	97	-	-	2	2	2	2	9	5	5	1	-	56
Narain Karthikeyan	IND	19	-	-	-	-	1	-	-	-	-	-	-	5
Christian Klien	A	31	-	-	-	-	-	1	1	1	3	-	-	12
Vitantonio Liuzzi	I	4	-	-	-	-	-	-	-	-	1	-	-	1
Felipe Massa	BR	52	-	-	-	-	2	2	3	3	5	-	-	27
Tiago Monteiro	P	19	-	-	-	1	-	-	-	-	1	-	-	7
Juan Pablo Montoya	CO	84	-	7	14	7	9	7	2	4	3	13	12	281
Antonio Pizzonia	BR	20	-	-	-	-	-	-	-	4	-	-	-	8
Kimi Räikkönen	FIN	86	-	9	13	8	7	2	4	4	3	8	16	281
Takuma Sato	J	51	-	-	-	1	2	3	4	-	3	-	-	40
Michael Schumacher	D	231	7	84	39	19	10	9	6	6	3	64	69	1248
Ralf Schumacher	D	145	-	6	6	14	18	17	10	9	5	6	8	304
Jarno Trulli	I	146	-	1	3	3	12	12	9	7	9	3	-	160
Jacques Villeneuve	CDN	151	1	11	5	7	10	6	9	8	9	13	9	228
Mark Webber	AUS	68	-	-	-	1	2	3	6	8	3	-	-	62
Alexander Wurz	A	53	-	-	-	2	5	3	1	7	1	-	1	32
Ricardo Zonta	BR	36	-	-	-	-	-	-	3	1	3	-	-	3

Note: As is now common practice, drivers retiring on the formation lap are not counted as having started. Where races have been subject to a restart, those retiring during an initial race are included as having started.

UNLAPPED: 2005
Number of cars on same lap as leader

Grand Prix	Starters	at ¼ distance	at ½ distance	at ¾ distance	at full distance
Australia	20	18	17	13	10
Malaysia	20	15	13	10	9
Bahrain	19	15	11	11	6
San Marino	20	16	14	9	11
Spain	18	14	13	12	6
Monaco	18	15	12	13	8
Europe	20	17	15	13	10
Canada	20	16	12	6	5
USA	6	6	4	3	2
France	20	15	10	4	3
Britain	20	18	14	9	9
Germany	20	15	12	10	9
Hungary	20	15	10	7	6
Turkey	20	15	11	8	9
Italy	20	18	15	15	10
Belgium	20	17	14	10	7
Brazil	20	17	12	8	6
Japan	20	17	17	13	12
China	20	20	17	15	12

LAP LEADERS: 2005

Grand Prix	Kimi Räikkönen	Fernando Alonso	Juan Pablo Montoya	Giancarlo Fisichella	Michael Schumacher	Rubens Barrichello	Ralf Schumacher	Jenson Button	Jarno Trulli	David Coulthard	Nick Heidfeld	Total
Australia	-	2	-	54	-	1	-	-	-	-	-	57
Malaysia	2	51	-	1	-	-	-	2	-	-	-	56
Bahrain	-	55	-	-	-	-	-	2	-	-	-	57
San Marino	8	46	-	-	3	-	5	-	-	-	-	62
Spain	66	-	-	-	-	-	-	-	-	-	-	66
Monaco	78	-	-	-	-	-	-	-	-	-	-	78
Europe	48	9	-	-	-	-	-	-	1	-	1	59
Canada	22	6	10	32	-	-	-	-	-	-	-	70
USA	-	-	-	-	51	22	-	-	-	-	-	73
France	-	70	-	-	-	-	-	-	-	-	-	70
Britain	-	7	51	2	-	-	-	-	-	-	-	60
Germany	35	32	-	-	-	-	-	-	-	-	-	67
Hungary	32	-	10	-	28	-	-	-	-	-	-	70
Turkey	58	-	-	-	-	-	-	-	-	-	-	58
Italy	-	-	53	-	-	-	-	-	-	-	-	53
Belgium	12	32	-	-	-	-	-	-	-	-	-	44
Brazil	8	2	61	-	-	-	-	-	-	-	-	71
Japan	6	-	-	27	3	-	12	4	-	1	-	53
China	-	56	-	-	-	-	-	-	-	-	-	56
Total	375	336	217	116	85	23	12	9	4	2	1	1180
(Per cent)	31.8	28.5	18.4	9.8	7.2	1.9	1.0	0.8	0.4	0.2	0.1	100.0

RETIREMENTS: 2005
Number of cars that retired

Grand Prix	Starters	at ¼ distance	at ½ distance	at ¾ distance	at full distance	% of finishers
Australia	20	1	1	3	5	75.0
Malaysia	20	3	4	6	7	65.0
Bahrain	19	3	5	5	7	65.0
San Marino	20	3	5	5	7	75.0
Spain	18	2	3	4	6	66.7
Monaco	18	1	3	3	4	77.8
Europe	20	1	1	2	3	85.0
Canada	20	0	2	8	9	52.7
USA	6	0	0	0	0	100.0
France	20	1	3	5	5	75.0
Britain	20	1	1	1	1	95.0
Germany	20	0	0	1	2	90.0
Hungary	20	2	3	4	6	70.0
Turkey	20	0	3	4	5	75.0
Italy	20	0	0	0	0	100.0
Belgium	20	1	4	4	7	65.0
Brazil	20	2	3	3	4	80.0
Japan	20	3	3	3	4	85.0
China	20	0	3	4	4	80.0

GP2 REVIEW
FAST and FURIOUS
by SIMON ARRON

Nico Rosberg emerged as a worthy champion of the GP Series. His performances led to a contract to race for Williams in F1 in 2006.
Photograph: GP2 Media Service

Near right: Hiroki Yoshimoto proved to be one of the revelations of the series.
Photograph: GP2 Media Service

Far right: Adam Carroll won at Monaco.
Photographs: LAT Photographic

Below: Ex-F1 driver Gianmaria Bruni won at Catalunya but, despite switching teams, all but disappeared from the points-scorers as the season progressed.
Photograph: James Moy/www.crash.net

MOTOR SPORT'S latest finishing school had been on public display for about 90 seconds when the promoters' faces turned a shade of red to match the pit exit light. Launched amid much fanfare as a replacement for the 20-season-old FIA Formula 3000 Championship, which had been axed in the face of increased competition and dwindling support, the Renault-backed GP2 Series could hardly have started more ignominiously. When the season's first free-practice session took place at Imola (Italy), 15 of the 24 competing cars ground to a halt before 30 minutes were up. Many, indeed, expired before they had completed so much as a lap. The problem? A rudimentary fuse-box, the kind of thing usually found on a Fiat Punto, rather than a cutting-edge 550-bhp racer, was tripping the electrics because it couldn't cope with the extreme vibration levels.

While F1 teams sat before banks of monitors in the neighbouring paddock, fretting over telemetry data, the GP2 fraternity was busily binding its trip switches with gaffer tape, to hold them in place. In the following afternoon's inaugural race, serious brake-wear issues became apparent and several drivers stopped voluntarily because they realised that to carry on was to court misadventure. The problem was so severe that an alternative supplier was drafted in overnight before Sunday morning's sprint event, which several teams had otherwise threatened to boycott. The racing was encouragingly effervescent in between breakdowns, but that couldn't mask the administrative discomfort.

Growing pains are an inevitable accompaniment to many new initiatives, yet these were fundamental cock-ups that shouldn't have arisen, not least because the GP2 prototype had been pounding around for several months beforehand. For the handful of teams that had transferred directly from the FIA F3000 series, it was a significant culture shock. They were accustomed to turning up, firing up and getting on with the job.

Their previous series had been hit by only two engine failures in nine seasons. Now they had something they felt they couldn't trust for nine laps. Furthermore, the initial format – two mandatory pit stops during the weekend's longer race, but no obligation to change tyres – made it extremely difficult for spectators to track competitors' progress (or, indeed, to understand why cars had peeled into the pits, stopped for no apparent reason and then driven back onto the circuit).

From this confusing, shambolic start, however, GP2 established itself as one of the brightest motor-sport innovations since the combustion engine. The format was fine-tuned – a single mandatory tyre stop was imposed in the main race from the second meeting onwards, to the benefit of public comprehension – and the racing was invariably captivating. This was partly because the top eight finishers in the first race lined up in reverse order at the front of the grid for the second, partly because a blend of brute force and restrictive technology (the sight of 24 cars departing beneath a veil of unfettered tyre smoke was a welcome anachronism) exposed driving flaws and created plentiful overtaking opportunities. Cutting-edge componentry was cast aside. The onus was on humans, with their many engaging frailties, and the result was all the better for it. A few technical glitches endured throughout the campaign, but their influence gradually diminished.

The destiny of the inaugural title was not settled until the Bahrain finale, the only event not to support a European grand prix. Renault test driver Heikki Kovalainen (Arden International) led the chase for most of the season, but Nico Rosberg's ART team fronted by Nicolas Todt, son of Ferrari sporting director Jean, found a clear performance advantage in the second half of the campaign and Rosberg edged ahead as the championship drew to its conclusion. Both men won five races (Rosberg three main events and two sprints, Kovalainen four main and one sprint), but the German's superior haul of fastest laps and pole positions, worth two points a time, gave him the upper hand. Victory in the first race in Bahrain, where he went on to become the first driver to score two wins in a weekend, put the issue beyond doubt.

Such was ART's mid-season momentum that the team was briefly suspected, privately at least, of malpractice. In Hungary the stewards ripped apart the cars of Rosberg and team-mate Alexandre Prémat and discovered an irregularity with the

Top: Although somewhat overshadowed by his team-mate Nico Rosberg, Alexandre Prémat proved a very able competitor.

Above: Scott Speed was unfortunate not to win a race but was sometimes among the very fastest runners. Expect him in F1 for 2006 with Squadra Toro Rosso, formerly Minardi.

Above right: Regular autograph sesions helped the fans to feel involved.

Right: Nelson Angelo Piquet blasting his car away from a pit stop.
Photographs: GP2 Media Service

steering-rack mounting points. The cars certainly didn't conform, but rival engineers accepted that the tweak might induce a little extra bump-steer but would not have a significant effect on overall performance. The reconfigured cars were sent to the back of the grid, from where they rose to fourth and fifth in the opening race and first and second in the sprint. After that, most rivals grudgingly accepted that ART had capitalised on the input of two strong drivers and was simply doing a better job.

Gracious in defeat, Kovalainen would have been just as worthy a champion as Rosberg. Part of Renault F1 linchpin Flavio Briatore's stable of emerging talent, Kovalainen is regarded as a likely candidate for a grand-prix seat by 2007 and will completely overturn the popular perception that racing Finns are spectacularly fast dullards. Bright and articulate, he shares with Rosberg the ability to drive quickly while retaining sufficient spare capacity to absorb the bigger picture.

The leading duo wasn't alone in having these skills. America's search to unearth its first F1 driver since 1993, when Michael Andretti made conspicuously poor use of a McLaren, finally appears to be over. Scott Speed (iSport) didn't win any races, although he was unjustly denied at least once by the inopportune appearance of a safety car, but he was part of a select group whose unfailing speed set it apart from the capable but undistinguished majority. In 2006, Red Bull support will springboard him into the drinks company's growing F1 armada, where his blunt, direct manner will provide a distinctive counterpoint to some of his future rivals' corporate correctness.

Northern Irishman Adam Carroll (Super Nova) had a softer, more measured manner off the track, but on it he emerged as one of GP2's most combative assets. He often made life hard for himself, stalling on the grid ahead of the Istanbul (Turkey) sprint race, for instance, yet his calm, instinctive race-craft invariably carried him back into contention. He went from 21st to second at the Nürburgring (Germany), 24th to second in Turkey and 24th to fifth at Spa (Belgium), and he scored three wins when he didn't saddle himself with unnecessary hurdles. He was the architect of many fine passing manoeuvres during a season that had its fair share, but his removal of Prémat from the lead at Imola's last chicane was perhaps the most exquisite.

Prémat ended up fourth in the final table, between Speed and Carroll. The Frenchman had a decent season and netted a couple of wins, but suffered simply because he was saddled with an even faster team-mate, Rosberg, as a yardstick.

Unlike everybody else in the field, Gianmaria Bruni (who began the year with Coloni before doing a lawyer-enriching flit to Durango) and Giorgio Pantano (Super Nova) were in effect on their way down the ladder, having competed (or driven, at least) in F1 the previous season. Both were as fast as their pedigree suggested they should be, but neither did enough to suggest further grand-prix opportunities will be forthcoming any time soon.

Bruni managed one win before falling out with Coloni. Pantano never really gave the impression that he wanted to be here – hardly surprising, given that he spent three years on the F3000 treadmill before his brief F1 cameo with Jordan. He suffered a string of technical problems but cheered up later in the season when he earned a chance to dip his toes into the Indy Racing League, a better career option than doing another lap at this level, where he has absolutely nothing to prove.

Swiss Neel Jani (Racing Engineering) was steady rather than spectacular, although he notched up a couple of wins in between carving a reputation as one of the series' most difficult people to pass. Much was expected of reigning British-F3 champion Nelson Piquet Jr (Hitech Piquet Sports), but the Brazilian was scuppered by unreliability, internal politics (his team underwent a mid-season management reshuffle) and his own gauche tactics. He eventually cobbled together a win at Spa, but that was marred by the manner of his delivery. He was in a position to challenge for victory only once he'd rammed Prémat off the track, but although the stewards found him culpable he was allowed to keep the points and was penalised only with a loss of ten slots on the grid for the following day's sprint. More often than not, he looked distinctly ordinary, intermittently fast, but immature with it.

Argentine Jose Maria Lopez (DAMS) started the season with a reputation for being fast but erratic, but embellished only the less desirable of those attributes. He won the Barcelona (Spain) sprint but spent most of the campaign driving into things. Like Kovalainen, he was a senior member of the Renault Driver Development programme. Unlike the Finn, he failed to make the most of this good fortune. Frenchman Olivier Pla (DPR) and Monegasque Clivio Piccione (Durango) completed the list of ten race winners, although both were generally fringe players.

Venezuelan Ernesto Viso (BCN) had a useful turn of speed but also proved to be woefully clumsy. His team-mate Hiroki Yoshimoto, however, emerged as the find of the season. He started the year as a virtual unknown (he was tenth in the 2003 Japanese F3 series, for instance), yet he took second place in the Magny-Cours (France) sprint and set seventh-fastest time in a wet qualifying session at Spa, a track he'd never seen before, and only inexperience denied him a string of decent finishes. The Osaka-born 25-year-old is a cosmopolitan character who spent his teenage years on Australia's Gold Coast and has a neat line in self-deprecatory humour. He has significant potential and is highly marketable with it.

As the season wore on and races became ever more keenly contested, several people suggested that GP2 was a perfect template for the way F1 ought to be. McLaren boss Ron Dennis retorted that a disparity in driving standards was the root cause of this new fad for overtaking. It's perfectly true that there was a sizeable gulf between those who could drive and those who were clinging on by their fingertips (much as there often is in F1, in fact), but that didn't explain why the genuinely talented blokes at the front of the field were able to race – and pass – each other with such vim.

That was the point.

Below: A moment to savour for the new GP2 champion Nico Rosberg as he stood on the podium in Bahrain.
Photograph: GP2 Media Service

A1 GP REVIEW
NATIONS UNITED
by CRAIG LLEWELLYN

Top: The field thundering away from the starting grid at the second round of this fledgling series at the Lausitzring.

Above: A1 GP will be represented in all corners of the world.
Photographs: Mike Weston/www.crash.net

Right: A rich mix of nations in the top three at Brands Hatch. Mexico's Salvador Durán (left), Brazil's Nelson Angelo Piquet (centre) and Australia's Will Power.
Photograph: Jakob Ebrey Motorsport Photography

Left: Drivers from countries such as Russia add to the intriguing mix.

Below: Dubai's Sheikh Maktoum, seen here at the opening race at Brands Hatch, was the man behind the vision for a 'World Cup of Motorsport'.
Photograph: Jakob Ebrey Motorsport Photography

Below centre: All of the cars are identical Lola-built machines. The livery – such as Ireland's distinctive green and orange, seen here – is the key to identification.

Bottom centre: Portugal's Alvaro Parente tucked into his car.
Photographs: Mike Weston/www.crash.net

THE world motor-sport arena was greeted by a new concept in 2005 when the A1 GP – the self-titled 'World Cup of Motorsport' – staged its impressive Brands Hatch debut late in September.

Twenty-five cars, resplendent in their national sporting colours, lined up for the first race watched by former F1 champions including Emerson Fittipaldi, John Surtees, Nelson Piquet, Alan Jones and Keke Rosberg, all of whom had an involvement in A1 GP in some form or other.

The brainchild of Sheikh Maktoum Hasher Maktoum Al Maktoum, A1 GP is a spec series (the cars are all the same)

with chassis by Lola, engines by Zytek and big wide slick tyres by Cooper. Fettling the machinery are squads ranging from the highly experienced in various formulae – such as DAMS, Carlin Motorsport, WSR (West Surrey Racing), Alan Docking Racing, Astromega, Dave Price Racing, SuperNova and Arden Motorsport – to the far less experienced squads put together using the home talent of the nations they represent.

'It's a business first and foremost,' explains Sheikh Maktoum of his new series. 'I started looking at motor sport as a concept. If I were a driver, I'd lose money; if I were a team, I'd lose money; if I were a series provider, I'd lose money – so there is something basically flawed in the business model and it's one of those things where you think there must be a better solution, and I said why don't I just restructure it?'

From within the motor-sport industry, there was a fair amount of healthy cynicism, as greets any new series, but the Sheikh was good to his word in getting 25 cars on the grid for the first event. Now the hard work transfers to the franchise holders to make the entries viable and sustainable operations. A quarter-season in and there is not the greatest amount of sponsorship on the sides of the cars, but it's still very early days.

The race calendar stretches over what is traditionally seen as the off-season. It began with Brands Hatch in the UK and includes trips to Germany's Lausitzring, Portugal's Estoril, Australia's Eastern Creek (Sydney), Malaysia's Sepang, the United Arab Emirates' Dubai, Indonesia's Sentul, South Africa's Durban, Brazil's Curitiba, Mexico's Monterrey, California's Laguna Seca (USA) and China's Shanghai.

Those circuits are hosting three-day race meetings with two one-hour practice sessions on the Friday and a third one-hour session on the Saturday, followed by an innovative qualifying format. The drivers are given four 15-minute sessions and are allowed to set a single flying lap per session. The top two times from each driver combine to make up the grid.

Race action follows on Sundays, with a rolling start for the sprint race, which lasts for around 30 minutes, and a standing-start feature race lasting twice that period and encompassing a compulsory pit stop. There is only an hour between the two races, making it critical to stay out of incidents in the first race.

Considering how much attention has been given to F1's qualifying format recently, A1 GP came up with a good variation for its show. The four open 15-minute sessions mean that drivers and teams still have to decide when to go out, taking into account when they'll find space on the track and when the track is at its fastest. Only a single flying lap may be set within each session, meaning that if a driver encounters traffic on his flyer, he can write off that session.

Winning through all of this for the first qualifying, at Brands Hatch, was 2004 British-F3 champion Nelson Piquet Jr, driving for Team Brazil. The son of the three-times F1 champion put in the then-best lap time of the weekend on his third flying lap, so it was no particular issue for him when he sat out the final qualifying run. The team cited a technical glitch, but Piquet was already assured of pole unless someone else did something

truly spectacular and, by not running in the final session, he saved a set of his allocated tyre allowance.

The qualifying session may have been tension-filled, but the first-ever sprint race was something of a let down. Despite the presence of PowerBoost buttons – which when pressed deliver extra power for a short period of time to increase a driver's chances of overtaking – and aerodynamics tailored to allow slipstreaming, the circuit and the drivers' anticipation of a second race just an hour away conspired to leave spectators wondering whether this race was just a display run to show off the cars, an extension of the opening ceremony that they had just witnessed.

Brazil won. Piquet's pole translated into an unchallenged run to the chequered flag, with Team France's DAMS-run Alex Prémat – who, like Piquet, raced in GP2 this year – in second place, having passed sports-car racer Matt Halliday in the WSR-run New Zealand car at the start, one of a scarcity of racing moves.

The second race was something altogether far more exciting. Nelson Piquet was once more the victor but dramas in the young Brazilian's pit stop meant that he exited in second place and had the Team Australia car of Will Power (World Series by Renault) up ahead. Helped by the fresh tyres that had gone unused in qualifying, Piquet closed in remorselessly and then capitalised on a mistake from Power at Graham Hill Bend to overtake in impressive fashion around the outside at Surtees.

There were spills as well as the thrills – most notably for the Team Lebanon car of Italian-F3 driver Kahlil Beschir, who came together with Italian Enrico Toccacelo (whose credits include F3000 and F1 testing with Minardi) turning into Paddock Hill Bend. He performed a barrel-roll demonstration of both the safety of the Lola chassis and the quality of the in-car television footage.

From Britain the series headed to Germany's Lausitzring and something of a scaling down of both the crowd and the spectacle surrounding the races. The French squad may have had a nightmare opening feature race at Brands Hatch due to a stall on the grid but, judging by its form in Germany two weeks later, the other nations will be hoping for more difficult events for the DAMS-run squad, which can call upon Alexandre Prémat and fellow GP2 driver Nicolas Lapierre for driving duties.

Lapierre was in the seat in Germany and he won both races. He was joined on the front row of the grid by Team USA's GP2 driver Scott Speed. In the sprint race, Lapierre was not seriously challenged. Speed and Team GBR's Robbie Kerr (2002 British-F3 champion) collided in an incident at the start that also proved terminal for the Netherlandish and Pakistani entries. France crossed the line leading Switzerland and Brazil, and New Zealand's Jonny Reid (Japanese F3) impressed with a run from 14th to fourth.

The Lausitzring feature race was an impressive affair. Lapierre made a relatively poor start and had to fight back into the lead, something that he achieved by the fourth lap. The Frenchman maintained his lead once the pit stops had worked out and led an impressive Robbie Kerr across the line. The Brit's squad had called Kerr in for an early stop from his back-of-the-grid start. Meanwhile Sean McIntosh (Formula Renault) took a fine third place for Canada.

Prémat did in Portugal as Lapierre had done in Germany and took a double victory.

Pole was Piquet's at Estoril, the Brazilian driver once more opting to miss one of the qualifying runs. Prémat started from third for the sprint race and all he needed at the rolling start was a blinding getaway – which was exactly what he got – to take the lead and go unchallenged to victory. Piquet and Switzerland's Neel Jani – another GP2 driver racing in A1 GP – took the other two podium spots and the Dutch cheered a fourth place for ex-F1 man Jos Verstappen, although he was some ten seconds adrift of the lead trio.

The feature race was Premat's and three safety-car periods didn't stop its being an easy result for the GP2 driver. It was an eventful race behind him, though he took victory by 7.517s from Jani with Ireland's sports-car racer Ralph Firman in third.

France may not have had an F1 race driver in the 2005 season but, if A1 GP can be used as a guide, Prémat and Lapierre are worthy of consideration – Lapierre continued the pattern in Australia and easily won both races.

With a quarter of the season over, the championship is in its early days. A few issues have emerged, such as the wheel nuts' causing problems for some teams in pit stops – but the battery problems encountered by some squads were found to be due to their using larger units than recommended; nothing that's going to bring the show to a stop. Lack of the income required to make the business model work, however, could be a concern and the departure of Team Japan from the line-up is evidence of this. There are, however, a lot of countries around the world and, on the evidence so far, A1 GP could have a strong future.

Above: Nelson Angelo Piquet proved a formidable competitor from the outset, winning for Brazil in the opening round at Brands Hatch.

Main: Adrian Sutil under ominously cloudy skies at Estoril, where Portugal's round of the A1 GP series took place.
Photographs: Mike Weston/www.crash.net

FORMULA 3 REVIEW

DOMINANT FORCES

by ANDY STOBART

Above: Adrian Sutil played second fiddle to Lewis Hamilton in the European series, two wins helping him to an eventual second place in the points tally.

Right: Lucas di Grassi had to be content with a single victory at Oschersleben.

Bottom: Sebastian Vettel was the Euro Series' top rookie, driving for ASL Mucke Motorsport. He is shown leading Giedo van der Garde's Team Rosberg Dallara-Opel.

Photographs: Marco Miltenberg/Racepictures.com

THERE were dominant performances in both the F3 Euro Series and the British F3 International Series in 2005 as Lewis Hamilton in the Euro Series and Alvaro Parente in the British took their respective crowns.

Hamilton opened up his season with an emphatic victory in the first race, at Germany's Hockenheim, and so it continued through the year, with only four races the British driver didn't win on the track – although he and six other drivers were later excluded from the first race of the weekend at Spa, Belgium, (which Hamilton had won) due to rear-diffuser-dimension discrepancies.

It was also a story of the superiority of the ASM squad and of the Mercedes engine over the Opel Spiess, but such a dominant performance by Hamilton pointed to more than just technical brilliance.

The five other victories went to Hamilton's team-mate Adrian Sutil, who took two; Manor Motorsport's Lucas di Grassi, who took one; and Signature's James Rossiter and rookie Guillaume Moreau, who took one apiece.

The champion took pole position 13 times in 20 races and seldom looked challenged, something reflected by his points tally at the year's end. Where Hamilton goes next will be interesting to see; another season of such domination would be quite some achievement. 'I delivered a fantastic season and I wouldn't mind if I could continue this way next year – no matter where I will be racing,' he admitted.

Second in the championship and with the unenviable task of attempting to measure up to his team-mate Hamilton on every race weekend, Adrian Sutil came home with two race wins and 94 points to Hamilton's 172. The wins came at Spa, where Hamilton had been disqualified for having one of the duff diffusers, and at the Nürburgring, Germany, where Hamilton and Di Resta had collided.

Paul di Resta finished in a lowly tenth place in the championship. He took his single win in the second race of the season, at Hockenheim. After that, things certainly didn't go to plan and he could manage only one other podium result, with a third place at the Norisring in Germany.

Moreau's race win was taken at the Dutch Zandvoort circuit, in the first race there. It was a case of right place, right time – ASM team-mates Hamilton and Sutil came together in the first corner of the opening lap and Moreau made the most of the safety-car restart. His only cause for concern, Paul di Resta, was penalised for his pass on Sebastian Vettel at the restart and given a drive-through penalty.

Lucas di Grassi's race win came at Oschersleben, Germany, where he had taken pole position and then allowed those behind him to make mistakes in a race that was restarted after rain brought out the red flags to stop the race early.

The Rookie Cup went the way of Sebastian Vettel, on 157 points to Esteban Guerrieri's 132, with Moreau – overall race-winner at Zandvoort – coming in third on 128.

When the renamed British F3 International Series lined up for its first race of 2005, its eventual champion – Alvaro Parente – was not on the grid. Nor was he when the series lined up for its season finale, but he didn't need to be because in the course of the 17 races that he had contested, he had a 50-percent success rate in his Dallara-Mugen, which was sufficient to bring the British-F3 title to the Carlin team.

Parente may have been a returnee to the championship, having finished in seventh place the year before, but that didn't account for his performance. He displayed impressive maturity and form all season long, never once showing any real chinks in his armoury.

'He's just been perfect ever since we put him in the car this year,' explained team boss Trevor Carlin after Parente sealed his title at the Nürburgring. 'I just think he needed an extra year in F3 to settle himself down and prove what he can do.'

Had the season-opener at Britain's Donington Park been a taste of things to come, it could have been a very different year. That two-race event led to a double victory from another returnee, Brazilian Danilo Dirani, driving for P1 Motorsport with a Lola chassis.

Alvaro's greatest challenge through the season came from an in-house Carlin pretender to the throne: the very impressive Charlie Kimball. Coming to F3 after a season in the British Formula Ford series, the American driver offered a refreshing maturity and a fantastic developing ability behind the wheel.

Other than Parente's, Kimball's and Dirani's, there were race wins for third-in-the-championship Mike Conway, who won at Croft; fifth-finishing Dan Clarke, who won at Castle Combe; Steven Kane, who finished a lowly ninth in the championship, despite showing frequent pace, and took a popular win for Lola at Mondello Park; and James Walker, who took a win in Germany but ended his year 11th in the points.

For 2005 the old scholarship class (for older cars) became the national class, creating a rather bizarre moniker: the British F3 International Series National Class. Australian Barton Mawer opened up the year well, initially entering on a race-by-race basis but later scraping together the money to complete the season. He led for much of it but, in the second half of the season, Mexican Salvador Durán truly came on song and took the title come the season's end.

These two series got together, to an extent, for the Marlboro Masters race at Zandvoort, the final event to be run under that moniker, due to Europe's new tobacco-advertising legislation. Only the best of the world's F3 drivers are invited to race at Zandvoort.

The Masters was run on the same Kumho tyres as the Euro Series used all year and Lewis Hamilton was on top form, taking pole and then driving off to an unchallenged victory. Steven Kane, from the British contingent but driving for the JB Motorsport squad in a Lola, qualified in fifth, but then had a high-speed accident in the warm-up and had to miss the race. Adrian Sutil came home second, some six and a half seconds adrift of Hamilton, with Lucas di Grassi right behind him. Mark Asmer, driving for Hitech, was the best of the British-series drivers, in seventh place.

As for the world's other F3 championships, the All Japan F3 title went to João Paulo de Oliveira at his second attempt, driving for the Tom's squad and notching up 270 points over the season to team-mate Kazuki Nakajima's 197. The Brazilian driver had been in the hunt to take the title in 2004, but an accident at the Mine circuit – where he clinched this year's title – had put him out of the running. This year he took seven wins over the course of the 20-race championship and scored points in all bar one race.

The German Recaro Cup was taken by Peter Elkmann with 150 points. He beat Ireland's Michael Devaney – who is racing in A1 GP and hopes to step up to GP2 or the World Series for Renault in 2006 – and Chinese driver Tung Ho-Pin, who was third on 88 points. Elkmann took six wins to Devaney's five. Six other drivers won races: two wins each went to Ho-Pin, Jan Seyffarth and Ferdinand Kool, and a win apiece to Frank Kechele, Julian Theobald and Martin Hippe.

In the Italian F3 Series, Luigi Ferrara took the title from Alex Müller with 180 points to the latter's 171. Ferrara took only half the race wins that Müller did (three to Müller's six), but was far more consistent than Müller. Paolo Maria Nocera matched the champion's race-win tally and came home third in a close-run championship with 168 points. No other driver won a race.

In Spain, there is one race meeting to go as AUTOCOURSE goes to press and José M Pérez Aicart leads with 99 points to Andy Soucek's 93, with Ricardo Risatti on 90. The Asian F3 Series has been won by Ananda Mikola and the South-American F3 championship has two rounds to go with Alberto Valério on 106 points to Zeca Cardoso's 89.

Insight F3 driver Aaron Caratti has dominated the Kumho Tyres Australian Formula 3 Championship, which has two rounds still to run, winning eight of the 12 races, including six consecutively. Team BRM's Michael Trimble has scored two wins and sits second in the series, but will need Caratti to have some fairly serious dramas at the end of the season if he is to have any chance of winning the championship.

Below left: Salvador Durán won the newly renamed national class of the British F3 series.

Below: Luigi Ferrara, the Italian F3 champion, in his Team Corbetta Dallara.
Photographs: Jakob Ebrey Motorsports Photography

Above: Bruno Senna drove for Räikkönen Roberston Racing in the British championship, following in the footsteps of his late uncle, Ayrton, who won the title in 1983.

Left: Dan Clarke competing against the changeable British weather.
Photographs: Jakob Ebrey Motorsports Photography

SPORTS & GT REVIEW

CHAMPION
PERFORMANCE

by GARY WATKINS

Above: The Le Mans-winning Champion
Audi of Tom Kristensen, JJ Lehto and
Marco Werner.
Photograph: Richard Dole/LAT Photographic

Left: The winning trio of drivers on the
podium. Kristensen was celebrating his
seventh win in the La Sarthe classic.
Photographs: Rainier Ehrhardt/www.crash.net

Above: World-Rally champion Sebastien Loeb joined the Pescarolo squad for the race, but he and his co-drivers Eric Helary and Soheil Ayari were eventually forced into retirement.

Top: The Emanuele Pirro/Allan McNish/ Frank Biela Champion Audi finished third after an off-track excursion stymied its chances of victory.

Photographs: Rainier Ehrhardt/www.crash.net

IT was the dream storyline for any sports-car fan worthy of the name: Tom Kristensen claimed a record seventh victory in the Le Mans 24 Hours and the Audi R8 bowed out from the great race with a fifth victory in six years. That outcome was no foregone conclusion in the run-up to the event, but before the race was even four hours old the Champion Racing entry that Kristensen shared with JJ Lehto and Marco Werner was sitting at the top of the leader board.

There was perhaps an inevitability about Kristensen's triumph, which moved him clear of Jacky Ickx in the all-time winners' table. Yet the Dane and his team-mates didn't have the fastest car around the Circuit de la Sarthe: the double penalty of 50 kg of ballast and a five-percent reduction in engine power applied to old-style LMP1 prototypes saw to that. It could even be argued that theirs wasn't the fastest of the three R8s present.

What they did have, however, was an incredible consistency, coupled with flawless reliability in temperatures in excess of 35°C. That set the winning entry apart from its opponents.

Kristensen and co had four genuine rivals for victory and perhaps the most remarkable thing was that all four of those cars ran into trouble before the race was much more than three hours old, allowing Lehto to take a lead that he and his team-mates would never relinquish.

The fastest of the challengers was the first to be delayed. Henri Pescarolo's pair of Judd-powered prototypes, now converted to the latest aerodynamic rules, easily had the edge on speed over the all-conquering R8. And not surprising: Le Mans's 2005 rule book decreed that the Pescarolo C60 was lighter, had more power and even had a bigger fuel tank. What's more, the Pescarolo drivers reckoned the team's designers had clawed back the downforce lost under the new regulations.

That explains why Emanuele Pirro, who initially led the Audi charge in the second Champion entry, suggested the French cars were 'in a different category'. After just two laps of the

8.48-mile Circuit de la Sarthe, the best of the Pescarolos, driven by Jean-Christophe Boullion, was nearly 15 seconds up on Pirro in fourth place. Seven laps in, that gap stood at more than half a minute.

If the Pescarolos could proceed through this race without drama – and one had run reliably to fourth place in 2004, remember – the Audis weren't going to get a look-in.

The Pescarolo Sport team hit trouble – and earlier than anyone could have expected. The car driven by World-Rally champion Sebastien Loeb, making his first appearance at La Sarthe, lost time in the hands of Soheil Ayari. A clash with a slower car before the race had reached the two-hour mark resulted in two stops for suspension repairs and briefly dropped the car out of the top ten. A second clash with a slower car in the night dropped Ayari, Loeb and Eric Helary out of contention and a third off shortly before midday on Sunday finally put the car out of the race.

The leading Pescarolo, meanwhile, made it as far as the end of the second hour before technical problems intervened. A gearbox glitch forced the team to change the internals with the loss of 26 minutes, or five laps.

Pescarolo's problems allowed Pirro in the second Champion Audi to take the lead, but he slid off the track in the third hour and lost around three minutes for repairs, allowing the Kristensen car to take up its position at the front.

The second Champion Audi, in which Pirro was joined by Allan McNish and Frank Biela, never fully recovered from this early delay. It briefly got within a minute of the leader on Sunday morning before a delaminated tyre sent McNish off the road at Indianapolis corner and from there back to the pits for attention to the suspension.

That allowed the lead Pescarolo, co-driven by Emmanuel Collard and Erik Comas, into second position. The car was still three laps down but such was its pace that the all-French crew had already clawed back two of the laps lost earlier.

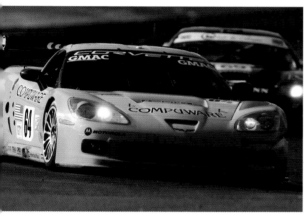

That gap briefly came down to under one lap, then Pescarolo realised the chase was in vain and, with the car's engine temperatures rising, decided to settle for second. 'I told my drivers to push,' said Pescarolo, 'and continued to do so until the final hour. The engine wasn't overheating, but it was a little too warm.'

The third Audi in the race, the French-run ORECA car, claimed fourth behind the Pirro/Biela/McNish car after twice being delayed by right-front suspension failure. The first was almost certainly caused by the car's running over some debris, but the second remained unexplained.

An unusually high rate of attrition among the prototypes allowed the GT1 class-winning Chevrolet Corvette C6.R driven by Oliver Gavin, Olivier Beretta and Jan Magnussen to claim fifth overall after a thrilling battle with the new Prodrive-built Aston Martin DBR9s that had trounced them in the American Le Mans Series opener at Sebring back in March.

GT2 honours fell to the BAM!/Alex Job Racing Porsche 911 GT3-RSR in which Mike Rockenfeller and Marc Lieb did all but a handful of laps (money-man Leo Hindrey took over for a brief stint early in the race). The two young Germans somehow kept the US-entered car ahead of the fancied Petersen/White Lightning entry of Jörg Bergmeister, Patrick Long and Timo Bernhard despite the heat.

It was a good day for the US teams. All bar the LMP2 prototype class, which was won by the British RML squad's MG-Lola, went to regulars from the American Le Mans Series (ALMS). Champion's victory ended a drought for teams from the other side of the Pond that stretched all the way back to 1966 and Shelby American's victory with Ford.

The Le Mans victory was the crowning moment of an amazing season for the Florida-based Champion squad. There was another ALMS title, sealed with a third straight victory in the Petit Le Mans 1,000-mile classic at Road Atlanta (Georgia), and a first win for the team in the Sebring 12 Hours (Florida).

Pirro and Biela may have missed out on a fourth triumph together at Le Mans, but victory in the second of those US enduros and a further three wins gave them each a second

Top left: The RML MG-Lola of Thomas Erdos, Mike Newton and Warren Hughes took the LMP2 class.

Centre left: The Alex Job Racing Porsche was the winner in the GT2 class.

Below left: The GT1 class-winning Chevrolet Corvette C6.R, driven by Oliver Gavin, Olivier Beretta and Jan Magnussen.

Below: The Pescarolo-Judd of Emmanuel Collard, Jean-Christophe Boullion and Erik Comas took pole position but had to settle for second place at the finish.
Photographs: Rainier Ehrhardt/www.crash.net

headed for its finale at Mexico City. The works-run Pontiac-powered Riley driven by Max Angelelli and Wayne Taylor held a clear advantage over the Lexus-engined version run by Chip Ganassi Racing for Scott Pruett and Luiz Diaz.

The level of competition also rose in the FIA GT Championship, even if grids were down. The ever-controversial Maserati MC12 emerged as the benchmark car in its first full season, though it was hit with a series of penalties that took the edge off its performance over the course of its campaign.

The new Vitaphone Racing squad, put together over the winter by former DTM touring-car driver Michael Bartels, emerged as the class act in the series. A hat trick of wins, including victory in the Spa 24 Hours (Belgium) for Bartels, regular team-mate Timo Scheider and local star Eric van de Poele, had a downside. The two Vitaphone Maseratis and the championship-leading JMB Racing entry driven by Andrea Bertolini and Karl Wendlinger were hit with a 40-kg weight penalty as the series left Europe for its three-race Asian run-in.

The Le Mans Endurance Series (LMES) was also due to climax outside Europe, albeit just over the Bosporus at the new Istanbul Park circuit (Turkey). The LMES attracted grids in excess of 40 cars in its second year and no one car dominated in any of the four classes. The top prototype division remained open going into the finale, with no fewer than five drivers in with a chance. At the top of the points was Japanese driver Hayanari Shimoda, who had won the series opener at Spa and round four at Germany's Nürburgring in the works-run Zytek 04S.

Audi's representative in the LMES, the French ORECA team, was a race winner but always remained an outsider in the championship chase after missing round two at Monza (Italy). It wasn't quite what the German manufacture had envisaged for one of the most successful sports cars of all time. But at least it signed off from Le Mans in style. And then some.

ALMS crown. Lehto and Marco Werner lost their chance of the championship when the former got himself involved a first-corner accident at Atlanta and was forced to limp back to the pits on three wheels.

The LMP1 entry again fell in the ALMS, whereas the Daytona Prototype (DP) class in the rival Grand American Sportscar Series went from strength to strength. The fields were always in excess of the 20-car mark – and that was without taking into account the GT cars that bulked out the grid.

The Riley MkXI maintained its position as the best DP car out there and was on course for a second straight title as the series

Left: The Porsche RS Spyder made its LMP2 début at the final ALMS round at Laguna Seca.
Photograph: Denis L Tanney/LAT Photographic

Below: Pedro Lamy strapped into his Ferrari 550 Maranello at Monza.
Photograph: Photo 4

Bottom: Allan McNish put in a storming drive in changeable conditions to win for Audi in the Le Mans Endurance Series round at Silverstone in August.
Photograph: Jakob Ebrey Motorsport Photography

TOURING CAR REVIEW

THE BEST OF BRITISH

by MATT SALISBURY

Top left: Andy Priaulx carried the fight for the World Touring Car crown to his fellow BMW driver and rival Dirk Müller.

Top: Fabrizio Giovanardi leading Augusto Farfus in an Alfa one-two at the head of the pack at Imola.

Above: Jordi Gené, leading team-mate Peter Terting, scored a first win for the new SEAT Leon at Valencia.

Left: Alex Zanardi continued to do remarkable things in his specially adapted BMW.

Far left: Dirk Müller was wheel-to-wheel with Priaulx for the WTCC crown going into the final race of the season.
Photographs: Photo 4

BRITISH racing drivers are the best in the world. That's certainly the case in terms of touring-car championships as AUTOCOURSE goes to press late in 2005. Brits stand as champions in their native British Touring Car Championship (BTCC) with Matt Neal, the German DTM with Gary Paffett and the European Touring Car Championship (ETCC) with Andy Priaulx, and even the Australian V8 Supercar Series is led by the London-born Russell Ingall.

The World Touring Car Championship (WTCC, successor to the ETCC) title is yet to be resolved, with ETCC champion Andy Priaulx one point off points-leading fellow-BMW driver Dirk Müller heading into the finale at Macau – and Alfa's lead charger Fabrizio Giovanardi is in with a shout of the title, too.

In its first year, the World Touring Car Championship has enjoyed grids of around the 30 mark and strong manufacturer backing from BMW, Alfa Romeo, SEAT, Chevrolet and, to a lesser extent, Ford. The series has been running on Eurosport's Super Racing Weekend package in conjunction with the FIA GT championship and crowd levels and TV viewing figures have been impressive, as has the action on-track, with a success-ballast structure ensuring the racing remains close.

The opening two rounds were dominated by the rear-wheel-drive BMWs, so the championship's front-wheel-drive (FWD) cars had 20 kg taken off their base weight ahead of the next round, at Britain's Silverstone. The front-wheel-drive Alfa Romeos promptly qualified in the top three spots and took the top four spots in the weekend's first race and SEAT took the second race. All of which illustrated the very difficult challenge of determining the most appropriate weight differences – the rear-wheel-drive BMWs always have a starting advantage which can often displace any lack of pace.

Ten drivers have taken race wins, including Giovanardi, who has four, Dirk and Jörg Müller, on three each, and Priaulx, a mere one win. The front-wheel-drive cars have taken ten wins. Alfa took seven of those, Gabriele Tarquini taking two and 2004 British Touring Car Champion James Thompson taking one, plus Giovanardi's tally. SEAT scored the other three FWD wins with Rickard Rydell, Peter Terting and Jordi Gené taking a win apiece. Gené's occurred in the new Leon, which the marque will campaign next season. Much like the 2004 ETCC battle, however, the title battle has been that between the lead BMW drivers and a solitary Alfa.

The organisers were quick to makes changes to ensure that the racing remained close and both Chevrolet and Alex Zanardi benefited from 10-kg weight breaks during the year. Zanardi, who took race victories in the Italian Supertourisme championship in 2005, scored an emotional first WTCC win at Oschersleben, Germany, during the race meeting in which Priaulx's solitary race win was achieved with maximum success ballast in his car.

'Dirk's been lucky enough to bounce off walls and carry on driving, whereas I've had quite a few races where I've failed to finish because I've not been in a position to carry on with the car,' said Priaulx before heading to Macau. 'If you look back over the year, I should really be leading the championship.

'If I want to win the championship, I have to beat Dirk in both races and if Giovanardi wants to win then he, realistically, has to win one of the races and hope Dirk and I finish down the order. All three of us have a chance of winning it but anyone who is confident going into the last race is stupid, because it can go to any of us.'

The 2006 season will bring the introduction of Yokohama tyres and racing on the streets of Helsinki, Finland, as well as the WTCC's running separately from the FIA GT championship because the two organisations were unable to reach an accommodation over appearing on the same race bill.

Above: Matt Neal drove a strongly strategic BTCC campaign to emerge victorious with his Team Dynamics Honda Integra.

Right: Neal celebrating his first BTTC title.

Below: Dan Eaves took third place in the standings with the second Halfords-backed car.

Photographs: Jakob Ebrey Motorsport Photography

In the Dunlop MSA British Touring Car Championship, a dominant performance from Team Halfords and its Team Dynamics-built and -run Honda Integra Type Rs took Matt Neal to his first overall BTCC drivers' title. The squad, under the watchful eye of Steve Neal (the driver's father), had played a blinder with its choice of car and, as an independent team, it had no marketing considerations such as Vauxhall had in going to the far larger new Astra.

It was a season in which 'the people's champ' Matt Neal became the overall champion – something not achieved by an independent runner in the series for over a decade. Neal's campaign started strongly, though he was pushed hard by team-mate Dan Eaves, who achieved a championship first by taking three wins in one day at Thruxton. Neal, however, drove with his sights firmly on the title and consolidating his points lead was the name of the game from early on.

Neal scored race wins at Donington, Brands Hatch, Oulton Park and Knockhill, and when he wasn't winning he was on the podium everywhere bar the Silverstone round. Yvan Muller took wins at Donington, Brands Hatch, Croft, Mondello and Knockhill, but the Astra just didn't have the pace with ballast to take the fight to the Integra, which performed admirably even when carrying full weight. 'This is not a massive team, but it's not one person who's won it; everyone in the team has won it,' said Neal of his championship win, the title taken from the manufacturer works drivers in emphatic fashion.

Muller came home second in the championship after a season of driving the wheels off the new Astra, just pipping Dan Eaves to the runners-up spot in the season finale at Brands Hatch. The Frenchman had no strong in-house challenge, as he had experienced in the past, and he was not battling for the title against someone in the same car. Whereas two-times champion James Thompson was in the team last year, taking the title from Muller with the slimmest of margins, lead 2005 team-mate Colin Turkington's season encompassed poles and race wins, but Turkington finished the year 99 points adrift of Muller, on 174 against the Frenchman's 273. Third VX Racing driver, Gavin Smith, took time to come to terms with the level of competition, but did have a race win to his name come the season's end.

Vauxhall did miss having two consistent challengers, as it has had in years gone by, and between Muller and Turkington in the final standings were Eaves, Jason Plato and Tom Chilton, Chilton having made a late switch to selected BTCC races after his DTM plans were aborted and he tailored his season around his sports-car campaign. It was a fast and not-quite-as-furious-as-in-the-past campaign from the developing 20-year-old. There was an extra challenge for the opposition, too, as Team Dynamics brought in Gareth Howell in a third car to great effect – he took a win at Silverstone.

SEAT's lead driver was once more Jason Plato, driving well but often on rather argumentative behaviour both off and on the track, with the weight equalisation for the S2000 cars his particular gripe. James Pickford in his début BTCC season was fast and feisty and certainly deserved better opportunities than he received; he was unlucky to miss out on a race win at the season finale at Brands Hatch, but insiders noted his talent. Luke Hines, meanwhile, had his second season with a works squad after his late switch from Vauxhall, but it was a season

that didn't deliver quite as the son of karting hero Martin Hines would have wanted.

WSR (West Surrey Racing) dusted off the MG ZS once more and, despite the departure of MG Rover from the automotive manufacturing arena, Rob Collard put in strong performances on occasion. The Hampshire driver is certainly no Anthony Reid, but he took victories at MG favourites Knockhill and Brands Hatch.

Elsewhere, the field was enlivened by the presence of a bioethanol-powered Astra driven by Fiona Leggate and a two-car-strong Lexus squad with former Renault Clio team-mates Richie Williams and Ian Curley. The series enjoyed unrivalled TV coverage and also staged street demonstrations across the UK.

The BTCC will run to the FIA's Super 2000 touring-car technical regulations from 2007, those used by the WTCC, and any new cars coming to the championship from that season will have to be based on a model that is readily available through authorised dealer networks across Europe, thus preventing any new strategies of the likes of Team Dynamics' successful 2005 tactic of using the personal-import-only Honda Integra.

Below far left: Allan Gow again played the role as the Bernie Ecclestone of the BTCC.

Below left: Jason Plato was his usual controversial self at the wheel of the SEAT.

Below: Fiona Legatte drove a bioethanol-powered Vauxhall Astra, which added to the technical variety of the BTCC series.

Bottom: High roller Yvan Muller put on a suitably spectacular two-wheeled show in his Vauxhall Astra.

Photographs: Jakob Ebrey Motorsport Photography

Above: Gary Paffett consolidated his reputation as potential F1 material by claiming the DTM title for Mercedes-Benz.

Right: There were aerodynamics aplenty on Pierre Kaffer's Audi.

Below: Joy for Mika Häkkinen as he celebrated his rebirth as a DTM star with victory at Spa-Francorchamps, the scene of his greatest F1 triumph.

Photographs: Marco Miltenberg/Racepictures.com

In the world of DTM, Gary Paffett achieved what he so nearly had in 2004 and took his first title in the popular German series. Paffett, driving for Mercedes, came to the season finale at Hockenheim with the title all but decided, needing only to finish in the top eight to secure the crown while defending champion, Audi's Mattias Ekstrom, needed to win with Paffett failing to score to stay champion.

It was an interesting season, in which Paffett took five race victories to Ekstrom's three. The only other drivers to win were all former F1 drivers: Jean Alesi, Mika Häkkinen and four-times DTM champion Bernd Schneider took a win each at Hockenheim, Spa (Belgium) and Hockenheim respectively.

Paffett and Ekstrom were once more the class of the field and both cemented their reputations. Paffett's wins came at the Lausitzring, Oschersleben, the Norisring, Zandvoort (Holland) and in the debut DTM race at Istanbul (Turkey), while Ekstrom's wins were at Brno, the Nürburgring and Lausitz. Third in the championship at the season's end was Le Mans legend Tom Kristensen in his second year of DTM with Audi, having taken pole at Oschersleben, where rain cancelled the single-flying-lap Superpole session for the top qualifying runners, which meant the qualifying times stood, and then setting the best Superpole lap at the next race for good measure too.

'It was an incredible feeling when I crossed the line,' said Paffett after coming home third in the final race of the year. 'During the race, I had no time at all to think about what it would be like to be the champion. This has been a nearly perfect season with some minor mistakes – and with a fantastic result. The battle with Mattias was big fun. The two final rounds turned out to be crucial. In those rounds, the team proved that it was able to deliver in superior style.'

Bernd Schneider ended the season in fourth place, the second of the Mercedes drivers, two points ahead of Häkkinen and three ahead of Jamie Green, who started from P1 twice during the course of the year. Alesi entertained the crowds as ever, though his season-opening win was not to be repeated.

Heinz-Harald Frentzen stood on the podium twice in Opel's final season but was looking for work at the end of the year, while Laurent Aiello finished in joint 11th place with Marcel Fässler and announced his retirement from motor sport.

As a footnote, there was very nearly a fourth manufacturer in the 2005 season – MG was poised for an entry with a Zytek-built and Arena Motorsport-run car with Tom Chilton and another, undecided, driver behind the wheel. Negotiations had even been conducted to get Johnny Herbert in the seat, but the British manufacturer's demise meant this never happened.

The Australian V8 Supercar Series goes from strength to strength and is arguably the closest and most competitive touring-car championship in the world. The 2004 season was settled in favour of Marcos Ambrose for Stones Brothers Racing, the Tasmanian driver making it two in a row for himself and for Ford. As AUTOCOURSE goes to press his team-mate, Russell Ingall, leads the 2005 championship with Triple Eight Engineering-run Craig Lowndes coming on strong over the latter events of the season.

The Australian championship visited China's Shanghai in 2005 and Bahrain joins the calendar from 2006 as the series branches out to new audiences with its Holden-v-Ford battle.

Left: Heinz-Harald Frentzen at Zandvoort.

Below left: Laurent Aiello called time on a long and distinguished career in single seaters and touring cars.

Below: Veteran DTM champion Bernd Schneider remained a competitive force, but the new generation put him under pressure.

Bottom: Tom Kristensen, seen here with his team-mate Matthias Ekström, piled on the Audi pressure to keep Mercedes on its toes.
Photographs: Marco Miltenberg/Racepictures.com

NEW HORIZONS

by GORDON KIRBY

Above: Champ car's revitalised spectator appeal continued to expand in 2005, a fixture at Edmonton being a new addition to its diverse North-American schedule.
Photograph: Mike Levitt/LAT Photographic

Far left: Paul Tracy remained one of the undisputed Champ car pace setters, but did not have quite the consistency to keep Sébastien Bourdais at bay.

Left: Bourdais took his second straight Champ car title after another impressive season for Newman/Haas.
Photographs: Phil Abbott/LAT Photographic

Right: Justin Wilson scored a rightly popular maiden Champ car victory through the streets of Toronto.
Photograph: Mike Levitt/LAT Photographic

IN an otherwise typical year for American motor sport – NASCAR (National Association for Stock Car Auto Racing) rolling along bigger and better than ever, the Indy 500 continuing its slow, steady decline, sports-car racing similarly disfigured and diminished – the big story was about Champ car's turnaround as the organisation reborn from CART's (Championship Auto Racing Teams) ashes in the winter of 2003–04 began to catch everyone's attention. There were successful new races, big crowds and an increasingly clear business plan from Champ car's primary owners Kevin Kalkhoven and Jerry Forsythe, enacted by Kalkhoven's long-time partner and business manager Dick Eidswick.

Kalkhoven and Forsythe had shown they were serious when they agreed to buy Cosworth in November 2004, thus securing the riddle of engine supply for the Champ Car World Series but also making a big commitment to motor sport as a whole and to the wider world of high-performance engineering.

They further demonstrated their commitment by buying the Long Beach Grand Prix from Dover Downs Entertainment in May 2005, once again outmanoeuvring Indianapolis Motor Speedway boss Tony George, as they had done 18 months earlier when George unsuccessfully tried to buy the bankrupt remains of CART. Then in October they completed a deal to buy Molstar, Molson's promotional and TV unit and promoter of the successful 20-year-old, mid-summer Toronto street race.

Late in the year Champ car announced its technical package for 2007–09 with a new, smaller, trimmer Panoz DP01 spec car replacing the venerable 2001-type Lola B2/00 that has dominated Champ car for the past four years, winning all but four races since 2002 and all races in the past two years.

The new Panoz will be built at Elan Motorsports Technologies outside Atlanta and will be powered by the familiar, traction control-free, 2.6-litre Ford-Cosworth XFE turbo V8 with the horsepower bumped up to more than 800 bhp. All the engines will continue to be supplied to the teams from a common pool.

And Champ car also announced a new Formula Atlantic for 2006 to replace Toyota Atlantic, after an 18-year run, with Swift chassis powered by 300-bhp, 2.3-litre, four-cylinder Cosworth-Ford Focus engines. There will also be a $2-million prize for the champion to spend on a Champ-car ride for the following year.

Never in the 40-year history of the formula – which made its debut in 1966 as Formula B and became Atlantic in 1974 – has any sanctioning body, least of all CART, properly embraced Formula Atlantic. But Kalkhoven and his group intend to promote the formula as the key step to Champ car and plan to announce sometime in 2006 a new FF2000/Formula BMW-like, Cosworth-powered entry-level series for 2007.

CHAMP CAR RISING

Champ car ran successful new races in 2005 in front of big crowds in Edmonton (Canada; 200,000 over three days), and San José (California; 160,000), and has plans for 2006 and beyond for new street races in Houston (Texas) and Philadelphia (Pennsylvania), as well as Ansan (South Korea), Beijing (China) and Otaru (a small resort city north of Sapporo, Japan. Street racing – so-called 'three-day urban festivals' – has become Champ car's mantra in a very clear differentiation from NASCAR and IRL.

'We've enjoyed successful downtown races for many years at Long Beach [California], Cleveland [Ohio], Toronto [Canada] and Surfers Paradise [Australia],' Kevin Kalkhoven commented. 'In recent years we've added great new events in Denver [Colorado] and Montreal [Canada] and this year in Edmonton and San José. These urban events are wonderful for spectators and are a perfect fit for our marketing strategy. It's clearly been proven that people love this type of event. People want to come to downtown events and our plan for downtown motor-racing festivals works. Champ car is alive and thriving.'

San José's inaugural street race in the shadow of Silicon Valley replaced nearby Laguna Seca on the Champ-car schedule and, as rough and 'Mickey Mouse' as the track may have been, the race generated plenty of coverage on TV and radio and in the newspapers throughout the Bay Area (which includes San Francisco, Oakland, San José and many other smaller cities with a combined population of eight million) unlike anything that Laguna Seca had ever generated.

It was sad to lose Laguna, but the politics of American open-wheeled racing and poor promotion had taken their tolls on both the crowd and the media coverage at the great old road course on the nearby Monterey Peninsula. In contrast, Kalkhoven said no fewer than 71 Silicon Valley companies came to the race in San José. 'If only 20 percent show an interest in sponsoring racing, we've made a good start,' he said.

Kalkhoven's plan is to maintain a balance, running half the races in the US and half in the rest of the world. With three successful races in Canada and two in Mexico, Champ car hopes to establish street races in Brazil or Argentina, but neither seems likely for a few years at least. The rest of the international focus is on the Pacific Rim with South Korea, China and Japan the primary targets.

An Australian who started his business career in London in the 1960s and made his fortune in Silicon Valley in the 1990s, Kalkhoven has impressed everyone with his aggressive approach, energy and sharp sense of humour. He and Jerry

Forsythe appear to be a perfect combination, Kalkhoven leading the charge and Forsythe quietly supporting him, splitting their investments 50-50 not only on Champ car, but on other purchases such as Cosworth, Long Beach and Molstar.

'I'm not surprised by the momentum,' Forsythe commented. 'A number of teams from other series have approached us and I'm very confident that several teams are going to join the Champ Car World Series for 2006.'

Forsythe said he believes it's probable that the field will be back to full strength with 24 or more cars when the new-generation Champ car replaces the current car in 2007. 'One of our goals is to see that happen,' he said.

The test for Champ car will be whether the new Formula Atlantic delivers in 2006 and 2007 and the new Champ-car formula delivers in 2007 and 2008, attracting the anticipated 24- or 26-car grids. If both these things happen, Champ car will be in great shape as a potential rival once again to F1 in the worldwide TV market with a fan base, a global business plan orchestrated by a pair of sharp operators and a proper ladder system focused on Formula Atlantic.

BOURDAIS'S SECOND TITLE

On the track in 2005, defending champions Sébastien Bourdais and Newman/Haas Racing demonstrated their mastery of Champ-car racing. Early in the year, Bourdais was challenged by 2003 champion Paul Tracy, but it all went wrong for Tracy after he ran out of fuel while leading at Toronto and then crashed while leading at Denver. In the end, it was all about Bourdais and Newman/Haas as the Frenchman won six races and romped to his second consecutive title while Oriol Servia made it one-two in the championship for Newman Haas.

Servia replaced the injured Bruno Junqueira in June and did a perfect job as stand-in, scoring his long-sought first Champ-car win at Montreal in August and taking second in the championship. After taking the lead by winning the year's second race in Monterrey, Mexico, Junqueira was badly injured

in the Indy 500 when he collided with the hapless AJ Foyt IV. Junqueira broke his back and was sidelined for the rest of the season. He hopes to race again in 2006.

When he was on form, Tracy was irresistible, as he was when he won at Milwaukee (Wisconsin) and Cleveland (Ohio) and led at Toronto, Denver and Las Vegas (Nevada), but he was no match for Bourdais's perfect finishing record. Tracy wound up slipping to fourth in the championship. Tracy's Forsythe team-mate Mario Dominguez was a solid number two, finishing ninth in the championship with second at Denver his best result.

Beating Tracy to third in the championship was Justin Wilson. For his second year in Champ car, Wilson moved to Carl Russo's RuSPORT team, paired with AJ Allmendinger. He had impressed in his rookie season and he looked even better in 2005, running away from the field at Portland in June before his engine's oil pump failed, then scoring his first win at Toronto in July and his second at Mexico City in November.

Team-mate Allmendinger responded to Wilson's gauntlet, finishing second to mentor Tracy at Milwaukee and Cleveland, and qualifying on the pole at Edmonton. In his second year in Champ car, Allmendinger finished fifth overall.

Kevin Kalkhoven's team, PKV Racing, upped its game for 2005, hiring returning 2001 CART champion Cristiano da Matta to partner Jimmy Vasser and taking on Champ car's most successful team manager/crew chief Jim McGee to run the team. PKV had its moments – Da Matta won at Portland (Oregon) and took the pole at Cleveland, and Vasser took pole at Milwaukee – but in many races they were merely also-rans. Much more is hoped for in 2006.

Champ car's top rookie in 2005 was German Timo Glock, who was very impressive in one of Paul Gentilozzi's Rocketsports cars. Glock showed himself to be an aggressive racer and easily won the rookie-of-the-year title while finishing eighth in the championship. Glock outshone his more experienced team-mate Ryan Hunter-Reay and beat a strong field of rookies, which included Swede Bjorn Wirdheim, French-Canadian Andrew Ranger and Dane Ronnie Bremer.

Left: Sébastien Bourdais leading the pack around the challenging San José circuit.
Photograph: Phil Abbott/LAT Photographic

Above: A winner at last. The likeable Oriol Servia deputised for Bruno Junqueira at Newman/Haas and proved his worth.
Photograph: Mark Horsburgh/LAT Photographic

Top: Oval tracks are again part of the varied Champ car format. Jimmy Vasser is shown refuelling at Las Vegas Speedway.
Photograph: Brad Bernstein/LAT Photographic

Above: **Dan Wheldon holding a commanding lead in the Indianapolis 500. He became the first Briton to win the race since Graham Hill did in 1966.**

Opposite top right: **Sam Hornish found that Toyota power for Penske usually left him struggling against the Honda-propelled Andretti-Green cars. Next year the Captain will be switching his cars to Honda power as well.**
Photographs: Phil Abbott/LAT Photographic

Opposite top left: **Wheldon and Dario Franchitti beckoned AGR team-mate Bryan Herta to the podium at St Petersburg.**
Photograph: Michael Kim/LAT Photographic

Opposite centre right: **Marco Andretti (centre) flanked by grandfather Mario (left) and father Michael.**
Photograph: LAT Photographic

Opposite centre left: **Tony Kanaan relinquished his IRL crown to Dan Wheldon, but at least the championship remained in the Andretti-Green domain.**

Opposite: **Danica Patrick nearly pulled off a remarkable victory in the Indianapolis 500 and understandably attracted considerable media attention.**
Photographs: Mike Levitt/LAT Photographic

WHELDON SWEEPS INDY 500 AND IRL

The Indy Racing League's big hopes for 2005 centred on the series' first venture into road racing, running a street race in St Petersburg (Florida) in April and two late-season road races at Sears Point (California) and Watkins Glen (New York). But whether it is racing on ovals, roads or street courses, the IRL still has a tough time pulling much of a crowd on anything but race day – and even then it's well short of Champ car's level.

In fact, in 2005 the IRL's public and media appeal was all about rookie lady driver Danica Patrick, who moved up to the IRL with Bobby Rahal's team after two years in Toyota Atlantic. Patrick caught the public's attention by finishing a lucky fourth at Indianapolis and there were hopes over the rest of the year that she could win a race, but it didn't come close to happening.

By mid summer, Toyota had confirmed that it was pulling out of the IRL after five years, at the end of 2006. Chevrolet also confirmed it was pulling out, but immediately, at the end of 2005, leaving Honda the only one of the IRL's three manufacturers spending serious money on development.

In fact, Honda spent lavishly on wind-tunnel work and friction reduction, with Andretti-Green in particular, but also with Bobby Rahal's and Adrian Fernandez's teams. As a result, Honda was superior to an even greater degree than in 2004 and at the end of the year it confirmed that it will continue in the series through to 2009, even if it has to be the IRL's sole engine supplier.

The series was dominated in 2005 by Andretti-Green Racing (AGR), which ran four cars with all four drivers winning at least once each for a total of 11 wins from 17 races. The team swept the championship, with Dan Wheldon winning the title and six races, including the Indy 500; 2004 champion Tony Kanaan finishing second in the championship with two wins; and Dario Franchitti finishing fourth in the points, also with two wins. Fourth AGR man Bryan Herta also managed to score a win. Wheldon's Indy-500 victory was the first for a Briton since Graham Hill won back in 1966, but Wheldon was upstaged by Ms Patrick, who got the lion's share of the media coverage on race day at Indianapolis and over the course of the season.

The only serious rival to AGR was Roger Penske's team. Penske is the only authorised outside rebuilder for Toyota engines and the team continued to develop its own engines, winning three races – two with Sam Hornish and one with Helio Castroneves. Hornish broke AGR's grip on the championship, finishing third in the points between Kanaan and Franchitti.

Other race winners were Tomas Scheckter, Scott Sharp and Scott Dixon. Driving one of the few Cosworth-based Chevrolets in the field, Scheckter was often quick and won at Texas in June. Sharp's lone win came at Kentucky in August and Dixon broke his own and Chip Ganassi's two-year IRL winless streak by winning at Watkins Glen in September. For most of the year, Ganassi's drivers were tail-end Charlies and endured a series of crashes: no fewer than 26. And IRL cars are uninsurable.

Based largely on the strength of her fourth place in the Indy 500, Danica Patrick was the IRL's rookie of the year and was said to have conducted more than 700 media interviews during 2005. Rahal's team leader and 2004 Indy-500 winner Buddy Rice missed the 2005 Indy 500 after crashing in practice and injuring his back. Rice soon returned to action but suffered a forgettable year. In fact, Rahal's best bet was third driver Brazilian Vitor Meira, who finished seventh in the championship.

Near the end of the year it was announced that Phoenix (Arizona), the California Speedway and Pike's Peak (Colorado) would not continue with the IRL in 2006, cutting the series' schedule from 17 to 14 races. Ten tracks have now given up on the IRL because of its inability to draw money-making crowds. The others were Atlanta (Georgia), Charlotte (North Carolina), Dover (Delaware), Las Vegas, New Hampshire, Nazareth (Pennsylvania) and Orlando (Florida). It is not a happy trend.

Early in the year, going into May, there was more fruitless talk about reunification between the IRL and Champ car. A series of meetings took place, the last in July when Kevin Kalkhoven flew to Indianapolis to meet Tony George. The meeting was over in less than five minutes when George told Kalkhoven, 'I don't like partners.' Kalkhoven thanked George for his time and flew home to California, shaking his head in bewilderment.

NASCAR'S MARKETING MACHINE

While Champ car attracted the attention of most of the local markets in which it raced and also caught the eyes of the enthusiast media and cognoscenti, there was no question that NASCAR continued its unabated motor-sports dominance of America's mass media and presence in the USA's popular culture. NASCAR means racing in America. All the top NASCAR stars are well known across the US and many of them sell or promote popular products on TV on a daily basis. Dale Earnhardt Jr may not have won a championship, but he is by far the most known and most popular racing driver in America and the public assumes he's every inch the match of four-times champion Jeff Gordon, NASCAR's most successful active driver.

Regularly, both inside and outside the sport, the question is asked: 'Is it racing or is it marketing?' It's about the latter, most people agree. 'NASCAR is a marketing machine,' says Champ-car star Paul Tracy. 'It specialises in marketing to the masses and neither Champ car nor the IRL has the dollars or the expertise or time to market the sport like NASCAR does.'

In NASCAR, 'the show' has always come first. This dictum was laid down by NASCAR's founder Bill France Sr more than 50 years ago and is put into play these days by third-generation boss Brian France. Brian is the grandson of Bill Sr and son of the equally tough, street-smart Bill Jr, who built soundly on his father's success through the last quarter of the 20th century.

Bill Jr passed on the reins to Brian in September 2003 and even though the grandson may be walking in some awfully large shoes, he has the support of a strong organisation with offices these days in New York and Los Angeles as well as Daytona Beach, Florida, and Charlotte. Meanwhile, Brian's father Bill Jr continues as vice-chairman, semi-retired at best, with Bill Jr's younger brother Jim continuing as vice-chairman and executive vice-president. Bill Jr's daughter and Brian's sister Lesa France Kennedy sits on NASCAR's board of directors and is president of the ISC (International Speedway Corporation), the publicly traded company that owns 12 racetracks and superspeedways across the US from Daytona and Talladega, Alabama, to the California Speedway and Watkins Glen.

In recent years, NASCAR has been America's fastest-growing sport. Crowd and TV numbers continue as strong as ever and the mainstream media following has gotten bigger than ever. Near the end of the year it was announced that ABC/ESPN had bought NASCAR's TV rights for the next three years, paying $280 million for the privilege after NBC/TNT decided not to renew its much-promoted $200-million deal because it was unable to make a profit televising NASCAR. Also, this was the second year that NASCAR's top series was known as the Nextel Cup, replacing long-time series sponsor Winston, but with Sprint's buying Nextel in the middle of the year, expect another renaming to Sprint Cup in 2007.

As usual, a number of drivers featured in the battle for the 2005 championship. Four-times champion Jeff Gordon won the season-opening Daytona 500 but then faded almost to also-ran status, failing to make 'the chase for the cup'. This was the second year of the chase, wherein the top ten drivers after 26 of 36 races qualify for a play-off for the championship over the season's final ten races. Neither Gordon nor Earnhardt Jr qualified for the chase, but TV and crowd numbers remained steady, proving that it was the show that mattered most.

Through the mid summer, 2002 champion Tony Stewart was the hot guy as he steamed into the championship lead, winning five races over a seven-race stretch from June to August, including the Brickyard 400. This was the first time that Indiana native Stewart had won at Indianapolis and, as the summer turned to autumn, Stewart seemed to hunker down, acting a little less volatile, a little more the seasoned old pro.

More than anyone else, 34-year-old Stewart was competitive in almost every race, a rare accomplishment over such a long season, and he stayed in the thick of the title fight all the way. Stewart has driven for NFL (National Football League) coaching legend Joe Gibbs' team since he moved to NASCAR from the IRL in 1999 and has established himself as one of stock-car racing's top stars beside Gordon and Earnhardt Jr.

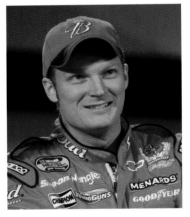

Top: Tony Stewart's Chevrolet Monte Carlo and Greg Biffle's Ford Taurus battling for the crown.

Above: Dale Earnhardt Jr had a less than memorable season.

Photographs: Robert LeSieur/LAT Photographic

Opposite: Roookie of the year Kyle Busch performed donuts after his win at Fontana.

Photograph: Lesley Ann Miller/LAT Photographic

In many ways, the story of the year was that neither Gordon nor Earnhardt made the ten-car field for the chase. In his 13th year in NASCAR's top league, Gordon, also 34, endured his least successful season on record. After winning three of the year's first nine races and looking like a serious contender for his fifth title, Gordon all but fell off the map, running into all manner of problems and often just plain off the pace.

Earnhardt Jr had an even worse time. In his sixth year racing Cup cars, he was less of a contender than Gordon and people wonder whether the 31-year-old son of NASCAR's greatest legend and his team – Dale Earnhardt Inc – can bounce back.

Five teams made the chase for the cup: the finalists included all five of Jack Roush's Fords, two of Penske South's three Dodges and one each from the multi-car Joe Gibbs (Chevrolet), Rick Hendrick (Chevrolet) and Ray Evernham (Dodge) teams. Roush's team comprised defending champion Kurt Busch, veteran Mark Martin, 2003 champion Matt Kenseth and newcomers Greg Biffle and Carl Edwards. Busch was often very

quick but rather luckless in 2005, winning some races but often getting caught up in incidents and accidents. Clearly one of NASCAR's best drivers, Busch decided in the second half of the season to leave Roush in 2007 for greener pastures with Roger Penske.

Meanwhile, in his third year with Roush, Biffle was often the team's strongest card, winning several races and leading the championship for a while. Oregonian Biffle won NASCAR's second-division Busch Grand National championship in 2002 and he stayed in the 2005 title battle all the way.

Carl Edwards could turn out to be the best of Roush's new generation of drivers. The 26-year-old Edwards ran a dozen Cup races as a rookie for Roush in 2004 and was often a front runner in 2005, his first full season. Edwards won a few races, including a dominant victory at Atlanta at the end of October that put him in the thick of the championship battle.

In his 18th year with Roush, 46-year-old Mark Martin was as competitive as ever, a frequent contender who easily made the

Below left: Despite winning the Daytona 500, Jeff Gordon had plenty to think about in a largely undistinguished 2005.

Below centre: Jimmie Johnson mounted another vigorous title bid for Rick Hendrick's team.

Below: The durable Mark Martin was always a contender.
Photographs: Robert LeSieur/LAT Photographic

Below: Carl Edwards did a backflip after scoring victory at Atlanta. The huge grandstands reflect the wealth and success of NASCAR as probably the most crucially important element of the US motor-racing scene.
Photograph: Robert LeSieur/LAT Photographic

Opposite top: Charles Zwolsman took the Toyota Atlantic championship in its final guise.
Photograph: Mike Levitt/LAT Photographic

Opposite centre left: Katherine Legge won three races and finished third in the Toyota Atlantic championship, earning an F1 test drive with Minardi at the end of the season.
Photograph: Gregg Feistman/LAT Photographic

Opposite centre right: The Infiniti Pro champion was Wade Cunningham, who saw off the more experienced Jeff Simmons.
Photograph: Lesley Ann Miller/LAT Photographic

championship play-off and also scored the 35th win of his career at the Kansas Speedway in October. Martin has never won the championship – he has finished second four times – and had intended to retire at the end of the year, but he was convinced by Roush to continue for one more season after Kurt Busch decided to leave his team. In mid-summer, Busch signed a lucrative multi-year contract with Penske South, where he will take over the retiring Rusty Wallace's seat in 2007.

Roger Penske's NASCAR team was surprisingly competitive in 2005 with relative newcomer Ryan Newman and veteran Rusty Wallace, but less so with rookie Travis Kvapil. In his fourth full year with Penske South, Newman was Tony Stewart's most serious rival. Newman was on the pole several times and frequently led races, but he found it difficult to win and fell out of the championship reckoning with three races to go.

The 49-year-old Wallace retired at the end of the year after completing his 22nd year on the Cup circuit and his 15th with Penske. Wallace stayed in the championship battle all the way.

Only one of Rick Hendrick's fleet of four Chevrolets made the chase and that was driven by fourth-year Hendrick driver Jimmie Johnson, runner-up in the title stakes in both 2003 and 2004. Johnson started the season well, leading the points for a time before tailing off in the second half of the year. He bounced back during the chase, however, and pulled even with Tony Stewart after winning his fourth race of the year at Charlotte in October.

One of Hendrick's cars was driven in 2005 by Kyle Busch, the 19-year-old brother of 2004 champion Kurt. Kyle took over the retired Terry Labonte's seat and was quick in some races. He proved himself when he won at the California Speedway in September, becoming at 20 years and four months old the youngest Cup winner in NASCAR history. In fact, NASCAR is infested with fresh-faced young kids these days, including Jaime

McMurray, Kasey Kahne and Carl Edwards; the latter also scored his first Cup win in 2005, driving for Jack Roush's team.

One of the grumbles made about NASCAR is that nothing changes, but there's a new look planned for introduction in 2007. For the first time in 30 years, a new chassis will be mandated, which will have a more centrally mounted seat and will be bigger and bulkier in an attempt to make the car less aerodynamically efficient. Another harbinger of change is the arrival of Toyota in NASCAR, starting off for the past two years in the third-division truck series. Toyota is expected to race in the Busch series next and the Cup series by 2007 or 2008.

Already the Japanese giant, intent on selling itself in America as an American-style company making jobs for Americans, has started pushing up the cost and politics. Kurt Busch's new contract with Penske, for example, is believed to be driven by Penske's long-term commitment to race Toyotas in the Cup series in the future and, with both General Motors and Ford in perilous financial waters these days, the worry is that Toyota will eventually spend the American dinosaurs out of the sport.

One of the things that remains persistently unchanged is the spectacle and danger of restrictor-plate racing at Daytona and Talladega: the cars are choked down from more than 800 bhp to about 450 bhp (by punctured plates between the carburettor and the intake manifold), reducing speeds from a theoretical 230 mph to 180 mph. The cars run flat-out, two and three abreast in a giant pack. The drivers hate it and at Talladega in September there were three big, multi-car wrecks.

Mark Martin was among those whose car was ruined in the first of these wrecks and the widely respected veteran pleaded to the fans on TV to do something about restrictor-plate racing. 'The fans are the only ones who can do anything about this,' Martin said. 'The drivers can't, the owners can't and NASCAR's not going to do anything about it. I doubt if the fans can, either.'

Protest the fans did, writing to newspapers and the motor-sports press. Inevitably, this was followed by a deafening silence from NASCAR. Restrictor plates will remain in effect at Daytona and Talladega and eventually will be used elsewhere, too. NASCAR remains firmly in control and it will be interesting in the years ahead to watch the wrestling match between the France-family empire and Toyota as GM and Ford, NASCAR's traditional partners, struggle for market share and survival.

Near the end of the season Brian France got everyone's attention by casually announcing to a group of reporters that NASCAR was considering limiting the number of cars that a team may run. Many people took this as a direct jab at Jack Roush after all five of his cars made the chase, but France said it was aimed at 'helping teams such as those of the Wood brothers, the Pettys and Cal Wells – independent teams that are finding themselves in increasing difficulties to compete'. He added, 'It will be much lower than five. It will be a cap.'

Unfortunately, we can't leave NASCAR without mentioning the remarkable number of tyre failures suffered during 2005 by Goodyear's spec tyre. Time and again, races were turned into lotteries with puncture after puncture putting cars into the wall. Both the May and October races at Charlotte were plagued by tyre failures and accidents, with a record 22 yellows in the spring race and 15 yellows in the autumn.

Goodyear blamed the epidemic on teams' under-inflating the tyres and a newly milled track surface at Charlotte in particular, but the problem did not reflect well on Goodyear, with its 40-plus years of experience in NASCAR, or on NASCAR itself.

OTHER RACING SERIES

Champ car's supporting Toyota Atlantic championship was won by Dane Charles Zwolsman, who took the title with three wins. Tonis Kasemets finished second, also winning three races, and 25-year-old Brit Katherine Legge surprised everyone by winning three races and finishing a strong third. When she took her first win, at Long Beach in April, Legge became the first woman to win an international single-seater race in more than 20 years.

Legge was sponsored by Kevin Kalkhoven and will continue under Kalkhoven's patronage in 2006, returning to the new Cosworth Atlantic series for her second year in the formula with hopes of moving up to Champ car in 2007.

The IRL's Infiniti Pro ladder-series championship was won by Wade Cunningham, who beat Jeff Simmons to the title. The American Formula BMW title went to 16-year-old French lad Richard Philippe, whose brother Nelson races Champ cars.

The American Le Mans sports-car championship was won by Frank Biela and Emanuele Pirro aboard a Champion Racing Audi R8. Champion ran a pair of Audis and battled for the title against Rob Dyson's pair of Lola B01s. The rival, NASCAR-backed Grand Am series for lower-tech, stock-block-powered cars was won by the Riley-Pontiac of Max Angelelli and Wayne Taylor.

And NASCAR's second-division Busch championship was taken by Martin Truex Jr, who dominated the series, handily outscoring another highly rated up-and-comer, Clint Bowyer. The Busch series, by the way, is America's second-most-watched racing series both at the gate and on TV.

The Sports Car Club of America's TransAm championship was won by Klaus Graf, a 36-year-old German who drove a Jaguar XKR for Gentilozzi's Rocketsports team. Graf beat Corvette-mounted Randy Ruhlman. Gentilozzi did not defend his title, focusing instead on running his Champ-car team.

Marco Andretti, the 18-year-old grandson of Mario and son of Michael, competed in the IPS and the Star Mazda series. He ran the entire Star Mazda series, finishing fifth in the points with a second place his best result. He was more successful in the IPS series, where he won three of the five races in which he participated. Bobby Rahal's 16-year-old son raced in the Star Mazda series after a year in Formula BMW and Rahal usually beat Andretti, taking fourth in the championship. The Star Mazda title was won by Brazilian Raphael Matos.

Above: A closely packed Grand Am field taking the start at Daytona.
Photograph: Denis L Tanney/LAT Photographic

Left: Klaus Graff steered one of Paul Gentilozzi's Jaguars to Trans Am glory.
Photograph: Dan Streck/LAT Photographic

MAJOR RESULTS

OTHER CHAMPIONSHIP RACING SERIES WORLDWIDE

Compiled by DAVID HAYHOE

GP2 Series

All cars are Dallara-Renault.

GP2 SERIES, Autodromo Enzo e Dino Ferrari, Imola, Italy, 23/24 April. Round 1. 37 and 17 laps of the 3.065-mile/4.933-km circuit.

Race 1 (113.266 miles/182.294 km).

1 Heikki Kovalainen, FIN, 1h 02m 15.934s, 109.145 mph/175.651 km/h; **2** José Maria López, RA, 1h 02m 22.736s; **3** Scott Speed, USA, 1h 02m 33.676s; **4** Gianmaria Bruni, I, 1h 02m 34.372s; **5** Adam Carroll, GB, 1h 02m 37.505s; **6** Neel Jani, CH, 1h 02m 58.941s; **7** Alexandre Prémat, F, 1h 03m 02.853s; **8** Nico Rosberg, D, 1h 03m 04.606s; **9** Olivier Pla, F, 1h 03m 12.013s; **10** Ernesto Viso, YV, 1h 03m 36.962s; **11** Sergio Hernández, E, 1h 03m 46.484s; **12** Mathias Lauda, A, 36 laps; **13** Giorgio Pantano, I, 35; **14** Nelson Angelo Piquet, BR, 35; **15** Clivio Piccione, MC, 35; **16** Can Artam, TR, 34; **17** Fairuz Fauzy, MAL, 33; **18** Borja Garcia, E, 30 (DNF-brakes); **19** Ferdinando Monfardini, I, 30 (DNF-brakes); **20** Juan Cruz Álvarez, RA, 23 (DNF-brakes); **21** Ryan Sharp, GB, 11 (DNF-brakes); **22** Hiroki Yoshimoto, J, 11 (DNF-steering); **23** Alexandre (Xandinho) Negrão, BR, 4 (DNF-brakes).

Did not start: Nicolas Lapierre, F, 0 (engine).

Fastest race lap: Viso, 1m 35.257s, 115.842 mph/186.430 km/h.

Fastest qualifying lap: Lapierre, 1m 33.505s, 118.013 mph/189.923 km/h.

Race 2 (51.962 miles/83.624 km).

1 Adam Carroll, GB, 28m 31.314s, 109.309 mph/175.915 km/h; **2** Alexandre Prémat, F, 28m 36.774s; **3** Heikki Kovalainen, FIN, 28m 38.029s; **4** Gianmaria Bruni, I, 28m 41.278s; **5** Olivier Pla, F, 28m 42.833s; **6** Nelson Angelo Piquet, BR, 28m 44.894s; **7** Juan Cruz Álvarez, RA, 28m 57.083s; **8** Sergio Hernández, E, 28m 59.051s; **9** Hiroki Yoshimoto, J, 29m 01.055s; **10** Borja Garcia, E, 29m 08.562s; **11** José Maria López, RA, 29m 08.796s; **12** Fairuz Fauzy, MAL, 29m 09.279s; **13** Alexandre (Xandinho) Negrão, BR, 29m 17.223s; **14** Ryan Sharp, GB, 29m 29.121s; **15** Neel Jani, CH, 16 laps; **16** Giorgio Pantano, I, 14 (DNF-tyre); **17** Nico Rosberg, D, 12 (DNF-brakes); **18** Nicolas Lapierre, F, 6 (DNF-withdrawn); **19** Mathias Lauda, A, 3 (DNF-brakes); **20** Can Artam, TR, 3 (DNF-brakes); **21** Scott Speed, USA, 2 (DNF-misfire); **22** Clivio Piccione, MC, 1 (DNF-fuel pump.

Did not start: Ernesto Viso, YV (brakes); Ferdinando Monfardini, I (clutch).

Fastest race lap: Lapierre, 1m 33.871s, 117.553 mph/189.183 km/h.

Pole position: Rosberg.

Championship points. Drivers: 1 Kovalainen, 14; **2** Carroll, 10; **3** López, 8; **4** Bruni 8; **5** Prémat, 7; **6** Speed, 6. **Teams: 1** Arden International, 18; **2** Super Nova International, 10; **3=** ART Grand Prix, 8; **3=** Coloni Motorsort, 8; **3=** DAMS, 8.

GP2 SERIES, Circuit de Catalunya, Montmeló, Barcelona, Spain, 7/8 May. Round 2. 39 and 18 laps of the 2.875-mile/4.627-km circuit.

Race 1 (112.050 miles/180.327 km).

1 Gianmaria Bruni, I, 58m 07.348s, 115.670 mph/186.152 km/h; **2** Scott Speed, USA, 58m 08.551s; **3** Heikki Kovalainen, FIN, 58m 15.137s; **4** Neel Jani, CH, 58m 25.513s; **5** Nelson Angelo Piquet, BR, 58m 30.942s; **6** José Maria López, RA, 58m 33.340s; **7** Adam Carroll, GB, 58m 41.088s; **8** Alexandre (Xandinho) Negrão, BR, 58m 44.229s; **9** Nico Rosberg, D, 58m 44.545s; **10** Alexandre Prémat, F, 58m 54.216s; **11** Nicolas Lapierre, F, 59m 13.500s; **12** Fairuz Fauzy, MAL, 59m 36.491s; **13** Giorgio Pantano, I, 38 laps; **14** Clivio Piccione, MC, 34 (DNF-spin); **15** Ryan Sharp, GB, 30 (DNF-engine); **16** Olivier Pla, F, 29 (DNF-spin); **17** Mathias Lauda, A, 28 (DNF-spin); **18** Can Artam, TR, 26 (DNF-gearbox); **19** Hiroki Yoshimoto, J, 19 (DNF-misfire); **20** Ernesto Viso, YV, 18 (DNF-transmission); **21** Sergio Hernández, E, 13 (DNF-engine); **22** Juan Cruz Álvarez, RA, 4 (DNF-spin); **23** Borja Garcia, E, 1 (DNF-accident); **24** Ferdinando Monfardini, I, 1 (DNF-spin).

Fastest race lap: Rosberg, 1m 25.875s, 120.528 mph/193.970 km/h.

Fastest qualifying lap: Speed, 1m 25.486s, 121.076 mph/194.852 km/h.

Race 2 (51.673 miles/83.160 km).

1 José Maria López, RA, 30m 10.213s, 102.763 mph/165.381 km/h; **2** Nelson Angelo Piquet, BR, 30m 13.182s; **3** Scott Speed, USA, 30m 13.492s; **4** Nico Rosberg, D, 30m 17.993s; **5** Neel Jani, CH, 30m 20.428s; **6** Adam Carroll, GB, 30m 21.453s; **7** Fairuz Fauzy, MAL, 30m 28.592s; **8** Clivio Piccione, MC, 30m 29.156s; **9** Nicolas Lapierre, F, 30m 29.905s; **10** Borja Garcia, E, 30m 31.441s; **11** Ferdinando Monfardini, I, 30m 34.462s; **12** Juan Cruz Álvarez, RA, 30m 34.874s; **13** Mathias Lauda, A, 30m 35.688s; **17** Hiroki Yoshimoto, J, 17 laps; **18** Sergio Hernández, E, 16; **19** Can Artam, TR, 11 (DNF-accident); **20** Gianmaria Bruni, I, 8 (DNF-accident); **21** Alexandre Prémat, F, 4 (DNF-spin); **22** Olivier Pla, F, 1 (DNF-spin); **23** Heikki Kovalainen, FIN, 0 (DNF-transmission); **24** Ernesto Viso, YV, 0 (DNF-engine).

Fastest race lap: Sharp, 1m 26.251s, 120.002 mph/193.124 km/h.

Pole position: Negrão.

Championship points. Drivers: 1= Kovalainen, 20; **1=** Speed, 20; **3** Bruni, 18; **4** Lopez, 17; **5** Carroll, 13; **6=** Piquet, 10; **6=** Jani, 10. **Teams: 1** Arden Intenational, 24; **2** iSport International, 20; **3** Coloni Motorsport, 18.

GP2 SERIES, Monte Carlo Street Circuit, Monaco, 21 May. Round 3. 44 laps of the 2.075-mile/3.340-km circuit, 91.317 miles/146.960 km.

1 Adam Carroll, GB, 1h 04m 41.326s, 84.698 mph/136.308 km/h; **2** Gianmaria Bruni, I, 1h 04m 41.983s; **3** Nico Rosberg, D, 1h 04m 42.427s; **4** Scott Speed, USA, 1h 04m 59.778s; **5** Heikki Kovalainen, FIN, 1h 05m 34.724s; **6** Mathias Lauda, A, 43 laps; **7** Can Artam, TR, 43; **8** Sergio Hernández, E, 42; **9** Olivier Pla, F, 41; **10** Borja Garcia, E, 40; **11** Nelson Angelo Piquet, BR, 40 (DNF-gearbox); **12** Alexandre (Xandinho) Negrão, BR, 40 (DNF-spin); **13** Nicolas Lapierre, F, 33 (DNF-spin); **14** Alexandre Prémat, F, 23 (DNF-spin); **15** Clivio Piccione, MC, 11 (DNF-accident); **16** Neel Jani, CH, 10 (DNF-brakes); **17** José Maria López, RA, 10 (DNF-gearbox); **18** Ryan Sharp, GB, 8 (DNF-gearbox); **19** Fairuz Fauzy, MAL, 6 (DNF-engine); **20** Giorgio Pantano, I, 0 (DNF-engine); **21** Juan Cruz Álvarez, RA, 0 (DNF-accident). Ernesto Viso, YV, competed 7 laps but was disqualified for exiting the pit lane under a red light.

Did not start: Ferdinando Monfardini, I (engine); Hiroki Yoshimoto, J (engine).

Fastest race lap: Kovalainen, 1m 23.864s, 89.089 mph/143.374 km/h.

Fastest qualifying lap: Kovalainen, 1m 24.665s, 88.246 mph/142.018 km/h.

Championship points. Drivers: 1 Kovalainen, 28; **2** Bruni, 26; **3** Speed, 25; **4** Carroll, 23; **5** Lopez, 17; **6** Rosberg, 12. **Teams: 1** Arden International, 32; **2** Coloni Motorsport, 29; **3** iSport International, 27.

GP2 SERIES, Nürburgring Grand Prix Circuit, Nürburg/Eifel, Germany, 28/29 May. Round 4. 33 and 24 laps of the 3.199-mile/5.148-km circuit.

Race 1 (105.550 miles/169.867 km).

1 Heikki Kovalainen, FIN, 1h 01m 43.066s, 102.613 mph/165.139 km/h; **2** Giorgio Pantano, I, 1h 01m 44.898s; **3** Nico Rosberg, D, 1h 02m 08.019s; **4** Alexandre Prémat, F, 1h 02m 23.586s; **5** Nelson Angelo Piquet, BR, 1h 02m 24.226s; **6** Neel Jani, CH, 1h 02m 32.103s; **7** Clivio Piccione, MC, 1h 02m 32.204s; **8** Gianmaria Bruni, I, 1h 02m 37.365s; **9** Ryan Sharp, GB, 1h 02m 50.985s; **10** Mathias Lauda, A, 1h 02m 51.758s; **11** Hiroki Yoshimoto, J, 1h 03m 00.538s; **12** Nicolas Lapierre, F, 1h 03m 03.063s; **13** José Maria López, RA, 1h 03m 03.816s; **14** Fairuz Fauzy, MAL, 1h 03m 08.570s; **15** Sergio Hernández, E, 1h 03m 15.176s; **16** Scott Speed, USA, 32 laps; **17** Can Artam, TR, 32; **18** Juan Cruz Álvarez, RA, 30 (DNF-accident); **19** Ernesto Viso, YV, 8 (DNF-wheel lost); **20** Olivier Pla, F, 0 (DNF-accident); **21** Adam Carroll, GB, 0 (DNF-accident); **22** Borja Garcia, E, 0 (DNF-accident); **23** Ferdinando Monfardini, I, 0 (DNF-accident); **24** Alexandre (Xandinho) Negrão, BR, 0 (DNF-accident).

Fastest race lap: Speed, 1m 44.992s, 109.682 mph/176.516 km/h.

Fastest qualifying lap: Pantano, 1m 43.862s, 110.875 mph/178.436 km/h.

Race 2 (76.761 miles/123.535 km).

1 Clivio Piccione, MC, 42m 42.210s, 107.852 mph/173.571 km/h; **2** Adam Carroll, GB, 42m 49.071s; **3** Nelson Angelo Piquet, BR, 42m 49.697s; **4** Nico Rosberg, D, 42m 49.937s; **5** Sergio Hernández, E, 42m 57.077s; **6** Ferdinando Monfardini, I, 42m 59.480s; **7** Giorgio Pantano, I, 43m 03.215s; **8** Olivier Pla, F, 43m 05.106s; **9** Ryan Sharp, GB, 43m 17.529s; **10** Fairuz Fauzy, MAL, 43m 38.441s; **11** Ernesto Viso, YV, 44m 03.120s; **12** Scott Speed, USA, 23 laps; **13** Neel Jani, CH, 22 laps (DNF-brakes); **14** José Maria López, RA, 22; **15** Juan Cruz Álvarez, RA, 22; **16** Can Artam, TR, 17 (DNF-spin); **17** Gianmaria Bruni, I, 16 (DNF-gearbox); **18** Alexandre (Xandinho) Negrão, BR, 6 (DNF-spin); **19** Heikki Kovalainen, FIN, 2 (DNF-accident); **20** Nicolas Lapierre, F, 1 (DNF-accident); **21** Alexandre Prémat, F, 1 (DNF-accident); **22** Mathias Lauda, A, 1 (DNF-accident); **23** Hiroki Yoshimoto, J, 0 (DNF-gearbox).

Did not start: Borja Garcia, E (injured in race 1 accident).

Fastest race lap: Speed, 1m 43.853s, 110.885 mph/178.452 km/h.

Pole position: Bruni.

Championship points. Drivers: 1 Kovalainen, 38; **2** Speed, 29; **3** Carroll, 28; **4** Bruni, 27; **5** Rosberg, 21; **6** Piquet, 18. **Teams: 1** Arden International, 42; **2** Super Nova International, 38; **3** ART Grand Prix, 33.

GP2 SERIES, Circuit de Nevers, Magny-Cours, France, 2/3 July. Round 5. 41 and 28 laps of the 2.741-mile/4.411-km circuit.

Race 1 (112.261 miles/180.667 km).

1 Heikki Kovalainen, FIN, 1h 02m 55.458s, 107.044 mph/172.270 km/h; **2** José Maria López, RA, 1h 02m 58.845s; **3** Nicolas Lapierre, F, 1h 03m 03.164s; **4** Adam Carroll, GB, 1h 03m 10.489s; **5** Neel Jani, CH, 1h 03m 18.068s; **6** Hiroki Yoshimoto, J, 1h 03m 18.600s; **7** Nico Rosberg, D, 1h 3m 18.805s; **8** Clivio Piccione, MC, 1h 03m 25.058s; **9** Alexandre Prémat, F, 1h 03m 28.555s; **10** Giorgio Pantano, I, 1h 03m 32.110s; **11** Ernesto Viso, YV, 1h 03m 32.558s; **12** Ferdinando Monfardini, I, 1h 03m 33.061s; **13** Sergio Hernández, E, 1h 03m 41.072s; **14** Fairuz Fauzy, MAL, 1h 03m 46.938s; **15** Scott Speed, USA, 1h 03m 48.030s; **16** Mathias Lauda, A, 1h 03m 56.954s; **17** Can Artam, TR, 1h 04m 24.256s; **18** Gianmaria Bruni, I, 40 laps; **19** Ryan Sharp, GB, 40; **20** Borja Garcia, E, 30 (DNF-gearbox); **21** Nelson Angelo Piquet, BR, 24 (DNF-engine); **22** Olivier Pla, F, 15 (DNF-spin); **23** Juan Cruz Álvarez, RA, 9 (DNF-suspension); **24** Alexandre (Xandinho) Negrão, BR, 1 (DNF-spin).

Fastest race lap: Bruni, 1m 27.809s, 112.370 mph/180.842 km/h.

Fastest qualifying lap: Prémat, 1m 25.132s, 115.904 mph/186.529 km/h.

Race 2 (76.630 miles/123.324 km).

1 Nico Rosberg, D, 41m 30.173s, 110.783 mph/178.287 km/h; **2** Hiroki Yoshimoto, J, 41m 55.539s; **3** Heikki Kovalainen, FIN, 41m 56.057s; **4** Neel Jani, CH, 42m 05.232s; **5** Nicolas Lapierre, F, 42m 09.579s; **6** Adam Carroll, GB, 42m 12.432s; **7** Giorgio Pantano, I, 42m 16.383s; **8** Ernesto Viso, YV, 42m 32.403s; **9** Olivier Pla, F, 42m 35.994s; **10** Fairuz Fauzy, MAL, 42m 36.597s; **11** Gianmaria Bruni, I, 42m 37.992s; **12** Borja Garcia, E, 42m 40.178s; **13** Alexandre (Xandinho) Negrão, BR, 42m 41.926s; **14** Sergio Hernández, E, 42m 50.489s; **15** Mathias Lauda, A, 42m 58.768s; **16** Can Artam, TR, 42m 01.959s; **17** Ferdinando Monfardini, I, 27 laps (DNF-accident); **18** Scott Speed, USA, 26; **19** Alexandre Prémat, F, 23 (DNF-accident); **20** José Maria López, RA, 22 (DNF-accident); **21** Ryan Sharp, GB, 6 (DNF-engine). Nelson Angelo Piquet, BR (27 laps), Clivio Piccione, MC (26 laps) and Juan Cruz Álvarez, RA (23 laps), were disqualified for tyre changing infringements.

Fastest race lap: Bruni, 1m 27.602s, 112.636 mph/181.269 km/h (originally Piquet in 1m 27.263s).

Pole position: Piccione.

Championship points. Drivers: 1 Kovalainen, 52; **2** Carroll, 34; **3** Bruni, 31; **4=** Rosberg, 29; **4=** Speed, 29; **6** Lopez, 25. **Teams: 1** Arden International, 64; **2** Super Nova International, 44; **3** ART Grand Prix, 43.

GP2 SERIES, Silverstone Grand Prix Circuit, Towcester, Northamptonshire, Great Britain, 9/10 July. Round 6. 36 and 24 laps of the 3.194-mile/5.141-km circuit.

Race 1 (114.936 miles/184.971 km).

1 Nico Rosberg, D, 58m 26.373s, 118.005 mph/189.910 km/h; **2** Heikki Kovalainen, FIN, 58m 26.937s; **3** Alexandre Prémat, F, 58m 52.674s; **4** Scott Speed, USA, 58m 56.092s; **5** Neel Jani, CH, 59m 16.919s; **6** Clivio Piccione, MC, 59m 17.428s; **7** Gianmaria Bruni, I, 59m 23.180s; **8** Olivier Pla, F, 59m 24.462s; **9** José Maria López, RA, 59m 24.758s; **10** Nicolas Lapierre, F, 59m 27.364s; **11** Juan Cruz Álvarez, RA, 59m 27.731s; **12** Giorgio Pantano, I, 59m 30.080s; **13** Hiroki Yoshimoto, J, 59m 30.740s; **14** Ferdinando Monfardini, I, 59m 32.542s; **15** Ernesto Viso, YV, 59m 45.356s; **16** Sergio Hernández, E, 59m 55.949s; **17** Borja Garcia, E, 1h 00m 01.461s; **18** Can Artam, TR, 35 laps; **19** Alexandre (Xandinho) Negrão, BR, 35; **20** Mathias Lauda, A, 35; **21** Adam Carroll, GB, 34 (DNF); **22** Fairuz Fauzy, MAL, 31 (DNF-gearbox); **23** Ryan Sharp, GB, 1 (DNF-transmission); **24** Nelson Angelo Piquet, BR, 0 (DNF-electrics).

Fastest race lap: Prémat, 1m 35.326s, 120.640 mph/194.150 km/h.

Fastest qualifying lap: Rosberg, 1m 31.509s, 125.672 mph/202.248 km/h.

Race 2 (76.602 miles/123.279 km).

1 Olivier Pla, F, 40m 09.933s, 114.429 mph/184.156 km/h; **2** Scott Speed, USA, 40m 10.480s; **3** Heikki Kovalainen, FIN, 40m 11.153s; **4** Nico Rosberg, D, 40m 11.819s; **5** Alexandre Prémat, F, 40m 15.482s; **6** Neel Jani, CH, 40m 16.716s; **7** Giorgio Pantano, I, 40m 18.353s; **8** Adam Carroll, GB, 40m 21.211s; **9** Borja Garcia, E, 40m 22.133s; **10** Ferdinando Monfardini, I, 40m 23.668s; **11** Gianmaria Bruni, I, 40m 25.427s; **12** Sergio Hernández, E, 40m 33.478s; **13** Ernesto Viso, YV, 40m 39.585s; **14** Can Artam, TR, 40m 47.812s; **15** Mathias Lauda, A, 40m 48.234s; **16** Alexandre (Xandinho) Negrão, BR, 23 laps; **17** Clivio Piccione, MC, 19 (DNF-steering); **18** Ryan Sharp, GB, 18; **19** Nicolas Lapierre, F, 16 (DNF-gearbox); **20** Nelson Angelo Piquet, BR, 8 (DNF-spin); **21** Juan Cruz Álvarez, RA, 5 (DNF-engine); **22** José Maria López, RA, 0 (DNF-engine); **23** Hiroki Yoshimoto, J, 0 (DNF-engine); **24** Fairuz Fauzy, MAL, 0 (DNF-engine).

Fastest race lap: Speed, 1m 35.092s, 120.936 mph/194.628 km/h.

Pole position: Pla.

Championship points. Drivers: 1 Kovalainen, 64; **2** Rosberg, 44; **3** Speed, 41; **4** Carroll, 34; **5** Bruni, 33; **6=** Lopez, 25, **6=** Jani, 25. **Teams: 1** Arden International, 76; **2** ART Grand Prix, 68; **3** Super Nova International, 44.

GP2 SERIES, Hockenheimring Grand Prix Circuit, Heidelberg, Germany, 23/24 July. Round 7. 40 and 27 laps of the 2.842-mile/4.574-km circuit.

Race 1 (113.686 miles/182.960 km).

1 Nico Rosberg, D, 59m 30.442s, 114.627 mph/184.474 km/h; **2** Alexandre Prémat, F, 59m 45.084s; **3** Nelson Angelo Piquet, BR, 59m 45.820s; **4** Scott Speed, USA, 59m 46.296s; **5** Heikki Kovalainen, FIN, 59m 55.086s; **6** Giorgio Pantano, I, 1h 00m 04.973s; **7** Borja Garcia, E, 1h 00m 11.765s; **8** Olivier Pla, F, 1h 00m 12.158s; **9** Nicolas Lapierre, F, 1h 00m 18.532s; **10** Juan Cruz Álvarez, RA, 1h 00m 18.758s; **11** Ryan Sharp, GB, 1h 00m 23.481s; **12** Hiroki Yoshimoto, J, 1h 00m 39.448s; **13** José Maria López, RA, 39 laps; **14** Mathias Lauda, A, 39; **15** Gianmaria Bruni, I, 20; **16** Can Artam, TR, 17 (DNF-gearbox); **17** Clivio Piccione, MC, 15 (DNF-gearbox); **18** Neel Jani, CH, 10 (DNF-gearbox); **19** Adam Carroll, GB, 7 (DNF-engine); **20** Fairuz Fauzy, MAL, 6 (DNF-spin); **21** Sergio Hernández, E, 4 (DNF-spin); **22** Ferdinando Monfardini, I, 1 (DNF-accident); **23** Alexandre (Xandinho) Negrão, BR, 0 (DNF-accident). Ernesto Viso, YV, finished 7th but was disqualified for car being under weight.

Fastest race lap: Rosberg, 1m 27.672s, 116.705 mph/187.818 km/h.

Fastest qualifying lap: Rosberg, 1m 24.691s, 120.813 mph/194.429 km/h.

Race 2 (76.738 miles/123.498 km).

1 Olivier Pla, F, 39m 54.758s, 115.359 mph/185.652 km/h; **2** Giorgio Pantano, I, 40m 01.698s; **3** Scott Speed, USA, 40m 02.146s; **4** Nico Rosberg, D, 40m 02.370s; **5** Borja Garcia, E, 40m 11.311s; **6** Heikki Kovalainen, FIN, 40m 12.497s; **7** Nicolas Lapierre, F, 40m 13.129s; **8** Nelson Angelo Piquet, BR, 40m 14.798s; **9** Alexandre Prémat, F, 40m 15.548s; **10** José Maria López, RA, 40m 16.456s; **11** Adam Carroll, GB, 40m 18.411s; **12** Ernesto Viso, YV, 40m 22.622s; **13** Ryan Sharp, GB, 40m 28732s; **14** Gianmaria Bruni, I, 40m 31.719s; **15** Ferdinando Monfardini, I, 40m 32.251s; **16** Fairuz Fauzy, MAL, 40m 41.736s; **17** Clivio Piccione, MC, 40m 42.694s **18** Alexandre (Xandinho) Negrão, BR, 40m 46.140s; **19** Sergio Hernández, E, 41m 00.227s; **20** Can Artam, TR, 41m 00.562s; **21** Mathias Lauda, A, 41m 03.292s; **22** Neel Jani, CH, 24 laps; **23** Hiroki Yoshimoto, J, 21 (DNF-gearbox); **24** Juan Cruz Álvarez, RA, 17 (DNF-suspension).

Fastest race lap: Rosberg, 1m 27.245s, 117.276 mph/188.737 km/h.

Pole position: Pla.

Championship points. Drivers: 1 Kovalainen, 69; **2** Rosberg, 63; **3** Speed, 50; **4** Carroll, 34; **5** Bruni, 33; **6** Prémat, 32. **Teams: 1** ART Grand Prix, 95; **2** Arden International, 81; **3=** Super Nova International, 52; **3=** iSport International, 52.

GP2 SERIES, Hungaroring, Mogyorod, Budapest, Hungary, 30/31 July. Round 8. 42 and 25 laps of the 2.722-mile/4.381-km circuit.

Race 1 (114.329 miles/183.995 km).

1 Neel Jani, CH, 1h 11m 11.253s, 96.362 mph/155.079 km/h; **2** Heikki Kovalainen, FIN, 1h 11m 11.683s; **3** Giorgio Pantano, I, 1h 11m 12.992s; **4** Alexandre Prémat, F, 1h 11m 18.555s; **5** Nico Rosberg, D, 1h 11m 21.724s; **6** Ernesto Viso, YV, 1h 11m 21.832s; **7** Olivier Pla, F, 1h 11m 22.531s; **8** Alexandre (Xandinho) Negrão, BR, 1h 11m 32.363s; **9** Adam Carroll, GB, 1h 11m 34.289s; **10** Gianmaria Bruni, I, 1h 11m 44.476s; **11** Borja Garcia, E, 1h 11m 50.684s; **12** Nicolas Lapierre, F, 41 laps; **13** Hiroki Yoshimoto, J, 41; **14** Can Artam, TR, 40; **15** Nelson Angelo Piquet, BR, 37 (DNF-hydraulics); **16** José Maria López, RA, 29 (DNF-accident); **17** Juan Cruz Álvarez, RA, 25 (DNF-gearbox); **18** Sergio Hernández, E, 24 (DNF-spin); **19** Ferdinando Monfardini, I, 21 (DNF-hydraulics); **20** Scott Speed, USA, 18 (DNF-hydraulics); **21** Mathias Lauda, A, 18 (DNF-gearbox); **22** Fairuz Fauzy, MAL, 16 (DNF-spin); **23** Giorgio Mondini, I, 11 (DNF-electrics); **24** Clivio Piccione, MC, 8 (DNF-hydraulics).

Fastest race lap: Yoshimoto, 1m 34.170s, 104.067mph/167.480 km/h.

Fastest qualifying lap: Jani, 1m 32.457s, 105.995 mph /170.583 km/h.

Race 2 (68.051 miles/109.518 km).

1 Alexandre Prémat, F, 45m 05.029s, 90.566 mph/145.752 km/h; **2** Nico Rosberg, D, 45m 05.433s; **3** Giorgio Pantano, I, 45m 07.013s; **4** Neel Jani, CH, 45m 08.683s; **5** Heikki Kovalainen, FIN, 45m 09.568s; **6** Nicolas Lapierre, F, 45m 10.378s; **7** Juan Cruz Álvarez, RA, 45m 11.003s; **8** Gianmaria Bruni, I, 45m 11.458s; **9** Adam Carroll, GB, 45m 12.162s; **10** Nelson Angelo Piquet, BR, 45m 13.057s; **11** Ferdinando Monfardini, I, 45m 13.569s; **12** Can Artam, TR, 45m 15.187s; **13** Fairuz Fauzy, MAL, 45m 17.902s; **14** Mathias Lauda, A, 45m 18.688s; **15** Alexandre (Xandinho) Negrão, BR, 45m 22.917s; **16** Clivio Piccione, MC, 45m 25.708s; **17** Hiroki Yoshimoto, J, 45m 28.770s; **18** Sergio Hernández, E, 24 laps; **19** Scott Speed, USA, 23; **20** Olivier Pla, F, 16 (DNF-electrics); **21** José Maria López, RA, 6 (DNF-spin); **22** Borja Garcia, E, 4 (DNF-accident); **23** Ernesto Viso, YV, 4 (DNF-gearbox); **24** Giorgio Mondini, I, 2 (DNF-accident damage).

Fastest race lap: Piccione, 1m 34.336s, 103.884 mph/167.185 km/h.

Pole position: Negrão.

Championship points. Drivers: 1 Kovalainen, 79; **2** Rosberg, 72; **3** Speed, 50; **4** Prémat, 43; **5** Jani, 40; **6** Carroll, 34. **Teams: 1** ART Grand Prix, 115; **2** Arden International, 92; **3** Super Nova International, 62.

GP2 SERIES, Istanbul Speed Park, Turkey, 20/21 August. Round 9. 34 and 23 laps of the 3.317-mile/5.338-km circuit.

Race 1 (112.645 miles/181.284 km).

1 Alexandre Prémat, F, 1h 01m 27.680s, 109.966 mph/176.973 km/h; **2** Giorgio Pantano, I, 1h 01m 28.016s; **3** Borja Garcia, E, 1h 01m 37.166s; **4** Nelson Angelo Piquet, BR, 1h 01m 38.667s; **5** Scott Speed, USA, 1h 01m 40.756s; **6** José Maria López, RA, 1h 01m 46.129s; **7** Adam Carroll, GB, 1h 01m 47.238s; **8** Hiroki Yoshimoto, J, 1h 01m 48.808s; **9** Olivier Pla, F, 1h 01m 49.295s; **10** Heikki Kovalainen, FIN, 1h 01m 56.310s; **11** Can Artam, TR, 1h 01m 58.262s; **12** Alexandre (Xandinho) Negrão, BR, 1h 02m 05.995s; **13** Giorgio Mondini, I, 1h 02m 07.713s; **14** Ernesto Viso, YV, 1h 02m 15.748s; **15** Juan Cruz Álvarez, RA, 1h 02m 18.104s; **16** Mathias Lauda, A, 1h 02m 20.088s; **17** Nico Rosberg, D, 32 laps; **18** Ferdinando Monfardini, I, 26 (DNF-accident); **19** Clivio Piccione, MC, 23 (DNF-spin); **20** Nicolas Lapierre, F, 16 (DNF-accident); **21** Gianmaria Bruni, I, 16 (DNF-accident); **22** Fairuz Fauzy, MAL, 10 (DNF-spin); **23** Sergio Hernández, E, 2 (DNF-engine); **24** Neel Jani, CH, 0 (DNF-accident).

Fastest race lap: Speed, 1m 38.288s, 121.488 mph/195.515 km/h.

Fastest qualifying lap: Rosberg, 1m 38.416s, 121.330 mph/195.260 km/h.

Race 2 (76.159 miles/122.566 km).

1 Heikki Kovalainen, FIN, 43m 48.581s, 104.304 mph/167.861 km/h; **2** Adam Carroll, GB, 43m 56.481s; **3** Nico Rosberg, D, 43m

57.137s; **4** Scott Speed, USA, 43m 57.909s; **5** Borja Garcia, E, 43m 59.922s; **6** Nelson Angelo Piquet, BR, 44m 06.941s; **7** José Maria López, RA, 44m 10.199s; **8** Giorgio Pantano, I, 44m 12.613s; **9** Gianmaria Bruni, I, 44m 14.299s; **10** Hiroki Yoshimoto, J, 44m 22.778s; **11** Clivio Piccione, MC, 44m 28.301s; **12** Ernesto Viso, YV, 44m 28.331s; **13** Nicolas Lapierre, F, 44m 28.676s; **14** Alexandre Prémat, F, 44m 51.993s; **15** Fairuz Fauzy, MAL, 45m 05.955s; **16** Can Artam, TR, 45m 17.380s*; **17** Olivier Pla, F, 45m 19.243s*; **18** Mathias Lauda, A, 22 laps; **19** Alexandre (Xandinho) Negrâo, BR, 22; **20** Sergio Hernández, E, 20; **21** Ferdinando Monfardini, I, 18 (DNF-spin); **22** Neel Jani, CH, 14 (DNF-accident); **23** Juan Cruz Álvarez, RA, 10 (DNF-hydraulics); **24** Giorgio Mondini, I, 2 (DNF-spin). *given a 25s penalty for changing tyres on the grid after the deadline.

Fastest race lap: Pla, 1m 41.209s, 117.981 mph/189.872 km/h.

Pole position: Yoshimoto.

Championship points. Drivers: 1 Kovalainen, 85; **2** Rosberg, 78; **3** Speed, 59; **4** Prémat, 53; **5** Carroll, 41; **6** Jani, 40. **Teams: 1** ART Grand Prix, 131; **2** Arden International, 98; **3** Super Nova International, 77.

GP2 SERIES, Autodromo Nazionale di Monza, Milan, Italy, 3/4 September. Round 10. 32 and 20 laps of the 3.600-mile/5.793-km circuit.

Race 1 (114.995 miles/185.067 km).

1 Heikki Kovalainen, FIN, 53m 55.234s, 127.961 mph/205.932 km/h; **2** Nico Rosberg, D, 53m 56.397s; **3** Nelson Angelo Piquet, BR, 54m 07.538s; **4** Nicolas Lapierre, F, 54m 25.214s; **5** Adam Carroll, GB, 54m 31.185s; **6** Giorgio Pantano, I, 54m 33.154s; **7** Neel Jani, CH, 54m 41.183s; **8** Ferdinando Monfardini, I, 54m 48.549s; **9** Can Artam, TR, 55m 04.269s; **10** Hiroki Yoshimoto, J, 55m 05.050s; **11** Clivio Piccione, MC, 55m 06.848s; **12** Juan Cruz Álvarez, RA, 55m 15.601s; **13** Mathias Lauda, A, 55m 26.323s; **14** Fairuz Fauzy, MAL, 55m 27.012s; **15** Toni Vilander, FIN, 30 laps; **16** Ernesto Viso, YV, 5 (DNF-accident); **17** Sergio Hernández, E, 5 (DNF-accident); **18** Alexandre (Xandinho) Negrâo, BR, 4 (DNF-accident); **19** Borja Garcia, E, 4 (DNF-accident); **20** Alexandre Prémat, F, 2 (DNF-accident); **21** Scott Speed, USA, 2 (DNF-engine); **22** José Maria López, RA, 2 (DNF-clutch); **23** Giorgio Mondini, I, 0 (DNF-accident); **24** Olivier Pla, F, 0 (DNF-accident).

Fastest race lap: Rosberg, 1m 36.315s, 131.544 mph/216.527 km/h.

Fastest qualifying lap: Kovalainen, 1m 33.725s, 138.262 mph/222.510 km/h.

Race 2 (71.800 miles/115.551 km).

1 Neel Jani, CH, 33m 54.148s, 127.071 mph/204.500 km/h; **2** Nico Rosberg, D, 33m 54.636s; **3** Giorgio Pantano, I, 33m 56.564s; **4** Ferdinando Monfardini, I, 34m 00.310s; **5** Heikki Kovalainen, FIN, 34m 00.355s; **6** Adam Carroll, GB, 34m 05.358s; **7** Sergio Hernández, E, 34m 09.210s; **8** Toni Vilander, FIN, 34m 21.198s; **9** Can Artam, TR, 34m 24.179s; **10** Borja Garcia, E, 34m 28.666s; **11** Fairuz Fauzy, MAL, 34m 32.994s; **12** Mathias Lauda, A, 34m 34.204s; **13** Alexandre (Xandinho) Negrâo, BR, 34m 34.805s; **14** Clivio Piccione, MC, 34m 35.050s; **15** Scott Speed, USA, 35m 15.518s; **16** Hiroki Yoshimoto, J, 35m 24.421s; **17** Juan Cruz Álvarez, RA, 19 laps; **18** Alexandre Prémat, F, 19; **19** Giorgio Mondini, I, 14 (DNF-gearbox); **20** Nicolas Lapierre, F, 8 (DNF-accident); **21** José Maria López, RA, 8 (DNF-accident); **22** Nelson Angelo Piquet, BR, 6 (DNF-accident); **23** Ernesto Viso, YV, 6 (DNF-spin); **24** Olivier Pla, F, 5 (DNF-spin).

Fastest race lap: Rosberg, 1m 35.881s, 135.153 mph/217.507 km/h. Speed set the fastest lap (1m 35.660s), but his time was removed for changing tyres which were damaged due to driver error.

Pole position: Monfardini.

Championship points. Drivers: 1 Kovalainen, 99; **2** Rosberg, 95; **3** Speed, 59; **4** Prémat, 53; **5** Jani, 48; **6** Carroll, 46. **Teams: 1** ART Grand Prix, 146; **2** Arden International, 117; **3** Super Nova International, 89.

GP2 SERIES, Circuit de Spa-Francorchamps, Stavelot, Belgium, 10/11 September. Round 11. 26 and 9 laps of the 4.335-mile/6.976-km circuit.

Race 1 (112.691 miles/181.359 km).

1 Nelson Angelo Piquet, BR, 1h 08m 13.224s, 99.112 mph/159.505 km/h; **2** Ernesto Viso, YV, 1h 08m 16.273s; **3** Nico Rosberg, D, 1h 08m 23.154s; **4** Scott Speed, USA, 1h 08m 29.139s; **5** Juan Cruz Álvarez, RA, 1h 08m 31.224s; **6** Borja Garcia, E, 1h 08m 32.200s; **7** Alexandre (Xandinho) Negrâo, BR, 1h 08m 48.289s; **8** Adam Carroll, GB, 1h 08m 55.487s; **9** Mathias Lauda, A, 1h 08m 56.561s; **10** José Maria López, RA, 1h 08m 57.352s; **11** Olivier Pla, F, 1h 09m 11.235s; **12** Clivio Piccione, MC, 1h 09m 11.826s; **13** Fairuz Fauzy, MAL, 1h 09m 31.503s; **14** Toni Vilander, FIN, 1h 10m 11.725s; **15** Heikki Kovalainen, FIN, 25 (DNF-spin); **16** Neel Jani, CH, 23; **17** Sergio Hernández, E, 22 (DNF-hydraulics); **18** Giorgio Pantano, I, 22; **19** Alexandre Prémat, F, 16 (DNF-accident); **20** Giorgio Mondini, I, 13 (DNF-accident); **21** Gianmaria Bruni, I, 8 (DNF-accident); **22** Hiroki Yoshimoto, J, 3 (DNF-accident); **23** Can Artam, TR, 3 (DNF-accident); **24** Nicolas Lapierre, F, 0 (DNF-gearbox).

Fastest race lap: Prémat, 2m 07.563s, 122.331 mph/196.872 km/h. (points for fastest lap awarded to Carroll).

Fastest qualifying lap: Bruni, 2m 14.273s, 116.217 mph/187.033 km/h.

Race 2 (39.002 miles/62.767 km).

1 Adam Carroll, GB, 21m 18.560s, 122.331 mph/176.731 km/h; **2** Borja Garcia, E, 21m 34.860s; **3** Ernesto Viso, YV, 21m 43.600s; **4** Scott Speed, USA, 21m 44.871s; **5** Nico Rosberg, D, 21m 49.730s; **6** Juan Cruz Álvarez, RA, 21m 53.226s; **7** Alexandre (Xandinho) Negrâo, BR, 21m 54.547s; **8** José Maria López, RA, 21m 56.619s; **9** Heikki Kovalainen, FIN, 21m 56.881s; **10** Olivier Pla, F, 22m 00.546s; **11** Giorgio Pantano, I, 22m 02.195s; **12** Alexandre Prémat, F, 22m 07.011s; **13** Toni Vilander, FIN, 22m 10.117s; **14** Nelson Angelo Piquet, BR, 22m 10.730s; **15** Fairuz Fauzy, MAL, 22m 13.436s; **16** Gianmaria Bruni, I, 22m 13.977s; **17** Hiroki Yoshimoto, J, 22m 14.479s; **18** Neel Jani, CH, 22m 16.015s; **19** Clivio Piccione, MC, 22m 17.775s; **20** Sergio Hernández, E, 22m 26.588s; **21** Giorgio Mondini, I, 22m 29.068s; **22** Can Artam, TR, 22m 34.963s; **23** Nicolas Lapierre, F, 22m 45.382s; **24** Mathias Lauda, A, 23m 02.665s. Race ended prematurely due to accidents.

Fastest race lap: Carroll, 2m 14.936s, 115.646 mph/186.114 km/h.

Pole position: Carroll.

Championship points. Drivers: 1 Rosberg, 102; **2** Kovalainen, 99; **3** Speed, 65.5; **4=** Carroll, 53; **4=** Prémat, 53; **6** Jani, 48. **Teams: 1** ART Grand Prix, 155; **2** Arden International, **3** 117; Super Nova International, 96.

GP2 SERIES, Bahrain International Circuit, Sakhir, Bahrain, 29/30 September. Round 12. 34 and 23 laps of the 3.363-mile/5.412-km circuit.

Race 1 (114.184 miles/183.762 km).

1 Nico Rosberg, D, 1h 03m 34.327, 107.768 mph/173.436 km/h; **2** Alexandre Prémat, F, 1h 0m 45.884s; **3** Heikki Kovalainen, FIN, 1h 03m 53.095s; **4** José Maria López, RA, 1h 04m 08.050s; **5** Giorgio Pantano, I, 1h 04m 12.675s; **6** Nicolas Lapierre, F, 1h 04m 18.257s; **7** Hiroki Yoshimoto, J, 1h 04m 28.404s; **8** Ernesto Viso, YV, 1h 04m 28.805s; **9** Adam Carroll, GB, 1h 04m 30.398s; **10** Juan Cruz Álvarez, RA, 1h 04m 42.039s; **11** Fairuz Fauzy, MAL, 1h 04m 43.743s; **12** Alexandre (Xandinho) Negrâo, BR, 1h 04m 44.343s; **13** Clivio Piccione, MC, 1h 04m 49.264s; **14** Mathias Lauda, A, 1h 04m 56.494s; **15** Sergio Hernández, E, 1h 05m 01.648s; **16** Neel Jani, CH, 1h 05m 07.506s; **17** Can Artam, TR, 1h 05m 11.320s; **18** Giorgio Mondini, I, 33 laps; **19** Borja Garcia, E, 31; **20** Olivier Pla, F, 29 (DNF-gearbox); **21** Ferdinando Monfardini, I, 20 (DNF-electrics); **22** Nelson Angelo Piquet, BR, 13 (DNF-hydraulics); **23** Scott Speed, USA, 10 (DNF-brakes); **24** Gianmaria Bruni, I, 7 (DNF-.gearbox).

Fastest race lap: Prémat, 1m 47.766s, 112.339 mph/180.791 km/h.

Fastest qualifying lap: Rosberg, 1m 44.643s, 115.691 mph/186.187 km/h.

Race 2 (77.193 miles/124.230 km).

1 Nico Rosberg, D, 41m 44.937s, 110.939 mph/178.538 km/h; **2** Ernesto Viso, YV, 41m 53.272s; **3** Alexandre Prémat, F, 41m 54.290s; **4** José Maria López, RA, 42m 01.197s; **5** Giorgio Pantano, I, 42m 07.586s; **6** Hiroki Yoshimoto, J, 42m 15.635s; **7** Clivio Piccione, MC, 42m 16.052s; **8** Adam Carroll, GB, 42m 17.911s; **9** Alexandre (Xandinho) Negrâo, BR, 42m 18.790s; **10** Fairuz Fauzy, MAL, 42m 19.508s; **11** Ferdinando Monfardini, I, 42m 19.781s; **12** Juan Cruz Álvarez, RA, 42m 20.339s; **13** Neel Jani, CH, 42m 22.964s; **14** Gianmaria Bruni, I, 42m 26.606s; **15** Nelson Angelo Piquet, BR, 42m 29.043s; **16** Can Artam, TR, 42m 34.489s; **17** Borja Garcia, E, 42m 35.180s; **18** Sergio Hernández, E, 43m 10.044s; **19** Scott Speed, USA, 22 laps; **20** Nicolas Lapierre, F, 22; **21** Mathias Lauda, A, 22; **22** Giorgio Mondini, I, 22; **23** Heikki Kovalainen, FIN, 0 (DNF-spin).

Did not start: Olivier Pla, F (gearbox in warm up).

Fastest race lap: Speed, 1m 47.401s, 112.721 mph/181.406 km/h.

Pole position: Viso.

Final championship points

Drivers: 1 Nico Rosberg, D, 120; **2** Heikki Kovalainen, FIN, 105; **3** Scott Speed, USA, 67.5; **4** Alexandre Prémat, F, 67; **5** Adam Carroll, GB, 53; **6** Giorgio Pantano, I, 49; **7** Neel Jani, CH, 48; **8** Nelson Angelo Piquet, BR, 46; **9** José Maria López, RA, 36; **10** Gianmaria Bruni, I, 35; **11=** Nicolas Lapierre, F, 21; **11=** Ernesto Viso, YV, 21; **13** Olivier Pla, F, 20; **14** Borja Garcia, E, 17.5; **15=** Clivio Piccione, MC, 14; **15=** Hiroki Yoshimoto, J, 14; **17** Ferdinando Monfardini, I, 5; **18** Juan Cruz Álvarez, RA, 4.5; **19** Alexandre (Xandinho) Negrâo, BR, 4; **20=** Sergio Hernández, E, 3; **20=** Mathias Lauda, A, 3; **22=** Can Artam, TR, 2; **22=** Ryan Sharp, GB, 2. **Teams: 1** ART Grand Prix, 187; **2** Arden International, 126; **3** Super Nova International, 102; **4** iSport International, 69.5; **5** Racing Engineering, 65.5; **6** Hitech Piquet Sports, 50; **7=** Coloni Motorsport, 36; **7=** DAMS, 36; **9** BCN Competicion, 35; **10** David Price Racing, 22; **11** Durango, 21; **12** Campos Racing, 7.5.

A1 Grand Prix of Nations

All cars are Lola with Zytek V8 engine.

A1 GRAND PRIX OF NATIONS, Brands Hatch Grand Prix Circuit, West Kingsdown, Dartford, Kent, Great Britain, 25 September. Round 1. 18 and 38 laps of the 2.423-mile/3.899-km circuit.

Sprint race (43.609 miles/70.182 km).

1 Brazil-Nelson Angelo Piquet, 23m 15.682s, 112.485 mph/181.026 km/h; **2** France-Alexandre Prémat, 23m 18.122s; **3** New Zealand-Matt Halliday, 23m 18.581s; **4** Australia-Will Power, 23m 27.139s; **5** Great Britain-Robbie Kerr, 23m 28.479s; **6** Mexico-Salvador Durán, 23m 32.955s; **7** Pakistan-Adam Khan, 23m 33.714s; **8** Portugal-Alvaro Parente, 23m 33.871s; **9** Switzerland-Neel Jani, 23m 36.533s; **10** Ireland-Michael Devaney, 23m 36.738s; **11** USA-Scott Speed, 23m 39.548s; **12** Japan-Ryo Fukuda, 23m 40.874s; **13** Malaysia-Fairuz Fauzy, 23m 41.033s; **14** Germany-Timo Scheider, 23m 41.587s; **15** India-Karun Chandhok, 23m 43.475s; **16** Italy-Enrico Toccacelo, 23m 51.203s; **17** Indonesia-Ananda Mikola, 23m 56.015s; **18** Czech Republic-Jan Charouz, 23m 56.028s; **19** Canada-Sean McIntosh, 23m 58.303s; **20** Austria-Mathias Lauda, 24m 10.975s; **21** China-Tengyi Jiang, 24m 13.876s; **22** Lebanon-Khalil Beschir, 24m 14.774s; **23** Russia-Alexei Vasiliev, 17 laps; **24** South Africa-Stephen Simpson, 17; **25** Netherlands-Jos Verstappen, 0 (DNF-accident).

Fastest race lap: France, 1m 17.143s, 113.09 mph/181.952 km/h.

Fastest qualifying lap: Brazil, 2m 30.789s, 115.682 mph/186.172 km/h (over 2 laps).

Feature race (92.064 miles/148.162 km).

1 Brazil-Nelson Angelo Piquet, 55m 01.910s, 100.375 mph/161.537 km/h; **2** Australia-Will Power, 55m 13.240s; **3** Mexico-Salvador Durán, 55m 25.035; **4** New Zealand-Matt Halliday, 55m 25.615s; **5** Malaysia-Alex Yoong, 55m 26.262s; **6** South Africa-Stephen Simpson, 55m 26.762s; **7** Netherlands-Jos Verstappen, 55m 27.540s; **8** Japan-Ryo Fukuda, 55m 28.129s; **9** Canada-Sean McIntosh, 55m 29.089s; **10** Germany-Timo Scheider, 37 laps; **11** Austria-Mathias Lauda, 37; **12** China-Tengyi Jiang, 37; **13** Pakistan-Adam Khan, 35; **14** Czech Republic-Jan Charouz, 24 (DNF-accident); **15** Russia-Alexei Vasiliev, 18 (DNF-spin); **16** Great Britain-Robbie Kerr, 17 (DNF-battery); **17** USA-Scott Speed, 14 (DNF-accident damage); **18** Lebanon-Khalil Beschir, 13 (DNF-accident); **19** Italy-Enrico Toccacelo, 13 (DNF-accident); **20** Portugal-Alvaro Parente, 1 (DNF-engine); **21** Switzerland-Neel Jani, 1 (DNF-accident); **22** Ireland-Michael Devaney, 0 (DNF-accident); **23** Indonesia-Ananda Mikola, 0 (DNF-accident).

Did not start: France-Alexandre Prémat (battery); India-Karun Chandhok (battery).

Fastest race lap: Brazil, 1m 16.547s, 113.941 mph/183.369 km/h.

Pole position: Brazil.

Championship points: 1 Brazil, 21; **2** Australia, 16; **3** New Zealand, 15; **4** Mexico, 13; **5** France, 9; **6=** Great Britain, 6; **6=** Malaysia, 6.

A1 GRAND PRIX OF NATIONS, EuroSpeedway Lausitz, Klettwitz, Dresden, Germany, 9 October. Round 2. 18 and 35 laps of the 2.817-mile/4.534-km circuit.

Sprint race (50.711 miles/81.612 km).

1 France-Nicolas Lapierre, 30m 10.429s, 100.838 mph/162.283 km/h; **2** Switzerland-Neel Jani, 30m 12.442s; **3** Brazil-Nelson Angelo Piquet, 30m 12.887s; **4** New Zealand-Jonny Reid, 30m 18.475s; **5** Germany-Timo Scheider, 30m 19.280s; **6** Malaysia-Alex Yoong, 30m 33.848s; **7** Canada-Sean McIntosh, 30m 34.438s; **8** Mexico-David Martinez, 30m 35.838s; **9** Ireland-Ralph Firman, 30m 37.010s; **10** Japan-Hideki Noda, 30m 38.271s; **11** Czech Republic-Tomás Enge, 30m 38.671s; **12** South Africa-Tomas Scheckter, 30m 50.690s; **13** Austria-Mathias Lauda, 30m 51.436s; **14** Indonesia-Ananda Mikola, 30m 53.064s; **15** Australia-Christian Jones, 30m 53.885s; **16** India-Karun Chandhok, 30m 54.308s; **17** Italy-Enrico Toccacelo, 30m 59.954s; **18** China-Tengyi Jiang, 16 laps; **19** Lebanon-Khalil Beschir, 7; **20** Portugal-Alvaro Parente, 3 (DNF-accident); **21** Pakistan-Adam Khan, 2 (DNF-accident); **22** Netherlands-Jos Verstappen, 1 (DNF-accident); **23** USA-Scott Speed, 0 (DNF-accident); **24** Great Britain-Robbie Kerr, 0 (DNF-accident). Italy finished 8th in 30m 34.454s, but was given a 25s penalty for overtaking under a waved yellow flag.

Fastest race lap: Brazil, 1m 34.736s, 107.058 mph/172.293 km/h.

Fastest qualifying lap: France, 3m 05.332s, 109.450 mph/176.142 km/h (over 2 laps).

Feature race (98.605 miles/158.690 km).

1 France-Nicolas Lapierre, 58m 45.700s, 100.683 mph/162.034 km/h; **2** Great Britain-Robbie Kerr, 58m 49.406s; **3** Canada-Sean McIntosh, 58m 51.158s; **4** New Zealand-Jonny Reid, 58m 51.674s; **5** Switzerland-Neel Jani, 58m 52.771s; **6** Ireland-Ralph Firman, 58m 53.781s; **7** Netherlands-Jos Verstappen, 58m 55.322s; **8** Indonesia-Ananda Mikola, 59m 02.406s; **9** Japan-Hideki Noda, 59m 05.044s; **10** Germany-Timo Scheider, 59m 07.560s; **11** Portugal-Alvaro Parente, 59m 10.440s; **12** Pakistan-Adam Khan, 59m 10.966s; **13** Mexico-David Martinez, 59m 14.878s; **14** Australia-Christian Jones, 59m 16.590s; **15** Austria-Mathias Lauda, 59m 16.832s; **16** Malaysia-Alex Yoong, 59m 31.081s; **17** China-Tengyi Jiang, 1h 00m 03.141s; **18** Lebanon-Khalil Beschir, 33 laps; **19** Czech Republic-Tomás Enge, 27 (DNF-accident); **20** Brazil-Nelson Angelo Piquet, 26 (DNF-accident); **21** India-Karun Chandhok, 19 (DNF-electrics); **22** South Africa-Tomas Scheckter, 15; **23** Italy-Enrico Toccacelo, 11 (DNF-electrics); **24** USA-Scott Speed, 4 (DNF-tyre).

Fastest race lap: Brazil-Nelson Angelo Piquet, 1m 34.856s, 106.923 mph/172.075 km/h.

Pole position: France.

Championship points: 1 Brazil, 30; **2=** France, 29; **2=** New Zealand, 29; **4** Switzerland, 17; **5=** Australia, 16; **5=** Mexico, 16.

A1 GRAND PRIX OF NATIONS, Autódromo Fernanda Pires da Silva, Alcabideche, Estoril, Portugal, 23 October. Round 3. 18 and 36 laps of the 2.599-mile/4.182-km circuit.

Sprint race (46.774 miles/75.276 km).

1 France-Alexandre Prémat, 27m 46.488s, 101.043 mph/162.613 km/h; **2** Brazil-Nelson Angelo Piquet, 27m 48.543s; **3** Switzerland-Neel Jani, 27m 49.777s; **4** Netherlands-Jos Verstappen, 27m 59.973s; **5** Czech Republic-Tomás Enge, 28m 00.416s; **6** Portugal-Alvaro Parente, 28m 05.149s; **7** Canada-Sean McIntosh, 28m 07.785s; **8** Malaysia-Fairuz Fauzy, 28m 18.541s; **9** Indonesia-Ananda Mikola, 28m 23.855s; **10** South Africa-Tomas Scheckter, 28m 26.210s; **11** Italy-Enrico Toccacelo, 28m 26.581s; **12** Germany-Adrian Sutil, 28m 28.314s; **13** USA-Scott Speed, 28m 28.403s; **14** New Zealand-Matt Halliday, 28m 29.666s; **15** Russia-Mikhail Aleshin, 28m 38.156s; **16** Austria-Mathias Lauda, 28m 53.21s; **17** India-Armaan Ebrahim, 28m 55.302s; **18** Lebanon-Basil Shaaban, 29m 02.510s; **19** Ireland-Ralph Firman, 17 laps; **20** Great Britain-Robbie Kerr, 5 (DNF-puncture); **21** China-Tengyi Jiang, 1 (DNF-accident); **22** Pakistan-Adam Khan, 0 (DNF-accident); **23** Mexico-Salvador Durán, 0 (DNF-accident); **24** Australia-Will Davison, 0 (DNF-accident).

Fastest race lap: France, 1m 31.992s, 101.692 mph/163.657 km/h.

Fastest qualifying lap: France, 3m 01.316s, 103.188 mph/166.065 km/h (over 2 laps).

Feature race (93.549 miles/150.552 km).

1 France-Alexandre Prémat, 1h 01m 05.454s, 91.878 mph/147.863 km/h; **2** Switzerland-Neel Jani, 1h 01m 12.971s; **3** Ireland-Ralph Firman, 1h 01m 21.387s; **4** USA-Scott Speed, 1h 01m 24.477s; **5** Portugal-Alvaro Parente, 1h 01m 32.774s; **6** Australia-Will Davison, 1h 01m 40.228s; **7** Italy-Enrico Toccacelo, 1h 01m 41.083s; **8** Brazil-Nelson Angelo Piquet, 1h 01m 41.719s; **9** Czech Republic-Tomás Enge, 1h 01m 43.184s; **10** Austria-Mathias Lauda, 1h 01 56.834s; **11** Lebanon-Basil Shaaban, 1h 02m 04.187s; **12** Great Britain-Robbie Kerr, 1h 02m 07.401s; **13** India-Armaan Ebrahim, 1h 02m 10.998s; **14** China-Tengyi Jiang, 1h 02m 16.035s; **15** Pakistan-Adam Khan, 1h 02m 21.971s; **16** New Zealand-Matt Halliday, 35 laps; **17** Russia-Mikhail Aleshin, 35; **18** Canada-Sean McIntosh, 20 (DNF-spin); **19** Netherlands-Jos Verstappen, 18 (DNF-accident); **20** Germany-Adrian Sutil, 17 (DNF-accident); **21** Malaysia-Fairuz Fauzy, 15 (DNF-spin); **22** South Africa-Tomas Scheckter, 14 (DNF-suspension); **23** Indonesia-Ananda Mikola, 11 (DNF-spin); **24** Mexico-Salvador Durán, 9 (DNF-accident).

Fastest race lap: France, 1m 31.106s, 102.681 mph/165.249 km/h.

Pole position: France.

Provisional championship points: 1 France, 50; **2** Brazil, 42; **3** Switzerland, 34; **4** New Zealand, 29; **5** Australia, 21; **6** Canada, 18; **7=** Ireland, 16; **7=** Mexico, 16; **9=** Great Britain, 15; **9=** Netherlands, 15; **11=** Malaysia, 14; **11=** Portugal, 14; **13=** Czech Republic, 8; **13=** Germany, 8; **15** USA, 7; **16=** Japan, 6; **16=** South Africa, 6; **18** Indonesia, 5; **19=** Italy, 4; **19=** Pakistan, 4; **21** Austria, 1.

Results of the remaining races will be given in AUTOCOURSE 2006–2007.

Trofeo Nazionale CSAI Formula 3000 (F3000 Italia)

F3000 ITALIA, Autodromo Adria International Raceway, Adria, Italy, 17 April. Round 1. 34 laps of the 1.679-mile/2.702-km circuit, 57.084 miles/91.868 km.

1 Alessandro 'Alex' Ciompi, I (Lola B02/50-Zytek), 40m 07.777s, 85.350 mph/137.356 km/h; **2** Fabrizio del Monte, I (Lola B02/50-Zytek), 40m 12.254s; **3** Luca Filippi, I (Lola B02/50-Zytek), 40m 12.851s; **4** Andrea Belicchi, I (Lola B99/50-Zytek), 40m 18.946s; **5** Juan Cáceres, U (Lola B02/50-Zytek), 40m 25.956s; **6** Jan Charouz, CZ (Lola B02/50-Zytek), 40m 26.456s; **7** Matias Russo, RA (Lola B02/50-Zytek), 40m 29.704s; **8** Stefano Gattuso, I (Lola B99/50-Zytek), 40m 57.856s; **9** Giuseppe Strano, I (Lola B99/50-Zytek), 41m 13.885s; **10** Matteo Grassotto, I (Lola B02/50-Zytek), 24 laps (DNF).

Fastest race lap: Ciompi, 1m 09.883s, 86.490 mph/139.192 km/h.

Fastest qualifying lap: Vilander, 1m 26.797, 69.636 mph/112.068 km/h.

F3000 ITALIA, Autodromo di Vallelunga, Campagnano di Roma, Italy, 8 May. Round 2. 32 laps of the 2.006-mile/3.228-km circuit, 64.185 miles/103.296 km.

1 Toni Vilander, FIN (Lola B02/50-Zytek), 39m 50.381s, 96.665 mph/155.567 km/h; **2** Jaroslav 'Jarek' Janis, CZ (Lola B02/50-Zytek), 39m 54.108s; **3** Giacomo Ricci, I (Lola B02/50-Zytek), 40m 03.150s; **4** Fabrizio del Monte, I (Lola B02/50-Zytek), 40m 14.761s; **5** Juan Cáceres, U (Lola B02/50-Zytek), 40m 17.528s; **6** Jan Charouz, CZ (Lola B02/50-Zytek), 40m 18.492s; **7** Stefano Gattuso, I (Lola B99/50-Zytek), 40m 19.016s; **8** Michael Vorba, CZ (Lola B02/50-Zytek), 40m 19.311s; **9** Giuseppe Strano, I (Lola B99/50-Zytek), 41m 00.100s; **10** Matias Russo, RA (Lola B02/50-Zytek), 30 laps.

Fastest race lap: Vilander, 1m 05.608s, 110.060 mph/177.124 km/h.

Fastest qualifying lap: Luca Filippi, I (B2/50-Zytek), 1m 05.272s, 110.627 mph/178.036 km/h.

F3000 ITALIA, Automotodrom Brno Masaryk Circuit, Brno, Czech Republic, 5 June. Round 3. 22 laps of the 3.357-mile/5.403-km circuit, 73.860 miles/118.866 km.

1 Luca Filippi, (Lola B02/50-Zytek), 40m 54.994s, 108.308 mph/174.305 km/h; **2** Giacomo Ricci, I (Lola B02/50-Zytek), 41m 12.686s; **3** Juan Cáceres, U (Lola B02/50-Zytek), 41m 22.943s; **4** Matteo Cressoni, I (Lola B02/50-Zytek), 41m 23.457s; **5** Bernhard Auinger, A (Lola B02/50-Zytek), 41m 25.016s; **6** Maro Engel, D (Lola B02/50-Zytek), 41m 30.030s; **7** Fabrizio del Monte, I (Lola B02/50-Zytek), 41m 38.941s; **8** Matias Russo, RA (Lola B02/50-Zytek), 41m 39.048s; **9** Stefano Gattuso, I (Lola B99/50-Zytek), 42m 09.757s; **10** Jan Charouz, CZ (Lola B02/50-Zytek), 42m 16.337s.

Fastest race lap: Engel, 1m 49.798s, 110.076 mph/177.150 km/h.

Fastest qualifying lap: Filippi, 1m 47.549s, 112.378 mph/180.855 km/h.

F3000 ITALIA, Autodromo Enzo e Dino Ferrari, Imola, Italy, 19 June. Round 4. 24 laps of the 3.065-mile/4.933-km circuit, 73.418 miles/118.155 km.

1 Luca Filippi, I (Lola B02/50-Zytek), 42m 22.661s, 103.948 mph/167.288 km/h; **2** Raffaele Giammaria, I (Lola B02/50-Zytek), 42m 27.213s; **3** Jaroslav 'Janek' Janis, CZ (Lola B02/50-Zytek), 42m 28.692s; **4** Maro Engel, D (Lola B02/50-Zytek), 42m 33.692s; **5** Jan Charouz, CZ (Lola B02/50-Zytek), 42m 52.954s; **6** Bernhard Auinger, A (Lola B02/50-Zytek), 42m 58.939s; **7** Giacomo Piccini, I (Lola B02/50-Zytek), 43m 01.002s; **8** Juan Cáceres, U (Lola B02/50-Zytek), 43m 09.554s; **9** Giacomo Ricci, I (Lola B02/50-Zytek), 43m 51.071s; **10** Stefano Gattuso, I (Lola B99/50-Zytek), 23 laps.

Fastest race lap: Filippi, 1m 41.588s, 108.623 mph/174.811 km/h.

Fastest qualifying lap: Filippi, 1m 39.778s, 110.594 mph/177.983 km/h.

F3000 ITALIA, Autodromo Internazionale del Mugello, Scarperia, Firenze (Florence), Italy, 3 July. Round 5. 24 laps of the 3.259-mile/5.245-km circuit, 78.218 miles/125.880 km.

1 Luca Filippi, I (Lola B02/50-Zytek), 43m 41.038s, 107.433 mph/172.896 km/h; **2** Alessandro 'Alex' Ciompi, I (Lola B02/50-Zytek), 43m 49.807s; **3** Giacomo Ricci, I (Lola B02/50-Zytek), 44m 07.941s; **4** Alex Lloyd, GB (Lola B02/50-Zytek), 44m 14.525s; **5** Matteo Cressoni, I (Lola B02/50-Zytek), 44m 16.374s; **6** Jaroslav 'Janek' Janis, CZ (Lola B02/50-Zytek), 44m 30.266s; **7** Pastor Maldonado, YV (Lola B02/50-Zytek), 44m 42.049s; **8** Giacomo Piccini, I (Lola B02/50-Zytek), 44m 49.503s; **9** Jan Charouz, CZ (Lola B02/50-Zytek), 44m 52.242s; **10** Stefano Gattuso, I (Lola B99/50-Zytek), 44m 52.334s.

Fastest race lap: Filippi, 1m 42.679s, 114.266 mph/183.893 km/h.

Fastest qualifying lap: Filippi, 1m 40.559s, 116.675 mph/187.770 km/h.

F3000 ITALIA, Autodromo Mario Umberto Borzacchini, Magione, Perugia, Italy, 24 July. Round 6. 30 laps of the 1.558-mile/2.507-km circuit, 46.733 miles/75.210 km.

1 Pastor Maldonado, YV (Lola B02/50-Zytek), 33m 36.305s, 83.440 mph/134.283 km/h; **2** Toni Vilander, FIN (Lola B02/50-Zytek), 33m 51.220s; **3** Jaroslav 'Janek' Janis, CZ (Lola B02/50-Zytek), 33m 51.495s; **4** Raffaele Giammaria, I (Lola B02/50-Zytek), 33m 52.897s; **5** Luca Filippi, I (Lola B02/50-Zytek), 33m 53.043s; **6** Maro Engel, D (Lola B02/50-Zytek), 33m 54.580s; **7** Giacomo Ricci, I (Lola B02/50-Zytek), 34m 02.247s; **8** Giacomo Piccini, I (Lola B02/50-Zytek), 34m 11.649s; **9** Juan

Cáceres, U (Lola B02/50-Zytek), 34m 18.306s; **10** Glauco Solieri, I (Lola B99/50-Zytek), 34m 18.810s.
Fastest race lap: Maldonado, 1m 06.282s, 84.608 mph/136.163 km/h.
Fastest qualifying lap: Maldonado, 1m 05.342s, 85.825 mph/138.122 km/h.

F3000 ITALIA, Autodromo Nazionale di Monza, Milan, Italy, 25 September. Round 7. 20 laps of the 3.600-mile/5.793-km circuit, 93.590 71.992 miles/115.860 km.
1 Luca Filippi, I (Lola B02/50-Zytek), 34m 01.412s, 126.957 mph/204.317 km/h; **2** Jaroslav 'Janek' Janis, CZ (Lola B02/50-Zytek),34m 03.329s; **3** Tuka Rocha, BR (Lola B02/50-Zytek), 34m 08.750s; **4** Maro Engel, D (Lola B02/50-Zytek), 34m 09.237s; **5** Giacomo Ricci, I (Lola B02/50-Zytek), 34m 23.855s; **6** Toni Vilander, FIN (Lola B02/50-Zytek), 34m 21.983s; **7** Giacomo Piccini, I (Lola B02/50-Zytek), 34m 34.122s; **8** Bernhard Auinger, A (Lola B02/50-Zytek), 34m 35.098s; **9** Alessandro 'Alex' Ciompi, I (Lola B02/50-Zytek), 34m 47.030s; **10** Juan Cáceres, U (Lola B02/50-Zytek), 34m 52.505s.
Fastest race lap: Filippi, 1m 41.088s, 128.191 mph/206.303 km/h.
Fastest qualifying lap: Janis, 1m 39.266s, 130.544 mph/210.090 km/h.

F3000 ITALIA, Autodromo Internazionale di Misano, Misano Adriatico, Rimini, Italy, 23 October. Round 8. 29 laps of the 2.523-mile/4.060-km circuit, 73.161 miles/117.740 km.
1 Jaroslav 'Janek' Janis, CZ (Lola B02/50-Zytek), 40m 27.829s, 108.482 mph/174.585 km/h; **2** Luca Filippi, I (Lola B02/50-Zytek), 40m 28.392s; **3** Giacomo Ricci, I (Lola B02/50-Zytek), 40m 36.44s; **4** Juan Cáceres, U (Lola B02/50-Zytek), 40m 57.860s; **5** Gabriele Lancieri, I (Lola B02/50-Zytek), 41m 08.624s; **6** Emilio de Villota Jr., E (Lola B02/50-Zytek), 41, 09.982s; **7** Stefano Gattuso, I (Lola B99/50-Zytek), 41m 21.324s; **8** Christian Danner, D (Lola B02/50-Zytek), 41m 31.542s; **9** Glauco Solieri, I (Lola B99/50-Zytek), 28 laps. **10** Alessandro 'Alex' Ciompi, I (Lola B02/50-Zytek),
Fastest race lap: Ricci, 1m 23.002s, 109.419 mph/176.092 km/h.
Fastest qualifying lap: Janis, 1m 22.287s, 110.369 mph/177.622 km/h.

Final championship points
1 Luca Filippi, I, 65; **2** Jaroslav 'Janek' Janis, CZ, 43; **3** Giacomo Ricci, I, 33; **4** Toni Vilander, FIN, 23; **5** Juan Cáceres, U, 20; **6** Alessandro 'Alex' Ciompi, I, 19; **7** Maro Engel, D, 17; **8** Fabrizio del Monte, I, 15; **9** Pastor Maldonado, YV, 14; **10** Raffaele Giammaria, I, 13; **11** Jan Charouz, CZ, 10; **12** Matteo Cressoni, I, 9; **13** Bernhard Auinger, A, 8; **14** Tuka Rocha, BR, 6; **15** Giacomo Piccini, I, 6; **16** Andrea Belicchi, I, 5; **17** Alex Lloyd, GB, 5; **18** Stefano Gattuso, I, 5; **19** Gabriele Lancieri, I, 4; **20=** Emilio de Villota Jr., E, 3; **20=** Matias Russo, RA, 3; **22=** Christian Danner, D, 1; **22=** Michael Vorba, CZ, 1.

Light Championship: 1 Stefano Gattuso.

3000 Pro Series

All cars are Lola B99/50-Zytek.

3000 PRO SERIES, Autodromo di Vallelunga, Campagnano di Roma, Italy, 10 April. Round 1. 18 laps of the 2.006-mile/3.228-km circuit, 36.104 miles/58.104 km.
1 Timo Lienemann, D, 29m 02.796s, 74.578 mph/120.022 km/h; **2** Fausto Ippoliti, BR, 29m 05.788s; **3** Dominik Jackson, GB, 29m 06.354s; **4** Tor Graves, GB, 29m 06.864s; **5** Olivier Tielemans, NL, 29m 11.704s; **6** Marco Mocci, I, 29m 17.459s; **7** Jean de Pourtales, F, 29m 30.305s; **8** Ignazio Belluardo, I, 29m 35.874s; **9** Stefano Attianese, I, 10 laps; **10** Sergio Ghiotto, I, 10.
Fastest race lap: Lienemann, 1m 20.602s, 89.586 mph/144.175 km/h.
Fastest qualifying lap: Norbert Siedler, A, 1m 07.461s, 107.037 mph/172.260 km/h.

3000 PRO SERIES, Autodromo Enzo e Dino Ferrari, Imola, Italy, 15 May. Round 2. 15 laps of the 3.065-mile/4.933-km circuit, 45.978 miles/73.995 km.
1 Norbert Siedler, A, 25m 45.472s, 107.101 mph/172.363 km/h; **2** Massimiliano 'Max' Busnelli, I, 25m 55.029s; **3** Timo Lienemann, D, 26m 04.875s; **4** Marco Mocci, I, 26m 09.061s; **5** Alessandro Bonetti, I, 26m 11.162s; **6** Scott Mansell, GB, 26m 28.421s; **7** Ignazio Belluardo, I, 26m 32.224s; **8** Fausto Ippoliti, BR, 26m 32.460s; **9** Basil Shaaban, RL, 26m 38.769s; **10** Glauco Solieri, I, 26m 51.208s.
Fastest race lap: Siedler, 1m 41.991s, 108.194 mph/174.121 km/h.
Fastest qualifying lap: Siedler, 1m 39.407s, 111.006 mph/178.647 km/h.

3000 PRO SERIES, Circuit de Spa-Francorchamps, Stavelot, Belgium, 12 June. Round 3. 11 laps of the 4.335-mile/6.976-km circuit, 47.682 miles/76.736 km.
1 Norbert Siedler, A, 27m 54.246s, 102.526 mph/164.999 km/h; **2** Massimiliano 'Max' Busnelli, I, 27m 57.434s; **3** Tor Graves, GB, 28m 00.999s; **4** Dominik Jackson, GB, 28m 04.336s; **5** Olivier Tielemans, NL, 28m 11.854s; **6** Marco Mocci, I, 28m 13.257s; **7** Alessandro Bonetti, I, 28m 13.919s; **8** Jean de Pourtales, F, 28m 21.518s; **9** Khalil Beschir, RL, 28m 21.749s; **10** Sergio Ghiotto, I, 28m 24.700s.
Fastest race lap: Siedler, 2m 08.653s, 121.294 mph/195.204 km/h.
Fastest qualifying lap: Siedler, 2m 06.581s, 123.280 mph/198.399 km/h.

3000 PRO SERIES, Autodromo Internazionale del Mugello, Scarperia, Firenze (Florence), Italy, 10 July. Round 4. 12 laps of the 3.259-mile/5.245-km circuit, 39.109 miles/62.940 km.
1 Massimiliano 'Max' Busnelli, I, 21m 16.076s, 110.333 mph/177.563 km/h; **2** Norbert Siedler, A, 21m 23.742s; **3** Alessandro Bonetti, I, 21m 32.918s; **4** Marco Mocci, I, 21m 37.195s; **5** Olivier Tielemans, NL, 21m 46.724s; **6** Tor Graves, GB, 21m 55.375s; **7** Ignazio Belluardo, I, 21m 57.963s; **8** Timo Lienemann, D, 21m 59.807s; **9** Sergio Ghiotto, I, 22m 05.013s; **10** Basil Shaaban, RL, 11 laps.
Fastest race lap: Tielemans.
Fastest qualifying lap: Busnelli, 1m 40.189s, 117.106 mph/188.464 km/h.

3000 PRO SERIES, Autodromo Internazionale di Misano, Misano Adriatico, Rimini, Italy, 24 July. Round 5. 19 laps of the 2.523-mile/4.060-km circuit, 47.933 miles/77.140 km.
1 Alessandro Bonetti, I, 27m 11.502s, 105.766 mph/170.214 km/h; **2** Norbert Siedler, A, 27m 11.858s; **3** Fausto Ippoliti, BR, 27m 13.419s; **4** Ignazio Belluardo, I, 27m 22.366s; **5** Olivier Tielemans, NL, 27m 29.587s; **6** Marco Mocci, I, 27m 31.482s; **7** Tor Graves, GB, 28m 03.330s; **8** Matteo Pellegrino, I, 28m 36.644s; **9** Timo Lienemann, D, 18 laps; **10** Massimiliano 'Max' Busnelli, I, 14.
Fastest qualifying lap: Busnelli, 1m 23.058s, 109.345 mph/175.973 km/h.

3000 PRO SERIES, EuroSpeedway Lausitz, Klettwitz, Dresden, Germany, 28 August. Round 6. 17 laps of the 2.523-mile/4.060-km circuit, 42.887 miles/69.020 km.
1 Robbie Kerr, GB, 27m 12.558s, 94.571 mph/152.198 km/h; **2** Timo Lienemann, D, 27m 12.971s; **3** Alessandro Bonetti, I, 27m 31.529s; **4** Massimiliano 'Max' Busnelli, I, 27m 41.853s; **5** Khalil Beschir, RL, 28m 01.005s; **6** Sergio Ghiotto, I, 28m 08.463s; **7** Ignazio Belluardo, I, 16 laps.
Fastest race lap: Kerr, 1m 34.877s, 95.724 mph/154.052 km/h.
Fastest qualifying lap: Kerr, 1m 33.167s, 97.480 mph/156.880 km/h.

3000 PRO SERIES, Autodromo Adria International Raceway, Adria, Italy, 25 September. Round 7. 27 laps of the 1.679-mile/2.702-km circuit, 45.332 miles/72.954 km.
1 Timo Lienemann, D, 32m 55.024s, 82.629 mph/132.978 km/h; **2** Massimiliano 'Max' Busnelli, I, 33m 02.775s; **3** Alessandro Bonetti, I, 33m 12.377s; **4** Norbert Siedler, A, 33m 13.681s; **5** Marco Mocci, I, 33m 31.835s; **6** Tor Graves, GB, 33m 38.202s; **7** Sergio Ghiotto, I; Ignazio Belluardo, I (DNF); Fausto Ippoliti, I (DNF).
Fastest qualifying lap: Siedler, 1m 08.189s, 88.639 mph/142.651 km/h.

3000 PRO SERIES, Autodromo Nazionale di Monza, Milan, Italy, 9 October. Round 8. 13 laps of the 3.600-mile/5.793-km circuit, 46.795 miles/75.309 km.
1 Massimiliano 'Max' Busnelli, I, 22m 23.851s, 125.357 mph/201.743 km/h; **2** Norbert Siedler, A, 22m 24.055s; **3** Timo Lienemann, D, 22m 24.786s; **4** Alessandro Bonetti, I, 22m 31.080s; **5** Tor Graves, GB, 22m 32.660s; **6** Davide Valsecchi, I, 22m 36.127s; **7** Fausto Ippoliti, BR, 22m 36.560s; **8** Luca Di Cienzo, I, 22m 48.931s; **9** Olivier Tielemans, NL, 22m 51.370s; **10** Sergey Zlobin, RUS, 12 laps.
Fastest qualifying lap: Siedler, 1m 41.489s, 127.684 mph/205.488 km/h.

Final championship points
1 Massimiliano 'Max' Busnelli, I, 49; **2** Norbert Siedler, A, 49; **3** Timo Lienemann, D, 41; **4** Alessandro Bonetti, I, 39; **5=** Marco Mocci, I, 23; **5=** Tor Graves, GB, 23; **7** Fausto Ippoliti, BR, 17; **8** Olivier Tielemans, NL, 16; **9** Ignazio Belluardo, I, 12; **10** Dominik Jackson, GB, 11; **11** Robbie Kerr, GB, 10; **12** Sergio Ghiotto, I, 5; **13** Khalil Beschir, RL, 4; **14=** Davide Valsecchi, I, 3; **14=** Scott Mansell, GB, 3; **14=** Jean de Pourtales, F, 3; **17=** Matteo Pellegrino, I, 1; **17=** Luca Di Cienzo, I, 1.

All-Japan Formula Nippon Championship

All cars are Lola B3/51-Mugen.

ALL-JAPAN FORMULA NIPPON CHAMPIONSHIP, Twin Ring Motegi, Motegi-machi, Haga-gun, Tochigi, Japan, 3 April. Round 1. 62 laps of the 2.983-mile/4.801-km circuit, 184.959 miles/297.662 km.
1 Richard Lyons, GB, 1h 44m 25.154s, 106.278 mph/171.039 km/h; **2** Yuji Ide, J, 1h 44m 29.802s; **3** Naoki Hattori, J, 1h 44m 55.986s; **4** Satoshi Motoyama, J, 1h 45m 01.604s; **5** Takeshi Tsuchiya, J, 1h 45m 01.974s; **6** Benoit Tréluyer, F, 1h 45m 02.289s; **7** Tatsuya Kataoka, J, 1h 45m 05.900s; **8** Katsuyuki Hiranaka, J, 1h 45m 19.652s; **9** Toranosuke Takagi, J, 1h 45m 55.785s; **10** Tsugio Matsuda, J, 61 laps.
Fastest race lap: Hiranaka, 1m 38.961s, 108.523 mph/174.651 km/h.
Fastest qualifying lap: Ide, 1m 35.221s, 112.785 mph/181.510 km/h.

ALL-JAPAN FORMULA NIPPON CHAMPIONSHIP, Suzuka International Racing Course, Suzuka-shi, Mie Prefecture, Japan, 17 April. Round 2. 51 laps of the 3.608-mile/5.807-km circuit, 184.023 miles/296.157 km.
1 Yuji Ide, J, 1h 35m 15.713s, 115.906 mph/186.532 km/h; **2** Tsugio Matsuda, J, 1h 35m 30.306s; **3** Takashi Kogure, J, 1h 35m 35.883s; **4** Satoshi Motoyama, J, 1h 35m 50.551s; **5** Richard Lyons, GB, 1h 35m 50.698s; **6** Naoki Hattori, J, 1h 36m 13.214s; **7** Jaroslav 'Janek' Janis, CZ, 1h 36m 31.356s; **8** Tatsuya Kataoka, J, 50 laps (DNF-accident); **9** Benoit Tréluyer, F, 46 (DNF-spin); **10** Andre Lotterer, D, 35 (DNF-accident).
Fastest race lap: Kogure, 1m 49.481s, 118.650 mph/190.948 km/h.
Fastest qualifying lap: Tréluyer, 1m 44.677s, 124.095 mph/199.711 km/h.

ALL-JAPAN FORMULA NIPPON CHAMPIONSHIP, Sportsland SUGO International Course, Shibata-gun, Miyagi Prefecture, Japan, 15 May. Round 3. 80 laps of the 2.302-mile/3.704-km circuit, 184.125 miles/296.32 km.
1 Satoshi Motoyama, J, 1h 45m 31.764s, 104.606 mph/168.476 km/h; **2** Richard Lyons, GB, 1h 45m 42.144s; **3** Takashi Kogure, J, 1h 45m 46.884s; **4** Takeshi Tsuchiya, J, 1h 46m 18.421s; **5** Yuji Ide, J, 79 laps; **6** Naoki Hattori, J, 79; **7** Jaroslav 'Janek' Janis, CZ, 79; **8** Tatsuya Kataoka, J, 79; **9** Andre Lotterer, D, 78; **10** Hideki Noda, J, 77.
Fastest race lap: Noda, 1m 11.571s, 115.768 mph/186.310 km/h.
Fastest qualifying lap: Kogure, 1m 09.320s, 119.527 mph/192.360 km/h.

ALL-JAPAN FORMULA NIPPON CHAMPIONSHIP, Fuji International Speedway, Sunto-gun, Shizuoka Prefecture, Japan, 5 June. Round 4. 62 laps of the 2.835-mile/4.563-km circuit, 175.790 miles/282.906 km.
1 Benoit Tréluyer, F, 1h 03m 40.504s, 165.644 mph/266.578 km/h; **2** Satoshi Motoyama, J, 1h 03m 47.765s; **3** Tsugio Matsuda, J, 1h 03m 50.489s; **4** Richard Lyons, GB, 1h 03m 58.185s; **5** Ronnie Quintarelli, I, 1h 03m 59.363s; **6** Katsuyuki Hiranaka, J, 1h 04m 03.258s; **7** Yuji Ide, J, 1h 04m 10.744s; **8** Takashi Kogure, J, 1h 04m 20.308s; **9** Toranosuke Takagi, J, 1h 04m 28.849s; **10** Naoki Hattori, J, 1h 05m 03.040s.
Fastest race lap: Matsuda, 1m 30.267s, 113.077 mph/181.980 km/h.
Fastest qualifying lap: Lyons, 1m 28.340s, 115.544 mph/185.950 km/h.

ALL-JAPAN FORMULA NIPPON CHAMPIONSHIP, Suzuka International Racing Course, Suzuka-shi, Mie Prefecture, Japan, 3 July. Round 5. 51 laps of the 3.608-mile/5.807-km circuit, 184.023 miles/296.157 km.
1 Satoshi Motoyama, J, 1h 58m 53.052s, 92.875 mph/149.468 km/h; **2** Takashi Kogure, J, 1h 58m 54.580s; **3** Richard Lyons, GB, 1h 58m 58.138s; **4** Sakon Yamamoto, J, 1h 59m 02.858s; **5** Ronnie Quintarelli, I, 1h 59m 06.484s; **6** Tsugio Matsuda, J, 1h 59m 07.147s; **7** Naoki Hattori, J, 1h 59m 14.831s; **8** Yuji Ide, J, 1h 59m 18.246s; **9** Hideki Noda, J, 50 laps; **10** Toranosuke Takagi, J, 50.
Fastest race lap: Ide, 2m 06.778s, 102.462 mph/164.896 km/h.
Fastest qualifying lap: Motoyama, 1m 46.901s, 121.513 mph/195.557 km/h.

ALL-JAPAN FORMULA NIPPON CHAMPIONSHIP, Mine Circuit, Nishi-Aho-cho, Mine City, Yamaguchi Prefecture, Japan, 31 July. Round 6. 75 laps of the 2.070-mile/3.331-km circuit, 155.234 miles/249.825 km.
1 Yuji Ide, J, 1h 46m 32.147s, 87.426 mph/140.699 km/h; **2** Ronnie Quintarelli, I, 1h 46m 47.041s; **3** Satoshi Motoyama, J, 1h 46m 52.345s; **4** Tsugio Matsuda, J, 1h 46m 54.668s; **5** Takeshi Tsuchiya, J, 1h 47m 10.460s; **6** Naoki Hattori, J, 1h 47m 10.989s; **7** Tatsuya Kataoka, J, 1h 47m 11.667s; **8** Sakon Yamamoto, J, 1h 47m 19.033s; **9** Toranosuke Takagi, J, 1h 47m 30.550s; **10** Andre Lotterer, D, 73 laps.
Fastest race lap: Ide, 1m 19.186s, 94.098 mph/151.436 km/h.
Fastest qualifying lap: Benoit Tréluyer, F, 1m 15.997s, 98.046 mph/157.790 km/h.

ALL-JAPAN FORMULA NIPPON CHAMPIONSHIP, Fuji International Speedway, Sunto-gun, Shizuoka Prefecture, Japan, 28 August. Round 7. 65 laps of the 2.835-mile/4.563-km circuit, 184.296 miles/296.595 km.
1 Andre Lotterer, D, 1h 40m 15.339s, 73.108 mph/117.656 km/h; **2** Tatsuya Kataoka, J, 1h 40m 18.230s; **3** Yuji Ide, J, 1h 40m 18.889s; **4** Richard Lyons, GB, 1h 40m 20.112s; **5** Takeshi Tsuchiya, J, 1h 40m 50.111s; **6** Katsuyuki Hiranaka, J, 1h 41m 00.899s; **7** Naoki Hattori, J, 1h 41m 02.195s; **8** Toranosuke Takagi, J, 1h 41m 25.389s; **9** Tsugio Matsuda, J, 1h 41m 26.590s; **10** Hideki Noda, J, 1h 41m 32.742s.
Fastest race lap: Satoshi Motoyama, J, 1m 30.769s, 112.452 mph/180.974 km/h.
Fastest qualifying lap: Lyons, 1m 29.372s, 114.210 mph/183.803 km/h.

ALL-JAPAN FORMULA NIPPON CHAMPIONSHIP, Twin Ring Motegi, Motegi-machi, Haga-gun, Tochigi, Japan, 23 October. Round 8. 62 laps of the 2.983-mile/4.801-km circuit, 184.959 miles/297.662 km.
1 Satoshi Motoyama, J, 1h 45m 51.073s, 104.841 mph/168.725 km/h; **2** Sakon Yamamoto, J, 1h 45m 51.680s; **3** Takeshi Tsuchiya, J, 1h 46m 08.791s; **4** Yuji Ide, J, 1h 46m 25.158s; **5** Ronnie Quintarelli, I, 1h 46m 26.988s; **6** Tatsuya Kataoka, J, 1h 46m 35.572s; **7** Naoki Hattori, J, 1h 46m 36.076s; **8** Hideki Noda, J, 1h 46m 36.377s; **9** Takashi Kogure, J, 1h 46m 43.529s; **10** Tsugio Matsuda, J, 1h 46m 44.010s.
Fastest race lap: Yamamoto, 1m 39.591s, 107.836 mph/173.546 km/h.
Fastest qualifying lap: Motoyama, 1m 52.124s, 95.783 mph/154.147 km/h.

Provisional championship points
1 Satoshi Motoyama, J, 46; **2** Yuji Ide, J, 35; **3** Richard Lyons, GB, 28; **4=** Takashi Kogure, J, 14; **4=** Tsugio Matsuda, J, 14; **6** Takeshi Tsuchiya, J, 13; **7** Ronnie Quintarelli, I, 12; **8** Benoit Tréluyer, F, 11; **9** Andre Lotterer, D, 10; **10** Sakon Yamamoto, J, 9; **11=** Tatsuya Kataoka, J, 7; **11=** Naoki Hattori, J, 7; **13** Katsuyuki Hiranaka, J, 2.

Result of the Suzuka race will be given in AUTOCOURSE 2006–2007.

British Formula 3 International Series

BRITISH FORMULA 3 INTERNATIONAL SERIES, Donington Park National Circuit, Castle Donington, Derbyshire, Great Britain, 3 April. 2 x 20 laps of the 1.9573-mile/3.150-km circuit.
Round 1 (39.146 miles/62.999 km).
1 Danilo Dirani, BR (Lola B05/30-Mugen), 25m 27.896s, 92.235 mph/148.439 km/h; **2** Mike Conway, GB (Dallara F305-Opel), 25m 29.677s; **3** Dan Clarke, GB (Dallara F305-Mugen), 25m 32.093s; **4** Ryan Lewis, GB (Dallara F305-Mugen), 25m 32.408s; **5** Christian Bakkerud, DK (Dallara F305-Mugen), 25m 37.507s; **6** Bruno Senna, BR (Dallara F305-Mugen), 25m 44.154s; **7** Steven Kane, GB (Lola B05/30-Mugen), 25m 45.390s; **8** Marko Asmer, EE (Dallara F305-Mugen), 25m 50.208s; **9** Susie Stoddart, GB (Dallara F305-Mugen), 25m 55.915s; **10** Josh Fisher, GB (Dallara F304-Mugen), 25m 56.902s (1st National class).
Fastest race lap: Lewis, 1m 02.682s, 112.413 mph/180.911 km/h.
Fastest qualifying lap: Dirani, 1m 02.784s, 112.231 mph/180.617 km/h.

Round 2 (39.146 miles/62.999 km).
1 Danilo Dirani, BR (Lola B05/30-Mugen), 25m 02.684s, 93.783 mph/150.928 km/h; **2** Marko Asmer, EE (Dallara F305-Mugen), 25m 07.489s; **3** Mike Conway, GB (Dallara F305-Opel), 25m 07.992s; **4** Dan Clarke, GB (Dallara F305-Mugen), 25m 08.663s; **5** Steven Kane, GB (Lola B05/30-Mugen), 25m 10.623s; **6** Christian Bakkerud, DK (Dallara F305-Mugen), 25m 13.381s; **7** Ryan Lewis, GB (Dallara F305-Mugen), 25m 18.514s; **8** James Walker, GB (Dallara F305-Opel), 25m 19.476s; **9** Tim Bridgeman, GB (Dallara F305-Mugen), 25m 24.030s; **10** Charlie Kimball, USA (Dallara F305-Mugen), 25m 27.834s. **National class winner:** Barton Mawer, AUS (Dallara F304-Mugen), 25m 30.675s (12th).
Fastest race lap: Asmer, 1m 03.215s, 111.465 mph/179.386 km/h.
Fastest qualifying lap: Asmer, 1m 03.094s, 111.679 mph/179.730 km/h.
Championship points: 1 Dirani, 40; **2** Conway, 27; **3** Clarke, 22; **4** Asmer, 19; **5** Lewis, 15; **6** Bakkerud, 14. **National Class: 1** Barton Mawer, AUS, 35; **2** Fisher, 32; **3=** Salvador Durán, MEX, 16; **3=**Juho Annala, FIN, 16.

The races scheduled for Spa-Francorchamps on 17 April were postponed due to fog and held at Monza (as round 13) and Silverstone (as round 14). Pole positions achieved at Spa are shown under those races.

BRITISH FORMULA 3 INTERNATIONAL SERIES, Croft Circuit, Croft-on-Tees, North Yorkshire, Great Britain, 8 May. 17 and 18 laps of the 2.127-mile/3.423-km circuit.
Round 3 (36.159 miles/58.192 km).
1 Mike Conway, GB (Dallara F305-Opel), 26m 30.701s, 81.833 mph/131.698 km/h; **2** Marko Asmer, EE (Dallara F305-Mugen), 26m 34.070s; **3** Alvaro Parente, P (Dallara F305-Mugen), 26m 34.605s; **4** Christian Bakkerud, DK (Dallara F305-Mugen), 26m 35.304s; **5** Salvador Durán, MEX (Dallara F304-Mugen), 26m 40.755s **(1st National class)**; **6** Barton Mawer, AUS (Dallara F304-Mugen), 26m 41.987s; **7** Ryan Lewis, GB (Dallara F305-Mugen), 26m 42.523s; **8** Josh Fisher, GB (Dallara F304-Mugen), 26m 44.052s; **9** Charlie Kimball, USA (Dallara F305-Mugen), 26m 44.957s; **10** Jonathan Kennard, GB (Dallara F304-Mugen), 26m 48.071s.
Fastest race lap: Conway, 1m 15.153s, 101.888 mph/163.973 km/h.
Fastest qualifying lap: Parente, 1m 14.251s, 103.126 mph/165.965 km/h.

Round 4 (38.286 miles/61.615 km).
1 Alvaro Parente, P (Dallara F305-Mugen), 29m 25.389s, 78.073 mph/125.647 km/h; **2** Christian Bakkerud, DK (Dallara F305-Mugen), 29m 26.925s; **3** Dan Clarke, GB (Dallara F305-Mugen), 29m 33.815s; **4** Ryan Lewis, GB (Dallara F305-Mugen), 29m 37.215s; **5** Bruno Senna, BR (Dallara F305-Mugen), 29m 39.220s; **6** Salvador Durán, MEX (Dallara F304-Mugen), 29m 40.626s (1st National class); **7** Marko Asmer, EE (Dallara F305-Mugen), 29m 43.318s; **8** James Walker, GB (Dallara F305-Opel), 29m 46.587s; **9** Steven Kane, GB (Lola B05/30-Mugen), 29m 50.201s; **10** Barton Mawer, AUS (Dallara F304-Mugen), 29m 53.227s.
Fastest race lap: Clarke, 1m 26.843s, 88.173 mph/141.901 km/h.
Fastest qualifying lap: Parente, 1m 14.639s, 102.590 mph/165.102 km/h.
Championship points: 1 Conway, 50; **2=** Dirani, 40; **2=** Asmer, 40; **4** Bakkerud, 39; **5** Clarke, 35; **6** Lewis, 33. **National Class: 1** Mawer, 65; **2** Durán, 57; **3** Fisher, 52.

BRITISH FORMULA 3 INTERNATIONAL SERIES, Knockhill Racing Circuit, By Dunfermline, Fife, Scotland, Great Britain, 22 May. 2 x 25 laps of the 1.2986-mile/2.090-km circuit.
Round 5 (32.465 miles/52.247 km).
1 Alvaro Parente, P (Dallara F305-Mugen), 22m 58.695s, 84.771 mph/136.426 km/h; **2** Ryan Lewis, GB (Dallara F305-Mugen), 23m 06.515s; **3** Mike Conway, GB (Dallara F305-Opel), 23m 07.475s; **4** Steven Kane, GB (Lola B05/30-Mugen), 23m 15.028s; **5** Danilo Dirani, BR (Lola B05/30-Mugen), 23m 18.223s; **6** Christian Bakkerud, DK (Dallara F305-Mugen), 23m 43.177s; **7** Charlie Hollings, GB (Dome F106/04-Mugen), 23m 45.225s (1st National class); **8** Salvador Durán, MEX (Dallara F304-Mugen), 23m 47.638s; **9** Josh Fisher, GB (Dallara F304-Mugen), 23m 49.964s; **10** Barton Mawer, AUS (Dallara F304-Mugen), 24 laps.
Fastest race lap: Kane, 54.025s, 86.533 mph/139.262 km/h.
Fastest qualifying lap: Parente, 46.923s, 99.630 mph/160.340 km/h.

Round 6 (32.465 miles/52.247 km).
1 Alvaro Parente, P (Dallara F305-Mugen), 20m 00.876s, 97.324 mph/156.628 km/h; **2** Marko Asmer, EE (Dallara F305-Mugen), 20m 09.062s **3** Charlie Kimball, USA (Dallara F305-Mugen), 20m 09.553s; **4** Steven Kane, GB (Lola B05/30-Mugen), 20m 09.921s; **5** Dan Clarke, GB (Dallara F305-Mugen), 20m 21.659s; **6** James Walker, GB (Dallara F305-Opel), 20m 24.100s; **7** Christian Bakkerud, DK (Dallara F305-Mugen), 20m 27.851s; **8** Ryan Lewis, GB (Dallara F305-Mugen), 20m 27.983s; **9** Danilo Dirani, BR (Lola B05/30-Mugen), 20m 29.829s; **10** Charlie Hollings, GB (Dome F106/04-Mugen), 20m 39.241s **(1st National class)**.
Fastest race lap: Lewis, 47.039s, 99.385 mph/159.944 km/h.
Fastest qualifying lap: Parente, 54.015s, 86.549 mph/139.288 km/h.
Championship points: 1 Parente, 72; **2** Conway, 62; **3** Asmer, 55; **4** Lewis, 52; **5** Dirani, 50; **6** Bakkerud, 49. **National Class: 1** Mawer, 91; **2** Durán, 81; **3** Fisher, 64.

BRITISH FORMULA 3 INTERNATIONAL SERIES, Thruxton Circuit, Andover, Hampshire, Great Britain, 29 May. 2 x 16 laps of the 2.356-mile/3.792-km circuit.
Round 7 (37.696 miles/60.666 km).
1 Charlie Kimball, USA (Dallara F305-Mugen), 18m 02.145s, 125.404 mph/201.819 km/h; **2** Marko Asmer, EE (Dallara F305-Mugen), 18m 05.808s; **3** Christian Bakkerud, DK (Dallara F305-Mugen), 18m 07.438s; **4** Mike Conway, GB (Dallara F305-Opel), 18m 08.135s; **5** Alvaro Parente, P (Dallara F305-Mugen), 18m 10.488s; **6** Ryan Lewis, GB (Dallara F305-Mugen), 18m 12.920s; **7** Danilo Dirani, BR (Lola B05/30-Mugen), 18m 13.362s; **8** Steven Kane, GB (Lola B05/30-Mugen), 18m 18.463s; **9** Dan Clarke, GB (Dallara F305-Mugen), 18m 22.758s; **10** James Walker, GB (Dallara F305-Opel), 18m 26.310s. **National class winner:** Barton Mawer, AUS (Dallara F304-Mugen), 18m 39.297s (14th).

Fastest race lap: Bakkerud, 1m 06.945s, 126.695 mph/203.896 km/h.
Fastest qualifying lap: Kimball, 1m 07.140s, 126.327 mph/203.304 km/h.

Round 8 (37.696 miles/60.666 km).
1 Charlie Kimball, USA (Dallara F305-Mugen), 20m 26.422s, 110.652 mph/178.077 km/h; **2** Marko Asmer, EE (Dallara F305-Mugen), 20m 31.239s; **3** Christian Bakkerud, DK (Dallara F305-Mugen), 20m 35.608s; **4** Ryan Lewis, GB (Dallara F305-Mugen), 20m 36.306s; **5** Dan Clarke, GB (Dallara F305-Mugen), 20m 43.874s; **6** Mike Conway, GB (Dallara F305-Opel), 20m 44.162s; **7** Steven Kane, GB (Lola B05/30-Mugen), 20m 44.518s; **8** James Walker, GB (Dallara F305-Opel), 20m 44.844s; **9** Barton Mawer, AUS (Dallara F304-Mugen), 20m 49.767s **(1st National class)**; **10** Stephen Jelley, GB (Dallara F305-Opel), 20m 50.650s.
Fastest race lap: Kimball, 1m 06.921s, 126.740 mph/203.969 km/h.
Fastest qualifying lap: Kimball, 1m 06.848s, 126.879 mph/204.192 km/h.
Championship points: 1 Asmer, 85; **2** Parente, 80; **3** Conway, 78; **4** Bakkerud, 74; **5** Lewis, 68; **6** Kennard, 60. **National Class: 1** Mawer, 132; **2** Durán, 91; **3** Hollings, 88.

BRITISH FORMULA 3 INTERNATIONAL SERIES, Castle Combe Circuit, Wiltshire, Great Britain, 26 June. 19 and 20 laps of the 1.850-mile/2.977-km circuit.
Round 9 (35.150 miles/56.568 km).
1 Dan Clarke, GB (Dallara F305-Mugen), 21m 28.508s, 98.207 mph/158.048 km/h; **2** Alvaro Parente, P (Dallara F305-Mugen), 21m 30.571s; **3** Charlie Kimball, USA (Dallara F305-Mugen), 21m 31.059s; **4** Ryan Lewis, GB (Dallara F305-Mugen), 21m 31.932s; **5** Danny Watts, GB (Dallara F305-Mugen), 21m 35.252s; **6** Mike Conway, GB (Dallara F305-Opel), 21m 35.765s; **7** Danilo Dirani, BR (Lola B05/30-Mugen), 21m 36.157s; **8** Christian Bakkerud, DK (Dallara F305-Mugen), 21m 39.134s; **9** Marko Asmer, EE (Dallara F305-Mugen), 21m 39.519s; **10** Steven Kane, GB (Lola B05/30-Mugen), 21m 39.850s. **National class winner:** Salvador Durán, MEX (Dallara F304-Mugen), 21m 46.092s (15th).
Fastest race lap: Clarke, 59.387s, 112.146 mph/180.481 km/h.
Fastest qualifying lap: Kimball, 59.100s, 112.690 mph/181.358 km/h.

Round 10 (37.000 miles/59.546 km).
1 Alvaro Parente, P (Dallara F305-Mugen), 24m 42.030s, 89.877 mph/144.643 km/h; **2** Danny Watts, GB (Dallara F305-Mugen), 24m 46.061s; **3** Dan Clarke, GB (Dallara F305-Mugen), 24m 46.580s; **4** Marko Asmer, EE (Dallara F305-Mugen), 24m 50.007s; **5** Danilo Dirani, BR (Lola B05/30-Mugen), 24m 51.469s; **6** Christian Bakkerud, DK (Dallara F305-Mugen), 24m 56.989s; **7** Mike Conway, GB (Dallara F305-Opel), 24m 58.124s; **8** James Walker, GB (Dallara F305-Opel), 24m 58.437s; **9** Stephen Jelley, GB (Dallara F305-Opel), 24m 58.795s; **10** Bruno Senna, BR (Dallara F305-Mugen), 25m 01.192s. **National class winner:** Barton Mawer, AUS (Dallara F304-Mugen), 25m 01.561s (11th).
Fastest race lap: Kimball, 59.897s, 111.191 mph/178.944 km/h.
Fastest qualifying lap: Parente, 58.994s, 112.893 mph/181.683 km/h.
Championship points: 1 Parente, 115; **2** Asmer, 97; **3** Conway, 88; **4** Clarke, 86; **5** Bakkerud, 83; **6** Lewis, 78. **National Class: 1** Mawer, 161; **2** Durán, 121; **3** Hollings, 106.

BRITISH FORMULA 3 INTERNATIONAL SERIES, Autodromo Nazionale di Monza, Milan, Italy, 9 July. 3 x 15 laps of the 3.600-mile/5.793-km circuit.
Round 11 (53.994 miles/86.895 km).
1 Alvaro Parente, P (Dallara F305-Mugen), 27m 21.294s, 118.430 mph/190.594 km/h; **2** Charlie Kimball, USA (Dallara F305-Mugen), 27m 21.700s; **3** Danilo Dirani, BR (Lola B05/30-Mugen), 27m 32.848s; **4** Mike Conway, GB (Dallara F305-Opel), 27m 34.927s; **5** Christian Bakkerud, DK (Dallara F305-Mugen), 27m 46.104s; **6** Ronayne O'Mahony, IRL (Dallara F305-Opel), 27m 50.786s; **7** Barton Mawer, AUS (Dallara F304-Mugen), 27m 51.855s; **8** Salvador Durán, MEX (Dallara F304-Mugen), 27m 54.544s); **9** Ben Clucas, GB (Lola F106/03-Mugen), 28m 11.626s; **10** Karl Reindler, AUS (Dallara F305-Mugen), 28m 12.257s.**National class winner:** Barton Mawer, AUS (Dallara F304-Mugen).
Fastest race lap: Kimball, 1m 48.594s, 119.330 mph/192.043 km/h.
Fastest qualifying lap: Kimball, 2m 03.295s, 105.102 mph/169.145 km/h.

Round 12 (53.994 miles/86.895 km).
1 Alvaro Parente, P (Dallara F305-Mugen), 27m 11.844s, 119.116 mph/191.698 km/h; **2** Charlie Kimball, USA (Dallara F305-Mugen), 27m 13.138s; **3** Danilo Dirani, BR (Lola B05/30-Mugen), 27m 24.790s; **4** Mike Conway, GB (Dallara F305-Opel), 27m 25.136s; **5** Ryan Lewis, GB (Dallara F305-Mugen), 27m 27.777s; **6** Bruno Senna, BR (Dallara F305-Mugen), 27m 31.020s; **7** Stephen Jelley, GB (Dallara F305-Opel), 27m 42.774s; **8** Steven Kane, GB (Lola B05/30-Mugen), 27m 48.816s; **9** Ben Clucas, GB (Lola F106/03-Mugen), 27m 49.913s **(1st National class)**; **10** Ronayne O'Mahony, IRL (Dallara F305-Opel), 27m 55.958s.
Fastest race lap: Parente, 1m 48.149s, 119.821 mph/192.833 km/h.
Fastest qualifying lap: Parente, 1m 47.021s, 121.084 mph/194.866 km/h.

Round 13 (53.994 miles/86.895 km).
Originally scheduled for Spa-Francorchamps, Belgium on 17 April but postponed due to fog.
1 Alvaro Parente, P (Dallara F305-Mugen), 27m 23.676s, 118.258 mph/190.318 km/h; **2** Charlie Kimball, USA (Dallara F305-Mugen), 27m 26.713s; **3** Christian Bakkerud, DK (Dallara F305-Mugen), 27m 32.685s; **4** Ryan Lewis, GB (Dallara F305-Mugen), 27m 35.357s; **5** Bruno Senna, BR (Dallara F305-Mugen), 27m 35.760s; **6** Marko Asmer, EE (Dallara F305-Mugen), 27m 44.430s; **7** Steven Kane, GB (Lola B05/30-Mugen), 27m 47.582s; **8** Stephen Jelley, GB (Dallara F305-Opel), 27m 49.269s; **9** Salvador Durán, MEX (Dallara F304-Mugen), 27m 55.105s (1st National class); **10** Josh Fisher, GB (Dallara F304-Mugen), 27m 56.549s.
Fastest race lap: Parente, 1m 48.175s, 119.793 mph/192.787 km/h.
Fastest qualifying lap: Parente, 2m 14.990s, 115.103 mph/185.240 km/h (achieved at Spa in April).
Championship points: 1 Parente, 177; **2** Kimball, 119; **3** Conway, 108; **4=** Asmer, 103; **4=** Bakkerud, 103; **6** Lewis, 97. **National Class: 1** Mawer, 193; **2** Durán, 172; **3** Fisher, 130.

BRITISH FORMULA 3 INTERNATIONAL SERIES, Silverstone Grand Prix Circuit, Towcester, Northamptonshire, Great Britain, 13/14 August. 15, 16 and 16 laps of the 3.194-mile/5.140-km circuit.
Round 14 (47.958 miles/77.181 km).
Originally scheduled for Spa-Francorchamps, Belgium on 17 April but postponed due to fog.
1 Charlie Kimball, USA (Dallara F305-Mugen), 30m 28.538s, 94.419 mph/151.953 km/h; **2** Alvaro Parente, P (Dallara F305-Mugen), 30m 32.874s; **3** Dan Clarke, GB (Dallara F305-Mugen), 30m 38.102s; **4** Danilo Dirani, BR (Lola B05/30-Mugen), 30m 38.774s; **5** Marko Asmer, EE (Dallara F305-Mugen), 30m 39.393s; **6** Mike Conway, GB (Dallara F305-Opel), 30m 40.347s; **7** Charlie Hollings, GB (Lola F106/04-Mugen), 30m 49.695s (1st National class); **8** Stephen Jelley, GB (Dallara F305-Opel), 30m 50.200s; **9** Keiko Ihara, J (Dallara F305-Mugen), 31m 10.062s; **10** Michael Herck, B (Dallara F305-Opel), 31m 10.224s.
Fastest race lap: Kimball, 1m 44.404s, 110.134 mph/177.243 km/h.
Fastest qualifying lap: Steven Kane, GB (Lola B05/30-Mugen), 2m 35.414s, 99.977 mph/160.896 km/h (achieved at Spa in April).

Round 15 (51.152 miles/82.321 km).
1 Alvaro Parente, P (Dallara F305-Mugen), 30m 51.402s, 99.464 mph/160.071 km/h; **2** Charlie Kimball, USA (Dallara F305-Mugen), 30m 54.336s; **3** Mike Conway, GB (Dallara F305-Opel), 31m 01.825s; **4** Marko Asmer, EE (Dallara F305-Mugen), 31m 02.500s; **5** Dan Clarke, GB (Dallara F305-Mugen), 31m 10.309s; **6** Danilo Dirani, BR (Lola B05/30-Mugen), 31m 11.249s; **7** Christian Bakkerud, DK (Dallara F305-Mugen), 31m 22.723s; **8** Tim Bridgeman, GB (Dallara F305-Mugen), 31m 23.119s; **9** James Walker, GB (Dallara F305-Opel), 31m 24.436s; **10** Ryan Lewis, GB (Dallara F305-Mugen), 31m 25.402s. **National class winner:** Salvador Durán, MEX (Dallara F304-Mugen), 31m 30.099s (12th).
Fastest race lap: Parente, 1m 43.877s, 110.692 mph/178.142 km/h.
Fastest qualifying lap: Parente, 1m 42.722s, 111.937 mph/180.145 km/h.

Round 16 (51.152 miles/82.321 km).
1 Alvaro Parente, P (Dallara F305-Mugen), 30m 54.693s, 99.276 mph/159.770 km/h; **2** Charlie Kimball, USA (Dallara F305-Mugen), 30m 56.710s; **3** Bruno Senna, BR (Dallara F305-Mugen), 31m 03.934s; **4** Steven Kane, GB (Lola B05/30-Mugen), 31m 07.815s; **5** Marko Asmer, EE (Dallara F305-Mugen), 31m 09.830s; **6** Dan Clarke, GB (Dallara F305-Mugen), 31m 11.310s; **7** Danilo Dirani, BR (Lola B05/30-Mugen), 31m 11.334s; **8** James Walker, GB (Dallara F305-Opel), 31m 11.869s; **9** Christian Bakkerud, DK (Dallara F305-Mugen), 31m 18.519s; **10** Stephen Jelley, GB (Dallara F305-Opel), 31m 26.282s. **National class winner:** Salvador Durán, MEX (Dallara F304-Mugen), 31m 26.872s (11th).
Fastest race lap: Parente, 1m 44.341s, 110.20016 mph/177.350 km/h.
Fastest qualifying lap: Asmer, 1m 42.891s, 111.753 mph/179.849 km/h.
Championship points: 1 Parente, 234; **2** Kimball, 170; **3** Asmer, 129; **4** Conway, 126; **5** Clarke, 114; **6** Bakkerud, 111. **National Class: 1** Durán, 213; **2** Mawer, 204; **3** Fisher, 162.

BRITISH FORMULA 3 INTERNATIONAL SERIES, Nürburgring Grand Prix Circuit, Nürburg/Eifel, Germany, 3 September. 2 x 14 laps of the 3.192-mile/5.137-km circuit.
Round 17 (44.688 miles/71.918 km).
1 James Walker, GB (Dallara F305-Opel), 26m 29.503s, 101.212 mph/162.884 km/h; **2** Mike Conway, GB (Dallara F305-Opel), 26m 31.116s; **3** Alvaro Parente, P (Dallara F305-Mugen), 26m 31.843s; **4** Danilo Dirani, BR (Lola B05/30-Mugen), 26m 32.258s; **5** Tim Bridgeman, GB (Dallara F305-Mugen), 26m 44.773s; **6** Marko Asmer, EE (Dallara F305-Mugen), 26m 45.084s; **7** Charlie Kimball, USA (Dallara F305-Mugen), 26m 46.478s; **8** Christian Bakkerud, DK (Dallara F305-Mugen), 26m 48.426s; **9** Dan Clarke, GB (Dallara F305-Mugen), 26m 48.712s; **10** Steven Kane, GB (Lola B05/30-Mugen), 26m 55.255s. **National class winner:** Salvador Durán, MEX (Dallara F304-Mugen), 27m 05.456 (12th).
Fastest race lap: Walker, 1m 52.283s, 102.341 mph/164.701 km/h.
Fastest qualifying lap: Parente, 1m 51.763s, 102.817 mph/165.467 km/h.

Round 18 (44.688 miles/71.918 km).
1 Alvaro Parente, P (Dallara F305-Mugen), 26m 26.953s, 101.374 mph/163.145 km/h; **2** Bruno Senna, BR (Dallara F305-Mugen), 26m 27.204s; **3** Dan Clarke, GB (Dallara F305-Mugen), 26m 28.735s; **4** Mike Conway, GB (Dallara F305-Opel), 26m 31.769s; **5** Charlie Kimball, USA (Dallara F305-Mugen), 26m 35.848s; **6** Marko Asmer, EE (Dallara F305-Mugen), 27m 37.623s; **7** Danilo Dirani, BR (Lola B05/30-Mugen), 27m 39.142s; **8** Ryan Lewis, GB (Dallara F305-Mugen), 27m 43.834s; **9** Tim Bridgeman, GB (Dallara F305-Mugen), 27m 44.038s; **10** Steven Kane, GB (Lola B05/30-Mugen), 27m 46.549s. **National class winner:** Michael Herck, B (Dallara F305-Opel), 26m 55.669s (12th).
Fastest race lap: Parente, 1m 52.532s, 102.114 mph/164.337 km/h.
Fastest qualifying lap: Senna, 1m 50.919s, 103.599 mph/166.727 km/h.
Championship points: 1 Parente, 267; **2** Kimball, 182; **3** Conway, 151; **4** Asmer, 141; **5** Clarke, 128; **6** Dirani, 124. **National Class: 1** Durán, 255; **2** Mawer, 224; **3** Fisher, 183.

BRITISH FORMULA 3 INTERNATIONAL SERIES, Mondello Park, Naas, County Kildare, Republic of Ireland, 18 September. 17 and 18 laps of the 2.177-mile/3.503-km circuit.
Round 19 (37.003 miles/59.551 km).
1 Alvaro Parente, P (Dallara F305-Mugen), 30m 29.358s, 72.819 mph/117.190 km/h; **2** Mike Conway, GB (Dallara F305-Opel), 30m 32.430s; **3** Steven Kane, GB (Lola B05/30-Mugen), 30m 38.777s; **4** Charlie Kimball, USA (Dallara F305-Mugen), 30m 40.686s; **5** Danilo Dirani, BR (Lola B05/30-Mugen), 30m 42.149s; **6** Dan Clarke, GB (Dallara F305-Mugen), 30m 47.838s; **7** Christian Bakkerud, DK (Dallara F305-Mugen), 30m 48.574s; **8** James Walker, GB (Dallara F305-Opel), 30m 50.882s; **9** Stephen Jelley, GB (Dallara F305-Opel), 30m 54.102s; **10** Ronayne O'Mahony, IRL (Dallara F305-Opel), 30m 55.138s. **National class winner:** Barton Mawer, AUS (Dallara F304-Mugen), 31m 10.964s (13th).
Fastest race lap: Parente, 1m 32.266s, 84.928 mph/136.678 km/h.
Fastest qualifying lap: Kane, 1m 31.507s, 85.633 mph/137.812 km/h.

Round 20 (39.180 miles/63.054 km).
1 Steven Kane, GB (Lola B05/30-Mugen), 31m 22.660s, 74.919 mph/120.571 km/h; **2** Ryan Lewis, GB (Dallara F305-Mugen), 31m 33.715s; **3** Charlie Kimball, USA (Dallara F305-Mugen), 31m 34.147s; **4** James Walker, GB (Dallara F305-Opel), 31m 35.945s; **5** Mike Conway, GB (Dallara F305-Opel), 31m 36.175s; **6** Dan Clarke, GB (Dallara F305-Mugen), 31m 40.505s; **7** Jonathan Kennard, GB (Dallara F304-Mugen), 31m 52.416s (1st National Class); **8** Charlie Hollings, GB (Lola F106/03-Mugen), 31m 54.288s; **9** Salvador Durán, MEX (Dallara F304-Mugen), 31m 54.989s; **10** Josh Fisher, GB (Dallara F304-Mugen), 31m 56.181s.
Fastest race lap: Alvaro Parente, P (Dallara F305-Mugen), 1m 32.321s, 84.878 mph/136.597 km/h.
Fastest qualifying lap: Kane, 1m 31.955s, 85.215 mph/137.140 km/h.
Championship points. 1 Parente, 289; **2** Kimball, 204; **3** Conway, 174; **4** Asmer, 141; **5** Clarke, 140; **6** Dirani, 132. **National Class: 1** Durán, 268; **2** Mawer, 244; **3** Kennard, 208.

BRITISH FORMULA 3 INTERNATIONAL SERIES, Silverstone International Circuit, Towcester, Northamptonshire, Great Britain, 9 October. 2 x 18 laps of the 2.249-mile/3.619-km circuit.
Round 21 (40.530 miles/65.227 km).
1 Charlie Kimball, USA (Dallara F305-Mugen), 25m 52.730s, 93.969 mph/151.228 km/h; **2** Danilo Dirani, BR (Lola B05/30-Mugen), 25m 53.173s; **3** Dan Clarke, GB (Dallara F305-Mugen), 25m 53.694s; **4** Marko Asmer, EE (Dallara F305-Mugen), 25m 54.792s; **5** Mike Conway, GB (Dallara F305-Opel), 25m 56.010s; **6** Christian Bakkerud, DK (Dallara F305-Mugen), 25m 56.661s; **7** Karl Reindler, AUS (Dallara F305-Mugen), 25m 57.207s; **8** Stephen Jelley, GB (Dallara F305-Opel), 25m 57.853s; **9** James Walker, GB (Dallara F305-Opel), 25m 58.102s; **10** Charlie Hollings, GB (Lola F106/04-Mugen), 25m 59.125s (1st National class).
Fastest race lap: Kimball, 1m 15.529s, 107.196 mph/172.515 mph.
Fastest qualifying lap: Kimball, 1m 15.176s, 107.699 mph/173.325 km/h.

Round 22 (40.530 miles/65.227 km).
1 Charlie Kimball, USA (Dallara F305-Mugen), 22m 58.217s, 105.867 mph/170.377 km/h; **2** Bruno Senna, BR (Dallara F305-Mugen), 23m 05.176s; **3** Marko Asmer, EE (Dallara F305-Mugen), 23m 09.492s; **4** Mike Conway, GB (Dallara F305-Opel), 23m 10.044s; **5** Dan Clarke, GB (Dallara F305-Mugen), 23m 10.981s; **6** Ryan Lewis, GB (Dallara F305-Mugen), 23m 15.379s; **7** James Walker, GB (Dallara F305-Opel), 23m 17.182s; **8** Danilo Dirani, BR (Lola B05/30-Mugen), 23m 18.874s; **9** Steven Kane, GB (Lola B05/30-Mugen), 23m 19.244s; **10** Tim Bridgeman, GB (Dallara F305-Mugen), 23m 21.622s. **National class winner:** Salvador Durán, MEX (Dallara F304-Mugen), 23m 33.691s (12th).
Fastest race lap: Kimball, 1m 15.356s, 107.442 mph/172.911 km/h.
Fastest qualifying lap: Kimball, 1m 15.436s, 107.328 mph/172.728 km/h.

Final championship points
1 Alvaro Parente, P, 289; **2** Charlie Kimball, USA, 246; **3** Mike Conway, GB, 192; **4** Marko Asmer, EE, 163; **5** Dan Clarke, GB, 160; **6** Danilo Dirani, BR, 150; **7** Christian Bakkerud, DK, 124; **8** Ryan Lewis, GB, 121; **9** Steven Kane, GB, 97; **10** Bruno Senna, BR, 75; **11** James Walker, GB, 69; **12** Stephen Jelley, GB, 30; **13** Danny Watts, GB, 23; **14** Ronayne O'Mahony, IRL, 21; **15** Tim Bridgeman, GB, 16; **16=** Karl Reindler, AUS, 12; **16=** Keiko Ihara, J, 12; **18** Susie Stoddart, GB, 2.
National Class
1 Salvador Durán, MEX, 300; **2** Barton Mawer, AUS, 256; **3** Jonathan Kennard, GB, 233; **4** Josh Fisher, GB, 221; **5** Charlie Hollings, GB, 216.

Formula 3 Euro Series

FORMULA 3 EURO SERIES, Hockenheimring Grand Prix Circuit, Heidelberg, Germany, 16/17 April. 18 and 17 laps of the 2.842-mile/4.574-km circuit.
Round 1 (51.159 miles/82.332 km).
1 Lewis Hamilton, GB (Dallara F305-Mercedes Benz), 28m 43.886s, 106.835 mph/171.934 km/h; **2** Adrian Sutil, D (Dallara F305-Mercedes Benz), 28m 50.018s; **3** Marco Bonanomi, I (Dallara F305-Opel), 29m 01.992s; **4** James Rossiter, GB (Dallara F305-Opel), 29m 02.683s; **5** Maximilian Götz, D (Dallara F305-Opel), 29m 11.237s; **6** Loïc Duval, F (Dallara F305-Opel), 29m 21.536s; **7** Ross Zwolsman, NL (Dallara F305-Opel), 29m 22.218s; **8** Atila Abreu, BR (Dallara F305-Mercedes Benz), 29m 25.785s; **9** Guillaume Moreau, F (Dallara F305-Opel), 29m 26.555s; **10** Richard Antinucci, USA (Dallara F305-TOM's Toyota), 29m 27.612s; Duval was originally given a 30s penalty for allegedly causing an accident, but this was later removed.
Fastest race lap: Hamilton, 1m 35.135s, 107.550 mph/173.084 km/h.
Fastest qualifying lap: Hamilton, 1m 37.725s, 104.699 mph/168.497 km/h.

Round 2 (48.317 miles/77.758 km).
1 James Rossiter, GB (Dallara F305-Opel), 31m 18.215s, 92.609 mph/149.039 km/h; **2** Loïc Duval, F (Dallara F305-Opel), 31m 32.407s; **3** Lewis Hamilton, GB (Dallara F305-Mercedes Benz), 31m 36.506s; **4** Giedo van der Garde, NL (Dallara F305-Opel), 31m 39.243s; **5** Sebastien Vettel, D (Dallara F305-Mercedes Benz), 31m 39.710s; **6** Esteban Guerrieri, RA (Dallara F305-TOM's Toyota), 31m 40.409s; **7** Richard Antinucci, USA (Dallara F305-TOM's Toyota), 31m 43.024s; **8** Franck Perera, F (Dallara F305-Opel), 31m 50.338s; **9** Atila Abreu, BR (Dallara F305-Mercedes Benz), 31m 50.409s; **10** Guillaume Moreau, F (Dallara F305-Opel), 31m 53.624s.
Fastest race lap: Antinucci, 1m 45.101s, 97.352 mph/156.672 km/h.
Fastest qualifying lap: Paul di Resta, GB (Dallara F305-Mercedes Benz), 2m 01.194s, 84.425 mph/135.868 km/h.

65th GRAND PRIX DE PAU, FIA FORMULA 3 EUROPE CUP, Circuit de Pau Ville, France. 7/8 May. 2 x 25 laps of the 1.715-mile/2.760-km circuit.
Round 3 (42.875 miles/69.000km).
1 Lewis Hamilton, GB (Dallara F305-Mercedes Benz), 30m 26.815s, 84.491 mph/135.974 km/h; **2** Loïc Duval, F (Dallara F305-Opel), 30m 36.205s; **3** James Rossiter, GB (Dallara F305-Opel), 30m 37.767s; **4** Guillaume Moreau, F (Dallara F305-Opel), 31m 00.235s; **5** Lucas di Grassi, BR (Dallara F305-Mercedes Benz), 31m 04.020s; **6** Giedo van der Garde, NL (Dallara F305-Opel), 31m 05.461s; **7** Sebastien Vettel, D (Dallara F305-Mercedes Benz), 31m 05.634s; **8** Richard Antinucci, USA (Dallara F305-TOM's Toyota), 31m 08.371s; **9** Alejandro Núnez, E (Dallara F305-Opel), 31m 14.888s; **10** Kohei Hirate, J (Dallara F305-Opel), 31m 17.069s.
Fastest race lap: Hamilton, 1m 11.353s, 86.527 mph/139.251 km/h.
Fastest qualifying lap: Hamilton, 1m 10.490s, 87.586 mph/140.956 km/h.

Round 4 (42.875 miles/69.000 km).
1 Lewis Hamilton, GB (Dallara F305-Mercedes Benz), 30m 15.999s, 84.994 mph/136.784 km/h; **2** Adrian Sutil, D (Dallara F305-Mercedes Benz), 30m 20.086s; **3** Loïc Duval, F (Dallara F305-Opel), 30m 23.262s; **4** James Rossiter, GB (Dallara F305-Opel), 30m 24.284s; **5** Fábio Carbone, BR (Signature SLC R1-Opel), 30m 33.581s; **6** Franck Perera, F (Dallara F305-Opel), 30m 35.952s; **7** Lucas di Grassi, BR (Dallara F305-Mercedes Benz), 30m 42.559s; **8** Guillaume Moreau, F (Dallara F305-Opel), 30m 43.568s; **9** Esteban Guerrieri, RA (Dallara F305-TOM's Toyota), 30m 54.497s; **10** Marco Bonanomi, I (Dallara F305-Opel), 31m 02.167s.
Fastest race lap: Hamilton, 1m 11.668s, 86.146 mph/138.639 km/h.
Fastest qualifying lap: Hamilton, 1m 11.021s, 86.931 mph/139.902 km/h.

FORMULA 3 EUROSERIES, Circuit de Spa-Francorchamps, Stavelot, Belgium, 14/15 May. 2 x 12 laps of the 4.335-mile/6.976-km circuit.
Round 5 (52.016 miles/83.712 km).
1 Adrian Sutil, D (Dallara F305-Mercedes Benz), 31m 21.675s, 99.517 mph/160.156 km/h; **2** James Rossiter, GB (Dallara F305-Opel), 31m 32.966s; **3** Guillaume Moreau, F (Dallara F305-Opel), 31m 39.591s; **4** Fábio Carbone, BR (Signature SLC R1-Opel), 31m 56.238s; **5** Kohei Hirate, J (Dallara F305-Opel), 31m 59.521s. **6** Franck Perera, F (Dallara F305-Opel), 32m 16.836s; **7** Esteban Guerrieri, RA (Dallara F305-TOM's Toyota), 32m 31.232s; **8** Maximilian Götz, D (Dallara F305-Opel), 32m 45.530s; **9** Alejandro Núnez, E (Dallara F305-Opel), 33m 03.977s; **10** Ross Zwolsman, NL (Dallara F305-Opel), 33m 06.826s.
Fastest race lap: Sutil, 2m 34.526s, 100.985 mph/162.520 km/h.
Fastest qualifying lap: Lewis Hamilton, GB (Dallara F305-Mercedes Benz), 2m 33.705s, 101.525 mph/163.388 km/h.

Round 6 (52.016 miles/83.712 km).
1 Lewis Hamilton, GB (Dallara F305-Mercedes Benz), 26m 56.524s, 115.840 mph/186.426 km/h; **2** Adrian Sutil, D (Dallara F305-Mercedes Benz), 26m 58.684s; **3** Lucas di Grassi, BR (Dallara F305-Mercedes Benz), 27m 14.086s; **4** Kohei Hirate, J (Dallara F305-Opel), 27m 17.663s; **5** Paul di Resta, GB (Dallara F305-Mercedes Benz), 27m 26.424s; **6** Franck Perera, F (Dallara F305-Opel), 27m 28.293s; **7** Greg Franchi, B (Dallara F305-Opel), 27m 29.092s; **8** James Rossiter, GB (Dallara F305-Opel), 27m 31.168s; **9** Hannes Neuhauser, A (Dallara F305-Mercedes Benz), 27m 33.882s; **10** Alejandro Núnez, E (Dallara F305-Opel), 27m 34.462s.
Fastest race lap: Hamilton, 2m 13.844s, 116.590 mph/187.633 km/h.
Fastest qualifying lap: Sutil, 2m 14.641s, 115.900 mph/186.522 km/h.

FORMULA 3 EUROSERIES, Monte Carlo Street Circuit, Monaco, 20/21 May. 18 and 26 laps of the 2.075-mile/3.340-km circuit.
Round 7 (37.357 miles/60.120 km).
1 Lewis Hamilton, GB (Dallara F305-Mercedes Benz), 28m 42.069s, 78.095 mph/125.681 km/h; **2** Adrian Sutil, D (Dallara F305-Mercedes Benz), 28m 43.846s; **3** Loïc Duval, F (Dallara F305-Opel), 28m 54.594s; **4** James Rossiter, GB (Dallara F305-Opel), 28m 55.583s; **5** Franck Perera, F (Dallara F305-Opel), 29m 00.609s; **6** Fábio Carbone, BR (Signature SLC R1-Opel), 29m 03.938s; **7** Lucas di Grassi, BR (Dallara F305-Mercedes Benz), 29m 06.190s; **8** Paul di Resta, GB (Dallara F305-Mercedes Benz), 29m 06.699s; **9** Richard Antinucci, USA (Dallara F305-TOM's Toyota), 29m 07.258s; **10** Alejandro Núnez, E (Dallara F305-Opel), 29m 09.375s.
Fastest race lap: Sutil, 1m 28.017s, 84.886 mph/136.609 km/h.
Fastest qualifying lap: Hamilton, 1m 28.593s, 84.334 mph/135.721 km/h.

Round 8 (53.960 miles/86.840 km).
1 Lewis Hamilton, GB (Dallara F305-Mercedes Benz), 39m 04.191s, 82.867 mph/133.361 km/h; **2** Loïc Duval, F (Dallara F305-Opel), 39m 11.835s; **3** Franck Perera, F (Dallara F305-Opel), 39m 14.704s; **4** James Rossiter, GB (Dallara F305-Opel), 39m 15.373s; **5** Lucas di Grassi, BR (Dallara F305-Mercedes Benz), 39m 39.924s; **6** Paul di Resta, GB (Dallara F305-Mercedes Benz), 39m 40.779s; **7** Maximilian Götz, D (Dallara F305-Opel), 39m 45.806s; **8** Alejandro Núnez, E (Dallara F305-Opel), 39m 51.031s; **9** Ross Zwolsman, NL (Dallara F305-Opel), 39m 51.738s; **10** Esteban Guerrieri, RA (Dallara F305-TOM's Toyota), 39m 53.851s.
Fastest race lap: Hamilton, 1m 28.797s, 84.140 mph/135.409 km/h.
Fastest qualifying lap: Hamilton, 1m 28.593s, 84.334 mph/135.721 km/h.

FORMULA 3 EUROSERIES, Motopark Arena Oschersleben, Germany, 25/26 June. 20 and 22 laps of the 2.279-mile/3.667-km circuit.
Round 9 (45.571 miles/73.340 km).
1 Lucas di Grassi, BR (Dallara F305-Mercedes Benz), 5h 01m 03.925s, 9.082 mph/14.616 km/h; **2** Adrian Sutil, D (Dallara F305-Mercedes Benz), 5h 01m 05.398s; **3** Lewis Hamilton, GB (Dallara F305-Mercedes Benz), 5h 01m 06.187s; **4** Paul di Resta, GB (Dallara F305-Mercedes Benz), 5h 01m 08.027s; **5** Sebastien Vettel, D (Dallara F305-Mercedes Benz), 5h 01m 13.024s; **6** Franck Perera, F (Dallara F305-Opel), 5h 01m 16.141s; **7** Guillaume Moreau, F (Dallara F305-Opel), 5h 01m 16.646s; **8** Atila Abreu, BR (Dallara F305-Mercedes Benz), 5h 01m 27.697s; **9** Fábio Carbone, BR (Signature SLC R1-Opel), 5h 01m 30.102s; **10** Alejandro Nú_ez, E (Dallara F305-Opel), 5h 01m 31.168s.
The race was stopped after 1 lap, due to a tropical storm and resumed four and a half hours later, after other qualifying, with lap 2 starting under a safety car.
Fastest race lap: Giedo van der Garde, NL (Dallara F305-Opel), 1m 19.384s, 103.331 mph/166.295 km/h.
Fastest qualifying lap: di Grassi, 1m 17.781s, 105.461 mph/169.722 km/h.

Round 10 (50.128 miles/80.674 km).
1 Lewis Hamilton, GB (Dallara F305-Mercedes Benz), 29m 18.523s, 102.622 mph/165.153 km/h; **2** Lucas di Grassi, BR (Dallara F305-Mercedes Benz), 29m 25.728s; **3** Adrian Sutil, D (Dallara F305-Mercedes Benz), 29m 26.741s; **4** Paul di Resta, GB (Dallara F305-Mercedes Benz), 29m 30.530s; **5** Sebastien Vettel, D (Dallara F305-Mercedes Benz), 29m 31.907s; **6** Giedo van der Garde, NL (Dallara F305-Opel), 29m 39.451s; **7** Esteban Guerrieri, RA (Dallara F305-TOM's Toyota), 29m 40.527s; **8** Loïc Duval, F (Dallara F305-Opel), 29m 41.715s; **9** Kohei Hirate, J (Dallara F305-Opel), 29m 44.671s; **10** Atila Abreu, BR (Dallara F305-Mercedes Benz), 29m 46.841s.
Fastest race lap: Hamilton, 1m 19.183s, 103.594 mph/166.717 km/h.
Fastest qualifying lap: Hamilton, 1m 17.747s, 105.507 mph/169.796 km/h.

FORMULA 3 EURO SERIES, Norisring, Nürnberg, Germany, 16/17 July. 34 and 35 laps of the 1.429-mile/2.300-km circuit.
Round 11 (48.591 miles/78.200 km).
1 Lewis Hamilton, GB (Dallara F305-Mercedes Benz), 30m 35.173s, 95.320 mph/153.402 km/h; **2** Sebastien Vettel, D (Dallara F305-Mercedes Benz), 30m 38.213s; **3** Paul di Resta, GB (Dallara F305-Mercedes Benz), 30m 39.780s; **4** Franck Perera, F (Dallara F305-Opel), 30m 40.859s; **5** Lucas di Grassi, BR (Dallara F305-Mercedes Benz), 30m 44.417s; **6** Marco Bonanomi, I (Dallara F305-Opel), 30m 45.863s; **7** Fábio Carbone, BR (Signature SLC R1-Opel), 30m 48.944s; **8** Guillaume Moreau, F (Dallara F305-Opel), 30m 52.925s; **9** Atila Abreu, BR (Dallara F305-Mercedes Benz), 30m 55.067s; **10** Alejandro Núnez, E (Dallara F305-Opel), 30m 58.054s.
Fastest race lap: Hamilton, 49.262s, 104.441 mph/168.080 km/h.
Fastest qualifying lap: Hamilton, 48.874s, 105.270 mph/169.415 km/h.

Round 12 (50.020 miles/80.500 km).
1 Lewis Hamilton, GB (Dallara F305-Mercedes Benz), 28m 51.233s, 104.015 mph/167.395 km/h; **2** Adrian Sutil, D (Dallara F305-Mercedes Benz), 28m 53.942s; **3** Franck Perera, F (Dallara F305-Opel), 29m 02.876s; **4** Sebastien Vettel, D (Dallara F305-Mercedes Benz), 29m 03.820s; **5** Loïc Duval, F (Dallara F305-Opel), 29m 07.256s; **6** Lucas di Grassi, BR (Dallara F305-Mercedes Benz), 29m 08.379s; **7** James Rossiter, GB (Dallara F305-Opel), 29m 08.779s; **8** Paul di Resta, GB (Dallara F305-Mercedes Benz), 29m 10.301s; **9** Esteban Guerrieri, RA (Dallara F305-TOM's Toyota), 29m 12.946s; **10** Atila Abreu, BR (Dallara F305-Mercedes Benz), 29m 26.748s.
Fastest race lap: Sutil, 49.035s, 104.924 mph/168.858 km/h.
Fastest qualifying lap: Hamilton, 49.038s, 104.918 mph/168.848 km/h.

FORMULA 3 EURO SERIES, Nürburgring Sprint Circuit, Nürburg/Eifel, Germany, 6/7 August. 22 and 21 laps of the 2.255-mile/3.629-km circuit.
Round 13 (49.609 miles/79.838 km).
1 Adrian Sutil, D (Dallara F305-Mercedes Benz), 30m 49.380s, 96.569 mph/155.412 km/h; **2** Lucas di Grassi, BR (Dallara F305-Mercedes Benz), 30m 49.974s; **3** Kohei Hirate, J (Dallara F305-Opel), 31m 05.596s; **4** Hannes Neuhauser, A (Dallara F305-Mercedes Benz), 31m 06.575s; **5** Franck Perera, F (Dallara F305-Opel), 31m 09.912s; **6** Loïc Duval, F (Dallara F305-Opel), 31m 16.030s; **7** Atila Abreu, BR (Dallara F305-Mercedes Benz), 31m 16.347s; **8** Giedo van der Garde, NL (Dallara F305-Opel), 31m 16.971s; **9** Marco Bonanomi, I (Dallara F305-Opel), 31m 18.179s; **10** James Rossiter, GB (Dallara F305-Opel), 31m 18.850s.
Fastest race lap: Paul di Resta, GB (Dallara F305-Mercedes Benz), 1m 23.147s, 97.632 mph/157.124 km/h.
Fastest qualifying lap: di Resta, 1m 22.463s, 98.442 mph/158.427 km/h.

Round 14 (47.354 miles/76.209 km).
1 Lewis Hamilton, GB (Dallara F305-Mercedes Benz), 30m 18.782s, 93.730 mph/150.844 km/h; **2** Sebastien Vettel, D (Dallara F305-Mercedes Benz), 30m 38.397s; **3** Adrian Sutil, D (Dallara F305-Mercedes Benz), 30m 41.193s; **4** Marco Bonanomi, I (Dallara F305-Opel), 30m 48.188s; **5** Giedo van der Garde, NL (Dallara F305-Opel), 30m 48.315s; **6** Franck Perera, F (Dallara F305-Opel), 30m 50.339s; **7** Kohei Hirate, J (Dallara F305-Opel), 30m 53.354s; **8** Guillaume Moreau, F (Dallara F305-Opel), 30m 54.519s; **9** Greg Franchi, B (Dallara F305-Opel), 30m 57.446s; **10** Loïc Duval, F (Dallara F305-Opel), 31m 00.637s.
Fastest race lap: Hamilton, 1m 22.744s, 98.108 mph/157.889 km/h.
Fastest qualifying lap: di Grassi, 1m 23.009s, 97.795 mph/157.385 km/h.

FORMULA 3 EURO SERIES, Circuit Park Zandvoort, Netherlands, 27/28 August. 16 and 19 laps of the 2.676-mile/4.307-km circuit.
Round 15 (42.820 miles/68.912 km).
1 Guillaume Moreau, F (Dallara F305-Opel), 30m 05.230s, 85.392 mph/137.424 km/h; **2** Sebastien Vettel, D (Dallara F305-Mercedes Benz), 30m 08.623s; **3** Franck Perera, F (Dallara F305-Opel), 30m 11.549s; **4** Greg Franchi, B (Dallara F305-Opel), 30m 16.572s; **5** Atila Abreu, BR (Dallara F305-Mercedes Benz), 30m 19.429s; **6** Esteban Guerrieri, RA (Dallara F305-TOM's Toyota), 30m 20.698s; **7** Hannes Neuhauser, A (Dallara F305-Mercedes Benz), 30m 21.272s; **8** Marco Bonanomi, I (Dallara F305-Opel), 30m 22.391s; **9** Alejandro Núnez, E (Dallara F305-Opel), 30m 26.675s; **10** Loïc Duval, F (Dallara F305-Opel), 30m 31.319s.
Fastest race lap: Paul di Resta, GB (Dallara F305-Mercedes Benz), 1m 33.497s, 103.046 mph/165.836 km/h.
Fastest qualifying lap: Lewis Hamilton, GB (Dallara F305-Mercedes Benz), 1m 31.259s, 105.573 mph/169.903 km/h.

Round 16 (50.849 miles/81.833 km).
1 Lewis Hamilton, GB (Dallara F305-Mercedes Benz), 30m 08.794s, 101.203 mph/162.870 km/h; **2** Sebastien Vettel, D (Dallara F305-Mercedes Benz), 30m 09.871s; **3** Giedo van der Garde, NL (Dallara F305-Opel), 30m 21.481s; **4** Guillaume Moreau, F (Dallara F305-Opel), 30m 22.085s; **5** Paul di Resta, GB (Dallara F305-Mercedes Benz), 30m 22.375s; **6** Franck Perera, F (Dallara F305-Opel), 30m 26.150s; **7** Greg Franchi, B (Dallara F305-Opel), 30m 27.047s; **8** Atila Abreu, BR (Dallara F305-Mercedes Benz), 30m 28.674s; **9** Marco Bonanomi, I (Dallara F305-Opel), 30m 29.349s; **10** James Rossiter, GB (Dallara F305-Opel), 30m 29.931s. Vettel was originally disqualified but was reinstated after a decision from court of appeal.
Fastest race lap: Lucas di Grassi, BR (Dallara F305-Mercedes Benz), 1m 34.134s, 102.349 mph/164.714 km/h.
Fastest qualifying lap: Hamilton, 1m 31.592s, 105.189 mph/169.285 km/h.

FORMULA 3 EURO SERIES, EuroSpeedway Lausitz, Klettwitz, Dresden, Germany, 17/18 September. 20 and 24 laps of the 2.139-mile/3.442 circuit.
Round 17 (42.775 miles/68.840 km).
1 Lewis Hamilton, GB (Dallara F305-Mercedes Benz), 31m 10.310s, 82.334 mph/132.504 km/h; **2** Giedo van der Garde, NL (Dallara F305-Opel), 31m 18.720s; **3** Sebastien Vettel, D (Dallara F305-Mercedes Benz), 31m 26.752s; **4** Adrian Sutil, D (Dallara F305-Mercedes Benz), 31m 28.300s; **5** Franck Perera, F (Dallara F305-Opel), 31m 34.401s; **6** Guillaume Moreau, F (Dallara F305-Opel), 31m 37.745s; **7** Atila Abreu, BR (Dallara F305-Mercedes Benz), 31m 42.623s; **8** Lucas di Grassi, BR (Dallara F305-Mercedes Benz), 31m 46.008s; **9** Hannes Neuhauser, A (Dallara F305-Mercedes Benz), 31m 46.587s; **10** Marco Bonanomi, I (Dallara F305-Opel), 31m 49.487s.
Fastest race lap: Esteban Guerrieri, RA (Dallara F305-TOM's Toyota), 1m 23.024s, 92.739 mph/149.248 km/h.
Fastest qualifying lap: van der Garde, 1m 20.813s, 95.276 mph/153.331 km/h.

Round 18 (51.330 miles/82.608 km).
1 Lewis Hamilton, GB (Dallara F305-Mercedes Benz), 30m 54.350s, 99.652 mph/160.373 km/h; **2** Adrian Sutil, D (Dallara F305-Mercedes Benz), 31m 05.527s; **3** Lucas di Grassi, BR (Dallara F305-Mercedes Benz), 31m 09.925s; **4** Guillaume Moreau, F (Dallara F305-Opel), 31m 13.441s; **5** Franck Perera, F (Dallara F305-Opel), 31m 17.940s; **6** Giedo van der Garde, NL (Dallara F305-Opel), 31m 23.984s; **7** Greg Franchi, B (Dallara F305-Opel), 31m 26.937s; **8** Kohei Hirate, J (Dallara F305-Opel), 31m 32.712s; **9** Loïc Duval, F (Dallara F305-Opel), 31m 34.025s; **10** Esteban Guerrieri, RA (Dallara F305-TOM's Toyota), 31m 34.921s. Paul di Resta, GB (Dallara F305-Mercedes Benz), finished 2nd in 31m 00.154s, but was disqualified.(Insifficient fuel in tank at end of race).
Fastest race lap: Hamilton, 1m 16.546s, 100.587 mph/161.879 km/h.
Fastest qualifying lap: di Resta, 1m 33.496s, 82.351 mph/132.531 km/h.

FORMULA 3 EURO SERIES, Hockenheimring Grand Prix Circuit, Heidelberg, Germany, 22/23 October. 17 and 18 laps of the 2.842-mile/4.574-km circuit.
Round 19 (48.317 miles/77.758 km).
1 Lewis Hamilton, GB (Dallara F305-Mercedes Benz), 31m 16.906s, 92.674 mph/149.143 km/h; **2** Lucas di Grassi, BR (Dallara F305-Mercedes Benz), 31m 31.136s; **3** Maximilian Götz, D (Dallara F305-Mercedes Benz), 31m 33.459s; **4** Franck Perera, F (Dallara F305-Opel), 31m 41.251s; **5** James Rossiter, GB (Dallara F305-Opel), 31m 45.429s; **6** Marco Bonanomi, I (Dallara F305-Opel), 31m 48.678s; **7** Esteban Guerrieri, RA (Dallara F305-TOM's Toyota), 31m 57.345s; **8** Atila Abreu, BR (Dallara F305-Mercedes Benz), 31m 58.513s; **9** Hannes Neuhauser, A (Dallara F305-Mercedes Benz), 32m 03.952s; **10** Greg Franchi, B (Dallara F305-Opel), 32m 13.846s.
Fastest race lap: Sebastien Vettel, D (Dallara F305-Mercedes Benz), 1m 47.439s, 95.233 mph/153.263 km/h.
Fastest qualifying lap: Hamilton, 1m 49.698s, 93.272 mph/150.107 km/h.

Round 20 (51.159 miles/82.332 km).
1 Lewis Hamilton, GB (Dallara F305-Mercedes Benz), 28m 37.411s, 107.238 mph/172.582 km/h; **2** Guillaume Moreau, F (Dallara F305-Opel), 28m 41.401s; **3** Seastien Vettel, D (Dallara F305-Mercedes Benz), 28m 43.183s; **4** Loïc Duval, F (Dallara F305-Opel), 28m 55.008s; **5** Franck Perera, F (Dallara F305-Opel), 28m 55.695s; **6** Marco Bonanomi, I (Dallara F305-Opel), 28m 58.912s; **7** Hannes Neuhauser, A (Dallara F305-Opel), 29m 03.286s; **8** Fábio Carbone, BR (Signature SLC R1-Opel), 29m 05.411s; **9** James Rossiter, GB (Dallara F305-Opel), 29m 09.597s; **10** Kohei Hirate, J (Dallara F305-Opel), 29m 10.794s.
Fastest race lap: Hamilton, 1m 34.528s, 108.240 mph/174.196 km/h.
Fastest qualifying lap: Hamilton, 1m 34.132s, 108.696 mph/174.929 km/h.

Final championship points
Drivers 1 Lewis Hamilton, GB, 172; **2** Adrian Sutil, D, 94; **3** Lucas di Grassi, BR, 68; **4** Franck Perera, F, 67; **5** Sebastien Vettel, D, 63; **6** Loïc Duval, F, 52; **7** James Rossiter, GB, 51; **8** Guillaume Moreau, F, 47; **9** Giedo van der Garde, NL, 34; **10** Paul di Resta, GB, 32; **11** Marco Bonanomi, I, 21; **12** Kohei Hirate, J, 18; **13** Fábio Carbone, BR, 15; **14** Maximilian Götz, D, 13; **15=** Atila Abreu, BR, 12; **15=** Esteban Guerrieri, RA, 12; **17** Greg Franchi, B, 11; **18** Hannes Neuhauser, A, 9; **19** Richard Antinucci, USA, 3; **20** Ross Zwolsman, NL, 2; **21** Alejandro Núnez, E, 1. **Rookie Cup 1** Sebastien Vettel; **2** Esteban Guerrieri; **3** Guillaume Moreau. **Teams 1** ASM Formula 3, 261; **2** Signature-Plus, 103; **3** Prema Powerteam, 98.
Nations' Cup 1 Great Britain, 237; **2** Germany, 170; **3** France, 161.

Recaro F3-Cup

RECARO F3-CUP, Motopark Arena Oschersleben, Germany, 23/24 April. 19 and 14 laps of the 2.279-mile/3.667-km circuit.
Round 1 (43.293 miles/69.673 km).
1 Ho-Pin Tung, PRC (Dallara F304-Opel), 26m 07.100s, 99.454 mph/160.055 km/h; **2** Peter Elkmann, D (Dallara F304-Opel), 26m 09.317s; **3** Frank Kechele, D (Dallara F304-Opel), 26m 12.732s; **4** Robert Kath, D (Dallara F304-Mercedes Benz), 26m 13.065s; **5** Paul Meijer, NL (Dallara F304-Opel), 26m 32.442s; **6** Franz Schmöller, D (Dallara F304-Opel), 26m 33.365s; **7** Ferdinand Kool, NL (Dallara F304-Opel), 26m 33.533s; **8** Michael Herck, B (Dallara F305-Opel), 26m 33.979s; **9** Martin Hippe, D (Dallara F304-Opel), 26m 34.000s; **10** Maxime Hodencq, B (Dallara F304-Opel), 26m 46.060s.
Fastest race lap: Elkmann, 1m 21.559s, 100.576 mph/161.861 km/h.
Fastest qualifying lap: Elkmann, 1m 20.632s, 101.732 mph/163.722 km/h.

Round 2 (31.900 miles/51.338 km).
1 Frank Kechele, D (Dallara F304-Opel), 19m 17.814s, 99.187 mph/159.626 km/h; **2** Robert Kath, D (Dallara F304-Mercedes Benz), 19m 18.961s; **3** Ho-Pin Tung, PRC (Dallara F304-Opel), 19m 22.246s; **4** Ferdinand Kool, NL (Dallara F304-Opel), 19m 26.447s; **5** Peter Elkmann, D (Dallara F304-Opel), 19m 26.828s; **6** Michael Herck, B (Dallara F305-Opel), 19m 27.373s; **7** Franz Schmöller, D (Dallara F304-Opel), 19m 27.761s; **8** Martin Hippe, D (Dallara F304-Opel), 19m 30.844s; **9** Paul Meijer, NL (Dallara F304-Opel), 19m 33.431s; **10** Pascal Kochem, D (Dallara F304-Mercedes Benz), 19m 33.991s.
Fastest race lap: Kechele, 1m 21.975s, 100.065 mph/161.039 km/h.
Fastest qualifying lap: Kechele, 1m 20.838s, 101.473 mph/163.304 km/h.

RECARO F3-CUP, Hockenheimring Grand Prix Circuit, Heidelberg, Germany, 21/22 May. 2 x 26 laps of the 1.616-mile/2.600-km circuit.
Round 3 (42.005 miles/67.600 km).
1 Michael Devaney, IRL (Dallara F304-Opel), 25m 38.863s, 98.265 mph/158.143 km/h; **2** Robert Kath, D (Dallara F304-Mercedes Benz), 25m 43.282s; **3** Pascal Kochem, D (Dallara F304-Mercedes Benz), 25m 44.090s; **4** Ho-Pin Tung, PRC (Dallara F304-Opel), 25m 44.893s; **5** Peter Elkmann, D (Dallara F304-Opel), 25m 45.945s; **6** Jochen Nerpel, D (Dallara F304-Mercedes Benz), 25m 46.817s; **7** Martin Hippe, D (Dallara F304-Opel), 25m 49.694s; **8** Frank Kechele, D (Dallara F304-Opel), 26m 01.509s; **9** Dominik Schraml, D (Dallara F304-Opel), 26m 05.926s; **10** Johannes Theobald, D (Dallara F304-Renault), 26m 19.409s.
Fastest race lap: Nerpel, 58.014s, 100.252 mph/161.340 km/h.
Fastest qualifying lap: Devaney, 58.374s, 99.634 mph/160.345 km/h.

Round 4 (42.005 miles/67.600 km).
1 Martin Hippe, D (Dallara F304-Opel), 25m 37.900s, 98.327 mph/158.242 km/h; **2** Peter Elkmann, D (Dallara F304-Opel), 25m 38.418s; **3** Ferdinand Kool, NL (Dallara F304-Opel), 25m 40.027s; **4** Ho-Pin Tung, PRC (Dallara F304-Opel), 25m 41.487s; **5** Jochen Nerpel, D (Dallara F304-Mercedes Benz), 25m 44.406s; **6** Pascal Kochem, D (Dallara F304-Mercedes Benz), 25m 44.842s; **7** Robert Kath, D (Dallara F304-Mercedes Benz), 25m 48.134s; **8** Frank Kechele, D (Dallara F304-Opel), 26m 03.001s; **9** Kevin Fank, D (Dallara F301-Opel), 26m 15.619s; **10** Julian Theobald, D (Dallara F304-Renault), 26m 23.950s.
Fastest race lap: Tung, 58.252s, 99.843 mph/160.681 km/h.
Fastest qualifying lap: Elkmann, 57.395s, 101.333 mph/163.080 km/h.

RECARO F3-CUP, Sachsenring, Oberlungwitz, Germany, 18/19 June. 2 x 20 laps of the 2.265-mile/3.645-km circuit.
Round 5 (45.298 miles/72.900 km).
1 Peter Elkmann, D (Dallara F304-Opel), 26m 06.157s, 104.123 mph/167.569 km/h; **2** Michael Devaney, IRL (Dallara F304-Opel), 26m 11.422s; **3** Pascal Kochem, D (Dallara F304-Mercedes Benz), 26m 12.313s; **4** Frank Kechele, D (Dallara F304-Opel), 26m 22.299s; **5** Jochen Nerpel, D (Dallara F304-Mercedes Benz), 26m 30.299s; **6** Franz Schmöller, D (Dallara F304-Opel), 26m 33.682s; **7** Ferdinand Kool, NL (Dallara F304-Opel), 26m 36.747s; **8** Martin Hippe, D (Dallara F304-Opel), 26m 47.119s; **9** Kevin Fank, D (Dallara F301-Opel), 27m 12.862s; **10** Johannes Theobald, D (Dallara F304-Renault), 27m 15.844s.
Fastest race lap: Elkmann, 1m 17.653s, 105.001 mph/168.983 km/h.
Fastest qualifying lap: Elkmann, 1m 17.350s, 105.412 mph/169.644 km/h.

Round 6 (45.298 miles/72.900 km).
1 Peter Elkmann, D (Dallara F304-Opel), 26m 13.746s, 103.621 mph/166.761 km/h; **2** Pascal Kochem, D (Dallara F304-Mercedes Benz), 26m 21.050s; **3** Frank Kechele, D (Dallara F304-Opel), 26m 29.772s; **4** Ferdinand Kool, NL (Dallara F304-Opel), 26m 29.797s; **5** Franz Schmöller, D (Dallara F304-Opel), 26m 37.634s; **6** Michael Devaney, IRL (Dallara F304-Opel), 26m 42.564s; **7** Robert Kath, D (Dallara F304-Mercedes Benz), 26m 43.027s; **8** Julian Theobald, D (Dallara F304-Renault), 27m 07.956s; **9** Johannes Theobald, D (Dallara F304-Renault), 27m 11.054s; **10** Christer Jöns, D (Dallara F301-Opel), 27m 11.986s.
Fastest race lap: Elkmann, 1m 17.969s, 104.575 mph/168.298 km/h.
Fastest qualifying lap: Kochem, 1m 16.866s, 106.076 mph/170.713 km/h.

RECARO F3-CUP, EuroSpeedway Lausitz (infield), Klettwitz, Dresden, Germany, 2/3 July, 19 and 18 laps of the 2.139-mile/3.442-km circuit.
Round 7 (40.636 miles/65.398 km).
1 Michael Devaney, IRL (Dallara F304-Opel), 25m 17.643s, 96.394 mph/155.131 km/h; **2** Martin Hippe, D (Dallara F304-Opel), 25m 26.256s; **3** Peter Elkmann, D (Dallara F304-Opel), 25m 26.835s; **4** Pascal Kochem, D (Dallara F304-Mercedes Benz), 25m 28.426s; **5** Ronny Wechselberger, D (Dallara F304-Opel), 25m 29.115s; **6** Franz Schmöller, D (Dallara F304-Opel), 25m 33.371s; **7** Jochen Nerpel, D (Dallara F304-Mercedes Benz), 25m 37.182s; **8** Adam Langley-Khan, GB (Dallara F304-Opel), 25m 49.952s; **9** Kevin Fank, D. (Dallara F301-Opel), 25m 50.450s; **10** Ferdinand Kool, NL (Dallara F304-Opel), 25m 51.081s.
Fastest race lap: Devaney, 1m 19.188s, 97.231 mph/156.478 km/h.
Fastest qualifying lap: Hippe, 1m 28.614s, 86.888 mph/139.833 km/h.

Round 8 (38.498 miles/61.956 km).
1 Peter Elkmann, D (Dallara F304-Opel), 25m 35.622s, 90.251 mph/145.245 km/h; **2** Michael Devaney, IRL (Dallara F304-Opel), 25m 37.645s; **3** Pascal Kochem, D (Dallara F304-Mercedes Benz), 25m 38.091s; **4** Frank Kechele, D (Dallara F304-Opel), 25m 39.029s; **5** Jochen Nerpel, D (Dallara F304-Mercedes Benz), 25m 41.301s; **6** Martin Hippe, D (Dallara F304-Opel), 25m 41.562s; **7** Ferdinand Kool, NL (Dallara F304-Opel), 25m 45.595s; **8** Franz Schmöller, D (Dallara F304-Opel), 25m 48.243s; **9** Dominik Schraml, D (Dallara F304-Opel), 25m 54.770s; **10** Ronny Wechselberger, D (Dallara F304-Opel), 25m 57.496s.
Fastest race lap: Elkmann, 1m 19.217s, 97.195 mph/156.421 km/h.
Fastest qualifying lap: Elkmann, 1m 18.365s, 98.252 mph/158.122 km/h.

RECARO F3-CUP, Nürburgring Sprint Circuit, Nürburg/Eifel, Germany, 9/10 July. 2 x 18 laps of the 2.248-mile/3.618-km circuit.
Round 9 (40.466 miles/65.124 km).
1 Peter Elkmann, D (Dallara F304-Opel), 25m 21.194s, 95.766 mph/154.120 km/h; **2** Frank Kechele, D (Dallara F304-Opel), 25m 29.376s; **3** Michael Devaney, IRL (Dallara F304-Opel), 25m 30.541s; **4** Ho-Pin Tung, PRC (Dallara F304-Opel), 25m 31.750s; **5** Pascal Kochem, D (Dallara F304-Mercedes Benz), 25m 32.173s; **6** Ferdinand Kool, NL (Dallara F304-Opel), 25m 38.284s; **7** Franz Schmöller, D (Dallara F304-Opel), 25m 48.587s; **8** Dominik Schraml, D (Dallara F304-Opel), 25m 51.228s; **9** Sven Barth, D (Dallara F304-Opel), 25m 51.682s; **10** Johannes Theobald, D (Dallara F304-Mercedes Benz), 26m 04.386s.
Fastest race lap: Elkmann, 1m 23.503s, 96.921 mph/155.980 km/h.
Fastest qualifying lap: Elkmann, 1m 23.210s, 97.263 mph/156.529 km/h.

Round 10 (40.466 miles/65.124 km).
1 Peter Elkmann, D (Dallara F304-Opel), 25m 20.667s, 95.799 mph/154.173 km/h; **2** Pascal Kochem, D (Dallara F304-Mercedes Benz), 25m 22.140s; **3** Ho-Pin Tung, PRC (Dallara F304-Opel), 25m 28.044s; **4** Michael Devaney, IRL (Dallara F304-Opel), 25m 30.711s; **5** Jochen Nerpel, D (Dallara F304-Mercedes Benz), 25m 36.580s; **6** Frank Kechele, D (Dallara F304-Opel), 25m 39.309s; **7** Martin Hippe, D (Dallara F304-Opel), 25m 41.535s; **8** Dominik Schraml, D (Dallara F304-Opel), 25m 54.259s; **9** Christer Jöns, D (Dallara F301-Opel), 26m 05.775s; **10** Tobias Blätter, CH (Dallara F301-Opel), 26m 14.214s.
Fastest race lap: Elkmann, 1m 23.496s, 96.930 mph/155.993 km/h.
Fastest qualifying lap: Elkmann, 1m 22.725s, 97.833 mph/157.447 km/h.

RECARO F3-CUP, Nürburgring Sprint Circuit, Nürburg/Eifel, Germany, 30/31 July. 2 x 18 laps of the 2.248-mile/3.618-km circuit.
Round 11 (40.466 miles/65.124 km).
1 Michael Devaney, IRL (Dallara F304-Opel), 25m 01.178s, 97.043 mph/156.175 km/h; **2** Peter Elkmann, D (Dallara F304-Opel), 25m 01.533s; **3** Pascal Kochem, D (Dallara F304-Mercedes Benz), 2m 14.715s; **4** Ho-Pin Tung, PRC (Dallara F304-Opel), 25m 16.317s; **5** Martin Hippe, D (Dallara F304-Opel), 25m 17.187s; **6** Ferdinand Kool, NL (Dallara F304-Opel), 25m 17.297s; **7** Dominik Schraml, D (Dallara F304-Opel), 25m 32.940s; **8** Franz Schmöller, D (Dallara F304-Opel), 25m 33.301s; **9** Tobias Blätter, CH (Dallara F301-Opel), 25m 41.396s; **10** Julian Theobald, D (Dallara F304-Mercedes Benz), 25m 41.634s.
Fastest race lap: Elkmann, 1m 22.529s, 98.065 mph/157.821 km/h.
Fastest qualifying lap: Elkmann, 1m 22.013s, 98.682 mph/158.814 km/h.

Round 12 (40.466 miles/65.124 km).
1 Michael Devaney, IRL (Dallara F304-Opel), 25m 18.236s, 95.952 mph/154.420 km/h; **2** Ho-Pin Tung, PRC (Dallara F304-Opel), 425m 22.444s; **3** Martin Hippe, D (Dallara F304-Opel), 25m 22.971s; **4** Peter Elkmann, D (Dallara F304-Opel), 25m 23.927s; **5** Frank Kechele, D (Dallara F304-Opel), 25m 24.331s; **6** Ferdinand Kool, NL (Dallara F304-Opel), 25m 29.744s; **7** Dominik Schraml, D (Dallara F304-Opel), 25m 46.646s; **8** Kevin Fank, D (Dallara F301-Opel), 25m 48.390s; **9** Franz Schmöller, D (Dallara F304-Opel), 25m 48.698s; **10** Johannes Theobald, D (Dallara F304-Mercedes Benz), 25m 53.584s.
Fastest race lap: Elkmann, 1m 23.234s, 97.235 mph/156.484 km/h.
Fastest qualifying lap: Michael Herck, B (Dallara F305-Opel), 1m 22.538s, 98.055 mph/157.804 km/h.

RECARO F3-CUP, Nationale Circuit Assen, Netherlands, 6/7 August. 18 and 19 laps of the 2.393-mile/3.851-km circuit.
Round 13 (43.072 miles/69.318 km).
1 Ferdinand Kool, NL (Dallara F304-Opel), 26m 25.179s, 97.819 mph/157.424 km/h; **2** Peter Elkmann, D (Dallara F304-Opel), 26m 28.178s; **3** Pascal Kochem, D (Dallara F304-Mercedes Benz), 26m 28.603s; **4** Davide Valsecchi, I (Dallara F304-Opel), 26m 32.281s; **5** Frank Kechele, D (Dallara F304-Opel), 26m 35.339s; **6** Ho-Pin Tung, PRC (Dallara F304-Opel), 26m 35.702s; **7** Christer Jöns, D (Dallara F301-Opel), 26m 59.595s; **8** Michael Devaney, IRL (Dallara F304-Opel), 27m 00.450s; **9** Joannes Theobald, D (Dallara F304-Mercedes Benz), 27m 01.223s; **10** Martin Hippe, D (Dallara F304-Opel), 27m 05.716s. Devaney finished 7th,

but was given a 3s penalty.
Fastest race lap: Tung, 1m 24.647s, 101769 mph/163.781 km/h.
Fastest qualifying lap: Kool, 1m 26.805s, 99.239 mph/159.710 km/h.

Round 14 (45.465 miles/73.169 km).
1 Michael Devaney, IRL (Dallara F304-Opel), 25m 25.417s, 107.298 mph/172.680 km/h; **2** Martin Hippe, D (Dallara F304-Opel), 25m 26.318s; **3** Peter Elkmann, D (Dallara F304-Opel), 25m 35.699s; **4** Frank Kechele, D (Dallara F304-Opel), 25m 36.266s; **5** Ho-Pin Tung, PRC (Dallara F304-Opel), 25m 42.306s; **6** Franz Schmöller, D (Dallara F304-Opel), 25m 47.891s; **7** Davide Valsecchi, I (Dallara F304-Opel), 25m 49.251s; **8** Johannes Theobald, D (Dallara F304-Mercedes Benz), 25m 59.865s; **9** Dominik Schraml, D (Dallara F304-Opel), 26m 00.133s; **10** Julian Theobald, D (Dallara F304-Mercedes Benz), 26m 11.249s.
Fastest race lap: Hippe, 1m 18.602s, 109.596 mph/176.377 km/h.
Fastest qualifying lap: Pascal Kochem, D (Dallara F304-Mercedes Benz), 1m 32.685s, 92.943 mph/149.578 km/h.

RECARO F3-CUP, EuroSpeedway Lausitz (oval), Klettwitz, Dresden, Germany, 27/28 August, 2 x 26 laps of the 2.020-mile/3.251-km circuit.
Round 15 (52.522 miles/84.526 km).
1 Jan Seyffarth, D (Dallara F304-Mercedes Benz), 25m 06.549s, 125.505 mph/201.981 km/h; **2** Ferdinand Kool, NL (Dallara F304-Opel), 25m 06.580s; **3** Peter Elkmann, D (Dallara F304-Opel), 25m 06.794s; **4** Pascal Kochem, D (Dallara F304-Mercedes Benz), 25m 06.909s; **5** Julian Theobald, D (Dallara F304-Mercedes Benz), 25m 09.315s; **6** Martin Hippe, D (Dallara F304-Opel), 25m 09.357s; **7** Frank Kechele, D (Dallara F304-Opel), 25m 10.179s; **8** Franz Schmöller, D (Dallara F304-Opel), 25m 10.248s; **9** Harald Schlegelmilch, LV (Dallara F304-Opel), 25m 10.613s; **10** Ronny Wechselberger, D (Dallara F304-Opel), 25m 14.095s.
Fastest race lap: Theobald (Julian), 46.828s, 155.298 mph/249.927 km/h.
Fastest qualifying lap: Kool, 46.846s, 155.238 mph/249.831 km/h.

Round 16 (52.522 miles/84.526 km).
1 Ferdinand Kool, NL (Dallara F304-Opel), 22m 09.192s, 142.251 mph/228.931 km/h; **2** Ho-Pin Tung, PRC (Dallara F304-Opel), 22m 09.673s; **3** Pascal Kochem, D (Dallara F304-Mercedes Benz), 22m 10.008s; **4** Michael Devaney, IRL (Dallara F304-Opel), 22m 10.348s; **5** Martin Hippe, D (Dallara F304-Opel), 22m 10.748s; **6** Julian Theobald, D (Dallara F304-Mercedes Benz), 22m 11.168s; **7** Franz Schmöller, D (Dallara F304-Opel), 22m 11.535s; **8** Ronny Wechselberger, D (Dallara F304-Opel), 22m 12.296s; **9** Frank Kechele, D (Dallara F304-Opel), 22m 13.103s; **10** Peter Elkmann, D (Dallara F304-Opel), 22m 13.541s.
Fastest race lap: Wechselberger, 46.664s, 155.843 mph/250.806 km/h.
Fastest qualifying lap: Elkmann, 46.487s, 156.437 mph/251.761 km/h.

RECARO F3-CUP, Motopark Arena Oschersleben, Germany, 8/9 October. 2 x 19 laps of the 2.279-mile/3.667-km circuit.
Round 17 (43.293 miles/69.673 km).
1 Peter Elkmann, D (Dallara F304-Opel), 26m 18.443s, 98.739 mph/158.905 km/h; **2** Ho-Pin Tung, PRC (Dallara F304-Opel), 26m 19.217s; **3** Michael Devaney, IRL (Dallara F304-Opel), 26m 19.655s; **4** Martin Hippe, D (Dallara F304-Opel), 26m 27.318s; **5** Pascal Kochem, D (Dallara F304-Mercedes Benz), 26m 28.314s; **6** Frank Kechele, D (Dallara F304-Toyota), 26m 34.717s; **7** Julian Theobald, D (Dallara F304-Mercedes Benz), 26m 35.983s; **8** Franz Schmöller, D (Dallara F304-Opel), 26m 49.475s; **9** Johannes Theobald, D (Dallara F304-Mercedes Benz), 26m 51.969s; **10** Kevin Fank, D (Dallara F301-Opel), 26m 55.488s.
Fastest race lap: Elkmann, 1m 21.993s, 100.043 mph/161.004 km/h.
Fastest qualifying lap: Elkmann, 1m 20.310s, 102.140 mph/164.378 km/h.

Round 18 (43.293 miles/69.673 km).
1 Ho-Pin Tung, PRC (Dallara F304-Opel), 26m 15.431s, 98.928 mph/159.209 km/h; **2** Peter Elkmann, D (Dallara F304-Opel), 26m 15.786s; **3** Michael Devaney, IRL (Dallara F304-Opel), 26m 27.506s; **4** Frank Kechele, D (Dallara F304-Toyota), 26m 27.813s; **5** Pascal Kochem, D (Dallara F304-Mercedes Benz), 26m 33.927s; **6** Martin Hippe, D (Dallara F304-Opel), 26m 34.858s; **7** Ferdinand Kool, NL (Dallara F304-Opel), 26m 42.875s; **8** Franz Schmöller, D (Dallara F304-Opel), 26m 42.882s; **9** Harald Schlegelmilch, LV (Dallara F304-Opel), 26m 47.841s; **10** Johannes Theobald, D (Dallara F304-Mercedes Benz), 26m 48.245s.
Fastest race lap: Elkmann, 1m 21.635s, 100.482 mph/161.710 km/h.
Fastest qualifying lap: Tung, 1m 21.399s, 100.773 mph/162.179 km/h.

Final championship points
1 Peter Elkmann, D, 150; **2** Michael Devaney, IRL, 101; **3** Ho-Pin Tung, PRC, 88; **4** Pascal Kochem, D, 79; **5** Frank Kechele, D, 71; **6** Martin Hippe, D, 64; **7** Ferdinand Kool, NL, 63; **8** Franz Schmöller, D, 28; **9** Robert Kath, D, 25; **10** Jochen Nerpel, D, 22; **11** Julian Theobald, D, 11; **12** Jan Seyffarth, D, 10; **13** Dominik Schraml, D, 7; **14** Ronny Wechselberger, D, 6; **15** Paul Meijer, NL, 5; **16=** Christer Jöns, D, 3; **16=** Johannes Theobald, D, 3; **18=** Adam Langley-Khan, GB, 1; **18=** Kevin Fank, D, 1.
Formel 3-Trophy 1 Kevin Fank, 127; **2** Christer Jöns, 116.
Rookie Cup 1 Pascal Kochem, 126; **2** Frank Kechele, 118; **3** Martin Hippe, 117.

Italian Formula 3 Championship

ITALIAN FORMULA 3 CHAMPIONSHIP, Autodromo Adria International Raceway, Adria, Italy, 17 April. Round 1. 28 laps of the 1.679-mile/2.702-km circuit, 47.010 miles/75.656 km.
1 Paolo Maria Nocera, I (Dallara F304-Opel), 34m 32.950s, 81.641 mph/131.388 km/h; **2** Luigi Ferrara, I (Dallara F304-Opel), 34m 34.550s; **3** Maurizio Ceresoli, I (Dallara F304-Opel), 34m 42.785s; **4** Riccardo Mari, I (Lola Dome F106-Opel), 34m 45.056s; **5** Giuseppe Termine, I (Dallara F304-Opel), 34m 47.881s; **6** Riccardo Azzoli, I (Dallara F304-Opel), 34m 48.638s; **7** Giacomo Piccini, I (Lola Dome F106-Opel), 34m 50.952s; **8** Massimo Torre, I (Dallara F304-Opel), 35m 09.621s; **9** Basil Shaaban, RL (Dallara F304-Mugen), 35m 10.229s; **10** Elias Papaelias, GR (Dallara F304-Opel), 35m 18.078s.
Fastest race lap: Nocera, 1m 12.849s, 82.969 mph/133.526 km/h.
Fastest qualifying lap: Ferrara, 1m 21.776s, 73.912 mph/118.949 km/h.

ITALIAN FORMULA 3 CHAMPIONSHIP, Autodromo di Vallelunga, Campagnano di Roma, Italy, 8 May. Round 2. 24 laps of the 2.006-mile/3.228-km circuit, 48.139 miles/77.472 km.
1 Alex Müller, D (Dallara F304-Mugen), 28m 00.201s, 103.142 mph/165.991 km/h; **2** Paolo Maria Nocera, I (Dallara F304-Opel), 28m 02.136s; **3** Luigi Ferrara, I (Dallara F304-Opel), 28m 03.224s; **4** Riccardo Azzoli, I (Dallara F304-Opel), 28m 15.548s; **5** Massimo Torre, I (Dallara F304-Opel), 28m 23.019s; **6** Giuseppe Termine, I (Dallara F304-Opel), 28m 31.589s; **7** Maurizio Ceresoli, I (Dallara F304-Opel), 15 laps; **8** Giacomo Piccini, I (Lola Dome F106-Opel), 5 (DNF).
Fastest race lap: Müller, 1m 09.203s, 104.343 mph/167.923 km/h.
Fastest qualifying lap: Nocera, 1m 09.083s, 104.524 mph/168.215 km/h.

ITALIAN FORMULA 3 CHAMPIONSHIP, Autodromo Internazionale Enzo e Dino Ferrari, Imola, Italy, 18/19 June. 2 x 13 laps of the 3.065-mile/4.933-km circuit.
Round 3 (39.848 miles/64.129 km).
1 Luigi Ferrara, I (Dallara F304-Opel), 23m 38.483s, 101.131 mph/162.754 km/h; **2** Paolo Maria Nocera, I (Dallara F304-Opel), 23m 39.065s; **3** Riccardo Azzoli, I (Dallara F304-Opel), 23m 43.808s; **4** Alex Müller, D (Dallara F304-Mugen), 23m 45.257s; **5** Massimo Torre, I (Dallara F304-Opel), 23m 55.724s; **6** Elias Papaelias, GR (Dallara F304-Opel), 23m 56.252s; **7** Imerio Brigliadori, I (Dallara F303-Opel), 24m 15.874s; **8** Maurizio Ceresoli, I (Dallara F304-Opel), 24m 23.764s; **9** Giuseppe Termine, I (Dallara F304-Opel), 24m 25.707s; **10** Nicola Ortolani, I (Dallara F399-Opel), 24m 57.174s.
Fastest race lap: Müller, 1m 47.910s, 102.259 mph/164.570 km/h.
Fastest qualifying lap: Nocera, 1m 46.790s, 103.322 mph/166.296 km/h.

Round 4 (39.848 miles/64.129 km).
1 Alex Müller, D (Dallara F304-Mugen), 23m 36.908s, 101.243 mph/162.935 km/h; **2** Paolo Maria Nocera, I (Dallara F304-Opel), 23m 37.737s; **3** Luigi Ferrara, I (Dallara F304-Opel), 23m 38.289s; **4** Riccardo Azzoli, I (Dallara F304-Opel), 23m 39.149s; **5** Elias Papaelias, GR (Dallara F304-Opel), 23m 55.825s; **6** Maurizio Ceresoli, I (Dallara F304-Opel), 24m 00.904s; **7** Imerio Brigliadori, I (Dallara F303-Opel), 24m 02.380s; **8** Nicola Ortolani, I (Dallara F399-Opel), 25m 06.281s; **9** Giuseppe Termine, I (Dallara F304-Opel), 6 laps.
Fastest race lap: Müller, 1m 48.168s, 102.015 mph/164.177 km/h.
Fastest qualifying lap: Müller, 1m 47.066s, 103.065 mph/165.867 km/h.

ITALIAN FORMULA 3 CHAMPIONSHIP, Autodromo Internazionale del Mugello, Scarperia, Firenze (Florence), Italy, 2/3 July. 2 x 12 laps of the 3.259-mile/5.245-km circuit.
Round 5 (39.109 miles/62.940 km).
1 Alex Müller, D (Dallara F304-Opel), 21m 57.985s, 106.824 mph/171.916 km/h; **2** Luigi Ferrara, I (Dallara F304-Opel), 22m 00.596s; **3** Riccardo Azzoli, I (Dallara F304-Opel), 22m 01.227s; **4** Davide Valsecchi, I (Dallara F304-Opel), 22m 12.619s; **5** Massimo Torre, I (Dallara F304-Opel), 22m 15.139s; **6** Elias Papaelias, GR (Dallara F304-Opel), 22m 17.162s; **7** Maurizio Ceresoli, I (Dallara F304-Opel), 22m 17.371s; **8** Paolo Maria Nocera, I (Dallara F304-Opel), 22m 18.705s; **9** Imerio Brigliadori, I (Dallara F303-Opel), 22m 48.370s; **10** Luca Di Cienzo, I (Dallara F399-FIAT), 23m 29.998s.
Fastest race lap: Azzoli, 1m 48.337s, 108.298 mph/174.289 km/h.
Fastest qualifying lap: Müller, 1m 45.102s, 111.632 mph/179.654 km/h.

Round 6 (39.109 miles/62.940 km).
1 Alex Müller, D (Dallara F304-Opel), 21m 59.275s, 106.720 mph/171.748 km/h; **2** Davide Valsecchi, I (Dallara F304-Opel), 22m 01.269s; **3** Luigi Ferrara, I (Dallara F304-Opel), 22m 02.080s; **4** Elias Papaelias, GR (Dallara F304-Opel), 22m 17.574s; **5** Maurizio Ceresoli, I (Dallara F304-Opel), 22m 17.583s; **6** Massimo Torre, I (Dallara F304-Opel), 22m 20.251s; **7** Riccardo Azzoli, I (Dallara F304-Opel), 22m 23.430s; **8** Paolo Maria Nocera, I (Dallara F304-Opel), 22m 33.282s; **9** Imerio Brigliadori, I (Dallara F303-Opel), 22m 34.939s; **10** Luca Di Cienzo, I (Dallara F399-FIAT), 5 laps (DNF).
Fastest race lap: Müller, 1m 49.088s, 107.553 mph/173.089 km/h.
Fastest qualifying lap: Müller, 1m 46.141s, 110.539 mph/177.895 km/h.

ITALIAN FORMULA 3 CHAMPIONSHIP, Autodromo Riccardo Paletti, Varano dei Melegari, Parma, Italy, 11 September. Round 7. 30 laps of the 1.476-mile/2.375-km circuit, 44.273 miles/71.250 km.
1 Paolo Maria Nocera, I (Dallara F304-Opel), 32m 09.473s, 82.604 mph/132.937 km/h; **2** Luigi Ferrara, I (Dallara F304-Opel), 32m 11.777s; **3** Riccardo Azzoli, I (Dallara F304-Opel), 32m 17.627s; **4** Davide Valsecchi, I (Dallara F304-Opel), 32m 29.974s; **5** Elias Papaelias, GR (Dallara F304-Opel), 32m 30.798s; **6** Alex Müller, D (Dallara F304-Mugen), 32m 31.184s; **7** Maurizio Ceresoli, I (Dallara F304-Opel), 32m 48.394s; **8** Marcello Puglisi, I (Lola Dome F106-Opel), 32m 52.070s; **9** Imerio Brigliadori, I (Dallara F303-Opel), 32m 57.124s; **10** Marco Cencetti, I (Dallara F304-Mugen), 29 laps.
Fastest race lap: Azzoli, 1m 03.611s, 83.519 mph/134.410 km/h.
Fastest qualifying lap: Nocera, 1m 02.608s, 84.857 mph/136.564 km/h.

ITALIAN FORMULA 3 CHAMPIONSHIP, Autodromo Nazionale di Monza, Milan, Italy, 24/25 September. 2 x 12 laps of the 3.600-mile/5.793-km circuit.
Round 8 (43.195 miles/69.516 km).
1 Luigi Ferrara, I (Dallara F304-Opel), 22m 01.647s, 117.658 mph/189.352 km/h; **2** Alex Müller, D (Dallara F304-Mugen), 22m 15.631s; **3** Maurizio Ceresoli, I (Dallara F304-Opel), 22m 18.024s; **4** Marco Barba, I (Dallara F302-Mugen), 22m 19.829s; **5** Paolo Maria Nocera, I (Dallara F302-Opel), 22m 20.665s; **6** Imerio Brigliadori, I (Dallara F303-Opel), 22m 59.594s; **7** Riccardo Azzoli, I (Dallara F304-Opel), 5 laps (DNF); **8** Elias Papaelias, GR (Dallara F304-Opel), 2 (DNF); **9** Giovanni Faraonio, I (Dallara F304-Opel), 0 (DNF).
Fastest race lap: Nocera, 1m 48.654s, 119.265 mph/191.937 km/h.
Fastest qualifying lap: Nocera, 1m 47.483s, 120.564 mph/194.028 km/h.

Round 9 (43.195 miles/69.516 km).
1 Paolo Maria Nocera, I (Dallara F302-Opel), 22m 10.965s, 116.835 mph/188.027 km/h; **2** Luigi Ferrara, I (Dallara F304-Opel), 22m 11.642s; **3** Riccardo Azzoli, I (Dallara F304-Opel), 22m 15.321s; **4** Elias Papaelias, GR (Dallara F304-Opel), 22m 19.372s; **5** Marco Barba, I (Dallara F302-Mugen), 22m 23.481s; **6** Maurizio Ceresoli, I (Dallara F304-Opel), 22m 26.758s; **7** Imerio Brigliadori, I (Dallara F303-Opel), 22m 42.247s; **8** Giovanni Faraonio, I (Dallara F304-Opel), 22m 57.700. Alex Müller, D (Dallara F304-Mugen), finished 1st in 22m 10.183s, but was disqualified.
Fastest race lap: Nocera, 1m 49.591s, 118.245 mph/190.296 km/h.
Fastest qualifying lap: Ferrara, 1m 47.985s, 120.003 mph/193.126 km/h.

ITALIAN FORMULA 3 CHAMPIONSHIP, Autodromo Adria International Raceway, Adria, Italy, 9 October. Round 10. 28 laps of the 1.679-mile/2.702-km circuit, 47.010 miles/75.656 km.
1 Alex Müller, D (Dallara F304-Mugen), 34m 15.935s, 82.317 mph/132.476 km/h; **2** Paolo Maria Nocera, I (Dallara F304-Opel), 34m 19.114s; **3** Luigi Ferrara, I (Dallara F304-Opel), 34m 43.977s; **4** Maurizio Ceresoli, I (Dallara F304-Opel), 34m 45.694s; **5** Elias Papaelias, GR (Dallara F304-Opel), 34m 50.048s; **6** Riccardo Azzoli, I (Dallara F304-Opel), 0 laps (DNF).
Fastest race lap: Nocera, 1m 12.312s, 83.585 mph/134.517 km/h.
Fastest qualifying lap: Ferrara, 1m 25.426s, 70.754 mph/113.867 km/h.

ITALIAN FORMULA 3 CHAMPIONSHIP, Autodromo Internazionale di Misano, Misano Adriatico, Rimini, Italy, 23 October. 2 x 16 laps of the 2.523-mile/4.060-km circuit.
Round 11 (40.364 miles/64.960 km).
1 Luigi Ferrara, I (Dallara F304-Opel), 23m 38.458s, 102.443 mph/164.866 km/h; **2** Riccardo Azzoli, I (Dallara F304-Opel), 23m 39.345s; **3** Alex Müller, D (Dallara F304-Mugen), 23m 42.192s; **4** Paolo Maria Nocera, I (Dallara F304-Opel), 23m 46.461s; **5** Maurizio Ceresoli, I (Dallara F304-Opel), 24m 06.307s; **6** Fabrizio Crestani, I (Dallara F304-Opel), 24m 08.509s; **7** Elias Papaelias, GR (Dallara F304-Opel), 7 laps.
Fastest race lap: Azzoli, 1m 27.512s, 103.780 mph/167.017 km/h.
Fastest qualifying lap: Ferrara, 1m 37.359s, 93.283 mph/150.124 km/h.

Round 12 (40.364 miles/64.960 km).
1 Alex Müller, D (Dallara F304-Mugen), 23m 31.520s, 102.947 mph/165.676 km/h; **2** Paolo Maria Nocera, I (Dallara F304-Opel), 23m 35.746s; **3** Riccardo Azzoli, I (Dallara F304-Opel), 23m 36.909s; **4** Elias Papaelias, GR (Dallara F304-Opel), 23m 38.075s; **5** Luigi Ferrara, I (Dallara F304-Opel), 23m 49.089s; **6** Maurizio Ceresoli, I (Dallara F304-Opel), 23m 55.378s; **7** Fabrizio Crestani, I (Dallara F304-Opel), 23m 56.583s.
Fastest race lap: Müller, 1m 27.481s, 103.816 mph/167.076 km/h.
Fastest qualifying lap: Nocera, 1m 26.701s, 104.750 mph/168.579 km/h.

Final championship points
1 Luigi Ferrara, I, 180; **2** Alex Müller, D, 171; **3** Paolo Maria Nocera, I, 168; **4** Riccardo Azzoli, I, 108; **5** Maurizio Ceresoli, I, 79; **6** Elias Papaelias, GR, 67; **7** Davide Valsecchi, I, 35; **8** Massimo Torre, I, 33; **9** Imerio Brigliadori, I, 24; **10** Marco Barba, I, 18; **11** Giuseppe Termine, I, 16; **12=** Riccardo Mari, I, 10; **12=** Fabrizio Crestani, I, 10; **14** Giacomo Piccini, I, 4; **15=** Marcello Puglisi, I, 3; **15=** Giovanni Faraonio, I, 3; **17** Basil Shaaban, RL, 2; **18** Marco Cencetti, I, 1.

All-Japan Formula 3 Championship

ALL-JAPAN FORMULA 3 CHAMPIONSHIP, Twin Ring Motegi, Motegi-machi, Haga-gun, Tochigi, Japan, 2/3 April. 14 and 20 laps of the 2.983-mile/4.801-km circuit.
Round 1 (41.765 miles/67.214 km).
1 João Paolo de Oliveira, BR (Dallara F305-Toyota), 25m 04.261s, 99.952 mph/160.856 km/h; **2** Paolo Montin, I (Dallara F305-Nissan), 25m 10.432s; **3** Naoki Yokomizo, J (Dallara F305-Nissan), 25m 18.386s; **4** Roberto Streit, BR (Dome F107-Toyota), 25m 19.450s; **5** Daisuke Ikeda, J (Dallara F305-Toyota), 25m 20.348s; **6** Jonny Reid, NZ (Dallara F303-Toyota), 25m 26.646s; **7** Taku Bamba, J (Dallara F305-Toyota), 25m 30.267s; **8** Yasuhiro Takasaki, J (Dome F107-Mugen), 25m 31.401s; **9** Ryo Orime, J (Dallara F304-Toyota), 25m 32.734s; **10** Hideto Yasuoka, J (Dome F107-Toyota), 25m 35.051s.
Fastest race lap: de Oliveira, 1m 46.502s, 100.839 mph/162.284 km/h.
Fastest qualifying lap: de Oliveira, 1m 45.571s, 101.728 mph/163.715 km/h.

Round 2 (59.664 miles/96.020 km).
1 Hideki Mutoh, J (Dome F107-Mugen), 36m 05.717s, 99.178 mph/159.610 km/h; **2** João Paolo de Oliveira, BR (Dallara F305-Toyota), 36m 06.326s; **3** Paolo Montin, I (Dallara F305-Nissan), 36m 14.953s; **4** Naoki Yokomizo, J (Dallara F305-Nissan), 36m 20.851s; **5** Daisuke Ikeda, J (Dallara F305-Toyota), 36m 22.511s; **6** Roberto Streit, BR (Dome F107-Toyota), 36m 27.160s; **7** Jonny Reid, NZ (Dallara F305-Toyota), 36m 30.098s; **8** Yasuhiro Takasaki, J (Dome F107-Mugen), 36m 37.030s; **9** Taku Bamba, J (Dallara F305-Toyota), 36m 37.526s; **10** Kouki Saga, J (Dallara F305-Toyota), 36m 51.715s.
Fastest race lap: Mutoh, 1m 47.616s, 99.795 mph/160.604 km/h.
Fastest qualifying lap: de Oliveira, 1m 45.269s, 102.020 mph/164.185 km/h.

ALL-JAPAN FORMULA 3 CHAMPIONSHIP, Suzuka International Racing Course, Suzuka-shi, Mie Prefecture, Japan, 16/17 April. 12 and 17 laps of the 3.608-mile/5.807-km circuit.
Round 3 (43.300 miles/69.684 km).
1 João Paolo de Oliveira, BR (Dallara F305-Toyota), 23m 29.163s, 110.618 mph/178.022 km/h; **2** Daisuke Ikeda, J (Dallara F305-Toyota), 23m 31.413s; **3** Kazuki Nakajima, J (Dallata F305-Toyota), 23m 32.937s; **4** Hideki Mutoh, J (Dome F107-Mugen), 23m 37.341s; **5** Roberto Streit, BR (Dome F107-Toyota), 23m 38.678s; **6** Taku Bamba, J (Dallara F305-Toyota), 23m 41.555s; **7** Jonny Reid, NZ (Dallara F305-Toyota), 23m 42.177s; **8** Naoki Yokomizo, J (Dallara F305-Nissan), 23 43.502s; **9** Paolo Montin, I (Dallara F305-Nissan), 23m 45.433s; **10** Yasuhiro Takasaki, J (Dome F107-Mugen), 23m 54.492s.
Fastest race lap: de Oliveira, 1m 56.922s, 111.099 mph/178.796 km/h.
Fastest qualifying lap: Ikeda, 1m 56.031s, 111.952 mph/180.169 km/h.

Round 4 (61.341 miles/98.719 km).
1 Hideki Mutoh, J (Dome F107-Mugen), 33m 37.737s, 109.443 mph/176.132 km/h; **2** João Paolo de Oliveira, BR (Dallara F305-Toyota), 33m 38.105s; **3** Kazuki Nakajima, J (Dallata F305-Toyota), 33m 42.228s; **4** Daisuke Ikeda, J (Dallara F305-Toyota), 33m 43.121s; **5** Jonny Reid, NZ (Dallara F303-Toyota), 33m 49.712s; **6** Paolo Montin, I (Dallara F305-Nissan), 33m 51.321s; **7** Yasuhiro Takasaki, J (Dome F107-Mugen), 33m 56.850s; **8** Naoki Yokomizo, J (Dallara F305-Nissan), 33m 57.211s; **9** Taku Bamba, J (Dallara F305-Toyota), 33m 59.046s; **10** Kouki Saga, J (Dallara F305-Toyota), 34m 10.781s.
Fastest race lap: de Oliveira, 1m 57.830s, 110.243 mph/177.418 km/h.
Fastest qualifying lap: de Oliveira, 1m 55.531s, 112.436 mph/180.948 km/h.

ALL-JAPAN FORMULA 3 CHAMPIONSHIP, Sportsland SUGO International Course, Shibata-gun, Miyagi Prefecture, Japan, 14/15 May. 18 and 25 laps of the 2.302-mile/3.704-km circuit.
Round 5 (41.428 miles/66.672 km).
1 Naoki Yokomizo, J (Dallara F305-Nissan), 23m 20.661s, 106.479 mph/171.361 km/h; **2** Jonny Reid, NZ (Dome F107-Toyota), 23m 25.885s; **3** Hideki Mutoh, J (Dome F107-Mugen), 23m 30.798s; **4** Kazuki Nakajima, J (Dallata F305-Toyota), 23m 31.578s; **5** Roberto Streit, BR (Dome F107-Toyota), 23m 41.432s; **6** Hiroki Kato, J (Dome F107-Toyota), 23m 41.593s; **7** Daisuke Ikeda, J (Dallara F305-Toyota), 23m 45.960s; **8** Taku Bamba, J (Dallara F305-Toyota), 23m 50.890s; **9** Paolo Montin, I (Dallara F305-Nissan), 23m 51.031s; **10** Ryo Orime, J (Dallara F304-Toyota), 24m 18.029s.
Fastest race lap: Reid, 1m 17.053s, 107.531 mph/173.054 km/h.
Fastest qualifying lap: Yokomizo, 1m 18.063s, 106.140 mph/170.815 km/h.

Round 6 (57.539 miles/92.600 km).
1 Naoki Yokomizo, J (Dallara F305-Nissan), 33m 59.499s, 101.564 mph/163.451 km/h; **2** João Paolo de Oliveira, BR (Dallara F305-Toyota), 34m 00.635s; **3** Kazuki Nakajima, J (Dallara F305-Toyota), 34m 01.755s; **4** Daisuke Ikeda, J (Dallara F305-Toyota), 34m 02.088s; **5** Roberto Streit, BR (Dome F107-Toyota), 34m 03.161s; **6** Jonny Reid, NZ (Dome F107-Toyota), 34m 07.53s; **7** Taku Bamba, J (Dallara F305-Toyota), 34m 12.896s; **8** Hideki Mutoh, J (Dome F107-Mugen), 34m 13.415s; **9** Hiroki Kato, J (Dome F107-Toyota), 34m 13.420s; **10** Yasuhiro Takasaki, J (Dome F107-Mugen), 34m 32.390s.
Fastest race lap: de Oliveira, 1m 18.237s, 105.904 mph/170.435 km/h.
Fastest qualifying lap: Yokomizo, 1m 17.287s, 107.206 mph/172.530 km/h.

ALL-JAPAN FORMULA 3 CHAMPIONSHIP, Fuji International Speedway, Sunto-gun, Shizuoka Prefecture, Japan, 4/5 June. 15 and 21 laps of the 2.835-mile/4.563-km circuit.
Round 7 (42.530 miles/68.445 km).
1 João Paolo de Oliveira, BR (Dallara F305-Toyota), 24m 27.406s, 104.339 mph/167.916 km/h; **2** Kazuki Nakajima, J (Dallata F305-Toyota), 24m 29.214s; **3** Naoki Yokomizo, J (Dallara F305-Nissan), 24m 43.900s; **4** Jonny Reid, NZ (Dome F107-Toyota), 24m 51.473s; **5** Hideki Mutoh, J (Dome F107-Mugen), 25m 00.931s; **6** Hideto Yasuoka, J (Dome F107-Toyota), 25m 04.667s; **7** Taku Bamba, J (Dallara F305-Toyota), 25m 09.627s; **8** Daisuke Ikeda, J (Dallara F305-Toyota), 25m 09.628s; **9** Yasuhiro Takasaki, J (Dome F107-Mugen); **10** Ryo Orime, J (Dallara F304-Toyota), 25m 16.052s.
Fastest race lap: Nakajima, 1m 37.406s, 104.790 mph/168.643 km/h.
Fastest qualifying lap: Yokomizo, 1m 37.625s, 104.555 mph/168.264 km/h.

Round 8 (59.542 miles/95.823 km).
1 João Paolo de Oliveira, BR (Dallara F305-Toyota), 34m 24.315s, 103.836 mph/167.107 km/h; **2** Kazuki Nakajima, J (Dallara F305-Toyota), 34m 30.440s; **3** Daisuke Ikeda, J (Dallara F305-Toyota), 34m 41.257s; **4** Naoki Yokomizo, J (Dallara F305-Nissan), 34m 58.312s; **5** Hideki Mutoh, J (Dome F107-Mugen), 35m 00.391s; **6** Yasuhiro Takasaki, J (Dome F107-Mugen), 35m 00.955s; **7** Roberto Streit, BR (Dome F107-Toyota), 35m 01.694s; **8** Paolo Montin, I (Dallara F305-Nissan), 35m 02.137s; **9** Jonny Reid, NZ (Dome F107-Toyota), 35m 03.797s; **10** Taku Bamba, J (Dallara F305-Toyota), 35m 04.695s.
Fastest race lap: de Oliveira, 1m 37.972s, 104.184 mph/167.668 km/h.

Fastest qualifying lap: Nakajima, 1m 37.487s, 14.703 mph/168.502 km/h.

ALL-JAPAN FORMULA 3 CHAMPIONSHIP, Okayama International Circuit (TI Circuit Aida), Aida Gun, Okayama Prefecture, Japan, 18/19 June. 18 and 25 laps of the 2.301-mile/3.703-km circuit.

Round 9 (41.417 miles/66.654 km).

1 Paolo Montin, I (Dallara F305-Nissan), 26m 36.175s, 93.411 mph/150.330 km/h; **2** João Paolo de Oliveira, BR (Dallara F305-Toyota), 26m 37.119s; **3** Daisuke Ikeda, J (Dallara F305-Toyota), 26m 45.468s; **4** Kazuki Nakajima, J (Dallara F305-Toyota), 26m 47.190s; **5** Roberto Streit, BR (Dome F107-Toyota), 26m 49.664s; **6** Naoki Yokomizo, J (Dallara F305-Nissan), 26m 55.257s; **7** Hideki Mutoh, J (Dome F107-Mugen), 26m 56.973s; **8** Jonny Reid, NZ (Dome F107-Toyota), 26m 59.427s; **9** Yasuhiro Takasaki, J (Dome F107-Mugen), 27m 00.618s; **10** Ryo Orime, J (Dallara F304-Toyota), 27m 09.306s.

Fastest race lap: de Oliveira, 1m 28.033s, 94.094 mph/151.429 km/h.

Fastest qualifying lap: de Oliveira, 1m 26.751s, 95.484 mph/153.667 km/h.

Round 10 (57.523 miles/92.575 km).

1 Naoki Yokomizo, J (Dallara F305-Nissan), 37m 05.538s, 93.049 mph/149.748 km/h; **2** Daisuke Ikeda, J (Dallara F305-Toyota), 37m 07.449s; **3** Paolo Montin, I (Dallara F305-Nissan), 37m 08.386s; **4** João Paolo de Oliveira, BR (Dallara F305-Toyota), 37m 08.927s; **5** Jonny Reid, NZ (Dome F107-Toyota), 37m 16.348s; **6** Roberto Streit, BR (Dome F107-Toyota), 37m 18.767s; **7** Hideki Mutoh, J (Dome F107-Mugen), 37m 21.654s; **8** Kazuki Nakajima, J (Dallara F305-Toyota), 37m 22.493s; **9** Yasuhiro Takasaki, J (Dome F107-Mugen), 37m 26.374s; **10** Taku Bamba, J (Dallara F305-Toyota), 37m 27.587s.

Fastest race lap: de Oliveira, 1m 27.970s, 94.161 mph/151.538 km/h.

Fastest qualifying lap: de Oliveira, 1m 26.287s, 95.998 mph/154.493 km/h.

ALL-JAPAN FORMULA 3 CHAMPIONSHIP, Suzuka International Racing Course, Suzuka City, Mie Prefecture, Japan, 2/3 July. 12 and 16 laps of the 3.608-mile/5.807-km circuit.

Round 11 (43.330 miles/69.684 km).

1 João Paolo de Oliveira, BR (Dallara F305-Toyota), 27m 18.568s, 95.131 mph/153.098 km/h; **2** Kazuki Nakajima, J (Dallara F305-Toyota), 27m 19.930s; **3** Daisuke Ikeda, J (Dallara F305-Toyota), 27m 27.056s; **4** Hideki Mutoh, J (Dome F107-Mugen), 27m 33.616s; **5** Roberto Streit, BR (Dome F107-Toyota), 27m 44.403s; **6** Taku Bamba, J (Dallara F305-Toyota), 27m 45.744s; **7** Paolo Montin, I (Dallara F305-Nissan), 27m 47.043s; **8** Naoki Yokomizo, J (Dallara F305-Nissan), 27m 47.445s; **9** Kouki Saga, J (Dallara F305-Toyota), 27m 57.783s; **10** Hideto Yasuoka, J (Dome F107-Toyota), 28m 03.759s.

Fastest race lap: Nakajima, 2m 14.073s, 96.887 mph/155.924 km/h.

Fastest qualifying lap: Ikeda, 1m 57.233s, 110.804 mph/178.321 km/h.

Round 12 (57.533 miles/92.912 km).

1 Roberto Streit, BR (Dome F107-Toyota), 36m 57.002s, 93.747 mph/150.871 km/h; **2** João Paolo de Oliveira, BR (Dallara F305-Toyota), 36m 59.468s; **3** Hideki Mutoh, J (Dome F107-Mugen), 37m 07.428s; **4** Paolo Montin, I (Dallara F305-Nissan), 37m 10.666s; **5** Kazuki Nakajima, J (Dallara F305-Toyota), 37m 11.122s; **6** Naoki Yokomizo, J (Dallara F305-Nissan), 37m 20.341s; **7** Taku Bamba, J (Dallara F305-Toyota), 37m 39.904s; **8** Kouki Saga, J (Dallara F305-Toyota), 37m 51.604s; **9** Ryo Orime, J (Dallara F304-Toyota), 38m 15.660s; **10** Motohiko Isozaki, J (Dallara F305-Toyota), 15 laps.

Fastest race lap: Nakajima, 2m 17.222s, 94.663 mph/152.345 km/h.

Fastest qualifying lap: de Oliveira, 1m 56.607s, 111.399 mph/179.279 km/h.

ALL-JAPAN FORMULA 3 CHAMPIONSHIP, Mine Circuit, Nishi-Aho-cho, Mine City, Yamaguchi Prefecture, Japan, 30/31 July. 20 and 30 laps of the 2.070-mile/3.331-km circuit.

Round 13 (41.396 miles/66.620km).

1 Kazuki Nakajima, J (Dallara F305-Toyota), 28m 11.981s, 88.077 mph/141.746 km/h; **2** João Paolo de Oliveira, BR (Dallara F305-Toyota), 28m 14.805s; **3** Roberto Streit, BR (Dome F107-Toyota), 28m 19.552s; **4** Paolo Montin, I (Dallara F305-Nissan), 28m 24.742s; **5** Hideki Mutoh, J (Dome F107-Mugen), 28m 25.249s; **6** Naoki Yokomizo, J (Dallara F305-Nissan), 28m 29.502s; **7** Jonny Reid, NZ (Dome F107-Toyota), 28m 29.759s; **8** Hideto Yasuoka, J (Dome F107-Toyota), 28m 32.714s; **9** Daisuke Ikeda, J (Dallara F305-Toyota), 28m 33.677s; **10** Kouki Saga, J (Dallara F305-Toyota), 28m 44.265s.

Fastest race lap: Nakajima, 1m 23.922s, 88.788 mph/142.890 km/h.

Fastest qualifying lap: de Oliveira, 1m 22.819s, 89.970 mph/144.793 km/h.

Round 14 (62.094 miles/99.930 km).

1 Kazuki Nakajima, J (Dallara F305-Toyota), 42m 56.311s, 86.766 mph/139.637 km/h; **2** Naoki Yokomizo, J (Dallara F305-Nissan), 43m 05.932s; **3** Paolo Montin, I (Dallara F305-Nissan), 43m 07.241s; **4** Hideto Yasuoka, J (Dome F107-Toyota), 43m 15.622s; **5** João Paolo de Oliveira, BR (Dallara F305-Toyota), 43m 32.177s; **6** Kouki Saga, J (Dallara F305-Toyota), 43m 56.786s; **7** Taku Bamba, J (Dallara F305-Toyota), 44m 03.424s; **8** Roberto Streit, BR (Dome F107-Toyota), 29 laps; **9** Hideki Mutoh, J (Dome F107-Mugen), 29; **10** Daisuke Ikeda, J (Dallara F305-Toyota), 29.

Fastest race lap: Streit, 1m 24.870s, 87.796 mph/141.293 km/h.

Fastest qualifying lap: Streit, 1m 22.311s, 90.525 mph/145.686 km/h.

ALL-JAPAN FORMULA 3 CHAMPIONSHIP, Fuji International Speedway, Sunto-gun, Shizuoka Prefecture, Japan, 27/28 August. 15 and 21 laps of the 2.835-mile/4.563-km circuit.

Round 15 (42.530 miles/68.445 km).

1 Paolo Montin, I (Dallara F305-Nissan), 24m 46.013s, 103.032 mph/165.814 km/h; **2** Kazuki Nakajima, J (Dallara F305-Toyota), 24m 46.676s; **3** Naoki Yokomizo, J (Dallara F305-Nissan), 24m 51.018s; **4** João Paolo de Oliveira, BR (Dallara F305-Toyota), 24m 51.543s; **5** Roberto Streit, BR (Dome F107-Toyota), 24m 57.561s; **6** Daisuke Ikeda, J (Dallara F305-Toyota), 24m 58.468s; **7** Jonny Reid, NZ (Dome F107-Toyota), 24m 59.492s; **8** Hideki Mutoh, J (Dome F107-Mugen), 25m 01.011s; **9** Taku Bamba, J (Dallara F305-Toyota), 25m 02.769s; **10** Kouki Saga, J (Dallara F305-Toyota), 25m 08.957s.

Fastest race lap: Nakajima, 1m 38.442s, 103.687 mph/166.868 km/h.

Fastest qualifying lap: Nakajima, 1m 38.373s, 103.760 mph/166.984 km/h.

Round 16 (59.542 miles/95.823 km).

1 João Paolo de Oliveira, BR (Dallara F305-Toyota), 34m 37.339s, 103.185 mph/166.059 km/h; **2** Kazuki Nakajima, J (Dallara F305-Toyota), 34m 37.645s; **3** Paolo Montin, I (Dallara F305-Nissan), 34m 44.307s; **4** Taku Bamba, J (Dallara F305-Toyota), 34m 56.005s; **5** Roberto Streit, BR (Dome F107-Toyota), 34m 56.253s; **6** Hideki Mutoh, J (Dome F107-Mugen), 34m 56.740s; **7** Koudai Tsukakoshi, J (Lola Dome F106-Mugen), 35m 00.982s; **8** Hideto Yasuoka, J (Dome F107-Toyota), 35m 10.264s; **9** Kouki Saga, J (Dallara F305-Toyota), 35m 11.728s; **10** Yasuhiro Takasaki, J (Dome F107-Mugen), 35m 11.856s.

Fastest race lap: Nakajima, 1m 38.478s, 103.649 mph/166.807 km/h.

Fastest qualifying lap: Nakajima, 1m 38.070s, 104.080 mph/167.500 km/h.

ALL-JAPAN FORMULA 3 CHAMPIONSHIP, Mine Circuit, Nishi-Aho-cho, Mine City, Yamaguchi Prefecture, Japan, 10/11 September. 20 and 30 laps of the 2.070-mile/3.331-km circuit.

Round 17 (41.396 miles/66.620 km).

1 Jonny Reid, NZ (Dome F107-Toyota), 30m 02.578s, 82.673 mph/133.049 km/h; **2** Hideki Mutoh, J (Dome F107-Mugen), 30m 02.870s; **3** João Paolo de Oliveira, BR (Dallara F305-Toyota), 30m 14.586s; **4** Naoki Yokomizo, J (Dallara F305-Nissan), 30m 33.095s; **5** Hideto Yasuoka, J (Dome F107-Toyota), 30m 33.467s; **6** Roberto Streit, BR (Dome F107-Toyota), 3m 45.072s; **7** Koudai Tsukakoshi, J (Lola Dome F106-Mugen), 30m 57.425s; **8** Taku Bamba, J (Dallara F305-Toyota), 31m 03.747s; **9** Hironari Kawachi, J (Lola Dome F106-Mugen), 31m 04.834s; **10** Motohiko Isozaki, J (Dallara F305-Toyota), 19 laps.

Fastest race lap: Kazuki Nakajima, J (Dallara F305-Toyota), 1m 23.551s, 89.182 mph/143.524 km/h.

Fastest qualifying lap: de Oliveira, 1m 22.903s, 89.879 mph/144.646 km/h.

Round 18 (62.094 miles/99.930 km).

1 João Paolo de Oliveira, BR (Dallara F305-Toyota), 42m 28.400s, 87.717 mph/141.166 km/h; **2** Kazuki Nakajima, J (Dallara F305-Toyota), 42m 36.150s; **3** Naoki Yokomizo, J (Dallara F305-Nissan), 42m 38.847s; **4** Hideki Mutoh, J (Dome F107-Mugen), 42m 39.663s; **5** Roberto Streit, BR (Dome F107-Toyota), 42m 43.188s; **6** Paolo Montin, I (Dallara F305-Nissan), 42m 48.232s; **7** Daisuke Ikeda, J (Dallara F305-Toyota), 42m 50.391s; **8** Koudai Tsukakoshi, J (Lola Dome F106-Mugen), 42m 54.281s; **9** Taku Bamba, J (Dallara F305-Toyota), 42m 56.723s; **10** Yasuhiro Takasaki, J (Dome F107-Mugen), 43m 00.676s.

Fastest race lap: de Oliveira, 1m 24.368s, 88.318 mph/142.134 km/h.

Fastest qualifying lap: Reid, 1m 21.967s, 90.905 mph/146.298 km/h.

ALL-JAPAN FORMULA 3 CHAMPIONSHIP, Twin Ring Motegi, Motegi-machi, Haga-gun, Tochigi, Japan, 22/23 October. 14 and 20 laps of the 2.983-mile/4.801-km circuit.

Round 19 (41.765 miles/67.214 km).

1 Hideki Mutoh, J (Dome F107-Mugen), 28m 15.025s, 88.703 mph/142.753 km/h; **2** João Paolo de Oliveira, BR (Dallara F305-Toyota), 28m 17.115s; **3** Kazuki Nakajima, J (Dallara F305-Toyota), 28m 30.011s; **4** Paolo Montin, I (Dallara F305-Nissan), 28m 36.784s; **5** Taku Bamba, J (Dallara F305-Toyota), 28m 41.414s; **6** Hiroki Kato, J (Dome F107-Toyota), 28m 51.188s; **7** Yasuhiro Takasaki, J (Dome F107-Mugen), 28m 51.922s; **8** Hideto Yasuoka, J (Dome F107-Toyota), 28m 55.336s; **9** Roberto Streit, BR (Dome F107-Toyota), 28m 55.839s; **10** Naoki Yokomizo, J (Dallara F305-Nissan), 29m 05.938s.

Fastest race lap: Mutoh, 2m 00.130s, 89.399 mph/143.874 km/h.

Fastest qualifying lap: Mutoh, 1m 47.385s, 100.010 mph/160.949 km/h.

Round 20 (59.664 miles/96.020 km).

1 Paolo Montin, I (Dallara F305-Nissan), 40m 52.769s, 87.571 mph/140.931 km/h. **2** João Paolo de Oliveira, BR (Dallara F305-Toyota), 40m 53.127s; **3** Hideki Mutoh, J (Dome F107-Mugen), 40m 53.581s; **4** Roberto Streit, BR (Dome F107-Toyota), 40m 58.387s; **5** Koudai Tsukakoshi, J (Lola Dome F106-Mugen), 41m 01.523s; **6** Hiroki Kato, J (Dome F107-Toyota), 41m 16.169s; **7** Daisuke Ikeda, J (Dallara F305-Toyota), 41m 17.020s; **8** Kouki Saga, J (Dallara F305-Toyota), 41m 41.490s; **9** Motohiko Isozaki, J (Dallara F305-Toyota), 42m 1.052s; **10** Hironari Kawachi, J (Lola Dome F106-Mugen), 42m 17.733s.

Fastest race lap: Streit, 1m 49.315s, 98.244 mph/158.108 km/h.

Fastest qualifying lap: Mutoh, 1m 49.687s, 97.911 mph/157.572 km/h.

Final championship points

1 João Paolo de Oliveira, BR, 300; **2** Kazuki Nakajima, J, 209; **3** Hideki Mutoh, J, 187; **4** Naoki Yokomizo, J, 181; **5** Paolo Montin, I, 176; **6** Roberto Streit, BR, 143; **7** Daisuke Ikeda, J, 126; **8** Jonny Reid, NZ, 94; **9** Taku Bamba, J, 66; **10** Hideto Yasuoka, J, 35; **11** Yasuhiro Takasaki, J, 30; **12=** Hiroki Kato, J, 20; **12=** Kouki Saga, J, 20; **14** Koudai Tsukakoshi, J, 19; **15** Ryu Orime, J, 7.

Major Non-Championship Formula 3 2004

The following races were run after AUTOOURSE 2004–2005 went to press.

FIA F3 WORLD CUP, 51st MACAU GP, Circuito Da Guia, Macau, 21 November. 10 and 11 laps of the 3.803-mile/6.120-km circuit.

Qualification Race (38.028 miles/61.200 km).

1 Lewis Hamilton, GB (Dallara F302-Mercedes Benz), 33m 16.057s, 68.585 mph/110.378 km/h; **2** Nico Rosberg, D (Dallara F303-Opel), 33m 18.341s; **3** Alexandre Prémat, F (Dallara F303-Mercedes Benz), 33m 20.039s; **4** Robert Kubica, PL (Dallara F303-Mercedes Benz), 33m 21.041s; **5** Jamie Green, GB (Dallara F303-Mercedes Benz), 33m 21.511s; **6** Fábio Carbone, BR (Dallara F303-Nissan), 33m 23.608s; **7** Loïc Duval, F (Dallara F302-Opel), 33m 33.346s; **8** Lucas di Grassi, BR (Dallara F302-Renault), 33m 34.945s; **9** James Rossiter, GB (Dallara F302-Opel), 33m 35.496s; **10** Danny Watts, GB (Dallara F302-Renault), 33m 36.570s.

Fastest race lap: Kubica, 2m 13.215s, 102.767 mph/165.387 km/h.

Fastest qualifying lap: Kubica, 2m 12.155, 103.591 mph/166.713 km/h.

Feature race (41.831 miles/67.320 km).

1 Alexandre Prémat, F (Dallara F303-Mercedes Benz), 37m 13.731s, 67.417 mph/108.497 km/h; **2** Robert Kubica, PL (Dallara F303-Mercedes Benz), 37m 14.406s; **3** Lucas di Grassi, BR (Dallara F302-Renault), 37m 14.909s; **4** Fábio Carbone, BR (Dallara F303-Nissan), 37m 15.153s; **5** Franck Perera, F (Dallara F304-Opel), 37m 15.553s; **6** Adam Carroll, GB (Dallara F302-Opel), 37m 15.950s; **7** Rob Austin, GB (Dallara F302-Opel), 37m 17.195s; **8** Ronnie Quintarelli, I (Dallara F302-Toyota), 37m 17.364s; **9** Richard Antinucci, USA (Dallara F304-Toyota), 37m 18.032s; **10** Nelson Angelo Piquet, BR (Dallara F303-Mugen), 37m 19.098s.

Fastest race lap: Hamilton, 2m 12.801s, 103.087 mph/165.902 km/h.

Pole position: Hamilton (leg 1 winner).

BAHRAIN F3 SUPER PRIX, Bahrain International Circuit, Sakhir, Bahrain, 10 December. 8 and 20 laps of the 3.340-mile/5.375-km circuit.

Qualifying Race (26.719 miles/43.000 km).

1 Jamie Green, GB (Dallara-Mercedes Benz), 15m 17.488s, 104.839 mph/168.722 km/h; **2** Fábio Carbone, BR (Dallara-Nissan), 15m 20.845s, **3** Nico Rosberg, D (Dallara-Opel), 15m 23.040s, **4** Marko Asmer, EE, (Dallara-Mugen), 15m 27.073s, **5** Richard Antinucci, USA (Dallara-TOM's Toyota), 15m 27.421s; **6** Paul di Resta, GB (Dallara-Mercedes Benz), 15m 28.130s; **7** Nelson Angelo Piquet, BR (Dallara-Mugen), 15m 29.035s, **8** Lucas di Grassi, BR (Dallara-Renault), 15m 29.892s; **9** Kazuki Nakajima, J (Dallara-TOM's Toyota), 15m 30.367s; **10** Ronnie Quintarelli, I (Dallara-TOM's Toyota), 15m 30.667s.

Fastest qualifying lap: Franck Perera, F (Dallara F304-Opel), 1m 53.938s, 105.527 mph/169.829 km/h.

Feature race (66.797 miles/107.500 km).

1 Lewis Hamilton, GB (Dallara-Mercedes Benz), 47m 11.528s, 84.926 mph/136.675 km/h; **2** Nico Rosberg, D (Dallara-Opel), 47m 12.322s; **3** Jamie Green, GB (Dallara-Mercedes Benz), 47m 16.229s; **4** James Rossiter, GB (Dallara-Opel), 47m 17.275s; **5** Fábio Carbone, BR (Dallara-Nissan), 47m 19.331s; **6** Marko Asmer, EE (Dallara-Mugen), 47m 19.391s; **7** Kazuki Nakajima, J (Dallara-TOM's Toyota), 47m 20.022s; **8** Loïc Duval, F (Dallara-Opel), 47m 20.961s; **9** Alexander Prémat, F (Dallara-Mercedes Benz), 47m 21.486s; **10** Ernesto Viso, YV (Dallara-Opel), 47m 21.672s.

Fastest race lap: Rosberg, 1m 54.168s, 105.314 mph/169.487 km/h.

2005

15th MARLBORO MASTERS OF FORMULA 3, Circuit Park Zandvoort, Netherlands, 12 June. 25 laps of the 2.677-mile/4.30748-km circuit, 66.914 miles/107.687 km.

1 Lewis Hamilton, GB (Dallara F305-Mercedes Benz), 39m 02.044s, 102.854 mph/165.528 km/h; **2** Adrian Sutil, D (Dallara F305-Mercedes Benz), 39m 08.521s; **3** Lucas di Grassi, BR (Dallara F305-Mercedes Benz), 39m 09.298s; **4** Paul di Resta, GB (Dallara F305-Mercedes Benz), 39m 10.112s; **5** Kohei Hirate, J (Dallara F305-Opel), 39m 28.961s; **6** Giedo van der Garde, NL (Dallara F305-Opel), 39m 32.994s; **7** Marko Asmer, EE (Dallara F305-Mugen), 39m 33.577s; **8** Franck Perera, F (Dallara F305-Opel), 39m 34.200s; **9** Hannes Neuhauser, A (Dallara F305-Mercedes Benz), 39m 35.700s; **10** Loïc Duval, F (Dallara F305-Opel), 39m 36.626s.

Fastest race lap: Hamilton, 1m 32.866s, 103.758 mph/166.982 km/h.

Fastest qualifying lap: Hamilton, 1m 31.200s, 105.653 mph/170.032 km/h.

Results of the Macau races will be given in AUTOCOURSE 2006–2007.

FIA GT Championship 2004

The following race was run after AUTOCOURSE 2004–2005 went to press.

FIA GT CHAMPIONSHIP, Zhuhai International Circuit, Zhuhai City, Guangdong Province, China, 12 November. Round 11. 113 laps of the 2.672-mile/4.300-km circuit, 301.924 miles/485.900 km.

1 Andrea Bertolini/Mika Salo, I/FIN (Maserati MC12), 3h 01m 11.193s, 99.982 mph/160.906 km/h; **2** Johnny Herbert/Fabrizio de Simone, GB/I (Maserati Benz MC12), 3h 01m 12.864s; **3** Matteo Bobbi/Gabriele Gardel, I/CH (Ferrari 550 Maranello), 3h 02m 04.646s; **4** Christophe Bouchut/Lilian Bryner/Enzo Calderari, F/CH/I (Ferrari 550 Maranello), 112 laps; **5** Karl Wendlinger/Tarso Marques/Iradj Alexander, A/BR/CH (Ferrari 575 M Maranello), 112; **6** Emanuele Naspetti/Philipp Peter, I/A (Ferrari 575 M Maranello), 111; **7** Chris Goodwin/Michael Mallock, GB/GB (Saleen S7-R), 111; **8** Gianni Morbidelli/Fabio Babini, I/I (Ferrari 575 M Maranello), 110; **9** Bert Longin/Maurizio Mediani/Sergey Zlobin, B/I/RUS (Ferrari 575 M Maranello), 109; **10** Christian Pescatori/Jaime Melo Jr., I/BR (Ferrari 360 Modena), 109 (1st N-GT class).

Fastest race lap: Bobbi, 1m 32.490s, 103.999 mph/167.369 km/h.

Fastest qualifying lap: Bobbi/Gardel, 1m 31.121, 105.561 mph/169.884 km/h.

Final championship points:

GT Drivers: 1= Fabrizio Gollin, I, 85; **1=** Luca Cappellari, I, 85; **3=** Matteo Bobbi, I, 74.5; **3=** Gabriele Gardel, CH, 74.5; **5=** Enzo Calderari, I, 55; **5=** Lilian Bryner, CH, 55; **7** Fabio Babini, I, 51; **8** Karl Wendlinger, A, 50.5; **9** Philipp Peter, A, 49; **10=** Uwe Alzen, D, 44; **10==** Michael Bartels, D, 44; **12** Stefano Livio, I, 36.5; **13** Mika Salo, FIN, 27; **14** Emanuele Naspetti, I, 21; **15** Jaime Melo Jr., BR, 20; **16** Vincent Vosse, B, 17; **17=** Jamie Campbell-Walter, GB, 16; **17=** Jamie Derbyshire, GB, 16; **19** Chris Goodwin, GB, 15; **20=** Mike Newton, GB, 14; **20=** Thomas Erdos, BR, 14; **20=** Robert Lechner, A, 14; **20=** Gianni Morbidelli, I, 14; **24** Bert Longin, B, 13.5; **25** Toto Wolff, A, 13; **26** Miguel Angel de Castro, E, 12.5; **27** Christophe Bouchut, F,11; **28=** Tarso Marques, BR, 10; **28=** Andrea Bertolini, 10; **30** Mike Hezemans, NL, 9.

GT Teams: 1 BMS Scuderia Italia, 159.5; **2** G.P.C. Giesse Squadra Corse, 72; **3** JMB Racing, 60; **4** Vitaphone Racing Team, 44; **5** Care Racing Development, 37.

N-GT Drivers: 1= Sascha Maassen, D, 93.5; **1=** Lucas Luhr, D, 93.5; **3=** Stéphane Ortelli, MC, 90; **3=** Emmanuel Collard, F, 90; **5** Christian Pescatori, I, 58; **6** Alexei Vasiliev, RUS, 48; **7=** Gerold Ried, D, 44; **7=** Christian Ried, D, 44; **9** Fabrizio de Simone, I, 36; **10** Nikolaj Fomenko, RUS, 26. **N-GT Teams: 1** Freisinger Yukos Motorsport, 138; **2** Freisinger Motorsport, 93.5; **3** G.P.C. Giesse Squadra Corse, 67; **4** Proton Competition, 45; **5** Gruppe M Europe, 19.5.

2005

FIA GT CHAMPIONSHIP, Autodromo Nazionale di Monza, Milan, Italy, 10 April. Round 1. 87 laps of the 3.600-mile/5.793-km circuit, 312.973 miles/503.682 km.

1 Pedro Lamy/Gabriele Gardel, P/CH (Ferrari 550 Maranello), 2h 40m 30.881s, 116.989 mph/188.275 km/h; **2** Michael Bartels/Timo Scheider, D/D (Maserati MC12), 2h 40m 31.802s; **3** Fabio Babini/Thomas Biagi, I/I (Maserati MC12), 2h 40m 32.337s; **4** Philipp Peter/Chris Buncombe/Roman Rusinov, A/GB/RUS (Maserati MC12), 86 laps; **5** Andrea Bertolini/Karl Wendlinger, I/A (Maserati MC12), 84; **6** Lilian Bryner/Enzo Calderari/Steve Zacchia, CH/I/CH (Ferrari 550 Maranello), 84; **7** Marc Lieb/Mike Rockenfeller, D/D (Porsche 996 GT3-RSR), 84 (1st GT2 class); **8** Emmanuel Collard/Tim Sugden, F/GB (Porsche 996 GT3-RSR), 84; **9** Justin Keen/Liz Halliday, GB/GB (Lister Storm GT), 83; **10** Paolo Ruberti/Joël Camathias, I/CH (Saleen S7R), 82.

Fastest race lap: Babini, 1m 46.077s, 122.162 mph/196.601 km/h.

Fastest qualifying lap: Peter/Buncombe/Rusinov, 1m 45.699s, 122.599 mph/197.304 km/h.

FIA GT CHAMPIONSHIP, Circuit de Nevers, Magny-Cours, France, 1 May. Round 2. 104 laps of the 2.741-mile/4.411-km circuit, 284.936 miles/458.560 km.

1 Andrea Bertolini/Karl Wendlinger, I/A (Maserati MC12), 3h 01m 20.442s, 94.276 mph/151.723 km/h; **2** Michael Bartels/Timo Scheider, D/D (Maserati MC12), 3h 01m 25.143s; **3** Fabio Babini/Thomas Biagi, I/I (Maserati MC12), 3h 01m 56.481s; **4** Bert Longin/Anthony Kumpen/Mike Hezemans, B/B/NL (Chevrolet Corvette C5-R), 3h 02m 47.900s; **5** Pedro Lamy/Gabriele Gardel, P/CH (Ferrari 550 Maranello), 102 laps; **6** Lilian Bryner/Enzo Calderari/Steve Zacchia, CH/I/CH (Ferrari 550 Maranello), 102; **7** Philipp Peter/Chris Buncombe/Roman Rusinov, A/GB/RUS (Maserati MC12), 101; **8** Christophe Bouchut/Nikolaj Fomenko/Alexei Vasiliev, F/RUS/RUS (Ferrari 550 Maranello), 100; **9** Emmanuel Collard/Tim Sugden, F/GB (Porsche 996 GT3-RSR), 100 (1st GT2 class); **10** Marc Lieb/Mike Rockenfeller, D/D (Porsche 996 GT3-RSR), 99.

Fastest race lap: Bertolini, 1m 38.826s, 99.843 mph/160.682 km/h.

Fastest qualifying lap: Bouchut/Fomenko/Vasiliev, 1m 36.580s, 102.165 mph/164.419 km/h.

FIA GT CHAMPIONSHIP, Silverstone International Circuit, Towcester, Northamptonshire, Great Britain, 15 May. Round 3. 134 laps of the 2.249-mile/3.620-km circuit, 301.415 miles/485.080 km.

1 Peter Kox/Pedro Lamy, NL/P (Aston Martin DBR9), 3h 00m 28.713s, 100.205 mph/161.265 km/h; **2** David Brabham/Darren Turner, AUS/GB (Aston Martin DBR9), 3h 00m 30.650s; **3** Fabio Babini/Thomas Biagi, I/I (Maserati MC12), 3h 00m 39.791s; **4** Andrea Bertolini/Karl Wendlinger, I/A (Maserati MC12), 133 laps; **5** Michael Bartels/Timo Scheider, D/D (Maserati MC12), 133; **6** Fabrizio Gollin/Gabriele Gardel, I/CH (Ferrari 550 Maranello), 133; **7** Andrea Piccini/Jean-Denis Deletraz, I/CH (Ferrari 575 Maranello GTC), 132; **8** Philipp Peter/Chris Buncombe/Roman Rusinov, A/GB/RUS (Maserati MC12), 132; **9** Marc Lieb/Mike Rockenfeller, D/D (Porsche 996 GT3-RSR), 129 (1st GT2 class); **10** Luca Pirri Ardizzone/Marco Panzavuota/Ryan Hooker, I/I/GB (Saleen S7R), 127.

Fastest race lap: Brabham, 1m 17.490s, 104.500 mph/168.177 km/h.

Fastest qualifying lap: Brabham/Turner, 1m 15.792s, 106.841 mph/171.944 km/h.

FIA GT CHAMPIONSHIP, Autodromo Enzo e Dino Ferrari, Imola, Italy, 29 May. Round 4. 97 laps of the 3.065-mile/4.933-km circuit, 297.327 miles/478.501 km.

1 Bert Longin/Anthony Kumpen/Mike Hezemans, B/B/NL (Chevrolet Corvette C5-R), 3h 01m 40.505s, 98.195 mph/158.030 km/h; **2** Pedro Lamy/Gabriele Gardel, P/CH (Ferrari 550 Maranello), 3h 01m 59.769s; **3** Fabio Babini/Thomas Biagi, I/I (Maserati MC12), 3h 02m 04.510s; **4** Andrea Bertolini/Karl Wendlinger, I/A (Maserati MC12), 3h 02m 34.262s; **5** Philipp Peter/Chris Buncombe/Roman Rusinov, A/GB/RUS (Maserati MC12), 96 laps; **6** Jaime Melo Jr./Jean-Philippe Belloc, BR/F (Ferrari 575 Maranello GTC), 94; **7** Emmanuel Collard/Tim Sugden, F/GB (Porsche 996 GT3-RSR), 94 (1st GT2 class); **8** Marc Lieb/Mike Rockenfeller, D/D (Porsche 996 GT3-RSR), 94; **9** Shaun Balfe/Jamie Derbyshire, GB/GB (Mosler MT900R), 89; **10** Enea Casoni/Edo Varini/Marco Panzavuota, I/I/I (Saleen S7R), 88.

Fastest race lap: Hezemans, 1m 47.868s, 102.299 mph/164.635 km/h.

Fastest qualifying lap: Longin/Kumpen/Hezemans, 1m 45.835s, 104.264 mph/167.797 km/h.

FIA GT CHAMPIONSHIP, Automotodrom Brno Masaryk Circuit, Brno, Czech Republic, 26 June. Round 5. 83 laps of the 3.357-mile/5.403-km circuit, 278.653 miles/448.449 km.
1 Pedro Lamy/Gabriele Gardel, P/CH (Ferrari 550 Maranello), 3h 01m 39.652s, 92.035 mph/148.116 km/h; **2** Andrea Bertolini/Karl Wendlinger, I/A (Maserati MC12), 3h 02m 37.688s; **3** Jaime Melo Jr./Jean-Philippe Belloc, BR/F (Ferrari 575 Maranello GTC), 3h 02m 39.515s; **4** Bert Longin/Anthony Kumpen/Mike Hezemans, B/B/NL (Chevrolet Corvette C5-R), 82 laps; **5** Michael Bartels/Timo Scheider, D/D (Maserati MC12), 82; **6** Philipp Peter/Chris Buncombe/Roman Rusinov, A/GB/RUS (Maserati MC12), 82; **7** Justin Keen/Liz Halliday, GB/GB (Lister Storm GT), 81; **8** Christophe Bouchut/Nikolaj Fomenko/Alexei Vasiliev, F/RUS/RUS (Ferrari 550 Maranello), 81; **9** Marc Lieb/Mike Rockenfeller, D/D (Porsche 996 GT3-RSR), 81 (1st GT2 class); **10** Andrea Montermini/Antonin Herbeck, I/CZ (Ferrari 575 Maranello GTC), 79.
Fastest race lap: Bartels, 1m 58.185s, 102.265 mph/164.579 km/h.
Fastest qualifying lap: Peter/Buncombe/Rusinov, 1m 56.322s, 103.903 mph/167.215 km/h.

SPA 24-HOURS, Circuit de Spa-Francorchamps, Stavelot, Belgium, 30-31 July. Round 6. 576 laps of the 4.316-mile/6.946-km circuit, 2486.042 miles/4000.896 km.
1 Timo Scheider/Eric van de Poele/Michael Bartels, D/B/D (Maserati MC12), 24h 00m 34.160s, 103.544 mph/166.638 km/h; **2** Andrea Bertolini/Karl Wendlinger/Philipp Peter, I/A/A (Maserati MC12), 574 laps; **3** Christophe Bouchut/Vincent Vosse/Kurt Mollekens/Gabriele Gardel, F/B/B/CH (Ferrari 550 Maranello), 567; **4** Lilian Bryner/Enzo Calderari/Steve Zacchia/Frederic Bouvy, CH/I/CH/B (Ferrari 550 Maranello), 562; **5** Peter Kox/Marc Goossens/Pedro Lamy, NL/B/P (Aston Martin DBR9), 557; **6** David Brabham/Darren Turner/Stéphane Sarrazin, AUS/GB/F (Asto Martin DBR9), 555; **7** Marc Lieb/Mike Rockenfeller/Lucas Luhr, D/D/D (Porsche 996 GT3-RSR), 541 (1st GT2 class); **8** Jos Menten/Marc Duez/Bruno Hernandez/Eric Cayrolle, NL/B/F/F (Chevrolet C5-R), 536; **9** Franco Groppi/Luigi Moccia/Joel Camathias, I/I/CH (Porsche 996 GT3-RSR), 535; **10** Thomas Erdos/Mike Newton/Michael Mallock/Phil Bennett, BR/GB/GB/GB (Saleen S7R), 529. DQ: Bert Longin/Anthony Kumpen/Mike Hezemans/Jeroen Bleekemolen, B/B/NL/NL (Chevrolet C5-R), 563 laps (data recording device not connected).
Fastest race lap: Jamie Davies, GB (Maserati MC12), 2m 15.598s, 114.587 mph/184.410 km/h.
Fastest qualifying lap: Scheider/van de Poele/Bartels, 2m 14.845s, 115.227 mph/185.440 km/h.

FIA GT CHAMPIONSHIP, Motopark Arena Oschersleben, Germany, 28 August. Round 7. 121 laps of the 2.279-mile/3.667-km circuit, 275.606 miles/443.545 km.
1 Fabio Babini/Thomas Biagi, I/I (Maserati MC12), 2h 58m 24.414s, 92.689 mph/149.169 km/h; **2** Andrea Bertolini/Karl Wendlinger, I/A (Maserati MC12), 2h 58m 44.704s; **3** Bert Longin/Anthony Kumpen/Mike Hezemans, B/B/NL (Chevrolet Corvette C5-R), 2h 58m 49.404s; **4** Robert Lechner/Jean-Marc Gounon, A/F (Saleen S7R), 2h 59m 22.516s; **5** Philipp Peter/Arjan van der Zwaan/Marcello Zani, A/NL/I (Maserati MC12), 2h 59m 39.647s; **6** Andrea Piccini/Jean-Denis Deletraz, I/CH (Ferrari 575 Maranello GTC), 120 laps; **7** Pedro Lamy/Gabriele Gardel, P/CH (Ferrari 550 Maranello), 120; **8** Peter Kox/Norman Simon, NL/D (Lamborghini Murcielago R-GT), 120; **9** Emmanuel Collard/Tim Sugden, F/GB (Porsche 996 GT3-RSR), 118 (1st GT2 class); **10** Marc Lieb/Mike Rockenfeller, D/D (Porsche 996 GT3-RSR), 117.
Fastest race lap: Hezemans, 1m 24.837s, 96.689 mph/155.607 km/h.
Fastest qualifying lap: Michael Bartels/Timo Scheider, D/D (Maserati MC12), 1m 22.991s, 98.840 mph/159.068 km/h.

FIA GT CHAMPIONSHIP, Istanbul Speed Park, Turkey, 18 September. Round 8. 59 laps of the 3.317-mile/5.338-km circuit, 195.567 miles/314.734 km.
1 Michael Bartels/Timo Scheider, D/D (Maserati MC12), 2h 00m 02.986s, 97.743 mph/157.302 km/h; **2** Fabio Babini/Thomas Biagi, I/I (Maserati MC12), 2h 00m 13.946s; **3** Andrea Bertolini/Karl Wendlinger, I/A (Maserati MC12), 2h 00m 29.973s; **4** Andrea Piccini/Jean-Denis Deletraz, I/CH (Ferrari 575 Maranello GTC), 2h 00m 59.457s; **5** Bert Longin/Anthony Kumpen/Mike Hezemans, B/B/NL (Chevrolet Corvette C5-R), 2h 01m 07.351s; **6** Pedro Lamy/Gabriele Gardel, P/CH (Ferrari 550 Maranello), 58 laps; **7** Emmanuel Collard/Tim Sugden, F/GB (Porsche 996 GT3-RSR), 58 (1st GT2 class); **8** Marc Lieb/Mike Rockenfeller, D/D (Porsche 996 GT3-RSR), 58; **9** Philipp Peter/Can Artam/Christophe Pillon, A/TR/CH (Maserati MC12), 58; **10** Christophe Bouchut/Nikolaj Fomenko/Alexei Vasiliev, F/RUS/RUS (Ferrari 550 Maranello), 57.
Fastest race lap: Babini, 1m 50.949s, 107.624 mph/173.204 km/h.
Fastest qualifying lap: Piccini/Deletraz, 1m 49.611s, 108.938 mph/175.318 km/h.

FIA GT CHAMPIONSHIP, Zhuhai International Circuit, Zhuhai City, Guangdong Province, China, 23 October. Round 9. 110 laps of the 2.672-mile/4.300-km circuit, 293.909 miles/473.000 km.
1 Bert Longin/Anthony Kumpen/Mike Hezemans, B/B/NL (Chevrolet Corvette C5-R), 3h 00m 21.567s, 97.774 mph/157.352 km/h; **2** Pedro Lamy/Gabriele Gardel, P/CH (Ferrari 550 Maranello), 3h 00m 28.727s; **3** Michael Bartels/Timo Scheider, D/D (Maserati MC12), 3h 01m 41.156s; **4** Fabio Babini/Thomas Biagi, I/I (Maserati MC12), 3h 01m 44.923s; **5** Andrea Piccini/Jean-Denis Deletraz, I/CH (Ferrari 575 Maranello GTC), 109 laps; **6** Andrea Bertolini/Karl Wendlinger, I/A (Maserati MC12), 109; **7** Marc Lieb/Mike Rockenfeller, D/D (Porsche 996 GT3-RSR), 107 (1st GT2 class); **8** Emmanuel Collard/Tim Sugden, F/GB (Porsche 996 GT3-RSR), 106; **9** Luigi Moccia/Cristian Passutti, I/I (Porsche 996 GT3-RSR), 104; **10** Matthew Marsh/Darryl O'Young, GB/CDN-PRC (Porsche 996 GT3-RSR), 103.
Fastest race lap: Lamy/Gardel, 1m 31.691s, 104.905 mph/168.828 km/h.
Fastest qualifying lap: Christophe Bouchut/Nikolaj Fomenko/Alexei Vasiliev, F/RUS/RUS (Ferrari 550 Maranello), 1m 30.661s, 106.097 mph/170.746 km/h.

Provisional championship points:
GT1 Drivers: 1= Karl Wendlinger, A, 66; **1=** Andrea Bertolini, I, 66; **3=** Timo Scheider, D, 62; **3=** Michael Bartels, D, 62; **5** Gabriele Gardel, CH, 60; **6=** Thomas Biagi, I, 59; **6=** Fabio Babini, I, 59; **8** Pedro Lamy, P, 45; **9=** Anthony Kumpen, B, 40; **9=** Bert Longin, B, 40; **9=** Mike Hezemans, NL, 40; **12** Philipp Peter, A, 37; **13** Eric van de Poele, B, 20; **14=** Chris Buncombe, GB, 17; **14=** Roman Rusinov, RUS, 17; **16=** Andrea Piccini, I, 16; **16=** Jean-Denis Deletraz, CH, 16; **18=** Enzo Calderari, I, 15; **18=** Lilian Bryner, CH, 15; **18=** Steve Zacchia, CH, 15. **GT1 Teams: 1** Vitaphone Racing Team, 121; **2** JMB Racing, 90; **3** Labre Compétition, 73; **4** GLPK-Carsport, 40; **5** G.P.C. Giesse Squadra Corse, 27.5. **GT1 Manufacturers: 1** Maserati, 210; **2** Ferrari, 102; **3** Corvette, 48.

GT2 Drivers: 1= Marc Lieb, D, 92; **1=** Mike Rockenfeller, D, 92; **3=** Emmanuel Collard, F, 64; **3=** Tim Sugden, GB, 64; **5** Luigi Moccia, I, 45; **6** Christian Ried, D, 39; **7** Gerold Ried, D, 39; **8** Jan Vonka, CZ, 27.5; **9** Emanuele Busnelli, I, 23; **10** Lucas Luhr, D, 20. **GT2 Teams: 1** GruppeM Racing, 156; **2** Proton Competition, 39; **3** Ebimotors, 29. **GT2 Manufacturers: 1** Porsche, 280; **2** Ferrari, 24; **3** TVR, 11.

Results of the Dubai and Bahrain races will be given in AUTOCOURSE 2006–2007.

Le Mans Endurance Series

1000km of SPA, Circuit de Spa-Francorchamps, Stavelot, Belgium, 17 April. Round 1. 132 laps of the 4.335-mile/6.976-km circuit, 572.178 miles/920.832 km.
1 Casper Elgaard/John Nielsen/Hayanari Shimoda, DK/DK/J (Zytek 04S), 6h 00m 48.389s, 95.150 mph/153.129 km/h; **2** Emmanuel Collard/Jean-Christophe Boullion/Erik Comas, F/F/F (Pescarolo C60-Judd), 131 laps; **3** Vanina Ickx/Rob Barff/Martin Short, B/GB/GB (Dallara LMP-Judd), 127; **4** Ryo Michigami/Juichi Wakisaka/Seiji Ara, J/J/J (Dome S101-Mugen), 126; **5** Bob Berridge/Gareth Evans/Peter Owen, GB/GB/GB (Lola B05/40-AER), 124; **6** Fabrizio Gollin/Matteo Cressoni/Miguel Ramos, I/I/P (Ferrari 550 Maranello), 123; **7** Christophe Tinseau/Christophe Pillon/Ni Amorim, F/CH/P (Courage C65-Mecachrome), 121; **8** Warren Hughes/Jonny Kane, GB/GB (TVR Tuscan T400R), 120; **9** Christophe Bouchut/Nikolaj Fomenko/Alexei Vasiliev, F/RUS/RUS (Ferrari 550 Maranello), 120; **10** Marc Hynes/Patrick Pearce/Jason Templemann, GB/GB/GB (TVR Tuscan T400R), 119.
Fastest race lap: Elgaard, 2m 10.270s, 119.788 mph/192.781 km/h.
Fastest qualifying lap: Boullion, 2m 21.076s, 110.613 mph/178.015 km/h.

1000km of MONZA, Autodromo Nazionale di Monza, Milan, Italy, 10 July. Round 2. 173 laps of the 3.600-mile/5.793-km circuit, 622.731 miles/1002.189 km.
1 Emmanuel Collard/Jean-Christophe Boullion/Erik Comas, F/F/F (Pescarolo C60-Judd), 5h 02m 32.220s, 123.502 mph/198.756 km/h; **2** Sam Hignett/John Stack/Haruki Kurosawa, GB/GB/J (Zytek 04S), 168 laps; **3** Vanina Ickx/João Barbosa/Martin Short, B/P/GB (Dallara LMP-Judd), 166; **4** Vincent Vosse/Claude-Yves Gosselin/Karim Ojjeh, B/F/ZA (Courage C65-AER), 165; **5** Bob Berridge/Gareth Evans/Peter Owen, GB/GB/GB (Lola B05/40-AER), 164; **6** Jean-Marc Gounon/Alexander Frei/Christian Vann, F/CH/GB (Courage C60 H-Judd), 161; **7** Nicolas Minassian/Jamie Campbell-Walter, F/GB (DBA 03S-Judd), 160; **8** Christian Pescatori/Michele Bartyan/Toni Seiler, I/I/CH (Ferrari 550 Maranello), 158; **9** Tomás Enge/Jaroslav 'Janek' Janis/Robert Pergl, CZ/CZ/CZ (Ferrari 550 Maranello), 158; **10** Hayanari Shimoda/Tom Chilton, J/GB (Zytek 04S), 157.
Fastest race lap: Shimoda, 1m 39.437s, 130.319 mph/209.729 km/h.
Fastest qualifying lap: Shimoda/Chilton, 1m 37.938s, 132.314 mph/212.938 km/h.

1000km of SILVERSTONE, Silverstone Grand Prix Circuit, Towcester, Northamptonshire, Great Britain, 13 August. Round 3. 151 laps of the 3.194-mile/5.140-km circuit, 482.294 miles/776.177 km.
1 Stéphane Ortelli/Allan McNish, MC/GB (Audi R8), 5h 51m 09.527s, 82.406 mph/132.620 km/h; **2** Nicolas Minassian/Jamie Campbell-Walter, F/GB (DBA 03S-Judd), 5h 51m 16.096s; **3** Vanina Ickx/João Barbosa/Martin Short, B/P/GB (Dallara LMP900-Judd), 144 laps; **4** Vincent Vosse/Claude-Yves Gosselin/Karim Ojjeh, B/F/ZA (Courage C65-AER), 143; **5** Peter Kox/Jaroslav 'Janek' Janis/Robert Pergl, NL/CZ/CZ (Ferrari 550 Maranello), 143; **6** Sam Hignett/John Stack/Haruki Kurosawa, GB/GB/J (Zytek 04S), 142; **7** Christophe Bouchut/Alexei Vasiliev, F/RUS (Ferrari 550 Maranello), 142; **8** Phil Bennett/Michael Vergers/Juan Barazi, DK/NL/DK (Courage C65-Judd), 141; **9** Xavier Pompidou/Marc Lieb, F/D (Porsche 996 GT3-RSR), 141; **10** Thomas Erdos/Mike Newton, BR/GB (MG Lola EX264-AER), 141.
Fastest race lap: Ortelli, 1m 53.635s, 101.187 mph/162.845 km/h.
Fastest qualifying lap: Minassian/Campbell-Walter, 1m 34.562s, 121.596 mph/195.600 km/h.

1000km of NÜRBURGRING, Nürburgring Grand Prix Circuit, Nürburg/Eifel, Germany, 4 September. Round 4. 193 laps of the 3.192-mile/5.137-km circuit, 616.053 miles/991.441 km.
1 Hayanari Shimoda/Tom Chilton, J/GB (Zytek 04S), 6h 01m 06.739s, 102.359 mph/164.731 km/h; **2** Stéphane Ortelli/Allan McNish, MC/GB (Audi R8), 6h 01m 17.506s; **3** Nicolas Minassian/Jamie Campbell-Walter, F/GB (DBA 03S-Judd), 6h 01m 31.262s; **4** Emmanuel Collard/Jean-Christophe Boullion, F/F (Pescarolo C60-Judd), 192 laps; **5** Vanina Ickx/João Barbosa/Martin Short, B/P/GB (Dallara LMP900-Judd), 187; **6** Sam Hignett/John Stack/Gregor Fisken, GB/GB/GB (Zytek 04S), 185; **7** Didier Theys/Eric van de Poele, B/B (Lola B05/40-AER), 184; **8** Jonathan Cochet/Alexander Frei, F/CH (Courage C60 H-Judd), 183; **9** Darren Turner/Rob Bell, GB/GB (Aston Martin DBR9), 179; **10** Matteo Cressoni/Matteo Malucelli/Miguel Ramos, I/I/P (Ferrari 550 Maranello), 178.
Fastest race lap: Shimoda, 1m 46.062s, 108.344 mph/174.362 km/h.
Fastest qualifying lap: Minassian/Campbell-Walter, 1m 44.965s, 109.476 mph/176.184 km/h (Shimoda/Chilton set the fastest lap of 1m 44.275s, 110.200 mph/177.350 km/h, but this was disallowed due to a technical abnormality).

Provisional championship points
P1 Drivers: 1 Hayanari Shimoda, J, 27; **2=** Jean-Christophe Boullion, F, 24; **2=** Emmanuel Collard, F, 24; **4=** Vanina Ickx, B, 22; **4=** Martin Short, GB, 22; **6=** Nicolas Minassian, F, 18; **6=** Jamie Campbell-Walter, GB, 18; **6=** Stéphane Ortelli, MC, 18; **6=** Allan McNish, GB, 18; **10** Tom Chilton, GB, 17; **11=** Sam Hignett, GB, 16; **11=** John Stack, GB, 16; **11=** João Barbosa, P, 16; **14** Haruki Kurosawa, J, 13; **15=** Casper Elgaard, DK, 10; **15=** John Nielsen, DK, 10; **15=** Alexander Frei, CH, 10; **15=** Christian Vann, GB, 10; **19** Erik Comas, F, 8; **20** Rob Barff, GB, 6; **21=** Seiji Ara, J, 5; **21=** Ryo Michigami, J, 5; **21=** Juichi Wakisaka, J, 5; **21=** Jean-Marc Gounon, F, 5; **21=** Jonathan Cochet, F, 5. **P1 Teams: 1** Zytek Motorsport, 27; **2** Pescarolo Sport, 24; **3** Rollcentre Racing, 22.

P2 Drivers: 1= Bob Berridge, GB, 26; **1=** Gareth Evans, GB, 26; **3=** Claude-Yves Gosselin, F, 23; **3=** Vincent Vosse, B, 23; **3=** Thomas Erdos, BR, 23; **3=** Mike Newton, GB, 23; **7** Peter Owen, GB, 18; **8** Didier Theys, B, 15; **9** Karim Ojjeh, ZA, 13; **10=** Ni Amorim, P, 10; **10=** Christophe Tinseau, F, 10; **10=** Eric van de Poele, B, 10; **10=** Paul Belmondo, F, 10; **10=** Didier André, F, 10. **P2 Teams: 1** Chamberlain Synergy Motorsport, 26; **2=** Paul Belmondo Racing, 23; **2=** RML, 23.

GT1 Drivers: 1 Matteo Cressoni, I, 27; **2=** Christophe Bouchut, F, 26; **2=** Alexei Vasiliev, RUS, 26; **4=** Michele Bartyan, I, 25; **4=** Christian Pescatori, I, 25; **4=** Toni Seiler, CH, 25. **GT1 Teams: 1** BMS Scuderia Italia (car no.52), 27; **2** Convers Team, 26; **3** BMS Scuderia Italia (car no.51), 25.

GT2 Drivers: 1= Xavier Pompidou, F, 30; **1=** Marc Lieb, D, 30; **3=** Franco Groppi, I, 20; **3=** Luigi Moccia, I, 20; **5=** Andrew Kirkcaldy, GB, 18; **5=** Nathan Kinch, GB, 18. **GT2 Teams: 1** Sebah Automotive, 30; **2** Autorlando Sport, 20; **3** Scuderia Ecosse, 18.

Result of the Istanbul race will be given in AUTOCOURSE 2006–2007

American Le Mans Series

MOBIL 1 12 HOURS OF SEBRING, Sebring International Raceway Florida, USA, 19 March. Round 1. 361 laps of the 3.700-mile/5.955-km circuit, 1335.700 miles/2149.601km.
1 JJ Lehto/Marco Werner/Tom Kristensen, FIN/D/DK (Audi R8), 12h 01m 49.211s, 111.028 mph/178.682 km/h, **2** Emanuele Pirro/Frank Biela/Allan McNish, I/D/GB (Audi R8), 12h 01m 55.576s; **3** James Weaver/Andy Wallace/Butch Leitzinger, GB/GB/USA (Lola EX257-AER), 341 laps; **4** Darren Turner/David Brabham/Stéphane Ortelli, GB/AUS/MC (Aston Martin DBR9), 338 (1st GT1 class); **5** Ron Fellows/Johnny O'Connell/Massimiliano 'Max' Papis, CDN/USA/I (Chevrolet Corvette C6-R), 337; **6** Oliver Gavin/Olivier Beretta/Jan Magnussen, GB/MC/DK (Chevrolette Corvette C6-R), 323; **7** Jörg Bergmeister/Patrick Long/Lucas Luhr, D/USA/D (Porsche 911 GT3-RSR), 321 (1st GT2 class); **8** Johnny Mowlem/Ralf Kelleners/Terry Borcheller, GB/D/USA (Saleen S7R), 318 (DNF-mechanical); **9** Andrea Bertolini/Fabrizio de Simone/Fabio Babini, I/I/I (Maserati MC12), 316; **10** Ryan Dalziel/Alex Figge/David Empringham, GB/USA/CDN (Chevrolet Corvette C5-R), 315.
Fastest race lap: Kristensen, 1m 48.580s, 122.675 mph/197.426 km/h.
Fastest qualifying lap: Lehto, 1m 49.723s, 121.397 mph/195.369 km/h. (based on practice times due to bad weather).

SPORTSBOOK.COM GRAND PRIX OF ATLANTA, Road Atlanta, Braselton, Georgia, USA, 17 April. Round 2. 112 laps of the 2.540-mile/4.088-km circuit, 284.480 miles/457.826 km.
1 Marco Werner/JJ Lehto, D/FIN (Audi R8), 2h 45m 27.420s, 103.162 mph/166.022 km/h; **2** Chris Dyson/Andy Wallace, USA/GB (Lola EX257-AER), 2h 46m 12.205s; **3** Emanuele Pirro/Frank Biela, I/D (Audi R8), 111 laps; **4** Jon Field/Clint Field, USA/USA (Lola B05/40-AER), 108 (1st P2 class); **5** Johnny O'Connell/Ron Fellows, USA/CDN (Chevrolet Corvette C6-R), 108 (1st GT1 class); **6** Olivier Beretta/Oliver Gavin, MC/GB (Chevrolet Corvette C6-R), 107; **7** Andrea Bertolini/Fabrizio de Simone, I/I (Maserati MC12), 107; **8** Johnny Mowlem/Terry Borcheller, GB/USA (Saleen S7R), 107; **9** Alex Figge/Ryan Dalziel, USA/GB (Chevrolet Corvette C5-R), 106; **10** James Weaver/Butch Leitzinger, GB/USA (Lola EX257-AER), 105 (DNF-fire).
Fastest race lap: Lehto, 1m 12.784s, 125.632 mph/202.185 km/h.
Fastest qualifying lap: Weaver/Leitzinger, 1m 11.241s, 128.353 mph/206.564 km/h.

AMERICAN LE MANS AT MID-OHIO, Mid-Ohio Sports Car Course, Lexington, Ohio, USA, 22 May. Round 3. 117 laps of the 2.258-mile/3.634-km circuit, 264.186 miles/425.166 km.
1 James Weaver/Butch Leitzinger, GB/USA (Lola EX257-AER), 2h 46m 05.925s, 95.432 mph/153.583 km/h; **2** Chris Dyson/Andy Wallace, USA/GB (Lola EX257-AER), 2h 46m 32.253s; **3** Emanuele Pirro/Frank Biela, I/D (Audi R8), 116 laps; **4** Hayanari Shimoda/Tom Chilton, J/GB (Zytek 04S), 113 (DNF); **5** Johnny O'Connell/Ron Fellows, USA/CDN (Chevrolet Corvette C6-R), 112 (1st GT1 class); **6** Olivier Beretta/Oliver Gavin, MC/GB (Chevrolet Corvette C6-R), 112; **7** Johnny Mowlem/Terry Borcheller, GB/USA (Saleen S7R), 112; **8** Alex Figge/Ryan Dalziel, USA/GB (Chevrolet Corvette C5-R), 110; **9** Timo Bernhard/Romain Dumas, D/F (Porsche 911 GT3-RSR), 109 (1st GT2 class); **10** Jörg Bergmeister/Patrick Long, D/USA (Porsche 911 GT3-RSR), 109.
Fastest race lap: Shimoda, 1m 12.592s, 111.979 mph/180.213 km/h.
Fastest qualifying lap: Shimoda, 1m 11.333s, 113.956 mph/183.394 km/h.

NEW ENGLAND GRAND PRIX, Lime Rock Park, Lakeville, Connecticut, USA, 4 July. Round 4. 165 laps of the 1.540-mile/2.478-km circuit, 254.100 miles/408.934 km.
1 JJ Lehto/Marco Werner, FIN/D (Audi R8), 2h 45m 48.079s, 91.953 mph/147.985 km/h; **2** Emanuele Pirro/Frank Biela, I/D (Audi R8), 2h 45m 49.796s; **3** Oliver Gavin/Olivier Beretta, GB/MC (Chevrolette Corvette C6-R), 159 laps (1ST GT1 class); **4** Ron Fellows/Johnny O'Connell, CDN/USA (Chevrolet Corvette C6-R), 157; **5** Johnny Mowlem/Terry Borcheller, GB/USA (Saleen S7R), 156; **6** Andrea Bertolini/Fabrizio de Simone, I/I (Maserati MC12), 156; **7** Alex Figge/Ryan Dalziel, USA/GB (Chevrolet Corvette C5-R), 155; **8** Timo Bernhard/Romain Dumas, D/F (Porsche 911 GT3-RSR), 154 (1st GT2 class); **9** John Macaluso/Chris McMurry/Jeff Bucknum, USA/USA/USA (Courage C65-AER), 154 (1st P2 class); **10** Jörg Bergmeister/Patrick Long/Michael Petersen, D/USA/USA (Porsche 911 GT3-RSR), 153.
Fastest race lap: Biela, 47.787s, 116.015 mph/186.700 km/h.
Fastest qualifying lap: Werner, 46.753s, 118.581 mph/190.837 km/h.

INFINEON GRAND PRIX OF SONOMA, Infineon Raceway, Sears Point, Sonoma, California, USA, 17 July. Round 5. 111 laps of the 2.530-mile/4.072-km circuit, 280.830 miles/451.952 km.
1 Emanuele Pirro/Frank Biela, I/D (Audi R8), 2h 46m 10.805s, 101.395 mph/163.179 km/h; **2** Chris Dyson/Andy Wallace, USA/GB (Lola EX257-AER), 2h 47m 35.377s; **3** JJ Lehto/Marco Werner, FIN/D (Audi R8), 110 laps; **4** Clint Field/Liz Halliday, USA/GB (Lola B05/40-AER), 105 (1st P2 class); **5** James Weaver/Butch Leitzinger, GB/USA (Lola EX257-AER), 105; **6** John Macaluso/Chris McMurry/Jeff Bucknum, USA/USA/USA (Courage C65-AER), 105; **7** Ron Fellows/Johnny O'Connell, CDN/USA (Chevrolet Corvette C6-R), 104 (1st GT1 class); **8** Olivier Beretta/Oliver Gavin, MC/GB (Chevrolet Corvette C6-R), 104; **9** Johnny Mowlem/Terry Borcheller, GB/USA (Saleen S7R), 104; **10** Jamie Bach/Guy Cosmo, USA/USA (Courage C65-Mazda), 102.
Fastest race lap: Werner, 1m 22.041s, 111.018 mph/178.666 km/h.
Fastest qualifying lap: Wallace, 1m 21.688s, 111.497 mph/179.438 km/h.

PORTLAND GRAND PRIX, Portland International Raceway, Oregon, USA, 30 July. Round 6. 137 laps of the 1.964-mile/3.161-km circuit, 269.068 miles/433.025 km.
1 Emanuele Pirro/Frank Biela, I/D (Audi R8), 2h 45m 06.409s, 97.780 mph/157.361 km/h; **2** Chris Dyson/Andy Wallace, USA/GB (Lola EX257-AER), 2h 45m 12.469s; **3** James Weaver/Butch Leitzinger, GB/USA (Lola-EX257-AER), 136 laps (DNF-mechanical); **4** Clint Field/Gregor Fisken, USA/GB (Lola B05/40-AER), 132 (1st P2 class); **5** Olivier Beretta/Oliver Gavin, MC/GB (Chevrolet Corvette C6-R), 131 (1st GT1 class); **6** Johnny O'Connell/Ron Fellows, USA/CDN (Chevrolet Corvette C6-R), 131; **7** Michael Lewis/Bryan Willman, USA/USA (Riley & Scott MkIIIC-Elan), 130; **8** Alex Figge/Ryan Dalziel, USA/GB (Chevrolet Corvette C5-R), 130; **9** Mika Salo/Fabrizio de Simone, FIN/I (Maserati MC12), 129; **10** Timo Bernhard/Romain Dumas, D/F (Porsche 911 GT3-RSR), 125 (1st GT2 class).
Fastest race lap: Wallace, 1m 04.271s, 110.009 mph/177.043 km/h.
Fastest qualifying lap: Wallace, 1m 02.712s, 112.744 mph/181.444 km/h.

GENERAC 500 AT ROAD AMERICA, Road America Circuit, Elkhart Lake, Wisconsin, USA, 21 August. Round 7. 72 laps of the 4.048-mile/6.515-km circuit, 291.456 miles/469.053 km.
1 Emanuele Pirro/Frank Biela, I/D (Audi R8), 2h 45m 46.441s, 105.489 mph/169.768 km/h; **2** Chris Dyson/Andy Wallace, USA/GB (Lola EX257-AER), 2h 45m 49.680s; **3** JJ Lehto/Marco Werner, FIN/D (Audi R8), 2h 45m 50.218s; **4** Olivier Beretta/Oliver Gavin, MC/GB (Chevrolet Corvette C6-R), 71 laps (1st GT1 class); **5** Ron Fellows/Johnny O'Connell, CDN/USA (Chevrolet Corvette C6-R), 71; **6** John Macaluso/Chris McMurry/Jeff Bucknum, USA/USA/USA (Courage C65-AER), 69 (1st P2 class); **7** Michael Lewis/Bryan Willman, USA/USA (Riley & Scott MkIIIC-Elan), 69; **8** Andrea Bertolini/Fabrizio de Simone, I/I (Maserati MC12), 69; **9** Jörg Bergmeister/Patrick Long, D/USA (Porsche 911 GT3-RSR), 69 (1st GT2 class); **10** Timo Bernhard/Romain Dumas, D/F (Porsche 911 GT3-RSR), 69.
Fastest race lap: Pirro, 1m 54.569s, 127.197 mph/204.703 km/h.
Fastest qualifying lap: James Weaver, GB (Lola EX257-AER), 1m 53.042s, 128.915 mph/207.468 km/h.

LABOUR DAY WEEKEND GRAND PRIX OF MOSPORT, Mosport Park, Bowmanville, Ontario, Canada, 4 September. Round 8. 127 laps of the 2.459-mile/3.957-km circuit, 312.293 miles/502.587 km.
1 James Weaver/Butch Leitzinger, GB/USA (Lola EX257-AER), 2h 31m 04.796s, 124.024 mph/199.598 km/h; **2** Marco Werner/JJ Lehto, D/FIN (Audi R8), 2h 31m 08.421s; **3** Emanuele Pirro/Frank Biela, I/D (Audi R8), 126 laps; **4** Chris Dyson/Andy Wallace, USA/GB (Lola EX257-AER), 125; **5** Clint Field/Liz Halliday/Jon Field, USA/GB/USA (Lola B05/40-AER), 120 (1st P2 class); **6** Olivier Beretta/Oliver Gavin, MC/GB (Chevrolet Corvette C6-R), 119 (1st GT1 class); **7** Ron Fellows/Johnny O'Connell, CDN/USA (Chevrolet Corvette C6-R), 119; **8** Johnny Mowlem/Terry Borcheller, GB/USA (Saleen S7R), 119; **9** Andrea Bertolini/Fabrizio de Simone, I/I (Maserati MC12), 118; **10** John Macaluso/Chris McMurry/Jeff Bucknum, USA/USA/USA (Courage C65-AER), 117.
Fastest race lap: Leitzinger, 1m 08.596s, 129.051 mph/207.688 km/h.
Fastest qualifying lap: Dyson, 1m 07.682s, 130.794 mph/210.493 km/h.

PETITE LE MANS, Road Atlanta, Braselton, Georgia, USA, 1 October. Round 9. 394 laps of the 2.540-mile/4.088-km circuit, 1000.760 miles/1610.567 km.
1 Emanuele Pirro/Frank Biela, I/D (Audi R8), 9h 16m 20.630s, 107.929 mph/173.695 km/h; **2** Chris Dyson/Guy Smith, USA/GB (Lola EX257-AER), 382 laps; **3** Oliver Gavin/Olivier Beretta/Jan Magnussen, GB/MC/DK (Chevrolette Corvette C6-R), 379 (1st GT2 class); **4** Darren Turner/David Brabham/Jonny Kane, GB/AUS/GB (Aston Martin DBR9), 378; **5** Clint Field/Liz Halliday/Jon Field, USA/GB/USA (Lola B05/40-AER), 375 (1st P2 class); **6** Johnny Mowlem/Ralf Kelleners/Terry Borcheller, GB/D/USA (Saleen S7R), 373; **7** JJ Lehto/Marco Werner, FIN/D (Audi R8), 372; **8** Andrea Bertolini/Fabrizio de Simone/Fabio Babini, I/I/I (Maserati MC12), 371; **9** Jörg Bergmeister/Patrick Long/Craig Stanton, D/USA/USA (Porsche 911 GT3-RSR), 364 (1st GT2 class); **10** Ian Baas/Emmanuel Collard/Marcel Tiemann, USA/F/D (Porsche 911 GT3-RSR), 363.
Fastest race lap: Lehto, 1m 12.958s, 125.332 mph/201.703 km/h.

Fastest qualifying lap: Hayanari Shimoda, J (Zytek 04S), 1m 10.781s, 129.187 mph/207.907 km/h.

MONTEREY SPORTS CAR CHAMPIONSHIPS, Mazda Raceway Laguna Seca, Monterey, California, USA, 16 October. Round 10. 164 laps of the 2.238-mile/3.602-km circuit, 367.032 miles/509.681 km.
1 Hayanari Shimoda/Tom Chilton, J/GB (Zytek 04S), 3h 59m 57.347s, 91.775 mph/147.697 km/h; **2** Emanuele Pirro/Frank Biela, I/D (Audi R8), 4h 01m 12.411s; **3** Chris Dyson/Andy Wallace, USA/GB (Lola EX257-AER), 163 laps; **4** JJ Lehto/Marco Werner, FIN/D (Audi R8), 163; **5** Sascha Maassen/Lucas Luhr, D/D (Porsche RS Spyder), 163 (1st P2 class); **6** James Weaver/Butch Leitzinger, GB/USA (Lola EX257-AER), 162; **7** Oliver Gavin/Olivier Beretta, GB/MC (Chevrolette Corvette C6-R), 158 (1st GT1 class); **8** Ron Fellows/Johnny O'Connell, CDN/USA (Chevrolet Corvette C6-R), 157; **9** Peter Kox/Pedro Lamy, NL/P (Aston Martin DBR9), 156; **10** Darren Turner/David Brabham, GB/AUS (Aston Martin DBR9), 155.
Fastest race lap: Shimoda, 1m 16.480s, 105.345 mph/169.537 km/h.
Fastest qualifying lap: Shimoda/Chilton, 1m 14.185s, 108.604 mph/174.781 km/h.

Final championship points:
P1 Drivers: 1= Frank Biela, D, 182; **1=** Emanuele Pirro, I, 182; **3** Chris Dyson, USA, 154; **4=** JJ Lehto, FIN, 148; **4=** Marco Werner, D, 148; **6** Andy Wallace, GB, 135; **7=** James Weaver, GB, 124; **7=** Butch Leitzinger, USA, 124; **9=** Michael Lewis, USA, 45; **9=** Bryan Willman, USA, 45; **11** Guy Smith, GB, 38; **12=** Hayanari Shimoda, J, 33; **12=** Tom Chilton, GB, 33; **14** Tom Kristensen, DK, 26; **15** Allan McNish, GB, 22. **P1 Teams: 1** ADT Champion Racing, 200; **2** Dyson Racing Team, 174. **P1 Chassis Manufacturers: 1** Audi, 200; **2** Lola, 174; **3** Riley & Scott, 45; **4** Zytek, 33. **P1 Engine Manufacturers: 1** Audi, 200; **2** AER, 174; **3** Elan, 45; **4** Zytek, 33.
P2 Drivers: 1 Clint Field, USA, 133; **2=** Chris McMurry, USA, 117; **2=** Jeff Bucknum, USA, 117; **4=** Guy Cosmo, USA, 116; **4=** Jamie Bach, USA, 116. **P2 Chassis Manufacturers: 1** Courage, 191; **2** Lola, 167. **P2 Engine Manufacturers: 1** AER, 207; **2** Mazda, 116. **P2 Teams: 1** Intersport Racing, 133; **2** Miracle Motorsports, 117; **3** B-K Motorsports Inc., 116.

GT1 Drivers: 1= Oliver Gavin, GB, 196; **1=** Olivier Beretta, MC, 196; **3=** Ron Fellows, CDN, 177; **3=** Johnny O'Connell, USA, 177; **5=** Terry Borcheller, USA, 114; **5=** Johnny Mowlem, GB, 114; **7=** Tom Weickardt, USA, 75; **7=** Michele Rugolo, I, 75; **9=** Alex Figge, USA, 65; **9=** Ryan Dalziel, GB, 65; **11=** David Brabham, AUS, 61; **11=** Darren Turner, GB, 61; **13** Jan Magnussen, DK, 45; **14=** Peter Kox, NL, 39; **14=** Pedro Lamy, P, 39; **16** Ralf Kelleners, D, 35; **17** Massimiliano 'Max' Papis, I, 34; **18** Jean-Philippe Belloc, F, 28; **19** Stéphane Ortelli, MC, 26; **20** Jonny Kane, GB, 22. **GT1 Automobile Manufacturers: 1** Chevrolet, 211; **2** Saleen, 114; **3** Dodge, 75. **GT1 Teams: 1** Corvette Racing, 211; **2** ACEMCO Motorsports, 114; **3** Carsport America, 75.

GT2 Drivers: 1= Patrick Long, USA, 179; **1=** Jörg Bergmeister, D, 179; **3=** Timo Bernhard, D, 145; **3=** Romain Dumas, F, 145; **5=** Johannes van Overbeeck, USA, 114; **5=** Jon Fogarty, USA, 114. **GT2 Automobile Manufacturers: 1** Porsche, 211; **2** Panoz, 85. **GT2 Teams: 1** Petersen/White Lightning Racing, 179; **2** Alex Job Racing, 161.

All-Japan (Super) GT Championship

OKAYAMA GT300 km, Okayama International Circuit (TI Circuit Aida), Aida Gun, Okayama Prefecture, Japan, 27 March. Round 1. 82 laps of the 2.301-mile/3.703-km circuit, 188.677 miles/303.646 km.
1 Manabu Orido/Dominik Schwager, J/D (Toyota Supra GT), 2h 02m 29.899s, 92.444 mph/148.727 km/h; **2** Takeshi Tsuchiya/James Courtney, J/GB (Toyota Supra GT), 2h 02m 33.393s; **3** Toshihiro Kaneishi/Erik Comas, J/F (Nissan Fairlady Z), 2h 02m 51.302s; **4** Daisuke Ito/Ralph Firman, J/GB (Honda NSX), 2h 03m 00.432s; **5** Tsugio Matsuda/Andre Lotterer, J/D (Honda NSX), 2h 03m 18.075s; **6** Tatsuya Kataoka/Sakon Yamamoto, J/J (Toyota Supra GT), 2h 03m 21310s; **7** Ryo Michigami/Takashi Kogure, J/J (Honda NSX), 2h 03m 35.940s; **8** Andre Couto/Ronnie Quintarelli, P/I (Toyota Supra GT), 81 laps; **9** Naoki Hattori/Shigekazu Wakisaka, J/J (Toyota Supra GT), 81; **10** Sébastien Philippe/Jérémie Dufour, F/F (Honda NSX), 81.
Fastest race lap: Satoshi Motoyama/Richard Lyons, J/GB (Nissan Fairlady Z), 1m 26.350s, 95.928 mph/154.381 km/h.
Fastest qualifying lap: Michael Krumm/Masataka Yanagida, D/J (Nissan Fairlady Z), 1m 23.999s, 98.613 mph/158.702 km/h.

FUJI GT 500km, Fuji International Speedway, Sunto-gun, Shizuoka Prefecture, Japan, 4 May. Round 2. 110 laps of the 2.835-mile/4.563-km circuit, 311.885 miles/501.930 km.
1 Yuji Tachikawa/Toranosuke Takagi, J/J (Toyota Supra GT), 2h 59m 16.717s, 104.380 mph/167.983 km/h; **2** Michael Krumm/Masataka Yanagida, D/J (Nissan Fairlady Z), 2h 59m 49.552s; **3** Naoki Hattori/Shigekazu Wakisaka, J/J (Toyota Supra GT), 2h 59m 49.657s; **4** Richard Lyons/Satoshi Motoyama, GB/J (Nissan Fairlady Z), 2h 59m 58.973s; **5** Juichi Wakisaka/Akira Iida, J/J (Toyota Supra GT), 3h 00m 13.331s; **6** Tatsuya Kataoka/Sakon Yamamoto, J/J (Toyota Supra GT), 3h 00m 26.465s; **7** Seiji Ara/Naoki Yokomizo, J/J (Toyota Supra GT), 3h 00m 45.247s; **8** Tsugio Matsuda/Andre Lotterer, J/D (Honda NSX), 109 laps; **9** Toshihiro Kaneishi/Erik Comas, J/F (Nissan Fairlady Z), 109; **10** Takeshi Tsuchiya/James Courtney, J/GB (Toyota Supra GT), 109.
Fastest race lap: Kataoka/Yamamoto, 1m 34.626s, 107.868 mph/173.597 km/h.
Fastest qualifying lap: Tachikawa/Takagi, 1m 33.070s, 109.672 mph/176.499 km/h.

JAPAN GT CHAMPIONSHIP MALAYSIA, Sepang Circuit, Kuala Lumpur, Malaysia, 26 June. Round 3. 54 laps of the 3.444-mile/5.543-km circuit, 185.990 miles/299.322 km.
1 Satoshi Motoyama/Richard Lyons, J/GB (Nissan Fairlady Z), 1h 52m 39.660s, 99.053 mph/159.410 km/h; **2** Daisuke Ito/Ralph Firman, J/GB (Honda NSX), 1h 52m 44.159s; **3** Takeshi Tsuchiya/James Courtney, J/GB (Toyota Supra GT), 1h 52m 55.035s; **4** Juichi Wakisaka/Akira Iida, J/J (Toyota Supra GT), 1h 53m 06.145s; **5** Tsugio Matsuda/Andre Lotterer, J/D (Honda NSX), 1h 53m 06.931s; **6** Michael Krumm/Masataka Yanagida, D/J (Nissan Fairlady Z), 1h 53m 13.347s; **7** Ryo Michigami/Takashi Kogure, J/J (Honda NSX), 1h 53m 13.612s; **8** Benoit Tréluyer/Yuji Ide, F/J (Nissan Fairlady Z), 1h 53m 30.055s; **9** Andre Couto/Ronnie Quintarelli, P/I (Toyota Supra GT), 1h 53m 33.129s; **10** Sébastien Philippe/Jérémie Dufour, F/F (Honda NSX), 1h 53m 46.27s.
Fastest race lap: Ito/Firman, 2m 00.888s, 102.569 mph/165.068 km/h.
Fastest qualifying lap: Ito/Firman, 1m 57.824s, 105.236 mph/169.361 km/h.

SUGO GT 300km, Sportsland SUGO International Course, Shibata-gun, Miyagi Prefecture, Japan, 24 July. Round 4. 78 laps of the 2.302-mile/3.704-km circuit, 179.522 miles/288.912 km.
Race staged over 2 sectors of 10 and 68 laps.
1 Tatsuya Kataoka/Sakon Yamamoto, J/J (Toyota Supra GT), 78 laps; **2** Andre Couto/Ronnie Quintarelli, P/I (Toyota Supra GT), 78; **3** Takeshi Tsuchiya/James Courtney, J/GB (Toyota Supra GT), 78; **4** Juichi Wakisaka/Akira Iida, J/J (Toyota Supra GT), 78; **5** Benoit Tréluyer/Yuji Ide, F/J (Nissan Fairlady Z), 78; **6** Daisuke Ito/Ralph Firman, J/GB (Honda NSX), 78; **7** Michael Krumm/Masataka Yanagida, D/J (Nissan Fairlady Z), 78; **8** Satoshi Motoyama/Richard Lyons, J/GB (Nissan Fairlady Z), 78; **9** Manabu Orido/Dominik Schwager, J/D (Toyota Supra GT), 78; **10** Naoki Hattori/Shigekazu Wakisaka, J/J (Toyota Supra GT), 78.
Fastest race lap: Tréluyer/Ide, 1m 17.571s, 106.813 mph/171.899 km/h.
Fastest qualifying lap: Tréluyer/Ide, 1m 15.994s, 109.030 mph/175.466 km/h.

MOTEGI GT 300km, Twin Ring Motegi, Motegi-machi, Haga-gun, Tochigi, Japan, 4 September. Round 5. 63 laps of the 2.983-mile/4.801-km circuit, 187.942 miles/302.463 km.
1 Sébastien Philippe/Jérémie Dufour, F/F (Honda NSX), 1h 56m 31.713s, 96.770 mph/155.737 km/h; **2** Ryo Michigami/Takashi Kogure, J/J (Honda NSX), 1h 56m 36.102s; **3** Benoit Tréluyer/Yuji Ide, F/J (Nissan Fairlady Z), 1h 56m 58.890s; **4** Michael Krumm/Masataka Yanagida, D/J (Nissan Fairlady Z), 1h 57m 33.511s; **5** Peter Dumbreck/Naoki Hattori, GB/J (Toyota Supra GT), 1h 57m 38.449s; **6** Richard Lyons/Satoshi Motoyama, GB/J (Nissan Fairlady Z), 1h 57m 48.646s; **7** Takeshi Tsuchiya/James Courtney, J/GB (Toyota Supra GT), 1h 57m 49.680s; **8** Tatsuya Kataoka/Sakon Yamamoto, J/J (Toyota Supra GT), 1h 58m 53.455s; **9** Juichi Wakisaka/Akira Iida, J/J (Toyota Supra GT), 63 laps; **10** Tsugio Matsuda/Andre Lotterer, J/D (Honda NSX), 62.
Fastest race lap: Michigami/Kogure, 1m 47.850s, 99.578 mph/160.256 km/h.
Fastest qualifying lap: Daisuke Ito/Ralph Firman, J/GB (Honda NSX), 1m 45.499s, 101.797 mph/163.827 km/h.

FUJI GT, Fuji International Speedway, Sunto-gun, Shizuoka Prefecture, Japan, 25 September. Round 6. 66 laps of the 2.835-mile/4.563-km circuit, 187.131 miles/301.158 km.
1 Yuji Tachikawa/Toranosuke Takagi, J/J (Toyota Supra GT), 1m 49m 02.070s, 102.975 mph/165.723 km/h; **2** Tsugio Matsuda/Andre Lotterer, J/D (Honda NSX), 1h 49m 03.759s; **3** Juichi Wakisaka/Akira Iida, J/J (Toyota Supra GT), 1h 49m 17.251s; **4** Toshihiro Kaneishi/Erik Comas, J/F (Nissan Fairlady Z), 1h 49m 20.280s; **5** Takeshi Tsuchiya/James Courtney, J/GB (Toyota Supra GT), 1h 49m 45.087s; **6** Peter Dumbreck/Naoki Hattori, GB/J (Toyota Supra GT), 1h 49m 47.056s; **7** Tatsuya Kataoka/Sakon Yamamoto, J/J (Toyota Supra GT), 1h 49m 47.228s; **8** Daisuke Ito/Ralph Firman, J/GB (Honda NSX), 1h 49m 47.757s; **9** Michael Krumm/Masataka Yanagida, D/J (Nissan Fairlady Z), 1h 49m 52.266s; **10** Satoshi Motoyama/Richard Lyons, J/GB (Nissan Fairlady Z), 1h 49m 53.398s.
Fastest race lap: Manabo Orido/Hideki Noda, J/J (Toyota Supra GT), 1m 35.999s, 106.325 mph/171.114 km/h.
Fastest qualifying lap: Matsuda/Lotterer, 1m 43.924s, 98.217 mph/158.066 km/h.

AUTOPOLIS GT, Autopolis International Racing Course, Kamit-sue-mura, Hita-gun, Oita Prefecture, Japan, 16 October. Round 7. 65 laps of the 2.904-mile/4.674-km circuit, 188.779 miles/303.810 km.
1 Daisuke Ito/Ralph Firman, J/GB (Honda NSX), 1h 56m 36.074s, 97.141 mph/156.333 km/h; **2** Michael Krumm/Masataka Yanagida, D/J (Nissan Fairlady Z), 1h 57m 39.058s; **3** Toshihiro Kaneishi/Erik Comas, J/F (Nissan Fairlady Z), 1h 57m 39.569s; **4** Benoit Tréluyer/Yuji Ide, F/J (Nissan Fairlady Z), 1h 57m 40.976s; **5** Ryo Michigami/Takashi Kogure, J/J (Honda NSX), 1h 57m 52.484s; **6** Satoshi Motoyama/Richard Lyons, J/GB (Nissan Fairlady Z), 1h 58m 12.584s; **7** Yuji Tachikawa/Toranosuke Takagi, J/J (Toyota Supra GT), 64 laps; **8** Takeshi Tsuchiya/James Courtney, J/GB (Toyota Supra GT), 64; **9** Peter Dumbreck/Naoki Hattori, GB/J (Toyota Supra GT), 64; **10** Juichi Wakisaka/Akira Iida, J/J (Toyota Supra GT), 64.
Fastest race lap: Ito/Firman, 1m 43.737s, 100.788 mph/162.202 km/h.
Fastest qualifying lap: Ito/Firman, 1m 53.328s, 92.258 mph/148.475 km/h.

Provisional championship points
1= Ralph Firman, GB, 58; **1=** Daisuke Ito, J, 58; **3=** Michael Krumm, D, 54; **3=** Masataka Yanagida, J, 54; **3=** James Courtney, GB, 54; **3=** Takeshi Tsuchiya, J, 54; **7=** Toranosuke Takagi, J, 47; **7=** Yuji Tachikawa, J, 47; **9=** Satoshi Motoyama, J, 45; **9=** Richard Lyons, GB, 45; **11=** Tatsuya Kataoka, J, 39; **11=** Sakon Yamamoto, J, 39; **13=** Akira Iida, J, 37; **13=** Juichi Wakisaka, J, 37; **15=** Tsugio Matsuda, J, 35; **15=** Andre Lotterer, D, 35; **17=** Erik Comas, F, 34; **17=** Toshihiro Kaneishi, J, 34; **19=** Yuji Ide, J, 33; **19=** Benoit Tréluyer, F, 33; **21=** Ryo Michigami, J, 31; **21=** Takashi Kogure, J, 31; **23** Naoki Hattori, J, 29; **24=** Sébastien Philippe, F, 25; **24=** Jérémie Dufour, F, 25; **24=** Manabu Orido, J, 25; **27** Dominik Schwager, D, 24; **28=** Andre Couto, P, 21; **28=** Ronnie Quintarelli, I, 21; **30** Shigekazu Wakisaka, J, 16.

Result of the Suzuka race will be given in AUTOCOURSE 2006-2007.

Other Sports Car races

33rd ADAC ZÜRICH 24 HOUR-RACE, Nürburgring Nordschleife Circuit, Nürburg/Eifel, Germany, 7-8 May. 139 laps of the 15.769-mile/25.378-km circuit, 2191.913 miles/3527.542 km.
1 Pedro Lamy/Boris Said/Duncan Huisman/Andy Priaulx, P/USA/NL/GB (BMW M3 GTR), 23h 58m 47.179s, 91.407 mph/147.105 km/h; **2** Dirk Müller/Jörg Müller/Hans-Joachim Stuck/Pedro Lamy, D/D/A/P (BMW M3 GTR), 134 laps; **3** Peter Zakowski/Robert Lechner/Sascha Bert, D/A/D (Dodge Viper GTS-R), 132; **4** Stefan Beil/Norbert Fischer/Paul Hulverscheid/Edgar Althoff, D/D/D/D (Porsche 911 GT3), 130; **5** Heinz-Josef Bermes/Thomas Koll/Heinz Dieter Schornstein/Andreas Bovensiepen, D/D/D/D (Porsche GT3 Cup), 130; **6** Vanina Ickx/Andre Duve/Jean Francois Hemroulie/Bert Lambrecht, B/B/B/B (Porsche GT3 Cup), 129; **7** Peter Schmidt/Friedrich Ney/Winfried Bär/Michael Irmgartz, D/D/D/D (Porsche 911 GT3 RS), 128; **8** Martin Morin/Henrik Morin/Anders Morin/Anders Levin, S/S/S/S (Porsche 996 GT3 Cup), 127; **9** Lucas Luhr/Timo Bernhard/Emmanuel Collard/Marcel Tiemann, D/D/F/D (Porsche 911 GT3-MR), 127; **10** Jürgen Alzen/Uwe Alzen/Klaus Ludwig/Peter Dumbreck, D/D/D/GB (Porsche 996 turbo), 126.
Fastest race lap: Müller/Müller/Stuck/Lamy, 8m 47.602s, 107.598 mph/173.162 km/h.
Fastest qualifying lap: Alzen (Uwe), 8m 30.846s, 111.127 mph/178.842 km/h.

73rd 24 HEURES DU MANS, Circuit International Du Mans, Les Raineries, Le Mans, France, 18-19 June. 370 laps of the 8.482-mile/13.650-km circuit, 3138.235 miles/5050.500 km.
1 JJ Lehto/Marco Werner/Tom Kristensen, FIN/D/DK (Audi R8), (1st LMP1 class), 24h 01m 31.038s, 130.622 mph/210.216 km/h; **2** Emmanuel Collard/Jean-Christophe Boullion/Erik Comas, F/F/F (Pescarolo C60-Judd), 368 laps; **3** Frank Biela/Emanuele Pirro/Allan McNish, D/I/GB (Audi R8), 364; **4** Franck Montagny/Jean-Marc Gounon/Stéphane Ortelli, F/F/MC (Audi R8), 362; **5** Oliver Gavin/Olivier Beretta/Jan Magnussen, GB/MC/DK (Chevrolet Corvette C6.R), 349 (1st GT1 class); **6** Ron Fellows/Johnny O'Connell/Massimiliano 'Max' Papis, CDN/USA/I (Chevrolet Corvette C6.R), 347; **7** Jan Lammers/Elton Julian/John Bosch, NL/USA/NL (Dome S101-Judd), 346; **8** Dominik Schwager/Christian Vann/Alexander Frei, D/GB/CH (Courage C60-H-Judd), 339; **9** David Brabham/Darren Turner/Stéphane Sarrazin, AUS/GB/F (Aston Martin DBR9), 333; **10** Mike Rockenfeller/Marc Lieb/Leo Hindery, D/D/USA (Porsche 911 GT3-RSR), 332 (1st GT2 class); **11** Timo Bernhard/Jörg Bergmeister/Patrick Long, D/D/USA (Porsche 911 GT3-RSR), 331; **12** Patrice Goueslard/Vincent Vosse/Olivier Dupard, F/B/F (Ferrari 550 Maranello), 324; **13** Johannes van Overbeek/Lonnie Pechnik/Seth Neiman, USA/USA/USA (Porsche 911 GT3-RSR), 323; **14** Nicolas Minassian/Jamie Campbell-Walter/Andy Wallace, F/GB/GB (DBA4 03S-Judd), 322; **15** Raymond Narac/Sébastien Dumez/Romain Dumas, F/F/F (Porsche 911 GT3-RSR), 322; **16** Martin Short/João Barbosa/Vanina Ickx, GB/P/B (Dallara LMP-Judd), 318; **17** Christophe Bouchut/Nikolaj Fomenko/Alexei Vasiliev, F/RUS/RUS (Ferrari 550 Maranello), 315; **18** Luc Alphand/Jérôme Policand/Christophe Campbell, F/F/F (Porsche 911 GT3-RS), 311; **19** Lars-Erik Nielsen/Thorkild Thyrring/Pierre Ehret, DK/DK/D (Porsche 911 GT3-RSR), 307; **20** Thomas Erdos/Warren Hughes/Mike Newton, BR/GB/GB (Lola B05/40-MG), 305 (1st LMP2 class); **21** Adam Sharpe/Karim Ojjeh/Claude-Yves Gosselin, GB/ZA/F (Courage C65-Ford), 300; **22** Paul Belmondo/Didier André/Rick Sutherland, F/F/USA (Courage C65-Ford), 294; **23** Philip Collin/David Shep/Horst Felbemayr, USA/CDN/A (Porsche 911 GT3-RSR), 274; **24** Phil Bennett/Ian Mitchell/Tim Mullen, GB/GB/GB (Courage C65-Judd), 268; **25** Sam Hignett/John Stack/Haruki Kurosawa, GB/GB/J (Zytek 04S), 325; **26** John Hartshorne/Richard Stanton/Piers Johnson, GB/GB/GB (TVR T400R), 256; **27** Yojiro Terada/Patrice Roussel/Bill Binnie, J/F/USA (WR LMP04-Peugeot), 137; **28** Peter Kox/Pedro Lamy/Tomás Enge, NL/P/CZ (Aston Martin DBR9), 327 (DNF-fuel pick-up); **29** Soheil Ayari/Éric Hélary/Sébastien Loeb, F/F/F (Pescarolo C60-Judd), 288 (DNF-accident); **30** Joe Macari/Stephane Eriksson/Rob Wilson, GB/S/NZ (Ferrari 360 Modena GTC), 218 (DNF-mechanical); **31** Ryo Michigami/Seiji Ara/Katsumoto Kaneishi, J/J/J (Dome S101-Hb-Mugen), 193 (DNF-gearbox); **32** Bryan Sellers/Marino Franchitti/Patrick Bourdais, USA/GB/F (Panoz Elan Esperante), 185 (DNF-transmission); **33** Val Hillebrand/Frank Hahn/Gavin Pickering, B/B/GB (Courage C65-Judd), 183 (DNF-engine); **34** Xavier Pompidou/Jean-Luc Blanchemain/Yutaka Yamagishi, F/F/J (Porsche 911 GT3-RS), 183 (DNF-accident); **35** Michael Krumm/Bobby Verdon-Roe/Harold Primat, D/GB/F (Dallara LMP-Nissan), 133 (DNF-withdrawn); **36** Sam Hancock/Gregor Fisken/Liz Halliday, GB/GB/GB (Lola B05/40-AER), 119 (DNF-withdrawn); **37** John Macaluso/Ian James/Andy Lally, USA/GB/USA (Courage C65-AER), 115 (DNF-disqualified); **38** Ni Amorim/Christophe Pillon/Romain Iannetta, P/CH/F (Courage C65-Mecachrome), 99 (DNF-gearbox); **39** Stéphane Daoudi/Jean-René de Fournoux/Jim Matthews, F/F/USA (Ferrari 575 GTC), 84 (DNF-engine); **40** Tom Coronel/Donny Crevels/Peter Van Merksteijn, NL/NL/NL (Spyker C8-Audi), 76 (DNF-engine); **41** Andrew Kirkcaldy/Nathan Kinch/Anthony Reid, GB/GB/GB (Ferrari 360 Modena GTC), 70 (DNF-accident damage); **42** Fabrizio Gollin/Christian Pescatori/Miguel Ramos, I/I/P (Ferrari 550 Maranello), 67 (DNF-accident); **43** Michele Bartyan/Matteo Malucelli/Toni Seiler, I/I/CH (Ferrari 550 Maranello), 60 (DNF-accident damage); **44** Jean-Bernard Bouvet/Sylvain Boulay/Bobby Julien, F/F/CDN (WR LMP04-Peugeot), 53 (DNF-spin); **45** Jonathan Cochet/Bruce Jouanny/Shinji Nakano, F/F/J (Courage C60-H-Judd), 52 (DNF-accident damage); **46** Pierre Bruneau/Philippe Haezerouck/Marc Rostan, F/F/F (Pilbeam MP93-JPX), 32 (DNF-clutch); **47** Sergey Zlobin/Bastien Briere/Juan Barazi, RUS/F/DK (Courage C65-AER), 30 (DNF-withdrawn); **48** Bob Berridge/Gareth Evans/Peter Owen, GB/GB/GB (Lola B05/40-AER), 30 (DNF-gearbox); **49** Bill Auberlen/Robin Liddell/Scott Maxwell, USA/GB/CDN (Panoz Elan Esperante), 27 (DNF-engine).
Fastest race lap: Boullion, 3m 34.968s, 142.041 mph/228.592 km/h.
Fastest qualifying lap: Collard, 3m 34.715s, 142.208 mph/228.862 km/h.

V8 Supercar Championship Series

CLIPSAL 500, Adelaide Street Circuit, Adelaide, South Australia, Australia, 19/20 March. Round 1. 2 x 78 laps of the 2.001-mile/3.220-km circuit.
Race 1 (156.064 miles/251.160 km).
1 Marcos Ambrose, AUS (Ford Falcon BA), 2h 06m 56.4343s, 73.765 mph/118.714 km/h; **2** Russell Ingall, AUS (Ford Falcon BA), 2h 06m 57.2670s; **3** Craig Lowndes, AUS (Ford Falcon BA), 2h 06m 59.4306s; **4** Steven Johnson, AUS (Ford Falcon BA), 2h 07m 07.5284s; **5** Steven Richards, AUS (Holden Commodore VY), 2h 07m 08.2073s; **6** Greg Murphy, AUS (Holden Commodore VZ), 2h 07m 09.4244s; **7** Garth Tander, AUS (Holden Commodore VZ), 2h 07m 12.1724s; **8** Todd Kelly, AUS (Holden Commodore VZ), 2h 07m 17.0386s; **9** Glenn Seton, AUS (Ford Falcon BA), 2h 07m 18.9745s; **10** Jamie Whincup, AUS (Holden Commodore VY), 2h 07m 19.3486s.
Fastest race lap: Mark Skaife, AUS (Holden Commodore VZ), 1m 23.1903s, 86.584 mph/139.343 km/h.
Fastest qualifying lap: Rick Kelly, AUS (Holden Commodore VZ), 1m 22.9438s, 86.841 mph/139.757 km/h.

Race 2 (156.064 miles/251.160 km).
1 Marcos Ambrose, AUS (Ford Falcon BA), 1h 59m 11.1013s, 78.565 mph/126.439 km/h; **2** Craig Lowndes, AUS (Ford Falcon BA), 1h 59m 17.4615s; **3** Mark Skaife, AUS (Holden Commodore VZ), 1h 59m 17.9126s; **4** Todd Kelly, AUS (Holden Commodore VZ), 1h 59m 33.3809s; **5** Paul Dumbrell, AUS (Holden Commodore VY), 1h 59m 37.6892s; **6** Cameron McConville, AUS (Holden Commodore VZ), 1h 59m 38.2501s; **7** Max Wilson, BR (Holden Commodore VZ), 1h 59m 40.8632s; **8** Paul Weel, AUS (Holden Commodore VZ), 1h 59m 47.9944s; **9** Rick Kelly, AUS (Holden Commodore VZ), 1h 59m 51.3224s; **10** Paul Radisich, NZ (Holden Commodore VZ), 1h 59m 54.5585s.
Fastest race lap: Ambrose, 1m 23.1359s, 86.640 mph/139.434 km/h.

PLACEMAKERS V8 INTERNATIONAL, Pukekohe Park Raceway, Auckland, New Zealand, 16/17 April. Round 2. 36, 50 and 47 laps of the 1.752-mile/2.820-km circuit.
Race 1 (63.082 miles/101.520 km).
1 Greg Murphy, AUS (Holden Commodore VZ), 34m 53.7573s, 108.462 mph/174.553 km/h; **2** Russell Ingall, AUS (Ford Falcon BA), 34m 56.8774s; **3** Mark Skaife, AUS (Holden Commodore VZ), 34m 58.4307s; **4** Steve Ellery, AUS (Ford Falcon BA), 35m 05.6801s; **5** Marcos Ambrose, AUS (Ford Falcon BA), 35m 08.6337s; **6** Paul Radisich, NZ (Holden Commodore VZ), 35m 09.1154s; **7** Jason Bright, AUS (Ford Falcon BA), 35m 09.5727s; **8** Todd Kelly, AUS (Holden Commodore VZ), 35m 13.6068s; **9** Paul Morris, AUS (Holden Commodore VZ), 35m 21.5482s; **10** Jamie Whincup, AUS (Holden Commodore VZ), 35m 21.5669s.
Fastest race lap: Murphy, 56.0781s, 112.489 mph/181.033 km/h.
Fastest qualifying lap: Craig Lowndes, AUS (Ford Falcon BA), 55.7367s, 113.178 mph/182.142 km/h.

Race 2 (87.613 miles/141.000 km).
1 Greg Murphy, AUS (Holden Commodore VZ), 52m 43.9734s, 99.687 mph/160.431 km/h; **2** Russell Ingall, AUS (Ford Falcon BA), 52m 44.7402s; **3** Marcos Ambrose, AUS (Ford Falcon BA), 52m 49.2836s; **4** Mark Skaife, AUS (Holden Commodore VZ), 52m 55.4886s; **5** Craig Lowndes, AUS (Ford Falcon BA), 52m 57.2547s; **6** Paul Radisich, NZ (Holden Commodore VZ), 52m 58.0662s; **7** Steve Ellery, AUS (Ford Falcon BA), 52m 58.6205s; **8** Steven Richards, AUS (Holden Commodore VY), 52m 59.3543s; **9** Paul Weel, AUS (Holden Commodore VZ), 53m 02.5594s; **10** John Bowe, AUS (Ford Falcon BA), 53m 08.3228s.
Fastest race lap: Murphy, 56.2953s, 112.055 mph/180.335 km/h.

Race 3 (82.357 miles/132.540 km).
1 Greg Murphy, AUS (Holden Commodore VZ), 1h 29m 16.4683s, 55.351 mph/89.078 km/h; **2** Russell Ingall, AUS (Ford Falcon BA), 1h 29m 17.2285s; **3** Steven Richards, AUS (Holden Commodore VY), 1h 29m 18.2505s; **4** Marcos Ambrose, AUS (Ford Falcon BA), 1h 29m 18.9172s; **5** Mark Skaife, AUS (Holden Commodore VZ), 1h 29m 22.5243s; **6** Paul Radisich, NZ (Holden Commodore VZ), 1h 29m 29.9604s; **7** Jason Bright, AUS (Ford Falcon BA), 1h 29m 30.0994s; **8** John Bowe, AUS (Ford Falcon BA), 1h 29m 30.6607s; **9** Garth Tander, AUS (Holden Commodore VZ), 1h 29m 35.7731s; **10** Paul Weel, AUS (Holden Commodore VZ), 1h 29m 36.2784s.
Fastest race lap: Skaife, 56.2424s, 112.160 mph/180.504 km/h.

PERTH V8 400, Barbagallo Raceway, Wanneroo, Perth, Western Australia, Australia, 7/8 May. Round 3. 50, 58 and 58 laps of the 1.501-mile/2.415-km circuit.
Race 1 (75.031 miles/120.750 km).
1 Mark Skaife, AUS (Holden Commodore VZ), 57m 21.4908s, 78.486 mph/126.312 km/h; **2** Marcos Ambrose, AUS (Ford Falcon BA), 57m 21.7754s; **3** Steven Richards, AUS (Holden Commodore VY), 57m 22.1566s; **4** Russell Ingall, AUS (Ford Falcon BA), 57m 24.3261s; **5** Greg Murphy, AUS (Holden Commodore VZ), 57m 24.5375s; **6** Paul Radisich, NZ (Holden Commodore VZ), 57m 26.3987s; **7** Jason Richards, AUS (Holden Commodore VZ), 57m 26.6588s; **8** Cameron McConville, AUS (Holden Commodore VZ), 57m 28.9344s; **9** Jason Bargwanna, AUS (Ford Falcon BA), 57m 29.4994s; **10** Paul Morris, AUS (Holden Commodore VZ), 57m 29.7679s.
Fastest race lap: Skaife, 56.3747s, 95.827 mph/154.218 km/h.
Fastest qualifying lap: Craig Lowndes, AUS (Ford Falcon BA), 55.6278s, 97.113 mph/156.289 km/h.

Race 2 (87.035 miles/140.070 km).
1 Steven Richards, AUS (Holden Commodore VY), 1h 03m 36.5838s, 82.096 mph/132.121 km/h; **2** Russell Ingall, AUS (Ford Falcon BA), 1h 03m 39.4225s; **3** Craig Lowndes, AUS (Ford Falcon BA), 1h 03m 41.3488s; **4** Steven Johnson, AUS (Ford Falcon BA), 1h 03m 42.6316s; **5** Marcos Ambrose, AUS (Ford Falcon BA), 1h 03m 42.9715s; **6** Paul Weel, AUS (Holden Commodore VZ), 1h 03m 43.3879s; **7** Jason Bright, AUS (Ford Falcon BA), 1h 03m 45.8864s; **8** Paul Radisich, NZ (Holden Commodore VZ), 1h 03m 47.4419s; **9** Cameron McConville, AUS (Holden Commodore VZ), 1h 03m 47.7031s, **10** Jason Bargwanna, AUS (Ford Falcon

BA), 1h 03m 50.7931s.

Fastest race lap: Ambrose, 56.5059s, 95.604 mph/153.860 km/h.

Race 3 (87.035 miles/140.070 km).

1 Russell Ingall, AUS (Ford Falcon BA), 1h 01m 18.0115s, 85.189 mph/137.099 km/h; **2** Steven Richards, AUS (Holden Commodore VY), 1h 01m 18.5308s; **3** Marcos Ambrose, AUS (Ford Falcon BA), 1h 01m 20.9407s; **4** Paul Weel, AUS (Holden Commodore VZ), h 01m 28.9143s; **5** Steven Johnson, AUS (Ford Falcon BA), 1h 01m 30.9488s; **6** Mark Skaife, AUS (Holden Commodore VZ), 1h 01m 31.1542s; **7** Todd Kelly, AUS (Holden Commodore VZ), 1h 01m 31.2430s; **8** John Bowe, AUS (Ford Falcon BA), 1h 01m 31.7532s; **9** Glenn Seton, AUS (Ford Falcon BA), 1h 01m 33.4733s; **10** Steve Ellery, AUS (Ford Falcon BA), 1h 01m 33.7492s.

Fastest race lap: Ambrose, 56.4974s, 95.619 mph/153.883 km/h.

V8 SUPERCAR CHAMPIONSHIP SERIES, Eastern Creek International Raceway, Sydney, New South Wales, Australia, 29 May. Round 4. 2 x 36 laps of the 2.442-mile/3.930-km circuit.

Race 1 (87.912 miles/141.480 km).

1 Marcos Ambrose, AUS (Ford Falcon BA), 1h 00m 28.5261s, 87.220 mph/140.368 km/h; **2** Craig Lowndes, AUS (Ford Falcon BA), 1h 00m 34.9890s; **3** Steven Richards, AUS (Holden Commodore VY), 1h 00m 52.5105s; **4** Greg Murphy, AUS (Holden Commodore VZ), 1h 00m 56.7161s; **5** Russell Ingall, AUS (Ford Falcon BA), 1h 00m 56.9899s; **6** Todd Kelly, AUS (Holden Commodore VZ), 1h 00m 57.3045s; **7** Mark Skaife, AUS (Holden Commodore VZ), 1h 00m 59.7814s; **8** Steve Ellery, AUS (Ford Falcon BA), 1h 01m 12.5716s; **9** Garth Tander, AUS (Holden Commodore VZ), 1h 01m 14.9572s; **10** Jason Richards, AUS (Holden Commodore VZ), 1h 01m 15.3356s.

Fastest race lap: Lowndes, 1m 32.8516s, 94.680 mph/152.372 km/h.

Fastest qualifying lap: Lowndes, 1m 31.5010s, 96.077 mph/154.621 km/h.

Race 2 (87.912 miles/141.480 km).

1 Craig Lowndes, AUS (Ford Falcon BA), 1h 01m 46.3894s, 85.388 mph/137.419 km/h; **2** Marcos Ambrose, AUS (Ford Falcon BA), 1h 01m 48.4061s; **3** Greg Murphy, AUS (Holden Commodore VZ), 1h 01m 48.6463s; **4** Todd Kelly, AUS (Holden Commodore VZ), 1h 01m 54.4820s; **5** Steven Richards, AUS (Holden Commodore VY), 1h 01m 55.6584s; **6** Russell Ingall, AUS (Ford Falcon BA), 1h 01m 56.1257s; **7** Mark Skaife, AUS (Holden Commodore VZ), 1h 02m 00.2053s; **8** John Bowe, AUS (Ford Falcon BA), 1h 02m 04.8012s; **9** Steven Johnson, AUS (Ford Falcon BA), 1h 02m 05.0887s; **10** Garth Tander, AUS (Holden Commodore VZ), 1h 02m 06.1373s.

Fastest race lap: Lowndes, 1m 32.9370s, 94.593 mph/152.232 km/h.

V8 SUPERCAR CHAMPIONSHIP SERIES, Shanghai International Circuit, Jiading, China, 11/12 June. Round 5. 22, 30 and 30 laps of the 3.387-mile/5.451-km circuit.

Race 1 (74.516 miles/119.922 km).

1 Todd Kelly, AUS (Holden Commodore VZ), 41m 49.4584s, 106.899 mph/172.037 km/h; **2** Steven Richards, AUS (Holden Commodore VY), 41m 50.5601s; **3** Mark Skaife, AUS (Holden Commodore VZ), 41m 53.4526s; **4** Craig Lowndes, AUS (Ford Falcon BA), 41m 53.8357s; **5** Marcos Ambrose, AUS (Ford Falcon BA), 41m 54.3447s; **6** Paul Radisich, NZ (Holden Commodore VZ), 41m 55.5014s; **7** Jason Bright, AUS (Ford Falcon BA), 41m 59.2969s; **8** Jason Richards, AUS (Holden Commodore VZ), 42m 01.1811s; **9** Jamie Whincup, AUS (Holden Commodore VZ), 42m 02.5905s; **10** Greg Murphy, AUS (Holden Commodore VZ), 42m 03.1965s.

Fastest race lap: Kelly (Todd), 1m 51.0737s, 109.779 mph/176.672 km/h.

Fastest qualifying lap: Skaife, 1m 49.8516s, 111.000 mph/178.637 km/h.

Race 2 (101.613 miles/163.530 km).

1 Mark Skaife, AUS (Holden Commodore VZ), 56m 55.5933s, 107.099 mph/172.359 km/h; **2** Steven Richards, AUS (Holden Commodore VY), 56m 58.2826s; **3** Todd Kelly, AUS (Holden Commodore VZ), 56m 58.6066s; **4** Marcos Ambrose, AUS (Ford Falcon BA), 57m 06.6939s; **5** Paul Radisich, NZ (Holden Commodore VZ), 57m 09.8069s; **6** Russell Ingall, AUS (Ford Falcon BA), 57m 13.3246s; **7** Glenn Seton, AUS (Ford Falcon BA), 57m 16.9595s; **8** Jamie Whincup, AUS (Holden Commodore VZ), 57m 26.4548s; **9** Cameron McConville, AUS (Holden Commodore VZ), 57m 31.3237s; **10** Greg Ritter, AUS (Ford Falcon BA), 57m 35.5618s.

Fastest race lap: Kelly (Todd), 1m 51.0557s, 109.797 mph/176.701 km/h.

Race 3 (101.613 miles/163.530 km).

1 Todd Kelly, AUS (Holden Commodore VZ), 59m 32.3831s, 102.398 mph/164.794 km/h; **2** Steven Richards, AUS (Holden Commodore VY), 59m 33.6256s; **3** Paul Radisich, NZ (Holden Commodore VZ), 59m 34.2887s; **4** Jamie Whincup, AUS (Holden Commodore VZ), 59m 34.5951s; **5** Max Wilson, BR (Holden Commodore VZ), 59m 38.4099s; **6** Jason Bright, AUS (Ford Falcon BA), 59m 41.3359s; **7** Greg Murphy, AUS (Holden Commodore VZ), 59m 41.5667s; **8** Greg Ritter, AUS (Ford Falcon BA), 59m 47.9806s; **9** Cameron McConville, AUS (Holden Commodore VZ), 59m 49.5888s; **10** Brad Jones, AUS (Ford Falcon BA), 59m 52.7604s.

Fastest race lap: Marcos Ambrose, AUS (Ford Falcon BA), 1m 51.1012s, 109.752 mph/176.628 km/h.

SKYCITY V8 SUPERCARS DARWIN, Hidden Valley Raceway, Darwin, Northern Territory, Australia, 2/3 July. Round 6. 17, 48 and 48 laps of the 1.802-mile/2.900-km circuit.

Race 1 (30.634 miles/49.300 km).

1 Todd Kelly, AUS (Holden Commodore VZ), 20m 08.1710s, 91.279 mph/146.900 km/h; **2** Mark Skaife, AUS (Holden Commodore VZ), 20m 08.8656s; **3** Craig Lowndes, AUS (Ford Falcon BA), 20m 09.2385s; **4** Marcos Ambrose, AUS (Ford Falcon BA), 20m 10.5154s; **5** Garth Tander, AUS (Holden Commodore VZ), 20m 19.1818s; **6** Paul Radisich, NZ (Holden Commodore VZ), 20m 20.1685s; **7** Paul Morris, AUS (Holden Commodore VZ), 20m 21.0836s; **8** Glenn Seton, AUS (Ford Falcon BA), 20m 22.7822s; **9** Rick Kelly, AUS (Holden Commodore VZ), 20m 26.8877s; **10** John Bowe, AUS (Ford Falcon BA), 20m 30.7146s.

Fastest race lap: Kelly (Todd), 1m 09.8544s, 92.866 mph/149.454 km/h.

Fastest qualifying lap: Skaife, 1m 08.7300s, 94.385 mph/151.899 km/h.

Race 2 (86.495 miles/139.200 km).

1 Todd Kelly, AUS (Holden Commodore VZ), 1h 00m 27.6924s, 85.835 mph/138.137 km/h; **2** Mark Skaife, AUS (Holden Commodore VZ), 1h 00m 28.4147s; **3** Garth Tander, AUS (Holden Commodore VZ), 1h 00m 30.5639s; **4** Russell Ingall, AUS (Ford Falcon BA), 1h 00m 31.2593s; **5** Rick Kelly, AUS (Holden Commodore VZ), 1h 00m 32.5621s; **6** Jason Richards, AUS (Holden Commodore VZ), 1h 00m 32.8892s; **7** Glenn Seton, AUS (Ford Falcon BA), 1h 00m 34.7750s; **8** Paul Radisich, NZ (Holden Commodore VZ), 1h 00m 36.0215s; **9** Jason Bright, AUS (Ford Falcon BA), 1h 00m 36.8438s; **10** John Bowe, AUS (Ford Falcon BA), 1h 00m 37.7845s.

Fastest race lap: Kelly (Todd), 1m 10.2408s, 92.355 mph/148.632 km/h.

Race 3 (86.495 miles/139.200 km).

1 Garth Tander, AUS (Holden Commodore VZ), 1h 01m 10.5109s, 84.833 mph/136.526 km/h; **2** Todd Kelly, AUS (Holden Commodore VZ), 1h 01m 10.8504s; **3** Rick Kelly, AUS (Holden Commodore VZ), 1h 01m 14.2439s; **4** Steven Richards, AUS (Holden Commodore VY), 1h 01m 14.7845s; **5** Glenn Seton, AUS (Ford Falcon BA), 1h 01m 17.1151s; **6** Steve Ellery, AUS (Ford Falcon BA), 1h 01m 19.1816s; **7** Steven Johnson, AUS (Ford Falcon BA), 1h 01m 20.6034s; **8** Jason Bright, AUS (Ford Falcon BA), 1h 01m 23.4493s; **9** Marcos Ambrose, AUS (Ford Falcon BA), 1h 01m 23.9741s; **10** Paul Dumbrell, AUS (Holden Commodore VY), 1h 01m 24.5520s.

Fastest race lap: Tander, 1m 10.4658s, 92.060 mph/148.157 km/h.

QUEENSLAND 300, Queensland Raceway, Brisbane, Queensland, Australia, 24 July. Round 7. 90 laps of the 1.942-mile/3.126-km circuit, 281.340 miles/174.817 km.

1 Craig Lowndes, AUS (Ford Falcon BA), 1h 57m 29.6514s, 89.272 mph/143.670 km/h; **2** Marcos Ambrose, AUS (Ford Falcon BA), 1h 57m 32.4526s; **3** Garth Tander, AUS (Holden Commodore VZ), 1h 57m 35.0978s; **4** Russell Ingall, AUS (Ford Falcon BA), 1h 57m 35.6251s; **5** Steven Richards, AUS (Holden Commodore VY), 1h 57m 36.2937s; **6** Todd Kelly, AUS (Holden Commodore VZ), 1h 57m 40.1539s; **7** Steve Ellery, AUS (Ford Falcon BA), 1h 57m 41.1502s; **8** Greg Murphy, AUS (Holden Commodore VZ), 1h 57m 44.4241s; **9** Jason Bright, AUS (Ford Falcon BA), 1h 57m 44.7792s; **10** Steven Johnson, AUS (Ford Falcon BA), 1h 57m 47.1180s.

Fastest race lap: Ambrose, 1m 11.1963s, 98.217 mph/158.064 km/h.

Fastest qualifying lap: Ambrose, 1m 10.2173s, 99.586 mph/160.268 km/h.

V8 SUPERCAR CHAMPIONSHIP SERIES, Oran Park Raceway, Narellan, Sydney, New South Wales, Australia, 14 August. Round 8. 2 x 54 laps of the 1.628-mile/2.620-km circuit.

Race 1 (87.912 miles/141.480 km).

1 Steven Richards, AUS (Holden Commodore VY), 1h 05m 18.7053s, 80.762 mph/129.974 km/h; **2** Russell Ingall, AUS (Ford Falcon BA), 1h 05m 20.0306s; **3** Greg Murphy, AUS (Holden Commodore VZ), 1h 05m 20.2563s; **4** Marcos Ambrose, AUS (Ford Falcon BA), 1h 05m 23.7366s; **5** Rick Kelly, AUS (Holden Commodore VZ), 1h 05m 24.0047s; **6** Jason Richards, AUS (Holden Commodore VZ), 1h 05m 26.6345s; **7** Jason Bright, AUS (Ford Falcon BA), 1h 05m 34.9164s; **8** Cameron McConville, AUS (Holden Commodore VZ), 1h 05m 38.4569s; **9** Craig Lowndes, AUS (Ford Falcon BA), 1h 05m 42.4892s; **10** Steven Johnson, AUS (Ford Falcon BA), 1h 05m 47.3013s.

Fastest race lap: Ambrose, 1m 09.4178s, 84.428 mph/135.873 km/h.

Fastest qualifying lap: Ambrose, 1m 08.3774s, 85.712 mph/137.940 km/h.

Race 2 (87.912 miles/141.480 km).

1 Russell Ingall, AUS (Ford Falcon BA), 1h 08m 50.5625s, 76.620 mph/123.307 km/h; **2** Marcos Ambrose, AUS (Ford Falcon BA), 1h 08m 56.7989s; **3** Greg Murphy, AUS (Holden Commodore VZ), 1h 08m 59.9637s; **4** Craig Lowndes, AUS (Ford Falcon BA), 1h 09m 01.6569s; **5** Garth Tander, AUS (Holden Commodore VZ), 1h 09m 03.2072s; **6** Rick Kelly, AUS (Holden Commodore VZ), 1h 09m 10.1073s; **7** Jason Bright, AUS (Ford Falcon BA), 1h 09m 18.3775s; **8** Cameron McConville, AUS (Holden Commodore VZ), 1h 09m 19.1035s; **9** Paul Radisich, NZ (Holden Commodore VZ), 1h 09m 19.3285s; **10** Max Wilson, BR (Holden Commodore VZ), 1h 09m 19.5809s.

Fastest race lap: Ambrose, 1m 09.9220s, 83.819 mph/134.893 km/h.

BETTA ELECTRICAL 500, Sandown International Motor Raceway, Melbourne, Victoria, Australia, 11 September. Round 9. 161 laps of the 1.926-mile/3.100-km circuit, 310.126 mile/499.100 km.

1 Craig Lowndes/Yvan Muller, AUS/F (Ford Falcon BA), 3h 30m 51.8944s, 88.244 mph/142.015 km/h; **2** Todd Kelly/Mark Skaife, AUS/AUS (Holden Commodore VZ), 3h 31m 27.5116s; **3** Jason Richards/Jamie Whincup, AUS/AUS (Holden Commodore VZ), 3h 31m 42.7831s; **4** Rick Kelly/Garth Tander, AUS/AUS (Holden Commodore VZ), 3h 31m 48.1352s; **5** Steve Ellery/Adam Macrow, AUS/AUS (Ford Falcon BA), 3h 31m 53.3849s; **6** David Brabham/Jason Bright, AUS/AUS (Ford Falcon BA), 160 laps; **7** Russell Ingall/Luke Youlden, AUS/AUS (Ford Falcon BA), 160; **8** Paul Morris/Paul Radisich, AUS/NZ (Holden Commodore VZ), 160; **9** John Bowe/Brad Jones, AUS/AUS (Ford Falcon BA), 160; **10** Cameron McConville/Andrew Jones, AUS/AUS (Holden Commodore VZ), 160.

Fastest race lap: Lowndes, 1m 11.7940s, 96.589 mph/155.445 km/h.

Fastest qualifying lap: Tander, 1m 10.8917s, 97.818 mph/157.423 km/h.

V8 SUPERCAR 1000, Mount Panorama, Bathurst, New South Wales, Australia, 9 October. Round 10. 161 laps of the 3.861-mile/6.213-km circuit, 621.553 miles/1000.298 km.

1 Todd Kelly/Mark Skaife, AUS/AUS (Holden Commodore VZ), 6h 37m 17.0012s, 93.871 mph/151.070 km/h; **2** Jason Richards/Jamie Whincup, AUS/AUS (Holden Commodore VZ), 6h 37m 19.4889s; **3** Steve Ellery/Adam Macrow, AUS/AUS (Ford Falcon BA), 6h 37m 32.8053s; **4** Cameron McConville/Andrew Jones, AUS/AUS (Holden Commodore VZ), 6h 37m 36.5767s; **5** Russell Ingall/Luke Youlden, AUS/AUS (Ford Falcon BA), 6h 37m 37.7586s; **6** Owen Kelly/Nathan Pretty, AUS/AUS (Holden Commodore VZ), 6h 38m 08.0591s; **7** Dale Brede/John Cleland, AUS/GB (Ford Falcon BA), 159 laps; **8** Craig Baird/David Besnard, AUS/AUS (Ford Falcon BA), 158; **9** Dean Canto/Glenn Seton, AUS/AUS (Ford Falcon BA), 158; **10** John Faulkner/Alan Gurr, AUS/AUS (Holden Commodore VZ), 158.

Fastest race lap: Kelly/Skaife, 2m 08.6515s, 108.029 mph/173.856 km/h.

Fastest qualifying lap: Craig Lowndes, AUS (Ford Falcon BA), 2m 08.5990s, 108.073 mph/173.927 km/h.

GILLETTE V8 SUPERCAR CHALLENGE, Surfer's Paradise street circuit, Queensland, Australia, 22/23 October. Round 11. 31, 22 and 22 laps of the 2.778-mile/4.470-km circuit.

Race 1 (86.103 miles/138.570 km).

1 Greg Murphy, AUS (Holden Commodore VZ), 59m 16.9355s, 61.845 mph/99.531 km/h; **2** Craig Lowndes, AUS (Ford Falcon BA), 59m 20.6521s; **3** Mark Skaife, AUS (Holden Commodore VZ), 59m 21.9886s; **4** Russell Ingall, AUS (Ford Falcon BA), 59m 26.5827s; **5** Cameron McConville, AUS (Holden Commodore VZ), 59m 28.2679s; **6** Jason Richards, AUS (Holden Commodore VZ), 59m 29.1210s; **7** Steve Ellery, AUS (Ford Falcon BA), 59m 35.6605s; **8** Jason Bright, AUS (Ford Falcon BA), 59m 59.7229s; **9** Rick Kelly, AUS (Holden Commodore VZ), 1h 00m 01.4653s; **10** Garth Tander, AUS (Holden Commodore VZ), 1h 00m 02.0853s.

Fastest race lap:: McConville, 1m 52.2280s, 89.096 mph/143.387 km/h.

Fastest qualifying lap: Murphy, 1m 51.3434s, 89.804 mph/144.526 km/h.

Race 2 (61.106 miles/98.340 km).

1 Craig Lowndes, AUS (Ford Falcon BA), 42m 02.6971s, 87.200 mph/140.336 km/h; **2** Greg Murphy, AUS (Holden Commodore VZ), 42m 05.4862s; **3** Mark Skaife, AUS (Holden Commodore VZ), 42m 06.2703s; **4** Garth Tander, AUS (Holden Commodore VZ), 42m 19.2772s; **5** Rick Kelly, AUS (Holden Commodore VZ), 42m 19.7789s; **6** Cameron McConville, AUS (Holden Commodore VZ), 42m 20.1694s; **7** Steve Ellery, AUS (Ford Falcon BA), 42m 30.0155s; **8** Jamie Whincup, AUS (Holden Commodore VZ), 42m 32.0979s; **9** Jason Bright, AUS (Ford Falcon BA), 42m 38.4102s; **10** Russell Ingall, AUS (Ford Falcon BA), 42m 42.5008s.

Fastest race lap: Ingall, 1 51.6246s, 89.578 mph/144.162 km/h.

Race 3 (61.106 miles/98.340 km).

1 Craig Lowndes, AUS (Ford Falcon BA), 43m 41.7737s, 83.905 mph/135.032 km/h; **2** Mark Skaife, AUS (Holden Commodore VZ), 43m 44.3204s; **3** Greg Murphy, AUS (Holden Commodore VZ), 43m 46.0829s; **4** Garth Tander, AUS (Holden Commodore VZ), 43m 48.5826s; **5** Cameron McConville, AUS (Holden Commodore VZ), 43m 49.0487s; **6** Rick Kelly, AUS (Holden Commodore VZ), 43m 50.2143s; **7** Steve Ellery, AUS (Ford Falcon BA), 43m 50.4891s; **8** Todd Kelly, AUS (Holden Commodore VZ), 43m 50.7234s; **9** Jason Bright, AUS (Ford Falcon BA), 43m 51.3967s; **10** Jamie Whincup, AUS (Holden Commodore VZ), 43m 52.0610s.

Fastest race lap: Lowndes, 1m 51.6328s, 89.571 mph/144.151 km/h.

Provisional championship points

1 Russell Ingall, AUS, 1610; **2** Marcos Ambrose, AUS, 1544; **3** Craig Lowndes, AUS, 1529; **4** Mark Skaife, AUS, 1516; **5** Todd Kelly, AUS, 1500; **6** Steven Richards, AUS, 1419; **7** Garth Tander, AUS, 1360; **8** Jason Bright, AUS, 1352; **9** Cameron McConville, AUS, 1303; **10** Rick Kelly, AUS, 1274; **11** Steven Johnson, AUS, 1232; **12** Glenn Seton, AUS, 1207; **13** Jamie Whincup, AUS, 1199; **14** Greg Murphy, AUS, 1194; **15** John Bowe, AUS, 1157; **16** Steve Ellery, AUS, 1156; **17** Paul Radisich, NZ, 1114; **18** Jason Richards, AUS, 1053; **19** Brad Jones, AUS, 907; **20** Craig Baird, AUS, 898.

Results of the Symmons Plains and Phillip Island races will be given in AUTOCOURSE 2006–2007.

Non Championship Australian V8 Supercar Race

FORMULA 1 SUPPORT RACES, Albert Park Lake Circuit, Melbourne, Victoria, Australia, 4/5/6 March. 10, 19 and 10 laps of the 3.295-mile/5.303-km circuit.

Race 1 (32.951 miles/53.030 km).

1 Todd Kelly, AUS (Holden Commodore VZ), 20m 03.3064s, 98.582 mph/158.653 km/h; **2** Marcos Ambrose, AUS (Ford Falcon BA), 20m 06.6157s; **3** Mark Skaife, AUS (Holden Commodore VZ), 20m 10.1400s; **4** Russell Ingall, AUS (Ford Falcon BA), 20m 12.8765s; **5** Jason Bright, AUS (Ford Falcon BA), 20m 15.1033s; **6** Cameron McConville, AUS (Holden Commodore VZ), 20m 15.6772s; **7** Paul Radisich, NZ (Holden Commodore VZ), 20m 17.0140s; **8** Steven Richards, AUS (Holden Commodore VY), 20m 17.6732s; **9** Greg Ritter, AUS (Ford Falcon BA), 20m 20.1688s; **10** Steven Johnson, AUS (Ford Falcon BA), 20m 20.9416s.

Fastest race lap: Ambrose, 1m 58.7812s, 99.868 mph/160.722 km/h.

Fastest qualifying lap: Kelly (Todd), 1m 57.7480s, 100.745 mph/162.133 km/h.

Race 2 (62.607 miles/100.757 km).

1 John Bowe, AUS (Ford Falcon BA), 48m 59.2305s, 76.682 mph/123.408 km/h; **2** Brad Jones, AUS (Ford Falcon BA), 49m 08.6683s; **3** Mark Skaife, AUS (Holden Commodore VZ), 49m 15.8024s; **4** Marcos Ambrose, AUS (Ford Falcon BA), 49m 16.3814s; **5** Russell Ingall, AUS (Ford Falcon BA), 49m 31.4081s; **6** Craig Lowndes, AUS (Ford Falcon BA), 49m 40.4726s; **7** Jason Bright, AUS (Ford Falcon BA), 49m 43.5295s; **8** Jamie Whincup, AUS (Holden Commodore VZ), 49m 43.9739s; **9** Steve Ellery, AUS (Ford Falcon BA), 49m 44.3750s; **10** Rick Kelly, AUS (Holden Commodore VZ), 49m 45.1310s.

Fastest race lap: Jones, 2m 04.5206s, 95.265 mph/153.314 km/h.

Race 3 (32.951 miles/53.030 km).

1 Mark Skaife, AUS (Holden Commodore VZ), 20m 10.7909s, 97.973 mph/157.672 km/h; **2** Marcos Ambrose, AUS (Ford Falcon BA), 20m 12.0825s; **3** Russell Ingall, AUS (Ford Falcon BA), 20m 12.4853s; **4** Craig Lowndes, AUS (Ford Falcon BA), 20m 21.8431s; **5** John Bowe, AUS (Ford Falcon BA), 20m 22.9665s; **6** Brad Jones, AUS (Ford Falcon BA), 20m 23.8694s; **7** Jamie Whincup, AUS (Holden Commodore VZ), 20m 29.0598s; **8** Jason Bargwanna, AUS (Ford Falcon BA), 20m 32.4452s; **9** Mark Winterbottom, AUS (Ford Falcon BA), 20m 33.6043s; **10** Jason Richards, AUS (Holden Commodore VZ), 20m 34.3552s.

Fastest race lap: Ambrose, 1m 59.5218s, 99.249 mph/159.727 km/h.

FIA World Touring Car Championship

FIA WORLD TOURING CAR CHAMPIONSHIP, Autodromo Nazionale di Monza, Milan, Italy, 10 April. 2 x 9 laps of the 3.600-mile/5.793-km circuit.

Round 1 (32.204 miles/51.828 km).

1 Dirk Müller, D (BMW 320i), 18m 03.203s, 107.031 mph/172.249 km/h; **2** Gabriele Tarquini, I (Alfa Romeo 156), 18m 05.668s; **3** Augusto Farfus Jr., BR (Alfa Romeo 156), 18m 07.057s; **4** Andy Priaulx, GB (BMW 320i), 18m 07.180s; **5** Antonio Garcia, E (BMW 320i), 18m 11.291s; **6** Fabrizio Giovanardi, I (Alfa Romeo 156), 18m 11.451s; **7** James Thompson, GB (Alfa Romeo 156), 18m 12.113s; **8** Rickard Rydell, S (SEAT Toledo Cupra), 18m 12.395s; **9** Jordi Gené, E (SEAT Toledo Cupra), 18m 12.617s; **10** Alessandro 'Alex' Zanardi, I (BMW 320i), 18m 18.046s.

Fastest race lap: Müller (Dirk), 1m 59.552s, 108.393 mph/174.441 km/h.

Fastest qualifying lap: Müller (Dirk), 1m 59.009s, 108.887 mph/175.237 km/h.

Round 2 (32.204 miles/51.828 km).

1 James Thompson, GB (Alfa Romeo 156), 18m 13.906s, 105.983 mph/170.564 km/h; **2** Dirk Müller, D (BMW 320i), 18m 14.436s; **3** Antonio Garcia, E (BMW 320i), 18m 14.671s; **4** Jörg Müller, D (BMW 320i), 18m 15.154s; **5** Andy Priaulx, GB (BMW 320i), 18m 15.373s; **6** Jordi Gené, E (SEAT Toledo Cupra), 18m 16.376s; **7** Alessandro 'Alex' Zanardi, I (BMW 320i), 18m 19.882s; **8** Fabrizio Giovanardi, I (Alfa Romeo 156), 18m 20.673s; **9** Augusto Farfus Jr., BR (Alfa Romeo 156), 18m 22.810s; **10** Marc Hennerici, D (BMW 320i), 18m 32.137s.

Fastest race lap: Müller (Jörg), 1m 59.058s, 108.843 mph/175.165 km/h.

Pole position: Rydell.

FIA WORLD TOURING CAR CHAMPIONSHIP, Circuit de Nevers, Magny-Cours, France, 1 May. 2 x 12 laps of the 2.741-mile/4.411-km circuit.

Round 3 (32.776 miles/52.748 km).

1 Jörg Müller, D (BMW 320i), 22m 19.545s, 88.085 mph/141.759 km/h; **2** Andy Priaulx, GB (BMW 320i), 22m 22.427s; **3** Rickard Rydell, S (SEAT Toledo Cupra), 22m 26.798s; **4** Gabriele Tarquini, I (Alfa Romeo 156), 22m 27.879s; **5** Antonio Garcia, E (BMW 320i), 22m 29.444s; **6** Dirk Müller, D (BMW 320i), 22m 32.457s; **7** Jordi Gené, E (SEAT Toledo Cupra), 22m 33.660s; **8** Augusto Farfus Jr., BR (Alfa Romeo 156), 22m 35.212s; **9** Peter Terting, D (SEAT Toledo Cupra), 22m 38.998s; **10** Fabrizio Giovanardi, I (Alfa Romeo 156), 22m 39.132s.

Fastest race lap: Müller (Jörg), 1m 50.826s, 89.033 mph/143.284 km/h.

Fastest qualifying lap: Müller (Jörg), 1m 49.486s, 90.122 mph/145.038 km/h.

Round 4 (32.776 miles/52.748 km).

1 Jörg Müller, D (BMW 320i), 22m 23.707s, 87.812 mph/141.320 km/h; **2** Dirk Müller, D (BMW 320i), 22m 28.710s; **3** Andy Priaulx, GB (BMW 320i), 22m 28.878s; **4** Antonio Garcia, E (BMW 320i), 22m 29.187s; **5** Augusto Farfus Jr., BR (Alfa Romeo 156), 22m 29.741s; **6** Jordi Gené, E (SEAT Toledo Cupra), 22m 32.586s; **7** Fabrizio Giovanardi, I (Alfa Romeo 156), 22m 34.245s; **8** Gabriele Tarquini, I (Alfa Romeo 156), 22m 34.535s; **9** James Thompson, GB (Alfa Romeo 156), 22m 40.842s; **10** Peter Terting, D (SEAT Toledo Cupra), 22m 42.764s.

Fastest race lap: Müller (Jörg), 1m 50.447s, 89.338 mph/143.776 km/h.

Pole position: Farfus Jr..

FIA WORLD TOURING CAR CHAMPIONSHIP, Silverstone International Circuit, Towcester, Northamptonshire, Great Britain, 15 May. 2 x 14 of the 2.249-mile/3.620-km circuit.

Round 5 (31.522 miles/50.730 km).

1 Gabriele Tarquini, I (Alfa Romeo 156), 20m 35.654s, 91.838 mph/147.799 km/h; **2** James Thompson, GB (Alfa Romeo 156), 20m 36.941s; **3** Fabrizio Giovanardi, I (Alfa Romeo 156), 20m 37.280s; **4** Augusto Farfus Jr., BR (Alfa Romeo 156), 20m 37.578s; **5** Andy Priaulx, GB (BMW 320i), 20m 40.040s; **6** Peter Terting, D (SEAT Toledo Cupra), 20m 41.249s; **7** Rickard Rydell, S (SEAT Toledo Cupra), 20m 41.673s; **8** Jason Plato, GB (SEAT Toledo Cupra), 20m 45.841s; **9** Jörg Müller, D (BMW 320i), 20m 47.265s; **10** Dirk Müller, D (BMW 320i), 20m 47.824s.

Fastest race lap: Giovanardi, 1m 26.969s, 93.110 mph/149.846 km/h.

Fastest qualifying lap: Tarquini, 1m 25.639s, 94.556 mph/152.174 km/h.

Round 6 (31.522 miles/50.730 km).

1 Rickard Rydell, S (SEAT Toledo Cupra), 21m 43.465s, 87.060 mph/140.110 km/h; **2** Jason Plato, GB (SEAT Toledo Cupra), 21m 48.174s; **3** Gabriele Tarquini, I (Alfa Romeo 156), 21m 48.514s; **4** Augusto Farfus Jr., BR (Alfa Romeo 156), 21m 49.022s; **5** Jordi Gené, E (SEAT Toledo Cupra), 21m 50.177s; **6** Dirk Müller, D

(BMW 320i), 21m 50.704s; **7** Jörg Müller, D (BMW 320i), 21m 58.081s; **8** Fabrizio Giovanardi, I (Alfa Romeo 156), 22m 03.064s; **9** Marc Hennerici, D (BMW 320i), 22m 07.150s; **10** Valle Mäkelä, FIN (SEAT Toledo Cupra), 22m 07.438s.
Fastest race lap: Priaulx, 1m 26.730s, 93.367 mph/150.259 km/h.
Pole position: Plato.

FIA WORLD TOURING CAR CHAMPIONSHIP, Autodromo Enzo e Dino Ferrari, Imola, Italy, 29 May. 2 x 11 laps of the 3.065-mile/4.933-km circuit.
Round 7 (33.570 miles/54.025 km).
1 Fabrizio Giovanardi, I (Alfa Romeo 156), 22m 12.202s, 90.715 mph/145.991 km/h; **2** Antonio Garcia, E (BMW 320i), 22m 15.348s; **3** Andy Priaulx, GB (BMW 320i), 22m 20.333s; **4** Dirk Müller, D (BMW 320i), 22m 21.328s; **5** Augusto Farfus Jr., BR (Alfa Romeo 156), 22m 24.501s; **6** Roberto Colciago, I (Honda Accord Euro R), 22m 27.377s; **7** James Thompson, GB (Alfa Romeo 156), 22m 29.197s; **8** Alessandro 'Alex' Zanardi, I (BMW 320i), 22m 29.678s; **9** Rickard Rydell, S (SEAT Toledo Cupra), 22m 30.176s; **10** Peter Terting, D (SEAT Toledo Cupra), 22m 30.543s.
Fastest race lap:: Giovanardi, 2m 00.208s, 91.798 mph/147.734 km/h.
Fastest qualifying lap: Giovanardi, 1m 58.573s, 93.063 mph/149.771 km/h.

Round 8 (33.570 miles/54.025 km).
1 Dirk Müller, D (BMW 320i), 22m 17.549s, 90.352 mph/145.408 km/h; **2** Andy Priaulx, GB (BMW 320i), 22m 19.576s; **3** Fabrizio Giovanardi, I (Alfa Romeo 156), 22m 23.371s; **4** Rickard Rydell, S (SEAT Toledo Cupra), 22m 24.335s; **5** Augusto Farfus Jr., BR (Alfa Romeo 156), 22m 26.344s; **6** Alessandro 'Alex' Zanardi, I (BMW 320i), 22m 27.996s; **7** Peter Terting, D (SEAT Toledo Cupra), 22m 28.262s; **8** Jason Plato, GB (SEAT Toledo Cupra), 22m 28.684s; **9** Antonio Garcia, E (BMW 320i), 22m 29.664s; **10** Gabriele Tarquini, I (Alfa Romeo 156), 22m 29.995s.
Fastest race lap: Giovanardi, 2m 00.625s, 91.480 mph/147.223 km/h.
Pole position: Zanardi.

FIA WORLD TOURING CAR CHAMPIONSHIP, Miguel E. Abed International Racetrack, Puebla, Mexico, 26 June. 2 x 17 laps of the 1.883-mile/3.030-km circuit.
Round 9 (32.007 miles/51.510 km).
1 Fabrizio Giovanardi, I (Alfa Romeo 156), 26m 06.219s, 73.569 mph/118.397 km/h; **2** Gabriele Tarquini, I (Alfa Romeo 156), 26m 08.391s; **3** Rickard Rydell, S (SEAT Toledo Cupra), 26m 17.744s; **4** James Thompson, GB (Alfa Romeo 156), 26m 19.517s; **5** Antonio Garcia, E (BMW 320i), 26m 19.991s; **6** Robert Huff, GB (Chevrolet Lacetti), 26m 21.877s; **7** Peter Terting, D (SEAT Toledo Cupra), 26m 24.773s; **8** Tom Coronel, NL (SEAT Toledo Cupra), 26m 28.099s; **9** Augusto Farfus Jr., BR (Alfa Romeo 156), 26m 30.706s; **10** Nicola Larini, I (Chevrolet Lacetti), 26m 31.291s.
Fastest race lap: Tarquini, 1m 30.587s, 74.822 mph/120.415 km/h.
Fastest qualifying lap: Giovanardi, 1m 29.993s, 75.316 mph/121.209 km/h. Roberto Colciago, I (Honda Accord Euro R), qualified 1st but was given a 10-place penalty.

Round 10 (32.007 miles/51.510 km).
1 Peter Terting, D (SEAT Toledo Cupra), 26m 10.825s, 73.353 mph/118.050 km/h; **2** Antonio Garcia, E (BMW 320i), 26m 11.518s; **3** Fabrizio Giovanardi, I (Alfa Romeo 156), 26m 18.403s; **4** James Thompson, GB (Alfa Romeo 156), 26m 22.446s; **5** Tom Coronel, NL (SEAT Toledo Cupra), 26m 23.863s; **6** Rickard Rydell, S (SEAT Toledo Cupra), 26m 24.455s; **7** Nicola Larini, I (Chevrolet Lacetti), 26m 27.916s; **8** Andy Priaulx, GB (BMW 320i), 26m 28.368s; **9** Giuseppe Cirò, I (BMW 320i), 2m 31.923s; **10** Augusto Farfus Jr., BR (Alfa Romeo 156), 26m 32.529s. Roberto Colciago, I (Honda Accord Euro R), finished 3rd in 23m 10.201s, but was given a 30s penalty for causing an accident.
Fastest race lap: Giovanardi, 1m 30.867s, 74.592 mph/120.044 km/h.
Pole position: Coronel.

FIA WORLD TOURING CAR CHAMPIONSHIP, Circuit de Spa-Francorchamps, Stavelot, Belgium, 30 July. 2 x 8 laps of the 4.316-mile/6.946-km circuit.
Round 11 (34.528 miles/55.568 km).
1 Dirk Müller, D (BMW 320i), 22m 58.706s, 90.159 mph/145.096 km/h; **2** Andy Priaulx, GB (BMW 320i), 22m 58.976s; **3** Jörg Müller, D (BMW 320i), 23m 04.154s; **4** Gabriele Tarquini, I (Alfa Romeo 156), 23m 04.418s; **5** James Thompson, GB (Alfa Romeo 156), 23m 04.565s; **6** Antonio Garcia, E (BMW 320i), 23m 09.400s; **7** Fabrizio Giovanardi, I (Alfa Romeo 156), 23m 10.003s; **8** Roberto Colciago, I (Honda Accord Euro R), 23m 10.201s; **9** Jason Plato, GB (SEAT Toledo Cupra), 23m 10.272s; **10** Peter Terting, D (SEAT Toledo Cupra), 23m 10.671s. Augusto Farfus Jr., BR (Alfa Romeo 156), finished 4th in 26m 32.529s but was disqualified for causing an accident.
Fastest race lap: Müller (Dirk), 2m 33.955s, 100.924 mph/162.421 km/h.
Fastest qualifying lap: Farfus Jr., 2m 33.158s, 101.449 mph/163.267 km/h.

Round 12 (34.528 miles/55.568 km).
1 Fabrizio Giovanardi, I (Alfa Romeo 156), 27m 49.757s, 74.443 mph/119.805 km/h; **2** Stefano d'Aste, I (BMW 320i), 27m 49.760s; **3** Tom Coronel, NL (SEAT Toledo Cupra), 27m 51.128s; **4** Augusto Farfus Jr., BR (Alfa Romeo 156), 27m 51.680s; **5** Dirk Müller, D (BMW 320i), 27m 53.807s; **6** Alain Menu, CH (Chevrolet Lacetti), 27m 57.376s; **7** James Thompson, GB (Alfa Romeo 156), 27m 59.564s; **8** Antonio Garcia, E (BMW 320i), 27m 59.826s; **9** Marc Hennerici, D (BMW 320i), 28m 00.335s; **10** Peter Terting, D (SEAT Toledo Cupra), 28m 03.963s.
Fastest race lap: Farfus Jr., 2m 42.690s, 95.505 mph/153.701 km/h.
Pole position: Colciago.

FIA WORLD TOURING CAR CHAMPIONSHIP, Motopark Arena Oschersleben, Germany, 28 August. 2 x 14 laps of the 2.279-mile/3.667-km circuit.
Round 13 (31.799 miles/51.176 km).
1 Andy Priaulx, GB (BMW 320i), 22m 05.714s, 86.352 mph/138.969 km/h; **2** Rickard Rydell, S (SEAT Toledo Cupra), 22m 08.952s; **3** Jörg Müller, D (BMW 320i), 22m 09.069s; **4** Dirk Müller, D (BMW 320i), 22m 09.354s; **5** Peter Terting, D (SEAT Toledo Cupra), 22m 10.522s; **6** Stéphane Ortelli, MC (SEAT Toledo Cupra), 22m 13.198s; **7** Jordi Gené, E (SEAT León), 22m 15.383s; **8** Alessandro 'Alex' Zanardi, I (BMW 320i), 22m 17.081s; **9** Augusto Farfus Jr., BR (Alfa Romeo 156), 22m 17.625s; **10** Thomas Klenke, D (Ford Focus), 22m 17.979s.
Fastest race lap: Müller (Jörg), 1m 34.063s, 87.206 mph/140.344 km/h.
Fastest qualifying lap: Müller (Jörg), 1m 31.772s, 89.383 mph/143.848 km/h.

Round 14 (31.799 miles/51.176 km).
1 Alessandro 'Alex' Zanardi, I (BMW 320i), 21m 59.901s, 86.732 mph/139.581 km/h; **2** Andy Priaulx, GB (BMW 320i), 22m 00.133s; **3** Jörg Müller, D (BMW 320i), 22m 00.425s; **4** Jordi Gené, E (SEAT León), 22m 01.428s; **5** Augusto Farfus Jr., BR (Alfa Romeo 156), 22m 02.191s; **6** Dirk Müller, D (BMW 320i), 22m 08.373s; **7** Rickard Rydell, S (SEAT Toledo Cupra), 22m 10.799s; **8** Alain Menu, CH (Chevrolet Lacetti), 22m 10.923s; **9** Antonio Garcia, E (BMW 320i), 22m 11.298s; **20** Michael Funke, D (Ford Focus), 22m 11.689s.
Fastest race lap: Gabriele Tarquini, I (Alfa Romeo 156), 1m 33.250s, 87.966 mph/141.568 km/h.
Pole position: Zanardi.

FIA WORLD TOURING CAR CHAMPIONSHIP, Istanbul Speed Park, Turkey, 18 September. 2 x 10 laps of the 3.317-mile/5.338-km circuit.
Round 15 (33.040 miles/53.172 km).
1 Fabrizio Giovanardi, I (Alfa Romeo 156), 21m 12.294s, 93.487 mph/150.452 km/h; **2** James Thompson, GB (Alfa Romeo 156), 21m 15.088s; **3** Andy Priaulx, GB (BMW 320i), 21m 18.428s; **4** Antonio Garcia, E (BMW 320i), 21m 19.187s; **5** Rickard Rydell, S (SEAT Toledo Cupra), 21m 20.312s; **6** Alessandro 'Alex' Zanardi, I (BMW 320i), 21m 21.807s; **7** Gabriele Tarquini, I (Alfa Romeo 156), 21m 26.789s; **8** Augusto Farfus Jr., BR (Alfa Romeo 156), 21m 32.005s; **9** Dirk Müller, D (BMW 320i), 21m 32.492s; **10** Alain Menu, CH (Chevrolet Lacetti), 21m 35.099s.
Fastest race lap: Thompson, 2m 05.942s, 94.812 mph/152.585 km/h.
Fastest qualifying lap: Tarquini, 2m 04.525s, 95.891 mph/154.32 km/h.

Round 16 (33.040 miles/53.172 km).
1 Gabriele Tarquini, I (Alfa Romeo 156), 21m 07.765s, 93.821 mph/150.989 km/h; **2** Augusto Farfus Jr., BR (Alfa Romeo 156), 21m 08.028s; **3** Alessandro 'Alex' Zanardi, I (BMW 320i), 21m 08.868s; **4** James Thompson, GB (Alfa Romeo 156), 21m 12.303s; **5** Dirk Müller, D (BMW 320i), 21m 13.188s; **6** Fabrizio Giovanardi, I (Alfa Romeo 156), 21m 17.129s; **7** Rickard Rydell, S (SEAT Toledo Cupra), 21m 19.173s; **8** Alain Menu, CH (Chevrolet Lacetti), 21m 19.302s; **9** Andy Priaulx, GB (BMW 320i), 21m 21.672s; **10** Peter Terting, D (SEAT Toledo Cupra), 21m 22.854s.
Fastest race lap: Tarquini, 2m 05.771s, 94.941 mph/152.792 km/h.
Pole position: Farfus Jr..

FIA WORLD TOURING CAR CHAMPIONSHIP, Circuit de la Comunitat Valenciana Ricardo Tormo, Cheste, Valencia, Spain, 2 October. 2 x 13 laps of the 2.489-mile/4.005-km circuit.
Round 17 (32.352 miles/52.065 km).
1 Jordi Gené, E (SEAT León), 22m 48.757s, 85.089 mph/136.937 km/h; **2** Dirk Müller, D (BMW 320i), 22m 52.045s; **3** Peter Terting, D (SEAT León), 22m 55.856s; **4** Andy Priaulx, GB (BMW 320i), 22m 57.174s; **5** Jörg Müller, D (BMW 320i), 22m 59.685s; **6** Fabrizio Giovanardi, I (Alfa Romeo 156), 23m 04.263s; **7** Nicola Larini, I (Chevrolet Lacetti), 23m 08.171s; **8** Alessandro 'Alex' Zanardi, I (BMW 320i), 23m 08.694s; **9** Stéphane Ortelli, MC (SEAT Toledo Cupra), 23m 14.042s; **10** Marc Carol, E (SEAT Toledo Cupra), 23m 14.971s.
Fastest race lap: Müller (Dirk), 1m 43.795s, 86.314 mph/138.908 km/h.
Fastest qualifying lap:: Gené, 1m 42.778s, 87.168 mph/140.283 km/h.

Round 18 (32.352 miles/52.065 km).
1 Jörg Müller, D (BMW 320i), 23m 00.510s, 84.365 mph/135.772 km/h; **2** Fabrizio Giovanardi, I (Alfa Romeo 156), 23m 08.270s; **3** Andy Priaulx, GB (BMW 320i), 23m 08.755s; **4** Dirk Müller, D (BMW 320i), 23m 08.990s; **5** Alessandro 'Alex' Zanardi, I (BMW 320i), 23m 09.676s; **6** Antonio Garcia, E (BMW 320i), 23m 09.874s; **7** Augusto Farfus Jr., BR (Alfa Romeo 156), 23m 10.316s; **8** Marc Carol, E (SEAT Toledo Cupra), 23m 11.633s; **9** Tomas Engström, S (Honda Accord Euro R), 23m 15.308s; **10** Giuseppe Cirò, I (BMW 320i), 23m 15.533s.
Fastest race lap Müller (Jörg), 1m 43.948s, 86.187 mph/138.704 km/h.
Pole position: Zanardi.

Provisional championship points
Drivers: 1 Dirk Müller, D, 86; **2** Andy Priaulx, GB, 85; **3** Fabrizio Giovanardi, I, 81; **4** Jörg Müller, D, 59; **5** Gabriele Tarquini, I, 55; **6=** James Thompson, GB, 51; **6=** Antonio Garcia, E, 51; **8=**Rickard Rydell, S, 49; **8=** Augusto Farfus Jr., BR, 49; **10** Alessandro 'Alex' Zanardi, I, 31; **11** Jordi Gené, E, 29; **12** Peter Terting, D, 27; **13** Tom Coronel, NL, 11; **14** Jason Plato, GB, 10; **15** Stefano d'Aste, I, 8; **16** Alain Menu, CH, 5; **17** Roberto Colciago, I, 4.

Independents' Trophy: 1 Marc Hennerici, D, 102; **2** Giuseppe Cirò, I, 87; **3** Tom Coronel, NL, 85; **4** Carl Rosenblad, S, 78; **5** Stefano d'Aste, I, 76.

Manufacturers: 1 BMW, 244; **2** Alfa Romeo, 219; **3** SEAT, 170; **4** Chevrolet, 57; **5** Ford, 10.
Teams: 1 Proteam Motorsport, 163; **2** GR Asia, 142; **3** Wiechers-Sport, 102; **4** Crawford Racing, 78; **5** JAS Motorsport, 71.

Results of the Macau races will be given in AUTOCOURSE 2006–2007.

German Touring Car Championship (DTM)

GERMAN TOURING CAR CHAMPIONSHIP, Hockenheimring Grand Prix Circuit, Heidelberg, Germany, 17 April. Round 1. 37 laps of the 2.842-mile/4.574-km circuit, 105.160 miles/169.238km.
1 Jean Alesi, F (Mercedes Benz C-class), 1h 04m 48.245s, 97.364 mph/156.691 km/h; **2** Gary Paffett, GB (Mercedes Benz C-class), 1h 04m 53.888s; **3** Bernd Schneider, D (Mercedes Benz C-class), 1h 04m 54.665s; **4** Christian Abt, D (Audi A4 DTM), 1h 04m 57.200s; **5** Mattias Ekström, S (Audi A4 DTM), 1h 05m 01.182s; **6** Jamie Green, GB (Mercedes Benz C-class), 1h 05m 04.666s; **7** Stefan Mücke, D (Mercedes Benz C-class), 1h 05m 08.810s; **8** Mika Häkkinen, FIN (Mercedes Benz C-class), 1h 05m 10.310s; **9** Marcel Fässler, CH (Opel Vectra GTS V8), 1h 05m 15.833s; **10** Frank Stippler, D (Audi A4 DTM), 1h 05m 16.247s.
Fastest race lap: Green, 1h 35.262s, 107.406 mph/172.853 km/h.
Pole position: Ekström, 1m 35.251s, 107.419 mph/172.873 km/h.

GERMAN TOURING CAR CHAMPIONSHIP, EuroSpeedway Lausitz, Klettwitz, Dresden, Germany, 1 May. Round 2. 48 laps of the 2.139-mile/3.442-km circuit, 102.660 miles/165.216 km.
1 Gary Paffett, GB (Mercedes Benz C-class), 1h 03m 21.071s, 97.230 mph/156.476 km/h; **2** Tom Kristensen, DK (Audi A4 DTM), 1h 03m 25.543s; **3** Mika Häkkinen, FIN (Mercedes Benz C-class), 1h 03m 27.146s; **4** Mattias Ekström, S (Audi A4 DTM), 1h 03m 55.927s; **5** Pierre Kaffer, D (Audi A4 DTM), 1h 03m 56.355s; **6** Frank Stippler, D (Audi A4 DTM), 1h 04m 03.370s; **7** Jean Alesi, F (Mercedes Benz C-class), 1h 04m 06.790s; **8** Stefan Mücke, D (Mercedes Benz C-class), 1h 04m 12.683s; **9** Christian Abt, D (Audi A4 DTM), 1h 04m 12.710s; **10** Laurent Aiello, F (Opel Vectra GTS V8), 1h 04m 15.447s.
Fastest race lap: Häkkinen, 1m 17.583s, 99.243 mph/159.715 km/h.
Pole position: Paffett, 1m 15.808s, 101.566 mph/163.455 km/h.

GERMAN TOURING CAR CHAMPIONSHIP, Circuit de Spa-Francorchamps, Stavelot, Belgium, 15 May. Round 3. 24 laps of the 4.335-mile/6.976-km circuit, 104.032 miles/167.424 km.
1 Mika Häkkinen, FIN (Mercedes Benz C-class), 54m 34.544s, 114.372 mph/184.064 km/h; **2** Mattias Ekström, S (Audi A4 DTM), 54m 38.802s; **3** Tom Kristensen, DK (Audi A4 DTM), 54m 40.520s; **4** Jean Alesi, F (Mercedes Benz C-class), 54m 44.632s; **5** Marcel Fässler, CH (Opel Vectra GTS V8), 55m 02.345s; **6** Martin Tomczyk, D (Audi A4 DTM), 55m 02.545s; **7** Laurent Aiello, F (Opel Vectra GTS V8), 55m 08.060s; **8** Gary Paffett, GB (Mercedes Benz C-class), 55m 08.060s; **9** Alexandros 'Alex' Margaritis, D (Mercedes Benz C-class), 55m 24.799s; **10** Christian Abt, D (Audi A4 DTM), 55m 25.400s.
Fastest race lap:: Häkkinen, 2m 13.134s, 117.212 mph/188.634 km/h.
Pole position: Häkkinen, 2m 32.729s, 102.174 mph/164.432 km/h.

GERMAN TOURING CAR CHAMPIONSHIP, Automotodrom Brno Masaryk Circuit, Brno, Czech Republic, 5 June. Round 4. 30 laps of the 3.357-mile/5.403-km circuit, 100.718 miles/162.090 km.
1 Mattias Ekström, S (Audi A4 DTM), 58m 52.558s, 102.641 mph/165.184 km/h; **2** Tom Kristensen, DK (Audi A4 DTM), 58m 52.846s; **3** Heinz-Harald Frentzen, D (Opel Vectra GTS V8), 59m 17.252s; **4** Gary Paffett, GB (Mercedes Benz C-class), 59m 21.061s; **5** Jamie Green, GB (Mercedes Benz C-class), 59m 23.555s; **6** Christian Abt, D (Audi A4 DTM), 59m 27.113s; **7** Allan McNish, GB (Audi A4 DTM), 59m 27.373s; **8** Frank Stippler, D (Audi A4 DTM), 59m 28.660s; **9** Jean Alesi, F (Mercedes Benz C-class), 59m 35.844s; **10** Rinaldo Capello, I (Audi A4 DTM), 59m 36.210s.
Fastest race lap: Martin Tomcyzk, D (Audi A4 DTM), 1m 54.786s, 105.293 mph/169.452 km/h.
Pole position: Paffett, 1m 52.191s, 107.728 mph/173.372 km/h.

GERMAN TOURING CAR CHAMPIONSHIP, Motopark Arena Oschersleben, Germany, 26 June. Round 5. 44 laps of the 2.279-mile/3.667-km circuit, 100.257 miles/161.348 km.
1 Gary Paffett, GB (Mercedes Benz C-class), 1h 01m 15.183s, 98.206 mph/158.047 km/h; **2** Mattias Ekström, S (Audi A4 DTM), 1h 01m 18.352s; **3** Jamie Green, GB (Mercedes Benz C-class), 1h 01m 25.643s; **4** Bernd Schneider, D (Mercedes Benz C-class), 1h 01m 39.841s; **5** Tom Kristensen, DK (Audi A4 DTM), 1h 01m 40.402s; **6** Allan McNish, GB (Audi A4 DTM), 1h 01m 41.314s; **7** Laurent Aiello, F (Opel Vectra GTS V8), 1h 01m 41.954s; **8** Marcel Fässler, CH (Opel Vectra GTS V8), 1h 01m 54.933s; **9** Frank Stippler, D (Audi A4 DTM), 1h 01m 55.505s; **10** Rinaldo Capello, I (Audi A4 DTM), 1h 01m 57.613s.
Fastest race lap: Ekström, 1m 20.791s, 101.532 mph/163.399 km/h.
Pole position: Kristensen, 1m 20.218s, 102.257 mph/164.566 km/h.

GERMAN TOURING CAR CHAMPIONSHIP, Norisring, Nürnberg, Germany, 17 July. Round 6. 72 laps of the 1.429-mile/2.300-km circuit, 102.899 miles/165.600 km.
1 Gary Paffett, GB (Mercedes Benz C-class), 1h 05m 58.262s, 93.586 mph/150.611 km/h; **2** Christian Abt, D (Audi A4 DTM), 1h 06m 01.889s; **3** Mattias Ekström, S (Audi A4 DTM), 1h 06m 04.531s; **4** Allan McNish, GB (Audi A4 DTM), 1h 06m 11.513s; **5** Martin Tomczyk, D (Auidi A4 DTM), 1h 06m 11.877s; **6** Heinz-Harald Frentzen, D (Opel Vectra GTS V8), 1h 06m 12.800s; **7** Tom Kristensen, DK (Audi A4 DTM), 1h 06m 20.179s; **8** Pierre Kaffer, D (Audi A4 DTM), 1h 06m 21.572s; **9** Manuel Reuter, D (Opel Vectra GTS V8), 1h 06m 32.512s; **10** Bernd Schneider, D (Mercedes Benz C-class), 1h 06m 54.274s.
Fastest race lap: Paffett, 48.922s, 105.166 mph/169.249 km/h.
Pole position: Kristensen, 48.446s, 106.200 mph/170.911 km/h.

GERMAN TOURING CAR CHAMPIONSHIP, Nürburgring Grand Prix Circuit, Nürburg/Eifel, Germany, 7 August. Round 7. 43 laps of the 2.255-mile/3.629-km circuit, 96.963 miles/156.047 km.
1 Mattias Ekström, S (Audi A4 DTM), 1h 05m 09.223s, 89.293 mph/143.703 km/h; **2** Tom Kristensen, DK (Audi A4 DTM), 1h 05m 10.311s; **3** Gary Paffett, GB (Mercedes Benz C-class), 1h 05m 13.808s; **4** Mika Häkkinen, FIN (Mercedes Benz C-class), 1h 05m 14.468s; **5** Bernd Schneider, D (Mercedes Benz C-class), 1h 05m 19.750s; **6** Allan McNish, GB (Audi A4 DTM), 1h 05m 26.929s; **7** Jean Alesi, F (Mercedes Benz C-class), 1h 05m 30.157s; **8** Jamie Green, GB (Mercedes Benz C-class), 1h 05m 33.875s; **9** Laurent Aïello, F (Opel Vectra GTS V8), 1h 05m 36.981s; **10** Christian Abt, D (Audi A4 DTM), 1h 05m 37.896s.
Fastest race lap: Paffett, 1m 24.442s, 96.135 mph/154.714 km/h.
Pole position: Paffett, 1m 23.161s, 97.616 mph/157.097 km/h.

GERMAN TOURING CAR CHAMPIONSHIP, Circuit Park Zandvoort, Netherlands, 28 August. Round 8. 38 laps of the 2.676-mile/4.307-km circuit, 101.697 miles/163.666 km.
1 Gary Paffett, GB (Mercedes Benz C-class), 1h 01m 59.421s, 98.452 mph/158.411 km/h; **2** Mattias Ekström, S (Audi A4 DTM), 1h 02m 11.436s; **3** Heinz-Harald Frentzen, D (Opel Vectra GTS V8), 1h 02m 16.153s; **4** Tom Kristensen, DK (Audi A4 DTM), 1h 02m 19.463s; **5** Marcel Fässler, CH (Opel Vectra GTS V8), 1h 02m 20.294s; **6** Martin Tomczyk, D (Auidi A4 DTM), 1h 02m 20.541s; **7** Jamie Green, GB (Mercedes Benz C-class), 1h 02m 22.857s; **8** Bernd Schneider, D (Mercedes Benz C-class), 1h 02m 30.342s; **9** Bruno Spengler, CDN (Mercedes Benz C-class), 1h 02m 35.909s; **10** Christian Abt, D (Audi A4 DTM), 1h 02m 37.140s.
Fastest race lap: Paffett, 1m 34.785s, 101.646 mph/163.582 km/h.
Pole position: Schneider, 1m 32.730s, 103.898 mph/167.208 km/h.

GERMAN TOURING CAR CHAMPIONSHIP, Eurospeedway Lausitz, Klettwitz, Dresden, Germany, 18 September. Round 9. 48 laps of the 2.139-mile/3.442-km circuit, 102.660 miles/165.216 km.
1 Mattias Ekström, S (Audi A4 DTM), 1h 03m 44.903s, 96.624 mph/155.501 km/h; **2** Gary Paffett, GB (Mercedes Benz C-class), 1h 03m 45.304s; **3** Tom Kristensen, DK (Audi A4 DTM), 1h 03m 47.965s; **4** Laurent Aiello, F (Opel Vectra GTS V8), 1h 03m 49.659s; **5** Manuel Reuter, D (Opel Vectra GTS V8), 1h 03m 50.985s; **6** Bruno Spengler, CDN (Mercedes Benz C-class), 1h 04m 03.665s; **7** Heinz-Harald Frentzen, D (Opel Vectra GTS V8), 1h 04m 06.271s; **8** Jean Alesi, F (Mercedes Benz C-class), 1h 04m 08.202s; **9** Allan McNish, GB (Audi A4 DTM), 1h 04m 14.669s; **10** Martin Tomczyk, D (Auidi A4 DTM), 1h 04m 15.101s.
Fastest race lap: Paffett, 1m 17.938s, 101.650 mph/158.987 km/h.
Pole position: Jamie Green, GB (Mercedes Benz C-class), 1m 17.489s, 99.363 mph/159.909 km/h.

GERMAN TOURING CAR CHAMPIONSHIP, Istanbul Speed Park, Turkey, 2 October. Round 10. 32 laps of the 3.317-mile/5.338-km circuit, 106.140 miles/170.816 km.
1 Gary Paffett, GB (Mercedes Benz C-class), 1h 05m 27.828s, 97.281 mph/156.559 km/h; **2** Mika Häkkinen, FIN (Mercedes Benz C-class), 1h 05m 31.050s; **3** Bernd Schneider, D (Mercedes Benz C-class), 1h 05m 31.379s; **4** Jamie Green, GB (Mercedes Benz C-class), 1h 05m 31.822s; **5** Tom Kristensen, DK (Audi A4 DTM), 1h 05m 58.717s; **6** Laurent Aiello, F (Opel Vectra GTS V8), 1h 06m 00.970s; **7** Jean Alesi, F (Mercedes Benz C-class), 1h 06m 04.362s; **8** Bruno Spengler, CDN (Mercedes Benz C-class), 1h 06m 05.369s; **9** Stefan Mücke, D (Mercedes Benz C-class), 1h 06m 13.453s; **10** Marcel Fässler, CH (Opel Vectra GTS V8), 1h 06m 20.309s.
Fastest race lap: Häkkinen, 2m 00.130s, 99.399 mph/159.966 km/h.
Pole position: Paffett, 1m 47.101s, 111.491 mph/179.426 km/h.

GERMAN TOURING CAR CHAMPIONSHIP, Hockenheimring Grand Prix Circuit, Heidelberg, Germany, 23 October. Round 11. 36 laps of the 2.842-mile/4.574-km circuit, 102.317 miles/164.664 km.
1 Bernd Schneider, D (Mercedes Benz C-class), 1h 02m 12.480s, 98.686 mph/158.819 km/h; **2** Jamie Green, GB (Mercedes Benz C-class), 1h 02m 20.556s; **3** Gary Paffett, GB (Mercedes Benz C-class), 1h 02m 28.466s; **4** Tom Kristensen, DK (Audi A4 DTM), 1h 02m 29.073s; **5** Frank Stippler, D (Audi A4 DTM), 1h 02m 39.298s; **6** Marcel Fässler, CH (Opel Vectra GTS V8), 1h 02m 55.391s; **7** Mattias Ekström, S (Audi A4 DTM), 1h 02m 56.971s; **8** Bruno Spengler, CDN (Mercedes Benz C-class), 1h 02m 58.236s; **9** Laurent Aïello, F (Opel Vectra GTS V8), 1h 03m 00.780s; **10** Pierre Kaffer, D (Audi A4 DTM), 1h 03m 02.508s.
Fastest race lap: Green, 1m 34.868s, 107.852 mph/173.571 km/h.
Pole position: Green, 1m 45.294s, 97.173 mph/156.384 km/h.

Final championship points
Drivers: 1 Gary Paffett, GB, 84; **2** Mattias Ekström, S, 71; **3** Tom Kristensen, DK, 56; **4** Bernd Schneider, D, 32; **5** Mika Häkkinen, FIN, 30; **6** Jamie Green, GB, 29; **7** Jean Alesi, F, 22; **8** Heinz-Harald Frentzen, D, 17; **9** Christian Abt, D, 16; **10** Allan McNish, GB, 13; **11=** Marcel Fässler, CH, 12; **11=** Laurent Aiello, F, 12; **13** Martin Tomczyk, D, 10; **14** Frank Stippler, D, 8; **15=** Pierre Kaffer, D, 5; **15=** Bruno Spengler, CDN, 5; **17** Manuel Reuter, D, 4; **18** Stefan Mücke, D, 3.
Teams: 1 DaimlerChrysler Bank AMG-Mercedes, 106; **2** Audi Sport Team Abt Sportsline, 81; **3** Audi Sport Team Abt, 69; **4** Vodafone-Sport Edition AMG-Mercedes, 62.
Manufacturers: 1 Mercedes, 205; **2** Audi, 179; **3** Opel, 45.

Other DTM Race

DTM RACE OF LEGENDS, Norisring, Nürnberg, Germany, 16 July. 1.429-mile/2.300-km circuit.
Session 1 fastest times:
1 Alain Prost, F (Audi TT), 49.920s; **2** Emerson Fittipaldi, BR (Mercedes Benz C-class), 51.381s; **3** Jody Scheckter, ZA (Audi A4), 51.631s; **4** Nigel Mansell, GB (Opel Vectra GTS V8), 51.740s; **5** Johnny Cecotto, YV (Opel Vectra GTS V8), 51.756s; **6** Mike Doohan, AUS (Mercedes Benz C-class), 53.128s.

Session 2 fastest times:
1 Alain Prost, F (Mercedes Benz C-class), 50.437s; **2** Johnny Cecotto, YV (Audi TT), 50.596; **3** Nigel Mansell, GB (Audi A4), 50.888s; **4** Jody Scheckter, ZA (Mercedes Benz C-class), 52.126s; **5** Emerson Fittipaldi, BR (Opel Vectra GTS V8), 52.190s; **6** Mike Doohan, AUS (Opel Vectra GTS V8), 52.367s.

Session 3 fastest times:
1 Emerson Fittipaldi, BR (Audi TT), 50.493s; **2** Johnny Cecotto, YV (Mercedes Benz C-class), 50.578s; **3** Alain Prost, F (Opel Vectra GTS V8), 50.667s; **4** Nigel Mansell, GB (Mercedes Benz C-class), 50.987s; **5** Mike Doohan, AUS (Audi A4), 52.154s; **6** Jody Scheckter, ZA (Opel Vectra GTS V8), no time.
Fastest overall lap: Prost, 49.920s, 113.064 mph/165.865 km/h.
Final score: 1 Prost, 8 points; **2** Fittipaldi, 7; **3** Cecotto, 6; **4** Mansell, 4, **5** Scheckter, 3; **6** Doohan, 2.

British Touring Car Championship

BRITISH TOURING CAR CHAMPIONSHIP, Donington Park National Circuit, Castle Donington, Derbyshire, Great Britain, 10 April. 3 x 16 laps of the 1.957-mile/3.149-km circuit.
Round 1 (31.312 miles/50.392 km).
1 Matt Neal, GB (Honda Integra), 19m 43.015s, 95.285 mph/153.346 km/h; **2** Yvan Muller, F (Vauxhall Astra Sport Hatch), 19m 43.354s; **3** Dan Eaves, GB (Honda Integra), 19m 51.156s; **4** Rob Collard, GB (MG ZS), 19m 52.631s; **5** Colin Turkington, GB (Vauxhall Astra Sport Hatch), 19m 55.248s; **6** Jason Plato, GB (SEAT Toledo Cupra), 19m 58.239s; **7** Luke Hines, GB (SEAT Toledo Cupra), 19m 58.413s; **8** Gavin Smith, IRL (Vauxhall Astra Sport Hatch), 19m 58.618s; **9** James Pickford, GB (SEAT Toledo Cupra), 20m 08.209s; **10** Mark Proctor, GB (Vauxhall Astra Coupé), 15 laps; **11** James Kaye, GB (Honda Civic Type-R), 13 (DNF-engine); **12** Richard Williams, GB (Lexus IS200),13.
Fastest race lap: Muller, 1m 12.889s, 96.657 mph/155.554 km/h.
Fastest qualifying lap: Turkington, 1m 12.092s, 97.725 mph/157.273 km/h.

Round 2 (31.312 miles/50.392 km).
1 Yvan Muller, F (Vauxhall Astra Sport Hatch), 19m 46.651s, 94.993 mph/152.876 km/h; **2** Rob Collard, GB (MG ZS), 19m 46.830s; **3** Matt Neal, GB (Honda Integra), 19m 47.951s; **4** Dan Eaves, GB (Honda Integra), 19m 52.831s; **5** Jason Plato, GB (SEAT Toledo Cupra), 19m 53.472s; **6** Gavin Smith, IRL (Vauxhall Astra Sport Hatch), 19m 53.687s; **7** James Pickford, GB (SEAT Toledo Cupra), 20m 00.955s; **8** Luke Hines, GB (SEAT Toledo Cupra), 20m 01.249s; **9** Richard Williams, GB (Lexus IS200), 19m 56.560s; **10** Mark Proctor, GB (Vauxhall Astra Coupé), 7 laps (DNF-suspension); **11** Colin Turkington, GB (Vauxhall Astra Sport Hatch), 2 (DNF-accident damage); **12** James Kaye, GB (Honda Civic Type-R), 1 (DNF-engine check).
Fastest race lap: Collard, 1m 13.229s, 96.208 mph/154.831 km/h.
Pole position: Neal.

Round 3 (31.312 miles/50.392 km).
1 Matt Neal, GB (Honda Integra), 19m 50.443s, 94.690 mph/152.389 km/h; **2** Dan Eaves, GB (Honda Integra), 19m 50.714s; **3** Yvan Muller, F (Vauxhall Astra Sport Hatch), 19m 52.397s; **4** Rob Collard, GB (MG ZS), 19m 56.396s; **5** Gavin Smith, IRL (Vauxhall Astra Sport Hatch), 19m 59.192s; **6** Jason Plato, GB (SEAT Toledo Cupra), 20m 02.311s; **7** James Pickford, GB (SEAT Toledo Cupra), 20m 02.600s; **8** Colin Turkington, GB (Vauxhall Astra Sport Hatch), 20m 07.231s; **9** Luke Hines, GB (SEAT Toledo Cupra), 20m 07.501s; **10** Mark Proctor, GB (Vauxhall Astra Coupé), 20m 36.120s; **11** Richard Williams, GB (Lexus IS200), 21m 01.485s; **12** James Kaye, GB (Honda Civic Type-R), 0 laps (DNF-spin).
Fastest race lap: Eaves, 1m 13.200s, 96.246 mph/154.893 km/h.
Pole position: Williams.

BRITISH TOURING CAR CHAMPIONSHIP, Thruxton Circuit, Andover, Hampshire, Great Britain, 1 May. 16, 16 and 18 laps of the 2.356-mile/3.792-km circuit.
Round 4 (37.696 miles/60.666 km).
1 Dan Eaves, GB (Honda Integra), 21m 33.222s, 104.936 mph/168.878 km/h; **2** Jason Plato, GB (SEAT Toledo Cupra), 21m 34.805s; **3** Matt Neal, GB (Honda Integra), 21m 36.028s; **4** Colin Turkington, GB (Vauxhall Astra Sport Hatch), 21m 41.066s; **5** Rob Collard, GB (MG ZS), 21m 49.838s; **6** Yvan Muller, F (Vauxhall Astra Sport Hatch), 21m 52.507s; **7** James Pickford, GB (SEAT Toledo Cupra), 21m 53.502s; **8** Luke Hines, GB (SEAT Toledo Cupra), 21m 55.953s; **9** Gavin Smith, IRL (Vauxhall Astra Sport Hatch), 22m 03.838s; **10** Tom Chilton, GB (Honda Civic Type-R), 22m 10.458s; **11** James Kaye, GB (Honda Civic Type-R), 4 laps (DNF-engine).
Did not start: Richard Williams, GB (Lexus IS200) - engine.
Fastest race lap: Chilton, 1m 18.658s, 107.829 mph/173.534 km/h.
Fastest qualifying lap: Chilton, 1m 17.011s, 110.135 mph/177.245 km/h.

Round 5 (37.696 miles/60.666 km).
1 Dan Eaves, GB (Honda Integra), 21m 35.659s, 104.739 mph/168.561 km/h; **2** Matt Neal, GB (Honda Integra), 21m 36.515s; **3** Yvan Muller, F (Vauxhall Astra Sport Hatch), 21m 38.166s; **4** James Pickford, GB (SEAT Toledo Cupra), 21m 39.485s; **5** Jason Plato, GB (SEAT Toledo Cupra), 21m 42.633s; **6** Tom Chilton, GB (Honda Civic Type-R), 21m 42.932s; **7** Colin Turkington, GB (Vauxhall Astra Sport Hatch), 21m 43.445s; **8** Luke Hines, GB (SEAT Toledo Cupra), 21m 50.669s; **9** James Kaye, GB (Honda Civic Type-R), 21m 56.462s; **10** Gavin Smith, IRL (Vauxhall Astra Sport Hatch), 21m 58.572s; **11** Rob Collard, GB (MG ZS), 22m 01.455s.
Did not start: Richard Williams, GB (Lexus IS200) - engine.
Fastest race lap: Eaves, 1m 19.302s, 106.953 mph/172.124 km/h.
Pole position: Eaves.

Round 6 (42.408 miles/68.249 km).
1 Dan Eaves, GB (Honda Integra), 26m 09.675s, 97.261 mph/156.527 km/h; **2** Colin Turkington, GB (Vauxhall Astra Sport Hatch), 26m 11.010s; **3** Yvan Muller, F (Vauxhall Astra Sport Hatch), 26m 11.700s; **4** Matt Neal, GB (Honda Integra), 26m 11.739s; **5** Jason Plato, GB (SEAT Toledo Cupra), 26m 12.054s; **6** James Pickford, GB (SEAT Toledo Cupra), 26m 12.393s; **7** James Kaye, GB (Honda Civic Type-R), 26m 13.018s; **8** Luke Hines, GB (SEAT Toledo Cupra), 26m 16.738s; **9** Rob Collard, GB (MG ZS), 13 laps (DNF-engine); **10** Gavin Smith, IRL (Vauxhall Astra Sport Hatch), 0 (DNF-accident); **11** Tom Chilton, GB (Honda Civic Type-R), 0 (DNF-accident).
Did not start: Richard Williams, GB (Lexus IS200) - engine.
Fastest race lap: Plato, 1m 19.445s, 106.761 mph/171.815 km/h.
Pole position: Smith.

BRITISH TOURING CAR CHAMPIONSHIP, Brands Hatch Indy Circuit, West Kingsdown, Dartford, Kent, Great Britain, 5 June. 24, 27 and 27 laps of the 1.2262-mile/1.973-km circuit.
Round 7 (29.429 miles/47.361 km).
1 Matt Neal, GB (Honda Integra), 20m 18.601s, 86.939 mph/139.914 km/h; **2** Colin Turkington, GB (Vauxhall Astra Sport Hatch), 20m 19.662s; **3** Yvan Muller, F (Vauxhall Astra Sport Hatch), 20m 19.905s; **4** Jason Plato, GB (SEAT Toledo Cupra), 20m 20.203s; **5** Luke Hines, GB (SEAT Toledo Cupra), 20m 21.399s; **6** Rob Collard, GB (MG ZS), 20m 21.924s; **7** Tom Chilton, GB (Honda Civic Type-R), 20m 22.776s; **8** James Kaye, GB (Honda Civic Type-R), 20m 22.780s; **9** James Pickford, GB (SEAT Toledo Cupra), 20m 25.229s; **10** Gavin Smith, IRL (Vauxhall Astra Sport Hatch), 20m 30.396s; **11** Richard Williams, GB (Lexus IS200), 15 laps (DNF-differential); **12** Mark Proctor, GB (Vauxhall Astra Coupé), 14 (DNF-alternator); **13** Ian Curley, GB (Lexus IS200), 11; **14** Dan Eaves, GB (Honda Integra), 9 (DNF-accident).
Fastest race lap: Pickford, 49.884s, 88.492 mph/142.414 km/h.
Fastest qualifying lap: Neal, 49.312s, 89.518 mph/144.066 km/h.

Round 8 (33.107 miles/53.281 km).
1 Matt Neal, GB (Honda Integra), 24m 35.608s, 80.771 mph/129.989 km/h; **2** Jason Plato, GB (SEAT Toledo Cupra), 24m 36.618s; **3** Dan Eaves, GB (Honda Integra), 24m 36.808s; **4** Yvan Muller, F (Vauxhall Astra Sport Hatch), 24m 37.956s; **5** Colin Turkington, GB (Vauxhall Astra Sport Hatch), 24m 38.362s; **6** Rob Collard, GB (MG ZS), 24m 38.596s; **7** Gavin Smith, IRL (Vauxhall Astra Sport Hatch), 24m 39.588s; **8** James Pickford, GB (SEAT Toledo Cupra), 24m 41.015s; **9** Ian Curley, GB (Lexus IS200), 25m 20.504s; **10** James Kaye, GB (Honda Civic Type-R), 26 laps (DNF-spin); **11** Tom Chilton, GB (Honda Civic Type-R), 6 (DNF); **12** Luke Hines, GB (SEAT Toledo Cupra), 2 (DNF-spin).
Did not start: Richard Williams, GB (Lexus IS200) - differential; Mark Proctor, GB (Vauxhall Astra Coupé) - alternator.
Fastest race lap: Eaves, 49.890s, 88.481 mph/142.396 km/h.
Pole position: Neal.

Round 9 (33.107 miles/53.281 km).
1 Yvan Muller, F (Vauxhall Astra Sport Hatch), 24m 30.175s, 81.070 mph/k130.469 m/h; **2** Dan Eaves, GB (Honda Integra), 24m 30.499s; **3** Jason Plato, GB (SEAT Toledo Cupra), 24m 32.027s; **4** James Kaye, GB (Honda Civic Type-R), 24m 35.794s; **5** Colin Turkington, GB (Vauxhall Astra Sport Hatch), 24m 37.068s; **6** Matt Neal, GB (Honda Integra), 24m 37.321s; **7** Tom Chilton, GB (Honda Civic Type-R), 24m 37.664s; **8** Mark Proctor, GB (Vauxhall Astra Coupé), 25m 17.392s; **9** Richard Williams, GB (Lexus IS200), 26 laps; **10** Ian Curley, GB (Lexus IS200), 22; **11** Luke Hines, GB (SEAT Toledo Cupra), 14 (DNF-suspension/accident); **12** Gavin Smith, IRL (Vauxhall Astra Sport Hatch), 8 (DNF-accident); **13** Rob Collard, GB (MG ZS), 0 (DNF-spin). James Pickford, GB (SEAT Toledo Cupra) finished 8th in 24m 44.014s but was disqualified for dangerous driving.
Fastest race lap: Chilton, 49.805s, 88.632 mph/142.639 km/h.
Pole position: Kaye.

BRITISH TOURING CAR CHAMPIONSHIP, Oulton Park Island Circuit, Tarporley, Cheshire, Great Britain, 19 June. 15, 15 and 18 laps of the 2.226-mile/3.582-km circuit.
Round 10 (33.390 miles/53.736 km).
1 Jason Plato, GB (SEAT Toledo Cupra), 22m 35.695s, 88.666 mph/142.694 km/h; **2** Matt Neal, GB (Honda Integra), 22m 35.979s; **3** Dan Eaves, GB (Honda Integra), 22m 39.061s; **4** Yvan Muller, F (Vauxhall Astra Sport Hatch), 22m 40.367s; **5** Tom Chilton, GB (Honda Civic Type-R), 22m 42.879s; **6** Gavin Smith, IRL (Vauxhall Astra Sport Hatch), 22m 47.567s; **7** Luke Hines, GB (SEAT Toledo Cupra), 22m 47.654s; **8** Rob Collard, GB (MG ZS), 22m 48.671s; **9** James Pickford, GB (SEAT Toledo Cupra), 22m 50.352s; **10** Colin Turkington, GB (Vauxhall Astra Sport Hatch), 22m 56.355s; **11** James Kaye, GB (Honda Civic Type-R), 23m 11.763s; **12** Mark Proctor, GB (Vauxhall Astra Coupé), 23m 44.633s; **13** Richard Williams, GB (Lexus IS200), 14 laps.
Did not start: Ian Curley, GB (Lexus IS200) - engine.
Fastest race lap: Neal, 1m 29.190s, 89.849 mph/144.597 km/h.
Fastest qualifying lap: Plato, 1m 28.958s, 90.083 mph/144.974 km/h.

Round 11 (33.390 miles/53.736 km).
1 Matt Neal, GB (Honda Integra), 22m 40.170s, 88.374 mph/142.225 km/h; **2** Yvan Muller, F (Vauxhall Astra Sport Hatch), 22m 40.673s; **3** Dan Eaves, GB (Honda Integra), 22m 42.738s; **4** Rob Collard, GB (MG ZS), 22m 43.549s; **5** Tom Chilton, GB (Honda Civic Type-R), 22m 45.592s; **6** Colin Turkington, GB (Vauxhall Astra Sport Hatch), 22m 48.277s; **7** James Pickford, GB (SEAT Toledo Cupra), 22m 58.721s; **8** Mark Proctor, GB (Vauxhall Astra Coupé), 23m 39.885s; **9** Richard Williams, GB (Lexus IS200), 23m 43.677s; **10** Jason Plato, GB (SEAT Toledo Cupra), 23m 58.864s; **11** Gavin Smith, IRL (Vauxhall Astra Sport Hatch), 23m 59.726s; **12** Luke Hines, GB (SEAT Toledo Cupra), 1 lap (DNF-driveshaft).
Did not start: James Kaye, GB (Honda Civic Type-R) - lost wheel on parade lap; Ian Curley, GB (Lexus IS200) - engine.
Fastest race lap: Neal, 1m 28.986s, 90.055 mph/144.929 km/h.
Pole position: Plato.

Round 12 (44.068 miles/64.483 km).
1 Tom Chilton, GB (Honda Civic Type-R), 33m 51.624s, 71.000 mph/114.263 km/h; **2** Matt Neal, GB (Honda Integra), 33m 54.361s; **3** Jason Plato, GB (SEAT Toledo Cupra), 33m 57.264s; **4** Rob Collard, GB (MG ZS), 34m 02.784s; **5** Luke Hines, GB (SEAT Toledo Cupra), 34m 06.045s; **6** Dan Eaves, GB (Honda Integra), 34m 09.231s; **7** James Pickford, GB (SEAT Toledo Cupra), 34m 15.398s; **8** James Kaye, GB (Honda Civic Type-R), 12 laps (DNF-electrics); **9** Gavin Smith, IRL (Vauxhall Astra Sport Hatch), 8 (DNF-accident damage); **10** Mark Proctor, GB (Vauxhall Astra Coupé), 1 (DNF-accident); **11** Yvan Muller, F (Vauxhall Astra Sport Hatch), 1 (DNF-accident damage); **12** Colin Turkington, GB (Vauxhall Astra Sport Hatch), 0 (DNF-accident); **13** Richard Williams, GB (Lexus IS200), 0 (DNF-accident).
Did not start: Ian Curley, GB (Lexus IS200) - engine.
Fastest race lap: Plato, 1m 39.532s, 80.513 mph/129.573 km/h.
Pole position: Plato.

BRITISH TOURING CAR CHAMPIONSHIP, Croft Racing Circuit, Croft-on-Tees, North Yorkshire, Great Britain, 17 July. 11, 15 and 15 laps of the 2.127-mile/3.423-km circuit.
Round 13 (23.397 miles/37.654 km).
1 Colin Turkington, GB (Vauxhall Astra Sport Hatch), 16m 06.290s, 87.168 mph/140.283 km/h; **2** Yvan Muller, F (Vauxhall Astra Sport Hatch), 16m 09.913s; **3** Matt Neal, GB (Honda Integra), 16m 10.507s; **4** Jason Plato, GB (SEAT Toledo Cupra), 16m 13.216s; **5** Dan Eaves, GB (Honda Integra), 16m 15.410s; **6** Tom Chilton, GB (Honda Civic Type-R), 16m 16.019s; **7** Rob Collard, GB (MG ZS), 16m 17.143s; **8** Gavin Smith, IRL (Vauxhall Astra Sport Hatch), 16m 23.933s; **9** James Kaye, GB (Honda Civic Type-R), 16m 26.399s; **10** James Pickford, GB (SEAT Toledo Cupra), 16m 39.999s; **11** Fiona Leggate, GB (Vauxhall Astra Coupé), 17m 47.299s; **12** Ian Curley, GB (Lexus IS200), 17m 47.757s; **13** Richard Williams, GB (Lexus IS200), 17m 48.302s; **14** Mark Proctor, GB (Vauxhall Astra Coupé), 9 laps (DNF-suspension/accident); **15** Luke Hines, GB (SEAT Toledo Cupra), 2 (DNF-accident).
Fastest race lap: Turkington, 1m 26.864s, 88.152 mph/141.866 km/h.
Fastest qualifying lap: Turkington, 1m 26.208s, 88.822 mph/142.946 km/h.

Round 14 (31.905 miles/51.346 km).
1 Yvan Muller, F (Vauxhall Astra Sport Hatch), 22m 09.067s, 86.420 mph/139.080 km/h; **2** Colin Turkington, GB (Vauxhall Astra Sport Hatch), 22m 13.095s; **3** Tom Chilton, GB (Honda Civic Type-R), 22m 13.525s; **4** Rob Collard, GB (MG ZS), 22m 16.216s; **5** James Kaye, GB (Honda Civic Type-R), 22m 18.235s; **6** Matt Neal, GB (Honda Integra), 22m 21.067s; **7** Gavin Smith, IRL (Vauxhall Astra Sport Hatch), 22m 25.085s; **8** James Pickford, GB (SEAT Toledo Cupra), 22m 34.547s; **9** Luke Hines, GB (SEAT Toledo Cupra), 22m 58.106s; **10** Dan Eaves, GB (Honda Integra), 22m 59.764s; **11** Ian Curley, GB (Lexus IS200), 23m 00.881s; **12** Richard Williams, GB (Lexus IS200), 23m 07.385s; **13** Jason Plato, GB (SEAT Toledo Cupra), 23m 08.439s; **14** Fiona Leggate, GB (Vauxhall Astra Coupé), 23m 10.868s.
Did not start: Mark Proctor, GB (Vauxhall Astra Coupé) - accident damage from race 1.
Fastest race lap: Muller, 1m 27.103s, 87.910 mph/141.477 km/h.
Pole position: Turkington.

Round 15 (31.905 miles/51.346 km).
1 Dan Eaves, GB (Honda Integra), 22m 04.317s, 86.730 mph/139.578 km/h; **2** Matt Neal, GB (Honda Integra), 22m 04.379s; **3** Jason Plato, GB (SEAT Toledo Cupra), 22m 18.407s; **4** James Pickford, GB (SEAT Toledo Cupra), 22m 19.352s; **5** Rob Collard, GB (MG ZS), 22m 20.835s; **6** Luke Hines, GB (SEAT Toledo Cupra), 22m 26.727s; **7** Colin Turkington, GB (Vauxhall Astra Sport Hatch), 22m 26.961s; **8** Yvan Muller, F (Vauxhall Astra Sport Hatch), 22m 28.237s; **9** Tom Chilton, GB (Honda Civic Type-R), 22m 28.747s; **10** Fiona Leggate, GB (Vauxhall Astra Coupé), 22m 59.968s; **11** James Kaye, GB (Honda Civic Type-R), 12 laps (DNF-engine); **12** Gavin Smith, IRL (Vauxhall Astra Sport Hatch), 9 (DNF-rear suspension); **13** Ian Curley, GB (Lexus IS200), 7 (DNF-gearbox); **14** Richard Williams, GB (Lexus IS200), 4 (DNF-gearbox).
Did not start: Mark Proctor, GB (Vauxhall Astra Coupé) - accident damage from race 1.
Fastest race lap: Eaves, 1m 26.468s, 88.555 mph/142.516 km/h.
Pole position: Eaves.

BRITISH TOURING CAR CHAMPIONSHIP, Mondello Park, Naas, County Kildare, Republic of Ireland, 24 July. 14, 14 and 15 laps of the 2.1764-mile/3.503-km circuit.
Round 16 (30.470 miles/49.037 km).
1 Yvan Muller, F (Vauxhall Astra Sport Hatch), 25m 15.139s, 72.396 mph/116.511 km/h; **2** Jason Plato, GB (SEAT Toledo Cupra), 25m 18.015s; **3** Matt Neal, GB (Honda Integra), 25m 18.328s; **4** Colin Turkington, GB (Vauxhall Astra Sport Hatch), 25m 21.726s; **5** Rob Collard, GB (MG ZS), 25m 22.535s; **6** Dan Eaves, GB (Honda Integra), 25m 29.390s; **7** Gavin Smith, IRL (Vauxhall Astra Sport Hatch), 25m 33.487s; **8** James Kaye, GB (Honda Civic Type-R), 25m 37.376s; **9** Tom Chilton, GB (Honda Civic Type-R), 25m 38.205s; **10** Jason Hughes, GB (MG ZS), 25m 38.724s; **11** James Pickford, GB (SEAT Toledo Cupra), 25m 48.095s; **12** Luke Hines, GB (SEAT Toledo Cupra), 26m 08.638s; **13** Fiona Leggate, GB (Vauxhall Astra Coupé), 26m 20.235s; **14** Mark Proctor, GB (Vauxhall Astra Coupé), 26m 32.611s; **15** Richard Williams, GB (Lexus IS200), 26m 37.525s; **16** Ian Curley, GB (Lexus IS200), 26m 39.113s.
Fastest race lap: Muller, 1m 47.063s, 73.182 mph/117.774 km/h.
Fastest qualifying lap: Muller, 1m 56.537s, 67.232 mph/108.200 km/h.

Round 17 (30.470 miles/49.037 km).
1 Colin Turkington, GB (Vauxhall Astra Sport Hatch), 26m 59.042s, 67.750 mph/109.034 km/h; **2** Dan Eaves, GB (Honda Integra), 27m 04.185s; **3** Matt Neal, GB (Honda Integra), 27m 10.668s; **4** Rob Collard, GB (MG ZS), 27m 26.540s; **5** Luke Hines, GB (SEAT Toledo Cupra), 27m 32.415s; **6** Yvan Muller, F (Vauxhall Astra Sport Hatch), 27m 50.337s; **7** Jason Hughes, GB (MG ZS), 27m 56.229s; **8** Tom Chilton, GB (Honda Civic Type-R), 27m 56.436s; **9** James Pickford, GB (SEAT Toledo Cupra), 28m 01.747s; **10** Jason Plato, GB (SEAT Toledo Cupra), 28m 04.111s; **11** Ian Curley, GB (Lexus IS200), 28m 44.422s; **12** Richard Williams, GB (Lexus IS200), 28m 45.128s; **13** Fiona Leggate, GB (Vauxhall Astra Coupé), 28m 54.469s; **14** Gavin Smith, IRL (Vauxhall Astra Sport Hatch), 12 laps (DNF-puncture); **15** James Kaye, GB (Honda Civic Type-R), 4 (DNF-spin); **16** Mark Proctor, GB (Vauxhall Astra Coupé), 4 (DNF-alternator/disqualified).
Fastest race lap: Neal, 1m 50.600s, 70.841 mph/114.008 km/h.
Pole position: Muller.

Round 18 (32.646 miles/52.539 km).
1 Yvan Muller, F (Vauxhall Astra Sport Hatch), 28m 01.018s, 69.913 mph/112.515 km/h; **2** Tom Chilton, GB (Honda Civic Type-R), 28m 02.119s; **3** Rob Collard, GB (MG ZS), 28m 06.788s; **4** Dan Eaves, GB (Honda Integra), 28m 07.962s; **5** Colin Turkington, GB (Vauxhall Astra Sport Hatch), 28m 08.300s; **6** Gavin Smith, IRL (Vauxhall Astra Sport Hatch), 28m 08.591s; **7** Matt Neal, GB (Honda Integra), 28m 09.427s; **8** Jason Hughes, GB (MG ZS), 28m 10.994s; **9** Fiona Leggate, GB (Vauxhall Astra Coupé), 28m 14.514s; **10** Mark Proctor, GB (Vauxhall Astra Coupé), 28m 21.160s; **11** James Kaye, GB (Honda Civic Type-R), 28m 30.825s; **12** Ian Curley, GB (Lexus IS200), 28m 31.030s; **13** Richard Williams, GB (Lexus IS200), 28m 31.415s; **14** Jason Plato, GB (SEAT Toledo Cupra), 8 laps (DNF-accident damage); **15** Luke Hines, GB (SEAT Toledo Cupra), 3 (DNF-accident damage); **16** James Pickford, GB (SEAT Toledo Cupra), 1 (DNF-steering).
Fastest race lap: Muller, 1 46.510s, 73.562 mph/118.386 km/h.
Pole position: Plato.

BRITISH TOURING CAR CHAMPIONSHIP, Snetterton Circuit, Thetford, Norfolk, Great Britain, 7 August. 3 x 16 laps of the 1.952-mile/3.141-km circuit.
Round 19 (31.232 miles/50.263 km).
1 Tom Chilton, GB (Honda Civic Type-R), 19m 28.318s, 96.237 mph/154.878 km/h; **2** Dan Eaves, GB (Honda Integra), 19m 30.684s; **3** Matt Neal, GB (Honda Integra), 19m 34.501s; **4** Yvan Muller, F (Vauxhall Astra Sport Hatch), 19m 36.193s; **5** Rob Collard, GB (MG ZS), 19m 36.380s; **6** James Pickford, GB (SEAT Toledo Cupra), 19m 37.948s; **7** Colin Turkington, GB (Vauxhall Astra Sport Hatch), 19m 40.131s; **8** James Kaye, GB (Honda Civic Type-R), 19m 44.377s; **9** Gavin Smith, IRL (Vauxhall Astra Sport Hatch), 19m 45.432s; **10** Luke Hines, GB (SEAT Toledo Cupra), 19m 57.449s; **11** Fiona Leggate, GB (Vauxhall Astra Coupé), 20m 10.162s; **12** Mark Proctor, GB (Vauxhall Astra Coupé), 20m 15.911s; **13** Richard Williams, GB (Lexus IS200), 20m 31.515s; **14** Ian Curley, GB (Lexus IS200), 20m 40.869s; **15** Jason Plato, GB (SEAT Toledo Cupra), 4 laps (DNF-engine).
Fastest race lap: Neal, 1m 12.249s, 97.264 mph/156.531 km/h.
Fastest qualifying lap: Chilton, 1m 11.835s, 97.824 mph/157.433 km/h.

Round 20 (31.232 miles/50.263 km).
1 Tom Chilton, GB (Honda Civic Type-R), 19m 33.769s, 95.790 mph/154.159 km/h; **2** Dan Eaves, GB (Honda Integra), 19m 34.761s; **3** Matt Neal, GB (Honda Integra), 19m 36.342s; **4** Yvan Muller, F (Vauxhall Astra Sport Hatch), 1m 36.747s; **5** Rob Collard, GB (MG ZS), 19m 37.408s; **6** James Kaye, GB (Honda Civic Type-R), 19m 44.477s; **7** Colin Turkington, GB (Vauxhall Astra Sport Hatch), 19m 45.050s; **8** Luke Hines, GB (SEAT Toledo Cupra), 19m 48.369s; **9** James Pickford, GB (SEAT Toledo Cupra), 19m 48.642s; **10** Jason Plato, GB (SEAT Toledo Cupra), 19m 49.010s; **11** Gavin Smith, IRL (Vauxhall Astra Sport Hatch), 19m 49.838s; **12** Richard Williams, GB (Lexus IS200), 20m 33.177s; **13** Fiona Leggate, GB (Vauxhall Astra Coupé), 15 laps; **14** Mark Proctor, GB (Vauxhall Astra Coupé), 14 (DNF-alternator); **15** Ian Curley, GB (Lexus IS200), 0 (DNF-driveshaft).
Fastest race lap: Neal, 1m 12.408s, 97.050 mph/156.187 km/h.
Pole position: Chilton.

Round 21 (31.232 miles/50.263 km).
1 Jason Plato, GB (SEAT Toledo Cupra), 19m 33.684s, 95.797 mph/154.170 km/h; **2** James Pickford, GB (SEAT Toledo Cupra), 19m 36.768s; **3** Yvan Muller, F (Vauxhall Astra Sport Hatch), 19m 37.469s; **4** Matt Neal, GB (Honda Integra), 19m 37.874s; **5** Dan Eaves, GB (Honda Integra), 19m 38.762s; **6** James Kaye, GB (Honda Civic Type-R), 19m 43.387s; **7** Tom Chilton, GB (Honda Civic Type-R), 19m 43.803s; **8** Gavin Smith, IRL (Vauxhall Astra Sport Hatch), 19m 47.545s; **9** Richard Williams, GB (Lexus IS200), 19m 54.878s; **10** Ian Curley, GB (Lexus IS200), 20m 42.663s; **11** Mark Proctor, GB (Vauxhall Astra Coupé), 20m 55.766s; **12** Rob Collard, GB (MG ZS), 15 laps; **13** Luke Hines, GB (SEAT Toledo Cupra), 13 (DNF-engine); **14** Colin Turkington, GB (Vauxhall Astra Sport Hatch), 7 (DNF-sump);
Did not start: Fiona Leggate, GB (Vauxhall Astra Coupé) - gearbox.
Fastest race lap: Muller, 1m 12.286s, 97.214 mph/156.451 km/h.
Pole position: Plato.

BRITISH TOURING CAR CHAMPIONSHIP, Knockhill Racing Circuit, By Dunfermline, Fife, Scotland, Great Britain, 28 August. 25, 24 and 25 laps of the 1.2986-mile/2.090-km circuit.
Round 22 (32.465 miles/52.247 km).
1 Yvan Muller, F (Vauxhall Astra Sport Hatch), 27m 30.191s, 70.825 mph/113.981 km/h; **2** Matt Neal, GB (Honda Integra), 27m 30.925s; **3** Colin Turkington, GB (Vauxhall Astra Sport Hatch), 27m 36.347s; **4** Dan Eaves, GB (Honda Integra), 27m 45.788s; **5** Tom Chilton, GB (Honda Civic Type-R), 27m 46.815s; **6** Jason Plato, GB (SEAT Toledo Cupra), 27m 47.562s; **7** Luke Hines, GB (SEAT Toledo Cupra), 27m 48.804s; **8** Gavin Smith, IRL (Vauxhall Astra Sport Hatch), 27m 51.301s; **9** Rob Collard, GB (MG ZS), 27m 52.129s; **10** James Kaye, GB (Honda Civic Type-R), 27m 53.175s; **11** Jason Hughes, GB (MG ZS), 28m 08.214s; **12** Ian Curley, GB (Lexus IS200), 28m 11.465s; **13** Mark Proctor, GB (Vauxhall Astra Coupé), 28m 28.576s; **14** Fiona Leggate, GB (Vauxhall Astra Coupé), 24 laps; **15** James Pickford, GB (SEAT Toledo Cupra), 10 (DNF-driveshaft); **16** Gareth Howell, GB (Honda Integra), 1 (DNF-accident);
Did not start: Richard Williams, GB (Lexus IS200) – driveshaft.
Fastest race lap: Neal, 59.861s, 78.097 mph/125.685 km/h.
Fastest qualifying lap: Turkington, 54.076s, 86.452 mph/139.130 km/h.

Round 23 (31.166 miles/50.157 km).
1 Matt Neal, GB (Honda Integra), 26m 16.364s, 71.176 mph/114.546 km/h; **2** Yvan Muller, F (Vauxhall Astra Sport Hatch), 26m 17.132s; **3** Tom Chilton, GB (Honda Civic Type-R), 26m 17.407s; **4** Colin Turkington, GB (Vauxhall Astra Sport Hatch), 26m 17.872s; **5** Luke Hines, GB (SEAT Toledo Cupra), 26m 18.546s; **6** Gareth Howell, GB (Honda Integra), 26m 20.875s; **7** Jason Hughes, GB (MG ZS), 26m 36.838s; **8** Jason Plato, GB (SEAT Toledo Cupra), 26m 41.721s; **9** Rob Collard, GB (MG ZS), 26m 42.220s; **10** Mark Proctor, GB (Vauxhall Astra Coupé), 26m 42.802s; **11** Fiona Leggate, GB (Vauxhall Astra Coupé), 26m 42.994s; **12** James Pickford, GB (SEAT Toledo Cupra), 26m 59.346s; **13** Gavin Smith, IRL (Vauxhall Astra Sport Hatch), 14 laps (DNF-radiator); **14** Richard Williams, GB (Lexus IS200), 14 (DNF-accident damage); **15** Ian Curley, GB (Lexus IS200), 15 (DNF-accident damage); **16** Dan Eaves, GB (Honda Integra), 11 (DNF-front suspension); **17** James Kaye, GB (Honda Civic Type-R), 1 (DNF-electrics).
Fastest race lap: Neal, 59.972s, 77.952 mph/125.452 km/h.
Pole position: Muller.

Round 24 (32.465 miles/52.247 km).
1 Rob Collard, GB (MG ZS), 27m 32.558s, 70.723 mph/113.818 km/h; **2** Matt Neal, GB (Honda Integra), 27m 34.258s; **3** Tom Chilton, GB (Honda Civic Type-R), 27m 39.138s; **4** Gareth Howell, GB (Honda Integra), 27m 41.421s; **5** Jason Plato, GB (SEAT Toledo Cupra), 27m 42.094s; **6** Dan Eaves, GB (Honda Integra), 27m 45.069s; **7** Colin Turkington, GB (Vauxhall Astra Sport Hatch), 27m 54.652s; **8** Jason Hughes, GB (MG ZS), 28m 06.423s; **9** Fiona Leggate, GB (Vauxhall Astra Coupé), 28m 25.132s; **10** Mark Proctor, GB (Vauxhall Astra Coupé), 28m 13.530s; **11** James Pickford, GB (SEAT Toledo Cupra), 21 laps (DNF-accident); **12** Yvan Muller, F (Vauxhall Astra Sport Hatch), 18 (DNF-engine); **13** Luke Hines, GB (SEAT Toledo Cupra), 17 (DNF-accident damage); **14** James Kaye, GB (Honda Civic Type-R), 2 (DNF-accident); **15** Gavin Smith, IRL (Vauxhall Astra Sport Hatch), 0 (DNF-accident).
Did not start: Ian Curley, GB (Lexus IS200) – accident damage; Richard Williams, GB (Lexus IS200) – accident damage.
Fastest race lap: Neal, 1m 00.328s, 77.492 mph/124.712 km/h.
Pole position: Proctor.

BRITISH TOURING CAR CHAMPIONSHIP, Silverstone National Circuit, Towcester, Northamptonshire, Great Britain, 18 September. 24, 22 and 25 laps of the 1.639-mile/2.638-km circuit.
Round 25 (39.383 miles/63.381 km).
1 Tom Chilton, GB (Honda Civic Type-R), 25m 26.083s, 92.904 mph/149.514 km/h; **2** James Pickford, GB (SEAT Toledo Cupra), 25m 27.588s; **3** Jason Plato, GB (SEAT Toledo Cupra), 25m 29.461s; **4** Yvan Muller, F (Vauxhall Astra Sport Hatch), 25m 32.774s; **5** Gareth Howell, GB (Honda Integra), 25m 33.342s; **6** Luke Hines, GB (SEAT Toledo Cupra), 25m 35.654s; **7** Colin Turkington, GB (Vauxhall Astra Sport Hatch), 25m 36.094s; **8** James Kaye, GB (Honda Civic Type-R), 25m 37.293s; **9** Matt Neal, GB (Honda Integra), 25m 39.366s; **10** Rob Collard, GB (MG ZS), 25m 39.576s; **11** Gavin Smith, IRL (Vauxhall Astra Sport Hatch), 25m 40.059s; **12** Richard Williams, GB (Lexus IS200), 26m 07.194s; **13** Fiona Leggate, GB (Vauxhall Astra Coupé), 26m 19.239s; **14** Ian Curley, GB (Lexus IS200), 26m 20.078s; **15** Mark Proctor, GB (Vauxhall Astra Coupé), 7 laps (DNF-clutch); **16** Dan Eaves, GB (Honda Integra), 2 (DNF-accident).
Fastest race lap: Plato, 1m 00.927s, 96.844 mph/155.855 km/h.
Fastest qualifying lap: Howell, 1m 00.270s, 97.899 mph/157.554 km/h.

Round 26 (36.105 miles/58.105 km).
1 Luke Hines, GB (SEAT Toledo Cupra), 22m 57.278s, 94.373 mph/151.879 km/h; **2** Gavin Smith, IRL (Vauxhall Astra Sport Hatch), 22m 57.941s; **3** Dan Eaves, GB (Honda Integra), 22m 58.087s; **4** Matt Neal, GB (Honda Integra), 23m 00.362s; **5** Fiona Leggate, GB (Vauxhall Astra Coupé), 23m 19.837s; **6** James Pickford, GB (SEAT Toledo Cupra), 23m 23.385s; **7** Richard Williams, GB (Lexus IS200), 23m 30.841s; **8** Tom Chilton, GB (Honda Civic Type-R), 23m 39.475s; **9** Mark Proctor, GB (Vauxhall Astra Coupé), 23m 40.966s; **10** Rob Collard, GB (MG ZS), 21 laps; **11** Ian Curley, GB (Lexus IS200), 20; **12** Gareth Howell, GB (Honda Integra), 19 (DNF-engine); **13** Yvan Muller, F (Vauxhall Astra Sport Hatch), 13 (DNF-driveshaft); **14** James Kaye, GB (Honda Civic Type-R), 10 (DNF-engine); **15** Colin Turkington, GB (Vauxhall Astra Sport Hatch), 3 (DNF-suspension). Jason Plato, GB (SEAT Toledo Cupra), finished 1st in 22m 46.155s but was disqualified. (causing Chilton to spin).
Fastest race lap: Howell, 1m 00.983s, 96.755 mph155.712 km/h. The fastest race lap set by Plato of 1m 00.976 was disallowed.
Pole position: Chilton.

Round 27 (41.022 miles/66.019 km).
1 Gareth Howell, GB (Honda Integra), 27m 16.356s, 90.249 mph/145.241 km/h; **2** Rob Collard, GB (MG ZS), 27m 18.043s; **3** Tom Chilton, GB (Honda Civic Type-R), 27m 18.330s; **4** Dan Eaves, GB (Honda Integra), 27m 18.972s; **5** Yvan Muller, F (Vauxhall Astra Sport Hatch), 27m 29.521s; **6** Jason Plato, GB (SEAT Toledo Cupra), 27m 20.891s; **7** Matt Neal, GB (Honda Integra), 27m 22.865s; **8** James Pickford, GB (SEAT Toledo Cupra), 27m 24.803s; **9** Colin Turkington, GB (Vauxhall Astra Sport Hatch), 27m 26.254s; **10** James Kaye, GB (Honda Civic Type-R), 27m 26.812s; **11** Gavin Smith, IRL (Vauxhall Astra Sport Hatch), 27m 35.581s; **12** Mark Proctor, GB (Vauxhall Astra Coupé), 28m 01.189s; **13** Fiona Leggate, GB (Vauxhall Astra Coupé), 28m 02.040s; **14** Ian Curley, GB (Lexus IS200), 28m 07.558s; **15** Luke Hines, GB (SEAT Toledo Cupra), 15 laps (DNF-accident/suspension); **16** Richard Williams, GB (Lexus IS200), 2 (DNF-spin).
Fastest race lap: Howell, 1m 01.191s, 96.426 mph/155.183 km/h.
Pole position: Collard.

BRITISH TOURING CAR CHAMPIONSHIP, Brands Hatch Grand Prix Circuit, West Kingsdown, Dartford, Kent, Great Britain, 2 October. 15, 14 and 17 laps of the 2.423-mile/3.899-km circuit.
Round 28 (36.345 miles/58.492 km).
1 Dan Eaves, GB (Honda Integra), 24m 35.507s, 88.676 mph/142.710 km/h; **2** Yvan Muller, F (Vauxhall Astra Sport Hatch), 24m 36.595s; **3** Jason Plato, GB (SEAT Toledo Cupra), 24m 36.937s; **4** Matt Neal, GB (Honda Integra), 24m 37.402s; **5** Gareth Howell, GB (Honda Integra), 24m 37.628s; **6** Gavin Smith, IRL (Vauxhall Astra Sport Hatch), 24m 39.187s; **7** Colin Turkington, GB (Vauxhall Astra Sport Hatch), 24m 39.550s; **8** James Kaye, GB (Honda Civic Type-R), 24m 40.573s; **9** James Pickford, GB (SEAT Toledo Cupra), 24m 40.773s; **10** Jason Hughes, GB (MG ZS), 24m 44.295s; **11** Richard Williams, GB (Lexus IS200), 24m 44.295s; **12** Andy Neate, GB (Vauxhall Astra Coupé), 24m 51.654s; **13** Fiona Leggate, GB (Vauxhall Astra Coupé), 24m 51.912s; **14** Ian Curley, GB (Lexus IS200), 24m 53.561s; **15** Luke Hines, GB (SEAT Toledo Cupra), 14 laps (DNF-engine); **16** Rob Collard, GB (MG ZS), 11 (DNF-accident); **17** Mark Proctor, GB (Vauxhall Astra Coupé), 11.
Fastest race lap: Eaves, 1m 33.178s, 93.614 mph/150.658 km/h.
Fastest qualifying lap: Eaves, 1m 32.586s, 94.213 mph/151.621 km/h.

Round 29 (33.922 miles/54.592 km).
1 Jason Plato, GB (SEAT Toledo Cupra), 22m 07.148s, 92.016 mph/148.086 km/h; **2** Dan Eaves, GB (Honda Integra), 22m 08.838s; **3** Matt Neal, GB (Honda Integra), 22m 09.262s; **4** Gavin Smith, IRL (Vauxhall Astra Sport Hatch), 22m 18.636s; **5** James Pickford, GB (SEAT Toledo Cupra), 22m 19.349s; **6** James Kaye, GB (Honda Civic Type-R), 22m 23.421s; **7** Luke Hines, GB (SEAT Toledo Cupra), 22m 48.417s; **8** Jason Hughes, GB (MG ZS), 22m 51.360s; **9** Rob Collard, GB (MG ZS), 2m 51.515s; **10** Andy Neate, GB (Vauxhall Astra Coupé), 22m 59.544s; **11** Yvan Muller, F (Vauxhall Astra Sport Hatch), 23m 07.679s; **12** Ian Curley, GB (Lexus IS200), 13 laps; **13** Fiona Leggate, GB (Vauxhall Astra Coupé), 11 (DNF-accident damage); **14** Richard Williams, GB (Lexus IS200), 6 (DNF-gearbox); **15** Mark Proctor, GB (Vauxhall Astra Coupé), 0 (DNF-power steering); **16** Colin Turkington, GB (Vauxhall Astra Sport Hatch), 0 (DNF-tyre). Gareth Howell, GB (Honda Integra), finished 4th in 22m 17.086s, but was disqualified for dangerous driving.
Fastest race lap: Neal, 1m 33.491s, 93.301 mph/150.153 km/h.
Pole position: Eaves.

Round 30 (41.191 miles/66.290 km).
1 Rob Collard, GB (MG ZS), 29m 25.626s, 83.986 mph/135.162 km/h; **2** James Pickford, GB (SEAT Toledo Cupra), 29m 27.540s; **3** Gavin Smith, IRL (Vauxhall Astra Sport Hatch), 29m 34.134s; **4** Gareth Howell, GB (Honda Integra), 29m 34.936s; **5** Matt Neal, GB (Honda Integra), 29m 38.762s; **6** Colin Turkington, GB (Vauxhall Astra Sport Hatch), 29m 38.986s; **7** James Kaye, GB (Honda Civic Type-R), 29m 40.252s; **8** Jason Hughes, GB (MG ZS), 29m 53.953s; **9** Richard Williams, GB (Lexus IS200), 29m 54.168s; **10** Fiona Leggate, GB (Vauxhall Astra Coupé), 29m 58.389s; **11** Andy Neate, GB (Vauxhall Astra Coupé), 30m 08.854s; **12** Ian Curley, GB (Lexus IS200), 30m 12.484s; **13** Mark Proctor, GB (Vauxhall Astra Coupé), 30m 12.656s; **14** Luke Hines, GB (SEAT Toledo Cupra), 16 laps (DNF-accident); **15** Dan Eaves, GB (Honda Integra), 1 (DNF-accident); **16** Yvan Muller, F (Vauxhall Astra Sport Hatch), 1 (DNF-accident); **17** Jason Plato, GB (SEAT Toledo Cupra), 1 (DNF-accident).
Fastest race lap: Collard, 1m 33.148s, 93.645 mph/150.706 km/h.
Pole position: Neate.

Final championship points
Drivers: 1 Matt Neal, GB, 316; **2** Yvan Muller, F, 273; **3** Dan Eaves, GB, 269; **4** Jason Plato, GB, 208; **5** Tom Chilton, GB, 175; **6** Colin Turkington, GB, 174; **7** Rob Collard, GB, 173; **8** James Pickford, GB, 116; **9** Luke Hines, GB, 87; **10** Gavin Smith, IRL, 86; **11** James Kaye, GB, 58; **12** Gareth Howell, GB, 54; **13** Jason Hughes, GB, 22; **14** Richard Williams, GB, 14; **15** Mark Proctor, GB, 13; **16** Fiona Leggate, GB, 12; **17** Ian Curley, GB, 3; **18** Andy Neate, GB, 1.
Independent Drivers: 1 Matt Neal, 367; **2** Dan Eaves, 313; **3** Rob Collard, 256; **4** Tom Chilton, 230; **5** James Kaye, 140.
Manufacturers: 1 Vauxhall, 781; **2** SEAT, 629. **Teams: 1** Team Halfords, 573; **2** VX Racing, 470; **3** SEAT Sport UK, 306; **4** WSR, 172; **5** Arena Motorsports, 157. **Independent Teams: 1** Team Halfords, 725; **2** WSR, 256; **3** Arena Motorsports, 230.

Indy Racing League (IRL) IndyCar Series

TOYOTA INDY 300, Homestead-Miami Speedway, Florida, USA, 6 March. Round 1. 200 laps of the 1.485-mile/2.390-km circuit, 297.000 miles/477.975 km.
1 Dan Wheldon, GB (Dallara-Honda), 2h 05m 27.8062s, 142.033 mph/228.581 km/h; **2** Sam Hornish Jr., USA (Dallara-Toyota), 2h 05m 31.4998s; **3** Tony Kanaan, BR (Dallara-Honda), 2h 05m 31.5095s; **4** Vitor Meira, BR (Panoz G Force-Honda), 2h 05m 31.5212s; **5** Hélio Castroneves, BR (Dallara-Toyota), 2h 05m 31.6570s; **6** Darren Manning, GB (Panoz G Force-Toyota), 2h 05m 39.2523s; **7** Patrick Carpentier, CDN (Dallara-Toyota), 2h 05m 39.4331s; **8** Alex Barron, USA (Dallara-Toyota), 199 laps; **9** A.J. Foyt IV, USA (Dallara-Toyota), 196; **10** Paul Dana, USA (Dallara-Toyota), 192; **11** Tomas Scheckter, ZA (Dallara-Chevrolet), 158 (DNF-accident); **12** Kosuke Matsuura, J (Panoz G Force-Honda), 158 (DNF-accident); **13** Scott Sharp, USA (Panoz G Force-Honda), 158 (DNF-accident); **14** Bryan Herta, USA (Dallara-Honda), 158 (DNF-accident); **15** Danica Patrick, USA (Panoz G Force-Honda), 158 (DNF-accident); **16** Scott Dixon, NZ (Panoz G Force-Toyota), 158 (DNF-accident); **17** Roger Yasukawa, USA (Dallara-Honda), 158 (DNF-accident); **18** Ed Carpenter, USA (Dallara-Toyota), 154 (DNF-accident); **19** Buddy Rice, USA (Panoz G Force-Honda), 92 (DNF-mechanical); **20** Ryan Briscoe, AUS (Panoz G Force-Toyota), 61 (DNF-accident); **21** Tomás Enge, CZ (Dallara-Chevrolet), 41 (DNF-mechanical); **22** Dario Franchitti, GB (Dallara-Honda), 12 (DNF-mechanical).
Most laps led: Wheldon, 158.
Fastest race lap: Rice, 24.9009s, 214.691 mph/345.512 km/h.
Fastest qualifying lap: Scheckter, 24.8518s, 215.115 mph/346.194 km/h.
Championship points: 1 Wheldon, 53; **2** Hornish Jr., 40; **3** Kanaan, 35; **4** Meira, 32; **5** Castroneves, 30; **6** Manning, 28.

XM SATELLITE RADIO INDY 200 PRESENTED BY ARGENT MORTGAGE, Phoenix International Raceway, Arizona, USA, 19 March. Round 2. 200 laps of the 1.000-mile/1.609-km circuit, 200.000 miles/321.869 km.
1 Sam Hornish Jr., USA (Dallara-Toyota), 1h 30m 23.6019s, 132.753 mph/213.645 km/h; **2** Hélio Castroneves, BR (Dallara-Toyota), 1h 30m 24.6427s; **3** Tony Kanaan, BR (Dallara-Honda), 1h 30m 25.8674s; **4** Dario Franchitti, GB (Dallara-Honda), 1h 30m 29.6783s; **5** Scott Sharp, USA (Panoz G Force-Honda), 1h 30m 30.2601s; **6** Dan Wheldon, GB (Dallara-Honda), 199 laps; **7** Bryan Herta, USA (Dallara-Honda), 199; **8** Darren Manning, GB (Panoz G Force-Toyota), 199; **9** Patrick Carpentier, CDN (Dallara-Toyota), 199; **10** Kosuke Matsuura, J (Panoz G Force-Honda), 198; **11** Vitor Meira, BR (Panoz G Force-Honda), 198; **12** Scott Dixon, NZ (Panoz G Force-Toyota), 198; **13** Alex Barron, USA (Dallara-Toyota), 198; **14** A.J. Foyt IV, USA (Dallara-Toyota), 195; **15** Danica Patrick, USA (Panoz G Force-Honda), 194; **16** Ed Carpenter, USA (Dallara-Toyota), 193; **17** Tomas Scheckter, ZA (Dallara-Chevrolet), 191 (DNF-accident); **18** Roger Yasukawa, USA (Dallara-Honda), 174 (DNF-mechanical); **19** Ryan Briscoe, AUS (Panoz G Force-Toyota), 112 (DNF-accident); **20** Tomás Enge, CZ (Dallara-Chevrolet), 74 (DNF-accident); **21** Paul Dana, USA (Dallara-Toyota), 33 (mechanical); **22** Buddy Rice, USA (Panoz G Force-Honda), 14 (DNF-accident).
Most laps led: Wheldon, 72.
Fastest race lap: Franchitti, 21.0872s, 170.720 mph/274.747 km/h.
Fastest qualifying lap: Herta, 20.3837s, 176.612 mph/284.229 km/h.
Championship points: 1 Hornish Jr., 90; **2** Wheldon, 84; **3=** Castroneves, 70; **3=** Kanaan, 70; **5** Manning, 52; **6** Meira, 51.

HONDA GRAND PRIX OF ST. PETERSBURG, Streets of St. Petersburg, Florida, USA, 3 April. Round 3. 100 laps of the 1.800-mile/2.897-km circuit, 180.000 miles/289.682 km.
1 Dan Wheldon, GB (Dallara-Honda), 2h 09m 54.1074s, 83.140 mph/133.800 km/h; **2** Tony Kanaan, BR (Dallara-Honda), 2h 09m 55.5651s; **3** Dario Franchitti, GB (Dallara-Honda), 2h 09m 59.0389s; **4** Bryan Herta, USA (Dallara-Honda), 2h 10m 13.1000s; **5** Vitor Meira, BR (Panoz G Force-Honda), 2h 10m 13.9576s; **6** Scott Dixon, NZ (Panoz G Force-Toyota), 2h 10m 14.3437s; **7** Buddy Rice, USA (Panoz G Force-Honda), 2h 10m 14.9112s; **8** Patrick Carpentier, CDN (Dallara-Toyota), 2h 10m 45.7153s; **9** Darren Manning, GB (Panoz G Force-Toyota), 99 laps; **10** Alex Barron, USA (Dallara-Toyota), 99; **11** Roger Yasukawa, USA (Dallara-Honda), 98; **12** Danica Patrick, USA (Panoz G Force-Honda), 95; **13** Kosuke Matsuura, J (Panoz G Force-Honda), 94 (DNF-mechanical); **14** Ryan Briscoe, AUS (Panoz G Force-Toyota), 91 (DNF-accident); **15** Sam Hornish Jr., USA (Dallara-Toyota), 85 (DNF-accident); **16** Tomás Enge, CZ (Dallara-Chevrolet), 85 (DNF-accident); **17** Tomas Scheckter, ZA (Dallara-Chevrolet), 77 (DNF-accident); **18** Scott Sharp, USA (Panoz G Force-Honda), 43 (DNF-accident); **19** Ed Carpenter, USA (Dallara-Toyota), 32 (DNF-accident); **20** Hélio Castroneves, BR (Dallara-Toyota), 12 (DNF-accident); **21** A.J. Foyt IV, USA (Dallara-Toyota), 11 (DNF-accident).
Most laps led: Briscoe, 43.
Fastest race lap: Franchitti, 1m 03.5606s, 101.950 mph/164.073 km/h.
Fastest qualifying lap: Herta, 1m 02.5096s, 103.664 mph/166.831 km/h.
Championship points: 1 Wheldon, 134; **2** Kanaan, 110; **3** Hornish Jr., 105; **4** Castroneves, 82; **5** Meira, 81; **6** Franchitti, 79.

INDY JAPAN 300, Twin Ring Motegi, Motegi-machi, Hagagun, Tochigi, Japan, 30 April. Round 4. 200 laps of the 1.520-mile/2.446-km circuit, 304.000 miles/489.241 km.
1 Dan Wheldon, GB (Dallara-Honda), 2h 16m 46.0711s, 133.365 mph/204.630 km/h; **2** Scott Sharp, USA (Panoz G Force-Honda), 2h 16m 49.5323s (under caution); **3** Buddy Rice, USA (Panoz G Force-Honda), 2h 17m 07.9550s; **4** Danica Patrick, USA (Panoz G Force-Honda), 2h 17m 08.2594s; **5** Bryan Herta, USA (Dallara-Honda), 2h 17m 15.5686s; **6** Tony Kanaan, BR (Dallara-Honda), 199 laps; **7** Sam Hornish Jr., USA (Dallara-Toyota), 199; **8** Darren Manning, GB (Panoz G Force-Toyota), 199; **9** Kosuke Matsuura, J (Panoz G Force-Honda), 199; **10** Tomas Scheckter, ZA (Dallara-Chevrolet), 198; **11** Hélio Castroneves, BR (Dallara-Toyota), 198; **12** Ryan Briscoe, AUS (Panoz G Force-Toyota), 197; **13** Patrick Carpentier, CDN (Dallara-Toyota), 196; **14** A.J. Foyt IV, USA (Dallara-Toyota), 196; **15** Vitor Meira, BR (Panoz G Force-Honda), 166; **16** Ed Carpenter, USA (Dallara-Toyota), 136 (DNF-accident); **17** Dario Franchitti, GB (Dallara-Honda), 123 (DNF-accident); **18** Roger Yasukawa, USA (Dallara-Honda), 112 (DNF-mechanical); **19** Alex Barron, USA (Dallara-Toyota), 57 (DNF-mecanical); **20** Paul Dana, USA (Dallara-Toyota), 56 (DNF-suspension); **21** Scott Dixon, NZ (Dallara-Toyota), 0 (DNF-accident); **22** Jeff Bucknum, USA (Dallara-Honda), 0 (DNF-accident).
Did not start: Tomás Enge, CZ (Dallara-Chevrolet) – injured during qualifying.
Most laps led: Franchitti, 67
Fastest race lap: Wheldon, 27.1846s, 201.290 mph/323.946 km/h.
Fastest qualifying lap: Hornish Jr., 26.7266s, 204.740 mph/329.497 km/h.
Championship points: 1 Wheldon, 184; **2** Kanaan, 138; **3** Hornish Jr., 131; **4** Herta, 104; **5** Castroneves, 101; **6** Sharp, 99.

89th INDIANAPOLIS 500, Indianapolis Motor Speedway, Speedway, Indiana, USA, 29 May. Round 5. 200 laps of the 2.500-mile/4.023-km circuit, 500.000 miles/804.672 km.
1 Dan Wheldon, GB (Dallara-Honda), 3h 10m 21.0769s, 157.603 mph/253.638 km/h; **2** Vitor Meira, BR (Panoz G Force-Honda), 3h 10m 21.2071s (under caution); **3** Bryan Herta, USA (Dallara-Honda), 3h 10m 21.2830s; **4** Danica Patrick, USA (Panoz G Force-Honda), 3h 10m 25.6284s; **5** Buddy Lazier, USA (Dallara-Chevrolet), 3h 0m 25.8816s; **6** Dario Franchitti, GB (Dallara-Honda), 3h 10m 26.2219s; **7** Scott Sharp, USA (Panoz G Force-Honda), 3h 10m 26.6564s; **8** Tony Kanaan, BR (Dallara-Honda), 3h 10m 27.4750s; **9** Hélio Castroneves, BR (Dallara-Toyota), 3h 10m 28.8456s; **10** Ryan Briscoe, AUS (Panoz G Force-Toyota), 199 laps; **11** Ed Carpenter, USA (Dallara-Toyota), 199; **12** Sébastien Bourdais, F (Panoz G Force-Honda), 198 (DNF-accident); **13** Alex Barron, USA (Dallara-Toyota), 197; **14** Adrian Fernandez, MEX (Panoz G Force-Honda), 197; **15** Felipe Giaffone, BR (Panoz G Force-Toyota), 194; **16** Jaques Lazier, USA (Panoz G Force-Toyota), 189; **17** Kosuke Matsuura, J (Panoz G Force-Honda), 186 (DNF-accident); **18** Roger Yasukawa, USA (Dallara-Honda), 167 (DNF-mechanical); **19** Tomás Enge, CZ (Dallara-Chevrolet), 155 (DNF-accident); **20** Tomas Scheckter, ZA (Dallara-Chevrolet), 154 (DNF-accident); **21** Patrick Carpentier, CDN (Dallara-Toyota), 153 (DNF-mechanical); **22** Jeff Bucknum, USA (Dallara-Honda), 150 (DNF-accident); **23** Sam Hornish Jr., USA (Dallara-Toyota), 146 (DNF-accident); **24** Scott Dixon, NZ (Panoz G Force-Toyota), 113 (DNF-accident); **25** Richie Hearn, USA (Panoz G Force-Chevrolet), 112 (DNF-accident); **26** Kenny Bräck, S Panoz G Force-Honda), 92 (DNF-mechanical); **27** Jeff Ward, USA (Dallara-Toyota), 92 (DNF-handling); **28** A.J. Foyt IV, USA (Dallara-Toyota), 84 (DNF-handling); **29** Darren Manning, GB (Panoz G Force-Toyota), 82 (DNF-mechanical); **30** Bruno Junqueira, BR (Panoz G Force-Honda), 76 (DNF-accident); **31** Marty Roth, CDN (Dallara-Chevrolet), 47 (DNF-handling); **32** Jimmy Kite, USA (Dallara-Toyota), 47 (DNF-handling); **33** Larry Foyt, USA (Dallara-Toyota), 14 (DNF-accident).
Did not qualify: Scott Mayer, USA (Dallara-Toyota); Arie Luyendyk Jr., USA (Dallara-Chevrolet); Buddy Rice, USA (Panoz G Force-Honda); Paul Dana, USA (Dallara-Toyota).
Most laps led: Hornish Jr., 77.
Fastest race lap: Kanaan, 39.4560s, 228.102 mph/367.095 km/h.
Fastest leading lap: Kanaan, 39.8533s, 225.828 mph/363.435 km/h.
Pole position/Fastest qualifying lap: Kanaan, 2m 38.1961s, 227.566 mph/366.232 km/h. (over four laps).
Championship points: 1 Wheldon, 234; **2** Kanaan, 162; **3** Hornish Jr., 146; **4** Herta, 139; **5** Meira, 136; **6** Sharp, 125.

BOMBARDIER LEARJET 500K, Texas Motor Speedway, Fort Worth, Texas, USA, 11 June. Round 6. 200 laps of the 1.455-mile/2.342-km circuit, 291.000 miles/468.319 km.
1 Tomas Scheckter, ZA (Dallara-Chevrolet), 1h 45m 47.2701s, 165.047 mph/265.618 km/h; **2** Sam Hornish Jr., USA (Dallara-Toyota), 1h 45m 47.3235s; **3** Tony Kanaan, BR (Dallara-Honda), 1h 45m 47.7719s; **4** Scott Sharp, USA (Panoz G Force-Honda), 1h 45m 47.8659s; **5** Hélio Castroneves, BR (Dallara-Toyota), 1h 45m 48.0956s; **6** Dan Wheldon, GB (Dallara-Honda), 1h 46m 00.4111s; **7** Kosuke Matsuura, J (Panoz G Force-Honda), 1h 46m 00.4416s; **8** Dario Franchitti, GB (Dallara-Honda), 1h 46m 00.5076s; **9** Vitor Meira, BR (Panoz G Force-Honda), 1h 46m 00.5812s; **10** Bryan Herta, USA (Dallara-Honda), 1h 46m 00.6499s; **11** Scott Dixon, NZ (Panoz G Force-Toyota), 1h 46m 01.0787s; **12** Ryan Briscoe, AUS (Panoz G Force-Toyota), 1h 46m 10.5800s; **13** Danica Patrick, USA (Panoz G Force-Honda), 1h 46m 10.6492s; **14** Alex Barron, USA (Dallara-Toyota), 199 laps; **15** Roger Yasukawa, USA (Dallara-Honda), 199; **16** Patrick Carpentier, CDN (Dallara-Toyota), 199; **17** Darren Manning, GB (Panoz G Force-Toyota), 199; **18** A.J. Foyt IV, USA (Dallara-Toyota), 198; **19** Tomás Enge, CZ (Dallara-Chevrolet), 194; **20** Ed Carpenter, USA (Dallara-Toyota), 63 (DNF-accident); **21** Buddy Rice, USA (Panoz G Force-Honda), 25 (DNF-mechanical); **22** Jimmy Kite, USA (Dallara-Toyota), 6 (DNF-accident).
Most laps led: Scheckter, 119.
Fastest race lap: Enge, 24.2294s, 216.184 mph/347.914 km/h.
Fastest qualifying lap: Scheckter, 24.4942s, 213.847 mph/344.153 km/h.
Championship points: 1 Wheldon, 262; **2** Kanaan, 197; **3** Hornish Jr., 186; **4** Herta, 159; **5** Meira, 158; **6** Sharp, 157.

SUNTRUST INDY CHALLENGE, Richmond International Raceway, Virginia, USA, 25 June. Round 7. 250 laps of the 0.750-mile/1.207-km circuit, 187.500 miles/301.752 km.
1 Hélio Castroneves, BR (Dallara-Toyota), 1h 38m 33.1105s, 114.153 mph/183.712 km/h; **2** Dario Franchitti, GB (Dallara-Honda), 1h 38m 33.6693s; **3** Patrick Carpentier, CDN (Dallara-Toyota), 1h 38m 34.9245s; **4** Tomas Scheckter, ZA (Dallara-Chevrolet), 1h 38m 36.1780s; **5** Dan Wheldon, GB (Dallara-Honda), 1h 38m 36.6505s; **6** Alex Barron, USA (Dallara-Toyota), 1h 38m 37.3481s; **7** Tomás Enge, CZ (Dallara-Chevrolet), 249 laps; **8** Bryan Herta, USA (Dallara-Honda), 249; **9** Kosuke Matsuura, J (Panoz G Force-Honda), 249; **10** Danica Patrick, USA (Panoz G Force-Honda), 247; **11** Buddy Rice, USA (Panoz G Force-Honda), 246; **12** Ed Carpenter, USA (Dallara-Toyota), 246; **13** Jimmy Kite, USA (Dallara-Toyota), 245; **14** A.J. Foyt IV, USA (Dallara-Toyota), 244; **15** Darren Manning, GB (Panoz G Force-Toyota), 240 (DNF-accident); **16** Roger Yasukawa, USA (Dallara-Honda), 235 (DNF-accident); **17** Scott Sharp, USA (Panoz G Force-Honda), 201 (DNF-accident); **18** Sam Hornish Jr., USA (Dallara-Toyota), 164 (DNF-accident); **19** Tony Kanaan, BR (Dallara-Honda), 150 (DNF-suspension); **20** Vitor Meira, BR (Panoz G Force-Honda), 145 (DNF-accident); **21** Ryan Briscoe, AUS (Panoz G Force-Toyota), 88 (DNF-accident); **22** Scott Dixon, NZ (Panoz G Force-Toyota), 37 (DNF-accident).
Most laps led: Castroneves, 112.
Fastest race lap: Enge, 16.1358s, 167.330 mph/269.291 km/h.
Fastest qualifying lap: Hornish Jr., 15.3197s, 176.244 mph/283.637 km/h.
Championship points: 1 Wheldon, 292; **2** Kanaan, 209; **3** Castroneves, 206; **4** Hornish Jr., 198; **5** Franchitti, 187; **6** Herta, 183.

ARGENT MORTGAGE INDY 300, Kansas Speedway, Kansas City, Kansas, USA, 3 July. Round 8. 200 laps of the 1.520-mile/2.446-km circuit, 304.000 miles/489.241 km.
1 Tony Kanaan, BR (Dallara-Honda), 1h 41m 03.0136s, 180.504 mph/290.494 km/h; **2** Dan Wheldon, GB (Dallara-Honda), 1h 41m 03.0256s; **3** Vitor Meira, BR (Panoz G Force-Honda), 1h 41m 03.0378s; **4** Dario Franchitti, GB (Dallara-Honda), 1h 41m 03.3955s; **5** Tomas Scheckter, ZA (Dallara-Chevrolet), 1h 41m 04.4870s; **6** Scott Sharp, USA (Panoz G Force-Honda), 1h 41m 04.6250s; **7** Darren Manning, GB (Panoz G Force-Toyota), 1h 41m 04.8422s; **8** Hélio Castroneves, BR (Dallara-Toyota), 1h 41m 05.0188s; **9** Danica Patrick, USA (Panoz G Force-Honda), 1h 41m 05.1802s; **10** Buddy Rice, USA (Panoz G Force-Honda), 1h 41m 06.8960s; **11** Tomás Enge, CZ (Dallara-Chevrolet), 1h 41m 09.0615s; **12** Sam Hornish Jr., USA (Dallara-Toyota), 1h 41m 12.5869s; **13** Alex Barron, USA (Dallara-Toyota), 1h 41m 15.3441s; **14** Patrick Carpentier, CDN (Dallara-Toyota), 1h 41m 15.3598s; **15** Bryan Herta, USA (Dallara-Honda), 1h 41m 24.3296s; **16** A.J. Foyt IV, USA (Dallara-Toyota), 1h 41m 24.6333s; **17** Ed Carpenter, USA (Dallara-Toyota), 1h 41m 26.2798s; **18** Scott Dixon, NZ (Panoz G Force-Toyota), 1h 41m 26.5264s; **19** Jimmy Kite, USA (Dallara-Toyota), 195 laps;

20 Kosuke Matsuura, J (Panoz G Force-Honda), 134 (DNF-mechanical); 21 Ryan Briscoe, AUS (Panoz G Force-Toyota), 113 (DNF-clutch); 22 Roger Yasukawa, USA (Dallara-Honda), 53 (DNF-accident).
Most laps led: Wheldon, 111.
Fastest race lap: Briscoe, 25.6518s, 213.318 mph/343.303 km/h.
Fastest qualifying lap: Patrick, 25.4905s, 214.668 mph/345.475 km/h.
Championship points: 1 Wheldon, 335; 2 Kanaan, 259; 3 Castroneves, 230; 4 Franchitti, 219; 5 Hornish Jr., 216; 6 Meira, 205.

FIRESTONE INDY 200, Nashville Superspeedway, Lebanon, Tennessee, USA, 16 July. Round 9. 200 laps of the 1.300-mile/2.092-km circuit, 260.000 miles/418.429 km.
1 Dario Franchitti, GB (Dallara-Honda), 1m 57m 12.9129s, 133.089 mph/214.185 km/h; 2 Sam Hornish Jr., USA (Dallara-Toyota), 1h 57m 14.2292s; 3 Patrick Carpentier, CDN (Dallara-Toyota), 1h 57m 14.5009s; 4 Scott Sharp, USA (Panoz G Force-Honda), 1h 57m 14.8642s; 5 Hélio Castroneves, BR (Dallara-Toyota), 1h 57m 15.4688s; 6 Scott Dixon, NZ (Panoz G Force-Toyota), 1h 57m 15.9724s; 7 Danica Patrick, USA (Panoz G Force-Honda), 1h 57m 16.2775s; 8 Ryan Briscoe, AUS (Panoz G Force-Toyota), 1h 57m 16.4365s; 9 Buddy Lazier, USA (Dallara-Chevrolet), 1h 57m 16.9097s; 10 Ed Carpenter, USA (Dallara-Toyota), 199 laps; 11 Roger Yasukawa, USA (Dallara-Honda), 199; 12 A.J. Foyt IV, USA (Dallara-Toyota), 199; 13 Jimmy Kite, USA (Dallara-Toyota), 195; 14 Kosuke Matsuura, J (Panoz G Force-Honda), 176 (DNF-accident); 15 Alex Barron, USA (Dallara-Toyota), 175 (DNF-accident); 16 Vitor Meira, BR (Panoz G Force-Honda), 175 (DNF-accident); 17 Tomas Scheckter, ZA (Dallara-Chevrolet), 160 (DNF-mechanical); 18 Buddy Rice, USA (Panoz G Force-Honda), 134 (DNF-half-shaft); 19 Tony Kanaan, BR (Dallara-Honda), 116 (DNF-accident); 20 Darren Manning, GB (Panoz G Force-Toyota), 115 (DNF-accident); 21 Dan Wheldon, GB (Dallara-Honda), 96 (DNF-suspension); 22 Bryan Herta, USA (Dallara-Honda), 75 (DNF-suspension); 23 Tomás Enge, CZ (Dallara-Chevrolet), 27 (DNF-accident).
Most laps led: Kanaan, 75.
Fastest race lap: Sharp, 23.2685s, 201.130 mph/323.688 km/h.
Fastest qualifying lap: Scheckter, 23.0409s, 203.117 mph/326.885 km/h.
Championship points: 1 Wheldon, 347; 2 Kanaan, 274; 3 Franchitti, 269; 4 Castroneves, 260; 5 Haornish Jr., 256; 6 Sharp, 230.

ABC SUPPLY CO. /A.J. FOYT 225, The Milwaukee Mile, Wisconsin State Fair Park, West Allis, Wisconsin, USA, 24 July. Round 10. 225 laps of the 1.015-mile/1.633-km circuit, 228.375 miles/367.534 km.
1 Sam Hornish Jr., USA (Dallara-Toyota), 1h 51m 38.6759s, 122.733 mph/197.520 km/h; 2 Dario Franchitti, GB (Dallara-Honda), 1h 51m 39.0595s; 3 Tomas Scheckter, ZA (Dallara-Chevrolet), 1h 51m 39.3261s; 4 Tony Kanaan, BR (Dallara-Honda), 1h 51m 43.1933s; 5 Dan Wheldon, GB (Dallara-Honda), 1h 51m 44.8029s; 6 Bryan Herta, USA (Dallara-Honda), 1h 51m 50.4608s; 7 Patrick Carpentier, CDN (Dallara-Toyota), 224 laps; 8 Alex Barron, USA (Dallara-Toyota), 224; 9 Vitor Meira, BR (Panoz G Force-Honda), 224; 10 Scott Sharp, USA (Panoz G Force-Honda), 221; 11 Kosuke Matsuura, J (Panoz G Force-Honda), 220; 12 Ed Carpenter, USA (Dallara-Toyota), 219; 13 Scott Dixon, NZ (Panoz G Force-Toyota), 219; 14 Jimmy Kite, USA (Dallara-Toyota), 218; 15 Roger Yasukawa, USA (Dallara-Honda), 212; 16 Hélio Castroneves, BR (Dallara-Toyota), 206; 17 Buddy Rice, USA (Panoz G Force-Honda), 164 (DNF-accident); 18 Buddy Lazier, USA (Dallara-Chevrolet), 129 (DNF-accident); 19 Danica Patrick, USA (Panoz G Force-Honda), 125 (DNF-accident); 20 Darren Manning, GB (Panoz G Force-Toyota), 34 (DNF-handling); 21 A.J. Foyt IV, USA (Dallara-Toyota), 19 (DNF-handling);
Did not start: Ryan Briscoe, AUS (Panoz G Force-Toyota).
Most laps led: Hornish Jr., 123.
Fastest race lap: Scheckter, 23.1415s, 157.898 mph/254.112 km/h.
Fastest qualifying lap: Hornish Jr., 21.4567s, 170.296 mph/274.066 km/h.
Championship points: 1 Wheldon, 377; 2= Hornish Jr., 309; 2=Franchitti, 309; 4 Kanaan, 306; 5 Castroneves, 274; 6 Sharp, 250.

FIRESTONE INDY 400, Michigan International Speedway, Brooklyn, Michigan, USA, 31 July. Round 11. 200 laps of the 2.000-mile/3.219-km circuit, 400.000 miles/643.738 km.
1 Bryan Herta, USA (Dallara-Honda), 2h 23m 32.5979s, 167.197 mph/269.077 km/h; 2 Dan Wheldon, GB (Dallara-Honda), 12h 23m 32.6353s; 3 Tomas Scheckter, ZA (Dallara-Chevrolet), 2h 23m 32.745s; 4 Tony Kanaan, BR (Dallara-Honda), 2h 23m 32.832s; 5 Sam Hornish Jr., USA (Dallara-Toyota), 2h 23m 33.064s; 6 Buddy Lazier, USA (Dallara-Chevrolet), 2h 23m 33.123s; 7 Scott Sharp, USA (Panoz G Force-Honda), 2h 23m 33.499s; 8 Dario Franchitti, GB (Dallara-Honda), 2h 23m 33.568s; 9 Patrick Carpentier, CDN (Dallara-Toyota), 199 laps; 10 Ryan Briscoe, AUS (Panoz G Force-Toyota), 199; 11 Alex Barron, USA (Dallara-Toyota), 199; 12 A.J. Foyt IV, USA (Dallara-Toyota), 198; 13 Jimmy Kite, USA (Dallara-Toyota), 197; 14 Vitor Meira, BR (Panoz G Force-Honda), 185 (DNF-electrics); 15 Townsend Bell, USA (Dallara-Chevrolet), 180 (DNF-accident); 16 Kosuke Matsuura, J (Panoz G Force-Honda), 180 (DNF-accident); 17 Jaques Lazier, USA (Panoz G Force-Toyota), 179 (DNF-accident); 18 Roger Yasukawa, USA (Dallara-Honda), 179 (DNF-accident); 19 Scott Dixon, NZ (Panoz G Force-Toyota), 166 (DNF-electrics); 20 Danica Patrick, USA (Panoz G Force-Honda), 163 (DNF-mechanical); 21 Hélio Castroneves, BR (Dallara-Toyota), 138 (DNF-mechanical); 22 Buddy Rice, USA (Panoz G Force-Honda), 126 (DNF-half-shaft); 23 Ed Carpenter, USA (Dallara-Toyota), 118 (DNF-mechanical).
Most laps led: Herta, 159.
Fastest race lap: Bell, 32.8055s, 219.475 mph/353.211 km/h.
Fastest qualifying lap: Herta, 32.8556s, 219.141 mph/352.673 km/h.
Championship points: 1 Wheldon, 417; 2 Hornish Jr., 339; 3 Kanaan, 338; 4 Franchitti, 333; 5 Herta, 291; 6 Castroneves, 286.

AMBER ALERT PORTAL INDY 300, Kentucky Speedway, Florence, Kentucky, USA. 14 August. Round 12. 200 laps of the 1.480-mile/2.382-km circuit, 296.000 miles/476.366 km.
1 Scott Sharp, USA (Panoz G Force-Honda), 1h 40m 55.1889s, 175.981 mph/283.214 km/h; 2 Vitor Meira, BR (Panoz G Force-Honda), 1h 40m 55.2668s; 3 Dan Wheldon, GB (Dallara-Honda), 1h 40m 55.7065s; 4 Alex Barron, USA (Dallara-Toyota), 1h 40m 56.3267s; 5 Hélio Castroneves, BR (Dallara-Toyota), 1h 41m 00.5497s; 6 Buddy Lazier, USA (Dallara-Chevrolet), 1h 41m 00.6718s; 7 Sam Hornish Jr., USA (Dallara-Toyota), 1h 41m 00.9360s; 8 Kosuke Matsuura, J (Panoz G Force-Honda), 1h 41m 01.4334s; 9 A.J. Foyt IV, USA (Dallara-Toyota), 1h 41m 01.5638s; 10 Jimmy Kite, USA (Dallara-Toyota), 1h 41m 01.7633s; 11 Tomás Enge, CZ (Dallara-Chevrolet), 1h 41m 01.8505s; 13 Patrick Carpentier, CDN (Dallara-Toyota), 1h 41m 02.0450s; 14 Ryan Briscoe, AUS (Panoz G Force-Toyota), 1h 41m 02.0700s, 15 Buddy Rice, USA (Panoz G Force-Honda), 199 laps; 16 Jaques Lazier, USA (Panoz G Force-Toyota), 197; 17 Danica Patrick, USA (Panoz G Force-Honda), 184; 18 Roger Yasukawa, USA (Dallara-Honda), 174 (DNF-gearbox); 19 Dario Franchitti, GB (Dallara-Honda), 169 (DNF-mechanical); 20 Bryan Herta, USA (Dallara-Honda), 144 (DNF-gearbox); 21 Tony Kanaan, BR (Dallara-Honda), 99 (DNF-wheel bearing); 22 Tomas Scheckter, ZA (Dallara-Chevrolet), 82 (DNF-mechanical); 23 Ed Carpenter, USA (Dallara-Toyota), 67 (DNF-accident); 24 Scott Dixon, NZ (Panoz G Force-Toyota), 27 (DNF-mechanical).
Most laps led: Wheldon, 104.
Fastest race lap: Patrick, 24.5663s, 216.882 mph/349.039 km/h.
Fastest qualifying lap: Patrick, 24.4947s, 217.516 mph/350.059 km/h.
Championship points: 1 Wheldon, 455; 2 Hornish Jr., 365; 3 Kanaan, 350; 4 Franchitti, 345; 5 Sharp, 326; 6 Castroneves, 316.

HONDA INDY 225, Pikes Peak International Raceway, Fountain, Colorado, USA, 21 August. Round 13. 225 laps of the 1.000-mile/1.609-km circuit, 225.000 miles/362.102 km.
1 Dan Wheldon, GB (Dallara-Honda), 1h 27m 46.9201s, 153.790 mph/247.501 km/h; 2 Sam Hornish Jr., USA (Dallara-Toyota), 1h 27m 59.3964s; 3 Tony Kanaan, BR (Dallara-Honda), 1h 28m 00.6840s; 4 Hélio Castroneves, BR (Dallara-Toyota), 224 laps; 5 Vitor Meira, BR (Panoz G Force-Honda), 224; 6 Tomás Enge, CZ (Dallara-Chevrolet), 224; 7 Dario Franchitti, GB (Dallara-Honda), 224; 8 Danica Patrick, USA (Panoz G Force-Honda), 223; 9 Scott Sharp, USA (Panoz G Force-Honda), 222; 10 Patrick Carpentier, CDN (Dallara-Toyota), 222; 11 Buddy Rice, USA (Panoz G Force-Honda), 222; 12 Bryan Herta, USA (Dallara-Honda), 222; 13 Kosuke Matsuura, J (Panoz G Force-Honda), 222; 14 Tomas Scheckter, ZA (Dallara-Chevrolet), 221; 15 Roger Yasukawa, USA (Dallara-Honda), 220; 16 Scott Dixon, NZ (Panoz G Force-Toyota), 220; 17 Jimmy Kite, USA (Dallara-Toyota), 219; 18 Alex Barron, USA (Dallara-Toyota), 219; 19 Ed Carpenter, USA (Dallara-Toyota), 217; 20 Ryan Briscoe, AUS (Panoz G Force-Toyota), 76 (DNF-accident); 21 A.J. Foyt IV, USA (Dallara-Toyota), 38 (DNF-handling).
Did not start: Jaques Lazier, USA (Panoz G Force-Toyota).
Most laps led: Hornish Jr., 71.
Fastest race lap: Franchitti, 21.1234s, 170.427 mph/247.276 km/h.
Fastest qualifying lap: Castroneves, 20.5218s, 175.423 mph/282.316 km/h.
Championship points: 1 Wheldon, 505; 2 Hornish Jr., 408; 3 Kanaan, 385; 4 Franchitti, 371; 5= Sharp, 348; 5= Castroneves, 348.

ARGENT MORTGAGE INDY GRAND PRIX, Infineon Raceway, Sears Point, Sonoma, California, USA, 28 August. Round 14. 80 laps of the 2.300-mile/3.701-km circuit, 184.000 miles/296.119 km.
1 Tony Kanaan, BR (Dallara-Honda), 2h 01m 15.9187s, 91.040 mph/146.515 km/h; 2 Buddy Rice, USA (Panoz G Force-Honda), 2h 01m 17.1013s; 3 Alex Barron, USA (Dallara-Toyota), 2h 01m 17.772s; 4 Patrick Carpentier, CDN (Dallara-Toyota), 2h 01m 18.582s; 5 Tomás Enge, CZ (Dallara-Chevrolet), 2h 01m 26.825s; 6 Kosuke Matsuura, J (Panoz G Force-Honda), 2h 01m 46.777s; 7 Scott Dixon, NZ (Panoz G Force-Toyota), 2h 01m 47.182s; 8 Dario Franchitti, GB (Dallara-Honda), 2h 01m 48.386s; 9 Vitor Meira, BR (Panoz G Force-Honda), 2h 01m 59.383s; 10 Jeff Bucknum, USA (Dallara-Chevrolet), 2h 02m 22.140s; 11 Roger Yasukawa, USA (Dallara-Honda), 2h 02m 49.973s; 12 Scott Sharp, USA (Panoz G Force-Honda), 2h 03m 40.973s; 13 Bryan Herta, USA (Dallara-Honda), 79 laps; 14 Giorgio Pantano, I (Panoz G Force-Toyota), 78 (DNF-accident); 15 Ed Carpenter, USA (Dallara-Toyota), 77; 16 Tomas Scheckter, ZA (Dallara-Chevrolet), 57 (DNF-suspension). 17 Sam Hornish Jr., USA (Dallara-Toyota), 56; 18 Dan Wheldon, GB (Dallara-Honda), 52 (DNF-fuel pump); 19 Ryan Briscoe, AUS (Panoz G Force-Toyota), 20 (DNF-accident); 20 Danica Patrick, USA (Panoz G Force-Honda), 19 (DNF-accident); 21 Hélio Castroneves, BR (Dallara-Toyota), 19 (DNF-accident);
Most laps led: Kanaan, 33.
Fastest race lap: Kanaan, 1m 18.3081s, 105.736 mph/170.166 km/h.
Fastest qualifying lap: Briscoe, 1m 16.4913s, 108.248 mph/174.208 km/h.
Championship points: 1 Wheldon, 517; 2 Kanaan, 438; 3 Hornish Jr., 421; 4 Franchitti, 395; 5 Sharp, 366; 6 Castroneves, 360.

PEAK ANTIFREEZE INDY 300 PRESENTED BY MR. CLEAN, Chicagoland Speedway, Chicago, Illinois, USA, 11 September. Round 15. 200 of the 1.520-mile/2.446-km circuit, 304.000 miles/489.241 km.
1 Dan Wheldon, GB (Dallara-Honda), 1h 47m 49.6126s, 169.160 mph/272.237 km/h; 2 Hélio Castroneves, BR (Dallara-Toyota), 1h 47m 49.6259s; 3 Sam Hornish Jr., USA (Dallara-Toyota), 1h 47m 49.6799s; 4 Tomas Scheckter, ZA (Dallara-Chevrolet), 1h 47m 49.8166s; 5 Tony Kanaan, BR (Dallara-Honda), 1h 47m 49.8370s; 6 Danica Patrick, USA (Panoz G Force-Honda), 1h 47m 50.0523s; 7 Vitor Meira, BR (Panoz G Force-Honda), 1h 47m 50.0650s; 8 Scott Sharp, USA (Panoz G Force-Honda), 1h 47m 50.2099s; 9 Patrick Carpentier, CDN (Dallara-Toyota), 1h 47m 50.2638s; 10 Buddy Lazier, USA (Dallara-Chevrolet), 1h 47m 50.5403s; 11 A.J. Foyt IV, USA (Dallara-Toyota), 1h 47m 50.5614s; 12 Dario Franchitti, GB (Dallara-Honda), 1h 47m 50.6546s; 13 Buddy Rice, USA (Panoz G Force-Honda), 1h 47m 50.7661s; 14 Bryan Herta, USA (Dallara-Honda), 1h 47m 50.9746s; 15 Roger Yasukawa, USA (Dallara-Honda), 1h 47m 51.7915s; 16 Jaques Lazier, USA (Panoz G Force-Toyota), 1h 47m 52.4481s; 17 Ed Carpenter, USA (Dallara-Toyota), 199 laps; 18 Jimmy Kite, USA (Dallara-Toyota), 199; 19 Scott Dixon, NZ (Panoz G Force-Toyota), 169 (DNF-gearbox); 20 Tomás Enge, CZ (Dallara-Chevrolet), 140 (DNF-suspension); 21 Alex Barron, USA (Dallara-Toyota), 19 (DNF-accident); 22 Ryan Briscoe, AUS (Panoz G Force-Toyota), 19 (DNF-accident); 23 Kosuke Matsuura, J (Panoz G Force-Honda), 19 (DNF-accident).
Most laps led: Wheldon, 88.
Fastest race lap: Franchitti, 24.9852s, 219.010 mph/352.462 km/h.
Fastest qualifying lap: Patrick, 25.3369s, 215.970 mph/347.569 km/h.
Championship points: 1 Wheldon, 570; 2 Kanaan, 468; 3 Hornish Jr., 456; 4 Franchitti, 413; 5 Castroneves, 400; 6 Sharp, 390.

WATKINS GLEN GRAND PRIX presented by ARGENT MORTGAGE, Watkins Glen International, Watkins Glen, New York, USA, 25 September. Round 16. 60 laps of the 3.370-mile/5.423-km circuit, 202.200 miles/325.409 km
1 Scott Dixon, NZ (Panoz G Force-Toyota), 1h 45m 42.3804s, 114.771 mph/184.706 km/h; 2 Tony Kanaan, BR (Dallara-Honda), 1h 45m 43.0344s (under caution); 3 Dario Franchitti, GB (Dallara-Honda), 1h 45m 43.5261s; 4 Giorgio Pantano, I (Panoz G Force-Toyota), 1h 45m 44.2603s; 5 Dan Wheldon, GB (Dallara-Honda), 1h 45m 44.5071s; 6 Kosuke Matsuura, J (Panoz G Force-Honda), 1h 45m 53.8242s; 7 Sam Hornish Jr., USA (Dallara-Toyota), 1h 45m 54.9456s; 8 Bryan Herta, USA (Dallara-Honda), 1h 46m 00.5616s; 9 Scott Sharp, USA (Panoz G Force-Honda), 1h 46m 00.7585s; 10 Patrick Carpentier, CDN (Dallara-Toyota), 1h 46m 22.1967s; 11 Jeff Bucknum, USA (Dallara-Chevrolet), 1h 46m 24.1986s; 12 Hélio Castroneves, BR (Dallara-Toyota), 59 laps (DNF-accident); 13 Tomás Enge, CZ (Dallara-Chevrolet), 59 (DNF-accident); 14 Ed Carpenter, USA (Dallara-Toyota), 59; 15 Roger Yasukawa, USA (Dallara-Honda), 58; 16 Danica Patrick, USA (Panoz G Force-Honda), 58; 17 Alex Barron, USA (Dallara-Toyota), 58; 18 Vitor Meira, BR (Panoz G Force-Honda), 48 (DNF-electrics); 19 Buddy Rice, USA (Panoz G Force-Honda), 27 (DNF-accident); 20 Tomas Scheckter, ZA (Dallara-Chevrolet), 4 (DNF-mechanical).
Most laps led: Dixon, 25.
Fastest race lap: Dixon, 1m 32.3466s, 131.375 mph/211.427 km/h.
Fastest qualifying lap: Castroneves, 1m 30.6688s, 133.806 mph/215.339 km/h.
Championship points: 1 Wheldon, 600; 2 Kanaan, 508; 3 Hornish Jr., 482; 4 Franchitti, 448; 5 Castroneves, 418; 6 Sharp, 412.

TOYOTA INDY 400, California Speedway, Fontana, California, USA, 16 October. Round 17. 200 laps of the 2.000-mile/3.219-km circuit, 400.000 miles/643.738 km.
1 Dario Franchitti, GB (Dallara-Honda), 2h 22m 22.6114s, 168.567 mph/271.282 km/h; 2 Tony Kanaan, BR (Dallara-Honda), 2h 22m 22.7231s; 3 Vitor Meira, BR (Panoz G Force-Honda), 2h 22m 23.5994s; 4 Scott Sharp, USA (Panoz G Force-Honda), 2h 22m 23.6988s; 5 Sam Hornish Jr., USA (Dallara-Toyota), 2h 22m 23.9825s; 6 Dan Wheldon, GB (Dallara-Honda), 2h 22m 24.3516s; 7 Tomas Scheckter, ZA (Dallara-Chevrolet), 2h 22m 24.9374s; 8 Tomás Enge, CZ (Dallara-Chevrolet), 2h 22m 27.0759s; 9 Hélio Castroneves, BR (Dallara-Toyota), 2h 22m 27.0832s; 10 Scott Dixon, NZ (Panoz G Force-Toyota), 2h 22m 29.2750s; 11 Bryan Herta, USA (Dallara-Honda), 2h 22m 30.7743s; 12 Buddy Rice, USA (Panoz G Force-Honda), 199; 13 Jimmy Kite, USA (Dallara-Toyota), 199; 14 Alex Barron, USA (Dallara-Toyota), 199; 15 Patrick Carpentier, CDN (Dallara-Toyota), 199; 16 Roger Yasukawa, USA (Dallara-Honda), 198; 17 Jaques Lazier, USA (Panoz G Force-Toyota), 184 (DNF-accident); 18 Danica Patrick, USA (Panoz G Force-Honda), 184 (DNF-accident); 19 Kosuke Matsuura, J (Panoz G Force-Honda), 168 (DNF-accident); 20 Ed Carpenter, USA (Dallara-Toyota), 133 (DNF-suspension); 21 A.J. Foyt IV, USA (Dallara-Toyota), 30 (DNF-accident).
Did not start: Thiago Medeiros, BR (Dallara-Honda).
Most laps led: Scheckter, 80.
Fastest race lap: Wheldon, 32.8041s, 219.485 mph/353.226 km/h.
Fastest qualifying lap: Franchitti, 32.8171s, 219.398 mph/353.087 km/h.

Final championship points
Drivers: 1 Dan Wheldon, GB, 628; 2 Tony Kanaan, BR, 548; 3 Sam Hornish Jr., USA, 512; 4 Dario Franchitti, GB, 498; 5 Scott Sharp, USA, 444; 6 Hélio Castroneves, BR, 440; 7 Vitor Meira, BR, 422; 8 Bryan Herta, USA, 397; 9 Tomas Scheckter, ZA, 390; 10 Patrick Carpentier, CDN, 376; 11 Alex Barron, USA, 329; 12 Danica Patrick, USA, 325; 13 Scott Dixon, NZ, 321; 14 Kosuke Matsuura, J, 320; 15 Buddy Rice, USA, 295; 16 Tomás Enge, CZ, 261; 17 Roger Yasukawa, USA, 246; 18 Ed Carpenter, USA, 244; 19 Ryan Briscoe, AUS, 232; 20 A.J. Foyt IV, USA, 231; 21 Darren Manning, GB, 186; 22 Jimmy Kite, USA, 163; 23 Buddy Lazier, USA, 140; 24 Jacques Lazier, USA, 81; 25 Jeff Bucknum, USA, 63; 26 Giorgio Pantano, I, 48; 27 Paul Dana, USA, 44; 28 Sébastien Bourdais, F, 18; 29 Adrian Fernandez, MEX, 16; 30= Felipe Giaffone, BR, 15; 30= Townsend Bell, USA, 15.
Bombardier Rookie of the Year: 1 Danica Patrick, 325; 2 Tomás Enge, 261; 3 Ryan Briscoe, 232.
Engine Manufacturers: 1 Honda, 153; 2 Toyota, 125; 3 Chevrolet, 96.
Chassis Manufacturers: 1 Dallara, 164; 2 Panoz G Force, 125.

Bridgestone presents The Champ Car World Series Powered by Ford

2004

The following race was run after AUTOCOURSE 2004–2005 went to press.

GRAN PREMIO TELMEX/GIGANTE PRESENTED BY BANAMEX/VISA, Autodromo Hermanos Rodriguez, Mexico City, Mexico, 7 November. Round 14. 63 laps of the 2.786-mile/4.484-km circuit, 175.518 miles/282.469 km.
1 Sébastien Bourdais, F (Lola B2/00-Ford Cosworth XFE), 1h 39m 02.662s, 106.327 mph/171.117 km/h; 2 Bruno Junqueira, BR (Lola B2/00-Ford Cosworth XFE), 1h 39m 07.266s; 3 A.J. Allmendinger, USA (Lola B2/00-Ford Cosworth XFE), 1h 39m 09.442s; 4 Justin Wilson, GB (Lola B2/00-Ford Cosworth XFE), 1h 39m 10.564s; 5 Jimmy Vasser, USA (Lola B2/00-Ford Cosworth XFE), 1h 39m 19.743s; 6 Patrick Carpentier, CDN (Lola B2/00-Ford Cosworth XFE), 1h 40m 00.450s; 7 Oriol Servia, E (Lola B2/00-Ford Cosworth XFE), 1h 40m 23.763s; 8 Mário Dominguez, MEX (Lola B2/00-Ford Cosworth XFE), 1h 40m 25.389s; 9 Michel Jourdain Jr., MEX (Lola B2/00-Ford Cosworth XFE), 1h 40m 34.561s; 10 Paul Tracy, CDN (Lola B2/00-Ford Cosworth XFE), 62 laps.
Most laps led: Bourdais, 63.
Fastest race lap: Bourdais, 1m 28.794s, 112.954 mph/181.781 km/h;
Fastest qualifying lap: Bourdais, 1m 25.919s, 116.733 mph/187.864 km/h.

Final championship points
Drivers: 1 Sébastien Bourdais, F, 369; 2 Bruno Junqueira, BR, 341; 3 Patrick Carpentier, CDN, 266; 4 Paul Tracy, CDN, 254; 5 Mário Dominguez, MEX, 244; 6 A.J. Allmendinger, USA, 229; 7 Alex Tagliani, CDN, 218; 8 Jimmy Vasser, USA, 201; 9= Ryan Hunter-Reay, USA, 199; 9= Oriol Servia, E, 199; 11 Justin Wilson, GB, 188; 12 Michel Jourdain Jr., MEX, 185; 13 Mario Haberfeld, BR, 157; 14 Rodolfo Lavin, MEX, 156; 15 Roberto Gonzalez, MEX, 136; 16 Nelson Philippe, F, 89; 17 Gaston Mazzacane, RA, 73; 18 Guy Smith, GB, 53; 19 Alex Sperafico, BR, 47; 20 David Besnard, AUS, 18; 21 Memo Gidley, USA, 15; 22 Tarso Marques, BR, 9; 23 Michael Valiante, CDN, 7; 24 Jaroslav 'Janek' Janis, CZ, 3.
Nation's Cup: 1 Canada, 361; 2= Brazil, 325; 2= France, 325; 4 United States, 285; 5 Mexico, 280; 6 Catalonia (Spain), 178; 7 England, 172; 8 Argentina, 73; 9 Australia, 17; 10 Czech Republic, 3.
Constructor's Cup: 1 Lola; 2 Reynard.
Rookie of the Year: 1 A.J. Allmendinger; 2 Justin Wilson; 3 Roberto Gonzalez.

2005

All cars are Lola B2/00 with Ford Cosworth XFE engines.

TOYOTA GRAND PRIX OF LONG BEACH, Long Beach Street Circuit, California, USA, 10 April. Round 1. 81 laps of the 1.968-mile/3.167-km circuit, 159.408 miles/256.542 km.
1 Sébastain Bourdais, F, 1h 46m 29.768s, 89.811 mph/144.536 km/h; 2 Paul Tracy, CDN, 1h 46m 33.906s; 3 Bruno Junqueira, BR, 1h 46m 35.215s; 4 Justin Wilson, GB, 1h 46m 36.039s; 5 Mário Dominguez, MEX, 1h 46m 37.685s; 6 Timo Glock, D, 1h 46m 38.269s; 7 Ronnie Bremer, DK, 1h 46m 38.767s; 8 A.J. Allmendinger, USA, 1h 46m 40.713s; 9 Jimmy Vasser, USA, 1h 46m 44.574s; 10 Cristiano da Matta, BR, 1h 46m 45.842s; 11 Oriol Servia, E, 1h 46m 48.487s; 12 Björn Wirdheim, S, 1h 46m 49.419s; 13 Ryan Hunter-Reay, USA, 1h 46m 49.803s; 14 Marcus Marshalll, AUS, 80 laps; 15 Alex Tagliani, CDN, 79; 16 Fabrizio del Monte, I, 74; 17 Andrew Ranger, CDN, 70 (DNF-accident); 18 Nelson Philippe, F, 61; 19 Ricardo Sperafico, BR, 41 (DNF-mechanical).
Most laps led: Bordais, 37.
Fastest race lap: Bourdais, 1m 09.171s, 102.424 mph/164.836 km/h.
Fastest qualifying lap: Tracy, 1m 07.485s, 104.983 mph/168.954 km/h.
Championship points: 1 Bourdais, 34; 2 Tracy, 29; 3 Junqueira, 27; 4 Wilson, 24; 5 Dominguez, 22; 6 Glock, 19.

TECATE/TELMEX MONTERREY GRAND PRIX PRESENTED BY ROSHFRANS, Parque Fundidora, Monterrey, Nuevo Leon, Mexico, 22 May. Round 2. 76 laps of the 2.104-mile/3.386-km circuit, 159.904 miles/257.341 km.
1 Bruno Junqueira, BR, 2h 03m 38.021s, 77.602 mph/124.889 km/h; 2 Andrew Ranger, CDN, 2h 03m 39.397s; 3 Alex Tagliani, CDN, 2h 03m 40.868s; 4 Justin Wilson, GB, 2h 03m 46.255s; 5 Sébastain Bourdais, F, 2h 03m 47.183s; 6 Cristiano da Matta, BR, 2h 03m 47.839s; 7 Ryan Hunter-Reay, USA, 2h 03m 49.579s; 8 Björn Wirdheim, S, 2h 03m 57.095s; 9 Oriol Servia, E, 2h 03m 58.988s; 10 A.J. Allmendinger, USA, 75 laps; 11 Timo Glock, D, 69 (DNF-accident); 12 Nelson Philippe, F, 68 (DNF-accident); 13 Mário Dominguez, MEX, 56 (DNF-accident); 14 Jimmy Vasser, USA, 54 (DNF-accident); 15 Paul Tracy, CDN, 49 (DNF-accident); 16 Marcus Marshalll, AUS, 39 (DNF-accident); 17 Ricardo Sperafico, BR, 28 (DNF-accident); 18 Jorge Goeters, MEX, 23 (DNF-mechanical); 19 Ronnie Bremer, DK, 13 (DNF-mechanical).
Most laps led: Philippe, 23.
Fastest race lap: Glock, 1m 15.307s, 100.580 mph/161.868 km/h.
Fastest qualifying lap: Bourdais, 1m 13.627s, 102.875 mph/165.562 km/h.
Championship points: 1 Junqueira, 59; 2 Bourdais, 58; 3 Wilson, 47; 4 Tracy, 36; 5 Ranger, 32; 6 Tagliani, 31.

TIME WARNER CABLE ROAD RUNNER 225 PRESENTED BY US BANK, The Milwaukee Mile, Wisconsin State Fair Park, West Allis, Wisconsin, USA, 4 June. Round 3. 221 laps of the 1.032-mile/1.661-km circuit, 228.072 miles/367.046 km.
1 Paul Tracy, CDN, 1h 45m 01.259s, 130.301 mph/209.699 km/h; 2 A.J. Allmendinger, USA, 1h 45m 04.629s; 3 Oriol Servia, E, 1h 45m 07.380s; 4 Justin Wilson, GB, 1h 45m 08.118s; 5 Jimmy Vasser, USA, 1h 45m 09.591s; 6 Sébastain Bourdais, F, 220 laps; 7 Mário Dominguez, MEX, 220; 8 Ronnie Bremer, DK, 220; 9 Timo Glock, D, 219; 10 Alex Tagliani, CDN, 218; 11 Cristiano da Matta, BR, 217; 12 Nelson Philippe, F, 216; 13 Marcus Marshalll, AUS, 216; 14 Ricardo Sperafico, BR, 211; 15 Björn Wirdheim, S, 174 (DNF-accident); 16 Andrew Ranger, CDN, 125 (DNF-accident); 17 Ryan Hunter-Reay, USA, 5 (DNF-accident).
Most laps led: Tracy, 192.
Fastest race lap: Tracy, 22.208s, 167.291 mph/269.229 km/h.
Fastest qualifying lap: Vasser, 21.081s, 176.235 mph/283.622 km/h.
Championship points: 1 Bourdais, 77; 2 Wilson, 70; 3 Tracy, 69; 4 Junqueira, 59; 5 Allmendinger, 53; 6= Servia, 48; 6= Dominguez, 48.

G.I. JOE'S PRESENTS THE CHAMP CAR GRAND PRIX OF PORTLAND, Portland International Raceway, Oregon, USA, 19 June. Round 4. 105 laps of the 1.964-mile/3.161-km circuit, 206.220 miles/331.879 km.
1 Cristiano da Matta, BR, 1h 51m 51.404s, 110.616 mph/178.020 km/h; **2** Sébastain Bourdais, F, 1h 52m 01.532s; **3** Paul Tracy, CDN, 1h 52m 08.974s; **4** Mário Dominguez, MEX, 1h 52m 10.044s; **5** A.J. Allmendinger, USA, 1h 52m 18.112s; **6** Jimmy Vasser, USA, 1h 52m 24.881s; **7** Andrew Ranger, CDN, 1h 52m 31.749s; **8** Ronnie Bremer, DK, 104 laps; **9** Björn Wirdheim, S, 104; **10** Timo Glock, D, 104; **11** Michael Valiante, CDN, 104; **12** Nelson Philippe, F, 104; **13** Ricardo Sperafico, BR, 104; **14** Marcus Marshalll, AUS, 103; **15** Ryan Hunter-Reay, USA, 103; **16** Oriol Servia, E, 79 (DNF-mechanical); **17** Justin Wilson, GB, 45 (DNF-mechanical); **18** Alex Tagliani, CDN, 8 (DNF-mechanical).
Most laps led: da Matta, 50.
Fastest race lap: Bourdais, 59.923s, 117.991 mph/189.889 km/h.
Fastest qualifying lap: Wilson, 57.597s, 122.756 mph/197.557 km/h.
Championship points: **1** Burdais, 106; **2** Tracy, 95; **3** Wilson, 77; **4** Allmendinger, 74; **5** da Matta, 73; **6** Dominguez, 71.

CHAMP CAR GRAND PRIX OF CLEVELAND PRESENTED BY U.S. BANK, Burke Lakefront Airport Circuit, Cleveland, Ohio, USA, 26 June. Round 5. 91 laps of the 2.106-mile/3.389-km circuit, 191.646 miles/308.424 km.
1 Paul Tracy, CDN, 1h 45m 43.856s, 108.755 mph/175.024 km/h; **2** A.J. Allmendinger, USA, 1h 45m 46.969s; **3** Oriol Servia, E, 1h 45m 47.770s; **4** Alex Tagliani, CDN, 1h 45m 54.041s; **5** Sébastain Bourdais, F, 1h 45m 57.118s; **6** Jimmy Vasser, USA, 1h 46m 04.217s; **7** Justin Wilson, GB, 1h 46m 07.345s; **8** Andrew Ranger, CDN, 1h 46m 09.068s; **9** Ricardo Sperafico, BR, 1h 46m 15.592s; **10** Timo Glock, D, 1h 46m 31.581s; **11** Tarso Marques, BR, 90 laps; **12** Marcus Marshalll, AUS, 89; **13** Nelson Philippe, F, 89; **14** Ronnie Bremer, DK, 80 (DNF-mechanical); **15** Björn Wirdheim, S, 51 (DNF-accident); **16** Cristiano da Matta, BR, 50 (DNF-accident); **17** Mário Dominguez, MEX, 38 (DNF-accident); **18** Ryan Hunter-Reay, USA, 1 (DNF-accident).
Most laps led: Tracy, 46.
Fastest race lap: Servia, 58.616s, 129.344 mph/208.158 km/h.
Fastest qualifying lap: Tracy, 57.419s, 132.040 mph/212.498 km/h.
Championship points: **1** Tracy, 128; **2** Bourdais, 127; **3** Allmendinger, 102; **4** Wilson, 95; **5** Vasser, 82; **6** da Matta, 80.

MOLSON INDY TORONTO, Canada National Exhibition Place Circuit, Toronto, Ontario, Canada, 10 July. Round 6. 86 laps of the 1.755-mile/2.824-km circuit, 150.930 miles/242.898 km.
1 Justin Wilson, GB, 1h 46m 10.177s, 85.296 mph/137.270 km/h; **2** Oriol Servia, E, 1h 46m 10.908s; **3** Alex Tagliani, CDN, 1h 46m 11.873s; **4** Jimmy Vasser, USA, 1h 46m 12.045s; **5** Sébastain Bourdais, F, 1h 46m 12.736s; **6** Ryan Hunter-Reay, USA, 1h 46m 13.411s; **7** Timo Glock, D, 1h 46m 14.876s; **8** Alex Sperafico, BR, 1h 46m 15.555s; **9** Ryan Dalziel, GB, 85 laps; **10** Nelson Philippe, F, 85; **11** Andrew Ranger, CDN, 83 (DNF-mechanical); **12** A.J. Allmendinger, USA, 80 (DNF-accident); **13** Mário Dominguez, MEX, 80 (DNF-accident); **14** Marcus Marshalll, AUS, 65 (DNF-accident); **15** Björn Wirdheim, S, 60 (DNF-accident); **16** Paul Tracy, CDN, 57 (DNF-mechanical); **17** Cristiano da Matta, BR, 56 (DNF-accident); **18** Ricardo Sperafico, BR, 55 (DNF-accident).
Most laps led: Bourdais, 34.
Fastest race lap: Wilson, 59.940s, 105.405 mph/169.634 km/h.
Fastest qualifying lap: Bourdais, 58.552s, 107.904 mph/173.655 km/h.
Championship points: **1** Bourdais, 150; **2** Tracy, 135; **3** Wilson, 128; **4** Allmendinger, 111; **5** Servia, 107; **6** Vasser, 105.

WEST EDMONTON MALL GRAND PRIX OF EDMONTON, Finning International Raceway, Edmonton, Alberta, Canada, 17 July. Round 7. 88 laps of the 1.973-mile/3.175-km circuit, 173.624 miles/279.421 km.
1 Sébastain Bourdais, F, 1h 38m 55.730s, 105.302 mph/169.468 km/h; **2** Oriol Servia, E, 1h 38m 56.326s; **3** Paul Tracy, CDN, 1h 38m 57.065s; **4** Justin Wilson, GB, 1h 38m 57.345s; **5** Mário Dominguez, MEX, 1h 39m 07.772s; **6** Ronnie Bremer, DK, 1h 39m 08.127s; **7** Alex Tagliani, CDN, 87 laps; **8** Marcus Marshalll, AUS, 87; **9** Nelson Philippe, F, 87; **10** Ricardo Sperafico, BR, 87; **11** Jimmy Vasser, USA, 86; **12** Alex Sperafico, BR, 86; **13** Timo Glock, D, 83 (DNF-accident); **14** A.J. Allmendinger, USA, 80 (DNF-accident); **15** Björn Wirdheim, S, 74 (DNF-accident); **16** Ryan Hunter-Reay, USA, 51 (DNF-electrics); **17** Cristiano da Matta, BR, 7 (DNF-mechanical); **18** Andrew Ranger, CDN, 3 (DNF-accident).
Most laps led: Allmendinger, 40.
Fastest race lap: Allmendinger, 59.900s, 118.578 mph/190.832 km/h.
Fastest qualifying lap: Allmendinger, 58.628s, 121.150 mph/194.973 km/h.
Championship points: **1** Bourdais, 182; **2** Tracy, 161; **3** Wilson, 152; **4** Servia, 135; **5** Allemdninger, 122; **6** Vasser, 115.

TAYLOR WOODROW GRAND PRIX OF SAN JOSÉ, San José Street Circuit, California, USA, 31 July. Round 8. 93 laps of the 1.448-mile/2.330-km circuit, 134.664 miles/216.721 km.
1 Sébastain Bourdais, F, 1h 45m 42.889s, 76.431 mph/123.003 km/h; **2** Paul Tracy, CDN, 1h 45m 46.613s; **3** Oriol Servia, E, 1h 45m 53.272s; **4** Justin Wilson, GB, 1h 45m 54.212s; **5** Mário Dominguez, MEX, 1h 45m 54.806s; **6** Timo Glock, D, 1h 45m 58.149s; **7** Ronnie Bremer, DK, 1h 45m 59.280s; **8** Björn Wirdheim, S, 1h 46m 02.332s; **9** Alex Tagliani, CDN, 89 laps; **10** Cristiano da Matta, BR, 77 (DNF-accident); **11** Jimmy Vasser, USA, 60 (DNF-mechanical); **12** Marcus Marshalll, AUS, 52 (DNF-mechanical); **13** Rodolfo Lavin, MEX, 40 (DNF-accident); **14** Ryan Hunter-Reay, USA, 36 (DNF-mechanical); **15** Nelson Philippe, F, 20 (DNF-mechanical); **16** Andrew Ranger, CDN, 13 (DNF-accident); **17** A.J. Allmendinger, USA, 12 (DNF-accident); **18** Ricardo Sperafico, BR, 0 (DNF-accident).
Most laps led: Bourdais, 63.
Fastest race lap: Bourdais, 55.083s, 94.635 mph/152.301 km/h.
Fastest qualifying lap: Bourdais, 54.243s, 96.101 mph/154.659 km/h.
Championship points: **1** Bourdais, 216; **2** Tracy, 188; **3** Wilson, 175; **4** Servia, 160; **5** Allmendinger, 126; **6** Dominguez, 125.

CENTRIX FINANCIAL GRAND PRIX OF DENVER PRESENTED BY PACIFICARE, Denver Street Circuit, Colorado, USA, 14 August. Round 9. 97 laps of the 1.657-mile/2.667-km circuit, 160.729 miles/258.668 km.
1 Sébastain Bourdais, F, 1h 49m 45.135s, 87.868 mph/141.410 km/h; **2** Mário Dominguez, MEX, 1h 50m 00.404s; **3** A.J. Allmendinger, USA, 1h 50m 02.342s; **4** Oriol Servia, E, 1h 50m 20.910s; **5** Rodolfo Lavin, MEX, 1h 50m 22.764s; **6** Ryan Hunter-Reay, USA, 1h 50m 28.372s; **7** Ronnie Bremer, DK, 1h 50m 32.622s; **8** Ricardo Sperafico, BR, 1h 50m 37.605s; **9** Nelson Philippe, F, 1h 50m 48.037s; **10** Andrew Ranger, CDN, 96 laps; **11** Björn Wirdheim, S, 96; **12** Marcus Marshalll, AUS, 94; **13** Timo Glock, D, 88 (DNF-in pit); **14** Alex Tagliani, CDN, 82; **15** Jimmy Vasser, USA, 65 (DNF-mechanical); **16** Paul Tracy, CDN, 62 (DNF-accident); **17** Justin Wilson, GB, 0 (DNF-accident); **18** Cristiano da Matta, BR, 0 (DNF-accident).
Most laps led: Tracy, 59.
Fastest race lap: Bourdais, 1m 00.574s, 98.478 mph/158.485 km/h.
Fastest qualifying lap: Tracy, 59.432s, 100.370 mph/161.530 km/h.
Championship points: **1** Bourdais, 249; **2** Tracy, 196; **3** Servia, 183; **4** Wilson, 179; **5** Dominguez, 152; **6** Allmendinger, 151.

MOLSON INDY MONTREAL, Circuit Gilles-Villeneuve, Ile-Notre-Dame, Montréal, Québec, Canada, 28 August. Round 10. 79 laps of the 2.709-mile/4.360-km circuit, 214.011 miles/344.417 km.
1 Oriol Servia, E, 1h 59m 10.516s, 107.746 mph/173.400 km/h; **2** Timo Glock, D, 1h 59m 11.516s; **3** Justin Wilson, GB, 1h 59m 11.932s; **4** Sébastain Bourdais, F, 1h 59m 12.153s; **5** Alex Tagliani, CDN, 1h 59m 13.737s; **6** Cristiano da Matta, BR, 1h 59m 14.968s; **7** Jimmy Vasser, USA, 1h 59m 15.827s; **8** Paul Tracy, CDN, 1h 59m 17.188s; **9** A.J. Allmendinger, USA, 1h 59m 17.729s; **10** Mário Dominguez, MEX, 1h 59m 18.194s; **11** Andrew Ranger, CDN, 1h 59m 23.130s; **12** Ryan Hunter-Reay, USA, 1h 59m 24.670s; **13** Björn Wirdheim, S, 1h 59m 26.620s; **14** Rodolfo Lavin, MEX, 1h 59m 27.491s; **15** Nelson Philippe, F, 1h 59m 55.875s; **16** Marcus Marshalll, AUS, 78 laps; **17** Ronnie Bremer, DK, 78; **18** Ricardo Sperafico, BR, 55 (DNF-accident).
Most laps led: Bourdais, 59.
Fastest race lap: Bourdais, 1m 21.667s, 119.417 mph/192.182 km/h.
Fastest qualifying lap: Bourdais, 1m 20.396s, 121.305 mph/195.221 km/h.
Championship points: **1** Bourdais, 276; **2** Servia, 215; **3** Tracy, 211; **4** Wilson, 24; **5** Allmendinger, 164; **6** Dominguez, 163.

CHAMP CAR GRAND PRIX OF LAS VEGAS, Las Vegas Motor Speedway, Nevada, USA, 24 September. Round 11. 166 laps of the 1.500-mile/2.414-km circuit, 249.000 miles/400.727 km.
1 Sébastain Bourdais, F, 1h 26m 22.636s, 172.962 mph/278.356 km/h; **2** Oriol Servia, E, 1h 26m 22.948s; **3** Jimmy Vasser, USA, 1h 26m 26.240s; **4** Mário Dominguez, MEX, 1h 26m 29.805s; **5** Rodolfo Lavin, MEX, 1h 26m 30.174s; **6** Björn Wirdheim, S, 1h 26m 30.191s; **7** Alex Tagliani, CDN, 1h 26m 30.798s; **8** Timo Glock, D, 165 laps; **9** Marcus Marshalll, AUS, 165; **10** Ryan Hunter-Reay, USA, 165; **11** Justin Wilson, GB, 164; **12** Cristiano da Matta, BR, 164; **13** A.J. Allmendinger, USA, 163; **14** Andrew Ranger, CDN, 162; **15** Ricardo Sperafico, BR, 161; **16** Nelson Philippe, F, 127 (DNF-accident); **17** Paul Tracy, CDN, 123 (DNF-accident); **18** Ronnie Bremer, DK, 41 (DNF-pit incident).
Most laps led: Tracy, 107.
Fastest race lap: Bourdais, 26.336s, 205.043 mph/329.984 km/h.
Fastest qualifying lap: Bourdais, 26.381s, 204.693 mph/329.421 km/h.
Championship points: **1** Bourdais, 310; **2** Servia, 243; **3** Tracy, 216; **4** Wilson, 214; **5** Dominguez, 186; **6=** Allmendinger, 173; **6=** Vasser, 173.

LEXMARK INDY 300, Surfer's Paradise street circuit, Queensland, Australia, 23 October. Round 12. 57 laps of the 2.795-mile/4.498-km circuit, 159.315 miles/256.393 km.
1 Sébastain Bourdais, F, 1h 39m 26.671s, 96.123 mph/154.695 km/h; **2** A.J. Allmendinger, USA, 1h 39m 35.801s; **3** Jimmy Vasser, USA, 1h 39m 58.523s; **4** Alex Tagliani, CDN, 1h 39m 43.091s; **5** Oriol Servia, E, 1h 40m 10.639s; **6** Timo Glock, D, 1h 40m 12.287s; **7** Justin Wilson, GB, 1h 40m 26.301s; **8** Ronnie Bremer, DK, 1h 40m 32.523s; **9** Ricardo Sperafico, BR, 1h 40m 42.963s; **10** Andrew Ranger, CDN, 1h 41m 00.159s; **11** Marcus Marshalll, AUS, 56 laps; **12** Michael McDowell, USA, 56; **13** Rodolfo Lavin, MEX, 53; **14** Nelson Philippe, F, 47 (DNF-off course); **15** Will Power, AUS, 29 (DNF-accident); **16** Fabrizio del Monte, I, 28 (DNF-accident); **17** Paul Tracy, CDN, 24 (DNF-mechanical); **18** Mário Dominguez, MEX, 1 (DNF-accident); **19** Cristiano da Matta, BR, 0 (DNF-accident).
Most laps led: Bourdais, 38.
Fastest race lap: Bourdais, 1m 32.063s, 109.295 mph/175.893 km/h.
Fastest qualifying lap: Servia, 1m 32.616s, 108.642 mph/174.843 km/h.

GRAN PREMIO TELMEX-TECATE, PRESENTED BY BANAMEX, Autodromo Hermanos Rodriguez, Mexico City, D.F., Mexico, 6 November. Round 13. 70 laps of the 2.786-mile/4.484-km circuit, 195.020 miles/313.854 km.
1 Justin Wilson, GB, 1h 58m 23.479s, 98.835 mph/158.136km/h; **2** A.J. Allmendinger, USA, 1h 58m 27.415s; **3** Paul Tracy, CDN, 1h 58m 30.263s; **4** Oriol Servia, E, 1h 58m 33.113s; **5** Timo Glock, D, 1h 58m 33.402s; **6** Jimmy Vasser, USA, 1h 58m 33.956s; **7** Nelson Philippe, F, 1h 58m 36.827s; **8** Alex Tagliani, CDN, 1h 58m 37.618s; **9** Andrew Ranger, CDN, 1h 58m 38.669s; **10** Will Power, AUS, 1h 58m 39.664s; **11** Michael McDowell, USA, 1h 58m 41.539s; **12** Mário Dominguez, MEX, 1h 58m 42.157s; **13** Charles Zwolsman, NL, 1h 58m 42.938s; **14** Cristiano da Matta, BR, 1h 58m 45.155s; **15** Rodolfo Lavin, 69; **16** Homero Richards, MEX, 69; **17** Sébastain Bourdais, F, 61 (DNF-accident); **18** Ricardo Sperafico, BR, 54 (DNF-suspension); **19** Ronnie Bremer, DK, 18 (DNF-accident);
Most laps led: Wilson, 65.
Fastest race lap: Wilson, 1m 28.479s, 113.356 mph/182.428 km/h.
Fastest qualifying lap: Wilson, 1m 26.602s, 115.813 mph/186.382 km/h.

Final championship points
Drivers: **1** Sébastain Bourdais, F, 348; **2** Oriol Servia, E, 288; **3** Justin Wilson, GB, 265; **4** Paul Tracy, CDN, 246 **5** A.J. Allmendinger, USA, 227; **6** Jimmy Vasser, USA, 217; **7** Alex Tagliani, CDN, 207; **8** Timo Glock, D, 202; **9** Mário Dominguez, MEX, 198; **10** Andrew Ranger, CDN, 140; **11** Cristiano da Matta, BR, 139; **12** Ronnie Bremer, DK, 139; **13** Nelson Philippe, F, 117; **14** Björn Wirdheim, S, 115; **15** Ryan Hunter-Reay, USA, 110; **16** Marcus Marshall, AUS, 104; **17** Ricardo Sperafico, BR, 92; **18** Rodolfo Lavin, MEX, 72; **19** Bruno Junqueira, BR, 59; **20** Alex Sperafico, BR, 24; **21** Michael McDowell, USA, 19; **22** Will Power, AUS, 17; **23** Ryan Dalziel, GB, 13; **24=** Tarso Marques, BR, 10; **24=** Michael Valiante, CDN, 10; **24=** Fabrizio del Monte, I, 10; **27** Charles Zwolsman, NL, 8; **28** Homero Richards, MEX, 5; **29** Jorge Goeters, MEX, 3.
Nations' Cup: **1** France, 346; **2** Canada, 322; **3** Spain, 283; **4** United States, 274; **5** England, 267; **6** Brazil, 211; **7** Mexico, 201; **8** Germany, 198; **9** Denmark, 133; **10** Australia, 115; **11** Sweden, 113; **12** Scotland, 13; **13** Italy, 10; **14** Netherlands, 8
Constructors' Cup: **1** Lola, 429.
Rookie of the Year: **1** Glock; **2** Ranger; **3** Bremer.

NASCAR Nextel Cup Series 2004

The following races were run after AUTOCOURSE 2004–2005 went to press.

CHECKER AUTO PARTS 500, Phoenix International Raceway, Arizona, USA, 7 November. Round 34. 315 laps of the 1.000-mile/1.609-km circuit, 315.000 miles/506.943 km.
1 Dale Earnhardt Jr., USA (Chevrolet Monte Carlo), 3h 19m 16.0s, 94.848 mph/152.643 km/h; **2** Ryan Newman, USA (Dodge Intrepid), 3h 19m 17.431s; **3** Jeff Gordon, USA (Chevrolet Monte Carlo), 315 laps; **4** Kevin Harvick, USA (Chevrolet Monte Carlo), 315; **5** Kasey Kahne, USA (Dodge Intrepid), 315; **6** Jimmie Johnson, USA (Chevrolet Monte Carlo), 315; **7** Rusty Wallace, USA (Dodge Intrepid), 315; **8** Tony Stewart, USA (Chevrolet Monte Carlo), 315; **9** Bobby Labonte, USA (Chevrolet Monte Carlo), 315; **10** Kurt Busch, USA (Ford Taurus), 315.
Pole position: Newman, 26.499s, 135.854 mph/218.636 km/h.
Drivers' championship points: **1** Busch, 6191; **2** Gordon (Jeff), 6150; **3** Earnhardt Jr., 6144; **4** Johnson, 6143; **5** Martin, 6089; **6** Stewart, 6049.

MOUNTAIN DEW SOUTHERN 500, Darlington Raceway, South Carolina, USA, 14 November. Round 35. 367 laps of the 1.366-mile/2.198-km circuit, 501.322 miles/806.800 km.
1 Jimmie Johnson, USA (Chevrolet Monte Carlo), 4h 00m 33.0s, 125.044 mph/201.239 km/h; **2** Mark Martin, USA (Ford Taurus), 4h 00m 33.959s; **3** Jeff Gordon, USA (Chevrolet Monte Carlo), 367 laps; **4** Jamie McMurray, USA (Dodge Intrepid), 367; **5** Kasey Kahne, USA (Dodge Intrepid), 367; **6** Kurt Busch, USA (Ford Taurus), 367; **7** Carl Edwards, USA (Ford Taurus), 367; **8** Joe Nemechek, USA (Chevrolet Monte Carlo), 367; **9** Bobby Labonte, USA (Chevrolet Monte Carlo), 367; **10** Mike Bliss, USA (Chevrolet Monte Carlo), 367.
Pole position: Busch (points leader - qualifying was cancelled due to bad weather).
Drivers' championship points: **1** Busch, 6346; **2** Johnson, 6328; **3** Gordon (Jeff), 6325; **4** Earnhardt Jr., 6274; **5** Martin, 6264; **6** Stewart, 6161.

FORD 400, Homestead-Miami Speedway, Florida, USA, 21 November. Round 36. 271 laps of the 1.500-mile/2.414-km circuit, 406.500 miles/654.198 km.
1 Greg Biffle, USA (Ford Taurus), 3h 50m 55.0s, 105.623 mph/169.983 km/h; **2** Jimmie Johnson, USA (Chevrolet Monte Carlo), 3h 50m 55.342s; **3** Jeff Gordon, USA (Chevrolet Monte Carlo), 271 laps; **4** Tony Stewart, USA (Chevrolet Monte Carlo), 271; **5** Kurt Busch, USA (Ford Taurus), 271; **6** Brendan Gaughan, USA (Dodge Intrepid), 271; **7** Jamie McMurray, USA (Dodge Intrepid), 271; **8** Rusty Wallace, USA (Dodge Intrepid), 271; **9** Ricky Rudd, USA (Ford Taurus), 271; **10** Kevin Harvick, USA (Chevrolet Monte Carlo), 271.
Pole position: Busch, 30.114s, 179.319 mph/288.585 km/h.

Final championship points
Drivers: **1** Kurt Busch, USA, 6506; **2** Jimmie Johnson, USA, 6498; **3** Jeff Gordon, USA, 6490; **4** Mark Martin, USA, 6399; **5** Dale Earnhardt Jr., USA, 6368; **6** Tony Stewart, USA, 6326; **7** Ryan Newman, USA, 6180; **8** Matt Kenseth, USA, 6069; **9** Elliott Sadler, USA, 6024; **10** Jeremy Mayfield, USA, 6000.

Not involved in 'Chase for the Nextel Cup'
11 Jamie McMurray, USA, 4597; **12** Bobby Labonte, USA, 4277; **13** Kasey Kahne, USA, 4274; **14** Kevin Harvick, USA, 4228; **15** Dale Jarrett, USA, 4214; **16** Rusty Wallace, USA, 3960; **17=** Greg Biffle, USA, 3902; **17=** Jeff Burton, USA, 3902; **19=** Joe Nemechek, USA, 3878; **19=** Michael Waltrip, USA, 3878; **21** Sterling Marlin, USA, 3857; **22** Casey Mears, USA, 3690; **23** Robby Gordon, USA, 3646; **24** Ricky Rudd, USA, 3615; **25** Brian Vickers, USA, 3521; **26** Terry Labonte, USA, 3519; **27** Scott Wimmer, USA, 3198; **28** Brendan Gaughan, USA, 3165; **29** Scott Riggs, USA, 3090; **30** Jeff Green, USA, 3054.
Raybestos Rookie of the Year: Kasey Kahne.
Manufacturers: **1** Chevrolet, 242; **2** Ford, 205; **3** Dodge, 180.
Bud Pole Award winner: Ryan Newman, 9 poles.

2005

46th DAYTONA 500, Daytona International Speedway, Daytona Beach, Florida, USA, 20 February. Round 1. 203 laps of the 2.500-mile/4.023-km circuit, 507.500 miles/816.742 km.
1 Jeff Gordon, USA (Chevrolet Monte Carlo), 3h 45m 16.0s, 135.173 mph/217.540 km/h; **2** Kurt Busch, USA (Ford Taurus), 3h 45m 16.158s; **3** Dale Earnhardt Jr., USA (Chevrolet Monte Carlo), 203 laps; **4** Scott Riggs, USA (Chevrolet Monte Carlo), 203; **5** Jimmie Johnson, USA (Chevrolet Monte Carlo), 203; **6** Mark Martin, USA (Ford Taurus), 203; **7** Tony Stewart, USA (Chevrolet Monte Carlo), 203; **8** Sterling Marlin, USA (Dodge Charger), 203; **9** Kevin Lepage, USA (Dodge Charger), 203; **10** Rusty Wallace, USA (Dodge Charger), 203.
Pole position: Dale Jarrett, USA (Ford Taurus).
Drivers' championship points: **1** Gordon (Jeff); **2** Busch (Kurt); **3** Earnhardt Jr.; **4** Riggs; **5** Johnson; **6** Martin.

AUTO CLUB 500, California Speedway, Fontana, California, USA, 27 February. Round 2. 250 laps of the 2.000-mile/3.219-km circuit, 500.000 miles/804.672 km.
1 Greg Biffle, USA (Ford Taurus), 3h 34m 45.0s, 139.697 mph/224.821 km/h; **2** Jimmie Johnson, USA (Chevrolet Monte Carlo), 3h 34m 45.231s; **3** Kurt Busch, USA (Ford Taurus), 250 laps; **4** Jamie McMurray, USA (Dodge Charger), 250; **5** Carl Edwards, USA (Ford Taurus), 250; **6** Kevin Harvick, USA (Chevrolet Monte Carlo), 250; **7** Mark Martin, USA (Ford Taurus), 250; **8** Elliott Sadler, USA (Ford Taurus), 250; **9** Ryan Newman, USA (Dodge Charger), 250; **10** Rusty Wallace, USA (Dodge Charger), 250.
Pole position: Kyle Busch, USA (Chevrolet Monte Carlo).
Drivers' championship points: **1** Busch, 340; **2** Johnson, 335; **3** Martin, 301; **4** Edwards, 287; **5** Biffle, 273; **6** Sadler, 272.

UAW-DAIMLERCHRYSLER 400, Las Vegas Motor Speedway, Nevada, USA, 13 March. Round 3. 267 laps of the 1.500-mile/2.414-km circuit, 400.500 miles/644.542 km.
1 Jimmie Johnson, USA (Chevrolet Monte Carlo), 3h 18m 32.0s, 121.038 mph/194.791 km/h; **2** Kyle Busch, USA (Chevrolet Monte Carlo), 3h 18m 33.661s; **3** Kurt Busch, USA (Ford Taurus), 267 laps; **4** Jeff Gordon, USA (Chevrolet Monte Carlo), 267; **5** Kevin Harvick, USA (Chevrolet Monte Carlo), 267; **6** Greg Biffle, USA (Ford Taurus), 267; **7** Casey Mears, USA (Dodge Charger), 267; **8** Matt Kenseth, USA (Ford Taurus), 267; **9** Ryan Newman, USA (Dodge Charger), 267; **10** Tony Stewart, USA (Chevrolet Monte Carlo), 267.
Pole position: Newman (Dodge Charger).
Drivers' championship points: **1** Johnson, 525; **2** Busch (Kurt), 510; **3** Biffle, 428; **4** Gordon, 418; **5** Edwards, 408; **6** Stewart, 406.

GOLDEN CORRAL 500, Atlanta Motor Speedway, Hampton, Georgia, USA, 20 March. Round 4. 325 laps of the 1.540-mile/2.478-km circuit, 500.000 miles/805.477 km.
1 Carl Edwards, USA (Ford Taurus), 3h 29m 18.0s, 143.478 mph/230.906 km/h; **2** Jimmie Johnson, USA (Chevrolet Monte Carlo), 3h 29m 18.028s; **3** Greg Biffle, USA (Ford Taurus), 325 laps; **4** Mark Martin, USA (Ford Taurus), 325; **5** Kasey Kahne, USA (Dodge Charger), 325; **6** Brian Vickers, USA (Chevrolet Monte Carlo), 325; **7** Michael Waltrip, USA (Chevrolet Monte Caro), 325; **8** Dave Blaney, USA (Chevrolet Monte Carlo), 325; **9** Scott Riggs, USA (Chevrolet Monte Carlo), 325; **10** Elliott Sadler, USA (Ford Taurus), 325.
Pole position: Ryan Newman, USA (Dodge Charger).
Drivers' championship points: **1** Johnson, 680; **2** Biffle, 598; **3** Edwards, 593; **4** Busch, 577; **5** Martin, 539; **6** Newman, 515.

FOOD CITY 500, Bristol Motor Speedway, Tennessee, USA, 3 April. Round 5. 500 laps of the 0.533-mile/0.858-km circuit, 266.500 miles/428.890 km.
1 Kevin Harvick, USA (Chevrolet Monte Carlo), 3h 26m 20.0s, 77.496 mph/124.718 km/h; **2** Elliott Sadler, USA (Ford Taurus), 3h 26m 24.652s; **3** Tony Stewart, USA (Chevrolet Monte Carlo), 500 laps; **4** Dale Earnhardt Jr., USA (Chevrolet Monte Carlo), 500; **5** Dale Jarrett, USA (Ford Taurus), 500; **6** Jimmie Johnson, USA (Chevrolet Monte Carlo), 500; **7** Travis Kvapil, USA (Dodge Charger), 500; **8** Kyle Petty, USA (Dodge Charger), 500; **9** Greg Biffle, USA (Ford Taurus), 500; **10** Scott Riggs, USA (Chevrolet Monte Carlo),
Pole position: Sadler (Ford Taurus).
Drivers' championship points: **1** Johnson, 835; **2** Biffle, 741; **3** Stewart, 679; **4** Edwards, 678; **5** Sadler, 657; **6** Harvick, 654.

ADVANCE AUTO PARTS 500, Martinsville Speedway, Virginia, USA, 10 April. Round 6. 500 laps of the 0.526-mile/0.847-km circuit, 263.000 miles/423.257 km.
1 Jeff Gordon, USA (Chevrolet Monte Carlo), 3h 38m 52.0s, 72.099 mph/116.032 km/h; **2** Kasey Kahne, USA (Dodge Charger), 3h 38m 52.593s; **3** Mark Martin, USA (Ford Taurus), 500 laps; **4** Ryan Newman, USA (Dodge Charger), 500; **5** Rusty Wallace, USA (Dodge Charger), 500; **6** Sterling Marlin, USA (Dodge Charger), 500; **7** Ricky Rudd, USA (Ford Taurus), 500; **8** Jimmie Johnson, USA (Chevrolet Monte Carlo), 500; **9** Elliott Sadler, USA (Ford Taurus), 500; **10** Joe Nemechek, USA (Chevrolet Monte Carlo), 500.
Pole position: Scott Riggs, USA (Chevrolet Monte Carlo).
Drivers' championship points: **1** Johnson, 977; **2** Biffle, 817; **3** Sadler, 795; **4** Martin, 779; **5** Stewart, 774; **6** Gordon, 772.

SAMSUNG/RADIO SHACK 500, Texas Motor Speedway, Fort Worth, Texas, USA, 17 April. Round 7. 334 laps of the 1.500-mile/2.414-km circuit, 501.000 miles/806.281 km.
1 Greg Biffle, USA (Ford Taurus), 3h 51m 08.0s, 130.055 mph/209.308 km/h; **2** Jamie McMurray, USA (Dodge Charger), 3h 51m 11.244s; **3** Jimmie Johnson, USA (Chevrolet Monte Carlo), 334 laps; **4** Casey Mears, USA (Dodge Charger), 334; **5** Sterling Marlin, USA (Dodge Charger), 334; **6** Michael Waltrip, USA (Chevrolet Monte Caro), 334; **7** Kurt Busch, USA (Ford Taurus), 334; **8** Ricky Rudd, USA (Ford Taurus), 334; **9** Dale Earnhardt Jr., USA (Chevrolet Monte Carlo), 334; **10** Rusty Wallace, USA (Dodge Charger), 334.
Pole position: Ryan Newman, USA (Dodge Charger).
Drivers' championship points: **1** Johnson, 1142; **2** Biffle, 1007; **3** Wallace, 905; **4** Busch (Kurt), 897; **5** Gordon (Jeff), 895; **6** Martin, 883.

SUBWAY FRESH 500, Phoenix International Raceway, Arizona, USA, 23 April. Round 8. 312 laps of the 1.000-mile/1.609-km circuit, 312.000 miles/502.115 km.
1 Kurt Busch, USA (Ford Taurus), 3h 02m 16.0s, 102.707 mph/165.290 km/h; **2** Michael Waltrip, USA (Chevrolet Monte Caro), 3h 02m 18.315s; **3** Jeff Burton, USA (Chevrolet Monte Carlo), 312 laps; **4** Dale Earnhardt Jr., USA (Chevrolet Monte Carlo), 312; **5** Brian Vickers, USA (Chevrolet Monte Carlo), 312; **6** Bobby Labonte, USA (Chevrolet Monte Carlo), 312; **7** Carl Edwards, USA (Ford Taurus), 312; **8** Kyle Busch, USA (Chevrolet Monte Carlo), 312; **9** Johnny Sauter, USA (Dodge Charger), 312; **10** Joe Nemechek, USA (Chevrolet Monte Carlo), 312.
Pole position: Jeff Gordon, USA (Chevrolet Monte Carlo).
Drivers' championship points: **1** Johnson, 1260; **2** Busch (Kurt),

1087; **3** Biffle, 1052; **4** Gordon (Jeff), 1027; **5** Sadler, 1009; **6** Martin, 997.

AARON'S 499, Talladega Superspeedway, Alabama, USA, 1 May. Round 9. 194 laps of the 2.660-mile/4.281-km circuit, 516.040 miles/830.486 km.
1 Jeff Gordon, USA (Chevrolet Monte Carlo), 3h 30m 46.0s, 146.904 mph/236.419 km/h; **2** Tony Stewart, USA (Chevrolet Monte Carlo), 3h 30m 46.193s; **3** Michael Waltrip, USA (Chevrolet Monte Caro), 194 laps; **4** Jeremy Mayfield, USA (Dodge Charger), 194; **5** Jamie McMurray, USA (Dodge Charger), 194; **6** Elliott Sadler, USA (Ford Taurus), 194; **7** Kurt Busch, USA (Ford Taurus), 194; **8** Ken Schrader, USA (Dodge Charger), 194; **9** Dale Jarrett, USA (Ford Taurus), 194; **10** Jeff Burton, USA (Chevrolet Monte Carlo), 194.
Pole position: Kevin Harvick, USA (Chevrolet Monte Carlo).
Drivers' championship points: 1 Johnson, 1368; **2** Busch (Kurt), 1238; **3** Gordon, 1217; **4** Biffle, 1181; **5** Sadler, 1164; **6** Stewart, 1088.

DODGE DEALERS 500, Darlington Raceway, South Carolina, USA, 7 May. Round 10. 370 laps of the 1.366-mile/2.198-km circuit, 505.420 miles/813.395 km.
1 Greg Biffle, USA (Ford Taurus), 4h 06m 29.0s, 123.031 mph/198.000 km/h; **2** Jeff Gordon, USA (Chevrolet Monte Carlo), 4h 06m 29.990s; **3** Kasey Kahne, USA (Dodge Charger), 370 laps; **4** Mark Martin, USA (Ford Taurus), 370; **5** Ryan Newman, USA (Dodge Charger), 370; **6** Jamie McMurray, USA (Dodge Charger), 370; **7** Jimmie Johnson, USA (Chevrolet Monte Carlo), 370; **8** Dale Earnhardt Jr., USA (Chevrolet Monte Carlo), 370; **9** Carl Edwards, USA (Ford Taurus), 370; **10** Tony Stewart, USA (Chevrolet Monte Carlo), 370.
Pole position: Kahne (Dodge Charger).
Drivers' championship points: 1 Johnson, 1519; **2** Gordon (Jeff), 1392; **3** Biffle, 1371; **4** Busch, 1290; **5** Sadler, 1267; **6** Martin, 1226.

CHEVY AMERICAN REVOLUTION 400, Richmond International Raceway, Virginia, USA, 14 May. Round 11. 400 laps of the 0.750-mile/1.207-km circuit, 300.000 miles/482.803 km.
1 Kasey Kahne, USA (Dodge Charger), 2h 59m 26.0s, 100.316 mph/161.443 km/h; **2** Tony Stewart, USA (Chevrolet Monte Carlo), 2h 59m 27.674s; **3** Ryan Newman, USA (Dodge Charger), 400 laps; **4** Kyle Busch, USA (Chevrolet Monte Carlo), 400; **5** Kevin Harvick, USA (Chevrolet Monte Carlo), 400; **6** Greg Biffle, USA (Ford Taurus), 400; **7** Elliott Sadler, USA (Ford Taurus), 400; **8** Bobby Labonte, USA (Chevrolet Monte Carlo), 400; **9** Michael Waltrip, USA (Chevrolet Monte Caro), 400; **10** Jamie McMurray, USA (Dodge Charger), 400.
Pole position: Kahne (Dodge Charger).
Drivers' championship points: 1 Johnson, 1562; **2** Biffle, 1521; **3** Gordon (Jeff), 1438; **4** Sadler, 1413; **5** Busch, 1407; **6** Stewart, 1397.

COCA-COLA 600, Lowe's Motor Speedway, Concord, Charlotte, North Carolina, USA, 29 May. Round 12. 400 laps of the 1.500-mile/2.414-km circuit, 600.000 miles/965.606 km.
1 Jimmie Johnson, USA (Chevrolet Monte Carlo), 5h 13m 52.0s, 114.698 mph/184.589 km/h; **2** Bobby Labonte, USA (Chevrolet Monte Carlo), 5h 13m 52.027s; **3** Carl Edwards, USA (Ford Taurus), 400 laps; **4** Jeremy Mayfield, USA (Dodge Charger), 400; **5** Ryan Newman, USA (Dodge Charger), 400; **6** Greg Biffle, USA (Ford Taurus), 400; **7** Martin Truex Jr., USA (Chevrolet Monte Carlo), 400; **8** Dale Jarrett, USA (Ford Taurus), 400; **9** Ken Schrader, USA (Dodge Charger), 400; **10** Rusty Wallace, USA (Dodge Charger), 400.
Pole position: Newman (Dodge Charger).
Drivers' championship points: 1 Johnson, 1747; **2** Biffle, 1676; **3** Sadler, 1542; **4** Newman, 1530; **5** Gordon (Jeff), 1516; **6** Stewart, 1488.

MBNA RACE POINTS 400, Dover International Speedway, Delaware, USA, 5 June. Round 13. 400 laps of the 1.000-mile/1.609-km circuit, 400.000 miles/643.738 km.
1 Greg Biffle, USA (Ford Taurus), 3h 15m 43.0s, 122.626 mph/197.348 km/h; **2** Kyle Busch, USA (Chevrolet Monte Carlo), 3h 15m 47.281s; **3** Mark Martin, USA (Ford Taurus), 400 laps; **4** Jimmie Johnson, USA (Chevrolet Monte Carlo), 400; **5** Rusty Wallace, USA (Dodge Charger), 400; **6** Brian Vickers, USA (Chevrolet Monte Carlo), 400; **7** Matt Kenseth, USA (Ford Taurus), 400; **8** Ryan Newman, USA (Dodge Charger), 400; **9** Kurt Busch, USA (Ford Taurus), 400; **10** Elliott Sadler, USA (Ford Taurus), 400;
Pole position: Johnson (Chevrolet Monte Carlo).
Drivers championship points: 1 Johnson, 1912; **2** Biffle, 1866; **3** Sadler, 1681; **4** Newman, 1672; **5** Stewart, 1606; **6** Martin, 1588.

POCONO 500, Pocono Raceway, Long Pond, Pennsylvania, USA, 12 June. Round 14. 201 laps of the 2.500-mile/4.023-km circuit, 502.500 miles/808.695 km.
1 Carl Edwards, USA (Ford Taurus), 3h 53m 24.0s, 129.177 mph/207.891 km/h; **2** Brian Vickers, USA (Chevrolet Monte Carlo), 201 laps (under caution); **3** Joe Nemechek, USA (Chevrolet Monte Carlo), 201; **4** Kyle Busch, USA (Chevrolet Monte Carlo), 201; **5** Michael Waltrip, USA (Chevrolet Monte Caro), 201; **6** Jimmie Johnson, USA (Chevrolet Monte Carlo), 201; **7** Mark Martin, USA (Ford Taurus), 201; **8** Kevin Harvick, USA (Chevrolet Monte Carlo), 201; **9** Jeff Gordon, USA (Chevrolet Monte Carlo), 201; **10** Jamie McMurray, USA (Dodge Charger), 201.
Pole position: Michael Waltrip (Chevrolet Monte Caro).
Drivers' championship points: 1 Johnson, 2062; **2** Biffle, 1939; **3** Sadler, 1781; **4** Edwards, 1759; **5** Martin, 1734; **6** Newman, 1733.

BATMAN BEGINS 400, Michigan International Speedway, Brooklyn, Michigan, USA, 19 June. Round 15. 200 laps of the 2.000-mile/3.219-km circuit, 400.000 miles/643.738 km.
1 Greg Biffle, USA (Ford Taurus), 2h 39m 22.0s, 150.596 mph/242.361 km/h; **2** Tony Stewart, USA (Chevrolet Monte Carlo), 2h 39m 23.675s; **3** Mark Martin, USA (Ford Taurus), 200 laps; **4** Matt Kenseth, USA (Ford Taurus), 200; **5** Carl Edwards, USA (Ford Taurus), 200; **6** Joe Nemechek, USA (Chevrolet Monte Carlo), 200; **7** Michael Waltrip, USA (Chevrolet Monte Caro), 200; **8** Elliott Sadler, USA (Ford Taurus), 200; **9** Kyle Busch, USA (Chevrolet Monte Carlo), 200; **10** Rusty Wallace, USA (Dodge Charger), 200.
Pole position: Ryan Newman, USA (Dodge Charger).
Drivers' championship points: 1 Johnson, 2173; **2** Biffle, 2124; **3** Sadler, 1923; **4** Edwards, 1914; **5** Martin, 1904; **6** Stewart, 1862.

DODGE/SAVE MART 350, Infineon Raceway, Sears Point, Sonoma, California, USA, 26 June. Round 16. 110 laps of the 1.990-mile/3.203-km circuit, 218.900 miles/352.285 km.
1 Tony Stewart, USA (Chevrolet Monte Carlo), 3h 00m 18.0s, 72.845 mph/117.233 km/h; **2** Ricky Rudd, USA (Ford Taurus), 3h 00m 20.266s; **3** Kurt Busch, USA (Ford Taurus), 110 laps; **4** Rusty Wallace, USA (Dodge Charger), 110; **5** Dale Jarrett, USA (Ford Taurus), 110; **6** Elliott Sadler, USA (Ford Taurus), 110; **7** Jeremy Mayfield, USA (Dodge Charger), 110; **8** Ron Fellows, CDN (Chevrolet Monte Carlo), 110; **9** Ryan Newman, USA (Dodge Charger), 110; **10** Brian Simo, USA (Chevrolet Monte Carlo), 110.
Pole position: Jeff Gordon, USA (Chevrolet Monte Carlo).
Drivers' championship points: 1 Biffle, 2250; **2** Johnson, 2228; **3** Sadler, 2073; **3** Stewart, 2052; **4** Martin, 2022; **5** Wallace, 2013.

PEPSI 400, Daytona International Speedway, Daytona Beach, Florida, USA, 2 July. Round 17. 160 laps of the 2.500-mile/4.023-km circuit, 400.000 miles/643.738 km.
1 Tony Stewart, USA (Chevrolet Monte Carlo), 3h 03m 11.0s, 131.016 mph/210.850 km/h; **2** Jamie McMurray, USA (Dodge Charger), 3h 03m 11.171s; **3** Dale Earnhardt Jr., USA (Chevrolet Monte Carlo), 160 laps; **4** Rusty Wallace, USA (Dodge Charger), 160; **5** Dale Jarrett, USA (Ford Taurus), 160; **6** Jimmie Johnson, USA (Chevrolet Monte Carlo), 160; **7** Jeff Gordon, USA (Chevrolet Monte Carlo), 160; **8** Mike Wallace, USA (Chevrolet Monte Carlo), 160; **9** Matt Kenseth, USA (Ford Taurus), 160; **10** Ken Schrader, USA (Dodge Charger), 160.
Pole position: Stewart.(Chevrolet Monte Carlo).
Drivers' championship points: 1 Johnson, 2378; **2** Biffle, 2305; **3** Stewart, 2242; **4** Sadler, 2178; **5** Wallace (Rusty), 2173; **6** Newman, 2115.

USG SHEETROCK 400, Chicagoland Speedway, Chicago, Illinois, USA, 10 July. Round 18. 267 of the 1.500-mile/2.414-km circuit, 400.500 miles/644.542 km.
1 Dale Earnhardt Jr., USA (Chevrolet Monte Carlo), 3h 08m 16.0s, 127.638 mph/205.414 km/h; **2** Matt Kenseth, USA (Ford Taurus), 3h 08m 16.291s; **3** Jimmie Johnson, USA (Chevrolet Monte Carlo), 267 laps; **4** Brian Vickers, USA (Chevrolet Monte Carlo), 267; **5** Tony Stewart, USA (Chevrolet Monte Carlo), 267; **6** Jeremy Mayfield, USA (Dodge Charger), 267; **7** Ricky Rudd, USA (Ford Taurus), 267; **8** Kurt Busch, USA (Ford Taurus), 267; **9** Casey Mears, USA (Dodge Charger), 267; **10** Mark Martin, USA (Ford Taurus), 267.
Pole position: Johnson (Chevrolet Monte Carlo).
Drivers' championship points: 1 Johnson, 2548; **2** Biffle, 2440; **3** Stewart, 2397; **4** Wallace (Rusty), 2300; **5** Sadler, 2230; **6** Martin, 2202.

NEW ENGLAND 300, New Hampshire International Speedway, Loudon, New Hampshire, USA, 17 July. Round 19. 300 laps of the 1.058-mile/1.703-km circuit, 317.400 miles/510.806 km.
1 Tony Stewart, USA (Chevrolet Monte Carlo), 3h 05m 36.0s, 102.608 mph/165.131 km/h; **2** Kurt Busch, USA (Ford Taurus), 3h 05m 36.851s; **3** Bobby Labonte, USA (Chevrolet Monte Carlo), 300 laps; **4** Kyle Busch, USA (Chevrolet Monte Carlo), 300; **5** Greg Biffle, USA (Ford Taurus), 300; **6** Kasey Kahne, USA (Dodge Charger), 300; **7** Ryan Newman, USA (Dodge Charger), 300; **8** Rusty Wallace, USA (Dodge Charger), 300; **9** Dale Earnhardt Jr., USA (Chevrolet Monte Carlo), 300; **10** Matt Kenseth, USA (Ford Taurus), 300.
Pole position: Brian Vickers, USA (Chevrolet Monte Carlo).
Drivers' championship points: 1 Johnson, 2672; **2** Biffle, 2595; **3** Stewart, 2587; **4** Wallace (Rusty), 2442; **5=** Busch (Kurt), 2347; **5=** Newman, 2347.

PENNSYLVANIA 500, Pocono Raceway, Long Pond, Pennsylvania, USA, 24 July. Round 20. 203 laps of the 2.500-mile/4.023-km circuit, 507.500 miles/816.742 km.
1 Kurt Busch, USA (Ford Taurus), 4h 03m 03.0s, 125.283 mph/201.623 km/h; **2** Rusty Wallace, USA (Dodge Charger), 203 laps (under caution); **3** Mark Martin, USA (Ford Taurus), 203; **4** Carl Edwards, USA (Ford Taurus), 203; **5** Ryan Newman, USA (Dodge Charger), 203; **6** Kevin Harvick, USA (Chevrolet Monte Carlo), 203; **7** Tony Stewart, USA (Chevrolet Monte Carlo), 203; **8** Bobby Labonte, USA (Chevrolet Monte Carlo), 203; **9** Mike Bliss, USA (Chevrolet Monte Carlo), 203; **10** Ricky Rudd, USA (Ford Taurus), 203.
Pole position: Jamie McMurray, (Dodge Charger).
Drivers' championship points: 1 Johnson, 2799; **2** Stewart, 2733; **3** Biffle, 2712; **4** Wallace (Rusty), 2617; **5** Busch (Kurt), 2537; **6** Newman, 2507.

ALLSTATE 400 AT THE BRICKYARD, Indianapolis Motor Speedway, Speedway, Indiana, USA, 7 August. Round 21. 160 laps of the 2.500-mile/4.023-km circuit, 400.000 miles/643.738 km.
1 Tony Stewart, USA (Chevrolet Monte Carlo), 3h 22m 03.0s, 118.782 mph/191.162 km/h; **2** Kasey Kahne, USA (Dodge Charger), 3h 22m 03.794s; **3** Brian Vickers, USA (Chevrolet Monte Carlo), 160 laps; **4** Jeremy Mayfield, USA (Dodge Charger), 160; **5** Matt Kenseth, USA (Ford Taurus), 160; **6** Casey Mears, USA (Dodge Charger), 160; **7** Mark Martin, USA (Ford Taurus), 160; **8** Jeff Gordon, USA (Chevrolet Monte Carlo), 160; **9** Sterling Marlin, USA (Dodge Charger), 160; **10** Kyle Busch, USA (Chevrolet Monte Carlo), 160.
Pole position: Elliott Sadler, (Ford Taurus).
Drivers' championship points: 1 Stewart, 2923; **2** Johnson, 2848; **3** Biffle, 2812; **4** Wallace (Rusty), 2705; **5** Busch (Kurt), 2646; **6** Martin, 2636.

SIRIUS SATELLITE RADIO AT THE GLEN, Watkins Glen International, New York, USA, 14 August. Round 22. 92 laps of the 2.450-mile/3.943-km circuit, 225.400 miles/362.746 km.
1 Tony Stewart, USA (Chevrolet Monte Carlo), 2h 35m 48.0s, 86.804 mph/139.697 km/h; **2** Robby Gordon, USA (Chevrolet Monte Carlo), 2h 35m 49.927s; **3** Boris Said, USA (Chevrolety Monte Carlo), 92 laps; **4** Scott Pruett, USA (Dodge Charger), 92; **5** Jimmie Johnson, USA (Chevrolet Monte Carlo), 92; **6** Rusty Wallace, USA (Dodge Charger), 92; **7** Mark Martin, USA (Ford Taurus), 92; **8** Brian Vickers, USA (Chevrolet Monte Carlo), 92; **9** Joe Nemechek, USA (Chevrolet Monte Carlo), 92; **10** Dale Earnhardt Jr., USA (Chevrolet Monte Carlo), 92.
Pole position: Stewart.
Drivers' championship points: 1 Stewart, 3113; **2** Johnson, 3008; **3** Biffle, 2861; **4** Wallace (Rusty), 2855; **5** Martin, 2782; **6** Busch (Kurt), 2692.

GFS MARKETPLACE 400, Michigan International Speedway, Brooklyn, Michigan, USA, 21 August. Round 23. 200 laps of the 2.000-mile/3.219-km circuit, 400.000 miles/643.738 km.
1 Jeremy Mayfield, USA (Dodge Charger), 2h 49m 33.0s, 141.551 mph/227.805 km/h; **2** Scott Riggs, USA (Chevrolet Monte Carlo), 2h 49m 31.974s; **3** Matt Kenseth, USA (Ford Taurus), 200 laps; **4** Carl Edwards, USA (Ford Taurus), 200; **5** Tony Stewart, USA (Chevrolet Monte Carlo), 200; **6** Greg Biffle, USA (Ford Taurus), 200; **7** Kurt Busch, USA (Ford Taurus), 200; **8** Joe Nemechek, USA (Chevrolet Monte Carlo), 200; **9** Brian Vickers, USA (Chevrolet Monte Carlo), 200; **10** Jimmie Johnson, USA (Chevrolet Monte Carlo), 200.
Pole position: Nemechek (Chevrolet Monte Carlo).
Drivers' championship points: 1 Stewart, 3268; **2** Johnson, 3142; **3** Biffle, 3016; **4** Wallace, 2979; **5** Martin, 2899; **7** Mayfield, 2869.

SHARPIE 500, Bristol Motor Speedway, Tennessee, USA, 27 August. Round 24. 500 laps of the 0.533-mile/0.858-km circuit, 266.500 miles/428.890 km.
1 Matt Kenseth, USA (Ford Taurus), 3h 08m 50.0s, 84.678 mph/136.276 km/h; **2** Jeff Burton, USA (Chevrolet Monte Carlo), 3h 08m 50.511s; **3** Greg Biffle, USA (Ford Taurus), 500 laps; **4** Ricky Rudd, USA (Ford Taurus), 500; **5** Rusty Wallace, USA (Dodge Charger), 500; **6** Jeff Gordon, USA (Chevrolet Monte Carlo), 500; **7** Mike Bliss, USA (Chevrolet Monte Carlo), 500; **8** Tony Stewart, USA (Chevrolet Monte Carlo), 500; **9** Dale Earnhardt Jr., USA (Chevrolet Monte Carlo), 500; **10** Kurt Busch, USA (Ford Taurus), 500.
Pole position: Kenseth (Ford Taurus).
Drivers' championship points: 1 Stewart, 3410; **2** Johnson, 3197; **3** Biffle, 3186; **4** Wallace (Rusty), 3139; **5** Martin, 3014; **6** Mayfield, 2983.

SONY HD 500, California Speedway, Fontana, California, USA, 4 September. Round 25. 254 laps of the 2.000-mile/3.219-km circuit, 508.000 miles/817.547 km.
1 Kyle Busch, USA (Chevrolet Monte Carlo), 3h 43m 32.0s, 136.356 mph/219.443 km/h; **2** Greg Biffle, USA (Ford Taurus), 3h 43m 32.554s; **3** Brian Vickers, USA (Chevrolet Monte Carlo), 254 laps; **4** Carl Edwards, USA (Ford Taurus), 254; **5** Tony Stewart, USA (Chevrolet Monte Carlo), 254; **6** Kasey Kahne, USA (Dodge Charger), 254; **7** Matt Kenseth, USA (Ford Taurus), 254; **8** Jamie McMurray, USA (Dodge Charger), 254; **9** Ricky Rudd, USA (Ford Taurus), 254; **10** Joe Nemechek, USA (Chevrolet Monte Carlo), 254.
Pole position: Edwards (Ford Taurus).
Drivers' championship points: 1 Stewart, 3570; **2** Biffle, 3361; **3** Johnson, 3312; **4** Wallace (Rusty), 3257; **5** Martin, 3149; **6** Busch (Kurt), 3114.

CHEVY ROCK & ROLL 400, Richmond International Raceway, Virginia, USA, 10 September. Round 26. 400 laps of the 0.750-mile/1.207-km circuit, 300.000 miles/482.803 km.
1 Kurt Busch, USA (Ford Taurus), 3h 02m 37.0s, 98.567 mph/158.628 km/h; **2** Matt Kenseth, USA (Ford Taurus), 3h 02m 37.899s; **3** Greg Biffle, USA (Ford Taurus), 400 laps; **4** Kyle Busch, USA (Chevrolet Monte Carlo), 400; **5** Rusty Wallace, USA (Dodge Charger), 400; **6** Jeremy Mayfield, USA (Dodge Charger), 400; **7** Tony Stewart, USA (Chevrolet Monte Carlo), 400; **8** Kasey Kahne, USA (Dodge Charger), 400; **9** Terry Labonte, USA (Chevrolet Monte Carlo), 400; **10** Kevin Harvick, USA (Chevrolet Monte Carlo), 400.
Pole position: Harvick (Chevrolet Monte Carlo).
Drivers' championship points: 1 Stewart, 3716; **2** Biffle, 3531; **3** Wallace (Rusty), 3412; **4** Johnson, 3400; **5** Busch (Kurt), 3304; **6** Martin, 3273.

SYLVANIA 300, New Hampshire International Speedway, Loudon, New Hampshire, USA, 18 September. Round 27. 300 laps of the 1.058-mile/1.703-km circuit, 317.400 miles/510.806 km.
1 Ryan Newman, USA (Dodge Charger), 3h 18m 36.0s, 95.891 mph/154.322 km/h; **2** Tony Stewart, USA (Chevrolet Monte Carlo), 3h 18m 36.292s; **3** Matt Kenseth, USA (Ford Taurus), 300 laps; **4** Greg Biffle, USA (Ford Taurus), 300; **5** Dale Earnhardt Jr., USA (Chevrolet Monte Carlo), 300; **6** Rusty Wallace, USA (Dodge Charger), 300; **7** Mark Martin, USA (Ford Taurus), 300; **8** Jimmie Johnson, USA (Chevrolet Monte Carlo), 300; **9** Jeff Burton, USA (Chevrolet Monte Carlo), 300; **10** Kevin Harvick, USA (Chevrolet Monte Carlo), 300.
Pole position: Stewart (Chevrolet Monte Carlo).
Drivers' championship points: 1 Stewart, 5230; **2** Biffle, 5210; **3** Newman, 5190; **4** Wallace (Rusty), 5190; **5** Kenseth, 5180; **6** Johnson, 5177.

MBNA RACE POINTS 400, Dover International Speedway, Dover, Delaware, USA, 25 September. Round 28. 404 laps of the 1.000-mile/1.609-km circuit, 404.000 miles/650.175 km.
1 Jimmie Johnson, USA (Chevrolet Monte Carlo), 3h 30m 41.0s, 115.054 mph/185.162 km/h; **2** Kyle Busch, USA (Chevrolet Monte Carlo), 3h 30m 41.080s; **3** Rusty Wallace, USA (Dodge Charger), 404 laps; **4** Mark Martin, USA (Ford Taurus), 404; **5** Ryan Newman, USA (Dodge Charger), 404; **6** Elliott Sadler, USA (Ford Taurus), 404; **7** Jeremy Mayfield, USA (Dodge Charger), 404; **8** Kyle Petty, USA (Dodge Charger), 404; **9** Carl Edwards, USA (Ford Taurus), 404; **10** Casey Mears, USA (Dodge Charger), 404.
Pole position: Newman (Dodge Charger).
Drivers' championship points: 1 Johnson, 5362; **2** Wallace (Rusty), 5355; **3** Newman, 5350; **4** Martin, 5341; **5=** Stewart, 5339; **5=** Biffle, 5339.

UAW-FORD 500, Talladega Superspeedway, Alabama, USA, 2 October. Round 29. 190 laps of the 2.660-mile/4.281-km circuit, 505.400 miles/813.362 km.
1 Dale Jarrett, USA (Ford Taurus), 3h 30m 51.0s, 143.818 mph/231.452 km/h; **2** Tony Stewart, USA (Chevrolet Monte Carlo), 190 laps (under caution); **3** Matt Kenseth, USA (Ford Taurus), 190; **4** Ryan Newman, USA (Dodge Charger), 190; **5** Carl Edwards, USA (Ford Taurus), 190; **6** Brian Vickers, USA (Chevrolet Monte Carlo), 190; **7** Sterling Marlin, USA (Dodge Charger), 190; **8** Kurt Busch, USA (Ford Taurus), 190; **9** Joe Nemechek, USA (Chevrolet Monte Carlo), 190; **10** Kevin Harvick, USA (Chevrolet Monte Carlo), 190.
Pole position: Elliott Sadler (Ford Taurus).
Drivers' championship points: 1 Stewart, 5519; **2** Newman, 5515; **3** Wallace (Rusty), 5443; **4** Johnson, 5437; **5** Biffle, 5421; **6** Edwards, 5419.

BANQUET 400 PRESENTED BY CONAGRA FOODS, Kansas Speedway, Kansas City, Kansas, USA, 9 October. Round 30. 267 laps of the 1.500-mile/2.414-km circuit, 400.500 miles/644.542 km.
1 Mark Martin, USA (Ford Taurus), 2h 54m 25.0s, 137.774 mph/221.725 km/h; **2** Greg Biffle, USA (Ford Taurus), 2h 54m 25.557s; **3** Carl Edwards, USA (Ford Taurus), 267 laps; **4** Tony Stewart, USA (Chevrolet Monte Carlo), 267; **5** Matt Kenseth, USA (Ford Taurus), 267; **6** Jimmie Johnson, USA (Chevrolet Monte Carlo), 267; **7** Rusty Wallace, USA (Dodge Charger), 267; **8** Casey Mears, USA (Dodge Charger), 267; **9** Ricky Rudd, USA (Ford Taurus), 267; **10** Jeff Gordon, USA (Chevrolet Monte Carlo), 267.
Pole position: Kenseth (Ford Taurus).
Drivers' championship points: 1 Stewart, 5684; **2** Newman, 5609; **3** Biffle, 5596; **4** Wallace (Rusty), 5594; **5** Johnson, 5592; **6** Edwards, 5589.

UAW-GM QUALITY 500, Lowe's Motor Speedway, Concord, Charlotte, North Carolina, USA, 16 October. Round 31. 336 laps of the 1.500-mile/2.414-km circuit, 504.000 miles/811.109 km.
1 Jimmie Johnson, USA (Chevrolet Monte Carlo), 4h 11m 18.0s, 120.334 mph/193.659 km/h; **2** Kurt Busch, USA (Ford Taurus), 4h 11m 18.309s; **3** Greg Biffle, USA (Ford Taurus), 336 laps; **4** Joe Nemechek, USA (Chevrolet Monte Carlo), 336; **5** Mark Martin, USA (Ford Taurus), 336; **6** Casey Mears, USA (Dodge Charger), 336; **7** Ryan Newman, USA (Dodge Charger), 336; **8** Denny Hamlin, USA (Chevrolet Monte Carlo), 336; **9** Ricky Rudd, USA (Ford Taurus), 336; **10** Carl Edwards, USA (Ford Taurus), 336.
Pole position: Eliott Sadler (Ford Taurus).
Drivers' championship points: 1= Stewart, 5777; **1=** Johnson, 5777; **3** Biffle, 5766; **4** Newman, 5760; **5** Martin, 5726; **6** Edwards, 5723.

SUBWAY 500, Martinsville Speedway, Virginia, USA, 23 October. Round 32. 500 laps of the 0.526-mile/0.847-km circuit, 263.000 miles/423.257 km.
1 Jeff Gordon, USA (Chevrolet Monte Carlo), 3h 46m 25.0s, 69.695 mph/112.162 km/h; **2** Tony Stewart, USA (Chevrolet Monte Carlo), 3h 46m 25.235; **3** Jimmie Johnson, USA (Chevrolet Monte Carlo), 500 laps; **4** Bobby Labonte, USA (Chevrolet Monte Carlo), 500; **5** Jeff Burton, USA (Chevrolet Monte Carlo), 500; **6** Kurt Busch, USA (Ford Taurus), 500; **7** Jamie McMurray, USA (Dodge Charger), 500; **8** Denny Hamlin, USA (Chevrolet Monte Carlo), 500; **9** Kyle Busch, USA (Chevrolet Monte Carlo), 500; **10** Ryan Newman, USA (Dodge Charger), 500.
Pole position: Stewart (Chevrolet Monte Carlo).
Drivers' championship points: 1 Stewart, 5957; **2** Johnson, 5942; **3** Newman, 5894; **4** Biffle, 5874; **5** Edwards, 5808; **6** Wallace (Rusty), 5791.

BASS PRO SHOPS MBNA 500, Atlanta Motor Speedway, Hampton, Georgia, USA, 30 October. Round 33. 325 laps of the 1.540-mile/2.478-km circuit, 500.500 miles/805.477 km.
1 Carl Edwards, USA (Ford Taurus), 3h 24m 31.0s, 146.834 mph/236.306 km/h; **2** Jeff Gordon, USA (Chevrolet Monte Carlo), 3h 24m 33.712s; **3** Mark Martin, USA (Ford Taurus), 325 laps; **4** Dale Earnhardt Jr., USA (Chevrolet Monte Carlo), 325; **5** Matt Kenseth, USA (Ford Taurus), 325; **6** Jamie McMurray, USA (Dodge Charger), 325; **7** Greg Biffle, USA (Ford Taurus), 325; **8** Jeff Burton, USA (Chevrolet Monte Carlo), 325; **9** Tony Stewart, USA (Chevrolet Monte Carlo), 325; **10** Elliott Sadler, USA (Ford Taurus), 325.
Pole position: Ryan Newman (Dodge Charger).

Provisional championship points
Drivers: 1 Tony Stewart, USA, 6100; **2** Jimmie Johnson, USA, 6057; **3** Greg Biffle, USA, 6025; **4=** Carl Edwards, USA, 5993; **4=** Ryan Newman, USA, 5993; **6** Mark Martin, USA, 5957; **7** Matt Kenseth, USA, 5945; **8** Rusty Wallace, USA, 5843; **9** Kurt Busch, USA, 5840; **30** Jeremy Mayfield, USA, 5790.

Not involved in 'Chase for the Nextel Cup'
11 Jamie McMurray, USA, 3782; **12** Jeff Gordon, USA, 3740; **13** Elliott Sadler, USA, 3722; **14** Kevin Harvick, USA, 3711; **15** Joe Nemechek, USA, 3693; **16** Brian Vickers, USA, 3617; **17** Dale Jarrett, USA, 3583; **18** Jeff Burton, USA, 3524; **19** Dale Earnhardt Jr., USA, 3489; **20** Kyle Busch, USA, 3485; **21** Ricky Rudd, USA, 3388; **22** Kasey Kahne, USA, 3377; **23** Michael Waltrip, USA, 3267; **24** Casey Mears, USA, 3215; **25** Bobby Labonte, USA, 3187; **26** Kyle Petty, USA, 2995; **27** Jeff Green, USA, 2980; **28** Dave Blaney, USA, 2967; **29** Mike Bliss, SA, 2953; **30** Sterling Marlin, USA, 2938.
Raybestos Rookie of the Year: Kyle Busch.
Manufacturers: 1 Chevrolet, 242; **2** Ford, 222; **3** Dodge, 163.
Bud Pole Award winner: Ryan Newman, 7 poles.

Results of the Texas, Phoenix and Homestead races will be given in AUTOCOURSE 2006–2007.

Other NASCAR Races

BUDWEISER SHOOTOUT, Daytona International Speedway, Daytona Beach, Florida, USA, 12 February, 70 laps of the 2.500-mile/4.023-km circuit, 175.000 miles/281.635 km.
1 Jimmie Johnson, USA (Chevrolet Monte Carlo), 70 laps; **2** Ryan Newman, USA (Dodge Charger), 70; **3** Jeff Gordon, USA (Chevrolet Monte Carlo), 70; **4** Tony Stewart, USA (Chevrolet Monte Carlo), 70; **5** Greg Biffle, USA (Ford Taurus), 70; **6** Kurt Busch, USA (Ford Taurus), 70; **7** Dale Earnhardt Jr., USA

(Chevrolet Monte Carlo), 70; **8** Mark Martin, USA (Ford Taurus), 70; **9** Kasey Kahne, USA (Dodge Charger), 70; **10** Bobby Labonte, USA (Chevrolet Monte Carlo), 70.
Pole position: Dale Jarrett (Ford Taurus).

NASCAR NEXTEL ALL-STAR CHALLENGE OPEN, Lowe's Motor Speedway, Concord, Charlotte, North Carolina, USA, 21 May. 90 laps of the 1.500-mile/2.414-km circuit, 135.000 miles/217.261 km.
1 Brian Vickers, USA (Chevrolet Monte Carlo), 90 laps; **2** Mike Bliss, USA (Chevrolet Monte Carlo), 90; **3** Travis Kvapil, USA (Dodge Charger), 90; **4** Kyle Busch, USA (Chevrolet Monte Carlo), 90; **5** Bobby Hamilton Jr., USA (Chevrolet Monte Carlo), 90; **6** Casey Mears, USA (Dodge Charger), 90; **7** Robby Gordon, USA (Chevrolet Monte Carlo), 90; **8** Ricky Rudd, USA (Ford Taurus), 90; **9** Ken Schrader, USA (Dodge Charger), 90; **10** Martin Truex Jr., USA (Chevrolet Monte Carlo), 90.
Pole position: Bliss (Chevrolet Monte Carlo).

NASCAR NEXTEL ALL-STAR CHALLENGE, Lowe's Motor Speedway, Concord, Charlotte, North Carolina, USA, 21 May. 90 laps of the 1.500-mile/2.414-km circuit, 135.000 miles/217.261 km.
Run over 3 segments of 30 laps each.
1 Mark Martin, USA (Ford Taurus), 90 laps; **2** Elliott Sadler, USA (Ford Taurus), 90; **3** Brian Vickers, USA (Chevrolet Monte Carlo), 90; **4** Jeff Gordon, USA (Chevrolet Monte Carlo), 90; **5** Jimmie Johnson, USA (Chevrolet Monte Carlo), 90; **6** Dale Jarrett, USA (Ford Taurus), 90; **7** Kurt Busch, USA (Ford Taurus), 90; **8** Jeremy Mayfield, USA (Dodge Charger), 90; **9** Bobby Labonte, USA (Chevrolet Monte Carlo), 90; **10** Dale Earnhardt Jr., USA (Chevrolet Monte Carlo), 90.
Pole position: Ryan Newman (Dodge Charger).

Indy Racing League (IRL) Menards Infiniti Pro Series

All cars are Dallara with 3.5 litre V8 Infiniti engine.

HOMESTEAD-MIAMI 100, Homestead-Miami Speedway, Florida, USA, 6 March. Round 1. 67 laps of the 1.485-mile/2.390-km circuit, 99.495 miles/160.122 km.
1 Travis Gregg, USA, 39m 32.0418s, 151.002 mph/243.013 km/h; **2** Jaime Camara, BR, 39m 32.1131s; **3** Jon Herb, USA, 67 laps; **4** Wade Cunningham, NZ, 67; **5** Jay Drake, USA, 67; **6** Nick Bussell, USA, 67; **7** Marty Roth, CDN, 67; **8** Mishael Abbott, USA, 67; **9** Jeff Simmons, USA, 67; **10** Chris Festa, USA, 34 (DNF-accident).
Most laps led: Gregg, 67.
Fastest race lap: Cunningham, 28.4151s, 188.139 mph/302.781 km/h.
Fastest qualifying lap: Gregg, 28.2475s, 189.256 mph/304.578 km/h.

PHOENIX 100, Phoenix International Raceway, Arizona, USA, 19 March. Round 2. 90 laps of the 1.000-mile/1.609-km circuit, 90.000 miles/144.841 km.
Race scheduled for 100 laps, but shortened after accidents.
1 Jon Herb, USA, 1h 00m 11.5901s, 89.711 mph/144.376 km/h; **2** Chris Festa, USA, 1h 00m 12.2953s; **3** Wade Cunningham, NZ, 90 laps; **4** Arie Luyendyk Jr., USA, 89; **5** Nick Bussell, USA, 89; **6** Travis Gregg, USA, 88; **7** Scott Mansell, GB, 87; **8** Al Unser III, USA, 40 (DNF-accident); **9** Mishael Abbott, USA, 31 (DNF-accident); **10** Marty Roth, CDN, 9 (DNF-accident).
Most laps led: Herb, 69.
Fastest race lap: Festa, 23.8122s, 151.183 mph/243.305 km/h.
Fastest qualifying lap: Gregg, 23.0334s, 156.295 mph/251.532 km/h.

MENARDS INFINITI PRO SERIES, Streets of St. Petersburg, Florida, USA, 3 April. Round 3. 40 laps of the 1.800-mile/2.897-km circuit, 72.000 miles/115.873 km.
1 Marco Andretti, USA, 49m 55.4666s, 86.531 mph/139.258 km/h; **2** Wade Cunningham, NZ, 1h 49m 56.8847s; **3** Nick Bussell, USA, 40 laps; **4** Al Unser III, USA, 40; **5** Arie Luyendyk Jr., USA, 40; **6** Travis Gregg, USA, 40; **7** P.J. Chesson, USA, 40; **8** Chris Festa, USA, 39; **9** Marty Roth, CDN, 39; **10** Jay Drake, USA, 27 (DNF-gearbox).
Most laps led: Andretti, 22.
Fastest race lap: Cunningham, 1m 08.4558s, 94.660 mph/152.340 km/h.
Fastest qualifying lap: Andretti, 1m 09.3256s, 93.472 mph/150.429 km/h.

FUTABA FREEDOM 100, Indianapolis Motor Speedway, Speedway, Indiana, USA, 27 May. Round 4. 40 laps of the 2.500-mile/4.023-km circuit, 100.000 miles/160.934 km.
1 Jaime Camara, BR, 40m 52.6390s, 146.780 mph/236.221 km/h; **2** Wade Cunningham, NZ, 40m 52.7709s; **3** Jay Drake, USA, 40 laps; **4** Al Unser III, USA, 40; **5** Marty Roth, CDN, 40; **6** Travis Gregg, USA, 40; **7** Jeff Simmons, USA, 40; **8** Chris Festa, USA, 40; **9** Taylor Fletcher, USA, 40; **10** German Quiroga, MEX, 40.
Most laps led: Camara, 33.
Fastest race lap: Jon Herb, USA, 47.3021s, 190.266 mph/306.204 km/h.
Pole position/fastest qualifying lap: Camara, 47.4009s, 189.870 mph/305.566 km/h. (over four laps).

FIRESTONE 100, Texas Motor Speedway, Fort Worth, Texas, USA, 11 June. Round 5. 67 laps of the 1.455-mile/2.342-km circuit, 97.485 miles/156.887 km.
1 Travis Gregg, USA, 34m 37.0057s, 168.967 mph/271.926 km/h; **2** Wade Cunningham, NZ, 34m 37.081s; **3** Chris Festa, USA, 67 laps; **4** Jay Drake, USA, 67; **5** Nick Bussell, USA, 67; **6** Marty Roth, CDN, 67; **7** Jon Herb, USA, 67; **8** Jeff Simmons, USA, 67; **9** Jaime Camara, BR, 67; **10** Arie Luyendyk Jr., USA, 67.
Most laps led: Gregg, 66.
Fastest race lap: Bussell, 27.7959s, 188.445 mph/303.273 km/h.
Fastest qualifying lap: Gregg, 27.9335s, 187.517 mph/301.779 km/h.

LIBERTY CHALLENGE, Indianapolis Motor Speedway (Road Course), Speedway, Indiana, USA, 18 June. Round 6. 25 laps of the 2.600-mile/4.184-km circuit, 65.000 miles/104.607 km.
1 Marco Andretti, USA, 35m 57.3780s, 108.465 mph/174.557 km/h; **2** Wade Cunningham, NZ, 36m 10.0830s; **3** Chris Festa, USA, 25 laps; **4** Nick Bussell, USA, 25; **5** Jaime Camara, BR, 25; **6** Arie Luyendyk Jr., USA, 25; **7** Travis Gregg, USA, 25; **8** Marty Roth, CDN, 25; **9** Jon Herb, USA, 25; **10** Jay Drake, USA, 25.
Most laps led: Andretti, 25.
Fastest race lap: Andretti, 1m 25.911s, 108.950 mph/175.338 km/h.
Fastest qualifying lap: Andretti, 1m 26.2363s, 108.539 mph/174.677 km/h.

CLEANEVENT 100, Nashville Superspeedway, Lebanon, Tennessee, USA, 16 July. Round 7. 77 laps of the 1.300-mile/2.092-km circuit, 100.100 miles/161.095 km.
1 Jaime Camara, BR, 43m 39.7982s, 137.553 mph/221.369 km/h; **2** Jeff Simmons, USA, 77 laps (under caution); **3** Jay Drake, USA, 77; **4** Wade Cunningham, NZ, 77; **5** Nick Bussell, USA, 77; **6** Jon Herb, USA, 77; **7** Chris Festa, USA, 77; **8** Arie Luyendyk Jr., USA, 77; **9** Jerry Coons Jr., USA, 76; **10** Travis Gregg, USA, 62 (DNF-accident).
Most laps led: Camara, 77.
Fastest race lap: Luyendyk Jr., 26.7546s, 174.923 mph/281.512 km/h.
Fastest qualifying lap: Camara, 26.1362s, 179.062 mph/288.172 km/h.

MILWAUKEE 100, The Milwaukee Mile, Wisconsin State Fair Park, West Allis, Wisconsin, USA, 24 July. Round 8. 100 laps of the 1.015-mile/1.633-km circuit, 101.500 miles/163.348 km.
1 Jeff Simmons, USA, 54m 55.4370s, 110.881 mph/178.445 km/h; **2** Wade Cunningham, NZ, 54m 57.2240s; **3** Nick Bussell, USA, 100 laps; **4** Jon Herb, USA, 100; **5** Jaime Camara, BR, 100; **6** Jay Drake, USA, 100; **7** Arie Luyendyk Jr., USA, 98; **8** Travis Gregg, USA, 98; **9** Marty Roth, CDN, 96; **10** Chris Festa, USA, 63 (DNF-accident).
Most laps led: Cunningham, 54.
Fastest race lap: Drake, 27.6847s, 131.986 mph/212.411 km/h.
Fastest qualifying lap: Camara, 25.5789s, 142.852 mph/229.898 km/h.

BLUEGRASS 100, Kentucky Speedway, Fort Mitchell, Kentucky, USA, 13 August. Round 9. 67 laps of the 1.480-mile/2.382-km circuit, 99.160 miles/159.583 km.
1 Travis Gregg, USA, 36m 58.9262s, 160.878 mph/258.908 km/h; **2** Wade Cunningham, NZ, 36m 00.6762s; **3** Marco Andretti, USA, 67 laps; **4** Jay Drake, USA, 67; **5** Jeff Simmons, USA, 67; **6** Nick Bussell, USA, 67; **7** Marty Roth, CDN, 67; **8** Jaime Camara, BR, 67; **9** Chris Festa, USA, 66; **10** Arie Luyendyk Jr., USA, 66.
Most laps led: Gregg, 67.
Fastest race lap: Drake, 28.3772s, 187.756 mph/302.165 km/h.
Fastest qualifying lap: Gregg, 28.3462s, 187.962 mph/302.495 km/h.

PIKES PEAK 100, Pikes Peak International Raceway, Fountain, Colorado, USA, 21 August. Round 10. 100 laps of the 1.000-mile/1.609-km circuit, 100.000 miles/160.934 km.
1 Jeff Simmons, USA, 41m 59.5213s, 142.884 mph/229.950 km/h; **2** Nick Bussell, USA, 41m 04.3978s; **3** Travis Gregg, USA, 100 laps; **4** Tom Wood, USA, 100; **5** Wade Cunningham, NZ, 99; **6** Chris Festa, USA, 99; **7** Marty Roth, CDN, 80 (DNF-handling); **8** Jay Drake, USA, 78 (DNF-handling); **9** Jaime Camara, BR, 66 (DNF-electrics); **10** Arie Luyendyk Jr., USA, 49 (DNF-handling);
Most laps led: Simmons, 99.
Fastest race lap: Gregg, 24.3340s, 147.941 mph/238.088 km/h.
Fastest qualifying lap: Gregg, 23.3418s, 154.230 mph/248.209 km/h.

SONOMA 100, Infineon Raceway, Sears Point, Sonoma, California, USA, 28 August. Round 11. 30 laps of the 2.300-mile/3.701-km circuit, 69.000 miles/111.045 km.
1 Marco Andretti, USA, 46m 40.3049s, 88.705 mph/142.756 km/h; **2** Wade Cunningham, NZ, 46m 41.3505s; **3** Jeff Simmons, USA, 30 laps; **4** Nick Bussell, USA, 30; **5** Chris Festa, USA, 30; **6** Travis Gregg, USA, 30; **7** Marty Roth, CDN, 30; **8** Jay Drake, USA, 29; **9** Jon Herb, USA, 29; **10** Scott Mansell, GB, 24 (DNF-mechanical).
Most laps led: Andretti, 30.
Fastest race lap: Simmons, 1m 24.6274s, 97.841 mph/157.459 km/h.
Fastest qualifying lap: Andretti, 1m 24.2259s, 98.307 mph/158.210 km/h.

CHICAGOLAND 100, Chicagoland Speedway, Chicago, Illinois, USA, 11 September. Round 12. 67 of the 1.520-mile/2.446-km circuit, 101.840 miles/163.896 km.
1 Jeff Simmons, USA, 40m 25.8974s, 151.129 mph/243.219 km/h; **2** Marty Roth, CDN, 40m 26.1280s; **3** Nick Bussell, USA, 67 laps; **4** Jon Herb, USA, 67; **5** Travis Gregg, USA, 67; **6** J aime Camara, BR, 67; **7** Jay Drake, USA, 55 (DNF-handling); **8** Bobby Wilson, USA, 6 (DNF-accident); **9** Sarah McCune, USA, 5 (DNF-accident); **10** Wade Cunningham, NZ, 5 (DNF-accident).
Most laps led: Simmons, 25.
Fastest race lap: Herb, 28.8068s, 189.955 mph/305.703 km/h.
Fastest qualifying lap: McCune, 29.1382s, 187.795 mph/302.226 km/h.

CORNING 100, Watkins Glen International, New York, USA, 25 September. Round 13. 29 laps of the 3.370-mile/5.423-km circuit, 97.730 miles/157.281 km
1 Jeff Simmons, USA, 51m 21.9152s, 114.159 mph/183.721 km/h; **2** Marco Andretti, USA, 51m 22.5468s; **3** Wade Cunningham, NZ, 29 laps; **4** Chris Festa, USA, 29; **5** Nick Bussell, USA, 29; **6** Phil Giebler, USA, 29; **7** Jaime Camara, BR, 29; **8** Larry Connor, USA, 29; **9** Bobby Wilson, USA, 29; **10** Marty Roth, CDN, 28
Most laps led: Andretti, 25.
Fastest race lap: Cunningham, 1m 40.7496s, 120.417 mph/193.793 km/h.
Fastest qualifying lap: Cunningham, 1m 39.6051s, 121.801 mph/196.020 km/h.

CALIFORNIA 100, California Speedway, Fontana, California, USA, 16 October. Round 14. 50 laps of the 2.000-mile/3.219-km circuit, 100.000 miles/160.934 km.
1 Wade Cunningham, NZ, 43m 06.744s, 139.170 mph/223.974 km/h; **2** Jeff Simmons, USA, 43m 06.8507s; **3** Travis Gregg, USA, 50 laps; **4** Chris Festa, USA, 50; **5** Nick Bussell, USA, 50; **6** Arie Luyendyk Jr., USA, 50; **7** Marty Roth, CDN, 50; **8** P.J. Abbott, USA, 49; **9** Jon Herb, USA, 47; **10** Jaime Camara, BR, 45.
Most laps led: Cunningham, 28.
Fastest race lap: Simmons, 37.4702s, 192.153 mph/309.240 km/h.
Fastest qualifying lap: Gregg, 38.1293s, 188.831 mph/303.894 km/h.

Final championship points: 1 Wade Cunningham, NZ, 519; **2** Jeff Simmons, USA, 474; **3** Travis Gregg, USA, 462; **4** Nick Bussell, USA, 430; **5** Jaime Camara, BR, 403; **6** Chris Festa, USA, 387; **7** Jon Herb, USA, 364; **8** Marty Roth, CDN, 355; **9** Jay Drake, USA, 341; **10** Marco Andretti, USA, 250; **11** Arie Luyendyk Jr., USA, 228; **12** Al Unser III, USA, 106; **13** Mishael Abbott, USA, 83; **14** Bobby Wilson, USA, 82; **15** Scott Mayer, USA, 80; **16** Tom Wood, USA, 68; **17** P.J. Chesson, USA, 61; **18** P.J. Abbott, USA, 43; **19** Taylor Fletcher, USA, 41; **20** Larry Connor, USA, 40.
Rookie of the Year: Wade Cunningham.

Champ Car Toyota Atlantic Championship Presented by Yokohama

All cars are Swift 014.a chassis with Toyota engine.

TOYOTA ATLANTIC CHAMPIONSHIP, Long Beach Street Circuit, California, USA, 10 April. Round 1. 32 laps of the 1.968-mile/3.167-km circuit, 62.976 miles/101.350 km.
1 Katherine Legge, GB, 47m 01.977s, 80.339 mph/129.292 km/h; **2** Antoine Bessette, CDN, 47m 02.484s; **3** Charles Zwolsman, NL, 47m 03.510s; **4** Chris Dyson, USA, 47m 33.847s; **5** Justin Sofio, USA, 48m 12.585s; **6** Dan Cobb, USA, 31 laps; **7** Dan Selznick, USA, 31; **8** Kyle Kelley, USA, 31; **9** Mark Ishikawa, USA, 31; **10** Rocky Moran Jr., USA, 30 (DNF-mechanical).
Most laps led: Bessette, 26.
Fastest race lap: Bessette, 1m 19.062s, 89.611 mph/144.214 km/h.
Fastest qualifying lap: Bessete, 1m 19.375s, 89.257 mph/143.646 km/h.

TOYOTA ATLANTIC CHAMPIONSHIP, Parque Fundidora, Monterrey, Nuevo Leon, Mexico, 22 May. Round 2. 32 laps of the 2.104-mile/3.386-km circuit, 67.328 miles/108.354 km.
1 Charles Zwolsman, NL, 46m 43.327s, 86.462 mph/139.147 km/h; **2** Tonis Kasemets, EST, 46m 44.559s; **3** David Martinez, MEX, 46m 56.357s; **4** Antoine Bessette, CDN, 46m 58.524s; **5** Katherine Legge, GB, 47m 09.540s; **6** Kyle Kelley, USA, 47m 45.722s; **7** Memo Rojas, MEX, 47m 56.631s; **8** Andreas Wirth, D, 48m 03.034s; **9** Tom Nastasi, USA, 31 laps; **10** Dan Cobb, USA, 31.
Most laps led: Zwolsman, 32.
Fastest race lap: Zwolsman, 1m 26.620s, 87.444 mph/140.727 km/h.
Fastest qualifying lap: Zwolsman, 1m 26.831s, 87.232 mph/140.386 km/h.

TOYOTA ATLANTIC CHAMPIONSHIP, Portland International Raceway, Oregon, USA, 18/19 June. 2 x 35 laps of the 1.964-mile/3.161-km circuit.
Round 3 (68.740 miles/110.626 km).
1 Tonis Kasemets, EST, 42m 38.821s, 96.710 mph/155.640 km/h; **2** Charles Zwolsman, NL, 42m 39.870s; **3** Andreas Wirth, D, 42m 54.806s; **4** Kyle Kelley, USA, 42m 57.949s; **5** Antoine Bessette, CDN, 42m 59.949s; **6** David Martinez, MEX, 43m 01.333s; **7** Al Unser III, USA, 43m 11.793s; **8** Chris Dyson, USA, 43m 12.104s; **9** Katherine Legge, GB, 43m 13.337s; **10** Dan Selznick, USA, 43m 50.085s.
Most laps led: Wirth, 24.
Fastest race lap: Zwolsman, 1m 09.269s, 102.072 mph/164.268 km/h.
Fastest qualifying lap: Wirth, 1m 08.546s, 103.148 mph/166.001 km/h.

Round 4 (68.740 miles/110.626 km).
1 Tonis Kasemets, EST, 40m 25.992s, 102.005 mph/164.162 km/h; **2** Andreas Wirth, D, 40m 37.756s; **3** Katherine Legge, GB, 40m 41.433s; **4** David Martinez, MEX, 40m 50.340s; **5** Antoine Bessette, CDN, 41m 07.219s; **6** Al Unser III, USA, 41m 38.050s; **7** Chris Dyson, USA, 34 laps; **8** Charles Zwolsman, NL, 34; **9** Lee Atkins, USA, 34; **10** Justin Sofio, USA, 34.
Most laps led: Kasemets, 35.
Fastest race lap: Kasemets, 1m 07.977s, 104.012 mph/167.391 km/h.
Fastest qualifying lap: Kasemets, 1m 09.152s, 102.244 mph/164.546 km/h.

TOYOTA ATLANTIC CHAMPIONSHIP, Burke Lakefront Airport, Cleveland, Ohio, USA, 25/26 June. 2 x 32 laps of the 2.106-mile/3.389-km circuit.
Round 5 (67.392 miles/108.457 km).
1 Charles Zwolsman, NL, 39m 28.711s, 102.423 mph/164.834 km/h; **2** Tonis Kasemets, EST, 39m 29.459s; **3** Andreas Wirth, D, 39m 51.265s; **4** Al Unser III, USA, 40m 06.125s; **5** Chris Dyson, USA, 40m 10.579s; **6** Tom Nastasi, USA, 40m 18.155s; **7** Justin Sofio, USA, 31 laps; **8** Rich Zober, USA, 30; **9** Dan Cobb, USA, 30; **10** Bob Siska, USA, 30.
Most laps led: Zwolsman, 32.
Fastest race lap: Kasemets, 1m 07.712s, 111.968 mph/180.196 km/h.
Fastest qualifying lap: Kasemets, 1m 07.932s, 111.606 mph/179.612 km/h.

Round 6 (67.392 miles/108.457 km).
1 Charles Zwolsman, NL, 36m 46.826s, 109.937 mph/176.926 km/h; **2** Antoine Bessette, CDN, 36m 57.191s; **3** Andreas Wirth, D, 37m 01.376s; **4** Tonis Kasemets, EST, 37m 02.044s; **5** Katherine Legge, GB, 37m 21.517s; **6** Chris Dyson, USA, 37m 35.804s; **7** Al Unser III, USA, 31 laps (DNF-off course); **8** David Martinez, MEX, 31; **9** Leonardo Maia, BR, 31; **10** Dan Selznick, USA, 31.
Most laps led: Zwolsman, 20.
Fastest race lap: Zwolsman, 1m 07.468s, 112.373 mph/180.847 km/h.
Fastest qualifying lap: Zwolsman, 1m 07.854s, 111.734 mph/179.818 km/h.

TOYOTA ATLANTIC CHAMPIONSHIP, Canada National Exhibition Place Circuit, Toronto, Ontario, Canada, 10 July. Round 7. 35 laps of the 1.755-mile/2.824-km circuit, 61.425 miles/98.854 km.
1 Antoine Bessette, CDN, 42m 58.149s, 85.771 mph/138.035 km/h; **2** David Martinez, MEX, 42m 59.430s; **3** Andreas Wirth, D, 42m 59.748s; **4** Al Unser III, USA, 43m 05.691s; **5** Eric Jensen, CDN, 43m 23.736s; **6** Katherine Legge, GB, 43m 31.301s; **7** Justin Sofio, USA, 43m 50.722s; **8** Tonis Kasemets, EST, 34 laps; **9** Daryl Leiski, CDN, 34; **10** Bob Siska, USA, 34.
Most laps led: Charles Zwolsman, NL, 23.
Fastest race lap: Zwolsman, 1m 07.835s, 93.138 mph/149.891 km/h.
Fastest qualifying lap: Zwolsman, 1m 07.335s, 93.829 mph/151.004 km/h.

NAPA AUTO PARTS PRESENTS THE TOYOTA ATLANTIC CHALLENGE, Finning International Speedway, Edmonton, Alberta, Canada, 17 July. Round 8. 32 laps of the 1.973-mile/3.175-km circuit, 63.136 miles/101.608 km.
1 Katherine Legge, GB, 39m 53.701s, 94.953 mph/152.812 km/h; **2** Charles Zwolsman, NL, 39m 53.921s; **3** Andreas Wirth, D, 39m 58.564s; **4** Antoine Bessette, CDN, 38m 58.692s; **5** Tonis Kasemets, EST, 39m 00.234s; **6** Al Unser III, USA, 39m 06.879s; **7** Eric Jensen, CDN, 39m 17.369s; **8** David Martinez, MEX, 31 laps; **9** Justin Sofio, USA, 31; **10** Dan Cobb, USA, 30.
Most laps led: Zwolsman, 18.
Fastest race lap: Zwolsman, 1m 07.828s, 104.718 mph/168.527 km/h.
Fastest qualifying lap: Zwolsman, 1m 07.628s, 105.028 mph/169.025 km/h.

TOYOTA ATLANTIC CHAMPIONSHIP, San José Street Circuit, California, USA, 31 July. Round 9. 45 laps of the 1.448-mile/2.330-km circuit, 65.160 miles/104.865 km.
1 Katherine Legge, GB, 48m 56.342s, 79.887 mph/128.566 km/h; **2** David Martinez, MEX, 48m 57.426s; **3** Charles Zwolsman, NL, 48m 59.524s; **4** Alan Sciuto, USA, 49m 00.048s; **5** Andreas Wirth, D, 49m 08.630s; **6** Al Unser III, USA, 49m 08.825s; **7** Grant Ryley, USA, 44 laps; **8** Phil Giebler, USA, 44; **9** Justin Sofio, USA, 44; **10** Dan Selznick, USA, 44. Most laps led: Zwolsman, 20.
Fastest race lap: Martinez, 1m 02.325s, 83.639 mph/134.604 km/h.
Fastest qualifying lap: Zwolsman, 1m 02.657s, 83.196 mph/133.891 km/h.

TOYOTA ATLANTIC CHAMPIONSHIP, Denver Street Circuit, Colorado, USA, 14 August. Round 10. 35 laps of the 1.657-mile/2.667-km circuit, 57.995 miles/93.374 km.
1 Andreas Wirth, D, 40m 29.856s, 85.924 mph/138.281 km/h; **2** Alan Sciuto, USA, 40m 36.343s; **3** Charles Zwolsman, NL, 40m 36.585s; **4** Antoine Bessette, CDN, 40m 36.934s; **5** David Martinez, MEX, 40m 47.814s; **6** Kyle Kelley, USA, 41m 15.302s; **7** Al Unser III, USA, 41m 17.434s; **8** Tonis Kasemets, EST, 42m 34.576s; **9** Dan Selznick, USA, 34 laps; **10** Justin Sofio, USA, 34.
Most laps led: Wirth, 35.
Fastest race lap: Kasemets, 1m 08.517s, 87.0620 mph/140.112 km/h.
Fastest qualifying lap: Sciuto, 1m 08.692s, 86.840 mph/139.755 km/h.

BOSPOKER.COM TOYOTA ATLANTIC GRAND PRIX OF ROAD AMERICA, Road America Circuit, Elkhart Lake, Wisconsin, USA, 21 August. Round 11. 17 laps of the 4.048-mile/6.515-km circuit, 68.816 miles/110.749 km.
1 Tonis Kasemets, EST, 35m 12.283s, 117.284 mph/188.751 km/h; **2** Katherine Legge, GB, 35m 14.831s; **3** David Martinez, MEX, 35m 28.621s; **4** Al Unser III, USA, 35m 36.938s; **5** Kyle Kelley, USA, 35m 37.993s; **6** Charles Zwolsman, NL, 35m 38.695s; **7** Alan Sciuto, USA, 35m 48.173s; **8** Daniel DiLeo, CDN, 35m 56.597s; **9** Chris Menninga, USA, 36m 29.432s; **10** Chris Souliotis, CDN, 37m 01.462s.
Most laps led: Kasemets, 17.
Fastest race lap: Kasemets, 2m 02.799s, 118.672 mph/190.984 km/h.
Fastest qualifying lap: Kasemets, 2m 01.747s, 119.697 mph/192.634 km/h.

TOYOTA ATLANTIC CHAMPIONSHIP, Circuit Gilles-Villeneuve, Ile-Notre-Dame, Montréal, Québec, Canada, 28 August. Round 12. 25 laps of the 2.709-mile/4.360-km circuit, 67.725 miles/108.993 km.
1 Antoine Bessette, CDN, 40m 47.532s, 99.615 mph/160.314 km/h; **2** Tonis Kasemets, EST, 40m 48.087s; **3** David Martinez, MEX, 40m 50.870s; **4** Katherine Legge, GB, 41m 03.411s; **5** Al Unser III, USA, 41m 17.044s; **6** Charles Zwolsman, NL, 41m 33.666s; **7** Dan Selznick, USA, 24 laps; **8** Eric Jensen, USA, 24; **9** Chris Souliotis, CDN, 24; **10** Daryl Leiski, CDN, 24.
Most laps led: Bessette, 22.
Fastest race lap: Martinez, 1m 35.648s, 101.961 mph/164.091 km/h.
Fastest qualifying lap: Martinez, 1m 35.084s, 102.566 mph/165.064 km/h.

Final championship points: 1 Charles Zwolsman, NL, 306; **2** Tonis Kasemets, EST, 289; **3=** Katherine Legge, GB, 267; **3=** Antoine Bessette, CDN, 267; **5** David Martinez, MEX, 238; **6** Andreas Wirth, D, 234; **7** Al Unser III, USA, 198; **8** Kyle Kelley, USA, 122; **9** Chris Souliotis, CDN, 115; **10** Dan Selznick, USA, 106; **11** Chris Dyson, USA, 95; **12** Alan Sciuto, USA, 69; **13** Brian McAtee, USA, 56; **14** Eric Jensen, CDN, 54; **15** Tom Nastasi, USA, 44; **16** Leonardo Maia, BR, 30; **17** Ryan Spencer-Smith, USA, 19; **18=** Memo Rojas, MEX, 17; **18=** Grant Ryley, USA, 17; **20=** Phil Giebler, USA, 15; **20=** Daniel DiLeo, CDN, 15.

C2 Class Championship winner: Juston Sofio, USA.
Rookie of the year: Charles Zwolsman, NL.